Small Business Management

An Entrepreneur's Guidebook

seventh edition

Mary Jane Byrd
University of Mobile

Leon C. Megginson
Emeritus
University of Mobile

 McGraw-Hill Irwin

The McGraw·Hill Companies

McGraw-Hill
Irwin

SMALL BUSINESS MANAGEMENT: AN ENTREPRENEUR'S GUIDEBOOK, SEVENTH EDITION

Published by McGraw-Hill, a business unit of The McGraw-Hill Companies, Inc., 1221 Avenue of the Americas, New York, NY 10020. Copyright © 2013 by The McGraw-Hill Companies, Inc. All rights reserved. Previous editions © 2009, 2006, and 2003. Printed in the United States of America. No part of this publication may be reproduced or distributed in any form or by any means, or stored in a database or retrieval system, without the prior written consent of The McGraw-Hill Companies, Inc., including, but not limited to, in any network or other electronic storage or transmission, or broadcast for distance learning.

Some ancillaries, including electronic and print components, may not be available to customers outside the United States.

This book is printed on acid-free paper.

1 2 3 4 5 6 7 8 9 0 RJE/RJE 1 0 9 8 7 6 5 4 3 2

ISBN 978–0–07–802909–7
MHID 0–07–802909–0

Vice President, General Manager: *Brent Gordon*
Managing Director: *Paul Ducham*
Brand Manager: *Anke Weekes*
Marketing Manager: *Michael Gedatus*
Managing Development Editor: *Laura Hurst Spell*
Buyer: *Nicole Baumgartner*
Project Manager: *Melissa M. Leick*
Cover Designer: *Studio Montage, St. Louis, MO*
Cover Image: *Getty Images*
Media Project Manager: *Prashanthi Nadipalli, Hurix Systems Pvt. Ltd.*
Typeface: *10/12 Times LT Std*
Compositor: *S4Carlisle Publishing Services*
Printer: *R. R. Donnelley*

All credits appearing on page or at the end of the book are considered to be an extension of the copyright page.

Library of Congress Cataloging-in-Publication Data

Byrd, Mary Jane.
Small business management: an entrepreneur's guidebook/Mary Jane Byrd,
Leon C. Megginson.—7th ed.
    p. cm.
    Includes index.
    ISBN 978-0-07-802909-7—ISBN 0-07-802909-0   1. Small business—Management. 2. Small business—Management—Case studies. I. Megginson, Leon C. II. Title.

    HD62.7.S5943 2013
    658.02'2—dc23

                                                                        2012030091

Leon C. Megginson
1921–2010

Mary Jane Byrd

Mary Jane Byrd (DBA, IPMA-CP) is professor of accounting and management at the University of Mobile, where she has been teaching for 27 years. She and her husband operate a small business that they founded in 1974. Dr. Byrd is certified by the International Public Management Association and participates with the Academy of Management, United States Association for Small Business and Entrepreneurship. She also serves on the editorial board for the International Journal of Public Administration and the boards of various local organizations. She has presented refereed papers both in the United States and in England, and has coauthored eight business textbooks. Her hobbies include water sports, reading, travel, and writing. She is married to Gerald Byrd, and they have three daughters: Kari, Juli, and Cori.

Leon C. Megginson

Leon Megginson had more than 15 years of managerial experience in the world of academics, practicing many of the skills found in this book. He served two years as associate dean of the business school at Louisiana State University (LSU), and he organized and served as chairman and dean of the School of Business at the University of Mobile for eight years. Although he had a short stay at the University of South Alabama, he received the Alumni Association's Research Professor of the Year award.

He served as operations officer of a squadron of more than 100 pilots and airmen in the 25th Bomb Squad, U.S. Air Force, during World War II. He was a Fulbright Research Scholar in Spain during the 1960s and a Ford Foundation Advisor in Pakistan from 1978 to 1979, assisting the Pakistani government in the area of management development. He is a fellow in the Academy of Management.

Dr. Megginson is the author or coauthor of 38 editions of 18 textbooks, several of which have won awards. He has spoken or taught in more than 50 countries, including Poland, Turkey, Germany, England, Switzerland, Iran, Iraq, Denmark, Canada, Italy, and Belgium. He has conducted management courses at the U.S. Military Academy at West Point and at the Pentagon in Washington, among other places. While at LSU, he chaired the committee that planned the University of New Orleans.

Preface

This is a stimulating and exciting time to be involved in small business—either as an owner or as a student studying to become an owner. Events since the publication of the Sixth Edition of *Small Business Management* have drastically changed the environment in which entrepreneurs and small business owners now operate—and especially the way they will operate during this twenty-first century!

While operating any business—small *or* large—will probably be complex and challenging, it should also provide more interesting, creative, and rewarding experiences. Current events indicate that the next few years will present ever more stimulating, challenging, and rewarding—and no doubt at times frustrating—opportunities to those millions of brave women and men who own and/or manage these essential enterprises.

Success will require desire, commitment, knowledge, and hard work on their part—plus a certain amount of luck, as in any endeavor. This text provides an overview of the knowledge required.

New to This Edition

The entire text has updated statistics, profiles, photos, Real-World Examples, and experiential exercises. Specific chapter updates include the following.

- Chapter 1 begins with a new profile of a company that was so successful as an Internet marketing group that they added their own production facility. This chapter also includes new information about the state-sponsored Self-Employment Assistance Program.

- Chapter 3 includes recent major organizational changes to the profile and a new Real-World Example about creating a not-for-profit organization.

- Chapter 4 has new information on how small business can practice conservation.

- Chapter 5 has a new example of a failed franchise. It also includes new topics: due diligence and the franchise trade show.

- Chapter 6 now includes information on choosing a financial advisor and the new topic of microloans.

- Chapter 7 contains some changes to the Profile regarding major expansions. Also new is information regarding existing businesses as a source of funds for a start-up.

- Chapter 9 Profile is updated to reflect a total organizational change in a continuing operation. Also included are misconceptions concerning foreign business.

- Chapter 12 now has a new topic: seasonal stores.

- Chapter 13 and the Profile reflect how changes in the economy and in technology have affected retailers and distribution.

- Chapter 14 Profile updates our classical example of a successful entrepreneur. It also includes the new topic and discussion of cost of goods sold.

- Chapter 16 now includes new examples of using current technology to safeguard inventory in the service sector. New topics include text marketing, Facebook and Twitter, and QR codes.

- Chapter 17 new topic is business insurance.

To the Student

This Seventh Edition of *Small Business Management: An Entrepreneur's Guidebook*—like the Sixth Edition—takes a practical, down-to-earth approach to conceiving, planning, organizing, and managing a small business. Based on extensive theory, research, and practice, the material in this edition is presented from a "how-to" perspective, with many practical examples and applications from the business world. Both authors have had meaningful experience in the "real world" as owner, manager, or employee of one or more small businesses.

The material in this text discusses the role and growing importance of small business. It explores the arguments both for and against owning a small firm. It presents up-to-date thinking about conceiving, preparing, starting, organizing, and operating a small business. And it explains how to achieve optimum benefits from the limited resources available to small firms and how to plan for growth and succession in a business.

The Profiles at the beginning of each chapter are especially useful examples from the real world that highlight actual entrepreneurs' experiences. Sometimes it may be as helpful to present the "how not to" as the "how to" of small business. Thus, the Profiles, and numerous other examples, look at all sides of small business issues and experiences. Web site addresses for organizations are given throughout.

Note that the websites included in this text are those that were in use at the time of writing and may or may not still be in use; however, they should give guidance as to what types of information can be gathered on the information superhighway.

Organization of the Book

Part 1, The Dynamic Role of Small Business, dramatizes the important role of small business in the United States and world economies; the chief characteristics of entrepreneurs and small business owners; the reasons why you should or should not own a small business; some current opportunities and challenges in small business; and the legal forms you can choose for your business. Also, the various issues and needs for today's family businesses' social responsibility and ethics are discussed.

Part 2, How to Plan and Organize a Business, explains in detail how to become the owner of a small business—including how to do strategic and operational planning—as well as the growing opportunities in franchising; how to prepare and present a winning business plan, along with a Sample Business Plan; and how to obtain the necessary financing for your business.

Part 3, How to Market Goods and Services, discusses how to develop marketing strategies for producing a product (either a good or service) and selling and distributing it. Included are discussions of developing global markets, marketing research, and other related activities.

Part 4, How to Organize, Manage, and Operate the Business, explains the important role played by human resources in a business. It shows how to recruit, select, train, and compensate the required number of capable employees. Students are encouraged to learn how to communicate with, motivate, and maintain good human relations with employees—and their union, when one is involved. It also deals with such important operating factors as locating and laying out facilities, purchasing and maintaining inventory, and assuring quality control.

Part 5, Basic Financial Planning and Control, explains what profit is, and how to plan for it; how to budget and control operations; and how to deal with taxes and recordkeeping. Also, much new information is provided concerning the use of computer technology and management information systems to do these things more effectively. Considerable insight is provided into the role and operation of the Internet. It also tells how to use insurance and crime prevention for better risk management and how to deal with laws affecting small businesses. It also discusses social responsibility and acting ethically.

Following Part 5, there is a Workbook for Developing a Successful Business Plan. The Workbook provides a discussion of what a business plan is and how to develop your own business plan. Instructions on how to use the Workbook to develop your own plan, using the case provided, or developing your own case are discussed. This Workbook should help you apply what you have learned from studying the text.

Aids to Learning

The text, which was written with the "millennial generation" in mind, provides many insightful visuals, including photos, tables, figures, charts, checklists, and cartoons to illustrate the concepts discussed. Throughout, real-life examples are provided, with their websites in many cases. Important terms or concepts that are defined in the chapter are boldfaced in the text for easy recognition and then defined in the margins. These terms are listed in a Glossary at the end of the book.

Each chapter begins with relevant, thought-provoking quotations, along with numbered Learning Objectives that set the stage for what should be learned in the chapter. A Profile is then presented. It describes an actual business and its business owner and how she or he operates that illustrates and gives a vivid, hands-on sense of the material to be covered.

Features at the end of the chapters include a summary—called "What You Should Have Learned"—which is coordinated with the numbered Learning Objectives at the chapter's beginning to help review the text material; Questions to test mastery of the chapter; interesting Cases and Experiential Exercises that analyze, amplify, and apply the material learned.

We think the Seventh Edition of *Small Business Management* will stimulate your interest in owning or managing a small business. We hope you will identify with the individuals in the Profiles, examples, and Cases and through them and their experiences learn to be a better owner or manager of a small firm yourself.

To the Instructor

As an instructor, you will find this Seventh Edition of *Small Business Management: An Entrepreneur's Guidebook* easy and interesting to teach from.

The outstanding strengths of this Edition include its simple, clear, and concise conversational writing style, numerous and varied visuals, and numerous and relevant examples throughout the text to reinforce the basic ideas being presented. The prevailing current topics of interest to small business owners, such as global issues, improving and expanding quality, franchising, computer operations, the Internet—and the mind-boggling implications it poses for small businesses—taxes and government regulations, estate planning, ethics and social responsibility, how to prepare and present a meaningful business plan, risk management, e-commerce, and—of course—how to plan for and make a profit, are discussed in sufficient depth to be meaningful to you and your students, while still being concise and short enough to be interesting and quickly comprehended.

At the start of each chapter there are philosophical, thought-provoking quotations to pique students' interest in the main concepts presented in the chapter. Then, Learning Objectives prepare students for what they should learn from the material in the chapter. These objectives are coordinated by number with the chapter-ending summary, entitled "What You Should Have Learned." The Learning Objectives are followed by a Profile, which is a close-up view of a business and its owner(s) or manager(s). The Profile and "real-world" Cases in each chapter give helpful and colorful portraits of actual small businesses in operation. The Profiles feature actual business situations and events in small firms, although some are small businesses that have become large. The Profile provides the tone and focus for the chapter, including a grounding for what is to follow in entrepreneurs' actual experiences.

All chapters contain many visuals, including photographs, figures, tables, and—where they give an appropriate touch to discussions—cartoons. In the text, examples, illustrations, and real-life vignettes are set apart from the text in order to show students how the material they are learning has been applied to actual business situations. The most important words and/or phrases defined in the text are boldfaced for easy recognition and the definitions are highlighted in the margins. These terms are then listed in a Glossary at the end of the book. Voluminous endnotes provide authority for—and cite the sources of—the material discussed so that readers can get further information if they choose. The endnotes are grouped at the end of the book to prevent "clutter" on the text pages.

Several end-of-chapter features aid learning. We have mentioned the summaries, called "What You Should Have Learned," that are coordinated with the numbered Learning Objectives to provide for a better review of the material. Short-answer and review Questions for Discussion can be used for student assignments, class discussion, or quizzes. Finally, pertinent and interesting Cases and Experiential Exercises at the end of each chapter help students analyze the text material from the point of view of real-world situations.

To help you plan, teach, and evaluate your course, we have put together a valuable package of supplements that includes the following:

Instructor Supplements: Website at www.mhhe.com/megginson7e

The website includes the following password protected downloadable supplements:

- Instructor's Manual with Chapter Overviews containing teaching suggestions, lecture outlines, answers to discussion questions, and numbered Learning Objectives which are coordinated with the end-of-chapter Summary;

- Test Bank containing true/false, multiple choice, and short-answer questions with the correct answers provided and page references made where the subject is discussed in the text;

- PowerPoint slides containing an overview of key points as well as figures and tables from the book.

Small Business and Entrepreneurship Video DVD Volume 2 ISBN 0077267958

Each of the videos brings important concepts to life by taking viewers on a field trip of sorts to these companies and to hear directly from these entrepreneurs. A new full-length film, *Boom Productions,* is also included on the DVD, which follows four young, aspiring entrepreneurs as they conceptualize and launch their new venture. Meet Ezra, Maria, Jake, and Susan along with all of the other characters they encounter. The film can be shown in its entirety or in shorter segments, which are structured around the 5 C's model for developing a business plan (concept, customers, competition, competence, and cash). A complete study guide for use with the film is included on the book's website.

Student Supplements: Website at www.mhhe.com/megginson7e

The website includes the following supplments:

- Self-grading chapter quizzes;

- Business plan templates.

- **Business Plan Pro** (ISBN: 0077637720): Palo Alto's *Business Plan Pro* helps students with its wizard-based environment step-by-step through the creation of a professional business plan. Sixty-eight sample plans provide guidance for students as they complete and integrate financials, real-world forecasting tools. There is also a grading sheet, built-in research data, all in an SBA-approved document format. This is a great option for instructors who incorporate a quarter/semester-long business plan project into their course. Purchasing *Business Plan Pro* with this text offers students a substantial savings over the academic pricing of the same software.

Important Current Issues Facing Small Business People

We have discussed many topics with which small business owners and managers will be concerned. These include taxes and their payment; business laws; social responsibility and managerial ethics; marketing and global marketing; developing and presenting a business plan; and the use of technology.

We have discussed from a practical, applications-oriented point of view the issues of location and purchasing, especially in retailing and services; the expanding roles of small businesses; franchising; diverse groups; and sources of financing. Finally, the functional areas of any business operation are covered from a small business perspective. These features of the text discussion make this an excellent, up-to-date teaching tool, relevant to the twenty-first century's changing environments.

An innovative feature of this text is the Workbook for Developing a Successful Business Plan at the end of the book. It provides a hands-on guide for developing an actual business plan. This is in addition to the Sample Business Plan, which is an Appendix to Chapter 6.

Acknowledgments

We wish to give our sincere thanks to those who contributed suggestions, cases, profiles, and examples to the text. Where appropriate, recognition is shown by the sources at the end of each Case or Profile. Our thanks also go to the many teachers, entrepreneurs, managers, and professional people, who made contributions.

Helpful comments and contributions from colleagues around the country and the following reviewers are gratefully acknowledged: Roosevelt Martin Jr., Chicago State University; Owen S. Sevier, University of Central Oklahoma; Vincent Weaver, Greenville Technical College; Dennis R. Williams, Pennsylvania College of Technology; Mary Wall, Atlantic Cape Community College; Dennis I. Levy, Bergen Community College; David W. Crain, Whittier College; Karl Baehr, Emerson College; Chandler Atkins, PhD, Adirondack Community College; and Roosevelt Martin, Chicago State University.

We are pleased and grateful for the support and encouragement given to us by our spouses, Jerry Byrd and Joclaire Megginson. We want to give special thanks and sincere appreciation to Martin Smith and Benjamin Smith for their tireless research and helpful preparations of Chapters 14, 15 and 16 and technology issues.

Also, thanks go to Hillary Holmes and Cori Byrd, who coordinated the logistics involved in copying and shipping the material to Irwin/McGraw-Hill. They also assisted in preparing the text materials. A special thanks goes to Alisha Britnell for overall editing and verifying materials.

Suzanne Hagan, Joseph Payne, and Darrell Waldrup made a great contribution with their preparation of the Sample Business Plan, which appears as an Appendix to Chapter 6.

Not enough can be said about the excellent and professional preparation of the *Instructor's Manual* by Sharon Page, William Rainey Harper College. It should be of considerable assistance to teachers in presenting the text material.

We would also like to express our thanks and appreciation to our supportive colleagues and friends at McGraw-Hill/Irwin. Special thanks to our book team for this edition: Anke Weekes, sponsoring editor, Laura Hurst Spell, managing development editor, Jean Smith, developmental editor, and Melissa Leick, project manager.

Finally, we would like to offer our thanks to the following people from the University of Mobile: Dr. Mark Foley, President; Dr. Audrey Eubanks, Vice President for Academic Affairs; and Dr. Jane Finley, Dean of the School of Business.

If we can be of assistance to you in developing your course, please contact jbyrd@umobile.edu.

Mary Jane Byrd

Brief Contents

Contents

Chapter 6

Planning, Organizing, and Managing a Small Business   126

APPENDIX:

Chapter 7

How to Obtain the Right Financing for Your Business   178

Chapter 15

Budgeting and Controlling Operations and Taxes   386

The Dynamic Role of Small Business

We are constantly being involved with small business, for it is everywhere! When we think of "business," we may think of large corporations—such as Fortune 500 companies—but if you look around you, where you work and live, you will realize that the vast majority of businesses are small. Not only are these small businesses numerically significant; they are also important as employers, as providers of needed (and often unique) goods and services, and as sources of satisfaction to their owners, employees, and customers. For these and many other reasons, there is hardly anyone who has not at some time or other been tempted to start a small business.

Part 1 of this text is designed to show what is involved in forming and/or owning a small business. Thus, the material covered should help you decide whether pursuing a career in small business is the right course of action for you.

The growing importance of small business is covered in Chapter 1. Chapter 2 describes the need for planned management succession and discusses family and manager problems. Then, the more popular forms of ownership available to small businesses are presented in Chapter 3. Chapter 4 looks at the relationship with government agencies and discusses the need for social responsibility and ethical practices. ●

Starting Your Small Business

The good health and strength of America's small businesses are a vital key to health and strength of our economy. . . . Indeed, small business is America.
—**Former President Ronald Reagan**

Guts, brains, and determination—key ingredients of the American entrepreneurial spirit—[have] sustained this nation through good times and bad, and launched it on an economic journey unlike any ever witnessed in history.
—**John Sloan, Jr., President and CEO, National Foundation of Independent Business**

Learning Objectives

After studying the material in this chapter, you should be able to:

1. Define what is meant by the term *business.*

2. Name some of the unique contributions of *small business.*

3. Explain some of the current problems small businesses face.

4. Discuss some of the current trends challenging entrepreneurs and small business owners.

5. Explain why people start small businesses.

6. Describe the characteristics of successful entrepreneurs.

7. Describe where the opportunities are for small businesses.

8. Identify some of the areas of concern for small business owners.

Filters-NOW.com, Inc.
Corporate Office
9800 I-65 Service Rd. N.
Creola, AL 36525
251-342-5004

PROFILE

Filters-Now

Chad Summerlin could not find an air filter for his home. Well, he figured if he could not find what he needed, surely others were in the same situation. Chad saw a need and figured out how to fill it. There were no real vendors in the marketplace that sold odd-sized air filters for individual use except large chain stores, such as Home Depot and Lowes. If you found a vendor, they sold only in large bulk numbers. Chad and financial planner Ronald Allen decided that they could buy in bulk and resell over the Internet to satisfy consumer needs and make a little profit. They entered the Internet market with Filters-NOW just when the Internet bubble burst. This niche was hard to establish because people did not yet trust Internet companies with credit cards or other payment methods.

Ron and Chad shared the startup cost of the company. They chose not to use outside funding such as loans. The only overhead was the storage unit they rented to store the filters. They bought from bulk manufacturers, separated the units, and sold online from a U-Store-It warehouse. They then took on another partner who specialized in designing websites.

In the beginning Ron and Chad did everything by themselves. Phones calls were taken at Ron's personal business and work was done manually. They personally unloaded the trucks, mailed filters, and took orders. Later they hired a part-time retired friend to help unload and pack during the day. This job grew from 20 hours a week to 70 or more. This quickly led to hiring more part-time workers to fill demand.

Filters-NOW is a true Internet-based business. Although 3M told the founders they were "wasting time" by selling on Internet, Chad and Ron thought consumers would enjoy finding a better selection on the web than in stores. They also have a store on Amazon.com. Filters-NOW sends out marketing e-mails on occasion to different target groups of customers, both new and previous customers who have not purchased in a while and customers who purchase specific products. These marketing e-mails offer discounts such as free shipping and a discount code for 10 or 20 percent off.

The company uses a variety of websites to continue to dominate the market: www.filters-now.com, www.airfilterexpress.com, www.airfilters.com, Amazon.com, and eBay. Another channel of Internet marketing Ron and Chad use is Facebook and Twitter. New friends on Facebook get a discount code for "liking" them. There are also statuses or tweets about the activities of the company. For example, they will tweet about what the weather is like at their home at Creola, Alabama, what activities the employees are doing, and the public relations events the company sponsors. This summer as a company they participated in a 5k run in order to increase awareness for the company and to participate in events in the community. Also, for breast cancer awareness employees got pink hair extensions or feathers.

In 2004 the company decided to start manufacturing their own product in addition to buying and breaking bulk. Currently they produce own brand of custom-sized air filters called Accumulair. They produce and sell more than 17,000 products and employ close to 100 people. Twenty-one people work in the office and the rest are in production, shipping, and receiving. Their warehouse is 50,000 square feet for the plant with 15,000 square feet in offsite storage. Additional storage trailers are on site.

The Filters-NOW product line includes air filters, humidifier filters, purifier filters, vacuum filters, water filters, water bottle filters, swamp coolers, aquarium filters, whole house filters, grill filters, air purifier and humidifier units, and many more miscellaneous items.

Filters-NOW made their first sale on May 15, 2000. By the end of 2003 their sales totaled $2.8 million, and they are projected to close out 2011 at $18 million.

Source: Personal interview of Chad Summerlin, MBA, by Epsie Long, October 28, 2011.

You have probably never heard of Chad Summerlin. But you have heard of companies such as Walmart, Sears, McDonald's, Dell Inc., Intel, and Microsoft. All of them were started as small businesses by then-unknown entrepreneurs such as Sam Walton, Richard Sears, Ray Kroc, Michael Dell, Andrew Grove, and Bill Gates. By capitalizing on their imagination, initiative, courage, dedication, hard work, and—often—luck, these entrepreneurs turned an idea into a small struggling business that became a large, successful one.

Now it is your turn to see if you can start (or restart) your career as an entrepreneur—by converting an idea into a small business. According to Joseph Nebesky, who has served as an adviser to the U.S. Agency for International Development, the Small Business Administration (SBA) (www.sba.gov), and the National Council on the Aging, these small firms "are the backbone of the American economy." He is right: Firms with fewer than 500 employees employ 53 percent of the total private nonfarm workforce, contribute 47 percent of all sales in the country, are responsible for 51 percent of the gross domestic product, and produce around two out of every three new jobs each year. They also account for more than half of U.S. gross domestic product. In 2009, almost 10 million people were self-employed with another 140,000 unpaid family workers.

It's an Interesting Time to Be Studying Small Business

This is indeed an interesting, challenging, and rewarding time to be studying small business. Owning and operating such a firm is one of the best ways to fulfill the "great American dream," and many Americans believe this is one of the best paths to riches in the United States.

The following are some reasons for the increased interest in small business:

- The number of small businesses is growing rapidly.
- Small firms generate most new private employment.
- The public favors small business.
- There is increasing interest in small business entrepreneurship at high schools and colleges.
- There is a growing trend toward self-employment.
- Entrepreneurship is attractive to people of all ages.

The Number of Small Businesses Is Growing Rapidly

The development of small business in the United States is truly an amazing story. The value of goods and services they produce and the new jobs they generate make the small business sector one of the greatest economic powers in the world, accounting for trillions of dollars' worth of commerce annually. There are about 23 million small businesses in the United States. These organizations create 75 percent of the new jobs and employ 50 percent of the country's private workforce. They also represent more than 99 percent of all employers and 97 percent of exporters.[1] Forty percent of current new business owners are self-employed and do not hire any workers. Of the remaining 60 percent, only about two-thirds employ more than 20 people. In 2003 there were 1.9 men for every woman entrepreneur. Today's typical entrepreneur is young, male (ethnically diverse), between the ages of 25 to 34, and has specialty expertise. It is also interesting to note that 5 out of every 100 adults have invested in someone else's business within the last three years. In 2003 informal investors provided more than $100 billion to 3.5 million startup and small businesses.[2]

The Public Favors Small Business

Generally, small business owners and managers believe in the free enterprise system, with its emphasis on indivßidual freedom, risk taking, initiative, thrift, frugality, and hard work. Indications of interest in small business and entrepreneurship can be explained by the large number of magazines aimed at that market. These include older ones, such as *Black Enterprise* (www .blackenterprise.com), *Entrepreneur, Inc.,* and *Hispanic Business* (www.hispanicbusiness.com), and many new ones such as *Fortune Small Business* (www.fsb.com). Some of these journals are targeted for specific markets. *Family Business* targets family-owned businesses; *Entrepreneurial Woman* aims at female business owners; and *Your Company,* sent free by American Express (www.americanexpress.com) to the millions or more holders of its small business corporate card, targets small firms. Other journals include *Journal of Small Business Management, International Small Business Journal* (www.isb.sagepub.com), *New Business Opportunities,* and *Business Week Newsletter for Family-Owned Businesses* (www.businessweek.com). Please note that the *BusinessWeek* site requires registration and a fee in order to view the entire file.

Interest Is Increasing at High Schools, Colleges, and Universities

Another indication of the growing popularity of small business is its acceptance as part of the mission of many high schools, colleges, and universities, where entrepreneurship and small business management are now academically respected disciplines. Virtually unheard of 20 years ago, courses in entrepreneurship are now offered at hundreds of U.S. colleges. Many university classes explore startups and business plans. Today more students think self-employment is a safer haven than working for big corporations. As for universities, they have discovered that by teaching entrepreneurship they are able to tap into a vast pool of funds to support such programs.[3] One survey has indicated that even teens between the ages of 13 and 18 see business as an ideal job. Thirteen percent of males and 10 percent of females are already aiming toward a business career.[4]

The considerable interest at colleges and universities is shown by the formation of many student organizations to encourage entrepreneurship. For example, the Association of Collegiate Entrepreneurs (ACE), founded in 1983 at Wichita State University, now has hundreds of chapters throughout the world. Other organizations include the University Entrepreneurial Association (UEA) and Students in Free Enterprise (SIFE) (www.sife.org).

Community colleges, especially, are now offering courses for small business owners. One study found that 90 percent of community colleges offer such courses, while 75 percent of public community colleges also provide training courses. This activity is one of the

TABLE 1.1 | Self-Employed by Industry

Agriculture, forestry, fishing, hunting	47%
Construction	27
Professional business services	21
Financial activities	12
Wholesale and retail trade	9
Leisure and hospitality	8
Education and health services	5[a]

[a]Richard A. Greenwald, "Solo Support," *The Wall Street Journal*, February 14, 2011, p. R8.

Source: U.S. Census Bureau, *Statistical Abstract of the United States: 2011* (130th ed.). Washington, DC, 2010, p. 387, table 604.

fastest-growing areas in the community college field. Many colleges and universities are now offering specialized business courses, such as programs in family business, franchising, and international operations, as well as job fairs and career days.

Trend Is toward Self-Employment

The growth rate for self-employment is greater than the growth rate of the general workforce.

In 2009 about 15.3 million or 11 percent of all U.S. workers were self-employed.[5] In 2011, however, there was a slight decline to about 14.5 million self-employed workers. Analysts attribute this slight dip to the recession.[6] Entrepreneurs are also feeling the economic funk. In 2010 there were about 500,000 new ventures that were only open less than one year.[7]

Working for oneself is a dream come true for many. Technology is available to help so many of us own and operate our businesses. Table 1.1 illustrates the number of self-employed by industry.[8]

Small business grew rapidly from the mid-1980s to the mid-1990s as investors became more willing to assume the risk of starting or revitalizing small businesses. Many of these were middle-aged executives from large corporations who were eager to put their management skills to work in reviving smaller companies in aging industries.

Real-World Example 1.1

William Zinke retired in his early sixties from a very demanding job in New York. He moved to Colorado to slow the pace of his life and created the nonprofit Center for Production Longevity (www.ctrpl.org). Now at the age of eighty he is still working and says that he "is fortunate to own his own business and to be able to set his own work schedule."[9]

This trend is still alive. For example, a national poll found that 55 percent of us want to be our own boss. Advances in technology have helped make this dream come true.[10] For example, there has been tremendous growth in the Internet and biotechnology industries, and they have attracted record amounts of venture capital financing.[11]

Entrepreneurship Is Attractive to All Ages

Entrepreneurship knows no age limits! From the very young to the very old, people are starting new businesses at a rapid rate. Particularly heartening is the large number of young people who are entrepreneurs. For example, 15-year-old Laima Tazmin is president of

LAVT LLC, a Web consulting company. She customizes computers and develops community-based online businesses. Laima turned her love for computers into a business plan that initially won a regional competition and then, with a few changes, won her top notch as "Young Entrepreneur" in a contest sponsored by Fleet Bank. This prize netted her $25,000 and broad media exposure. Laima says "Entrepreneurship is about planning for the future. . . . I want to grow myself."[12]

Real-World Example 1.2

Age is not a requirement for success in starting small businesses. Megan Crump is a good example of a young entrepreneur. At age seven she found an exciting way to make money. After a successful evening of trick-or-treating, Megan took all her candy to school and sold it to her schoolmates for a handsome profit of $3 the first day and $1 the second day. She later held a yard sale where, among other things, she sold her sister's used bicycle for $9. The resourcefulness of youngsters such as Megan should continue to stimulate our economy well into the twenty-first century.[13]

College entrepreneurs find many areas for opening a business. These include reselling textbooks, importing and selling crafts from home, renting mini fridges and microwaves, dorm cleaning services, and transportation. The most difficult problem for these students to solve is what to do with their business after they graduate.

Older people are also involved in forming new companies, as small businesses offer the most opportunities and flexibility to retirees or those terminated from their regular employment. For example, after spending 20 years climbing the corporate ladder, Andrea Papa was laid off in March 2001. With little severance pay and no future income, she started her own media and marketing consulting firm. Now she is at home to welcome her son home from school.[14]

Several states now have the Self-Employment Assistance (SEA) program. This lets people launch their new business while collecting state unemployment checks. Currently SEA is offered in New York, New Jersey, Oregon, Washington, and Maine. About 2,000 are now in the program, which has a federal cap of 5 percent.

Real-World Example 1.3

Rose Rios started a medical communications and market research company named KOLComm LLC after losing her previous job. She started her business at home where she was able to both care for her new baby and develop her software. She has brought in over $2.5 million and employs three full-time people as well as outsourcing to freelancers.[15]

Twenty-something entrepreneurs know no fear. This group believes "failure" is relative, and if you fail—learn from it—the lesson can speed you up the ladder of the next venture.

More and more seasoned professionals, unemployed due to layoffs or early retirement, are turning to creating small businesses they can manage from home. This allows them to spend more time with their families.

Real-World Example 1.4

Jeremy Kahn and Henry Rich noticed that every time someone needed a cigarette the phrase "oral fixation" came up. One thing led to another and Oral Fixation Mints were born. This wacky idea has produced sleek tins of candy that can be purchased at Miami's Mandarin Oriental Hotel and New York City's Whitney Museum of Modern Art.

It is interesting to note that more than half of the million-plus independent workers in New York City are usually college educated and are 25 to 40 years old.[16] A recent survey of small business owners reinforces the boldness of new entrepreneurs. Eighty-four percent of those polled are certain they have properly planned for their businesses' future needs. They are "not worried about the future."[17]

Many groups, such as the American Association of Retired Persons (AARP) (www.aarp.org), colleges, and private consultants now offer classes—and, more important, support groups—specifically for retirement-aged potential and actual entrepreneurs. Also, 40 percent of those who form new businesses each year already have some management experience, and one-fourth of them have managed or owned a business before.

A word of caution is needed at this point. If you start a business, you cannot just "turn it on and off" like a light switch; that is, you cannot take time off whenever you want. If your business is to succeed, you cannot shut down for holidays or vacations or when things are not going well. As one discouraged small business owner said at a recent conference, "A small business is wonderful: You only have to work half a day—and you get to choose which 12 hours it is that you will work!"

Defining Small Business—No Easy Task

Now that we have seen how much interest there is in small business, what *is* small business? There is no simple definition, but let's look at some definitions that are frequently used.

What Is Small?

At first, this question appears easy to answer. Many places of business that you patronize—such as independent neighborhood grocery stores, fast-food restaurants, hair stylists, dry cleaners, video or music shops, and the veterinarian—are examples of small businesses.

Qualitative factors are also important in describing small businesses. To be classified as "small," *a small business must have at least two of the following features:*

• Management is independent, because the manager usually owns the business.

• Capital is supplied and ownership is held by an individual or a few individuals.

• The area of operations is primarily local, although the market is not necessarily local.

• The business is small in comparison with the larger competitors in its industry.

Perhaps the best definition of small business is the one used by Congress in the Small Business Act of 1953, which states that *a small business is one that is independently owned and operated and is not dominant in its field of operation.* We'll use that definition in this text, unless otherwise indicated.

As will be shown in Chapter 7, the SBA, for loan purposes, uses different size criteria by industry. In general, however, it uses the size classification shown in Table 1.2. In Europe small firms are considered different from country to country. In the European Union (EU), about 34 percent of the workforce is employed in firms with 10 or fewer employees.[18]

Distinguishing between Entrepreneurial Ventures and Small Businesses

We also need to distinguish between small businesses and entrepreneurial ventures. The rapidity of the rate of growth of a business is one useful way to distinguish between small business owners and entrepreneurs.

An **entrepreneurial venture** is one in which the principal objectives of the entrepreneur are profitability and growth. Thus, the business is characterized by innovative strategic practices and/or products. The entrepreneurs and their financial backers are usually seeking rapid growth, immediate—and high—profits, and a quick sellout with (possibly) large capital gains.

A **small business,** sometimes called a micro business, on the other hand, is any business that is independently owned and operated and is not dominant in its field. It may never grow large, and the owners may not want it to, as they prefer a more relaxed and less aggressive approach to running the business. They manage their business in a normal way, expecting normal sales, profits, and growth. In other words, they seek a certain degree of freedom and—ideally—a certain degree of financial independence.

These businesses are often run from the owner's home. They account for more than 60 percent of the nation's 5.6 million employers and more than $100 billion in annual spending.[19] A survey in 1999 found that 1 in 12 adults was trying to found a new business.[20]

It is not always easy to distinguish between a small business owner and an entrepreneur; the distinction hinges on their intentions. In general, a **small business owner** establishes a business for the principal purpose of furthering personal goals, which *may* include

In an **entrepreneurial venture,** the principal objectives of the owner are profitability and growth.

A **small business** is independently owned and operated and is not dominant in its field.

A **small business owner** establishes a business primarily to further personal goals, including making a profit.

TABLE 1.2 | Classification of Business by Size, According to SBA

Under 20 employees	Very small
20–99	Small
100–499	Medium
500 or more	Large

Source: Small Business Administration.

making a profit. Thus, the owner may perceive the business as being an extension of his or her personality, which is interwoven with family needs and desires. On the other hand, the **entrepreneur** starts and manages a business for many reasons, including achievement, profit, and growth. Such a person is characterized principally by innovative behavior and will employ strategic management practices in the business. Of course, the owner's intentions sometimes change, and what started out as a small business may become an entrepreneurial venture.

Some Unique Contributions of Small Business

As indicated throughout this chapter, small firms differ from their larger competitors. Let's look at some major contributions made by small businesses that set them apart from larger firms. Smaller firms tend to:

- Encourage innovation and flexibility.
- Maintain close relationships with customers and the community.
- Keep larger firms competitive.
- Provide employees with comprehensive learning experience.
- Develop risk takers.
- Generate new employment.
- Provide greater employee job satisfaction.

Encourage Innovation and Flexibility

Smaller businesses are often sources of new ideas, materials, processes, and services that larger firms may be unable or reluctant to provide. In small businesses, experiments can be conducted, innovations initiated, and new operations started or expanded. In fact, small firms produce 55 percent of all innovations,[21] and in 2009 there were 191,900 patents issued by the U.S. Patent and Trademark Office.[22] It is interesting to note that the United States leads the globe in patent applications.[23] If we apply the 55 percent innovation rate, we can say that more than 105,500 patents were issued to small businesses. This trend is especially true in the computer field, where most initial developments have been carried on in small companies.

Real-World Example 1.5

For example, it is no coincidence that IBM did not produce the first electronic computer, as it already owned 97 percent of the then-popular punched-card equipment, which the computer would tend to make obsolete. Instead, the Univac was conceived and produced by a small firm formed by John Mauchly and J. Presper Eckert. However, while they were design experts, they lacked production and marketing skills, so they sold out to Remington Rand, which controlled the remaining 3 percent of the punched-card business. Thus, the first giant computers at organizations such as the U.S. Census Bureau and General Electric's Appliance Park in Kentucky in January 1954 were Univacs. Nonetheless, IBM's marketing expertise overcame Remington's production expertise, and IBM soon dominated the computer industry.

Also, it is no coincidence that two design geniuses, Steven Jobs (age 21) and Steve Wozniak (age 19) essentially started the PC industry by founding Apple Computer in 1976 with capital obtained by selling Job's Volkswagen microbus and Wozniak's Hewlett-Packard scientific calculator. And Michael Dell (age 19) started Dell Inc. by selling computer parts from his dorm room at the University of Texas. He started out to "make it big."

Maintain Close Relationship with Customers and Community

Small businesses tend to be in close touch with their communities and customers. They can do a more individualized job than big firms can, thereby attracting customers on the basis of specialty products, quality, and personal services rather than solely on the basis of price. While competitive prices and a reputation for honesty are important, an atmosphere of friendliness makes people feel good about patronizing the business and encourages them to continue shopping there.

There are more than 1,600 Main Street programs (mainstreet.org). These programs are designed to encourage community revitalization, economic development, historic preservation, and downtown revitalization. Each year the National Trust for Historic Preservation recognizes only five cities as winners. One eye opener was when one small community was ready to give up when Walmart opened; instead, they all pulled together and were able to compete—and survive—by providing better customer service and products that were unique.

Real-World Example 1.6

For example, Mike and Carol Hamilton's Chutters General Store (chutters.com) has 111 feet of candy jars, making them the home of the world's largest candy counter according to the *Guiness Book of World Records*. Their store is one of the stars in Littleton, NH, which received the 2003 Great American Main Street Award.[24]

Keep Larger Firms Competitive

Smaller companies have become a controlling factor in the American economy by keeping the bigger concerns on their toes. With the introduction of new products and services, small businesses encourage competition, if not in price, then at least in design and efficiency, as happened in the area of California now called Silicon Valley, where the personal computer was developed.

Provide Employees with Comprehensive Learning Experience

A small business provides employees with a variety of learning experiences not open to individuals holding more specialized jobs in larger companies. Along with performing a greater variety of functions, small business employees also have more freedom to make decisions, which can lend zest and interest to their work experience. Small businesses train people to become better leaders and managers and to develop their talents and energies more effectively. This reality has led more college graduates to seek full-time jobs with small businesses, according to a survey by the National Association of Colleges and Employers. The reason for this trend is that small companies "tend to offer broader experiences because of their small staffs." Thus, employees "get more responsibility, more quickly," according to one graduate applicant.

Develop Risk Takers

Small businesses provide one of the basic American freedoms—risk taking, with its consequent rewards and punishments. Small business owners have relative freedom to enter or leave a business at will, to start small and grow big, to expand or contract, and to succeed or fail, which is the basis of our free enterprise system. Yet founding a business in an uncertain environment is risky, so much planning and study must be done before startup.

Generate New Employment

As repeatedly emphasized throughout this chapter, small businesses generate employment by creating job opportunities. Small firms also serve as a training ground for employees, who, because of their more comprehensive learning experience, their emphasis on risk taking, and their exposure to innovation and flexibility, become valued employees of larger companies.

> **Real-World Example 1.7**
>
> According to Brynn Albretsen (profile, Chapter 5), "The best advice I can give as to how to start your own business: Be a student, always. Continue to learn new things, try new things, read new things, and stay current on business and technology. Be a sponge and learn as much as you can from those around you, teachers, business professionals, and others. Take off the blinders, do not get stuck in a rut of 'this is how it has always been done,' make a concerted effort to see things from different perspectives and challenge yourself to think outside the box."

Provide Greater Job Satisfaction

Small companies also provide greater employee job satisfaction. For example, an *Inc.*/Gallup survey of American workers found that employees in smaller workplaces have higher job satisfaction than those in larger firms. But the greatest satisfaction comes to those who own their own workplaces.

Some Current Problems Facing Small Businesses

Just as small companies make unique contributions, there are special problems that affect them more than larger businesses. These problems can result in limited profitability and growth, the decision to voluntarily close the business, or financial failure.

There is a great deal of conflicting data on the failure rate of small businesses. Most statistics err on the optimistic side, which can be explained by the huge number of small businesses that never make it into the reporting system. Today, the biggest worries facing small business owners, according to a 2003 survey, are:

- Recession/current economic issues.
- Retirement or transition.
- Capital or financing issues.
- Unexpected growth.
- Succession.[25]

Over time we see repeated areas that create problems for small business owners and entrepreneurs. These areas include inadequate financing, inadequate management, and burdensome government regulations and paperwork.

Inadequate Financing

In the preceding list, inadequate financing is the primary cause of new business failure. *It cannot be stressed enough that a shortage of capital is the greatest problem facing small business owners.* Without adequate funds, the small business owner is unable to acquire and maintain facilities, hire and reward capable employees, produce and market a product, or do the other things necessary to run a successful business.

Inadequate Management

Inadequate management—in the forms of limited business knowledge, poor management, inadequate planning, and inexperience—is the second problem facing small firms. Many owners tend to rely on one-person management and seem reluctant to vary from this managerial pattern. They tend to guard their position very jealously and may not select qualified employees, or may fail to give them enough authority and responsibility to manage adequately. Most small businesses are started because someone is good at a specific activity or trade, not because she or he has managerial skill.

Managers of small firms must be generalists rather than specialists. Because they must make their own decisions and then live with those choices, managers are faced with a dilemma. Because the business's resources are limited, it cannot afford to make costly mistakes; yet because the organization is so small, the owner cannot afford to pay for managerial assistance to prevent bad decisions.

Burdensome Government Regulations and Paperwork

If you want to upset small business managers, just mention government regulations and paperwork. That is one of their least favorite subjects—and with good reason. At one time, smaller firms were exempt from many federal regulations and even some state and local ones. Now, small firms are subject to many of the same regulations as their larger competitors. These regulations are often complex and contradictory, which explains why small business managers find it so difficult to comply with governmental requirements. While most businesspeople do not purposely evade the issues or disobey the law, they are often unaware of all pertinent regulations and requirements. As will be shown in Chapter 4, however, small businesses often benefit from many of these regulations.

Some Current Trends Challenging Small Business Owners

Small firms, like large ones, are now experiencing fundamental changes and new trends in the way business is conducted and people are being employed. If small businesses are to overcome the problems just discussed, they must be prepared to recognize and cope with

FIGURE 1.1 | Declining Job Types by 2018

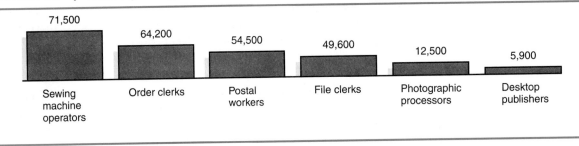

Source: BLS Occupational Employment Statistics and Division of Occupational Outlook Handbook, 2010–2011 Edition (www.bls.gov).

current trends that are potentially rewarding but that will challenge them and require their best performance. The most important trends are exploding technology, occupational and industry shifts, and global challenges.

Exploding Technology

Few jobs in small firms are unaffected by improvements in communications and computer technology. Small business management is being drastically changed as automated robotics are introduced in production departments, as accounting departments become heavily dependent on computer support, and as marketing people use computer-aided promotional and sales programs.

The primary challenge of exploding technology for small companies will be to improve the selection and training of workers and overcome their resistance to change. Therefore, owners and managers must keep up to date themselves on the latest technologies so they can effectively train their people to use these technologies, including telecommuting. Chapter 15 will introduce you to many examples of computer software and new technology available for the small business owner. According to the Office of Advocacy, U.S. Small Business Administration, 38 percent of all jobs in the high-tech sector are through small business.[26] Figure 1.1 projects the areas of decline for the next five years.

Occupational and Industry Shifts

Technological advances in automation, computers, robotics, and electronic communication, along with changing markets resulting from cultural, demographic, and economic changes, have affected traditional "smokestack" industries. These changes have caused a concurrent shift toward more people-related activities to which small business enterprise is exceptionally well suited, such as health care, banking and financial services, retail trade, transportation, and computer services.

Among these shifts, **reinvention,** particularly including a reduction in the size and markets for businesses, has led to fewer job opportunities for those who are less well-trained and educated. At the same time, many larger companies have **reengineered** their activities, which has involved wiping the slate clean as far as current operations are concerned and asking, "If we blew this place up and started over, what would we do differently? What should we eliminate? What can we do that would make things easier for our customer?" The result is **downsizing** (sometimes called **rightsizing**), whereby an organization reduces the number of people it employs as it strives to become leaner and meaner and consolidates departments and work groups.

Reinvention is the fundamental redesign of a business, often resulting in reduction in size and markets.

Reengineering is the redesign of operations, starting from scratch.

Downsizing (rightsizing) is reducing the number of employees to increase efficiency.

This movement is giving people more responsibility for making decisions and the chance to escape acting like automatons—but they must work harder, and they are under more pressure. *These shifts help smaller firms, as many highly skilled workers and managers leave to join the ranks of small business owners and managers.*

Global Challenges

The trend in business is to become more active globally, and those interested in small business management need to understand at least what the challenge is and what the rewards may be. We are entering an age of global competition and a one-world market. Consequently, *we estimate that up to half of all today's college graduates will work in some type of global activities in the future.* Small businesses today represent 96 percent of all U.S. exporters.[27]

One result of this global challenge is the growing number of large and small U.S. businesses that are or become foreign owned. These foreign-owned companies tend to have different management styles from their original American owners, which means small business owners and managers must learn to adjust and adapt to nontraditional styles. While foreign ownership may lead to new management styles, the American consumer may not realize the change.

Real-World Example 1.8

At one time, for example, few Americans knew or cared that consumer products for sale with RCA and GE brand names were owned by a French company, Thompson S.A. Magnavox and Sylvania were owned by Philips Electronics of The Netherlands, and Quasar was made by Japan's Matsushita Electric Industries. Even Zenith, the last television sets to be "Made in America," are made in South Korea by L. G. Electronics. But it really doesn't seem to make that much difference to consumers.

Why People Start Small Businesses

One cause of the explosion of new entrepreneurs is the current trend of today's corporate professionals who leave their large companies to start their own businesses. The changing environment in large firms is leaving employees frustrated and uncertain about their future. Thus, they leave to find a better job or—as many are now doing—to start their own company, using the expertise they learned at the larger firm.

As these employees who go out on their own are aware, owning a small business provides an excellent opportunity to satisfy personal objectives while achieving the firm's business objectives. Probably in no other occupation or profession is this as true. But there are almost as many different reasons for starting small businesses as there are small business owners. However, those reasons can be summarized as (1) satisfying personal objectives and (2) achieving business objectives.

Satisfy Personal Objectives

Small business owners have the potential to fulfill many personal goals. In fact, owning a small business tends to satisfy most of our work goals. According to a survey by Padgett Business Services USA Inc. (www.smallbizpros.com), the best things about owning a small business are independence (cited by 72 percent of those surveyed), control (10 percent), satisfaction (10 percent), and other factors (8 percent). The worst parts of such ownership are the long hours (mentioned by 23 percent of respondents), taxes (22 percent), risk (17 percent), responsibility (17 percent), and other factors (12 percent).

Similar results were found in a study by the National Bureau of Economic Research in Great Britain, where 46 percent of the self-employed were "very satisfied," versus 29 percent of those working for others. In the United States, the numbers were 63 percent versus 27 percent. Victoria Neal said, "It is our youth who've happened upon the realization that they would be a heck of a lot better off just working for themselves."[28]

The personal objectives of owners of small businesses differ from those of managers of larger firms. Managers of large companies tend to seek security, place, power, prestige, high income, and benefits. By contrast, the primary objectives of small business owners are as follows:

- Achieve independence.
- Obtain additional income.
- Help their families.
- Provide products not available elsewhere.

In summary, the personal objectives of small business owners tend to be achievement oriented, as opposed to those of managers of large firms, who tend to be power and prestige oriented. How these personal objectives are achieved depends on the knowledge, skills, and personal traits these owners bring to the business. A good checklist for aspiring entrepreneurs according to Duncan Cheatle of the U.K. includes these thoughts:

- Do it for passion not money.
- Do something you know about.
- Don't give up too early.
- Have a mentor.
- Have appropriate funding.
- Be a good cash manager.
- Build sales first.
- Don't try to rush.
- Be wary of bad advice or suppliers.[29]

Achieve Independence   The new business owner's primary motive is usually independence, that is, freedom from interference or control by superiors. Small business owners tend to want autonomy to exercise their initiative and ambition; this freedom often results in innovations and leads to greater flexibility, which is one of the virtues of small businesses. People who operate small firms know they are running a risk when they strike out on their own, but they hope to realize their goal of independence. In essence, owning your own business provides a feeling of satisfaction that may be missing if you work for someone else. As you can see from Figure 1.2, this is the choice the prospective entrepreneur must make.

Obtain Additional Income   Many people start a business to obtain needed income. This need obviously varies with different people in different life stages or situations. For example, a retired person may want to earn just enough to supplement Social Security payments

FIGURE 1.2 |
Which Road to Take?

and possibly provide a few luxuries. Such a person may be content with a business that provides a small supplement to retirement income.

On the other hand, owning a business can provide the opportunity to make a great deal of money and to take advantage of certain tax benefits. (You should consult your lawyers and tax accountants, though, to make sure you stay on the right side of tax laws, which have been modified to remove many of these benefits.) Not all small business owners and managers make a lot of money, nor do they all intend to.

As we said at the outset, people sometimes start small businesses after being unable to find employment elsewhere or after being discharged from a larger firm. Professional athletes, whose bodies are a wasting asset and who must retire early, often find a second career in small businesses they have formed. For example, Earvin "Magic" Johnson, the former Los Angeles Lakers star player, has invested in inner cities that have been ignored or abandoned by other entrepreneurs. His Magic Johnson Theaters have created at least 100 new jobs at each of their locations in Atlanta, Houston, New York, Ohio, and Los Angeles. His mission is "to revitalize the underserved communities." The result has been one of the highest-grossing theater complexes in the nation. This group has now merged with AMC Entertainment, Inc., to create a combined total of 185 years of successful operations.

Help Their Families   Small business owners are probably motivated as much by personal and family considerations as by the desire for profit. Students may return home to operate the family business so their parents can retire or take life easier. They may take over the firm on the death of a parent or form a business to help their family financially. According to a recent study, there are over 1 million women-led businesses generating in excess of $300 billion in revenues, or about 3 percent of the U.S. Gross National Product. These companies play a big role in providing flextime, allowing mothers to be "stay at home moms."

Provide Products Not Available Elsewhere   The saying "Necessity is the mother of invention" applies to the beginning of many small firms. In fact, most American economic development has resulted from innovations born in small firms. Relative to the number of people employed, small firms produce two-and-a-half times as many new ideas and products as large firms. The first air conditioner, airplane, automobile, instant camera, jet engine, helicopter, office copier, heart pacemaker, foam fire extinguisher, quick-frozen foods, sliced and wrapped bread, vacuum tube, zipper, and safety razor—not to mention the first giant computer, as well as many other breakthroughs—either resulted from the creativity found in small companies or led to the creation of a new business, as the following example illustrates.

Real-World Example 1.9

Lloyd Mandel recognized a need for more economical funerals. As most funeral homes began to offer more services, such as expensive seals and elaborate ceremonies, he identified a growing need for basic rituals. Mandel opened such a "funeral store" in a Skokie, Illinois, mall 12 years ago.

He was so successful that he was bought out by the huge Service Corporation International (SCI). He is now a regional vice president who does research and similar ventures for Service Corp.

Achieve Business Objectives

Objectives are the goals toward which the activities of the business are directed.

One of the most important functions any business owner must perform is setting **objectives,** which are the ends toward which all the activities of the company should be aimed. Essentially, objectives determine the character of the firm because they give the business its direction and provide standards by which to measure individual performance.

Among the objectives that are important to a business are service, profit, social, and growth objectives. These objectives tend to be interrelated. For example, the service objective must be achieved to attain the profit objective. Yet profits must be made if the business is to continue to reach its social and service objectives. Growth depends on attaining both profit *and* social objectives, which are not necessarily incompatible.

Service Objective In general, the objective of a business is to serve customers by producing and selling goods or services (or the satisfactions associated with them) at a cost that will ensure a fair price to the consumer and adequate profits for the owners. Thus, a person who aspires to operate a small business *must set service as the primary objective— but seek to make a profit as a natural consequence.* The pragmatic test for a small firm is this: If the firm ceases to give service, it will go out of business; if there are no profits, the owners will cease operations.

Profit is the revenue received by a business in excess of the expenses paid.

Profit Objective **Profit** is the revenue received by a business in excess of the expenses paid. We expect a private business to receive a profit from its operations because profit is acceptable in a free-enterprise economy and is considered to be in the public interest. Simply stated, the **profit motive** is entering a business to make a profit, which is the reward for taking risks. Profits are not self-generating, however; goods or services must be produced

The **profit motive** is expecting to make a profit as the reward for taking the risk of starting and running the business.

at a cost low enough to permit the firm to make a profit while charging customers a price they are willing and able to pay.

Profits, then, are the reward for accepting business risks and performing an economic service. They are needed to ensure the continuity of a business.

Social objectives are goals regarding assisting groups in the community and protecting the environment.

Social Objective   As will be discussed further in Chapter 4, successful small businesses must have **social objectives,** which means helping various groups in the community, including customers, employees, suppliers, the government, and the community itself. Even small firms have a responsibility to protect the interest of all parties as well as to make a profit. Profit and social objectives are not necessarily incompatible.

Growth Objective   Owners of small firms should be concerned with growth and should select a growth objective, which will depend on answers to questions such as: "Will I be satisfied for my business to remain small?", "Do I want it to grow and challenge larger firms?", and "Do I seek a profit that is only 'satisfactory,' considering my effort and investment, or do I seek to maximize profits?"

Need to Mesh Objectives

Personal and business objectives can be integrated in a small business. In fact, there is often a close connection between profitability, customer satisfaction, manager satisfaction, and nonfinancial rewards. Also there is an increased chance of success when the objectives of the business—service at a profit—are meshed with the owner's personal objectives.

Characteristics of Successful Entrepreneurs

The abilities and personal characteristics of the owner(s) exert a powerful influence on the success of a small company. Also, the methods and procedures adopted in a small firm should be designed not only to offset any personal deficiencies the owner may have but also to build on his or her strengths.

A recent study found that almost one-third of all U.S. millionaires are entrepreneurs or business owners. And 57 percent indicate that the most important factors leading to their success were "being honest with all people" and "being well disciplined."[30] Another characteristic of successful entrepreneurs is persistence. For example, the National Federation of Independent Business found that 16 percent of new business owners had been in business before. In fact, nearly 10 percent of them had had six or more operations.[31] Finally, even though the year 2000 was not a very prosperous time in the United States, nearly 1 out of every 10 Americans (9.8 percent) tried to start a business during the year.[32]

Entrepreneurship is not limited to the United States. In fact, the United States ranks second in the world. The top 10 best countries for entrepreneurs include

1. New Zealand
2. United States
3. Canada
4. Australia
5. Singapore
6. Hong Kong
7. Britain
8. Ireland
9. Denmark
10. Iceland[33]

From these and many other sources, we conclude that the characteristics of successful owners of small businesses are that they

- Desire independence.
- Have a strong sense of initiative.
- Are motivated by personal and family considerations.
- Expect quick and concrete results.
- Are able to react quickly.
- Are dedicated to their businesses.
- Enter business as much by chance as by design.

Desire Independence

As shown earlier in the chapter, those people who start small businesses seek independence and want to be free of outside control. They enjoy the freedom that comes from "doing their own thing" and making their own decisions—for better or for worse.

Have a Strong Sense of Initiative

Owners of small businesses have a strong sense of initiative that gives them a desire to use their ideas, abilities, and aspirations to the greatest degree possible. They are able to conceive, plan, and carry to a successful conclusion ideas for a new product. This is not always true in a larger organization.

Another aspect of initiative usually seen in small business owners is their willingness to work long, hard hours to reach their goals. They tend to be capable, ambitious, persevering individuals.

Are Motivated by Personal and Family Considerations

As shown earlier, small business owners are often motivated as much by personal and family considerations as by the profit motive. They start and operate their businesses to help their parents, children, and other family members. The flexibility afforded small business owners is a great advantage in planning family activities.

There now seems to be a trend toward children helping their parents—financially and otherwise—by putting them on their payroll. We will discuss this trend further in Chapter 2. This trend builds on the past practice of parents helping their children. As society enjoys longer healthier lives, many retirees are looking for new challenges and sometimes new careers.

Expect Quick and Concrete Results

Small business owners expect quick and concrete results from their investment of time and capital. Instead of engaging in the long-range planning that is common in large businesses, they seek a quick return on their capital, and they become impatient and discouraged when these results are slow in coming.

Are Able to React Quickly

Small businesses have an advantage over larger firms in that they can react more quickly to changes occurring both inside and outside the company. For example, one characteristic of a small business is its vulnerability to technological and environmental changes. Because the business is small, such changes have a great effect on its operations and profitability. A small business owner must therefore have the ability to react quickly. Also, we are experiencing a "Fifth" migration to new regions. These are bedroom communities within commuting distance to large urban areas. Services follow these moves and create many needs such as house cleaning, day care, and transportation.

Are Dedicated to Their Businesses

Small business owners tend to be fiercely dedicated to their companies. With so much time, energy, money, and emotions invested in it, they want to ensure that nothing harms their "baby." Consequently, they have a zeal, devotion, and ardor often missing in managers of big companies.

Enter Business as Much by Chance as by Design

An interesting characteristic of many small business owners is that they get into business as much by chance as by design. These are the owners who quite frequently ask for assistance in the form of management training and development. This type of individual differs sharply from those who attend college with the ambition to become professional managers and who gear their programs toward that end.

> **Real-World Example 1.10**
>
> For example, 17-year-old Levi Strauss emigrated from Bavaria to America in 1847. After peddling clothing and household items from door to door in New York for three years, he sailed by clipper ship to California with a load of denim to make tents for gold miners. There was little demand for tents but great demand for durable working clothes, so the ever-adaptable Strauss had a tailor make the unsold cloth into waist-high overalls, called them "Levi's," and was in business (www.levistrauss.com).[34]

What Leads to Success in Managing a Small Business?

Although it is difficult to determine precisely what leads to success in managing a small business, the following are some important factors:

- Serving an adequate and well-defined market for the product.
- Acquiring sufficient capital.
- Recruiting and using human resources effectively.
- Obtaining and using timely information.
- Coping effectively with government regulations.
- Having expertise in the field on the part of both the owner and the employees.
- Being flexible.

Doing an Introspective Personal Analysis

Now that you have seen some characteristics of successful small business owners, do you think you have enough of those characteristics to be successful? The following personal evaluation will help you decide this important question. None of these items is more important than any other; rather, you need to determine whether the combination of qualities you have will help you succeed as a small business owner:

- Analyze your values.
- Analyze your mental abilities.
- Analyze your attitudes.

Where Are the Opportunities for Small Business?

Up to this point, we have shown you the challenges of becoming an entrepreneur and explained the requirements for succeeding as the owner of a small business. Now it is time to explain what your opportunities are.

What Are the Fastest-Growing Industries?

Most of the growing industries are dominated by small private companies. According to the SBA's Office of Advocacy (www.sba.gov), only construction and personnel/supply services tend to be dominated by larger businesses.

Professional and related occupations are expected to have 11.9 million job openings generated by 2018 closely followed by services at 7.6 million. The occupation with the fastest growth overall is health care. With advances in technology, many tasks are now performed by lower-paid workers such as assistants and aides. About 24 percent of all new jobs will be in the health care industry (see Figure 1.3).[35]

Factors Affecting the Future of an Industry or a Business

Many changes are now occurring that will affect the future of an industry or business, and small business owners should study them intently in order to adjust to them. These changes can cause slow-growing industries to speed up or fast-growing ones to slow down. For instance, one recent study found that the more professional technicians or other "knowledge workers" an industry has, the greater the chance that it will create new jobs. The study defined such **high-knowledge industries** as those in which 40 percent or more of workers are high-knowledge workers.[36]

High-knowledge industries are those in which 40 percent or more of human resources are professionals, technicians, or other "knowledge workers."

Another important reality to consider is that a change that provides an opportunity for one industry or business may pose a threat to others. For example, aging of the population may increase the need for retirement facilities but hurt industries supplying baby needs.

Figure 1.4 shows some selected examples of factors that affect various industries and businesses. These factors will be discussed in Chapters 5 and 6.

FIGURE 1.3 |
Where the New Jobs Will Be

These industries are expected to produce the most new jobs by the year 2018.

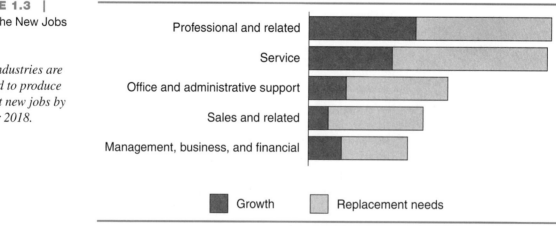

Source: U.S. Department of Labor, Bureau of Labor Statistics, www.bls.gov, accessed September 29, 2011.

FIGURE 1.4 |

Examples of Factors Affecting Industry and Business Trends

1. *Economics*—gross national product (GNP), interest rates, inflation rates, stages of the business cycle, employment levels, size and characteristics of business firms and not-for-profit organizations, and opportunities in foreign markets.

2. *Technology*—artificial intelligence, thinking machines, laser beams, new energy sources, amount of spending for research and development, and issuance of patents and their protection.

3. *Lifestyle*—career expectations, consumer activism, health concerns, desire to upgrade education and climb the socioeconomic ladder, and need for psychological services.

4. *Political-legal*–antitrust regulations, environmental protection laws, foreign trade regulations, tax changes, immigration laws, child care legislation, and the attitude of governments and society toward the particular type of industry and business.

5. *Demographics*—population growth rate, age and regional shifts, ethnic moves and life expectancy, number and distribution of firms within the industry, and size and character of markets.

Some Practical Ideas for Small Businesses

Recent Bureau of Labor Statistics figures indicate that around 71 percent of future employment in the fastest-growing industries (such as medical care, business services, and the environment) will likely come from small businesses—and these are areas where small firms are quite competitive. One reason for this is that entrepreneurs tend to be innovative and to develop new ideas. Some innovative ideas currently being developed, such as the following, could lead to the big businesses of tomorrow:

- Career counseling.
- Catering.
- Computer and office machine repair.
- Day care.
- Educational services and products.
- Financial planning.
- Home health care.
- Marketing, promotion, and public relations.
- Senior fitness and recreation.
- Specialized delivery services.

Real-World Example 1.11

For example, Cuisine Express (www.westchestermenu.com) provides fast, effective home or office delivery of meals from 40 restaurants in Westchester County, New York. Customers choose the restaurant and meal they desire and place an order with Cuisine Express's operator or via the Internet. The meal is ordered from the restaurant. A driver then picks it up, delivers it, and collects payments by cash, Visa, MasterCard, American Express, Discover, or Diner's Club.

Some Areas of Concern for Small Business Owners

So far, we have indicated that opportunities abound for anyone with a good idea, the courage to take a chance and try something new, and some money to invest. That's what small business is all about. But, as shown in this chapter, the success of smaller firms tends to be limited by factors such as inadequate management, shortages of capital, government regulation and paperwork, and lack of proper recordkeeping. Two other concerns are poorly planned growth and the threat of failure.

Poorly Planned Growth

Poorly planned growth appears to be a built-in obstacle facing many small businesses. Clearly, if the owners are incapable, inefficient, or lacking in initiative, their businesses may flounder and eventually fail, or if the owners are mediocre, their businesses remain small. However, if the owners are efficient and capable and their organizations succeed and grow, but in a poorly planned way, they risk losing the very things they seek from their companies.

For instance, as small businesses succeed, their owners may begin to feel trapped. Instead of feeling on top of the world, they feel like prisoners of long hours and hard work. Todd Logan, who owned and operated a publishing and trade show company, cites five core symptoms that entrepreneurs must understand and change if they are to deal with this syndrome:

1. Despair over the loss of closeness in important personal relationships.
2. Unshakable anxiety despite accomplishments.
3. Anger toward family, employees, and customers.
4. Frustration that the lack of significant current progress is preventing forward movement.
5. The paradox itself: You own your business, yet you don't enjoy it.[37]

Loss of Independence or Control   With growth, owners must please more people, including employees, customers, and the public. There are new problems, such as hiring and rewarding managers and supervising other people, exercising the very authority small business owners may resent in others.

Many otherwise creative entrepreneurs are poor managers. They can generate ideas and found the business but are unable to manage it on a day-to-day basis. If the firm becomes large enough to require outside capital for future success and growth, the owner may lose control over the company.

Typical Growth Pattern   Historically, the ownership and management of small businesses have tended to follow a growth pattern similar to that shown in Figure 1.5. During stage 1, owners manage the business and do all the work. In stage 2, the owners still manage their companies but hire employees to help with routine and/or management activities. In stage 3, the owners hire managers to run the firms. The length of service of professional managers (as opposed to owner-managers) in small businesses tends to be relatively short; they move from one company to another as they progress upward in rank and earnings. Often, owners must give managers a financial interest in the business to hold them. Thus, the business takes on the form, the characteristics, and many of the problems of a big business. If entrepreneurs plan poorly, and fail to foresee these growth patterns, they may run into trouble.

FIGURE 1.5 |
Stages in the
Development of a
Small Business

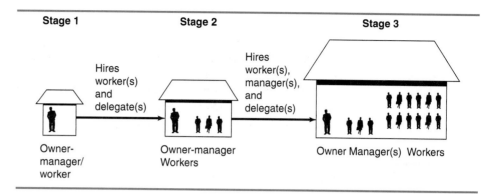

Threat of Failure

The threat of failure and discontinuance is a reality for many small businesses. A **discontinuance** is a voluntary decision to quit. A discontinuance may result from any of several factors, including health, changes in family situation, and the apparent advantages of working for some else. A **failure** results from inability to make a go of the business; things just do not work out as planned. There are two types of failure: (1) **formal failures,** which end up in court with some kind of loss to the creditors, and (2) **personal (informal) failures,** where the owner cannot make it financially and so voluntarily calls it quits. Personal failures are far more numerous than formal ones. People put their money, time, and effort into a business only to see losses wipe out the investment. Creditors usually do not suffer, as the owners tend to absorb the losses. The owners are the ones who pack up, close the door, and say "That's it!"

Studies of the behavior of people who choose careers in small business show that, all too often, discontinuance or failure results from one or more of the following weaknesses: (1) too much was left to chance, (2) too many decisions were based on a hunch or intuition, (3) crucial obstacles went unnoticed for too long, (4) the amount of time and/or physical effort demanded of the small business manager was not recognized and/or planned for, and (5) the amount of capital needed was either not estimated or grossly underestimated.

Underestimating the difficulty of business startups is one of the most common roads to disaster. Some say failure is usually caused by:

- lack of managerial experience
- lack of financial backing
- poor location
- unexpected growth
- communication skills.

One source to help avoid startup disaster is the National Business Incubation Association (NBIA). **Business Incubators** nurture young firms and help them to survive and grow during the startup period when they are most vulnerable. Hands-on management assistance, access to financing, and orchestrated exposure to critical business or technical support services are provided. Incubators offer entrepreneurial firms shared office services, access to equipment, flexible leases, and expandable space—all under one roof.

The main goal of an incubation program is to produce successful graduates, that is, businesses that are financially viable and freestanding when they leave the incubator. While the usual incubation period is two to three years, 30 percent of incubator clients typically graduate each year.

A **discontinuance** is a voluntary decision to terminate a business.

A **failure** results from inability to succeed in running a business.

Formal failures are failures ending up in court with loss to creditors.

In **personal (informal) failures,** the owner who cannot succeed voluntarily terminates the business.

Business incubators nurture young firms and help them to survive and grow during the startup period when they are most vulnerable.

Tom Segwald, Director,
Center for Entrepreneurial
Excellence.

Today there are about 1,900 business incubators in 60 nations: 60 percent are self-sufficient; others are subsidized. In 1997 only 13 percent could stand alone. Incubators now have about an 80 percent success rate. It is also interesting to note that 84 percent of incubators are not-for-profit organizations. Incubators are sponsored by academic institutions, government, economic development organizations, and for-profit entities (www.niba.org).

The Center for Entrepreneurial Excellence (www.ceebic.org) operates in a former school building. The classrooms are perfect for startup businesses and large meeting rooms. It is a community partnership with the city, county, and chamber of commerce. It provides secretarial support, office equipment, on-premises business consulting, classes and seminars, conference and classrooms, shipping services, and graphic design with flexible rental space and controlled overhead.[38]

While looking for data on failure rates and trends in failure rates, the latest available information seems to indicate a decrease. The data available is sketchy at best due to the lack of consistent collection vehicles. For example, many hobbyists, mom-and-pop ventures, and other small undertakings open and close every day without any documentation for tracking their success or failure rate. Many fail to consult with the Small Business Administration, obtain licensing, or report results to the Internal Revenue Service, which makes tracking the nonsurviving entities next to impossible.

What You Should Have Learned

1. Defining *small business* is difficult because the definition of smallness varies widely. In general, a small business is independently owned and operated and is not dominant in its field of operation. It is difficult to draw a clear distinction between a *small business* and an *entrepreneurial venture,* as the distinction depends on the intentions of the owners. If they start a small business and want it to stay small, it is a small business. If, on the other hand, they start small but plan to grow big, it is an entrepreneurial venture. Although small businesses generate only 12 percent of the total receipts each year, according to the IRS, around 96 percent of U.S. businesses are small, and firms with fewer than 500 employees account for 80 percent of existing jobs.

2. Small firms differ from larger ones in many ways, but their unique contributions include (*a*) flexibility and room for innovation; (*b*) the ability to maintain close relationships with customers and the community; (*c*) the competition they provide, which forces larger companies to remain competitive; (*d*) the opportunity they give employees to gain experience in many areas; (*e*) the challenge and freedom they offer to risk takers; (*f*) the employment opportunities they generate; and (*g*) the job satisfaction they provide.

3. Some current problems that plague small companies more than larger ones—and limit their development—are (*a*) inadequate financing, (*b*) inadequate management (especially as the firm grows), and (*c*) burdensome government regulation and paperwork.

4. Some current trends challenging small businesses are (*a*) exploding technology, (*b*) occupational and industry shifts, and (*c*) the move to global operations.

5. People start businesses for many personal and business reasons. While income is an important consideration, the primary reason is to achieve independence. The need to exercise initiative and creativity also leads entrepreneurs to take the risk involved in striking out on their own. Many small business owners are also motivated by family considerations, such as taking over a family business to permit parents to retire or starting a family business to have more time with their families. Also, some people start businesses chiefly to provide a product or service not readily available elsewhere. Finally, some entrepreneurs start businesses to achieve business objectives such as providing services to their customers; making a profit; providing social benefits to society; and growing into large, profitable organizations.

6. The characteristics most typical of the more successful business owners are that they (*a*) desire independence, (*b*) have a strong sense of enterprise, (*c*) tend to be motivated by personal and family considerations, (*d*) expect quick and concrete results, (*e*) are able to react quickly to change, (*f*) are dedicated to their businesses, and (*g*) often enter business as much by chance as by design.

7. There are many opportunities for prospective small business owners, especially in eating and drinking establishments, offices of health practitioners, and nursing and personal care facilities. The best opportunities are found in small firms, limited in scope, that involve long, hard hours working to satisfy basic human needs.

8. Poorly planned growth and the threat of failure should concern small business owners. Failure to grow can mean the death of a business, but poorly planned growth and the failure to foresee the stages of growth a typical company may go through can also pose a real problem.

   Some businesses discontinue for health, family, or other personal reasons, while others fail. Although relatively few failures are formal failures, personal failures resulting from unprofitability or general discouragement can be just as devastating for small business owners.

Key Terms

business incubators 25
discontinuance 25
downsizing (rightsizing) 14
entrepreneur 10
entrepreneurial venture 9
failure 25
formal failures 25
high-knowledge industries 22
objectives 18
personal (informal) failures 25
profit 18
profit motive 18
reengineering 14
reinvention 14
small business 9
small business owner 9
social objectives 19

Questions for Discussion

1. Do you agree that this is an interesting time to be studying small business? Why are you doing so?

2. All of us have had personal experiences with small business—as an owner, employee, friend, or relative of an owner, or in other relationships. Explain one or more such experience(s) you have recently had.

3. What comes to your mind when you think of a small business? How does your concept differ from the definition given in this chapter?

4. Distinguish between a small business and an entrepreneurial venture. If you were to start your own business, which would you wish it to be? Why?

5. How do you explain the growing interest young people have in small business? Relate this to your personal small business experience.

6. What are the unique contributions of small businesses? Give examples of each from your own experience of owning or working in a small business or from small businesses that you patronize.

7. What are some problems facing small businesses? Again, give example from your experience.

8. Discuss the four personal objectives that people seek when starting a new business.

9. Explain the interrelationship between the *service* and *profit* objectives.

10. How does success cause concern for small businesses? Can you give examples from your experience or suggest ways to avoid the problems of growth?

Case 1.1

The Big Wash

Henry Gibson, a 68-year-old retired file clerk, enjoyed sitting on his front porch on Belmont Street in Washington, D.C., on summer evenings watching his neighbors go by. But the sight of them lugging their laundry to two coin-operated laundries a half-mile on each side of him—one uphill, one downhill—caused him distress. With no business education or experience, nevertheless he had an idea: Why not start a laundry in the neighborhood?

Gibson knew he could not do this alone, especially raising the $250,000 needed to set up a good-sized coin laundry business. So he sought the help of Reuben McCornack, an adviser with Hope Housing, a nonprofit group located in the same block. Together they formed the Belmont Investment Group (BIG) and started selling 300 shares at $100 per share. Many investors came from the Community of Hope Church, where Gibson is an usher. Two shareholders sing in its choir. Some bought only one share, while others bought up to 50. (One neighbor invested his life's savings in 50 shares.)

Once the two men had sold 600 shares ($60,000), McCornack raised $60,000 in grants from seven foundations. With this backing, the two men were able to get a loan from a local bank and a District of Columbia government agency for a total of $300,000.

The Big Wash (the "Big" comes from the initials of their investment group) opened during the summer of 1995 in a well-designed and refurbished building on the same block where Gibson lives. (Even with its inner-city location, but without bars or a roll-down iron fence, the place had not been robbed or vandalized by early 1998.) The laundry has much going in its favor, especially the official criterion for success, according to the Coin Laundry Association: a densely populated neighborhood, with lots of kids and renters.

With 30 washers, 28 dryers, and 8 staff members—four of whom are paid attendants—operating from 7 A.M. to midnight, Big Wash usually grosses over $20,000 a month. This puts it in the top ranks of all the 35,000 self-service coin-operated laundries in the United States, which gross between $15,000 and $300,000 a year.

Since its opening in 1995, each of the laundry's shareholders has received $175 back on his or her $100 investment. For most of them, this is the first experience receiving dividend checks, which are issued quarterly by the investment group.

Questions

1. Evaluate Henry Gibson's approach to starting a new business.
2. Could there have been another source of funding? Explain.
3. How do you explain the fact that Big Wash has not been robbed?

Source: Prepared by Leon C. Megginson from various sources, including "Odds and Ends: It Took a Laundry to Clean the Area," *Mobile* (Alabama) *Register,* February 13, 1998, p. 2A. Used by permission of Newhouse News Service.

Case 1.2

The American Dream

Ugo and Gina Benincasa own and operate a small upscale hotel and restaurant in Lexington, Virginia. The both immigrated to the United States from Italy in the early 1960s. Several years ago Ugo renovated a historic building on Main Street in Lexington and opened an Italian restaurant. After a few years he and his wife had the opportunity to purchase the old abandoned livery stable across the street. The old circa 1887 structure was refurbished and converted into a small upscale hotel with nine rooms and three

suites. Interestingly, the original builders of the livery were also immigrants; they were from Ireland.

The restaurant, outdoor café, and lounge are housed in the rear of the hotel overlooking an open courtyard with a beautiful overhead vista of the local mountains. It also has a large banquet room for special occasions and meetings. Frankie Benincasa, who is Ugo and Gina's son, is the head chef. The restaurant features lunch and dinner seven days a week and has a varied menu of appetizers, soups, salads, and entrees to satisfy all tastes. A continental breakfast is served to guests of the Inn.

The Sheridan Livery Inn is truly the culmination of the American Dream. It is a successful small business that is family owned and operated. The Benincasa family work hard and give meaning to the phrase "24/7." As natives of Italy, they have felt the effects of cultural diversity. Mr. Benincasa attributes his success to hard work and a policy of political uninvolvement.

It is located in the heart of the historic district and within walking distance of Washington and Lee University and Virginia Military Institute.

Mr. Benincasa believes that small business is a "spider web" and can fall down at the whim of big business. He also believes that the American Dream is diminishing.

Questions

1. Do you believe in the American Dream? Why? Or Why not?

2. Do you think ethnicity is still a problem for small business owners in the mainstream? Why? Or Why not?

Source: Interviews and correspondence with the Benincasa family, October 2007.

Experientials

1. Ask your professor to plan a trip to the nearest business incubator. If you do not have one nearby, go to the chamber of commerce and inquire about startup facilities.

2. Talk to your fellow students and see what services are needed on your campus.

Family-Owned Businesses

Time present and time past
Are perhaps both contained in time future,
And time future contained in time past.
> —T. S. Eliot

Either you shape the future or the future will shape you.
> —John W. Teets, chairman and CEO, Dial Corporation

Learning Objectives

After studying the material in this chapter, you should be able to:

1. Discuss some problems involved in organizing and operating small family-owned businesses.

2. Explain how family relationships can affect the business.

3. Describe the activities needed to prepare the next generation to enter the firm.

4. Discuss the importance and method of preparing for management succession.

5. Discuss the need for tax and estate planning in small companies.

Farris-Feuerborn Memorial Chapel

Reuben Feuerborn is a third-generation funeral director/embalmer. If you ask him why he chose this particular career, he will tell you that he has "just always liked the service provided to families." Mr. Feuerborn assumed the leadership position in his family business located in Anderson County, Kansas on January 1, 2007, after joining his father in 1999. Reuben has three children and if one of them should follow in his footsteps, he or she would become the fourth generation to work in the business.

The history of Feuerborn dates prior to 1900, with E. E. Varner who died in 1906. He was the undertaker in the county whose business was purchased by brothers J. B. and O. G. Farris in January 1907. J. B. Farris took the examination and received his license after buying the business. J. B. and O. G. continued until 1910, when J. B. moved to the county seat in Garnett, Kansas, and purchased the R. L. Adams Undertaking Company from R. L. Adams, who had owned and operated the business since May 11, 1900, when he had purchased it from J. W. Lewis.

O. G. Farris continued in business in Colony and was later joined in business by his son, Eugene L. Farris, and his daughter, Frances Farris. In 1924, Marie Feuerborn began working for the Farris family in their home and later in the funeral home. Her husband Reuben began working for the funeral home in 1941 as funeral director and embalmer. After O. G.'s death, his son, Eugene, continued with the business in Colony until his death in 1965, when the Colony business was purchased by R. W. Farris, son of J. B. Farris, and consolidated with the Garnett business.

In 1975, the corporation consisting of the Garnett and Colony businesses was purchased by Dudley Reuben and Carol Ann Feuerborn. Today the business is an S corporation and still operates both of the facilities. In 1995, a new funeral home was built to replace the old one in Garnett; in 1998 the same was done in Colony. The company employs three full-time employees; two are licensed embalmers and funeral directors. A third site was added in Moran, Kansas, in July 2005.

Preneed burial policies, which are prefunded funeral plans, are sold at all locations. In October 2011, Mr. Feuerborn estimated that about 35–40 percent of the funerals that he provided are prefunded to some extent.

Regulatory compliance is always an issue in any business—large or small—and funeral homes are no exception. In addition to all zoning, business license, and other state and local requirements, the premises of funeral homes are regularly inspected by OSHA and the State Board of Mortuary Arts. The board also inspects prefunded policies, of which Kansas state law requires that each policy be placed in a separate account. The board regulates the renewal of professional licensing for funeral

Reuben and Dudley (3) 1944.

Reuben and Peyton (3) 2000.

Dudley and Reuben (3) 1977.

directors, funeral establishments, and embalmers. In turn, the Federal Trade Commission requires all funeral homes to provide a "general price list," which includes all available services along with their itemized prices. A copy of this list must be provided to anyone who asks for it or before any funeral arrangements are made.

When asked about ethical issues in the profession, Mr. Feuerborn said, "Nearly every issue is an ethical one that some unscrupulous undertaker has violated at some point in time. There are no questionable issues if you treat every family as if they were your own." Dudley Feuerborn states that today's funerals are "events" and funeral directors fall into the category of event planners specializing in care giving.

Currently, the average cost for a funeral, according to the National Association of Funeral Directors (NFDA) is $13,000 including the burial fee[1]. If cremation is chosen, then you may subtract another few hundred dollars. Approximately 90 percent of NFDA member funeral homes are owned and operated as family businesses, and the average life of those operations is 65 years. The other 10 percent, or about 2,200 funeral homes, are owned by four publicly traded corporations.[2]

According to the American Board of Funeral Service Education, approximately 51 percent of 2003 funeral service graduates were women, up from 14.5 percent in 1985, with an average age in the late twenties, and two-thirds of all graduates had no prior family relationships in funeral services. The American Board of Funeral Service

Education tracks statistics for the 48 accredited colleges and 5 other colleges that are currently applying for accreditation in the United States that offer degrees in mortuary science. Statistics indicate that more students are enrolled in mortuary science than ever before.

Gordon Bigelow, executive director of the American Board of Funeral Service Education in Brunswick, Maine, does not know why enrollment is increasing, but he feels that it is probably due to the fact that there are more job openings than professionals to fill them. He said, "Most students are surprised to find that over 90 percent of a Funeral Director's time is spent working with the living; less than 10 percent is actual preparation time with the dead."

Sources: Conversations and correspondence with Reuben Feuerborn.

The Profile of the Farris-Feuerborn Memorial Chapel is a good illustration of a successful family business that has survived several generations. Not only has the business survived, but it also maintains its original purpose and market niche. The world's oldest family business closed in 2006, after operating for 1,400 years. Kongo Gumi temple builders closed because of excess debt and unfavorable business climate. This family business was successful because, instead of handing down to the oldest son, the reins were given to the one that exhibited the best health, responsibility, and job talent. This selective method worked for 14 centuries and 40 generations.[3] The lesson here is to pick a stable industry and create flexible succession policies.

Role of the Family-Owned Business

The Family Firm Institute of Boston estimates that around 90 percent of all U.S. companies are family owned. That means that there are approximately 14 million such firms. And these are predominantly small companies, the majority of which have fewer than 20 employees.

Also, the Institute estimates that only about 30 percent of these small companies survive to the second generation of family members. Only 12 percent survive to the third generation, and 3 percent to the fourth generation and beyond. The Institute blames this high mortality rate primarily on the high estate tax (which will be discussed later in this chapter).[4]

More than 46 million Americans work in home-based businesses, and while family-owned businesses provide a living and personal satisfaction for many people, they must be managed just like any other small firms if they are to succeed.

Family businesses are the backbone of America, but they can also be a source of unresolved family tensions and conflicts, which can create obstacles to achieving even the most basic business goals. When close relatives work together, emotions often interfere with business decisions. Also, unique problems, such as the departure of the founder-owner, develop in family-owned firms. When more than one family member is involved, emotions and differing value systems can cause conflicts between members. In fact, most people-related challenges faced by family businesses—small or large—result from the interactions of business necessity with family values and relationships.[5]

Occasionally family-run businesses get a bad rap that is totally underserved. A family member may receive a lot of bad publicity for various reasons, and the public tends to attach a negative feeling toward the family name attached to the small business. Or the company may be part of a scandal that tends to tarnish the family as a whole.

The Family and the Business

All businesses require a well-thought-out and appropriate mission statement (Chapter 6) for successful operations. Families who own and operate family businesses need a family mission statement to provide direction for coping with the 24/7 necessities of operation. As business occurs we tend to get caught up in business activities and delay attention to our families while concentrating on the financial needs. In a recent article in *USA Today*, M. R. dellaCava states that the family should put in writing a mission statement for those family members who own and operate a small business. He acknowledges that it is important that the children be included in making decisions and setting goals. When the entire family is included, they become a family again. Family discussions also help parents stay in touch with each other and not lose sight of family values. For the family mission example, he cited the Franklin Covey Website. This site has suggestions such as

> Start from a family foundation of trust and openness, where everyone feels welcome to participate.
>
> Once everyone agrees on a final draft that truly summarizes the family's values and vision, make copies available to all.
>
> Avoid rushing your family, favoring one's agenda, or forgetting your purpose.[6]

We usually think of family businesses as being started, owned, and operated by the parents, with children helping out and later taking over. This has been the normal pattern, as many examples in the text will show.

Now, though, two contrary trends are developing. First, many young people are going into business for themselves—and tapping their parents for funds to finance their ventures. In return, the children often give one or both parents an executive position in the company, including a seat on the company's board. In fact, the average age of those involved in home-based businesses is 48.[7] Also, many retirees want to work part time for their children's businesses, without assuming a lot of responsibility.

Real-World Example 2.1

For example, the two brothers who run the Levy Organization in Chicago employ their mother as a hostess at one of their restaurants. They even named a deli after her and use her recipes. According to Mark Levy, the company's vice chairman, "My mom is a very integral part of our business."

On her birthday in 2011, her sons said, "The heart that beats behind our passion for great food and warm hospitality is our Company Mom Eadie Levy. More than 30 years ago she brought her family recipes and shared her knack for welcoming every guest with open arms and a big heart. She has been an inspiration to all of us at Levy Restaurants from the very first day, and she continues to share her love of food and people with everyone she meets." As a mother, grandmother, and great grandmother, Eadie believes that her proudest accomplishment is her sons' "entrepreneurialism and creativity in making Levy Restaurants a successful company."[8]

Another trend is the large number of spouses doing business together. This trend is indicated by a recent survey that shows that 18 percent of all U.S. businesses are equally owned by both men and women.[9]

Actually about one-third of all family businesses are husband and wife teams. These are referred to as *copreneurs*. One group recommends that before copreneurs start their business they should consider the following:

- Jot down what each hopes to accomplish and see if their goals are compatible.
- Find trusted employees or advisors to help settle disputes.
- Consider talking to a marriage counselor about how this will affect their relationship.
- Let each spouse take the role he or she fills best.
- Schedule personal time.
- Don't hold grudges.
- Don't have one spouse work for another as an employee.
- Don't let business arguments get personal.
- Don't make major decisions without consulting your spouse.
- Don't start a business in the first place unless the relationship is strong.[10]

Real-World Example 2.2

Jim and Eva Sisler satisfied their desire to see new places after their children were grown and before they retired. Jim enrolled in a six-week course in truck driver training and suggested Eva do the same. Last year they earned over $100,000 while seeing new places. Asked about spending so much time so closely together, Jim replied, "We know how to get on each others nerves, how to get off—and when."[11]

Willie Foster, inspired by a desire to make biscuits that tasted as good as his aunt's, opened the very successful Biscuit King Café. When phenomenal sales growth necessitated adding another person, Willie's wife, Nancy, joined him in the operation. The Fosters say the key to their success was starting small and working hard.

The second business presented in the example is the kind of family business we traditionally think of: a married couple running a small neighborhood store, toiling long hours for a modest living. Now, though, a new breed of husband-and-wife entrepreneurs has emerged. They typically run a service enterprise out of their home using computers, modems, and phone lines—even websites—as the tools of their trade. Figure 2.1 offers some tips on how to get along with your spouse while running a joint business.

FIGURE 2.1 | Making It in Business with Your Spouse

Following are some tips for spouses to follow in running a jointly owned business:

- Don't be blinded by romance; follow all the rules.
- Define each person's role and accentuate each other's talents.
- Don't ignore business conflicts in an attempt to spare a personal relationship.
- Agree to disagree—set the ground rules.
- Be clear and specific about your expectations of each other.
- Set aside family time, and stick to it.
- Set up a system for recognizing and rewarding hard work done by family members.

Source: Adapted from Paula Ancona, "Define Partners' Role in Family-Run Business," *Mobile* (Alabama) *Register,* June 6, 1993, p. 4-F. Reprinted by permission of Newspaper Enterprise Association, Inc.

A word of caution is needed at this point. While most modern marriages are built on a consensus model, with the assumption that neither spouse can make important decisions unilaterally, this is not practical in a business. Instead, one person should be clearly in charge, at least in a given management area, especially if other employees are involved. In business, a clearly defined chain of command is needed and expected.

It is interesting to note that in the last five years, family businesses controlled by women are almost twice as efficient as those controlled by men.[12] A study by the Babson College and MassMutual Financial group also found that female-owned firms averaged nearly the same revenue as those of male-controlled firms in the same areas, but had only half the number of workers. Female family business owners have increased by about 37 percent in the last five years. For business ownership in general, women now own 40 percent of all U.S. businesses.[13]

Although ownership of a small firm is usually controlled by one or a few family members, many others in the larger family are often involved. The spouse and children are vitally interested because the business is usually the source of their livelihood. In addition, some relatives may be employed by the firm, some may have investments in it, and some may perform various services for it. Involvement of family members should always be based on sound business practices.

(Source: © 1989 Doug Blackwell, Blackwell Cartoon Service. Used by permission.)

The founder-owner may set any one or more of a variety of goals, such as adequate income and perpetuation of the business, high sales, service to the community, and production of an unusual product, just to name a few. This variety of goals exists in all companies, but in family firms strong family ties can improve the chances of consensus and support, while dissension can lead to disagreement and/or disruption of activities.

According to Leslie Dashaw, founder of the Human Side of Enterprise, an organizational development consulting firm, more and more women are taking over the family business. Historically, leadership has passed from the father to the son, but that is changing.

Patricia Estess suggests that daughters who are interested in leading the family business should:

- Express interest.
- Gain experience outside of the family business.
- Learn from the senior generation.
- Be sensitive to the parent.
- Get involved and ask questions.
- Meet with women who lead family businesses.
- Define yourself.
- Develop a company vision.[14]

Think about Reuben Feuerborn's oldest child (see Profile), Peyton. Reuben has no issues whatsoever with the idea that she may someday become a mortician/funeral director. Reuben says, "It's the talent and interest in people that is so important, if Peyton wants to do it, we'll have no problem including her in our family business."

Another interesting father-daughter story is that of Larry Strassner and Lauren Russell. After retirement he agreed to help his daughter start a custom-made furniture business—Russell and McKenna, Inc. Mrs. Russell says it works because she and her father are family and therefore have a similar temperament. They talk business all the time, "There is really no off switch; we're workaholics."[15]

Family Interactions

Usually the founder—or a close descendant—is the head of a small business. Relatives may be placed in high positions in the company, while other positions are filled by nonfamily members. In some cases, it is expected that the next head of the firm will be a family member and other members will move up through the ranks, according to their position in the family, as the following example illustrates.

Real-World Example 2.3

Asplundh Tree Expert Company (www.asplundh.com) is such a business. Asplundh defines itself as "a bunch of tree cutters." That may be true, but this "bunch" now operates in all 50 states and eight foreign countries. Outsourcing has enabled Asplundh to remain a family business since 1928. There are 65 members in the fourth generation, and a few will work in the company and help carry on the family work. When asked why they do not go public, Chris Asplundh replied, "Then we'd just have money—that isn't what this family is about."[16] In 2008 Asplundh celebrated its 80th anniversary.

Family members' sense of "ownership" can be a strong, positive motivator in building the business and leading to greater cooperation. The opposite can also be true, however. Conflicts can occur because various relatives look at the business from a different perspective. Relatives who are silent partners, stockholders, or directors may see only dollar signs when judging capital expenditures, growth, and other important matters. On the other hand, relatives involved in daily operations may judge those matters from the viewpoint of marketing, operations, and personnel necessary to make the firm successful.

How to Deal with Incompetent Family Members   A related problem can be the inability of family members to make objective decisions about one another's skills and abilities. Unfortunately, their quarrels and ill feelings may spread to include nonfamily employees. One possible solution is to convince family members, as well as nonfamily employees, that their interests are best served by a profitable firm with strong leadership.

Some members want to become the head of the business but do not have the talents or training needed. Others may have the talents, but because of their youth or inexperience, these talents may not be recognized by other family members.

Family members with little ability to contribute to the firm can be placed in jobs in which they do not disturb other employees. Sometimes, though, relatives can demoralize the business by their dealings with other employees or customers or by loafing on the job, avoiding unpleasant tasks, or taking special privileges. They may be responsible for the high turnover rate of top-notch nonfamily managers and employees. Such relatives should be assigned to jobs allowing minimal contact with other employees. In some cases, attitudes may be changed by formal or informal education.

How to Compensate Family Members   Compensating family members and dividing profits among them can also be difficult because some of them may feel they contribute more to the success of the firm than others. Compensation should be based on job performance, not family position. When a family business decides to hire every relative who wants to work for the company—regardless of ability—it quickly becomes a welfare fund instead of a profit-making entity.

Fringe benefits can be useful as financial rewards, but they must conform to those given to nonfamily employees. Stock can be established as part of the compensation plan. Deferred profit-sharing plans, pension plans, insurance programs, and stock purchase programs can all be effective in placating disgruntled family members, as can a managerial title—if deserved!

When success leads a company into the second generation, titles start to matter to the younger relatives. A title is perceived as a confirmation of a job well done and also tends to serve as a motivator. This technique must be used carefully, however, to avoid counterproductive behavior in the future.

Family Limitations

Entrepreneurs tend to be specialists in an activity such as marketing, production, or finance, so they usually do not make good general managers. While managerial skills can be developed through training and/or experience, the skill of sometimes saying "no" to family members wanting to enter the business may still be missing.

Another problem is that family managers may feel it is necessary to clear routine matters with the top family member, regardless of his or her position or ability. Also, bottlenecks that work against efficient operations can be caused by personality clashes and emotional reactions. Therefore, lines of authority and responsibility in the company must be clear and separated from those within the family circle. This is an important distinction, because a person's age often determines the lines of authority in a family, while *ability* must be the primary guide in any business.

The number of competent family members from whom to choose the managers of the company is usually limited. Some members do not want to join—or are not capable of joining—the company in any position; some are capable of filling only lower-level jobs; and some are not willing to take the time or expend the effort to prepare themselves for a management position. So it is amazing that so many family businesses do in fact have such good leadership—family and nonfamily. As the leader grows older, however, he or she must keep up with the times and guard against letting past successes lead to trying to maintain the status quo.

Real-World Example 2.4

For example, the five stockholders of Donald & Asby, engineers, established a policy of encouraging growth. One of the younger stockholders suggested using media advertising to obtain new business. But Donald, who had helped found the firm 30 years earlier, said this would produce an undesirable type of growth. He suggested that they continue to depend on the company's reputation to expand requests for job proposals. How do you think the stockholders decided? Why?

Some families organize their businesses into corporations and hire professional managers to run them when no family members are in a position to manage, or no agreement can be reached on who should run the company. This solution has the advantages of using professional management, freeing family time for other purposes, reducing friction, and having employees treated more fairly.

The disadvantages of this arrangement, however, may be reduced family employment, lower income, concentration of power in small cliques, difficulties in finding and keeping a good management team, and loss of the "personal touch."

Now that divorce is an unfortunate reality for more than 50 percent of U.S. couples, it poses special problems for the quarter-million husband-and-wife–run U.S. businesses. If

(Source: Reprinted with special permission of King Features Syndicate.)

you are going through a divorce, your primary goal is to protect what is rightfully yours, based on your contribution to the business since its inception. You can best do this by (1) having the business appraised, (2) negotiating a buyout agreement, and (3) deciding what to do with any stock you might hold in the business, and consulting competent professionals for help in tax issues. This is an area where preplanning can really help. For example, written ownership agreements at the time the business opens, such as buy or sell, can be used in corporations. Pre- or post-nuptial agreements are also good.

Divorce financial specialist Jaffrey Landers suggests the following as a checklist for a pre- or postnuptial agreement:

- Each party should be represented by their own separate attorney.
- The agreement should be in writing, not oral.
- The agreement must be voluntary for each party.
- Each party must provide full disclosure of all assets and liabilities.
- The agreement must be fair and reasonable.
- Both parties should execute the agreement, ideally before witnesses or a notary.
- The agreement should be formatted so that each party to the contract declares or avows their own act of making the agreement.[17]

Single individuals may decide to transfer ownership into a self-settled trust. This also works as a safety net for unmarried children.

Culture and the Family Business

There is also a cultural-based growth in family businesses. The Mormon culture encourages women to stay at home and care for their children. Many families are large, making day care costs very expensive. These women agree that, "Everyone is better off when Mom stays at home." In Utah this is 70 percent of the state's population. The stay-at-home moms refine craftwork and turn many hobbies into home-based businesses.

Real-World Example 2.5

For example, when Laura Savages husband's construction business collapsed when she was pregnant with her sixth child, she discovered her home business was the key to her family's survival.

She expanded her line of refrigerator magnets, notepads, and stickers that were sold at conventions. She also created dress-up outfits for children.

In our "family-friendly" business environment many businesses are cutting back on flextime, job sharing, and paid family leave in order to continue to be profitable. This is a major reason mothers are quitting their current jobs and positions. One study of 400 employers indicates job sharing has decreased by 7 percent, four-day workweeks have decreased by 9 percent, and telecommuting is also decreasing. This creates an incentive for working moms to establish a home-based business.

Real-World Example 2.6

Diane St. James, a mortgage underwriter, went into business for herself so she could stay at home with her two daughters. She says now they have time to talk.

After leaving a sales job, Krista Sweeney decided not to look for another corporate position but to launch her own website as a resource for others, and she is selling health care benefits from home.[18]

There are many home-based businesses for stay-at-home moms: Avon, Pampered Chef, Tupperware, and lingerie to name a few. Stay-at-home dads are still a minority, but the latest statistics indicate that there are 159,000 fathers and 5.6 million mothers who stay at home to care for children. "Dadpreneurs" can access many online resources for support. For example: AtHomeDad.com is a network for primary-care dads who want to start or join activities to help connect at-home dads.[19]

According to the Bureau of Labor Statistics (www.bls.gov), in 2010 about 15 percent of Americans worked from home; that's over 22 million people! This can be explained in part by the 55 percent of working mothers who have infants.[20]

Family Resources

The amount of capital available within the family may limit expansion. While family resources and contacts may be adequate for a small business, as the company grows the borrowing power is limited by the amount of family assets. Then, family members may disagree about such issues as the following: Should money be obtained by borrowing, issuing stock, selling assets, or other financial techniques? Should planning be for the short or long run? Because of the diversity of opinion, even the choice of a consultant can be controversial.

Preparing the Next Generation

It might be assumed that children (or grandchildren) will automatically want to enter the family business. But this is not always true. A growing problem facing many small family businesses today is apathy on the part of offspring. Often, children who are reared in a small business become bored or uninterested, or simply lack the drive and desire to succeed that had motivated their parents. They may feel that since the business has supported them in the past, it will continue to do so in the future.

What leads children to follow in their parents' footsteps? In a significant early study, Nancy Bowman-Upton of Baylor University found that the two primary reasons were "to make money" and that they "like the business."[21] Helping children to "like the business" requires helping them discover what things they like to do and then matching those individual interests to the needs of the family business. The concept of doing what one likes is a motivator to meet the challenge of joining any business.[22]

Start at Part-Time or Full-Time Jobs?   One way to prepare children to take over the family business is to let them work on simple jobs, or on a part-time basis, which provides insights that may influence them into—or away from—the company. The experience often encourages them to finish their education to be better prepared when it's their turn to run the business.

Another form of preparation is working for another company to broaden their training and background. Such experience helps justify moving a family member into the family business at a higher level.

Start at Entry-Level or Higher-Level Positions?   Should a family member start in an entry-level job to learn the business from the ground up? There is some disagreement on this point, but none about the need for knowing the business, regardless of how it's done. The following are some techniques that should work for you:

- Never allow a child to work in senior management until he or she has worked for someone else for at least two years.
- Rotate the person in varying positions within your business.
- Give promotions only as they are earned.
- Devote at least half an hour each day to face-to-face teaching and training.
- Do not take business matters home.
- If the newcomer is ready to learn the business, true responsibility must be given. Otherwise, the person cannot learn to manage the business, as the following example shows.

Real-World Example 2.7

One family affair that has flourished for the past 60 years is Lee Patterson Co. of Orlando, Florida. Originally Lee sold paints and accessories on the road with his wife June at his side. Young son Gary also worked with Dad. Lee Patterson Co. has evolved over the years into specializing in equipment used in specialized paint jobs with revenues in excess of $3 million. This company remains in the same location with many expansions. Gary operated the business from 1979 until 2000. Now his daughter Kimberly (Lee's granddaughter) and her husband run the business. Gary's wife Nancy handles accounts receivable and personnel. This is a good example of a family business that has evolved from a corner store into a major supplier.[23]

Preparing for Management Succession

Any business must anticipate changes in its top management. It is not enough just to select a person to step into the top job when it becomes vacant. That key job requires much training and experience because the decisions the person makes can vitally affect the company and its future. Thus, every transfer of ownership and power is an invitation to disaster. To prevent that from happening, the owner should do two things: *Plan early and carefully,* and *groom a successor!*

Why Succession Is a Problem

When preparing someone for management succession, many small business owners have concerns about passing the business on to their children. In the Profile at the beginning of this chapter, two things are evident. The next generation not only needs the ability to operate the business but also needs the education, certifications, talent, and desire to carry on the service.

Real-World Example 2.8

Reuben Feuerborn's father has a brother who chose politics and retailing for a career rather than funeral services. Bill Feuerborn represents their area in the Kansas State Legislature and owns various small retail establishments in their hometown.[24]

One survey found that the main concern was how to treat all children fairly; another was the reaction of nonfamily employees. And several respondents mentioned family communication, conflict, and estate taxes as concerns.

Another trend is for two or more children to follow the parent in running the business. A classic survey of owners of family-owned businesses with two or more children working for the company revealed that some groom one child from an early age to take over, while others plan to let children compete and to choose one or more successors with or without help from the board of directors. Still others plan to form an "executive committee" of two or more children, or let the children choose their own leader(s). In essence, however, an early study found that more than half the respondents wanted to include two or more children in future ownership and management.[25]

If family members are going to be used to run the business, rather than bring in outsiders, ongoing training should begin early. One or more replacements should be started early on the path toward taking over the reins of the firm. This process sometimes does not work, but, as shown in the following example, sometimes it can work well.

Real-World Example 2.9

In 1914, Marie and Albert Cottaze created a company called French Hand Laundry and Dry Cleaning. This company now specializes in cleaning and restoring vintage clothing. Susan McManigal is now the owner and operator of French Hand, which employs 30 people. After graduating from college and beginning law school, Susan decided to follow in her mother's footsteps after she was asked to fill a sudden vacancy created by the illness of the company's staff accountant. From this point on she learned the company from the ground up. Susan recalls the oldest garment she ever worked on as being a "sampler" from the 1700s. Most of the older garments that pass through the French Hand Laundry are priceless. "When needed, repairs are made with the same or similar vintage and antique fabric from our personal collection so not to compromise the integrity of the garment."

Last December Susan's mother Virginia passed away, but her memory and dedication still motivates current employees. "She was highly respected in the community . . . and we're all working harder to keep all of those values and standards as high as they possibly can be." While Susan still misses her mom, she is not worried about the future of the family business. "I'm just from a very strong line of women and have been very fortunate to be in a line of business that I really enjoy."[26]

When the choice of replacements is limited, the owner may consider reorganizing the present assignments and using present managers more effectively. The job specifications for a new manager may be written more broadly to widen the range of choices. All present managers—family and nonfamily—should participate in this planning so they feel they have contributed to the decision. However, in some cases there is no heir to whom the business may be passed.

> ### Real-World Example 2.10
>
> A classic example of this trend is Jimmy Callis, who cleans and reshapes hats at Bon Ton Hatters in downtown Birmingham, Alabama. Callis is the third generation of his family to run the business of cleaning and reshaping hats.
>
> The business began as a shoe-cobbling shop in the early 1900s by an immigrant from Greece. Hat cleaning, dry cleaning, and pressing were added after 1914.
>
> By the year 2001, the future of Bon Ton looked dim. There would be no fourth generation to run the business, as his 16-year-old daughter is training to be a pediatric intensive care nurse.[27]

An Overlooked Problem

In most firms, the development of managerial personnel and the provision for management succession are greatly neglected, often until it is too late to do anything about it. Research studies indicate that most entrepreneurs simply do not want to face the inevitable.

But this trend is changing. A growing number of entrepreneurs are turning to formal succession plans to save their heirs endless squabbles, according to Massachusetts Mutual Life Insurance Company (www.massmutual.com). Its annual survey of more than 1,000 family business owners found that 44 percent of them had written plans to guide the next generation's succession to control.

Plan Ahead!

Management succession occurs when the family leader (1) dies, (2) becomes incapacitated, (3) leaves the company (voluntarily or otherwise), or (4) retires. To avoid family succession problems, entrepreneurs should start planning early for their replacements. A comprehensive succession plan involves more than just laying out the role of the younger generation in the business and ownership of the business. Instead, operating authority must pass from one generation to the next. These plans should be flexible enough to include (1) a sudden departure or (2) a planned one.

Sudden Departure

A successful business must continue to operate even when the owner-manager leaves. Plans can easily be made for vacations because they are of short duration, they require a limited number of decisions, and the vacationer is available if needed. When the owner takes a vacation, a form of on-the-job training is provided for those left in charge. Those persons can take over temporarily under those circumstances.

However, the sudden death or incapacity of the owner can be very disruptive if not adequately provided for. If the owner has left no will or instructions on what to do, family members will probably have conflicting opinions about what should be done. For this reason, an owner should make a will and keep it current, including instructions about what should be done in—or with—the business.

As shown in Chapter 17, the firm can take out life insurance on the owners, the proceeds from which will go to the company in case of death. This money can be used to help the business operate until it recovers from the loss of its owner-manager.

Planned Departure

When owners plan to leave or retire they have a number of options, as shown in Figure 2.2. If the company is a corporation, there will probably be less controversy because the replacement top officer should be known by the time the owner departs, and the transition

FIGURE 2.2 |

Options for Replacing
Family Management

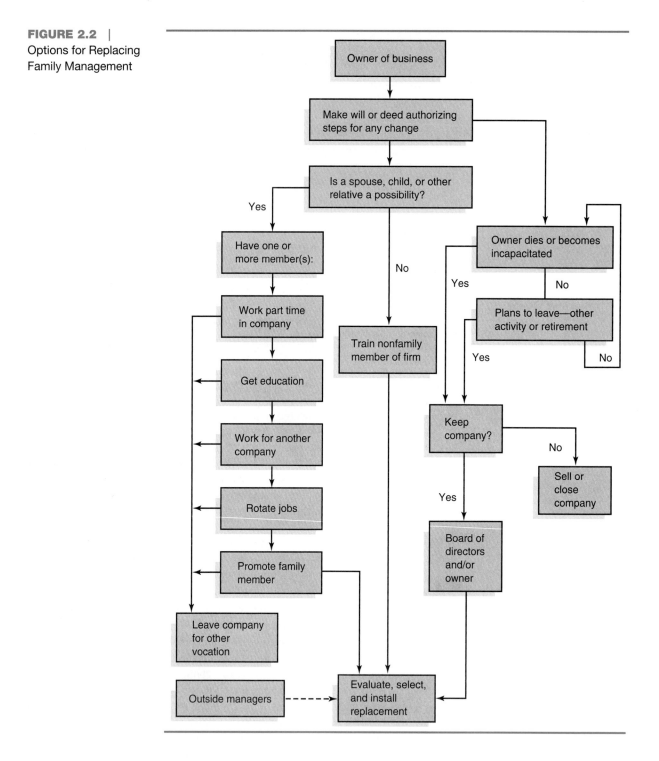

should go smoothly. The board of directors can select a family or nonfamily employee, or an outsider, for the top job. The handling of the stock can be delayed, but stock retention may give the new key executive the feeling that the departed one is still looking over his or her shoulder.

The entire family tends to become involved in the replacement decision in proprietorships and partnerships. Therefore, in planning for departure, the owner should look for someone in the family able and willing to take over. This person may already be recognized as the "heir apparent."

Selling to Family Members

If the transition is to be complete, the business should be sold to the offspring so that full responsibility is handed over to them. The advantages of this type of change for the original owner are as follows:

- The business stays in the family.

- It provides a source of employment for family members.

- The family's stature is maintained.

- The former owner is free to relax or travel.

- There is pleasure when the successor is successful.

- It can strengthen family bonds rather than produce additional family friction.

Real-World Example 2.11

For example, Dudley Feuerborn sold to Reuben on January 1, 2007, and can be quoted as saying, "his (Reuben's) success is my retirement." Dudley has a new 40' motor home and plans to do lots of traveling, specifically all the way around the boundaries of the United States.

Sometimes however, the business is sold to outsiders and later repurchased by one or more family members. This may occur when the owner wants to retire and the children are too young, or lack interest, skills, or the funds needed to purchase the company.

Real-World Example 2.12

For example, Charles Alfieri sold his hair replacement business to a Japanese company with a long-term employment contract. After disagreements with management, he retired from the firm.

Nine years later the company was preparing to close, and Charles's cousin Andy (who had stayed on at the firm) bought the operation. Now, after 40 years, Andy Alfieri is at the helm of the organization where he worked and learned from his cousin Charles while still in high school (www.alfieri.com).

Selling to Outsiders

If no relative will assume responsibility for the running of the business, the owner can sell out to a partner or an outsider, or can even close the business. Many small businesses are now being sold and moved offshore. Sometimes companies will see an opportunity for expansion in other countries, open businesses there, and later sell the established fledglings to locals. Mexico, where American interests continue to grow, is a good example.

There are many advantages to turning the reins over to an outsider. Among these are assured income, lack of worry about what subsequently happens, possible opportunity to consult, release of family tension, and relief from further responsibility. Selling to someone outside the family can mean loss of family identification and resulting sadness, since it marks the end of years of effort and the loss of something the founder built. Still, selling to outsiders can have a beneficial effect on family relationships, as the following example illustrates.

Real-World Example 2.13

When a troubled family business was sold, the reaction of one child was this: "A number of financially enmeshed families were liberated to pursue individual courses. A company had shed its burdensome past and could look forward to a renewal under new leadership. Ray, Joyce, and I are no longer wrangling siblings polarized in an ugly triad. We are free to be friends."[28]

Making the Transition Easier

What preparations should you make when you plan to turn the business over to someone else? Too often, a small firm suffers under these circumstances, and sales may decrease, or production lag.

To make transitions easier for themselves, owners need to broaden their focus. The narrower the owners' experience and skills, the more difficult it will be to make a smooth transition to other activities after leaving their business. Owners should begin to devote more time to hobbies and outside group activities, which should help them develop a sense of worth apart from the business. Finally, the transition can be made in phases, by gradually turning part of the business over to the successor(s).

Tax and Estate Planning

As shown in Chapter 15, in projecting the future of your business, planning is needed to minimize estate taxes. A business and its assets may appreciate in value much more than the owners are aware, and inheritance taxes can be devastating. Therefore, estate plans should be reviewed frequently, along with possible estate tax liability and the provisions for paying such taxes.

Tax Planning

In planning your firm's future activities, consider the influence taxes will have on profits and the business's capital structure. Because tax laws and regulations change frequently, stay current in the knowledge of these matters. You should probably have annual planning conferences with a CPA well versed in business tax matters.

Estate Planning

Estate planning is preparing for the orderly transfer of the owner's equity in the business when death occurs.

Estate planning is preparing for the orderly transfer of the owner's equity when death occurs. The major concerns are usually the perpetuation of a family business and maintaining liquidity. Without sufficient cash to pay estate taxes, heirs may have little choice but to siphon cash from the business or even sell it.

Tax rates on estates are now such that the assets bequeathed to beneficiaries may be needed to pay taxes, resulting in the eliminating of equity from a business. By planning for the transition, this problem can be minimized.

From the small firm's standpoint, estate planning can (1) reduce the need for beneficiaries to withdraw funds, (2) help maintain beneficiaries' interest in keeping funds in the firm, and (3) provide for a smooth transition. Estate planning for the above objectives can

TABLE 2.1 | Buy/Sell Effectiveness

Internal Revenue Code Section 2803 regulations concerning buy-sell agreements:

- It must be a bona fide business arrangement.
- It must not be a device to transfer property to members of the decedent's family for less than full and adequate consideration.
- It is similar to comparable arm's-length transactions.

In addition, applicable case law has established several rules that must be followed:

- The estate must be obligated to sell at death.
- The agreement must have a fixed and determined sale price or a method for determining the price.

The owner cannot sell the property during his or her lifetime without first offering it to the other owners.

- The price must be fair and adequate when the agreement is made.

A buy-sell agreement benefits both heirs and surviving owners.

Benefits to heirs

- Freedom from business worries.
- Guarantee of a fair purchase price.
- Possibility of avoiding probate delays.

Benefits to surviving owners

- Relief from concern about new and possibly unwanted partners.
- Advance knowledge of the purchase price.
- Retention of good relations with creditors and clients through a smooth transition of ownership.

Source: Author's conversations and correspondence with Alfred C. Corina, CLU, ChFC.

A **family limited partnership** allows business owners to pass assets to heirs with a minimum of income and estate tax costs while retaining control of assets during their lifetime.

be in the form of (1) gifts to children, (2) stock sales to family members, (3) living trusts, and (4) **family limited partnerships.** This type of partnership allows business owners to pass assets to heirs with a minimum of income and estate tax costs—while retaining control of the assets during their lifetime.

In carrying out those planning steps, appropriate actions should be taken to assure compliance with IRS regulations, especially the valuation of the business. Three methods for determining the true value of a business are (1) determining the value of a comparable business that is publicly traded, (2) ascertaining the business's value by capitalizing its earnings, and (3) estimating the business's value by determining its book value.

A **buy-sell agreement** provides for the corporation to buy back a shareholder's stock when he or she leaves the company.

Certain actions are possible to ensure that the IRS is bound by a predetermined agreement. One way of accomplishing this is to use a predetermined shareholder **buy-sell agreement,** whereby the corporation agrees to buy back the stock or sell it for the shareholder. Such an agreement becomes binding on the IRS; however, it must be in writing. Table 2.1 gives the regulations for a valid buy-sell agreement. In addition, a properly prepared buy-sell agreement assures a market for the stock. It also provides protection for the minority stockholder. If such a stockholder is terminated without such an agreement, he or she may be placed at a serious disadvantage, as the following example illustrates.

Real-World Example 2.14

A young woman held 28 percent of the stock in her employer's corporation; a majority of her personal assets were tied up in the stock. Without warning, she lost her job, and her unsympathetic ex-employer was unwilling to redeem the stock.

A number of references may be used to aid in estate and tax planning, but we recommend using the services of a lawyer, accountant, and/or professional tax planner as well. If you wish to do your own planning, there are many software packages that can be of assistance.

Estate Planning to Minimize Taxes

No one wants to pay more taxes than necessary, especially when you are trying to pass the benefits of the estate you have built up over the years to your family. You want to reduce taxes to the minimum so they will get the maximum. Because family business owners frequently do not have the financial skills needed for estate planning, they should rely on a Certified Financial Planner (CFP). In 2005, there were 39,481 estate-tax returns with an excess of $1.5 million; only about half of these were taxable.[29]

Estate Planning Issues

For entrepreneurs, several issues are involved in estate planning. The most important of these are (1) trying to minimize taxes, (2) retaining control of the business, and (3) maintaining flexibility of operations.

Estate Planning Techniques

While it is impossible to avoid all estate taxes, the following can be used to minimize them: (1) family gifts, (2) family partnerships, (3) stock sales to family members, and (4) living trusts.

Make Gifts to Family   One way to reduce taxes on your estate is to start giving parts of it to your family as soon as feasible. The rules are as follows:

- The gifts must be of "present interest," such as a direct cash gift, rather than a "future interest," such as gifts of cash that go into a trust fund for later distribution.
- The first $13,000 given by each spouse to each person during the year is tax free.
- Under current law, a lifetime maximum of $3,500,000 can be given away free of the estate tax.
- The gifts, which are based on the fair market value of the property, can be cash, bonds, real estate, the family business, interest in a partnership, and so forth.

Establish a Family Limited Partnership   You can form a family limited partnership to take money out of your company at lower tax rates. It must be a passive partnership that owns some type of property but does not operate the business. For example, a business owner may elect to set up a family limited partnership, retaining at least 2 percent of the stock as a general partner and giving the balance to the children as limited partners, subject only to gift tax. *Because this type of tax shelter is very complex, do not try to establish it by yourself; get professional help.*

Sell Stock to Children   You can also sell all or part of your business to your children, but, like establishing a family partnership, this is complicated. First, your children will need a source of income to make nondeductible payments to you for the stock. And second, you must pay capital gains tax on the stock you sell. You may want to combine this method with gifts to the family. If the value of your business is greater than the amount you can give as gifts during your lifetime, you may want to give up to the maximum and sell stock for the rest of the business.

A **living trust** resembles a will but, in addition to providing for distributing personal assets on the maker's death, it also contains instructions for managing those assets should the person become disabled.

Establish a Living Trust   A **living trust** resembles a will, but, in addition to providing for distributing personal assets on the maker's death, it also contains instructions for managing those assets should the person become disabled. You can put property into a living trust while you are still alive. Then, when you die, the property automatically goes to the designated heirs without having to go through probate court, saving considerable time and expense.

But there are some disadvantages of a living trust. First, when you establish such a trust, you must also change the title on all real estate, securities, and other assets to the name of your trust. From a legal point of view, you no longer own these properties, so there is nothing to probate when it becomes time to distribute your assets. In addition, beneficiaries are still taxed and it may be expensive to set up the trust. You (and your spouse) may find it advantageous to become joint trustees in order to bypass the probate process. Finally, if you need to refinance your home or other assets, some lenders may refuse to refinance it if it is in a trust.

To avoid the many pitfalls of this device, hire an experienced trust attorney and select a capable and trustworthy trustee. Also, carefully weigh the benefits against the time and effort required.

What You Should Have Learned

1. This chapter shows that members of family-owned firms have different viewpoints depending on their relationships in the family and the business. Founders expect that some family members, especially their children, will follow them into the firm.

2. To the extent feasible, ownership and management should be separated from family affairs in order to be fair to nonfamily employees and to reduce friction. Accepted upward movement of family and other employees in the business can generate positive motivation, but evaluation of family members' skills is often difficult. Disruptive members should be isolated, delegation should be practiced, and compensation should be based on job performance—not personal or family relationships—if possible.

3. Family businesses are usually limited in the number and caliber of people from whom to choose managers, and in the money available for such purposes. Age may hamper the progress of younger family members and may lead to disagreements on money matters. Forming a corporation tends to lessen

family stress within the company. Ongoing training, including early employment in the business and personal contact with the owner, is recommended for developing younger members.

4. Start planning for succession early in the game to help smooth any sudden transition. If the new CEO is known early, planning has been good; if not, selection may have to be made under adverse conditions. Transfer of the firm to other family members has many advantages, including continuity and family support.

5. Planning for the future should also include estate planning to minimize the tax burden of the business owner's heirs. Strategies to reduce the beneficiaries' need to withdraw funds, maintain their interest in leaving funds in the firm, and provide for a smooth transition include gifts to children, selling stock to family members, setting up a living trust, and setting up a family limited partnership. In all such planning, owners are advised to consult professionals such as lawyers, accountants, or professional tax planners, and to ensure that IRS regulations are met.

Key Terms

buy-sell agreement 49   family limited   living trust 51
estate planning 48   partnership 49

Questions for Discussion

1. Why is management succession an important issue for any small firm? For a family firm?
2. Why is it often difficult to make reasonable decisions in a family business? What problems are caused by a family organization structure?
3. What problems face a company when a key officer leaves suddenly?
4. If you start a business when you are in your twenties or thirties, should you do anything about your replacement? Explain.
5. Suppose you have a successful business now but decide you want to leave it. What might be some reasons for leaving it? What alternatives do you have for the business?
6. How important is estate planning? How can you do it?

Case 2.1

Tire Rack—www.tirerack.com

Somebody ought to stock a few of every tire, sell them over the phone, and ship them, thought Mike Joines when he had trouble finding the right performance tires for his sports coupe.

When Joines approached his father-in-law, Peter Veldman, with the idea, Veldman instead asked Joines to help him open a retail tire store that now sells more than 2 million tires each year. After seven years, the two were taking so many phone orders, they closed the store and added phone lines.

Veldman is now president and patriarch of Tire Rack, a family-owned Internet and mail-order tire retailer. His wife, Wilma, four of their six children, and two sons-in-law also work for Tire Rack. The family members who work at the firm live within five miles of each other, and Matt Edmonds, marketing vice president and Veldman's son-in-law, describes the working relationship as almost "impossibly pleasant." While they "have their moments," the family gets along very well. So well that they want the company "to feel like a family" to all 401 employees.

Tire Rack sells name-brand tires to consumers and to other retailers who don't want to wait more than two days for delivery. For consumers, Tire Rack ships to its network of recommended installers, to their homes, or to the service shop of their choice. Tires account for 85 percent of its business; the rest comes from sales of wheels, springs, and similar parts.

According to Joines, Veldman has been the company's biggest growth proponent, pushing hard for the company to adopt an Internet strategy in 1996 when few were taking the plunge. Now, the Internet business accounts for almost half of sales, and most phone customers have used the Web site for research.

Customer service is Tire Rack's priority. Joines says the goal is offering the "best product at the right price in the shortest amount of time." He feels that educating consumers on the best tire for their car helps the firm win and retain customers. They probably benefit from being the seller of multiple brands, so there is no appearance of pushing one brand. Sales staff tests different tires with varying states of wear on ice, water, and dry pavement to better help customers. Customers can pull their cars into one of the service bays at Tire Rack that they have ordered by phone or the Internet where they can have tires installed.

Edmonds says, "Word of mouth and references are still our biggest source of new customers." The company, which has more than a million square feet of warehouse space in four locations, says it sells more than 2 million tires a year, or a set for every 100 people who buy tires. Its Web site gets 2.4 million visitors a month, more than any other tire company, and more than many automakers, according to Alexa Internet, an Amazon.com company that ranks web traffic.

Questions

1. Why is management succession so important in a family firm?
2. Why is it often difficult to make decisions in a family-run business?
3. What qualities have contributed to the success of Tire Rack?

Source: Abstracted from Jayne O'Donnell, "Family Rolling to Success on Tire Rack," *USA Today*, December 8, 2003, p. 3B. Copyright 12/8/2003. Reprinted by permission.

Experientials

1. Locate three (3) family businesses in your community and interview the owner. Write a brief report including, but not limited to, the age of the business, why it was started, and how many hours per week the owner dedicates to the operation.
2. Call or e-mail a specific chamber of commerce and ask if they have any statistics on local family businesses.

CHAPTER 3

Forms of Ownership of Small Businesses

Good order is the foundation of all good things.
   —Edmund Burke
To me, going public [incorporating] would be like selling my soul.
   —Carlton Cadwell, manufacturer

Learning Objectives

After studying the material in this chapter, you should be able to:

1. Name the legal forms of ownership a small business can have.

2. Explain the reasons for and against forming a proprietorship.

3. Explain the reasons for and against forming a partnership.

4. Explain the reasons for and against forming a corporation.

5. Discuss some other legal forms a business can take.

Spring Hill Kitchens, LLC

Barkley Shreve and her two sisters grew up eating their mother's delicious cheese wafers. The sisters often said that frozen cheese wafer dough would be a great retail product! They talked on and off for years about marketing the wafers, but since they all had families and lived in three different cities, the idea never seemed to get off the ground. At one point, a brother-in-law laughingly said, "All you girls do is eat cheese wafers—I don't think you're ever going to sell them."

However, in spring 2003, this changed. While at a party eating cheese wafers, Shreve told her idea to a close friend, Susan Thompson. They then began discussing the idea of starting a business together. They were both ready for a change. Thompson had always worked for law firms and had reached a point where she wanted to try something different. Shreve was working at the time on her Master of Arts with the thought of teaching, but the idea of marketing the wafers was always in the back of her mind.

Sometime before that, Thompson had read a magazine article about two friends who launched what is now a successful specialty food product business and decided, "They sounded just like us—real, normal people who had a good product." Thompson was the motivator, Shreve says, as a few days later, she called her and said, "Let's do it!"

They soon found that all the issues involved in starting a new business were quite daunting. Legal issues, accounting needs, and insurance decisions were a few of the matters to be resolved. They would also need equipment, a commercial kitchen, packaging, boxes, tubing, labels, fasteners, and business forms. They had to find the right formula for large-scale adjustments to the recipe. However, naming their product was the easy part. They decided "Mamie's Famous Cheese Wafers" would be appropriate as the recipe belonged to Shreve's mother, Mary (known as "Mamie" to Shreve's children).

Their next step was to consult an attorney as to the form of business they should pursue. He suggested they go with a limited liability company (LLC). Many small business owners and entrepreneurs prefer LLCs because they combine the limited liability protection of a corporation with the "pass-through" taxation of a sole proprietorship or partnership and allow greater flexibility in management and business organization.

Shreve and Thompson contacted the local chamber of commerce for information about the group called SCORE (Service Corp of Retired Executives) but were told there was no one locally who had experience in the food area. Therefore, their main sources of information concerning starting a small business came from people already in the field who proved to be very generous with their time, advice, and counseling.

"Really, our 'guardian angel' was Walne Donald at Mobile Fixtures," said Shreve. "We went to see him, explained what we wanted to do, and asked if he thought we could do it. If Walne had been discouraging, we were at the point where we might have been talked out of it. But, he confidently assured us we could succeed."

"We were having a horrible time finding a kitchen large enough for our needs," said Thompson. "After talking to Walne concerning the cost of the equipment, and talking to the Board of Health concerning their requirements, we realized it would have been a different level of start-up if we had to build our own kitchen." Donald knew of a local restaurant with the requirements they needed that wasn't using one of their large buildings to full capacity. Shreve and Thompson then contacted the manager of the restaurant, Joe Duralde, to work out an arrangement for use of those facilities. Duralde, who had many years of experience in the restaurant business, was extremely encouraging. Being "up front and honest," he would tell them what they were doing right and what they were doing wrong. He was not shy about offering suggestions, trained them on how to use a lot of their equipment, and showed them shortcuts. He then told them that he was just going to leave them alone and let them figure it out.

Increasing the ingredients to make large batches of dough was an extremely frustrating task. "It's really chemistry," said Thompson. "You can't take a recipe for one batch and just double, triple, or quadruple it, as it would be too greasy, or the texture was wrong, or it was too spicy, and so forth. Again, Joe suggested we cut back on one item or add more of another. We were at a point that we forgot how the original wafers tasted. At Joe's suggestion, we went home, made one batch to compare the taste. We then began adjusting ingredients to get it right. It took a little while, but we finally solved the problem."

Probably the second biggest challenge, they stated, was finding the right machine to load the finished dough into freezer-ready packaging. Thompson spoke with a manager at a local grocery store, and he suggested that they use a sausage stuffer, which is a much cheaper piece of equipment than the "extruder" they thought was needed. Everyone suggested they go to another city in an adjacent state to purchase equipment. While there, they were able to process a batch of dough through the machine to see if it would work. "It was a really happy day," said Thompson. "We came back thinking that this relatively inexpensive piece of equipment was going to work perfectly."

Shreve and Thompson invested equally to buy their equipment. Because that used up much of the money,

they set up a relationship with a banker and applied for a line of credit. In the beginning, they used the line of credit occasionally to buy their ingredients and pay their rent. After the first seven months, they had reached the breakeven point, and were even making a small profit. "And, everyone tells us that, for a business to break even in that period of time is unusual," states Shreve. As the business grows, the concentration remains on the volume needed to achieve further financial growth. In 2010, Shreve bought out her partner but retained the LLC with her husband. The product is now outsourced for production to Tanner's Pecans & Candy, Inc. (www .tannerpecan.com), where Shreve maintains her offices and is available to oversee production and quality control.

Their cheese wafers are now selling in the Southeast nationally and specifically target consumers over thirty, those who entertain a lot, and those who appreciate the convenience of the product.

Mamie's Famous Cheese Wafers can be found at over 100 Fresh Market Grocery Stores, multiple gourmet and specialty stores, William-Sonoma catalog, and Internet sales to individuals through their website www .mamieswafers.com. Also, Mamie's Famous Cheese Wafers can be found on Facebook and Twitter. The product is delivered in freezer trucks by the pallet. A pallet contains 105 cases. Smaller orders are packed with frozen gel packs in Styrofoam coolers and shipped FedEx ground.

Shreve feels that one of the things that has made the venture so much fun has been the people she has met—and learning something new has been great. Shreve's husband, a CPA, has been advising her on certain points of the business and takes care of their bookkeeping by computerizing data entry for easy access. "I could not have done it without him."

Some travel is required for sampling at store openings, new accounts, and various marketing. Shreve's business is a member of the "Buy Alabama's Best" organization, which not only increases the business's visibility but also is an excellent networking tool. She states that sales were negatively impacted by the recession in 2010, when many of her regular accounts went out of business. But 2011 is proving to see a great increase in both sales and new accounts. Shreve did not let the downturn crush her spirit and credits her positive attitude for continuing success.

Source: Conversations with Barkley Shreve.

Selecting the Right Legal Form

Going into business for yourself and being your own boss is a dream that can become either a pleasant reality or a nightmare. Although it may be satisfying to give the orders, run the show, and receive the income, other factors must be considered when choosing the legal form to use for the business. One of the first decisions you must make that has long-term implications is how to structure your company. You may want to consult with an accountant and/or attorney at this point. Spring Hill Kitchens LLC, the Profile at the beginning of this chapter, is a very good example of structure choices. Income tax considerations, the amount of free time available, responsibility for others, and family wishes—as well as the amount of available funds—must also be considered in choosing a proprietorship, partnership, corporation, or other legal form for the business. According to Thomas A. Stewart, "the modern corporation, like modern art, is over. We're seeing more and more mutant forms of company organization."[1]

Factors to Consider

When choosing the proper legal form for your business, you should take into account the following:

- Your vision regarding the size of your business.
- The nature of your business.
- The level of control you desire.
- The level of structure desired.
- Business vulnerability to lawsuits.
- Tax implications of different ownership structures.
- Expected profit (or loss).
- Earnings reinvestment.
- Personal cash needs. www.sba.gov

For example, to what extent is your family able to endure the physical, psychological, and emotional strains associated with running the business? Second, how easy is it to start, operate, and transfer to others your interest in the company? Third, to what extent are you and your family willing to accept the financial risks involved, including being responsible for not only your own losses and debts but also those of other people? Finally, how much information about yourself, your family, and your economic status are you willing to make public? For example, if you choose the corporate form, information about the business—including profits and/or losses—may have to be made public knowledge.

The choice of legal form does not have to be final. The usual progression is to start as a proprietorship or partnership and then move into a corporation. For example, in the

FIGURE 3.1 |
Relative Position of
U.S. Proprietorships,
Partnerships, and
Corporations

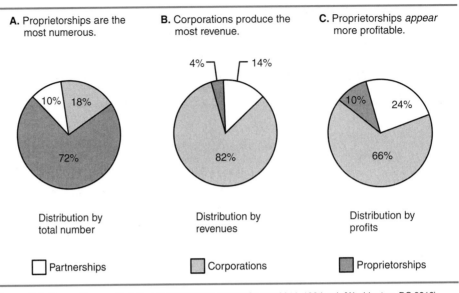

A. Proprietorships are the most numerous.

B. Corporations produce the most revenue.

C. Proprietorships *appear* more profitable.

Distribution by total number

Distribution by revenues

Distribution by profits

☐ Partnerships   ▢ Corporations   ▆ Proprietorships

Source: U.S. Census Bureau, *Statistical Abstract of the United States: 2011,* 130th ed. (Washington, DC 2010), Table 743, p. 491.

Clean-Drum case from the workbook at the end of this text, Sue Ley started her business as a proprietorship, but when she needed extra capital, she brought in a partner.

Relative Importance of Each Form

As you can see from Figure 3.1, the proprietorship is by far the most popular form of business in the United States. Around 72 percent of all businesses are proprietorships, while only 18 percent are corporations, and 10 percent are partnerships. Notice in Table 3.1 that the proprietorship is most popular in all industries. Finance, insurance, and real estate use the partnership more frequently than do the other industries.

While the proprietorship is the most popular form, it accounts for only a small share of total revenues. As Figure 3.1 shows, proprietorships generate only around 4 percent of all revenues, while corporations account for about 82 percent, and partnerships provide around 14 percent.

Table 3.1 shows that corporations dominate the business receipts in all areas. Proprietorships account for significant revenues in services, trade, and construction.

TABLE 3.1 | Comparison of Proprietorships, Partnerships, and Corporations in Selected Industries

Industry	Percentage of Firms in the Industry			Percentage of Industry's Business in Receipts		
	Proprietorships	Partnerships	Corporations	Proprietorships	Partnerships	Corporations
Services	76	4	20	11	23	66
Trade	70	6	24	3	11	86
Construction	77	4	19	13	12	75
Finance, insurance, real estate	44	37	19	3	18	79
Manufacturing	53	7	40	*	11	89

*Less than 1 percent.

Source: U.S. Census Bureau, *Statistical Abstract of the United States: 2011,* 130th ed. (2010), Table 745, p. 492.

TABLE 3.2 | Forms of Ownership

Structure	Typical Owner	Liability	Taxable Profits	Paperwork of Origin
Proprietorship	Individual	Individual	Individual	None
General partnership	2 or more	Individual	Individual as per Partnership agreement	Partnership agreement
Limited partnership	2 or more 1 general Partner	General partner	Individual as per Partnership agreement	Partnership agreement
Joint venture	2 or more companies	Business purpose only	As per agreement	Partnership agreement
Corporation	No limit of owner	Corporate entity	Corporate and declared Dividends to individuals	Charter, Articles of Inc.
S corporation	100 max	Corporate entity	Owners	Charter, Articles of Inc.
Professional service corporation	All owners in same profession	Individual liability only	Owners	Charter, Articles of Inc.

Sources: Various.

Figure 3.1 shows that proprietorships appear to be the most profitable form; they received 10 percent of profits on only about 4 percent of revenues. Partnerships accounted for 6 percent of revenues and 24 percent of profits. Corporations received only 66 percent of the profits on about 82 percent of the sales. These numbers should be interpreted with caution, however, because proprietorship "profits" include net financial return to owners. In a corporation, much of that return would be included in wage and salary expense and deducted from profit. Table 3.2 briefly explains some typical structures in use by businesses.

Why Form a Proprietorship?

A **proprietorship** is a business that is owned by one person. The vast majority of small businesses start out as sole proprietorships. These firms are owned by one person, usually the individual who has day-to-day responsibility for running the business. Sole proprietors own all the assets of the business and the profits generated by it. They also assume complete responsibility for any of its liabilities or debts. In the eyes of the law and the public, you are one in the same with the business.[2] It is the oldest and most prevalent form of ownership, as well as the least expensive to start. Most small business owners prefer the proprietorship because it is simple to enter, operate, and terminate and provides for relative freedom of action and control—as shown in Figure 3.2. Finally, the proprietorship has a favorable tax status. As will be shown in Chapter 15, it is taxed at the owner's personal income tax rate. In these respects, you may find it an attractive form to use, as millions of proprietors now do.

Real-World Example 3.1

Sanford Bryant creates his own line of high-fashion custom-designed menswear for celebrities. He spent a lot of time learning the "not-so-glamorous" side of the business before opening the Sanford Bryant Co. in 1999. His previous experience in the fashion industry helped prepare him to deal not only with clients but also maintain industry connections. Bryant continued to consult for other people to create a positive cash flow while in the development stage of Sanford Bryant Co. Since its launch, the company focus has shifted to "affordable, custom-made luxury clothing for average consumers."[3] In 2006, the company added women's wear to their offerings. (www.sanfordbryant.com)

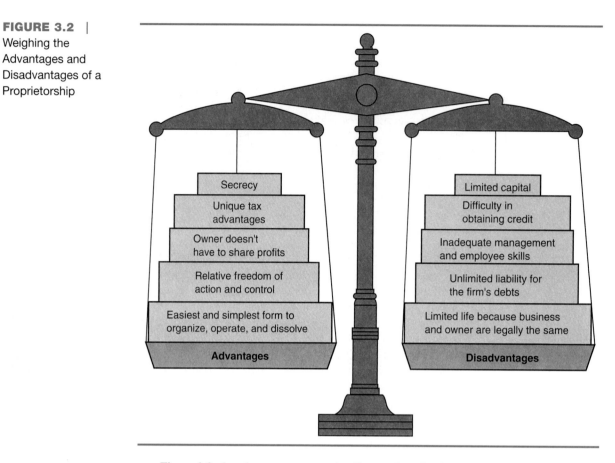

Figure 3.2 also shows some negative factors that should be considered. First, from a legal point of view, the business and its owner are one and the same and cannot be separated. Consequently, the business legally ends with the proprietor's death, and some legal action must be taken to restart it. Second, if the business does not have enough funds to pay its obligations, the owner must use personal assets to pay them. The figure summarizes the major advantages and disadvantages of owning a proprietorship. A partial list of federal tax filings for a sole proprietorship is provided here:

Form 1040: Individual Income Tax Return.

Schedule C: Profit and Loss from Business.

Schedule SE: Self-Employment Tax.

Form 1040EZ: Estimated Tax for Individuals.

Form 4562: Depreciation and Amortization.

Form 8829: Expenses for Business Use of Your Home.

Employment Tax Forms. www.sba.gov/smallbusinessplanner

Why Form a Partnership?

A **partnership** is a
business owned by two or
more persons who have
unlimited liability for its
debts and obligations.

A **partnership** is a voluntary association of two or more persons to carry on as co-owners of a business for profit.

In a partnership, two or more people share ownership of a single business. Like proprietorships, the law does not distinguish between the business and its owners. The partners

FIGURE 3.3 |
Weighing the
Advantages and
Disadvantages of a
Partnership

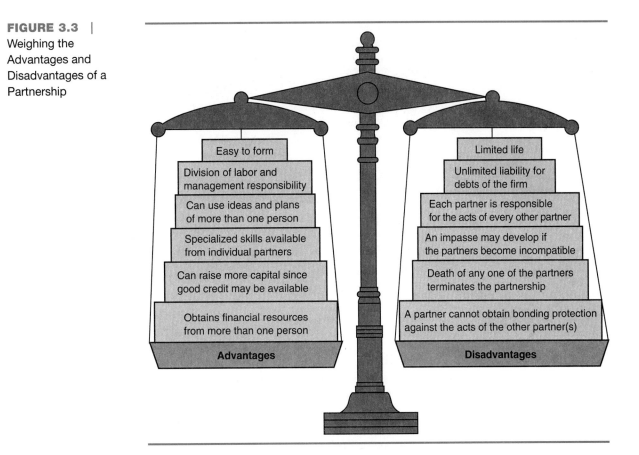

should have a legal agreement that sets forth how decisions will be made, how profits will be shared, how disputes will be resolved, how future partners will be admitted to the partnership, how partners can be bought out, and what steps will be taken to dissolve the partnership when needed. Yes, it is hard to think about a "breakup" when the business is just getting started, but many partnerships split up at crisis times, and unless there is a defined process, there will be even greater problems. They also must decide up front how much time and capital each will contribute.[4] As shown in Figure 3.3, the partnership is similar to the proprietorship but is more difficult to form, operate, and terminate. As with the proprietorship, profits are taxed only once—on each partner's share of the income—not twice, as in the corporation. Partnerships, however, are generally more effective than proprietorships in raising funds and in obtaining better ideas, management, and credit.

According to Paul Lemberg, an equal partnership is an entrepreneurial mistake that can kill your company. In a 50/50 partnership, no one has a final say and decision-making bogs down quickly. Good advice—make it 51/49.[5]

Real-World Example 3.2

Business partners can be found in some of the strangest places. For example: Mary Kumble and Paige Tolmach, founders of Swoon, a home décor company in Los Angeles, met on a plane to New Orleans. Both were products of the entertainment field and wanted a change. Both were ready to redecorate their homes, which led to their new business, Swoon.

> Brian Reynolds and Jason Moody met while trying to get a seat in a boat race at the U.S. Rowing Nationals Championship. After several long car rides together to matches, they discovered a common interest and founded PowerHouse Timing.
>
> Boardwalk Auto Group cofounders Bobby Rodriquez and Scott Ginsburg met when former sales manager Bobby was approached by Scott, who was in the market to buy a car. After negotiations started, they decided they would succeed in their own business and soon the new Audi, Porsche, and Volkswagen dealerships were born.[6]

Figure 3.3 also shows that the partnership has many drawbacks. For example, the death of any one of the partners legally terminates the business, and legal action is needed to revive it. This disadvantage may be overcome, however, by an agreement among the partners stating that the remaining partner(s) will purchase the interest of the deceased partner. Further, the partnership itself usually carries insurance to cover this contingency.

How a Partnership Operates

The Uniform Partnership Act (UPA) governs the operations of partnerships *in the absence of other expressed agreements.* The Act has done much to reduce controversies in integrating the laws relating to partnerships.

Each partner is responsible for the acts of all the other partners. Thus, all partners—except in a limited partnership (see next section)—are liable for all the debts of the firm; even the personal property of each partner can be used to satisfy the debts of the partnership. Nor can a partner obtain bonding protection against the acts of the other partner(s). Therefore, each partner is bound by the actions of the other partners.

An impasse can easily develop if the partners cannot agree on basic issues. Consequently, the business may become inoperative (or even dissolve). Unfortunately you cannot simply vote a partner off like you can in some popular television shows. According to *Inc.* magazine, "Extracting yourself from a bad partnership is like defusing a bomb. Sudden moves can set the whole thing off. Compromise should be the goal, and negotiation the means."[7]

Types of Partnerships

In a **general partnership,** each partner actively participates as an equal in managing the business and being liable for the acts of other partners.

In a **limited partnership,** one or more general partners conduct the business, while one or more limited partners contribute capital but do not participate in management and are not held liable for debts of the general partners.

Partnerships may be general or limited. In a **general partnership,** each partner is known to the public and held liable for the acts of the other partners. In a **limited partnership,** there are one or more general partners and one or more limited partners, whose identity is not generally known. The firm is managed by the general partners, who have unlimited personal liability for the partnership's debt. The personal liability of the limited partners is limited to the amount of capital they have contributed. Limited partners may be employees of the company but may not participate in its management.

Rights of Partners

If there is no agreement to the contrary, each general partner has an equal voice in running the business, which can lead to difficulties between the partners, as shown in Figure 3.3. While each of the partners may make decisions pertaining to the operations of the business, the consent of all partners is required to make fundamental changes in the structure itself. The partners' share of the profits is presumed to be their only compensation; in the absence of

"How come they have to swear in the witness but not the lawyer?"

(Source: © 2005 Reprinted courtesy of Bunny Hoest and PARADE magazine.)

articles of copartnership are drawn up during the preoperating period to show rights, duties, and responsibilities of each partner.

A **corporation** is a business formed and owned by a group of people, called stockholders, given special rights, privileges, and limited liabilities by law.

The **C corporation** is a regular corporation that provides the protection of limited liability for shareholders, but its earnings are taxed at both the corporate and shareholder levels.

any agreement otherwise, profits and losses are distributed equally.

Ordinarily, the rights, duties, and responsibilities of the partners are detailed in the **articles of copartnership.** These should be agreed on during the preoperating period and should spell out the authority, duties, and responsibilities of each partner.

A partnership is required to file Form 1065 with the IRS (www.irs.gov) for information purposes. The IRS can, and sometimes does, challenge the status of a partnership and may attempt to tax it as a separate legal entity. Other forms that may be required are

- Form 1065 K-1: Partner's Share of Income, Credit, Deductions.
- Form 4562: Depreciation.
- Form 1040: Individual Income Tax Return.
- Schedule E: Supplemental Income and Loss.
- Schedule SE: Self-Employment Tax.
- Form 1040-ES: Estimated Tax for Individuals.
- Employment Tax Forms. (www.sba.gov)

Why Form a Corporation?

In one of the earliest decisions of the U.S. Supreme Court, a corporation was defined as "an artificial being, invisible, intangible, and existing only in contemplation of the law." In other words, a **corporation** is a legal entity whose life exists at the pleasure of the courts. The traditional form of the corporation is called a **C corporation** (Inc. or Ltd.).

A corporation, chartered by the state in which it is headquartered, is considered by law to be a unique entity, separate and apart from those who own it. A corporation can be taxed; it can be sued; it can enter into contractual agreements. The owners of a corporation are its shareholders. The shareholders elect a *board of directors* to oversee the major policies and decisions. The corporation has a life of its own and does not dissolve when ownership changes.

According to Joseph Nocera, "the corporation is really quite a remarkable thing when you stop to think about it." Corporations are said to be the vehicle that "made the world safe for investment."[8]

The formation of a corporation is more formal and complex than that of the other legal forms of business. The minimum number of persons required as stockholders varies with individual state laws, but it usually ranges from three to five. The procedure for formation is usually legally defined and requires the services of an attorney. Incorporation fees are normally based on the corporation's amount of capital.

The corporate form offers several advantages, as shown in Figure 3.4. Because the corporation is separate and distinct from the owners as individuals, the death of one stockholder does not affect its life. Also, each owner's liability for the firm's debts is limited to the amount invested, so personal property cannot be taken to pay the debts of the business (with certain limited restrictions, such as loan guarantees, nonpayment of taxes, and malfeasance). Finally, because the owners are not required to help run the firm's operations, large amounts of capital can be raised relatively easily.

FIGURE 3.4 |
Weighing the
Advantages and
Disadvantages of a
Corporation

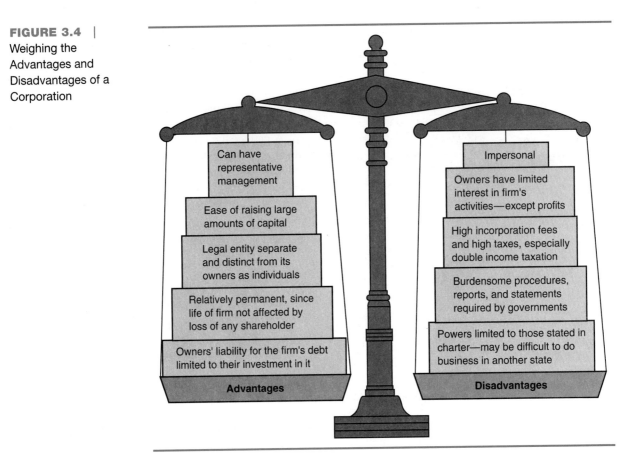

The many disadvantages of the corporation, also shown in Figure 3.4, might keep you from choosing it for your business. The main problem is double taxation, as the corporation pays taxes on its profit, and then individual owners pay taxes on their dividends. (As will be shown later, this is one reason for using an S corporation.) A partial list of federal income tax forms is provided here:

- Form 1120 or 1120-A: Corporation Income Tax Return.
- Form 1120-W: Estimated Tax for Corporation.
- Form 8109-B: Deposit Coupon.
- Form 4625: Depreciation.
- Employment tax forms.
- Other forms as needed for capital gains, sale of assets, alternative minimum tax, etc.
  www.sba.gov

Also, note the area of operations is limited by the corporation's charter, and the process of incorporation is complex and costly.

How to Form a Corporation

**articles of
incorporation** are the
instrument by which a
corporation is formed
under the corporation laws
of a given state.

A **corporate charter**
states what the business
can do and provides other
organizational and financial
information.

To form a corporation, **articles of incorporation** must be prepared and filed with the state in exchange for a **corporate charter,** which states what the business can do and provides other information. Also, the procedures, reports, and statements required for operating a corporation are cumbersome, and because the owners' powers are limited to those stated in the charter, it may be difficult for the corporation to do business in another state. Unlike corporations, LLCs have a limited life. The articles of organization must specify the dates of the LLC's existence; they also dissolve at the death, withdrawal, resignation, expulsion, or bankruptcy of a member.

Because the legal requirements for incorporating vary from state to state, it might be advantageous to incorporate in a state favorable to business, such as Delaware. Delaware's incorporation requirements are so lenient that, despite its small size, it charters more corporations than any other state. Texas, however, has fewer filing requirements and simpler forms than any other state.

The articles of incorporation contain eleven key areas: corporation's name, names of the organizers, stock or no stock, organization "will," purpose, profit or not-for-profit, U.S. corporation must file with Internal Revenue Service, stock authorization, initial board members, initial directors, and home office location. A sample can be found at <u>www .managementhelp.org/</u>.

One danger in any business is that one of the owners will leave and start a competing business. Even if trade secrets are not stolen, the new competitor will have acquired business knowledge at the corporation's expense. It may not be possible to prevent such defections, but incorporators can make provisions during the incorporation process for recovering damages for any loss the firm suffers.

One way is to include a **buy-sell agreement** in the articles of incorporation. This arrangement details the terms by which stockholders can buy out each other's interest. Also, if the success of the venture is dependent on key people, insurance should be carried on them. This type of insurance protects the resources of the firm in the event of the loss of these people (see Chapter 17).

Adequate bond and insurance coverage should be maintained against losses that result from the acts of employees and others.

A **buy-sell agreement** explains how stockholders can buy out each other's interest.

How a Corporation Is Governed

The initial incorporators usually operate the corporation after it is formed. But they are assisted by other stockholders, directors, officers, and executives.

Stockholders   The stockholders are the corporation's owners. In a small company, one or a few people may own most of the stock and therefore be able to control it. In a large corporation, however, holders of as little as 10 percent may be able to control the company. Often, the founders have the controlling interest and can pick the people to be on the board of directors.

Board of Directors   The board of directors represents the stockholders in managing the company. Board members can help set goals and plan marketing, production, and financing strategies. However, some owners prefer to run the company alone, without someone "looking over their shoulder."

There are many sources of effective outside directors, such as experienced businesspeople, investors, bankers, and professionals such as attorneys, CPAs, or business consultants. It is becoming difficult, however, to obtain competent outsiders to serve on boards—especially of small companies—because of liability suits.

Corporate Officers   While their titles and duties vary, corporate officers usually include the chairman, president, secretary, and treasurer. Within limits set by stockholders and the board, these officers direct the day-to-day operations of the business. As the business grows, others are often added to constitute an executive committee, which performs this function.

The S Corporation

A form of business ownership receiving growing attention in recent years is the **S corporation,** a special type of corporation with fewer than 100 shareholders, that is exempt from multiple taxation and excessive paperwork.

If the income from corporate operations is distributed to the stockholders of an S corporation, they pay taxes on it at their individual rates. While the payment process is similar to that of a partnership, the corporation must file a special federal income tax return. A partial list of federal tax forms required includes the following:

- Form 1120S: Income Tax Return for S Corporation.
- Form 1120S K-1: Shareholder's Share of Income, Credit, Deductions.
- Form 4625: Depreciation.
- Employment tax forms.
- Form 1040: Individual Income Tax Return.
- Schedule E: Supplemental Income and Loss.
- Schedule SE: Self-Employment Tax.
- Form 1040ES: Estimated Tax for Individuals.
- Other forms as needed for capital gains, sale of assets, alternative minimum tax, etc. www.sba.gov

There are, however, significant costs to electing S corporation status. These corporations can issue only one class of stock—common. This may limit equity financing in some cases, because other forms of stock, which cannot be issued by the S corporation, are preferred by many venture capitalists. Another disadvantage is that all shareholders must be individuals, estates, or some type of personal trust. Therefore, no other corporation, nonresident alien, LLC, or partnership may invest in the company. Also, only shareholders who are individuals or estates and are U.S. citizens or permanent residents can belong. Finally, tax rules for S corporations are very tough and confusing.

As an indication of the popularity of this form, the IRS received 3.99 million S corporation tax returns in 2007, compared with 2.86 million in 2000. S corporation returns account for 68 percent of all corporate returns filed in 2007 as compared to 42 percent recorded in 2000.[9]

Other Forms of Business

Other legal forms can be used by a small business owner. The most popular of these are the limited liability company (LLC), the limited liability partnership (LLP), the family limited liability partnership (FLP), the professional service corporation (PSC), the nonprofit corporation, the cooperative, the joint venture, and fractional ownership.

The Limited-Liability Company (LLC)

Limited-liability companies (LLCs) are formed to help entrepreneurs gain the benefit of limited liability provided by the corporation along with the tax advantages of a partnership. LLCs provide benefits similar to the S corporation, without the special eligibility requirements. The limited liability company is a type of hybrid business structure that is now permissible in all states. It is designed to provide the limited liability features of a corporation and the tax efficiencies and operational flexibility of a partnership. Formation is more complex and formal than that of a general partnership. The owners are members, and the duration of the LLC is usually determined when the organization papers are filed. The time limit can be continued if desired by a vote of the members at the time of expiration. LLCs must not have more than two of the four characteristics that define corporations: limited liability to the extent of assets, continuity of life, centralization of management, or free transferability of ownership interests. Taxed as a partnership in most cases, corporation forms must be used if there are more than two of the four corporate characteristics, as just described.

Billed as the "business entity of the future," the LLC is attractive to many small business owners, for without some shield from personal liability, an owner can be held personally liable for the company's debts, which is a major deterrent to prospective proprietors and partners (see the Profile at the beginning of this chapter). Like a partnership, an LLC distributes profits and losses directly to owners and investors, who must report them on their personal income tax return. But, like a corporation, it provides limited liability for members even if they participate in management.

However, as far as federal tax liability, an LLC may elect to be taxed as a sole proprietorship, partnership, or corporation. If the LLC decides to file as a corporation it must file Form 1120 and pay the appropriate amount of tax on its earnings annually.

Advantages of an LLC include limited personal liability, income can be allocated differently than portion of ownership, and IRS rules allow type of taxation. The disadvantages include the expense to form one is higher than that of a partnership or proprietorship, and state laws for forming an LLC may not include the latest federal tax changes.

The Limited Liability Partnership (LLP)

A **limited liability partnership (LLP)** is organized to protect individual partners from personal liability for the negligent acts of other partners or employees not under their direct control. LLPs are not recognized by every state; those states that do sometimes limit LLPs to organizations that provide a professional service, such as medicine or law, for which each partner is licensed. Partners report their share of profits and losses on their personal tax returns. Check with your Secretary of State's office to see if your state recognizes LLPs and, if so, which occupations qualify.[10]

The Family Limited Partnership (FLP)

In a **family limited partnership (FLP),** the majority of the partners are related to each other as spouses, parents, grandparents, siblings, cousins, nieces, or nephews. The most common type of industry for this type of organization is agriculture, or family farms. The FLP offers the same advantages as other LLPs. In some states, this style has many additional benefits; for example, in Iowa they enjoy an exemption from real estate transfer taxes when the exchange of ownership is between the partners.[11]

The Professional Service Corporation (PSC)

A **professional service corporation** must be organized for the sole purpose of providing a professional service for which each shareholder is licensed. The advantage here is limited personal liability for shareholders. This option is available to certain professionals, such as doctors, lawyers, and accountants. Check with your Secretary of State's office to find out which occupations qualify.

Nonprofit Corporations

These are formed for civic, educational, charitable, and religious purposes and enjoy tax-exempt status and limited personal liability. **Nonprofit corporations** are managed by a board of directors or trustees. Assets must be transferred to another nonprofit group if the corporation is dissolved.

A **limited liability partnership (LLP)** is organized to protect individual partners from personal liability for the negligent acts of other partners or employees.

A **family limited partnership (FLP)** is the organizational type where the majority of the partners are related to each other as spouses, parents, grandparents, siblings, cousins, nieces, or nephews.

A **professional service corporation (PSC)** must be organized for the sole purpose of providing a professional service for which each shareholder is licensed.

A **nonprofit corporation** is formed for civic, educational, charitable, and religious purposes.

Real-World Example 3.3

A group of citizens petitioned their city council for a dog park to be built in an unused portion of a large city park. The city refused due to lack of available funds. The dog owners got busy and began the process of getting the approvals to do this on their own. A 501(c)3 (not for profit) organization was created, funds were raised, and the dog park became a reality.[10] It is interesting to note that 4 percent of all not-for-profit corporations are formed for environmental or animal purposes.[11]

The Cooperative

A **cooperative** is a business owned by and operated for the benefit of patrons using its services.

A **cooperative** is a business composed of independent producers, wholesalers, retailers, or consumers that acts collectively to buy or sell for its clients. Usually the cooperative's net profit is returned to the patrons at the end of each year, resulting in no profits and no taxes to it. To receive the advantages of a cooperative, a business must meet certain requirements of federal and state governments. The cooperative form of business is usually associated with farm products—purchasing, selling, and financing farm equipment and materials, and/or processing and marketing farm products.

Real-World Example 3.4

Delta Pride Catfish Inc. (www.deltapride.com) of Indianola, Mississippi, the farm-raised catfish capital of the United States, is such a cooperative. Catfish farming, the nation's largest aquaculture industry, is done primarily by small farmers who don't have the expertise or resources to do their own marketing. So they join cooperatives that provide aggressive marketing and financing. Delta Pride, the largest U.S. processor of fresh fish, is a farmer-owned cooperative with nearly 200 members, each of whom receives one share of stock for each acre of land in production. Delta Pride's members own 64,000 acres of catfish ponds.

The Joint Venture

A **joint venture** is a form of temporary partnership whereby two or more firms join in a single endeavor to make a profit.

Working relationships between noncompeting companies are quite popular these days and may become even more so in the future. The usual arrangement is a **joint venture,** which is a form of temporary partnership whereby two or more firms join in a single endeavor to make a profit. For example, two or more investors may combine their finances, buy a piece of land, develop it, and sell it. At that time, the joint venture is dissolved.

Many small businesses are using their research and development capabilities to form joint ventures with larger companies that provide them with marketing and financial clout, as well as other expertise. Joint ventures are becoming quite popular in both domestic and global operations, as shown in this example:

Real-World Example 3.5

BHP Billington Ltd. and four Chinese steel mills are planning to set up a joint venture to acquire $9 billion in iron-ore sales from Australia to China throughout 2029. China's fast-paced economic growth has created a serious need for raw materials. This agreement requires approval from both the Chinese and the Australian authorities.[12]

In summary, in an endeavor where neither party can achieve its purpose alone, a joint venture becomes a viable option. Usually, income derived from a joint venture is taxed as if the organization were a partnership.

Fractional Ownership

fractional ownership can be defined as a percentage share of an expensive asset.

Fractional ownership can be defined as a percentage share of an expensive asset. Usually the owners employ a management company to oversee the usage of the asset. Most often this form of structure is used for aircraft, sports cars, and real property. Fractional ownership in aviation began in 1984 and is referred to as "Time shares in the sky." Conceptually, fractional ownership is not the same as time shares since the purchaser owns part of the title to the asset. For example, three pilots want to own their own private airplane, but they cannot afford it alone. They decide to get together and each purchase one third of the aircraft. All general expenses are divided equally and each pays an hourly rate for their personal flight time.

After hurricane Katrina devastated the Gulf Coast, new housing began to boom. Now you can buy one-eighth interest in a condo using the fractional method. No longer must you take complete responsibility for your vacation home. Instead of paying $1.5 million for a vacation home, you could pay about $200,000 for a one-eighth fractional ownership. The key to successful fractional ownership is good, honest co-owners and careful scheduling for usage.

How to Evaluate the Legal Form of Organization

A small business may change its legal form many times during its life. There are many and varied factors that influence these decisions. Figure 3.5 provides a checklist that owners of small firms should consider using when making this type of decision.

FIGURE 3.5 |
Checklist for Evaluating Legal Forms of Organization

- Under what legal form of organization is the firm now operating?
- What are the major risks to which the firm is subjected?
- Does the legal form of organization give the proper protection against these risks?
- Does the firm supplement its legal form of protection with public liability insurance?
- Is unlimited liability a serious potential problem?
- Has the present form limited financial needs in any way?
- What is the relative incidence of the firm's major risks?
- Are there tax advantages available by changing the legal form of organization?
- Have you considered the management advantages of alternative legal forms?
- Are you aware of the features of a Subchapter S corporation? Would they be beneficial?
- Is the company using all the advantages of the present legal form of organization?

Source: Verona Beguin, ed., *Small Business Institute Student Consultant's Manual* (Washington, DC: U.S. Small Business Administration, 1992), Appendix F5. Used by permission of the author.

What You Should Have Learned

1. Although your choice of legal form is important, it is not final, for many businesses progress from one form to another. While most small businesses are proprietorships, they generate only a small proportion of business revenues; yet they seem to be quite profitable. Most other U.S. businesses are corporations and partnerships. Corporations account for most of the revenues and profits.

2. A proprietorship is a business owned by one person. It is simple to organize, operate, and dissolve and gives the proprietor a great deal of freedom. The owner gets all the profits (if any), is not required to share information with anyone, and has some unique tax advantages. Because the business is legally inseparable from its owner, it ends when he or she dies. As the owner is personally liable for all the debts of the business, he or she may find it hard to raise money or get credit.

3. A partnership is jointly owned by two or more people and is automatically dissolved by the death of any partner. The partners share its profits, its management, and its liabilities. The partnership can combine the resources of several people but can also be difficult to manage if the partners disagree. Moreover, except for limited partners, all partners bear responsibility for the actions of the other partners, and bonding protection against such actions is not available.

4. A corporation is a legal entity separate from its owners. Because owners are not personally responsible for its liabilities, the corporate form makes it possible to raise large amounts of capital, provides representative management, and ensures the continuity of the business regardless of what happens to individual owners. Its main disadvantages are double taxation, the expense and paperwork of incorporation, and the limitations of its charter, which may make it difficult to operate in another state.

   Stockholders have the right to make decisions submitted to them for a vote but may be dominated by a majority of the owners. The board of directors, which is elected by the stockholders, is responsible for running the company, but day-to-day operations are directed by company management.

   For simple businesses, with 100 or fewer shareholders and no corporate shareholders, the S corporation offers relief from multiple taxation and some of the burdensome paperwork required of the traditional C corporation.

5. Other forms of business include limited-liability companies (LLCs), limited liability partnerships (LLPs), family limited partnerships (FLPs), professional service corporations (PSC), nonprofit corporations, cooperatives, joint ventures, and fractional ownerships.

Key Terms

articles of copartnership 63
articles of incorporation 64
buy-sell agreement 65
C corporation 63
cooperative 68
corporate charter 64
corporation 63

family limited partnership (FLP) 67
fractional ownership 69
general partnership 62
joint venture 68
limited-liability company (LLC) 66
limited-liability partnership (LLP) 67

limited partnership 62
nonprofit corporation 67
partnership 60
professional service corporation (PSC) 67
proprietorship 59
S corporation 66

Questions for Discussion

1. What are some basic questions to ask when deciding on the legal form to choose for a small business?
2. Define proprietorship, partnership, corporation, limited-liability company, cooperative, and joint venture.
3. What are some advantages and disadvantages of a proprietorship?
4. What are some advantages and disadvantages of a partnership?
5. What are some advantages and disadvantages of a corporation?
6. Distinguish between a general partnership and a limited partnership.
7. Distinguish between a C corporation, an S corporation, and a limited-liability company (LLC).
8. What is the most likely form of business for family farms? Why?

Case 3.1

The Martin Family Grows a Business

In 1989, Dot and Jiggs Martin, along with their married daughters, Michele Statkewicz and Renee Thompson, started a small business—named Bloomin' Lollipops, Inc.—to supplement their retirement income and provide future income for their children—and grandchildren, one of whom worked in the business. They specialized in making chocolate flowers, hard candy lollipops, candy animals, a caramel-chocolate-pecan dipped gourmet apple "drizzled" with white chocolate, and eight varieties of gourmet popcorn. These were arranged in gift baskets, mugs, vases, and other containers. Their unique arrangements were sold in the store, delivered by van within a 15-mile radius, and shipped beyond that range by UPS. The owners advertised on local radio and TV and in local upscale magazines.

The aspiring entrepreneurs did extensive research for about six months before opening their store. The family members worked closely together on all aspects of organizing, promoting, opening, and operating the store. They searched for and tried many recipes for candy, then developed their own by combining the best aspects of the ones they liked. Although each person specialized in one particular job—such as making candy, arranging items creatively in containers, serving customers and answering the phone, or delivering the wrapped items—each one helped in all the activities as demand dictated.

The organizers also studied what form of ownership would be best. They wanted to form an S corporation but for technical reasons decided on a C corporation with the Martins holding 50 percent of the stock (25 percent each), Michelle 30 percent, and Renee 20 percent. There was a buyout clause in the charter, which permitted the other stockholders to buy the stock of anyone leaving the business. This occurred a few years later when Renee left to return to her "first love," being a dental technician.

The business grew so rapidly that the stockholders opened a satellite location, which was immediately successful, and expanded into wholesaling on a limited basis. Even with the normal growing pains, the family not only did an outstanding job of running the business but also enjoyed social interaction with each other and the employees, many of whom were friends or relatives.

A few years ago, however, the volume of business and the resulting recordkeeping were so great that something had to be done. The family realized they would either have to sell out or hire more people, build a separate "kitchen" to make the products, and expand the wholesaling activities. Because she had a growing family, Michele had little time to give to the business, and Jiggs and Dot did not look forward to at least five more years of "working around the clock" before Michele could return to full-time employment. For these and other reasons, they sold the business.

While Dot is enjoying the role of grandmother to her many grandchildren, Jiggs and Michele have started another small business. They provide a select group of high-volume service stations with car-washing machinery, sophisticated automobile vacuum cleaners, and coin-operated pneumatic tire pumps. Michele and Jiggs buy the equipment and provide it to their clients under a lease, profit-sharing, or financing arrangement.

As a result of the Martin family's vision, enterprise, and hard work, Bloomin' Lollipops has continued to expand and prosper. By 1999, its new owners had a kiosk in one of the city's shopping malls and have built a new production facility and expanded their wholesaling operation to include major retailers in New York and other large cities.

Questions

1. Do you think the Martins did the right thing in selling out? Why or why not?

2. Do you think the decision to incorporate as a C corporation rather than an S corporation was correct? Explain.

3. What—if anything—would you have done differently from the Martins?

Source: Author's conversations with members of the Martin family.

Case 3.2

DB Bikes

David recently opened a small bike shop after completing a course in small business management at a local community college. At first he needed no assistance as business was slow and he had all the skills needed to run the business. As the business began to flourish, however, he could no longer do everything himself. Also, he was frequently in a financial bind.

To solve both problems—but especially to gain more capital—David asked Becky to join him in the venture. They formed DB Bikes as a general partnership. They each had an equal share in the business and drew the same amount of salary. They used the profits from operations to expand the business. They also shared liabilities equally as they arose.

As the business continued to expand, however, they realized they could not manage it alone, as they did not have enough funds to meet the growing customer demand. So they decided to incorporate and sell shares to the public. Because there were only 15 stockholders, David and Becky decided to become an S corporation. The business became DB Bikes Inc.

Questions

1. What form of business was DB Bikes when David owned it alone?

2. What kind of business did it become when Becky joined the business?

3. What kind of partnership did David and Becky have? Explain the difference between this and other kinds of partnerships.

4. What kind of business did it become when they sold shares and became an S corporation? Do you think they made the proper decision? Why or why not?

Experientials

1. Locate a small business with a buy-sell agreement and request a copy to share with the class.

2. Obtain articles of incorporation for a not-for-profit small business.

3. Rejena and Carlos met in college and soon learned they were a success as study partners, but they both enjoy totally different lifestyles. They both wanted to own and operate their own old-fashioned family drugstore, a small business with the basic health aids, a pharmacy, and an old-fashioned soda shop. Rejena inherited an old building in a rapidly revitalizing and growing urban tourist area. Carlos has a large maturing trust fund. They believe they can pool their resources and capture this opportunity to open their store. After studying the legal formations for businesses, what would be the best type for Rejena and Carlos? Explain and defend your choice.

CHAPTER 4

Maintaining Good Government Relations and Business Ethics

If you have integrity, nothing else matters. If you don't have integrity, nothing else matters.
 —**Alan K. Simpson**

Exercise caution in your business affairs, for the world is full of trickery. But let this not blind you to what virtue there is.
 —**"Desiderata," plaque found in Old St. Paul's Church, Baltimore, Maryland**

The dominant issues are the small business person's access to capital; and, second, the burden of regulation.
 —**Philip Lader, SBA**

Learning Objectives

After studying the material in this chapter, you should be able to:

1. Understand the legal system in which small businesses operate, and explain some basic business laws affecting them.

2. Discuss the role played by government assistance.

3. Describe some burdensome aspects of government regulations and paperwork.

4. Explain how to choose a lawyer.

5. Describe what is ethical and socially responsible behavior.

BSI: Forty Years and Still Going

BSI is a small subchapter S land surveying corporation established in 1974. It employs between 20 and 25 people, two of which are certified professionals. Its primary business is subdivision development and boundary surveys, but the firm also does mortgage loan surveys, percolation tests, and construction layout work.

Gerald Byrd, the president and CEO, is licensed in Alabama, Florida, and Mississippi. The Board of Licensure in each state oversees ethical professional practices. As in any professional service organization, ethics is a main concern, and many forms of advertising are not considered ethical for this industry. Opportunities for marketing the services are few because professional associations are used to get the word out about the business and its services.

BSI belongs to the local chamber of commerce, Mortgage Bankers Association (where Byrd serves as a director of the local chapter), and various state professional land surveyors organizations. He is also "Associate Council Director Emeritus" of the homebuilders association and is active in the realtors association.

Byrd is very active in and a past president of the Alabama Society of Professional Land Surveyors. He is also treasurer of the local chapter, a state director, and a member of the Professional Standards Committee. In addition, he serves as a technical adviser for the Alabama Board of Registration for Professional Engineers and Land Surveyors. As a result of his work with various planning and zoning groups, such as the Mobile City Planning Commission, Gerald Byrd, CEO, has been appointed county surveyor.

Such professional memberships can mean many extra hours of service and hard work. Because its membership is a marketing tool, however, BSI employees are always active and working members, serving on the various boards and attending all meetings and organizational functions. These associations hold many charitable activities, from fishing rodeos to actual construction of buildings and homes. Active members provide services, supplies, and labor for many causes.

To maintain an image of friendly professionalism, Byrd also personally delivers many of his finished jobs. This is a follow-up prospecting function. During this visit to the client, questions can be answered and new projects brainstormed. This is also a very good opportunity to make sure that all work completed was done so in a professional manner. Pricing, timing, and criteria may also be discussed one-to-one at this time of personal contact. It is also very important that all phone calls and "drop-ins" be treated with courtesy and respect. "Let's not forget the quality of the finished product," Byrd says. His business creed is, "A satisfied client is a continuing client."

Despite all the hours necessary to own and manage a small business, Byrd still finds time to pursue his favorite hobby—flying!

Source: Prepared by W. Jay Megginson from conversations with Gerald Byrd, his associates, and fellow professionals.

TABLE 4.1 | Selected Basic Legal Terminology

Common law	Unwritten law derived from judicial decisions based on customs and usages accepted by the people.
Statutory law	Body of laws passed by federal, state, and local governments.
Interstate commerce clause	Gives Congress the right to "regulate commerce with foreign nations, and among the several states."
Police power	States' right to regulate business, including the right to use the force of the state to promote the general welfare of citizens. All laws must be based on the federal or a state constitution.
Due process	Implies that everyone is entitled to a day in court, and all processes must be equal and fair.
Legislative branch of government	The U.S. Congress, state legislature, county/city council, or any other body that passes laws.
Executive branch of government	President, governor, mayor, or any other who enforces the laws through regulatory agencies and decrees.
Judicial branch of government	The court system, or those who interpret the laws and supervise enforcement.
Public law	Deals with the rights and powers of the government.
Criminal law	Deals with punishing those who commit illegal acts.
Private law	Is administered between two or more citizens.
Civil law	Deals with violations against another person who has been harmed in some way.

Throughout the book, we talk about the operation of a small business within the framework of government assistance and regulation. We will look at some of the most important government laws and regulations affecting small firms, as well as show how governments provide assistance and control. Almost unlimited information can be found from more than 63 small business developement centers funded by the Small Business Administration (www.sba.gov). Then we will discuss how to choose a lawyer and how to maintain ethical and socially responsible behavior.

Understanding the Legal Environment

Because it is so important to know and obey government laws and regulations, we will give you an overview of the subject. For further coverage, you should obtain competent legal assistance from someone familiar with local business conditions.

You are already familiar with some of the most basic legal principles, such as *Everyone is equal under the law, Everyone is entitled to his or her day in court,* and *A person is presumed innocent until proven guilty.* Table 4.1 provides a closer look at some basic legal principles and terminology.

All laws affecting small businesses are based on the federal or a state constitution. However, the making, administering, and interpreting of laws are separated into three distinct branches of government: legislative, executive, and judicial. Moreover, laws are made at all levels of our government, including federal, state, county, and municipal levels. These levels are generally referred to as *multiple levels of government,* and each level administers its own laws. Occasionally some of these laws are contradictory, and they are often complex, so be prepared to retain competent legal representation, and practice the lesson shown in Figure 4.1.

FIGURE 4.1 |
Good Advice

Source: Courtesy of Schieffelin & Somerset Co.

Some Basic Laws Affecting Small Business

It is beyond the scope of this book to name—much less explain—all of the many complex and often contradictory laws, old and new, affecting owners of small businesses, but we will hit the highlights. First we will discuss the Uniform Commercial Code, then torts and bankruptcy.

The Uniform Commercial Code

The **Uniform Commercial Code (UCC)** is a set of uniform model statutes to govern business and commercial transactions in all states.

Because laws affecting business vary greatly from state to state, massive efforts have been made by the National Conference of Commissioners on Uniform State Laws to draft a set of uniform model statutes to govern business and commercial transactions in all 50 states. The result is the **Uniform Commercial Code (UCC),** consisting of nine parts. The Code has been adopted in 52 jurisdictions, including all 50 states, the District of Columbia, and the Virgin Islands. Louisiana, however, with laws still based on the Code Napoléon—the French civil code that has been in effect since the Louisiana Purchase in 1803—has adopted only Articles 1, 3, 4, 7, 8, and 9.

The Code's nine articles are (1) General Provisions, (2) Sales, (3) Commercial Paper, (4) Bank Deposits and Collections, (5) Letters of Credit, (6) Bulk Transfers, (7) Documents of Title, (8) Investment Securities, and (9) Secured Transactions, including sales of accounts and chattel paper. Because of the complexity of these articles, we will not try to discuss them in detail. Instead, we refer you to any good basic business law text.

Torts

A **tort** is a wrongful act by one party, not covered by criminal law, that results in injury to a second party's person, property, or reputation, for which the first party is liable.

A **tort** is a wrongful act by one party that results in injury to a second party's person, property, or reputation, for which the first party is liable. In essence, tort law provides a means by which society compensates those who have suffered an injury as a result of wrongful action(s) by others.

Laws dealing with torts provide for the performance of duties and compensation for the physical, mental, or economic injuries resulting from faulty products or actions of others. This usually involves some form of economic restitution (monetary payment) for damages or losses incurred.

Bankruptcy

Bankruptcy is a formal legal condition of inability to repay debts. People or businesses can petition the courts to be relieved of this financial obligation.

Under **bankruptcy** law, people or businesses can petition the courts to be relieved of the obligation to pay debts they cannot repay. There are two types of bankruptcy: *ordinary,* or *straight, bankruptcy,* and *Chapter 11 bankruptcy,* or *reorganization.* Ordinary bankruptcy occurs when a debtor files an application with a court claiming that debts exceed assets and asks to be declared bankrupt. When one or more creditors file the bankruptcy petition against the debtor, it's called *involuntary bankruptcy.*

In 2004, Martha Stewart was sent to a federal prison for convictions on four counts of obstruction of justice. At the time of her conviction, Martha Stewart Living Omnimedia Stock fell more than 20 percent. That was bad news for the company and shareholders. If not for a $180 million stockpile of cash and no debt, the company could have plunged into bankruptcy.[1]

Chapter 11 provides for reorganizing a bankrupt business, whether the bankruptcy petition is filed voluntarily or involuntarily.

Chapter 11 of the Bankruptcy Reform Act of 1978 contains a provision for reorganizing the bankrupt business, whether the bankruptcy petition is filed voluntarily or involuntarily. Thus, the firm can continue to operate while its debts are being repaid. If the business is so far gone that it cannot keep operating, it must be liquidated.

You should consult a lawyer as soon as possible if your business is ever faced with a bankruptcy situation. See "Choosing and Using a Lawyer" later in this chapter for more details.

Government Help for Small Businesses

Many examples of assistance to small businesses have been given throughout this text. Because most such help is provided by the SBA (www.sbaonline.sba.gov) and the U.S. Department of Commerce (www.doc.gov), their assistance will be summarized.

Small Business Administration (SBA)

As shown in Chapter 6, the SBA provides many types of direct and guaranteed loans for small firms. The SBA also provides help for small firms through publications such as its series of Management Aids, local workshops, small business development centers, and small business institutes. Information on overseas marketing is also provided. As shown in Figure 4.2, the SBA now has an "SBA Answer Desk" with a toll-free number.

In addition, the SBA sponsors the Service Corps of Retired Executives (SCORE). SCORE (www.score.org) is made up of volunteer members who specialize in helping people develop their business ideas. SCORE can match one or more of these counselors to a specific business. It can also call on its extensive roster of public relations experts, bankers, lawyers, and the like to answer the important and detailed questions you might have about setting up a business. They will even work with you as long as you need after you start your business. Some clients consult with SCORE counselors for several years.

Another way the SBA helps is by encouraging small business owners to try to perform more effectively. It does this by making state and national awards for the "Small Business Persons of the Year." The current President of the United States announces the winners and presents the awards at the White House.

FIGURE 4.2 |
SBA Answer Desk

SBA ANSWER DESK
1-800-U-ASK-SBA (800-827-5722) or e-mail www.sba.gov (click on "Answer Desk")

The information listed above is for the small business information and referral service being offered by the U.S. Small Business Administration. Call for information on starting a new business or for sources of technical and financial assistance for an already existing business.

Small Business Development Centers (SBDCs)

Small Business Development Centers deliver up-to-date counseling, training, and technical assistance in all aspects of small business management (www.sba.gov). Services include assistance with financial, marketing, production, organization, engineering and feasibility studies, and help with international trade (see Chapter 9). SBDCs are funded in part by the SBA. There are presently over 1,100 locations to meet small business needs serving over 1.25 million clients annually and generating $500 million in new tax revenues (asbdc-us.org). The Association of Small Business Development Centers was established through a public/private partnership by Congress.

SBDCs operate in every state with 63 lead centers. These lead centers are the basis for the network of local centers housed in colleges, chambers of commerce, economic development corporations, and universities.

Real-World Example 4.1

Dr. Fred Ware at Valdosta State University relates that the SBDC at the University of Georgia in Athens is a very important resource. He states it provides major networking to a number of state and federal agencies such as Georgia's Trade Division of the Georgia Department of Economic Development. A local center is also housed at Valdosta State University.[2]

U.S. Department of Commerce

As indicated in earlier chapters, the U.S. Department of Commerce also offers assistance through its International Trade Administration (ITA), its U.S. and Foreign Commercial Service Agency (USFCSA), and its Minority Business Development Agency (MBDA). Finally, the department's Census Bureau furnishes much demographic information. For small firms in a hurry, data may be obtained electronically.

Other Government Agencies

Among the other agencies helping small business is the U.S. Department of Agriculture, which provides assistance through the Cooperative Extension Service, the Federal Land Bank Association, the Production Credit Association, and the Farmers Home Administration.

Real-World Example 4.2

For example, when the North American Free Trade Agreement (NAFTA) went into effect, the SBA, in cooperation with USDA, started a program to guarantee hundreds of millions of dollars' worth of small business loans in 35 selected areas where NAFTA had led to job losses. The North American Development Bank (NADB), an international financial institution jointly capitalized and governed by Mexico and the United States, is coordinating the program. Small businesses in those areas can also apply to NADB for loans.[3]

Handling Government Regulations and Paperwork

As we mentioned in Chapter 1, if you want to see a small business person become incensed, mention government regulations and paperwork, which are a growing problem. At one time, smaller firms were exempt from many federal regulations and even some state and local ones. Today, though, these firms tend to be regulated the same as their larger competitors. While most small business owners are willing to comply with government regulations, compliance is often complex, costly, and time-consuming, and regulations are often confusing or contradictory.

Dealing with Regulatory Agencies

In theory, a regulatory agency is more flexible and sensitive to the needs of society than Congress can be, since less time is needed for an agency to develop and issue new regulations than for Congress to enact new legislation. Experience, however, does not seem to support this theory. Many small business managers believe that on occasion an agency's findings may be arbitrary or may protect its own security or that of the industry it is supposed to regulate, as the following example illustrates.

Real-World Example 4.3

The Public Transit Authority of New York City refused to allow van or jitney services to operate in competition with established bus routes. Vincent Cummings started Brooklyn Van Lines to provide door-to-door service in his area. Although he won the approval of the Taxi and Limousine Commission (TLC) after five years of effort, his application was unanimously rejected by a New York City Council Committee.

When he brought his case before the City Council, he was told there would be no vote because the TLC had withdrawn its approval because of the ". . . manner of operating of the vans and the effect on mass transit." In effect, *the city's transit monopoly must be preserved.*

After Cummings took his case to court, the City Council reversed course and permitted him to operate 20 vans. His vans, which had to meet all insurance requirements and pass safety inspections, would give 40 people employment in order to take passengers to and from production jobs.[4] He now operates as BRD 24/7 with hundreds of vehicles and drivers.[5]

Some Benefits of Government Regulation

Do the benefits of government regulation outweigh the costs? Because there is no profit mechanism to measure this, as there is in private business, and because both costs and benefits are hard to determine, estimates must be made. Even with these measurement limitations, though, it's been shown that some regulations are truly cost-effective.

Real-World Example 4.4

For example, air pollution requirements have provided economic benefits that far outweigh the costs of complying with them, according to the White House Council on Environmental Quality.[6]

"Sparky's found a way to get a bite back out of the government."

(Source: ©1996 by Margaret P. Megginson. Reprinted with permission.)

When regulations are imposed on one industry or business they often generate opportunities for other small entrepreneurs.

Real-World Example 4.5

When the EPA announced standards for replacements for automobile catalytic converters several years ago, it created a market for replacement models that could be made more cheaply because they did not have to last as long. Perfection Automotive Products Corporation of Livonia, Michigan, broadened its product line to make them. It added nearly 100 employees, doubling its previous work force, to serve the market.[7]

Some Problems with Government Regulation

There are at least four areas of concern that small firms have with government regulations. The first problem is *the difficulty of understanding some of the regulations.* Many of them are often confusing and very restrictive.

Real-World Example 4.6

Steve Forbes, editor-in-chief of *Forbes* (www.forbes.com) magazine, offered the following comment on our complex income tax system: "The Gettysburg Address runs to about 200 words. The Declaration of Independence has around 1,300 words. And the Holy Bible has about 773,000 words. But the U.S. federal income tax code has about seven million words and is growing longer every year."[8]

A second problem is *the enormous amount of paperwork involved in preparing and handling the reports needed to comply with government regulations and in maintaining the records needed to satisfy the regulators.* In 1996, Congress tried to help small businesses by passing the Small Business Regulatory Enforcement Fairness Act. The act requires each federal agency to set up compliance centers to help small businesses deal with pending legislation. The main thrust of the act is to get small business input as agencies are formulating new regulations, as it is easier to change a rule before it is written than after.

Real-World Example 4.7

Karen V. Brown has been doing this for years at the Environmental Protection Agency. For instance, she has helped the wood-processing industry comply with regulations so they can get bank financing. And she recently wrote a memo—approved by the EPA's chief of regulators management—requiring EPA regulators to prepare simplified one-page explanations of 28 regulatory matters to be used in meetings with 25 small trade associations.[9] She is now small business ombudsman for the EPA and recommends "Environmental Assistance Services for Small Business," which can be found at www.epa.gov.[10]

A third problem is *the difficulty and cost of complying with the regulations.* National Federation of Independent Business (www.nfib.com) president and CEO Dan Danner told Fox Business News that the costs small businesses face stemming from government regulations can amount to $10,000 per employee to stay in line with government rules. In August 2011 there were more than 4,200 new environmental, financial, labor, and other regulations pending at the federal level. One senator declared that these proposals were causing uncertainty and ultimately harming small businesses and their ability to create jobs. According to a report conducted for the Small Business Administration's office of advocacy last year, government regulations currently cost the U.S. economy $1.75 trillion a year, or more than 12 percent of our national GDP. In the last five years, there has been a 60 percent increase in pending federal regulations that are defined as "major" or "economically significant"—costing the economy $100 million or more.

Finally, a fourth problem is that *regulations tend to discourage small firms from hiring more workers as their employment approaches the cutoffs set by federal laws and regulations.* The following laws apply to small companies with the number of employees shown:

Occupational Safety and Health Act	10
Federal civil rights laws	15 or more
Americans with Disabilities Act	15
Family and Medical Leave Act	50
Worker Adjustment and Retraining Act	100

How Owners of Small Firms Can Cope with Government Regulations

What can small business managers and owners do about burdensome government regulations and paperwork? There are several approaches to consider.

1. Learn as much as you can about the law, particularly if it is possible that a law can help you. For example, The General Accounting Office reports that small businesses are more likely to have compliance problems based on the several layers of tax law filing, reporting, and deposit requirements. Brian Gloe of Ross Lithographing in

Kansas City, Missouri, said that his company has to file more than 180 IRS forms annually. Some of the required forms are merely to verify the filing of other forms.[11]

2. Challenge detrimental or harmful laws, perhaps by joining organizations such as the National Federation of Independent Business, the National Small Business Association, or National Small Business United. At the very least, you can get your message across to your elected representatives. For businesspeople too busy to write to officials, there are other entrepreneurs who will do it for them—for a price.

3. Become involved in the legal-political system to elect officials of your choosing who will help change the laws.

4. Find a better legal environment, if possible, even if it means moving to a different city, county, or state.

5. Learn to live with the laws and regulations, even if it means forming an alliance with other companies or organizations.

Dealing with Private Regulators

Governments are not alone in posing a problem for small firms: Many professional organizations also establish standards of practice for their members. The guidelines are created to ensure professional conduct in various areas. Some of these areas include ethics, technical knowledge, competence, and compliance.

History indicates that government regulations are legislated when the business world neglects to regulate itself. However, sometimes the private regulators need to be regulated.

Choosing and Using a Lawyer

You can see from the previous discussion that, from a legal point of view, it is not easy to start and operate a small business. Therefore, one of the first things you should do when forming a business is to retain a competent lawyer. Actually, your attorney should be retained at the time you are developing your business plan, as well as when you are obtaining financing—not when you get into trouble.

Even though the decisions are for the small business owners to make, lawyers can be an excellent resource. A lawyer brings more to the table than just legal expertise. Your lawyer has several roles:

- Education.
- Knowledge of the law.
- Ability to see the big picture.
- Talent for weighing alternatives.

Consultations do cost money, but good decision making saves money.[12]

Choosing the Lawyer

You should choose a lawyer as you would a consultant, an accountant, or anyone else who provides services. Comparison shop! Check the credentials of different attorneys! Discuss fees with them candidly! And, whatever you do, do not forget to talk with them about the wisdom of retaining legal counsel. For example, does it make sense to spend $500 in legal fees and court costs to recover a $300 bad debt?

Where to Look   How do you look for a lawyer? The first and most obvious step is to define the nature of your legal problem. Once you have defined the problem, there are a number of ways to find a lawyer to help you with it. The American Bar Association recommends four sources:[13]

1. *Personal referral* from someone whose opinion you value, such as your banker, your minister, a relative, or another lawyer.
2. The *Martindale-Hubbell Law Directory* (www.martindale.com), which includes professional biographies of most of the attorneys engaged in private practice throughout the United States.
3. *Lawyer Referral and Information Services (LRS),* which are provided by most bar associations in larger cities.
4. *Advertising,* because lawyers can now advertise certain information in newspapers and the Yellow Pages and on radio and television. (Very few do, however, except personal injury and workers' compensation attorneys.)

What to Look For   First, look for appropriate experience with your type of small business. While you may not necessarily rely on the lawyer for business advice, the one chosen should at least have sufficient background knowledge and information about the particulars of your business and its problems to represent you effectively.

Second, because there should be compatibility between lawyer and client, observe the lawyer's demeanor, the style and atmosphere of his or her office, and any clients—if possible—before making your choice. Does the lawyer represent a competitor?

Third, does the lawyer have time for you and your business? For example, if you have difficulty getting an appointment or are repeatedly kept waiting on the phone, you should probably look elsewhere.

Finally, because cost is an important consideration, do not hesitate to discuss fees with the prospective attorney, for performance must be balanced against the cost of the service provided. Lawyers' time is expensive!

Maintaining Relationships with Lawyers

Lawyers usually have three basic ways of charging for their services. First, a flat fee may be charged for a specific assignment. Thus, the cost of the service is known, and funds can be allocated for it. Second, the lawyer may charge an hourly fee based on the type of activities to be performed and the amount of staff assistance required. Third, a contingency fee may be set. If the stakes are really high, and if time and risks are involved, the attorney may charge a percentage (say 30 percent) of the negotiated settlement, or even more if the amount is obtained through a trial (as high as 50 percent), as shown in the sample contract in Figure 4.3. Also, the lawyer will expect to be reimbursed for expenses. In long, involved cases, the lawyer should provide periodic reports, including a statement of expenses.

Socially and Ethically Responsible Behavior

While most small business people have long accepted—and practiced—social responsibility and ethical behavior, considerable external emphasis is now being placed on these topics. Sometimes, however, small businesses are put at a disadvantage when they try to capitalize on being socially responsible, as the following example illustrates.

FIGURE 4.3 | A Sample Contract for a Lawyer's Services

I, John Doe, hereby agree to employ the law firm of Ruth Roe to represent me and act on my behalf and in my best interest in presenting a claim for any and all damages, including my personal injury, resulting from an accident which occurred on or about June 29,1993, near Bethesda, Maryland.

I agree to pay to said firm an amount equal to 30 percent of any and all sums collected by way of settlement or from legal action. In the event of trial (as determined as of the time a jury is impaneled), I agree to pay said firm an amount equal to 50 percent of any amounts received.

Be it further understood that no settlement will be made without consent of client. It is understood that if nothing is obtained on client's behalf, then client owes nothing to said law firm, except for the expenses associated with handling this case.

Said law firm agrees to act on client's behalf with all due diligence and in client's best interest at all times in prosecuting said claims.

DATED this _____ day of _____, 20_____

John Doe _____

Ruth Roe, by: _____

Source: Copyright 1998, *USA Today*, Reprinted with permission.

Real-World Example 4.8

A few years ago, Gabreiella Melchionda weighed a deal that could have made her then $76,000 skin care business a small fortune. But she turned down the $2 million contract to sell her all-natural "Lip Lubes" abroad because the exporter also sold weapons. Her "feel good" business practices did pay off, however, as her business picked up to over $300,000 in the year 2000.[14]

The role of small business in civic responsibility includes much more than charitable donations. A recent Cone Corporate Citizenship Study indicates that 78 percent of Americans expect companies to support causes, and 84 percent said they decide which companies they want in their area based on the company's commitment to social issues. One successful entrepreneur said, "If you've had any kind of success, you should give back to help those who are less fortunate get to the same level you're at." Sometimes, getting involved with the community is just as rewarding for the entrepreneur as for the people who are helped.[15]

Social Responsibility

Social responsibility is a business's obligation to follow desirable courses of action in terms of society's values and objectives.

Social responsibility is a business's obligation to set policies, make decisions, and follow actions that are desirable in terms of the values and objectives of society. Whether that term is used or not, it means the business acts with the best interests of society in mind, as well as those of the business.

Socially responsible behavior can best be illustrated in terms of specific action programs that management undertakes. Thus, social responsibility as practiced by small firms usually takes the form of (1) consumerism, (2) employee relations, including providing equal employment opportunity to former unemployables, (3) environmental protection, and (4) community relations.

Consumerism   While the old saying that ". . . the customer is always right . . . " may not always be true, small business managers are now truly concerned about consumer needs

Consumerism is the organized efforts of independent, government, and business groups to protect consumers from undesirable effects of poorly designed and produced products.

and wishes. The movement to protect the valid interests of consumers (consumerism) is a major force in small business today.

Consumerism is the organized efforts of independent, government, and business groups to protect consumers from undesirable effects of poorly designed and poorly produced products. The consumerism movement became popular during the 1960s and 1970s. The Child Protection and Toy Safety Act set up the Consumer Product Safety Commission (CPSC) to set safety standards, require warning labels on potentially unsafe products, and require recall of products found to be harmful. "Truth in advertising" is now also of paramount interest to small business owners.

Enlightened **employee relations** is showing interest in and concern for employees' rights.

Employee Relations   Enlightened **employee relations** involves a concern for employee rights, especially as to meaningful employment; training, development, and promotions; pay; and health and safety. As shown in Chapter 10, there is now a greater effort to hire qualified persons without regard to race, sex, religion, color, creed, age, or disabilities. While much is still to be done, small and large firms have made tremendous strides in this area.

Other areas of employee relations include sexual harassment, family leave, care for children and elderly family members, and drug testing. While the courts and legislators are sorting out the legal aspects of these affairs, business owners must consider the ethical aspects.

Now that men and women are working alongside one another in almost equal circumstances, an emerging problem for managers is what to do about "office romances." A survey of firms of all sizes by the American Management Association found that more than 30 percent of employees reported having been involved with a coworker at least once during their employment. While this situation poses a dilemma for managers, a rule of thumb is: *If it appears in any way to involve sexual harassment, step in forcefully to prevent it.*[16]

Environmental protection tries to maintain a healthy balance between people and their environment.

Pollution control is the effort to prevent the contamination or destruction of the natural environment.

Environmental Protection   **Environmental protection** is trying to maintain a healthy balance between people and their environment. It takes two forms: (1) controlling pollution, and (2) conserving natural resources.

Pollution control is trying to prevent the contamination or destruction of the natural environment. It is one of the most difficult problems facing not only small business but also all others in society. While efforts are being made to prevent—or control—air, soil, and water pollution, the problem is very complex. It involves balancing our current use of natural resources and conserving them for future use. The real problem—from a small business perspective—is balancing environmental needs with economic ones. This is becoming increasingly difficult; for example, court rulings have held that banks may be liable when their customers pollute, so banks have started demanding an environmental audit and proof that customers have never polluted.

Real-World Example 4.9

The Environmental Protection Agency (EPA) is also stepping up enforcement of such laws. For example, in August 2001, the EPA put General Electric on notice that it will probably have to pay $500 million to clean up the Hudson River because its toxins damaged fish, animals, and the boating industry.[17]

Conservation means practicing the most effective use of resources, while considering society's current and future needs.

Conservation means practicing the most effective use of resources, while considering society's current and future needs. Conservation is also known as the "green" movement. A recent survey indicates 36 percent of people are concerned about the planet they are

Recycling is reprocessing used items for future use.

leaving for future generations.[18] One form of conservation is **recycling,** which is reprocessing used items for future use. For example, BSI (see the profile this chapter) practices recycling by collecting all paper and taking it to the local recycling center. In addition, with rapidly changing technology, many tools of the trade constantly need to be updated or replaced leaving piles of old junk. Most communities have special drives or drop-off spots for disposal or recycling of the old technological products. Batteries present a serious threat to our environment and should be included in technological recycling.

There are many things that the business owner can do to help conserve our environment. These include reduce waste, recycle, reduce energy (adjust the thermostat), purchase recycled products, carpool, and encourage others to follow your lead in conserving our environment. Do your research and keep up with green trends.

Community Relations   There are several other areas of social responsibility in which small firms participate: (1) educational and medical assistance, (2) urban development and renewal, and (3) the arts, culture, and recreation.

Entrepreneurs and small business owners are very active in providing assistance to educational and medical institutions. The following example shows what one socially responsible owner is doing.

Real-World Example 4.10

Truett Cathy, founder and CEO of Atlanta-based Chick-fil-A, Inc. (www.chick-fil-a.com), offers $1,000 college scholarships to all restaurant employees who have worked at least 20 hours per week for two consecutive years. Since 1973, Chick-fil-A has awarded more than $13 million in more than 10,000 scholarships at over 1,200 institutions.

Another unique feature of Chick-fil-A is Cathy's refusal to open on Sundays. His "never on Sunday" policy gives him an edge in attracting and retaining a high-quality staff to his nearly 900 restaurants.

Small business owners are particularly interested in urban development and renewal. First, it helps improve the environment in which they operate. Second, it helps provide them with a higher purpose.

Most companies—from mom-and-pop stores to large corporations—contribute in some way to hometown arts, cultural, and recreational activities. These efforts include such activities as art workshops for children, civic orchestras or ballet or opera companies, and youth sports teams.

Industry trade associations are good ways for the small business owner to participate in community and charitable activities. For example, a local homebuilders association promotes activities that donate all proceeds to the local shelter for abused women and their children. By doing this the business owner can make a stronger impact than by making a single donation. Strength in numbers.

Business Ethics

Business ethics are the standards used to judge the rightness or wrongness of a business's and its personnel's relations to others.

Business ethics are the standards used to judge the rightness or wrongness of a business's and its personnel's relations to others. Small business people are expected to deal ethically with employees, customers, competitors, and others. Ethical behavior is expected in decisions concerning cases of bribery, industrial theft and espionage, collusion, tax evasion, false and/or misleading advertising, and conflicts of interest, as well as in all personnel's conduct generally—loyalty, confidentiality, respect for others' privacy, and truthfulness are all expected. Yet a study by the Society for Human Resource Management and the Ethics Resource Center found that 54 percent of human resource professionals ". . . had observed employees running afoul of the law or of workplace standards."[19]

Young people today are becoming concerned about ethical behavior. One survey of youths, 13 to 18 years old, indicated that they were very skeptical of our business leaders. It reflected the facts that 45 percent believe that business leaders are not ethical, with another 38 percent unsure.[20]

One ethical dilemma of our current age is junk food. The World Health Organization (WHO) is very concerned about the multimillion-dollar junk food market that is glutting the world. In addition to preventing obesity, it is about stopping people from getting sick, protecting children, and wealth. Bad diets are making millions for many. For example, Disney now has guidelines that call for limiting calories, fat, saturated fat, and sugar for producers using Disney characters in packaging children's food. The challenge is the determination of "unhealthy food." McDonald's now offers children's meals with apples and low-fat milk.[21] In the United States alone, obesity costs $147 billion per year in health care costs, which amounts to about 9 percent of all medical spending.[22] It is interesting to note that fast-food advertising aimed at children costs restaurant owners over $10 billion per year.

According to the Institute of Business Ethics (www.ibe.org), companies with clear commitments to proper ethical conduct outperform others financially and provide direction for long-term success and growth.

Many large and small companies are embracing business ethics to be socially responsible, while others do it to enhance profits. Does practicing social responsibility and ethical behavior affect profits?

Real-World Example 4.11

This relationship is particularly appealing to women. One recent study found that U.S. mutual funds that invest only in companies deemed socially responsible returned an average of 14.7 percent a year compared with only 13.51 percent for funds that did not make such a distinction.[23]

In general, if you launch a business ethics program solely to enhance profits—*or* only to be socially responsible—the program will fail. Instead, socially responsible behavior and profits are *both* needed.

What course are you to follow, then? There are at least three levels of ethical behavior. At the lowest level is obeying the laws of the land. This is the very least that can be expected of the owners and managers of small businesses—as well as of large ones. The second level is governed by any codes of ethics issued by groups to which the business owner belongs. Finally, at the top level is the individual's **personal ethic.** This is the person's own belief system that tells him or her what to do if, as, or when the laws and/or any pertinent

One's **personal ethic** is one's own belief system that tells one what to do if or when the laws and/or any pertinent codes of ethics are silent.

codes of ethics are silent. Ethical behavior is your choice, and, to help you, Dave Anderson suggests four points to consider:

1. *You can control your attitude* (about 80 percent of what you hear is negative); reinforce your attitude by setting and reviewing goals.

2. *You can control your associations;* choose to associate with and listen to ethical winners.

3. *You can control your disciplines;* "When you start doing the things you ought to do, when you ought to do them, the day will come when you can do the things you want to do, when you want to do them." Ruts are the results of repeated errors.

4. *You can choose to work on yourself;* failure is never an accident, you set yourself up for it. You are not a victim; choose your behaviors.[24]

As a minimum, the public expects small business owners and managers to obey both the letter and the spirit of laws affecting their operations. Finally, they should go beyond laws and social responsibility to behavior based solely on ethical considerations. Sometimes, it may seem difficult for the small business to act ethically and still satisfy the customer. For example, Robin Liss developed her consumer information website (www.reviewed.com) while in high school, which earns all its revenue from ads. One company accused her of taking bribes and told her they had reported her to the FBI. Her ethic policy includes (but not limited to) buy, borrow and return, or donate samples being examined to charity, and we always pay our own way to conventions and manufacturing facilities. "Ethics is our selling point" (see www .reviewed.com/Ethics.html). She later asked the accusing company if they really reported her to the FBI and was told yes, but she was only found guilty of a passion to build a reliable company.[25] Your company's reputation is too important to ignore and must be deliberately honed. Do not take a passive approach, but develop reputation-building strategies. Small companies generally do a poor job at building an image. Find what you do well and build on it.[26]

Perhaps your best test of ethical behavior is Rotary International's "Four-Way Test" of the things we think, say, or do:

1. Is it the TRUTH?
2. Is it FAIR to ALL concerned?
3. Will it build GOODWILL and Better Friendships?
4. Will it be BENEFICIAL to ALL concerned?

The great entrepreneur James Cash Penney, who became a Rotarian in 1942, tried a practical application of this test—even before Rotary was founded in 1905. In 1902, he opened his first Golden Rule Store—later known as J. C. Penney Company (www.jcpenney.com)—to provide top-quality customer service, treat his employees fairly, and apply ethical standards of the golden rule to business.

In 1913, he formalized his beliefs into the "The Penney Idea," which is spelled out as follows:[27]

•   To serve the public, as nearly as we can, to its complete satisfaction.

•   To expect for the service we render a fair remuneration and not all the profit the traffic will bear.

•   To do all in our power to pack the customer's dollar full of value, quality, and satisfaction.

- To continue to train ourselves and our associates so that the service we give will be more and more intelligently performed.

- To improve constantly the human factor in our business.

- To reward men and women in our organization through participation in what the business produces.

- To test our every policy, method, and act in this wise: "Does it square with what is right and just?"

For small businesses to live and lead with honor, their leadership integrity must be firmly grounded in the company's values and integrated into individual employee values. We must understand that ethics statements and codes of conduct are like the white lines on either side of the road: They give us freedom and indicate boundaries. People make mistakes, but when it is a mistake in judgment, the costs can stagger a small company.

Real-World Example 4.12

For example, consider the employee who worked several years at a builder's supply/lumber company. He was very active in the local Homebuilders Association (HBA) and had a large following of customers. He and two investors decided to open their own store and became extremely successful. Consequently, the successful lumber company went bankrupt when he went into the homebuilding business competing against his own customers! They did not like it and took their business elsewhere.[28]

Companies in trouble can look to the Federal Sentencing Guidelines for Organizations (FSGO). These guidelines outline programs for effective ethics and by successfully following them the company can reduce federal fines by up to 95 percent. The FSGO outlines a minimum framework that includes

- Clear standards.

- Ethics training for employees.

- A reporting system for misconduct.

- Establishing a track record of disciplining violators.[29]

What You Should Have Learned

1. The U.S. legal system is based on principles of fairness, including (a) everyone is equal under the law, (b) everyone is entitled to a day in court, and (c) a person is presumed innocent until proven guilty. As there are multiple levels of government which create and administer the laws, small business owners may confront a body of complex and sometimes contradictory laws. The most important areas of business law for small firms are (a) sales, including leases; (b) commercial paper; (c) bank deposits and collections; (d) letters of credit; (e) bulk transfers; (f) warehouse receipts; (g) investment securities; and (h) secured transactions. Many of these laws, which differ in the various states, have been codified into the Uniform Commercial Code. Torts are wrongful injuries for

which the law sets punishments and compensation. There are two types of bankruptcy: ordinary and Chapter 11.

2. Both the federal and local governments provide considerable assistance for small businesses. The SBA, U.S. Department of Commerce, U.S. Department of Agriculture, and other agencies provide assistance.

3. There is considerable regulation and paperwork from government agencies, which causes problems for small firms, including (*a*) the difficulty of understanding some of the regulations, which may be confusing and even contradictory; (*b*) the enormous amounts of paperwork needed to comply with them; (*c*) the difficulty and cost of complying with the regulations; and (*d*) that regulations tend to discourage small firms from hiring more workers as they near the cutoffs set by laws and regulations. However, government also provides many benefits to small businesses.

   Small firms can cope with regulation by (*a*) learning about the laws and using them for their benefit; (*b*) challenging detrimental or harmful laws and trying to get them modified or repealed; (*c*) becoming involved in the legal-political system; (*d*) finding a better legal environment, if possible; and (*e*) learning to live with the laws.

4. In choosing a lawyer, look for one who is familiar with small business activities, as well as with the problems you are facing. You can use a local or national lawyer referral service, talk to friends, or use word of mouth in searching for a competent lawyer. Some criteria for choosing a lawyer are to be sure that (*a*) the lawyer is knowledgeable about your type of business, (*b*) you and the lawyer are compatible, (*c*) the lawyer has time to deal with you and your business, and (*d*) the costs are not prohibitive.

5. Small businesses are expected to act in an ethical and socially responsible manner in dealing with employees, customers, and the public, and to consider not only the owners but also others in making decisions that affect them. Most small businesses have always acted ethically and responsibly, and continue to do so. At a minimum, small business owners are expected to obey both the letter and the spirit of laws affecting them. Further, they should adhere to any code(s) of ethics of groups to which they belong. Finally, their own personal ethic should guide their actions.

Key Terms

bankruptcy 78	employee relations 86	recycling 87
business ethics 87	environmental	social responsibility 85
Chapter 11 78	protection 86	tort 77
conservation 86	personal ethic 88	Uniform Commercial
consumerism 86	pollution control 86	Code (UCC) 77

Questions for Discussion

1. (*a*) What is the Uniform Commercial Code? (*b*) Explain what is included in it.
2. What is a tort?
3. Distinguish between (*a*) ordinary, or straight, bankruptcy and (*b*) Chapter 11 bankruptcy.
4. Describe some of the assistance available to small firms from government agencies.
5. Describe some of the problems involved in handling government regulations and paperwork.
6. Explain five ways in which small firms can cope with regulations.
7. (*a*) Describe the characteristics you should look for in a lawyer. (*b*) How would you find such a lawyer? (*c*) How are lawyers compensated for their services?

8. (*a*) What is social responsibility? (*b*) Why is it important to small firms?

9. (*a*) What are business ethics? (*b*) Why are they so important? (*c*) Quote Rotary International's "Four-Way Test."

Case 4.1

"Hannadowns"

Gun and Tom Denhart left the East Coast to found a new company in Portland, Oregon, to produce high-quality, high-priced children's clothing. They were neither inexperienced nor naïve. Gun, who was from Sweden, had the equivalent of an MBA from her country's Lund University. Also, she had been a systems analyst, controller, and business law teacher for 15 years. Tom was an art director at a prestigious New York advertising agency.

The idea to produce a high-quality line of children's clothing came to Gun when people stopped her on the street to ask where she had gotten her son's colorful cotton clothes. In fact, they had been sent from Sweden by his grandparents. Gun decided to start producing a similar line of clothing.

The couple decided on the mail-order approach for Hanna Andersson, the Swedish name they chose for their new company. To counter the "sticker shock" caused by the high price, the company set out to demonstrate that the clothes would wear well enough to be passed from child to child. This was done by inviting customers to mail back outgrown clothing in good condition. Customers would receive a credit amounting to 20 percent of the garment's average retail price.

The program was so successful that "less than 1 percent" of the garments returned were rejected for recycling because of "poor quality." Hanna Andersson donates the usable returned clothing to needy children. In one year alone the program—called "Hannadowns"—shipped 133,000 garments and accessories to the company's warehouse in Louisville, Kentucky. They were promptly distributed to organizations for the needy, such as nonprofit schools, charities, and shelters.

After several years, Hanna Andersson was doing quite well. It had 230 employees, five retail stores in four states, and a prosperous mail-order business in Japan, where it was considering opening retail stores as well.

The company is known for its enlightened employee program. In fact, *Working Mother* magazine has honored the company for six consecutive years for offering flextime to its employees. The company also pays 40 percent of employees' child care costs.

According to Gun Denhart, who is quite involved in philanthropic activities, the company is primarily a for-profit organization. The original idea for "Hannadowns," she says, was not "How can we save the world?" but a way to prove that her clothes were "really, really good."

Questions

1. Evaluate Gun Denhart's observation that her company's program of donating used clothes to needy children originated from the profit motive rather than considerations of social responsibility.

2. Do you think the company can continue the "Hannadown" program if it pursues its plan to expand its retail operation in Japan? Why or why not?

3. Would you say the company is following responsible business practices? Why or why not?

Source: Abstracted from Annette Spence, "Heroes in Our Time: Hannadowns," *Sky,* May 1998, pp. 107–11. Annette Spence is a writer and editor who lives in Knoxville, TN. Used by permission of the author.

Case 4.2

What to Do?

Matt Snipes has been with the Turner Foods grocery store chain for one year. During that time he has gone from assistant manager to manager of his own store in five months. The company is now promoting Matt to a store twice as big that does twice as many sales. Matt is 26 years old, married, and has one son. This company has been good to Matt and feels that he has a promising career with the company. Matt is hoping to move into the corporate office once he has his degree, which he is working on at night.

Bob Lindsey is the manager of another Turner Foods store in the district. Matt and Bob have become friends, and their families get together as often as their schedules permit. Bob may not be as good a manager as Matt, but he tries. Bob and his wife have two children, with another on the way. They want to buy a bigger house and feel that, if they cut back and budget, they can afford an increase in house payments. Bob has worked with this company for seven years and doesn't have a lot of career options.

While visiting with the district manager, Matt was told that Bob was probably going to be demoted back to assistant manager. Matt feels that because Bob is his friend he should warn him. If Matt does this, however, he could lose his job.

Questions

1. What would be Matt's appropriate ethical action?
2. Should Matt have been privy to such information?
3. What responsibility does Matt have to Bob?

Experientials

1. Contact three separate small companies and ask:
    *   Do you use an attorney in your business?
    *   How did you go about selecting your attorney?
2. Research your community newspaper archives and locate one small business in your area that is green. Write a report to share with your class explaining what the selected company does to be socially responsible.

PART 2

How to Plan and Organize a Business

Part 1 showed some opportunities in small business, as well as the characteristics of small businesses and their owners. It included some thoughts on studying the economic environment in order to increase the chances of success, but those suggestions presented general ideas rather than precise details. In Part 2, more specific ideas for planning and organizing a small business are covered. The information presented is considerably more detailed, taking a practical "how to" approach to the activities involved in starting such a business.

Owners and managers of small firms must get things done through others, allocate scarce resources, and make decisions so that their objectives are reached. In doing these things, they perform the same five functions as managers in an organization of any size: planning, organizing, staffing, leading, and controlling. Some business textbooks organize individual chapters around these functions, but we will discuss them all in their proper context throughout the text.

We will, however, devote specific chapters to detailed discussion of the more important activities involved in starting a business. Chapter 5 explains how to become a small business owner; Chapter 6 shows how to do strategic and operational planning; and Chapter 7 discusses ways of obtaining the proper financing for the business. ●

CHAPTER 5

Becoming the Owner of a Small Business

There is no such thing as growth industries. There are only companies organized and operated to create and capitalize on growth opportunities.
    —Theodore Levitt

Buying a franchise is probably the quickest, easiest, and most successful way of becoming an entrepreneur.
    —Harlan Sanders, founder of Kentucky Fried Chicken

A butterfly will never fly . . . thinking like a caterpillar.
    —George W. Byfield

Learning Objectives

After studying the material in this chapter, you should be able to:

1. Explain how to go into business for yourself.

2. Describe the steps involved in the procedure recommended for going into business.

3. Describe how to search for and identify a product needed by the public—that is, how to find your niche.

4. Decide whether to start a new business, buy an existing one, or buy a franchise.

5. Describe the growing opportunities in franchising.

6. Explain how to tell if a franchise is right for you.

7. Explain the future of franchising.

Photo: Courtesy of Brynn Albretsen

Brynn Albretsen, Chick-Fil-A Franchise Owner

Brynn Albretsen began working at Chick-Fil-A at the young age of 15. She quickly realized she enjoyed her job and wanted to pursue a career in the thriving franchise. She began to work toward her goal and was promoted to team leader in 1998, and the following year she was given a manager position. Brynn transferred stores when she moved to Mobile, Alabama, for college. She continued to be a manager at Chick-Fil-A while studying Business Administration in school.

In 2001 Brynn helped with the grand opening of a new store where she also became the manager. This position brought lots of responsibility. A few of these responsibilities included labor scheduling, inventory management, and money management. In September of 2002, Brynn began school at Rutgers University under a semester exchange program. She transferred to Chick-Fil-A at Menlo Park Mall as store manager. Her boss, Chad Maynor, helped her develop goals and leadership skills by teaching her all areas of the business. Together, they developed a plan for Brynn to continue her education and patiently wait to gain ownership of the Chick-Fil-A at Menlo Park Mall.

In 2004, after 7 years of serving as an employee in the Chick-Fil-A business, Brynn began the application process of having her own franchise. The process took approximately two and a half months, including a 13-page application and an extensive interview process. Even though Brynn had been with the company for several years, the competition was tough. Chick-Fill A receives 10,000 applications every year for franchises and opens approximately 80 new stores per year. There is also a minimal payment of $5,000 to get started. Brynn gained her financial support and encouragement from her father and previous owners who helped her reach her goals throughout the years. She also received knowledgeable advice from female business owner Raleigh Burgess about being a woman in the business world and issues she would face. "Owning your own franchise brings difficulties and benefits." Some of the difficulties Brynn encountered were gaining respect as a young female business woman, hiring good employees at a minimum wage type job, staying focused on growing a business and not strictly controlling costs, and taking on the weight of owning your own business. There are also great benefits in owning a franchise. Brynn can set her own working hours, take vacation when she pleases, and she does not have to answer to anyone. She is also rewarded by her efforts and hard work, and she gets great support from the head corporate office.

Brynn, at the age of 22, now owned her own franchise at the Menlo Park Mall where she achieved the company's "Symbol of Success," the highest award given, for the same store sales increase of 15 percent in a calendar year with totals of more than $1 million. In 2008, Brynn and her husband moved to Florence, Alabama, to be closer to family. In order to relocate she had to give up her Menlo Park site. She currently owns and operates Chick-fil-A at Regency Square (www .chick-fil-a.com/regencysquaredto). This store has no dining room, but is a double lane drive thru. Again she has achieved the "Symbol of Success" by increasing sales 18 percent in a year; and, was one of only nineteen that reached this goal from about 1400 Chick-fil-A stores.

In 2010, sales increased by 8.3 percent. So did Her family—they welcomed their first child, a daughter and named her Rane.

The best advice she can give to entrepreneurs who are looking to start a business is to always be a student. Continue to learn, try new things, and think outside the box. It is also very important to stay current in business issues and new technology. Brynn's final advice is to learn from others and always challenge yourself to view things in a different perspective.[1]

FIGURE 5.1 |

How a Business Is Formed and Operates

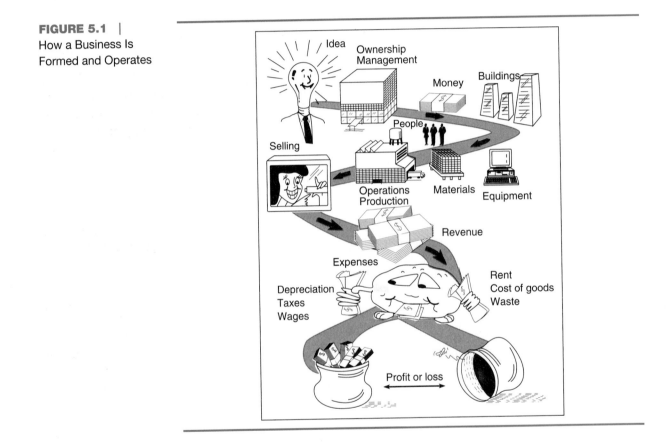

As you can see from the Profile, many opportunities exist for enterprising people to go into business for themselves. As shown in Figure 5.1, the process begins when you have an idea for a new product, such as an innovative computer game. Technically, a product can be either a physical good or a service. To prevent repetition, we will use the term *product* to mean both. Then you decide on the ownership and management of the business and obtain resources—in the form of people, buildings and equipment, materials and supplies, and the money to finance them. You then begin producing and selling the product to obtain revenues to pay expenses and provide you with a profit, so you can repeat the cycle.

While the concept is simple, the actual process is not as easy as it may appear from the figure. In fact, the actual process of choosing a business to enter is quite complex, as will be shown in this and the following chapters.

How to Go into Business for Yourself: Steps in Starting a Business

Chapter 1 cites many reasons for starting a small business and describes some available opportunities. Those who decide to take the important step of starting their own business must do extensive planning in order to increase their chances of success. Now we would like to explain how to actually go into business—if that is what you would like to do.[2]

Once the decision is made to go into business, proper planning becomes essential. While there is no one tried-and-true procedure that will work for everyone, you should at least follow some logical, well-thought-out procedure.[3]

If you *really want to start a new business, how do you do it?* We have tried to compress all the details into the following eight steps:

1. Search for and identify a needed product.

2. Study the market for the product, using as many sources of information as feasible.

3. Decide whether to start a new business, buy an existing one, or buy a franchise.

4. Make strategic plans, including setting your mission, strategic objectives, and strategies.

5. Make operational plans, including setting policies, budgets, standards, procedures, and methods, and planning the many aspects of producing and marketing the product.

6. Make financial plans, including estimating income and expenses, estimating initial investment, and locating sources of funds.

7. Develop these plans into a detailed business plan.

8. Implement the plan.

The first three of these steps are covered in this chapter. Steps 4 through 8 are covered in Chapter 6. Implementing the business plan is also covered throughout the text.

Finding Your Niche by Identifying a Needed Product

Many business owners fail because they see the glamour of some businesses—and the apparent ease with which they are run—and think, "I know I can make a lot of money if I start my own business." While a few do succeed without adequate preparation, the majority fail. Although proper planning does not ensure success, it does improve the chances of succeeding.

Planning starts with searching for a good or service to sell. According to William A. Sahlman, who teaches entrepreneurial finance at Harvard, "Being bright-eyed and bushy-tailed is not necessarily a barometer of success. If people succeed, it's because they really understand an industry and perceive some need or service that no one else has seen." So first find your product!

The list of possible products is almost unlimited, considering the variety of goods and services offered by the over 32 million U.S. businesses. What types of businesses are available? Not all the fields are open, but there is very likely a potential new business; you just have to find it. The best place to start searching is to find your appropriate market niche. This process is called **niche marketing,** which is the process of finding a small—but profitable—demand for something, then producing a custom-made product for that market, as the following examples illustrate.

Niche marketing is the process of finding a small—but profitable—demand for something and producing a custom-made product for that market.

Real-World Example 5.1

Sales were expected to reach a sweet $2.2 million for Brad Oberwager and his new company Sandia. He found his niche while painstakingly researching the branding market for watermelons. His company provides brand stickers (required by retailers on produce) for the estimated 1,070 watermelon growers. In addition, Oberwager produces watermelon-based juices which can already be found in several thousand retail locations.[4]

Real-World Example 5.2

Scott Altman mentioned to his wife Pam that builders always griped about poor service from trash pickup companies. At that point Pam and her friend Cheryl Alley put up $30,000 each and created She Can. They purchased 25 trash bins and borrowed $114,000 from a local bank to buy a truck. Pink dumpsters are now the signature of success for this million-dollar-a-year company.

In addition to their successful company, they also provide community service in several areas such as speaking to women's groups, mentoring girls, and work on community projects. They also sponsor a men's softball team, "We love seeing those big guys in our pink tee shirts."[5]

Real-World Example 5.3

Richard Heinichen moved to the Texas Hill Country 13 years ago. Unable to tolerate the sulfur-smelling well water, he began collecting rainwater in a custom fiberglass tank. A neighbor's request for a similar system was the inspiration for his business, which now includes bottled rainwater. Heinichen now considers himself the mayor of "Tank Town."[6]

Real-World Example 5.4

Keurig Inc., after eight years of development, released an industrial-strength, single-serving coffee machine that delivers a perfect cup of coffee or tea each time. Founders Peter Dragone and John Sylvan created their machine to target office workers. Every day office workers in the United States and Canada brew about 800,000 cups of Keurig coffee with sales in excess of $25 million this year.[7]

Some of the most successful small firms find a "niche within a niche" and never deviate from it. This is what Ray Kroc did with McDonald's.

How to Decide on a Product

How can the right product be found? Most new businesses were at one time uncommon or innovative, such as selling front pouches for parents to carry children in, selling or renting videotapes, and selling computer software. Talking to large companies may help you identify opportunities that can be handled better by a small business. Newspapers are filled with advertisements for "business opportunities"—businesses for sale, new products for sale by their inventors, and other opportunities to become one's own boss. Bear in mind, though, that *these ideas are not always feasible, so proceed with caution.*

Do not forget to look to the past for a "new" product. Consumer tastes run in cycles, so it may be time to reintroduce an old product.

Hobbies, recreation, and working at home require study, training, and practice that can lead to products of new design or characteristics. In addition, the subject of needed products and services often comes up in social conversation. Bankers, consultants, salespeople, and anyone else can be good sources of ideas. But it takes observation, study, vision, and luck to recognize the appropriate product for your business.

The search for and identification of a product requires innovative and original thinking, including putting the ideas together in an organized form. For example, if the chosen product is now being provided by competitors, what change is necessary for you to compete successfully or avoid competition?

Looking into the future requires extensive reading and making contacts with a wide variety of people. Constant questioning of changes that are occurring and critical analysis of products and services being received provide ideas. Innovation is alive and well and will continue its surge ahead. Each new idea spawns other ideas for new businesses. The Federal Small Business Administration's web site (www.sba.com) has what it calls a Small Business Startup Kit to help prospective entrepreneurs focus on some of the factors they need to consider. You can view this online or order your own hard-copy version.

Choosing the Business to Enter

In choosing the business to enter, first eliminate the least attractive ideas from consideration and then concentrate on selecting the most desirable one. It is important to eliminate ideas that will not provide the challenges, opportunities, and rewards—financial and personal—that you are seeking. Be ruthless in asking, "What's in it for me?" as well as, "What can I do to be of service to others?" Questions like those in Figure 5.2 will be helpful. Also, concentrate on the thing(s) you would like to do—and can do—not on what someone else wants for you.

After eliminating the unattractive ideas, get down to the serious business of selecting the business to which you plan to devote your energy and resources. One way of doing this is to talk to friends, various small business owners, relatives, financial advisers, or lawyers to find out what kinds of products are needed but not available. Try to get them to identify not only existing types of businesses but also new kinds. Then consider the market for the kinds of products and businesses they have suggested.

Several self-help groups of entrepreneurs in various parts of the country can be called on at this stage, as well as later stages. These groups help potential entrepreneurs find their niche and then assist them in surviving startup, operating, and even personal problems. **Service Corps of Retired Executives (SCORE)** members can also be important sources of information. In addition to its Washington, DC, headquarters office, SCORE now has about

SCORE (Service Corps of Retired Executives) is a group of retired—but active—managers from all walks of life who help people develop their business ideas.

FIGURE 5.2 |
Questions to Ask to Help Eliminate Possible Businesses That Are Wrong for You

- How much capital is required to enter and compete successfully in this business?
- How long will it take to recoup my investment?
- How long will it take to reach an acceptable level of income?
- How will I live until that time?
- What degree of risk is involved? Am I willing to take that risk?
- Can I make it on my own, or will I need the help of my family or others?
- How much work is involved in getting the business going? In running it? Am I willing to put out that much effort?
- Do I want to acquire a franchise from an established company, or do I want to start from scratch and go it on my own?
- What is the potential of this type of business? What are my chances of achieving that potential?
- Is sufficient information available to permit reaching a meaningful decision? If so, what are the sources of information?
- Is it something I would enjoy?

364 chapters located in the United States and its territories. With about 13,000 volunteers and 16 permanent employees, SCORE has advised over 7 million aspiring entrepreneurs since it was founded in 1964.

It is a good idea for all prospective business owners to get help and advice from as many people as possible. The following are good sources of information:

- Small Business Administration.
- State Economic Development Agencies.
- *Directory of Trade Associations in the United States.*
- U.S. Department of Commerce (Office of International Trade).
- Local colleges.
- Public libraries.
- Chambers of commerce.

The last of these—chambers of commerce—are particularly effective sources of information. Being private associations of local (or regional) business and professional people, they are usually quite familiar with the area's needs. Also, the members have a vested interest in expanding business opportunities.

When obtaining advice from outsiders, though, remember it is your resources that are at stake when the commitment is made, so the ultimate decision must be yours. *Do not let someone talk you into something you are uncomfortable with.*

After discussing the need for the product with other people, select the business that seems best for you. To be more methodical and objective in your evaluation, you might prepare a checklist similar to the one in Figure 5.3. It is used by a consultant with the MIT Enterprise Forum (mitef.org) to help people decide what business to enter. You could use these criteria to help you decide whether suggestions you have received are appropriate for you. If not, make other lists until you find an idea that matches your ability, training, experience, personality, and interests.

Initially you may want to make more than one choice and leave yourself some options. Remember to consider your personal attributes and objectives in order to best utilize your capabilities. Let your mind—not your emotions—govern your decisions.

Studying the Market for the Product

After selecting the product and business, look at the market potential for each one. If a market does not exist—or cannot be developed—do not pursue the project any further. On the other hand, there may be a market in a particular location or a segment of the population that needs your product.

FIGURE 5.3 |
Business Selection
Survey Checklist

Capital required	Degree of risk involved	Amount of work involved	Independent ownership or franchise	Potential of the business	Source of data

> ### Real-World Example 5.5
>
> For example, a number of entrepreneurs have discovered a market that has not been adequately served—"plus-sized" individuals. Having discovered that there was a 9 percent increase in the number of overweight people, who were being forced to accept clothing and other products designed for average-sized customers, many companies are now developing products and services especially for this market.
>
> In one case, Jan Herrick, a large-sized person herself, began publishing *Royal Resources,* a sort of Yellow Pages for plus-sized products and services. It includes more than 1,200 items ranging from "dating services and toilet seats to wigs and motorized gear."
>
> In another instance, Ann Kelly enjoyed working out at the gym, but was tired of trying to find plus-sized activewear. To compensate, she developed a catalog carrying all types of athletic items.[8]

Small businesses usually select one segment of the population for their customers, or choose one product niche because they do not have sufficient resources to cover the whole market. Also, small businesses cannot include as large a variety of products in their efforts as large businesses can. Hence, a small business must concentrate its efforts on the customers it can serve most effectively.

Methods of Obtaining Information about the Market

Market research is the systematic gathering, recording, and analyzing of data related to the marketing of goods and services.

There are many ways to identify a market, and all can be generally classified as marketing research. As will be discussed in Chapter 8, **market research** consists of gathering, recording, classifying, analyzing, and interpreting data related to the marketing of goods and services. Formal research programs can be very valuable in giving direction, but they can also be expensive. Computers are helping to increase the amount of information gathered while reducing the cost.

Another means of collecting data is a search of existing literature. The first places to look in a library are the "technical section" and the "government documents section." You should examine Census Bureau data on subjects such as population, business, and housing.

The U.S. Department of Commerce is another good source of information, as its district offices have well-stocked libraries of census data. The department publishes many useful books on planning and organizing small businesses.

Methods Used to Study the Market

There are three things you need to do when estimating your sales and market share. First, determine the size of the industry and market segment you want to enter. Second, estimate your competition and determine how you stack up against it. Finally, estimate your own share of the market.

Estimating the Size of the Market   Before launching a business, you should find out, by asking questions similar to the following, whether the market for it is large enough to accommodate a newcomer:

- How large is the industry?
- Where is the market for the company, and how large is it?
- Are sales to be made to a selected age group, and, if so, how large is that group?

- What are the size and distribution of income within the population?
- Is the sales volume for this kind of business growing, remaining stable, or declining?
- What are the number and size of competitors?
- What is the success rate for competing businesses?
- What are the technical aspects (state of the art) of the industry?

Estimating the Competition   In studying the market area, the number of similar businesses that have gone out of business or merged with a competitor should be determined. A high number of these activities usually signals market weakness. Analysis of competitors' activities may also indicate how effectively a new company can compete. Is the market large enough for another firm? What features—such as lower price, better product, or more promotion—will attract business? Can these features be developed for the new firm? For example, Tomi Sue Rusling did extensive research in the specialty coffee retail industry before she opened Carpe Diem (see Profile, Chapter 14).

While the biggest worry for small businesses is their large national or global competitors, the natural advantage goes to the "excellent" companies—large *or* small—that strive for low overhead, use no-frills assets, and look for a better real estate deal. Small, growing companies should stay out of the path of focused market leaders and deliver unprecedented value to the chosen customers in their market niche.

Estimating Your Share of the Market   By now, you should be able to arrive at a ballpark figure for your sales volume and share of the market. First, determine the geographic boundaries of the market area and estimate how much of your product might be purchased. Finally, make an educated guess as to what part of this market you might attract as your share.

Deciding Whether to Start a New Business, Buy an Existing One, or Buy a Franchise

By now, you have probably decided what type of industry you want to enter and have done an economic feasibility study of that industry and the potential business. The next step is to decide whether to start a new business from scratch, buy an established business, or buy a franchise. As shown in Figure 5.4, many prospective business owners find themselves in a quandary over which direction to take. The material in this section may be helpful in making the choice more effectively.

To Start a New Business?

Many successful small business owners start a new business because they want others to recognize that the success is all theirs. Often, the idea selected is new, and the businesses for sale at the time do not fit the desired mold. Also, the size of the company, fresh inventory, new personnel, and a new location can be chosen to fit the new venture.

All this is exciting and—when successful—satisfying. But the venture is also challenging because everything about it is new, it demands new ideas, and it must overcome difficulties. Moreover, because everything is newer, a larger investment may be required.

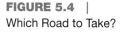

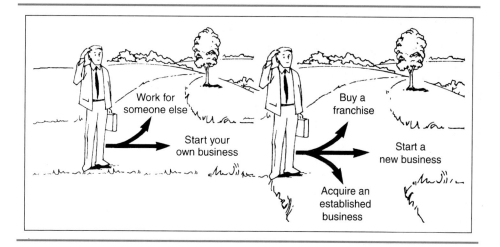

Reasons FOR Starting a New Business   Some reasons for starting a new business lie in the owner's freedom to

- Define the nature of the business.
- Create the preferred type of physical facilities.
- Obtain fresh inventory.
- Have a free hand in selecting and developing personnel.
- Take advantage of the latest technology, equipment, materials, and tools to cover a void in acceptable products available.
- Select a competitive environment.

Real-World Example 5.6

For example, Cindy and Bob Maynard started Vermont Country Cyclers and in 11 years, the business had grown too big—bringing in $2 million a year by taking 6,000 people on bike trips throughout the world. The Maynards felt that cycling was falling behind the times. Also, the population was aging, and people wanted to get back to basics. So the couple sold the business.

They then founded Country Walkers (www.countrywalkers.com) which in 2011 offered vacations in the United States and 37 other countries with 85 destinations. In 2006 they opened First Step Store, now CW store, offering functional clothing and accessories for the tours. The CW (walk.newheadings.com) Store is operated as a partnership with New Headings LLC.

Reasons for NOT Starting a New Business   Some reasons for not starting a new business are

- Problems in finding the right business.
- Problems associated with assembling the resources, including the location, building, equipment, materials, and workforce.
- Lack of an established product line.

- Production problems associated with starting a new business.
- Lack of an established market and channels of distribution.
- Problems in establishing basic management systems and controls.
- The risk of failure is higher in small business start-ups than in acquiring a franchise or even buying an existing business.

To Buy an Existing Business?

Buying a business can mean different things to different people. It may mean acquiring the total ownership of an entire business, or it may mean acquiring only a firm's assets, its name, or certain parts of it. Keep this point in mind as you study the following material. Also remember that many entrepreneurs find that taking over an existing business is not always a "piece of cake."

Reasons FOR Buying an Existing Business   Some reasons for buying an established business are

- Personnel are already working.
- The facilities are already available.
- A product is already being produced for an existing market.
- The location may be desirable.
- Relationships have been established with banks and trade creditors.
- Revenues and profits are being generated, and goodwill exists.

Reasons for NOT Buying an Existing Business   Some reasons for not buying an ongoing business are

- The physical facilities may be old or obsolete.
- The employees may have a poor production record or attitude.
- The accounts receivable may be past due or uncollectible.
- The location may be bad.
- The financial condition and relations with financial institutions may be poor.
- The inventory may be obsolete or of poor quality.

Some Questions to Ask before Buying   *A word of caution is needed here.* Even if there are several businesses to choose from, the evaluation finally comes down to one business that must be thoroughly evaluated before the final decision is made. Past success or failure is not sufficient foundation for a decision about whether or not to buy a given business. Instead, you must make a thorough analysis of its present condition and an appraisal of what the business might do in the future. Table 5.1 suggests some important questions to be asked when making the decision to buy an ongoing business.

To Buy a Franchise?

As you will see later in this chapter, franchising is expanding rapidly and appears to be very successful. Yet franchisers have failed, and some franchisees have suffered severe losses. So the decision to buy a franchise is a serious one.

TABLE 5.1 | Questions to Ask before Buying an Existing Business

- **Why is the business available for purchase?** This question should help establish the validity of the owner's stated reason for selling the business. Some reasons suggest a challenging opportunity.

- **What are the intentions of the present owners?** After selling a business, former owners are free to do what they wish unless restricted by contract. What has been said before the sale and what happens afterward may not be the same. Some questions needing answers are: Will the present owner remain in competition? Does he or she want to retire or leave the area?

- **Are environmental factors changing?** The demand for a firm's product may rise or fall, or the niche may change, because of such factors as changes in population characteristics, neighborhood, consumer habits, zoning, traffic patterns, environment, tax law, or technology.

- **Are physical facilities suitable for present and future operations?** To be suitable, facilities must be properly planned and laid out, effectively maintained, and up-to-date.

- **Is the business operating efficiently?** Will the business need to be "whipped into shape" after purchase? Are the personnel effective? Is waste excessive or under control? Is the quality of the product satisfactory, and is the inventory at the proper level and up-to-date?

- **What is the financial condition of the firm?** Will the business be a good financial risk? This can be determined by checking variables such as the validity of financial statements, the cash position, the cash flow, various financial ratios, the amount and terms of debt, and the adequacy of cost data.

- **How much investment is needed?** Remember, the investment includes not only the purchase price of the existing firm but also capital needed for renovations, improvements, and start-up activities.

- **What is the estimated return on investment?** This estimate should be realistic and not based on wishful thinking. It should include potential losses as well as potential gains.

- **Is the price right?** One important factor that should always be considered is the price asked for the firm. Sometimes, a successful ongoing business can be bought at a fraction of its value. But while you may be lucky enough to get such a bargain, be wary of pitfalls. For example, a retailer may offer to sell a business for "the current price of assets—less liabilities." But the accounts receivable may be in arrears, while the inventory consists of unsalable goods.

- **Do you have the necessary managerial ability?** Some people have a special talent for acquiring ongoing businesses that are in economic difficulty and turning them around. If you have—or can develop—this special talent, the ability is valuable to society and profitable to you, the new entrepreneur.

Reasons FOR Buying a Franchise   Franchise agreements normally spell out what both the franchiser and franchisee are responsible for and must do. Each party usually desires the success of the other. The franchiser brings proven and successful methods of operation and business images to aid the franchisee. If you decide to become a business owner, you can obtain guidance from experienced people by obtaining a franchise. Franchises are available in a wide range of endeavors, so you may be able to find one that combines your talents and desires, as the following example shows.

Real-World Example 5.7

SCORE volunteer Hap Appleman assisted his son-in-law, Tom Scherwitz, with his search for a new career after his involvement in two corporate downsizings. Tom went through a listening and assessment process to find a business that would suit his skills and interests. This led to a franchise for a UPS Store in metropolitan San

Antonio. With the help of other SCORE volunteers, Tom secured an SBA loan, set up an accounting system, secured a lease, and underwent franchise training. He opened his store in October 2005.[9]

Another reason for buying a franchise is that it probably has many of the requirements for success. The market niche has been identified, and sales activities are in place. Also, the business may already be located, managed, and running. The questions to ask about franchises are: How much help do I need? Can a franchise help me enough to more than cover the costs of the franchise?

Most potential small business owners do not have the competencies or resources to get started successfully. But the franchiser can provide supplemental help through its experience and concentrated study of the field. These talents come from both successes and failures in the past. A study of the services listed in the contract, in relation to your needs, shows the value to you. For example, the qualifications for a Chick-Fil-A franchise include

- Hands on/active leader.
- Visionary.
- Accountability for
  - Sales growth.
  - Financial return.
  - Operation excellence.
  - Human resources.
- People developer.
- Community leader.
- Upholder of Chick-Fil-A brand.
- Free of any other business venture.
- Be in business for yourself, not by yourself.[10]

Reasons for NOT Buying a Franchise   Buying a successful franchise is probably beyond the means of the ordinary entrepreneur, as the best ones are quite costly. Expenses include initial investments and fees, as well as royalty payments.

According to Jeff Elgin, franchises tend to fail for three main reasons:

1. Not having enough money to cover all needs (including personal funds).
2. Unsuccessful marketing.
3. Issues affecting the franchisee understanding their role in the responsibilities of operating the franchise.[11]

Real-World Example 5.8

John and Katherine Tait had dreams of starting a Bruster's Real Ice Cream franchise in January 2004 and began the franchise training. By July they had opened their franchise; greeted by immediate success, they very much enjoyed it. Then things began to go wrong. Katherine said that they had three main problems with their franchise: "the downturn in the economy, increased cost of goods sold, and high overhead costs such as city code ordinances and building regulations."

In October 2009 they had to leave their franchise due to low profit margins. During their experiences of owing the franchise, the husband and wife worked well together as a team but were careful to divide the duties and responsibilities and set up boundaries. John did the accounting, inventory, and made the ice cream, while Katherine handled the employees, sales, and catering. A few words of advice she would pass on to others desiring to open a franchise are to research and to speak to many current owners—not just the ones the franchisor tells you about. Also, look for hidden expenses not revealed in the franchisor's projected financial statements The Taits have now moved on to pursue careers in real estate.[12]

The costs may outweigh the benefits from its purchase. It may not fit the owner's desires or direction, or it may not give the franchisee enough independence. Finally, over-priced, poorly run, uninteresting, and "white elephant" franchises are potentially disastrous, as the following example illustrates.

Real-World Example 5.9

An enterprising young woman and her younger brother put up $2,000 as a guaranteed investment for candy machines after the franchiser promised to find good locations for them. These failed to materialize, however, because all the desirable locations were already in use. The franchiser disappeared, and the entrepreneurs lost their $2,000.

One way to help avoid franchise scams is to carefully review the franchisers disclosure document and then "do your homework." The reason many franchise scams still exist today is because people continue to invest in "good ideas" without examining the franchiser and the market.[13]

Even under the best of conditions, franchisers tend to hold an advantage, as shown in Table 5.2. Usually, this relates to operating standards, supply and material purchase agreements, and agreements relating to the repurchase of the franchise. Also, there are constraints as to the size of the territory and the specific location. Moreover, you sometimes have no choice about the layout and decor. However, careful study of franchisers' past records and contract offerings can lead to selection of a potentially successful franchise operation.

Growing Opportunities in Franchising

The Profile of Brynn Albretsen illustrates the many exciting opportunities in one of the fastest-growing and most important segments of U.S. business: franchising. As Harlan

TABLE 5.2 | How Franchising Benefits Both Franchisee and Franchiser

Selected Benefits to the Franchisee	Selected Benefits to the Franchiser
1. Brand recognition	1. Faster expansion and penetration
2. Management training and/or assistance	2. Franchisee motivation
3. Economies of large-scale buying	3. Franchisee attention to detail
4. Financial assistance	4. Lower operating costs
5. Share in local or national promotion	

Sanders indicates in one of the opening quotations, this alternative to starting a new business has helped tens of thousands of entrepreneurs achieve their dream of owning a business of their own. However, while many franchising opportunities exist, they do not automatically spell success. Caution is called for, especially in dealing with franchisers who promise a guaranteed return on your investment. Contracts with elusive or vanished companies often prove worthless. According to overall industry statistics in *Bond's Franchise Guide,* there are about 2,552 franchise companies operating in the United States, and they include 75 different industries.[14] A trip to the local shopping mall is all the proof you need that franchising is a good business opportunity. Many can be researched through the International Franchise Association's (IFA) website at www.franchise.org. It is also interesting to note that less than 1 percent of franchise ideas ever get off the ground.[15]

What Is Franchising?

We will define franchising by describing the process and parties involved, and then discuss the two most popular types of franchises. These are (1) product and trademark franchising and (2) business format franchising.

Franchising is a marketing system based on a legal arrangement that permits one party—the franchisee—to conduct business as an individual owner while abiding by the terms and conditions set by the second party—the franchiser.

The **franchise** is the agreement granting the right to do business and specifying the terms and conditions under which the business will be conducted. The **franchiser** is the company that owns the franchise's name and distinctive elements (such as signs, symbols, and patents) and that grants others the right to sell its product. The **franchisee** is usually an independent local businessperson who agrees with the franchise owner to operate the business on a local or regional basis. While the franchisee is given the right to market the franchiser's designated goods or services, that marketing must be done according to the terms of the licensing agreement. The contract specifies what the franchisee can and cannot do and prescribes certain penalties for noncompliance.

Extent of Franchising

According to Arthur Karp, chairman of the International Franchise Association (IFA) (www.franchise.org), the only international trade association serving franchisers in more than 53 countries in 2001, U.S. franchises create around 300,000 *new jobs* each year, and employ more than 8 million people,[16] as each new franchise creates about 8 to 10 new jobs, many of which go to younger and older workers who otherwise would be unable to find jobs. In 2006 one in seven jobs in the United States were with a franchise.

The IFA also estimates that a new franchised business opens in the United States every eight minutes. These franchises are responsible for generating more than $1.5 trillion in annual sales.[17]

Types of Franchising Systems

Figure 5.5 shows the two main types of franchising systems: product and trademark franchising; and business format franchising. **Product and trademark franchising** is an arrangement under which the franchisee is granted the right to sell a widely recognized product or brand. Most such franchisees concentrate on handling one franchiser's product line and identify their business with that firm. Familiar examples include automobile and truck dealerships, gasoline service stations, and soft-drink bottlers. The franchiser exercises very little control over the franchisee's operations; what control there is has to do with maintaining the integrity of the product, not with the franchisee's business operations.

Franchising is a marketing system whereby an individual owner conducts business according to the terms and conditions set by the franchiser.

A **franchise** is an agreement whereby an independent businessperson is given exclusive rights to sell a specified good or service.

The **franchiser** owns the franchise's name and distinctive elements and licenses others to sell its products.

The **franchisee** is an independent businessperson who agrees to sell the product according to the franchiser's requirements.

Product and trademark franchising grants the franchisee the right to sell a widely recognized product or brand.

FIGURE 5.5 |

Types of Franchising
Systems

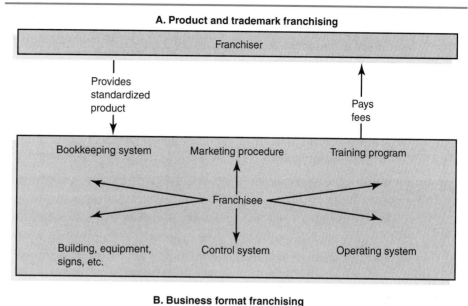

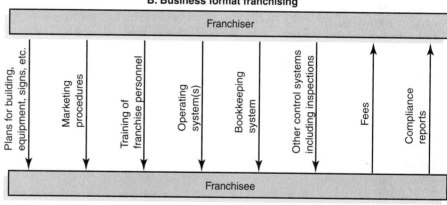

FIGURE 5.5 |

Types of Franchising Systems

Business format franchising grants a franchisee the right to market the product and trademark and to use a complete operating system.

Business format franchising is a relationship in which the franchisee is granted the right to use an entire marketing system, along with ongoing assistance and guidance from the franchiser. The industry groups with the largest volume of sales in this type of franchising are restaurants, retailing (nonfood), hotels and motels, business aids and services, automotive products and services, and convenience stores.

Why Franchising Is Growing in Importance

Franchising has been one of the fastest-growing areas of U.S. business during the past decade or so. And if you think of all the franchises you have interfaced with during the past week, you can see why they are growing in importance.

Recent Rapid Growth

The number of franchise establishments has rapidly increased over the last few years, and this trend is expected to continue during the twenty-first century. Business format franchising has accounted for most of this growth. Earlier, product and trademark franchising dominated the franchise field, but its role has declined rapidly during the past two decades as business format franchising has skyrocketed.

Causes of Rapid Growth

There are many reasons franchising, especially business format franchising, has become so popular. First, a franchiser has already identified a consumer need and created a product to meet that need, as well as a convenient and economical method of marketing it. For example, in single-parent or dual-career homes, few people want to spend precious time preparing meals, so they head for a fast-food outlet such as Wendy's. Reluctance to make dental or doctor's appointments far in advance—with a good chance of spending hours in the waiting room—has led to franchising of walk-in health care services, such as LensCrafters (www.lenscrafters.com) and United Surgical Centers. Increasing leisure time has resulted in franchising of recreational and exercise activities, such as Jazzercise (www.jazzercise.com). In other words, franchises have emerged to cater to many consumer and business needs that were not being recognized or satisfied elsewhere.

Second, as Harlan (Colonel) Sanders said in the chapter's opening quotation, one of the best ways to succeed in small business is to buy an established franchise. This is because, according to the Department of Commerce, 80 percent of independent businesses fail in the first five years; however, the International Franchise Associations estimate only 5 percent of franchised businesses fail.[18]

A third reason for franchising's popularity is that franchisees have the support of established management systems for bookkeeping, marketing, operations, and control. These systems give franchisees the benefit of business experience without their having to acquire it for themselves. This is also explained by the use of technology which has made it easier for franchisers to replicate and spread their systems. Franchisees find ease in keeping track of their units from offsite at any time with the help of laptops and pda's.[19]

A major drawback to franchising, though, is the voluminous paperwork needed to provide disclosure documents to potential franchisees. These statements, required by the Federal Trade Commission (FTC) (www.ftc.gov), provide background and financial position information about the franchiser and the franchise offering.

How to Tell Whether a Franchise Is Right for You

While franchising opportunities abound, intensive study and evaluation are needed before you enter into such an arrangement. When you buy a franchise, you are relying not only on your own business expertise and experience but also on the franchiser's business ideas, skills, capital, and ethics. While nothing is guaranteed to protect you in buying a franchise, you can reduce your risks by taking the actions discussed in this section. At this time **due diligence** is needed to evaluate each company of interest. This means you should thoroughly research and analyze to determine which franchise could be appropriate for your specific circumstances. See Figure 5.6 for specific questions to ask when checking out a potential franchise.

In investigating franchises, learn which ones are growing the fastest so as to get in on growth possibilities. You can do this by studying such sources as *Entrepreneur* magazine's annual listing of the best performers, the SBA's New Franchise Registry (www.franchiseregistry.com), and the U.S. Commerce Department's *Franchise Opportunities Handbook,* published annually. Also, your local SBA office or SCORE chapter, schools with small business development centers, chambers of commerce, and libraries can be of great help.

See What the Franchise Can Do for You

While you may cherish your freedom to operate as you choose, you might prefer to receive the management training and assistance provided by the franchiser. You should consider

Due diligence is the research and analysis of the company that is done before a business transaction.

FIGURE 5.6 |

How to Check Out a Franchise

The Franchise

1. Does your lawyer approve of the franchise contract being considered?
2. Does the franchise call on you to take any steps that your lawyer considers unwise or illegal?
3. Does the franchise agreement provide you an exclusive territory for the length of the franchise, or can the franchiser sell a second or third franchise in the territory?
4. Is the franchiser connected in any way with any other franchise handling similar merchandise or services?
5. If the answer to question 4 is yes, what is your protection against the second franchiser?
6. Under what circumstances and at what cost can you terminate the franchise contract if you decide to cancel it?
7. If you sell your franchise, will you be compensated for goodwill?

The Franchiser

8. How many years has the franchiser been operating?
9. Has it a reputation among local franchisees for honesty and fair dealing?
10. Has the franchiser shown you any certified figures indicating net profit of one or more franchisees that you have personally checked?
11. Will the franchiser assist with

    a. A management training program?   d. Capital?
    b. An employee training program?   e. Credit?
    c. A public relations program?   f. Merchandising ideas?

12. Will the franchiser help find a good location for the new business?
13. Is the franchiser adequately financed to implement its stated plan of financial assistance and expansion?
14. Does the franchiser have an experienced management team trained in depth?
15. Exactly what can the franchiser do for you that you can't do for yourself?
16. Has the franchiser investigated you carefully enough to be sure of your qualifications?
17. Does your state have a law regulating the sales of franchises, and has the franchiser complied with that law?

The Franchisee

18. How much equity capital will you need to purchase the franchise and operate it until it reaches the break-even point? Where are you going to obtain it?
19. Are you prepared to give up some independence to secure the advantages offered by the franchise?
20. Do you really believe you have the qualifications to succeed as a franchisee?
21. Are you ready to spend much or all of your remaining business life with this franchise company?

The Market

22. Have you determined that an adequate market exists in your territory for the good or service at the prices you will have to charge for it?
23. Is the population in the territory expected to increase, remain the same, or decrease over the next five years?
24. Will the good or service be in greater, about the same, or less demand five years from now than it is today?
25. What is the competition in the territory for the good or service

    a. From nonfranchised firms?
    b. From franchised firms?

Source: *Franchising Opportunities Handbook* (Washington, DC: U.S. Department of Commerce, January 1988), pp. xxxii–xxxiv.

whether you are willing to give up some of your independence in exchange for such training and assistance. For entrepreneurs with little business experience, the assistance they can get from the franchiser justifies some sacrifice of their independence.

When you buy a franchise, you will pay up front to buy a building or rent space, renovate a store or office, lease or buy equipment, buy inventory, and receive other facilities. Then you will pay the franchiser a one-time **franchise fee,** which gives the franchisee the right to open and operate a business using the franchiser's business ideas or products, and pay regular **royalty fees.** For these fees and costs—ranging from around 3 to 10 percent— you can expect the kind of help shown in Figure 5.7. Those considering buying a franchise should ask themselves if they are willing to pay these fees, accept the franchiser's regulations, and give up a certain amount of their independence. For example, the initial financial commitment of $5,000 is needed to gain the opportunity to become a selected Chick-Fil-A franchisee. Royalty fees for operation are 15 percent of gross sales and 50 percent of net profits every month. Chick-Fil-A develops all national and point of sale advertising materials and assists operators through its corporate staff.[20]

Investigate the Franchise

You should investigate the franchiser and the franchise business as thoroughly as possible. First, be sure to look at more than one franchise and investigate similar franchises in the same line of business. Review the brief descriptions of franchises in the Commerce Department's *Franchise Opportunities Handbook,* and consult other guides and literature available from your library or the other sources mentioned above. According to the Franchise King (www.thefranchisekingblog.com), the top 10 websites for searching out franchise opportunities are: entrepreneur.com, franchisedirect.com, franchisegator.com, franchise.org, franchise opportunities.com, americasbestfranchises.com, bizbuysell.com, franchising.com, azfranches.com, and globalbx.com.

The Federal Trade Commission requires that a franchise give prospective franchisees a formal agreement and a Uniform Franchise Offering Circular (UFOC) at least 10 days before the contract is executed or before any money is paid. This **prospectus** or **disclosure statement**

A **franchise fee** is one-time fee paid by the franchisee to the franchiser for the business concept, rights to use of trademarks, management assistance, and other related services from the franchiser.

A **royalty fee** is continuous fee paid by the franchisee to the franchiser usually based on a percentage of the franchisee's gross revenue.

A **prospectus** or **disclosure statement,** sometimes called an offering circular, is a document that provides information on 20 items required by the Federal Trade Commission.

FIGURE 5.7 |

Services Provided by Competent Franchisers

- Startup assistance, such as market information, site location, building and equipment design and purchase, and financial advice.
- A proven and successful system for operating the business.
- A standardized accounting and cost control system for business records. These records are audited periodically by the franchiser's staff. In many instances, standard monthly operating statements are required. The franchiser develops a set of standard performance figures based on composite figures of reporting franchisees and returns a comparative analysis to the franchisee as a managerial aid.
- In some instances, financial assistance to cover land, building, equipment, inventory, and working capital needs.
- Assistance in the purchase of the site and the construction of a standardized structure with a design identified with the franchise.
- A training program to help prepare employees to operate and manage the unit. (The more successful franchisers have their own special training schools, such as McDonald's Hamburger University and the Holiday Inn University.)
- A well-planned and well-implemented national or regional advertising program to establish and maintain a uniform image.
- A set of customer service standards created by the franchiser and its professional staff, who make regular inspection visits to ensure compliance by the franchisee.
- Sensitivity and responsiveness to changing market opportunities.
- The advantage of discounts for buying in large quantities.

should provide background on the franchiser and its financial position; the financial requirements for a franchisee; and the restrictions, protections, and estimated earnings of the franchise. A franchiser's formal offering circular can be downloaded from the World Wide Web.

Contact several of the franchise owners listed in the disclosure statement and ask about their franchising experiences. Preferably, seek those who have been in the business for several years. They should be able to give the best advice about what to expect in the first year of operation—typically the period during which the success or failure of a new franchise is determined.

Obtain Professional Advice

The legal requirements of franchising are such that both franchiser and franchisee should work with a franchise attorney from day one. The potential franchisee especially should obtain professional assistance in reviewing and evaluating any franchise under consideration. The financial statements will reveal to a professional accountant, banker, or financial analyst whether the franchiser's financial condition is sound or whether there is a risk that it will be unable to meet its financial and other obligations. It is also important to check to see whether you will be required to stock items that you do not need or can not sell, or whether the contract can be terminated for insufficient reason. Incidentally, while some terms of a franchise agreement are negotiable, *some are not.* For example, *trademarks, royalty rates, and assignment or termination provisions are usually not negotiable.*

Legal advice is the most important professional assistance you need before investing in a franchise. A lawyer can advise you about your legal rights and obligations in relation to the franchise agreement and may be able to suggest important changes in it that will protect your interest better. A lawyer should also tell you of any laws that may affect the franchise, especially taxation and personal liability aspects. However, Russ Moserowitz, founder and managing director of Franchise Insights, recommends that both franchisers and franchisees exercise caution when using attorneys as business advisers. He claims that generally "attorneys are critical to the success of any business."[21] Although they may play a critical role, there is much more to building a successful franchise than the legal side.

Know Your Legal and Ethical Rights

The IFA, mentioned earlier, has a code of ethics that covers a franchiser's obligations to its franchisees. Each member company pledges to comply with all applicable laws and to make sure its disclosure statements are complete, accurate, and not misleading. Furthermore, it pledges that all important matters affecting its franchise will be contained in written agreements and that it will accept only those franchisees who appear to possess the qualifications needed to conduct the franchise successfully. The franchiser agrees to base the franchisee's compensation on the sale of the product, not on the recruitment of new franchisees.

In considering the franchisee's rights, what happens if the franchiser attempts to buy back the franchise when it becomes very profitable? Should the franchisee be required to sell, as happened in the following example?

Real-World Example 5.10

One of the contract provisions of Subway's tight control of franchisees was so restrictive that the SBA intervened. In an unusual action, the SBA refused to guarantee loans to buyers who signed what had become the standard contract offered by Doctor's Associates Inc., Subway's franchiser (www.subway.com).

> The offending provision, apparently unprecedented in the contracts of other large franchisers, gave Doctor's the right to repurchase franchises "at any time." It also made it easier to oust "difficult" or "underperforming" franchisees. Critics said it "drastically undermines franchisees' ownership rights." Doctor's agreed to amend the provision, but only for those who seek SBA assistance.[22] There are now 34,000 locations in 100 countries. Doctor's is owned by Subway cofounders DeLuca and Buck.

Other possible problem areas for franchisees include (1) the high price of supplies that must be bought from the franchiser, (2) inadequate servicing, (3) slashing technical support and services, (4) fraud, and (5) encroachment, whereby a franchiser opens another outlet "too close."

Real-World Example 5.11

Franchise outlets, especially fast-food restaurants, are multiplying so rapidly that new ones occasionally open just a mile or so away from an established one. While the franchisers and courts have tended to ignore the problem in the past, franchisees were given hope by a recent ruling by the Ninth U.S. Circuit Court of Appeals (www.ce9.uscourts.gov). A three-member panel concluded that Naugles Inc., a Mexican restaurant chain, "breached its covenant of good faith and fair dealing" with franchisee Vylene Enterprise Inc. by building a new site [only] 1.4 miles from Vylene's restaurant.[23] The court upheld a lower court's award of $2.2 million in damages, plus attorney's fees and other costs of $550,000.

Franchisees got another boost in October 1994, when Congress passed a law requiring the SBA to provide clients with information on the risks and benefits of franchising. However, the agency has been slow complying with the law.

The Future of Franchising

The future of franchising is indeed bright, and the number and variety of U.S. franchises are expected to continue to grow. Franchises now account for nearly 41 percent of all retail trade, and the Commerce Department expects this figure to increase to 50 percent.

Franchise Trade Shows When searching out the appropriate franchise for you, you should consider attending franchise trade shows. At these sites franchisors display their products and are available to discuss the various issues with you. The largest is sponsored by the International Franchise Association (IFA) annual convention and is endorsed by the Department of Commerce. While attending, you will find many seminars and sessions available to attend and meet the experts. In order to get the most value from trade shows, it is best to investigate their offerings before you go so you will have an idea what companies will be represented. This makes it easier to locate the ones you are most interested in. After the show is over it is a good idea to sort and prioritize your materials while it is all still fresh in your mind.

Expected Areas of Growth

The industries that especially lend themselves to franchising are restaurants; motels; convenience stores; electronics; and automotive parts, accessories, and servicing. Not all franchises in these categories are of a quality worthy of selection, nor are these categories the only ones worthy of consideration; but they do appear to be good growth areas.

Today's two-career married couples are working 700 more hours each year. The greatest increase has come in families with children under the age of three. Paid hours in single-parent households increased 28 percent, and working families now have 22 fewer hours a week to spend together. This has created a huge consumer demand for fast foods and businesses catering to time-pressed consumers. These new franchise areas are referred to as "Fast Franchises."[24]

Restaurants   The success of restaurants, especially those offering fast foods, is related to many variables, including demographic factors such as the high percentage of young adults and singles in the population and the increasing number of women working outside the home.

Real-World Example 5.12

For example, Buck's Pizza is a pick-up/delivery type of pizza franchise, and franchisees Andy and Terri King saw an opportunity to locate their franchise in a renewing urban area that needed to include a dining room. They were able to adapt their franchise agreement to locate in a large historical building and include not only a dining room but also a bar. Thanks to tourist traffic and downtown renewal they operate a successful franchise. Their unique franchise agreement allows them to expand their menu items for the on-site dining. They also deliver to the local downtown hotels.

According to the National Restaurant Association, industry sales were projected at $604 billion in 2011.

Other factors that seem to have had a positive influence on franchised restaurant success are product appeal to a growing segment of the market, fast service, a sanitary environment, and buildings and signs that are easily recognizable. As a new defense, established franchises such as McDonald's (www.mcdonalds.com) and Burger King (www.burgerking.com) are offering new dieting selections such as fresh apples in children's meals to replace french fries. Subway is seeing success with "low-carb" sandwiches,[25] and Krispy Kreme's earnings have slipped since the low-carb diet phase.[26]

Motels   The motel industry has experienced explosive growth since the interstate highway system began in 1956 and the growing affluence and mobility of Americans created a market for quality motels. The industry has grown from mom-and-pop units (with an often questionable image) to one dominated by large corporate empires. These corporations not only sell franchises to independent businesspeople but also operate some of the most profitable units themselves. Best Western is considered to have the largest number of establishments.

Convenience Stores   While the term *convenience store* is usually associated with food outlets, it can cover other types of specialty shops. Some examples of these franchises are the Bread Basket, T-Shirts Plus, and Health Mart.

Technology   With the rapid growth in electronics fields such as music, video, TV, and computers, franchising has naturally followed. Some other well-known franchises are Best Buy (www.bestbuy.com), Babbage's (www.babbages-etc.com), and Muzak (www.muzak.com). Today most businesses in the United States own at least one computer which indicates tremendous opportunities for franchises.

Real-World Example 5.13

For example, Georgia Jones found herself helping friends and neighbors get comfortable with their first computers. She helped them shop, buy, and set up their systems. Before long, she had expanded her business into Computer Moms (www.computermoms.com), a franchise that offers customized one-on-one computer training and support services to customers in their homes or offices.[27]

Lonnie Henderson turned his idea of a mobile computer repair into what is now the successful Computer Doctor franchise. Computer Doctor claims to be the only national franchise to actively pursue computer service business for its franchisees.[28]

Helen Greiner and Colin Angle founded iRobot (www.irobot.com) in 1990 as a college project to refine robotics as a useful tool for safety. Their products were used for search and rescue at Ground Zero World Trade Center. They also have toy robots and believe that "robots will eventually have almost human levels of intelligence."[29] In 2010 iRobot generated more than $4 million in revenue. Is franchising next for Helen and Colin?

Automotive Parts, Accessories, and Servicing   Automotive franchises have been around for a long time as retail outlets for parts and accessories. Some of the units have been affiliated with nationally known tire manufacturers such as General Tire (www.generaltire.com). A comparatively recent entry into the automotive franchise field is the specialty service shop. Some examples are shops specializing in muffler and shock absorber repairs and parts, such as Midas International (www.midas.com); shops providing technical assistance and specialized parts for "customizing" vans; and diagnostic centers with sophisticated computerized electronic equipment. Also, the number of automotive service franchises, such as Precision Tune (www.precision-tune.com) and Jiffy Lube (www.jiffylube.com), has been growing as gasoline stations shift from full service to self-service, and many of these franchises use former service station facilities. According to the president of Valvoline Instant Oil Change Franchising Inc. (www.vioc.com), "It was the decline of the neighborhood service station that gave rise to our business. . . . Many of the original sites used for our centers were such stations."[30]

Other Areas of Expected Development

A growing number of small business owners are finding that they do not have the expertise, the resources, or the time to package and ship their wares. This trend has led to the expansion of franchises to address these needs for local outlets. In addition to packaging and shipping, these franchises offer other services, such as private mailbox rentals, faxing, photocopying, and quick printing.

Changing demographics are also creating a need for new franchises. There have been many franchises for health care and fitness. Now there is a need to merge these activities, as there are more single parents and less physical activity on the streets and playgrounds.

Another trend is toward mergers of franchises in related fields. These mergers can result in stronger and more powerful franchises.

There is a growing emphasis on **synergy** among U.S. small businesses as they try to *reengineer* and *rightsize* themselves. Another way to think about synergy is that the whole becomes greater than the sum of its parts. One way they are doing this is by combining noncompeting franchises into one location. This latest rage in franchising goes by many names, such as **combination franchising, multiformat franchising, dual branding,** and **complementary branding.** The concept, however, is the same by any name: Big-name franchise operations team up with each other to offer both companies' products under the same roof.

There can, however, be "cultural clashes" that lead to the breakup of these arrangements.

> ### Real-World Example 5.14
>
> For example, when Arby's (www.arbys.com) and ZuZu Inc. planned to share at least 85 of their restaurants, they thought they had "a winner." But only "a handful" of the two-menu restaurants ever appeared, and they were short-lived because of "cultural clashes from the start." Arby's sandwiches came in simple paper wrappings, but ZuZu dishes came on crockery plates with metal utensils. Some customers, confused by the difference, threw ZuZu's plates and utensils in the trash along with Arby's paper.

Another aspect of synergy is the trend toward ownership of a large number of franchise outlets. Franchisers find it speeds their growth and simplifies their work to place multiple units in the hands of "big boys," as those owning 20 or more stores are called. This trend has led to the practice of some franchisers shunning "mom-and-pop" franchisees entirely.[31]

Global Franchising

The success achieved by some U.S. franchises has resulted in growing global interest and opportunity. One survey found that an estimated 20 percent of U.S. franchisers operate internationally by means of company units, master licenses, individual franchises, or joint ventures.

Franchises also help the U.S. balance of trade. Germany, Canada, Japan, the United Kingdom, and Mexico are our biggest sources of export revenue.

Global operations also help the franchisers. For example, McDonald's revenues from foreign sales topped 50 percent of the total, and that figure was expected to be 60 percent by the next few years. They operate in 117 counties and employ 1.7 million. McDonald's is obviously committed to global expansion.

Synergy is the concept that two or more people, working together in a coordinated way, can accomplish more than the sum of their independent efforts.

In **combination franchising (multiformat franchising, dual branding, complementary branding)** big-name franchise operations offer both companies' products under the same roof.

TABLE 5.3 | 2010 Top Global Franchises

	United States	Foreign	Start-up Costs ($)	Franchise Fee ($)	Royalty Percentage
1. Hampton Hotels	1,705	18	3,716,000–13,148,800	50,000	5
2. ampm	1,199	1,978	1,786,929–7,596,688	30,000–70,000	5
3. McDonald's	12,477	12,764	1,057,200–1,885,000	45,000	12.5
4. Supercuts	986	0	119,350–196,000	22,500	6
5. Days Inn	1677	94	192,291–6,479,764	36,000–37,500	5.5
6. Vanguard Cleaning Systems	1734	0	8,200–38,100	7,650–37,000	5
7. Subway	24,211	7,337	84,300–258,300	15,000	8
8. Denny's Inc.	1,296	28	1,125,609–2,396,000	40,000	4
9. Jan-Pro Franchising Int'l. Inc.	10,266	39	5,000–50,000	950–14,000	8
10. Hardee's	1,225	203	1,100,000–1,500,000	25,000	4

Another global operator is KFC International (formerly Kentucky Fried Chicken) (www.kfc.com), which has close to 11,000 restaurants in 80 countries on six continents outside the United States. Although it owns more than 1,000 of those units, KFC's global units are operated primarily through franchise and joint venture arrangements. In these arrangements, KFC holds an equity stake in the operations, from which it earns a percentage of profits.

U.S. franchisers have been quite successful in Eastern Europe. Many U.S. law firms specializing in franchising are already setting up branches abroad, such as East Europe Law Ltd., in Budapest, Hungary.

Fast-food franchises have been particularly successful abroad. Because the fast-food industry is not as well developed in other countries, U.S. franchises have a great opportunity to be leaders in many markets. For example, franchises such as McDonald's, Pizza Hut (www.pizzahut.com), and Pepsi (www.pepsi.com) are flourishing in Eastern European countries and Russia.

Table 5.3 illustrates the 10 Top Global Franchises, the costs involved, and the number of units. When you do your homework on foreign-based franchises be sure to examine the culture of the prospective market and make sure of a "good fit."

Growing franchise industries also include maid and personal services; home improvements; business aids and services (such as accounting, collections, and personnel services); automobile products and services; weight-control centers; hair salons and services; and private postal services, Global franchises sales were excepted to grow 5 percent in 2011.

Turning Your Dream into a Reality

We've presented much information to help you decide whether or not you want to go into franchising. You've also been told how to investigate whether a franchise is right for you or not. Figure 5.8 provides a step-by-step review of what is required for you to become a franchisee. It also estimates the time required for each of the steps. While all these steps may not be required, and the time spans are not universal, the information is a good overview of the activities required by many franchisers and the time it takes to do each of them.

FIGURE 5.8 | What's Needed to Become a Franchise Owner

Step-by-step review of what needs to be done and how long it will take to turn the dream of owning your own business into the reality of opening day.

Phase	1 Decide to become a franchisee	2 Make decision and invest $___	3 Real estate	4 Construction	5 Equipment and inventory
Action items	Investigate and select your franchise	Decide, buy, sign contract; pay $___	Look for proper store site: a. Storefront type b. Build to specs, freestanding	Conform to franchise contract: a. Leasehold improvements b. Construct building per drawings	Order and install all equipment; order opening inventory—goods
Time span	3 months to 2 years	3 months	2 to 12 months	3 to 11 months	1 to 3 months

Phase	6 Hiring	7 Training	8 Preopening final check	9 Opening and operations	10 Contract term
Action items	Hire manager or assistant manager; hire crew; fill out state and federal forms	Get your training in franchiser's school; learn procedures and methods	Construction; punch list; permits; bank accounts; marketing plan; inventory	First soft opening; later grand opening Employee daily work schedule Daily sales reports Cash register tapes, money Deposit cash in bank nightly Insurance accuracy Pay royalty and advertising fees	Work and manage your own franchise
Time span	2 to 6 weeks	2 weeks to 2 months	1 day to 2 weeks	Select a Friday, Saturday, or Sunday	

Source: Ralph J. Weiger, "Franchise Investigation Time Span," *Franchising World,* March/April 1989, p. 18. Reprinted with permission of the International Franchise Association.

What You Should Have Learned

1. The first thing to do in becoming a small business owner is to decide whether it is what you *really want to do.* Then, proper planning becomes essential to chart your new venture. The time of starting your new business is also important.

2. Although there is no set procedure for starting a business, there are steps that can be taken to help ensure success. They are (*a*) search for a needed product; (*b*) study the market for the product; (*c*) decide whether to start a new business, buy an existing one, or buy a franchise; (*d*) make strategic plans, including setting a mission, objectives, and strategies; (*e*) make operational plans, including setting up policies, budgets, procedures, and plans for operating the business; (*f*) make financial plans, including estimating income, expenses, and initial investment, and locating sources

of funds; (g) prepare a business plan; and (h) implement the plan. The first three steps were discussed in this chapter.

3. The product to sell can be found by (a) reading books, papers, and other information; (b) having social and business conversations with friends, support groups, businesspeople, and others; and (c) using checklists, questioning people, and doing marketing research. You should then study the market to estimate (a) its size, (b) the competition and its share of the market, and (c) your own share of the market.

4. Next, you should decide whether to (a) start a new business, (b) buy an existing one, or (c) buy a franchise. There are compelling arguments for and against each of these alternatives. Starting a new business means it is your own, but the process is time consuming and quite risky.

   When you buy an existing business, you acquire established markets, facilities, and employees. But you must be sure when you buy that all aspects of the business are in good shape and that you are not inheriting someone else's problems.

   Buying a franchise may help bring success in a hurry, since it provides successful management and operating procedures to guide the business. But you must be able to succeed on your own, for a franchise does not ensure success. Also, the cost may be high, or the franchiser may not perform satisfactorily.

5. Franchising is a marketing system that permits the franchisee to conduct business as an individual owner under the terms and conditions set by the franchiser. The two most common franchising systems are (a) product and trademark franchising and (b) business format franchising. In the first, franchisees acquire the right to sell the franchiser's product and use its trademark, but they are relatively free to use their own operating methods. In the second, the franchiser determines virtually every aspect of the franchisee's operations, including management policies, accounting methods, reporting forms, designs, and furnishings. The number of product and trademark franchises has declined, particularly in auto dealerships and gasoline service stations. Business format franchising has increased steadily because it provides a ready market and management system, and the failure rate is lower than for independent businesses. Franchising sales have more than doubled in the last decade, and the number of establishments is also increasing.

6. Franchising is a good way for someone to enter business. But you should carefully research the industry and investigate the particular franchise to determine whether the assistance provided by the franchiser is worth the sacrifice of independence. You should study the franchise offering circular, check with existing franchisees, and obtain professional advice to understand your rights and obligations. Franchisers who belong to the International Franchise Association (IFA) subscribe to a code of ethics that provides protection to their franchisees.

7. The future of franchising looks good, especially for restaurants; motels; convenience stores; electronics; automotive parts, accessories, and servicing; packaging and shipping; health care and fitness; combination franchising; and catering to home-based small businesses. International franchising is one of the fastest growing areas of franchising. Minority ownership of franchises is also growing, and special efforts are being made to encourage minority franchising.

Key Terms

business format franchising 111	franchisee 110	prospectus/disclosure statement 114
combination franchising 119	franchiser 110	royalty fee 114
due diligence 112	franchising 103	SCORE (Service Corps of Retired Executives) 101
franchise 110	market research 104	
franchise fee 114	niche marketing 99	synergy 119
	product and trademark franchising 110	

Questions for Discussion

1. What are some important factors to consider in choosing the type of business to enter?

2. How can you identify a business you would like to own? What characteristics do you have that would help make that business successful?

3. How do you determine the market for a product? Your share of that market?

4. What are some characteristics you should consider in studying the potential market for a proposed business?

5. *a.* What are some reasons for and against starting a new business?

    b. What are some reasons for and against buying an existing business?

    c. What are some reasons for and against buying a franchise?

6. What distinguishes a franchise from an independent small business?

7. What are the two most important forms of franchising? Describe each.

8. Describe why franchising is growing in importance.

9. What are some expected areas of growth for franchising in the future?

10. Why is franchising growing globally?

Case 5.1

Tim Lewis Fills a Niche

Tim Lewis owns T. A. Lewis and Associates in Birmingham, Alabama, a consulting firm that designs telephone, data, and video systems. In this information age, Lewis's success might seem inevitable, but it is based on experience, hard work, and finding a market niche.

The Lewis story begins in his hometown of Tuscaloosa, about 35 miles southwest of Birmingham, where Lewis gained both business and technical skills. While in high school he worked as a salesman at a local shoe store and served as business manager for the James Brown Singers, a local community choir.

After earning an electrical engineering degree from the University of Alabama, Lewis became an account manager and sales trainer for TMC, a new and growing long-distance phone company. When he went to companies such as Rust Engineering in Birmingham to sell long-distance service, executives would ask him many questions and seek his advice. The buyers wanted his opinion on fax machines, voice-mail systems, and copy machines. They wanted some knowledgeable person to give them fair and unbiased answers. Lewis offered suggestions, and most of the time his advice turned out to be right, so they kept asking him.

It occurred to Lewis that a market niche might exist that no one was filling. When he studied the market, he learned that it was very difficult for small to medium-sized firms to get objective information on products. Most "consultants" were representatives of particular manufacturers; if clients weren't interested in buying the products they were selling, they weren't interested in giving advice.

After about 18 months of research, Lewis prepared a comprehensive business plan. Then, with the help of the Birmingham Business Assistance Network (an incubator organization for small businesses), he took the plunge and ventured out on his own. The contacts he had made while working with TMC provided a springboard. When he left TMC, he had accounts at seven Birmingham-area hospitals, and the business he got from them spread. That's why a third of his customers are in the health care industry.

He now has 18 full-time employees and is planning to expand by adding a training facility.

Lewis continues to live in Tuscaloosa and drives 90 minutes to and from his facility in Birmingham. Of this commuting time, he says, "I've got a cellular phone and a beeper, so I can work on the way up and work on the way back."

Questions

1. What do you think of Lewis's method of finding an unfilled niche?
2. What growth possibilities are there for him in this expanding technological age?
3. What suggestions would you make to him as to where to live? Explain.

Source: Gilbert Nicholson, "Filling a Niche," *The Tuscaloosa* (Alabama) *News*, October 22, 1995, p. 1E. Used by permission.

Case 5.2

Failed Franchise

Herb has been in the aviation business of some sort since he was 18, when he took his first flying lesson. Shortly thereafter he began selling planes. As soon as he got his license, he worked ferrying, washing, and polishing aircraft in exchange for flying time in someone else's plane. Herb was drafted into the military, and when he returned, the market was flooded with pilots and jobs were scarce. He then utilized an eight-passenger Beech and organized a commuter airline to fly to regional major cities before the interstate system was complete. "He flew all day and performed maintenance on the craft all night." On weekends he chartered. A former airline handled baggage and ticketing for him through the various airports. The airline then requested he acquire a larger plane and fly their routes. At that point he leased a 16-passenger plane that eventually developed so many mechanical problems that it led to the demise of his company.

The next career move was the purchase of an east ramp airport hanger built in the 1940s, and his first Fixed-Base Operation (FBO) was born. An FBO is essentially a refueling facility for aircraft that offers a variety of aviation-related services. This service survived for five years until a contractual agreement expired. He then continued selling airplanes, dabbled in the rental car business and with oil interests, and encountered problems when the economy took a downturn and interest rates soared. His next venture was a commuter airline and it was the very first "nonsmoking" commercial flight. He started with three planes and served 11 cities. This carrier was controlled by outside investors and was shut down because it was successful. The major investors had funded this company for a tax write-off only. Needless to say, he was extremely upset and disappointed.

For the next several years, Herb did a lot of freelance flying and served as a flight instructor for FedEx 727 pilots—real, paying jobs. Then the bug bit him again. He studied the market, examined locations, and spent five years putting together a new venture. He encountered a successful local competitor who had a monopoly at the airport, and eventually won the right to operate in his selected location by filing a complaint with the Federal Aviation Administration (FAA). Personal funds were the basis for a new FBO franchise. An additional investor was brought in for startup, and the business was opened June 16, 2001. The franchise operated as an S corporation. "It was not easy getting up and going because the tragedy of September 11, 2001, happened shortly after and the entire industry encountered an extremely serious downturn." He hung in there and slowly grew his operation. Today a larger percentage of affluent individuals and companies are utilizing private aviation instead of facing uncertainties, inconvenience, and safety issues associated with commercial travel. His franchise contract addressed every aspect of operating an FBO, ranging from hiring employees to operational guidelines to ethics.

Unfortunately, his competitor next door diluted the market and captured most of the clients. Hindsight reflects that the market was too small for more than one FBO at the airport.

Questions

1. Do you think Herb was really cut out to operate this FBO?
2. Discuss the "small market" implication of this case.

Experientials

1. In teams, survey your classmates who live in the dorms for services they would purchase (*hint*: cleaning services) and why. Report the number one request to the class.
2. Evaluate three franchise offerings and critique the contractual agreement. Would you choose any of the companies you evaluated: 1) to operate, and/or 2) to consume the product or service.

CHAPTER 6

Planning, Organizing, and Managing a Small Business

Businesses don't plan to fail, they just fail to plan.

—Old business adage

A completed business plan is a guide that illustrates where you are going, and how to get there.

—Charles J. Bodenstab

A business is not defined by its name, statutes, or articles of incorporation. It is defined by the business mission. Only a clear definition of the mission and purpose of the organization makes possible clear and realistic business objectives.

—Peter Drucker

Learning Objectives

After studying the material in this chapter, you should be able to:

1. Tell why planning is so important—yet so neglected—in small businesses.

2. Explain the role of strategic and operational planning, and give some examples.

3. Explain the role of financial planning, and give some examples of it.

4. Tell why a business plan is needed and what purpose it should serve.

5. Prepare a sample business plan.

Sam and Teresa Davis Do Their Homework before Launch

When Sam and Teresa Davis decided it was time for a career change, they opted to start their own business rather than work for someone else. After considering the options, Sam, who had 18 years of marketing and managing experience with a large regional department store, and Teresa, who was a veteran teacher, chose to open a school supply store in Northport, near the university. Knowing that many small businesses fail because of poor planning the Davises chose to start their venture the right way—by doing extensive strategic and operational planning.

One of the first steps the Davises took early in their endeavor was to seek the services of the university's Small Business Development Center. "They were very helpful and supportive," says Sam. "It's tough getting started . . . but we felt we had done enough background work" to start the business successfully.[1] Sam cites the Center's *Small Business Handbook* as an invaluable asset that answered questions concerning such important details as taxes, business licenses, zoning problems, and advertising.

Before getting in over their heads the Davises knew they had to do extensive research and write a comprehensive business plan. This step would not only assist their fund-raising efforts, but also serve as a blueprint for the process of making their dream a reality. The key word, according to Sam, was research. "The biggest problem was gathering the facts to write a detailed business plan."

The Davises did their homework well. First, they made numerous trips to school supply stores in surrounding cities. They also took their idea directly to their potential clients—teachers and school administrators. Finally, after carefully assembling the needed information, they wrote a detailed business plan.

One thing the Davises learned from their research was that there was little or no diversity among school supply stores. To avoid being just another run-of-the-mill school supply store—and risk market saturation—they needed to find a unique twist, something to set their store apart from the others. They found their niche by adding a work area that includes a letter and shape cutter, a laminator, and a copier to produce transparencies.

This unique idea proved to be the solution to one of the most difficult problems new businesses face—getting customers in the door. "Sometimes we have as many as six university students at a time working on some school project here," Teresa says. Others using the center include junior and senior high school students working on science and social studies projects, as well as church workers. Through their research the Davises also discovered that the growing home schooling trend had been virtually ignored by other supply stores; this opened a new market for their products. The Davises cite this as another key factor in their success.

As a result of their painstaking research and creative ideas the Davises' store, Learning Experiences, has been tremendously successful. They are open until late afternoon and on weekends so that teachers and parents can take advantage of what the store has to offer.[2] Now, as they advise potential entrepreneurs, the Davises emphasize two points about formulating a good business plan and running an effective business: (1) entreprenuers *must* have firsthand knowledge of the product or service they plan to offer, and (2) they must create a distinctive niche by making the business unique in some fashion. Now after eighteen years they have more than doubled their size in square footage. This was accomplished when a neighboring tenant moved out. The author asked Teresa how she liked having a small business, and she said, "I love it! Check out our website at www.learningexperiences123.com."

The Profile illustrates some of the problems and steps involved in planning, organizing, and developing a new business. The first three of those steps were discussed in Chapter 5, and others will be explained in detail in this chapter.

Why Is Planning So Important to Small Businesses?

To become an effective business owner-manager *you must look ahead.* In selecting the business to enter, as discussed in Chapter 5, you are doing just that—planning for the future. As shown in Figure 6.1, planning should be the first step in performing a series of managerial functions because it sets the future course of action for all aspects of the business. **Planning,** which is the process of setting objectives and devising actions to achieve those objectives, answers such questions as these: What business am I in? What finances do I need? What is my sales strategy? Where can I find needed personnel? How much profit can I expect?

> **Planning** is the process of setting objectives and determining actions to reach them.

For example, business owner Terry Thomas says that after 15 years of ups and downs he has identified a set of criteria to follow:

- Be prepared.
- Be patient.
- Know when to get help.
- Form your own support system.
- Know the power of vertical integration.
- Never rest on your own laurels.[3]

Stan Caplan, a successful operator of several high-volume dry cleaning and laundry plants, says that business plans can be likened to U.S. military plans. Market research is akin to know your enemy and all military operations begin with a mission. Estimated enemy situations include evaluations of strengths, weaknesses, opportunities, and threats. Military plans for combat service support encompass all administrative and service support such as employees, supplies, maintenance, and so on. And finally, the military is always giving orders (communicating with employees) when implementing a mission (plan).[4] New venture Weinstein Co. is a present day multifaceted media company operated by Harvey and Bob Weinstein, formerly of Disney's Miramax Film, operating out of Manhattan. The brothers have developed a strategy for their startup. According to a recent interview, the strategy is of a boutique multimedia company with a "business plan that is very specific, prudent . . . , and makes sense in the world we live in today."

Why Small Business Owners *Need* to Plan

Planning is one of the most difficult activities you must do. Yet it is essential that you do it because, before taking action, you must know where you are going and how to get there.

FIGURE 6.1 |
How Planning Relates
to Other Managerial
Functions

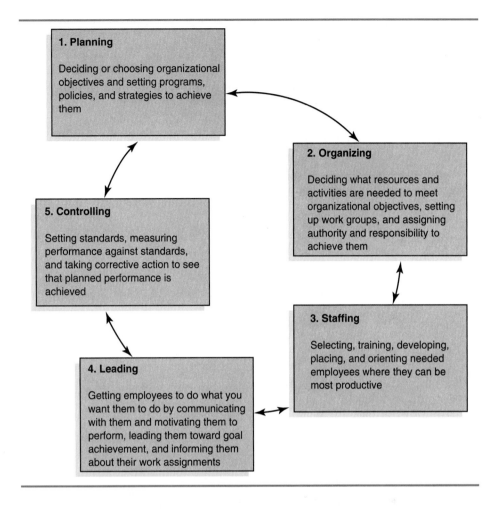

1. Planning

Deciding or choosing organizational
objectives and setting programs,
policies, and strategies to achieve
them

2. Organizing

Deciding what resources and
activities are needed to meet
organizational objectives, setting
up work groups, and assigning
authority and responsibility to
achieve them

5. Controlling

Setting standards, measuring
performance against standards,
and taking corrective action to see
that planned performance is
achieved

3. Staffing

Selecting, training, developing,
placing, and orienting needed
employees where they can be
most productive

4. Leading

Getting employees to do what you
want them to do by communicating
with them and motivating them to
perform, leading them toward goal
achievement, and informing them
about their work assignments

Outsiders who invest or lend money need to know your chances of success. Plans provide
courses of action, information to others, bases for change, and a means of delegating work.
In summary, well-developed plans can (1) interest moneyed people in investing in your
business, (2) guide the owner and managers in operating the business, (3) give direction to
and motivate employees, and (4) provide an environment to attract customers and prospective employees.

Why Small Business Owners *Neglect* Planning

Although planning is so important, it is one of the most difficult managerial activities
to perform. Many small business owners neglect planning because (1) day-to-day activities leave them little or no time for planning, (2) they fear the problems and weaknesses
planning may reveal, (3) they lack knowledge of how to plan, and (4) they feel that future
changes cannot be planned for.

Planning requires original thinking, takes time, and is difficult to do, but it does help
one prepare to take advantage of promising opportunities and cope with unexpected problems. Table 6.1 illustrates and explains strategic planning.

TABLE 6.1 | Some of the Most Important Types of Plans and Planning Functions

Types of Plans and Planning Functions	Examples
Strategic Planning:	
Mission: The long-term direction of the business.	To provide financial security at low cost.
Objectives: Shorter-term ends to help achieve the mission.	
For total firm.	Earn a 20% return on investment in 2013.
For functional area.	Increase penetration of market by 25% by 2014.
Strategies: Means to achieve an end, or courses of action needed to achieve objectives.	
For total firm.	Establish control procedures to control costs by 2013.
For functional area.	Use 1 percent of sales to improve and expand service.
Operational Planning:	
Policies: Guides to action that provide consistency in decision making, particularly in repetitive situations.	*Personnel policy:* Promote from within, giving preference to promotions for present employees.
Methods and procedures: Prescribed manner of accomplishing desired output.	*Employee selection procedure*: Complete application form, test, interview, investigate, select.
Budgets and standards: Plans for future activities using measures for control.	*Cash budget:* For planning use of money.

The Role of Strategic Planning

Strategic planning
provides comprehensive
long-term direction to
help a business
accomplish its mission.

Strategic planning provides comprehensive long-term direction to help a business accomplish its mission. Table 6.1 shows that strategic planning consists of two parts: the firm's mission and objectives, and its strategies. Small business owners need to seek help with strategic planning as the business grows and prospers. Forte Group, a management consulting firm, suggests you ask yourself the following questions:

- Do I have the ability to develop a comprehensive strategic plan to take the company to the next level?
- Do I have the experience and life lessons necessary for furthering the strategic vision of the company?
- Do I have the leadership skills the organization needs to grow?
- Do the investors relate to and trust me?[5]

The following are some examples of strategic planning:

- Selecting the type of business to enter.
- Formulating the mission of the company.
- Deciding whether to start a new business, buy an existing one, or buy a franchise.
- Choosing the product or service to sell.
- Deciding on the market niche to exploit.
- Choosing the type of organization to use.

- Determining financial needs.
- Selecting the location for the business.

Real-World Example 6.1

For example, a recent study by three CPAs indicated the significance of location to small businesses. They studied which small firms in their areas were succeeding and which were failing.

Jacqueline L. Babicky's consulting group found that the types of business doing well in the Portland, Oregon, area were those that had taken steps to differentiate themselves and/or their products from others in the mainstream. Larry Field's firm found a growing number of small high-tech businesses were moving into the Phoenix, Arizona, region to provide secondary parts to larger manufacturers.

Ann Adams, owner of Aloha by Ana, specializes in wedding and event planning and shipping in fresh leis from Hawaii. She feels her "mission is to introduce the aloha spirit" to her marketing area (alohabyana@aol.com).[6]

SWOT Analysis

A SWOT (Strengths, Weaknesses, Opportunities, and Threats) is one tool that most strategic planners use to scan the business's environments and base objectives. SWOT analysis allows the owner to identify new markets and to prepare for perceived downturns or competitions. SWOT analysis is a useful tool to aid the process of strategic planning and can be organized into the form of a matrix. A study is made of the opportunities and threats in the external environment and the strengths and weaknesses in the internal environment. The key is to be able to eliminate weaknesses and threats and to capitalize on the strengths and opportunities. A simple listing within cells is a good basis for analysis.

Strengths	Weaknesses
1.	1.
2.	2.
3.	3.
4.	4.
5.	5.
Opportunities	Threats
1.	1.
2.	2.
3.	3.
4.	4.
5.	5.

This format allows you to reach a basic understanding of your business and the environment in which it operates.

FIGURE 6.2 |
Strategic Umbrella

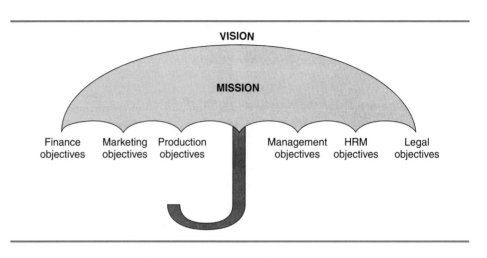

Mission and Objectives

A business's **mission**
statement defines the
present business scope
and broadly describes
the organization's present
capabilities, focus, and
activities.

A business's **mission** statement defines the present business scope and broadly describes the organization's present capabilities, focus, and activities. It is concerned with broad concepts such as the firm's image, with the basic services the firm plans to perform (e.g., "entertainment" instead of just "movies"), and with long-term financial success. Once set, missions are rarely revised.

A clear definition of your mission enables you to design *results-oriented objectives and strategies.* A good mission statement defines exactly the identity of your business and allows all of your planning to flow from it. Figure 6.2 illustrates the "umbrella" structure of strategic planning. The umbrella shows graphically how important it is to have a mission statement and major objectives that will interrelate and provide guidance for a cohesive and meaningful organizational structure.

Frequently when small business owners are closely tied to their business, the mission becomes very personal.

Real-World Example 6.2

Carpe's Mission Statement: To deliver to our customers the finest quality products and service available, to offer to the community a comfortable and enjoyable gathering place for all to share and, above all, to give back through our community service and support.[7] Profile, Chapter 14.

Objectives are the
purposes, goals, and
desired results for the
business and its parts.

Objectives are the goals that give shorter-term direction to the business and serve as benchmarks for measuring performance. Examples of objectives might include: "To increase total sales by 8 percent a year" and "To introduce within the next two years a new product aimed at the middle-class consumer." Notice in Figure 6.2 how the objectives flow from the mission statement. Objectives are more specific than missions and are revised more frequently. Table 6.2 illustrates how objectives can be set. Creating the mission and defining objectives for a small business involve two important considerations: the business's external environment and the internal resources that give it a competitive edge.

TABLE 6.2 | Example of How Objectives Can Be Set

Firm's Objectives	2014	2015	2016	2017
Total net profit (income) after taxes	$____	$____	$____	$____
Return on investment (ROI) (net income after taxes/total assets)	____	____	____	____
Return on equity (ROE) (net income after taxes/equity)	____	____	____	____
Total sales volume (units)	____	____	____	____
Total sales volume ($)	____	____	____	____
Return on sales (ROS) (net income after taxes/sales)	____	____	____	____

To attain a _____ percent share of market by the end of 2015.

To have a _____ percent debt-to-equity ratio in the capital structure initially, declining to _____ percent debt-equity at the end of 2016.

To develop a new product by the end of the year 2017.

The External Environment Many consultants and other advisers are pushing small companies to give more emphasis to their external environment. In a study of 100 companies, the Futures Group of Glastonbury, Connecticut (www.tfg.com) found that "managers who spend more time evaluating external factors such as their competitors, the U.S. market climate, and emerging technology can better manage and forecast business than those who focus on internal factors."[8] This practice was found to improve their strategic plans.

Some other external environmental factors to consider include clients, the economy, legal and political factors, changing demographics, foreign competition, and many other influences. This examination is part of a SWOT analysis. Changes caused by the introduction of videotapes, computer hardware and software, lasers, and population aging, for example, have been a blessing to some companies and a death warrant to others. For example, the population of the Baby Boomer generation is almost twice that of the next generation—Generation X. As Boomers begin to retire, there will be fewer workers to replace them. Because of this shortage, more firms will ask retirees to remain.[9] The expanding communication and transportation systems require that even the smallest companies keep abreast of a constantly widening range of events.

Internal Resources and Competitive Edge The internal resources found in small businesses include those listed below and also examines strengths and weaknesses of a SWOT analysis. Also, to be competitive, the resources must include the characteristics listed:

Human resources are the personnel that make up the business's work force.

1. **Human resources** include both management and nonmanagement people and include key operating employees such as production supervisors, sales personnel, financial analysts, and engineers. To keep the company competitive, these people must be motivated, imaginative, qualified, and dedicated.

Physical resources are the buildings, tools and equipment, and service and distribution facilities that are needed to carry on the business.

2. **Physical resources** include buildings, tools and equipment, and service and distribution facilities. For the company to be competitive, these resources must be strategically located, be productive, be low in operating costs, be effective distributors, and make the proper product.

Financial resources include the cash flow, debt capacity, and equity available to finance operations.

3. **Financial resources** include cash flow, debt capacity, and equity available to run the business. To make the company competitive, company finances must be adequate to maintain current levels of activities and to take advantage of future opportunities.

FIGURE 6.3 |
Mission/Strategy of
John Smith, General
Agent, Tulsa,
Oklahoma

Mission: To provide the maximum amount of personal financial security at the lowest possible cost while maintaining the highest quality of individualized service.

Objective: To serve the financial needs of businesses, individuals, and their families in the Tulsa area through guaranteed income to meet loss from death or disability, through these services and policy coverages.

- Estate tax planning
- Qualified pension and profit sharing
- Group life and health
- Ordinary life
- Business interruption

Many accountants suggest that aspiring entrepreneurs get their financial house in order before starting. This includes setting aside funds for taxes and Social Security and as a cushion against financial reversals.[10]

A **competitive edge** is a particular characteristic that makes a firm more attractive to customers than are its rivals.

If a small firm has exceptionally good resources that are effectively used, it can have a **competitive edge** over its rivals. Therefore, a proper evaluation of available resources may permit you to focus on your customers and provide them with a little something extra, which gives you a competitive edge. Thus, a small business must align its mission, objectives, and resources with its environment if it is to be effective. The proper evaluation of its competitive edge can make a small firm's planning more realistic and lead to greater profitability.

Strategies

Strategies are the means by which a business achieves its objectives and fulfills its mission.

Strategies are the means by which the mission and objectives sought by a small business can be achieved. A basic question in setting strategies is how should the business be managed to achieve its objectives and fulfill its mission? To be most effective, strategies should give a business a competitive advantage in the marketplace. They should combine the activities such as marketing, production or operations, research and development, finance, and personnel in order to use the firm's resources most effectively.

Figure 6.3 shows how a strategy can be set up to fulfill the mission of a small business. Notice that John Smith will provide certain services and policy coverage to clients so they will have maximum personal financial security at the lowest possible cost.

As we discussed in Chapter 1, an effort is now being made to encourage owners of small businesses to rethink and redesign the way their organization operates. Thus, while top management must still be involved, lower levels of managers and workers seem to be more involved in integrating their company's vision, mission, objectives, and strategies into their strategic planning.

The Role of Operational Planning

Why do so many small businesses fail? As shown in Chapter 1, the underlying reason in most cases is lack of proper strategic and operational planning. These types of planning are vital because they help potential and new entrepreneurs avoid costly blunders, save time, and result in a more polished final product. Three types of planning will improve a small business owner's chances of success: (1) strategic planning before starting the business; (2) a business plan to attract investors, financiers, and prospective employees; and (3) continuous operational planning and control before and after the business starts operating.

Setting Up Policies, Methods, Procedures, and Budgets

Operational planning sets policies, procedures, and standards for achieving objectives.

Policies are general statements that serve as guides to managerial decision making and supervisory activities.

Methods and **procedures** provide standing instructions to employees on how to perform their jobs.

Budgets are detailed plans, expressed in monetary terms, of the results expected from officially recognized programs for a given future period.

As you can see from Table 6.1, **operational planning** starts with setting policies, methods and procedures, and budgets, which together form the basis for the other part of operational methods and planning.

   Policies guide action. They exist so that managers can delegate work and employees will make decisions based on the thinking and wishes of the business owner. **Methods** and **procedures** provide employees with standing instructions for performing their jobs. They comprise detailed explanations of how to do the work properly, and in what order it should be done. **Budgets** set the requirements needed to follow the strategies and accomplish the objectives. For example, a cash budget shows the amount and dates of cash income and outgo. It helps the manager determine when and how much to borrow.

Planning to Operate the Business

The second part of operational planning—planning to operate the business—includes[11]:

- Choosing your location.
- Planning operations and physical facilities.
- Developing sources of supply for goods and materials.
- Planning your human resource requirements.
- Setting up the legal and organizational structure.
- Determining your approach to the market.
- Establishing an efficient records system.
- Setting up a time schedule.

Choosing a Location   The type of business influences most of your location decisions, as they relate to access to customers, suppliers, employees, utilities, and transportation, as well as compliance with zoning regulations and other laws. The mission of the business is also a basic consideration in seeking the right location. As will be shown in Chapter 12, each type of firm has its own factors to consider and gives priority to those that most affect the business.

   For example, landlords across the United States are seeking nonretail occupants for failing department store spaces. Those taking advantage include telemarketers, warehouses, dining establishments, and office space.[12]

Planning Operations and Physical Facilities   A firm's ability to sell its product is based on its ability to produce that good or service, as well as on its market potential. Good selection and efficient arrangement of physical facilities, then, are important. Too much capacity increases costs, which can reduce the company's competitive position; too little capacity reduces the availability of goods and causes loss of sales. Therefore, a proper balance between production and sales volume is needed. Planning starts with the estimate of sales and the operations needed to produce the product(s). Using these estimates, the machines and personnel needed for the demand can be determined.

   Another important decision is whether to buy facilities or lease them. Any such choice between purchase and lease is based on differences in initial investment cost, operating performance and expense, and tax considerations. A photocopier is an example of an item that should probably be leased rather than purchased. Because of rapid improvements—and the need for prompt and proper maintenance—leased copiers will probably give more dependable service than purchased ones. Chapter 12 provides more details on locating and laying out facilities.

Developing Sources of Supply for Goods and Materials   The largest expense for companies selling products usually is purchasing materials, supplies, and/or goods; this cost is often more than 50 percent of the cost of products sold. Therefore, the ability to purchase these essentials at favorable prices can lead to profitability—or vice versa. Lowest-cost materials do not necessarily mean inferior quality, and small firms should take every opportunity to reduce costs. But small businesses usually find it difficult to compete with large ones on the basis of price alone. Instead, they can more successfully compete on the basis of better quality, service, delivery, and so forth. And, as will be shown in Chapter 13, the business must be sure to have sources of supply that meet its standards in all ways, including competitive prices.

Human resource planning is the process of converting the business's plans and programs into an effective work force.

Planning Human Resource Requirements   **Human resource planning** can be one of the most frustrating tasks facing small businesses when such businesses are not big enough to easily hire the specialized people needed. Therefore, you, as a small businessperson, need to estimate how much time you will spend in the business, for the less time you can devote to the business, the more important it will be to have capable employees who must be able to work with less supervision than in larger firms. The issue arises of obtaining good employees. Some important questions to ask yourself are: How many workers are needed? Where will they be obtained? How much must I pay them? These and similar questions are discussed in Chapters 10 and 11.

Setting Up the Legal and Organizational Structure   Your organizational structure must be developed taking into consideration the legal and administrative aspects of the business. Both legal and administrative structures offer several options, so you must select the structure that best serves your needs. Many small business owners, especially if they have started as sole proprietors, may have difficulty envisioning a management structure beyond the boss/employee relationship shown in Figure 6.4. Retaining too much authority is one of the best ways to kill your small business, so be aware of setting up too rigid an organizational structure.

The legal form of a business, as discussed in Chapter 3, may be a proprietorship, partnership, corporation (C corporation or S Corporation), limited-liability company (LLC), cooperative, or joint venture. Other forms of business may include limited liability partnership (LLP),

FIGURE 6.4 |
An Oversimplified
Organizational
Structure

"As you see, we are a highly centralized organization."

family limited liability partnership (FLP), professional service corporation (PSC), nonprofit corporation, and fractional ownership. The administrative structure of a small business should be based on factors such as (1) the strategic plan, including the business mission and objectives; (2) the owner's personal and business objectives; (3) the plans, programs, policies, and practices that will achieve those objectives; and (4) the authority and responsibility relationships that will accomplish the mission or purpose of the firm.

Determining Approach to Market   The volume of sales and income of a small firm depends on its marketing strategies and activities. If a study of the environment determines that there is a sufficiently large market for the firm's product(s), plans must be made to capture enough of that market to be successful. Even if your company's service is the best you must tell potential customers about it. Many methods of marketing are in use; the ones used must be chosen for the particular business.

Real-World Example 6.3

For example, a number of years ago, a man living in New England conceived of a rubber, instead of metal, dustpan. He had a dozen samples of the new product custom-made in a variety of colors and headed to Boston to hawk his wares in Filene's and Jordan Marsh. Neither seemed interested in the dustpan.

Still, because he was sure that homemakers would buy his product, he decided to test-market the dustpan by calling on them. Pulling into a residential street, he parked his car and set out to ring doorbells. Just 45 minutes later, he returned to his car with only two pans left. Convinced that his idea was good, Earl Tupper developed a company—Tupperware (www.tupperware.com)—to market the product directly to consumers.

Once a target market is chosen you must provide for sales promotion and distribution to it. The product to be offered should again be studied carefully to determine answers to the following questions: What qualities make it special to the customer? Are there unique or distinct features to emphasize, such as ease of installation or low maintenance? Should the company use newspaper advertising or mailings to publicize the product? These and other marketing questions are discussed in more detail in Chapters 8 and 9.

Establishing an Efficient Records System   Even in a small business simple records and information systems must be used. But they must be designed to help you control your business by keeping track of activities and obligations and also to collect certain types of information demanded by outside organizations such as government agencies. For example, you must maintain records of such data as (1) the date each employee is hired, the number of hours each one works, and the wages and benefits paid; (2) inventories, accounts receivable, and accounts payable; (3) taxes paid and owed (see Chapter 15); and (4) units of each product sold.

Many records are needed to help make the small business operate successfully. Management information systems, covered in Chapter 16, should be selected and designed to aid management in this respect.

Setting Up a Time Schedule   Once you decide to go ahead with the formation of the business, you should establish a time schedule to provide an orderly and coordinated program. The schedule should probably include the prior planning steps. Many of these steps can be and often are performed simultaneously. A SCORE representative can provide valuable assistance.

The Role of Financial Planning

Financial planning can be quite simple or very complex, as shown in Chapters 7, 14, and 15, but it should involve at least the following:

1. Estimating income and expenses.
2. Estimating initial investment required.
3. Locating sources of funds.

When choosing a financial advisor, there is an "alphabet soup" of credentials for you to sift through. Some designations represent certifications and some require passing one or more Regulatory Board tests. Table 6.3 presents a few. In 2010, there were 87,222 complaints against financial advisors. Information about financial advisors can be found at BrightScope Advisor pages (www.brightscope.com).

Estimating Income and Expenses

The steps described so far set the stage for determining the profit (or loss) from operating your new business. Income from sales (also called *revenue*) can be estimated by studying the market, and expenses (also called *costs*) can be calculated from past experience and other sources, such as knowledgeable people, a library, or a trade association. After all costs have been estimated, they can be totaled and subtracted from the estimated sales income to obtain the expected **net profit** (or loss), as shown in the worksheet for Dover Enterprises* in Figure 6.5. Remember two key points when making your estimates. First, these expense and income (or loss) estimates are usually for only the first year of operations. However, if you also make an income analysis for an expected typical year in the future as well as for the first year, the exercise can provide valuable information for planning purposes. For example, Jim Benson was a rocket entrepreneur and planned to send his customers into space. His space tourism business operated as Benson Space Company and wanted to start regular trips outside our atmosphere. Tickets for each of the six passengers were estimated at between $100,000 and $300,000. It would cost $20 million for tourists to go to the International Space Station aboard the Russian Soyez.

Second, while total expenses do move up and down with sales volume, they do not vary as much. Some expenses, such as materials, which rise in direct proportion to increases in sales volume and drop as sales volume drops, are called **variable expenses.**

TABLE 6.3 |

CFA	Certified Financial Planner
NAPFA	Fee-only financial advisors
CFA	Chartered Financial Analyst
CPA/PFS	Certified Public Accountant/ Personal Financial Specialist
ChFC	Chartered Financial Consultant
CRPS	Chartered Retirement Plans Specialist
RIA	Registered Investment Advisor
CMFC	Chartered Mutual Fund Counselor
CRC	Certified Retirement Counselor
CDFA	Certified Divorce Financial Analyst
AEP	Accredited Estate Planner

Source: Christine Dugas, "Deciphering Financial Advisors' Credentials," *USA Today,* April 29, 2011, p. 4B.

―――――――
*An actual company, but the name is disguised at the owner's request.

FIGURE 6.5

DOVER ENTERPRISES
Worksheet for Estimated Annual Income,
Expenses, and Profit (Loss)*

	Units Sold					
	10,000		**20,000**		**30,000**	
Income						
Sales income ($5/unit)		$50,000		$100,000		$150,000
Cost of goods sold:						
Production cost ($1.62/unit)	$16,200		$32,400		$48,600	
Shipping boxes and labels ($0.04/unit)	400		800		1,200	
Depreciation (mold)	2,500		2,500		2,500	
Total production expenses		19,100		35,700		52,300
Gross profit		30,900		64,300		97,700
Other operating expenses						
Salaries	30,000		30,000		30,000	
Telephone	3,000		3,500		4,000	
Rent	2,100		2,100		2,100	
Insurance	400		400		400	
Office expense	1,000		1,100		1,200	
Sales promotion	7,000		8,000		9,000	
Freight	1,000		2,000		3,000	
Travel	4,000		4,000		4,000	
Taxes and licenses	4,000		4,000		4,000	
Miscellaneous	1,000		2,000		3,000	
Total operating expenses		53,500		57,100		60,700
Net profit (loss)		($22,600)		$ 7,200		$ 37,000

*Projections for three levels of sales.

Fixed expenses do not vary with output, but remain the same.

Other expenses, such as depreciation on buildings, which do not vary in value as sales volume rises or falls, are called **fixed expenses.** Also, there are some expenses, such as supervision, that combine variable and fixed costs.

Changes in sales volume drastically affect the amount of net profit: As sales volume rises (say, from 10,000 to 20,000 units), losses are reduced and profits may rise; as sales volume drops (say, from 20,000 to 10,000), profits drop and losses may occur.

Don't forget to prepare a personal budget! As Robert Caldwell, a New York financial planner, emphasizes, "Living below your means is never a mistake, and that is even more true with a startup business." Therefore, you—and your family—must have enough income to live on during the time you are moving from being an employee to being an employer. If your standard of living drops too drastically it will probably be devastating to your family. So, in addition to determining the expected income and expenses of the business, also estimate your continuing needs and where you will get the resources to satisfy them.

Estimating Initial Investment

You will need money and/or credit to start your business. You must pay for items such as buildings, equipment, materials, personnel, inventory, machines, business forms, and sales promotion at the outset before income from sales starts providing the means to pay these expenses from internal sources. Credit may be extended to help sell the products, but this only adds to operating expenses.

The worksheet in Figure 6.6 provides a logical method of calculating the initial cash needs of a new business such as Dover Enterprises. The figures in column 1 are estimates that have already been made for the income statement for the first year. The amount of cash needed is some multiple of each of the values in column 1, as shown in column 3. The total of these multiple values is an estimate of the money needed to start the business and is shown in column 2. This sum can be considerable.

Note that the cash needed to start the business—shown in column 2—represents the delay between paying money out for expenses and receiving it back as revenue. The item called *starting inventory* is an illustration of buying goods in one period and selling them in another. But inventories of goods and supplies—in the form of purchases and recurring inventories—continue to exist for the life of the business. Therefore, funds obtained from investments in the business or from loans must continue for its life unless they are paid off.

Because cash does not produce revenue, it should not sit idle but should be used to earn income. The amount of cash a business needs, and has, will vary during the year, since most businesses have busy and slack periods. To keep the investment and borrowing low, **cash flow** projections must be made. The worksheet in Chapter 15 (Figure 15.1) is a form that can be used to make such projections, which can then be compared with what actually happens. You might contact your nearest SBA office to get information to help you estimate your startup costs. Also, various financial firms and certified public accountants have computed some helpful standard figures.

Locating Sources of Funds

Once the amount of funds needed is known, you must find sources for those funds. The many sources from which to obtain funds to start and operate a business boil down to two: the owner and others. These two sources will be discussed in detail in Chapter 7, so only the highlights are discussed here. Before approaching a funding source, decide how much money you and others will put into the business and how much should come from other sources.

For example, when looking for startup capital, consider all possibilities. Dozens of resources exist to fund home-based entrepreneurial endeavors. If you have a good business idea, you should be able to find the money you need to make your dream come true. Pursue all the resources available to you and you will be on your way to greater home-based success.[13]

Using Your Own Funds   Some small business owners prefer to invest only their personal funds and not borrow to start or operate a business. Others believe they should use little of their own money and instead make as much profit as possible by using their interest in the business as security when obtaining funds from others. Normally owners control a company; they take the risks of failure but also make the decisions. To maintain control you must continue to invest more personal funds than all the other investors combined. Moreover, you can maintain control only so long as lenders do not become worried about the safety of their money.

For example, with your own capital, you can lend money to your home business, set loan conditions, and then pay the loan off to yourself with interest. Another way you can personally finance your home business is by keeping your current full-time job and working your home business around it on a part-time basis.

Your credit cards can also help fund startup business expenses and purchase equipment and supplies. The price one pays for easy access to credit can be relatively high interest rates, often exceeding twice those on a business loan secured through a bank.[14]

Using Funds from Others   There are several sources of outside funds. These can be generally divided into **equity investors,** who actually become part owners of the business,

Cash flow is the amount of cash available at a given time to pay expenses.

Equity investors are those who actually become part owners of the business.

FIGURE 6.6

DOVER ENTERPRISES
Estimated Monthly Expenses and Starting Costs
January 1, 20__

Estimated Monthly Expenses

Item	(1) Estimate of monthly expenses based on sales of $100,000 per year	(2) Estimate of how much cash you need to start your business (see column 3)	(3) What to put in (2) (Multipliers are typical for one kind of business. You must decide how many months to allow for in your business.)
Salary of owner-manager	$2,500	$5,000	2 times column 1
All other salaries and wages	—	—	3 times column 1
Rent	175	525	3 times column 1
Travel		1,000	As required
Advertising	700	2,100	3 times column 1
Delivery expense	100	300	3 times column 1
Supplies	100	300	3 times column 1
Recurring inventory and purchases	—	—	Check with suppliers for estimate
Telephone and telegraph	300	900	3 times column 1
Other utilities	—	—	3 times column 1
Insurance		400	Payment required by insurance company
Taxes, including Social Security	325	1,300	4 times column 1
Interest	—	—	3 times column 1
Maintenance	—	—	3 times column 1
Legal and other professional fees	—	—	3 times column 1
Miscellaneous	200	600	3 times column 1

Starting Costs You Have to Pay Only Once

Fixtures and equipment: Telephone, $203; mold, $11,280; computer, $750	$12,233	Enter total from separate list
Decorating and remodeling	—	Talk it over with a contractor
Installation of fixtures and equipment	—	Talk to suppliers from whom you wish to buy these
Starting inventory	5,000	Suppliers will probably help you estimate this
Deposits with public utilities	—	Find out from utilities companies
Legal and other professional fees	—	Lawyer, accountant, and so on
Licenses and permits	(Part of taxes above)	Find out from city offices what you have to have
Advertising and promotion for opening	(Part of advertising above)	Estimate what you'll use
Accounts receivable	1,200	What you need to buy more stock until credit customers pay
Cash	1,000	For unexpected expenses or losses, special purchases, etc.
Other		Make a separate list and enter total
Total estimated cash you need to start with	$31,858	Add up all the numbers in column 2

Source: This basic worksheet is based in *Checklist for Going into Business*, Management Aids No. 2.016 (Washington, DC: Small Business Administration), p. 4.

Lenders are those outsiders who provide business owners money for a limited time at a fixed rate of interest.

Microloans is a small short term loan provided by the SBA through intermediaries.

and **lenders,** who provide money for a limited time at a fixed rate of interest. Both run the risk of losing their money if the business fails, but this gamble is offset for investors by the possibility of large returns if the business is successful. Because the rate of return for lenders is fixed, some security is usually given to offset their risk.

Microloan are small short term loans for small businesses that are provided by the SBA through intermediaries. The maximum amount is $50,000 and the average is $13,000.

Real-World Example 6.4

Lucy Valena obtained $4,000 to help launch her coffee business, Voltage Coffee, through the Samuel Davis Brewing the American Dream program. This is a program that provides microloans to food, beverage, and hospitality entrepreneurs.[15]

You may be able to find investors interested in a venture opportunity. Such people might be found among relatives, friends, attorneys, bankers, or securities dealers. Building multiple bank relationships early on in your business is important. But you must have a well-prepared business plan and an advocate in the bank on your side.

Special types of investors—venture capitalists—capitalize a business startup in return for partial ownership. They seek high-risk businesses that show the potential for high profit. The flip side of the coin for high risk is, of course, a greater likelihood of a loss. A venture capitalist may have plans to publicly sell shares of stock of the successful venture. If your home-based business is involved with new technology, website design, software development, computer training, or software consulting, venture capitalists may be interested. To reach potential venture capitalists and other investors, share information about your home business opportunity and startup capital needs on the Internet, in networking organizations such as your city's chamber of commerce, and in advertisements placed in a local or national newspaper.

The Role of the Business Plan in Strategic and Operational Planning

As the Davises discovered in the opening Profile, a new business results from the prospective owner(s) having both a good idea for producing and selling a product and the ability to carry out the idea. Yet other things—such as buildings and machines, human resources, materials and supplies, and finances—are also needed. These needs are developed from the strategic, operational, and financial planning. And all that planning needs to be formalized into a **business plan,** which is a formal plan to serve as a tool for attracting the other components of the business formation package—the people and the money. A well-developed and well-presented business plan can provide small business owners with a much greater chance of success—and reduce their chances of failing.

A **business plan** is a formal plan prepared to serve as a tool for attracting the other components of the business formation package, including people and money.

Purposes of the Plan

The business plan could be the most useful and important document you, as an entrepreneur, ever put together. When you are up to your ears in the details of starting the business, the plan keeps your thinking on target, keeps your creativity on track, and concentrates your power on reaching your goal.

The plan can be a useful money-raising tool to attract venture capital for those entrepreneurs who are willing to dilute control of their company. Although few owners use a plan to attract venture funds, many more use a formal business plan to obtain loans from lending agencies.

But an effective plan does more than just help convince prospective investors that the new business is sound. It provides a detailed blueprint for the activities needed to finance the business, develop the product, market it, and otherwise manage the new business. Business plans are also used for planning the continuing operations of a firm, as the following example illustrates.

Real-World Example 6.5

Craig Knouf, the CEO of Associated Business Systems, figures he's revised his plan about 120 times since the founding of his company. He refers to his plan monthly, quarterly, and annually and says running the company any other way "would be like driving a car with no steering wheel." With society and the economy in constant change, he must be prepared to satisfy his customers' needs by being aware of new trends. In addition, the changing business plan provides a detailed, written record of his company's evolution. Lenders love this type of information.[16]

What the Plan Should Include

Because an effective business plan helps determine the feasibility of an idea, it should include a detailed analysis of factors such as the following:

- The proposed product.
- The expected market for it.
- The strengths and weaknesses of the industry.
- Planned marketing policies, such as price, promotion, and distribution.
- Operations or production methods and facilities.
- Financial aspects, including expected income, expenses, profits (or losses), investment needed, and expected cash flow.

In addition, a properly developed, well-written business plan should answer questions such as the following:

- Is the business formation package complete?
- Would it be attractive to potential investors?
- Does the proposed business have a reasonable chance for success at the start?
- Does it have any long-run competitive advantages to the owner? To investors? To employees?
- Can the product be produced efficiently?
- Can it be marketed effectively?
- Can the production and marketing of the product be economically financed?
- Can the new company's business functions—operations, distribution, finance, and human resources—be properly managed?
- Are the needed employees available?

In summary, a properly developed and written plan provides more than mere facts. It serves as (1) an effective communication tool to convey ideas, research findings, and proposed plans to others, especially financiers; (2) the basis for managing the new venture; and (3) a measuring device by which to gauge progress and evaluate needed changes. Developing and writing a business plan takes much time, effort, and money, but the results can make the difference between the company's success and failure. There are several websites you can use to help design your business plan such as: www.sba.gov, and www.score.org.

Preparing the Plan

When developing a business plan you should consider the firm's background, origins, philosophy, mission, and objectives, as well as the means of fulfilling that mission and attaining those objectives.[17] A sound approach is to (1) determine where the business is by

FIGURE 6.7 |

How to Prepare a
Business Plan

- Survey consumer demands for your product(s) and decide how to satisfy those demands.
- Ask questions that cover everything from the firm's target market to its competitive position.
- Establish a long-range strategic plan for the entire business.
- Develop short-term, detailed plans for all those involved with the business, including the owner(s), managers, and employees.
- Plan for every part of the venture, including operations, marketing, general and administrative functions, and distribution.
- Prepare a plan that uses staff time sparingly.

recognizing its current status; (2) decide where you would like to be by clarifying your philosophy about doing business, developing the firm's mission, and setting objectives; and (3) determine how to get to where you want to be by identifying the best strategies for accomplishing the business's objectives.

Figure 6.7 shows one approach to preparing a business plan. It is the one we recommend for those who are serious about succeeding in small business ownership.

Who Should Prepare the Plan?

If the prospective owner is the only one involved in the business, he or she should prepare the plan, with the advice and counsel of competent advisers. But if the business is to be organized and run by more than one person, it should be a team effort. You might encourage each manager to prepare a part of the plan. We also recommend having other key employees help in the planning stage, as this will improve communication and motivation. Dennis Winans, director of Central California Small Business Center, said, "What we see commonly is a lack of planning, undercapitalization, not doing enough research."[18]

Real-World Example 6.6

For example, N. C. Tognazzini compares his business plan to a restaurant. "A business plan is solid, consistent, and thorough with a few grease stains here and there." Composing your own plan gives you a valuable vantage point on the pros and cons of your business. He says, "A well-written plan can adapt to changes, good or bad. Without a plan, the foundation of your business can crumble like bacon hot off the griddle."[19]

There are many software packages available to assist one in planning and preparing the business plan. Ideally such a system should include several key characteristics. To begin with, it should be user-friendly and have plenty of examples to help you. Spreadsheet-like templates for individual data input and automated integration between the modules or sections are also needed. You must remember that a software package is only a helpful tool and that you must formalize your plan. The software provided with this text is a good place to start.

Developing Action Steps

You can collect needed information from the steps discussed in Chapter 5 and earlier in this chapter, as well as from business associates and from legal, management, and financial consultants. Discussions with people both inside and outside the business are useful in gathering and evaluating this information.

The focus of the plan should be on future developments for the business with steps set up to deal with specific aspects, such as product development, marketing, production or operations, finance, and management. Realistic, measurable objectives should be set, and the plan's steps should be delegated, monitored, and reported regularly.

Questions such as the following are useful in developing action steps: Who will be responsible for each course of action? What is the time frame for achieving each objective? What are the barriers to achieving the objectives? How can those barriers be overcome? Have the necessary controls been considered?

Components of the Plan

Because the business plan is such an important document it should be arranged logically and presented clearly to save the reader time and effort, as well as to ensure understanding. While the information that should be included tends to be standardized, the format to be used is not. (Figure 6.8 presents a typical format.)

Regardless of the specific format chosen, any plan should include at least the following elements: cover sheet, executive summary, table of contents, history of the (proposed) business, description of the business, definition of the market, description of the product(s), management structure, objectives and goals, financial data, and appendixes.

FIGURE 6.8 |
Typical Business Plan Format

1. Cover sheet
   - Business name, address, and phone number
   - Principals
   - Date
2. Executive summary
   - Abstract—mission statement
   - Objectives
   - Description of products or services
   - Marketing plan
   - Financial budget
3. Table of contents
4. History
   - Background of principals, or company origins
   - History of products or services
   - Organization structure
   - Company history in brief
5. Description of the business
6. Definition of the market
   - Target market/area
   - Market analysis
   - Competitor analysis
   - Industry analysis
7. Description of products or services
   - What is to be developed or produced
   - Status of research and development
   - Status of patents, trademarks, copyrights
8. Management structure
   - Who will enact plan
   - Organizational chart
   - Communication flowchart
   - Employee policies

9. Objectives and goals
   - Profit plan
   - Marketing plans
   - Manufacturing plans
   - Quality control plans
   - Financial plans
10. Financial data
    - Pro forma income statements (three years)
    - Pro forma cash flow analyses (first year, by months)
    - Pro forma balance sheets (three years)
    - Cost-volume-profit analyses where appropriate
11. Appendixes
    - Narrative history of firm in detail
    - Résumés of key employees
    - Major environmental assumptions
    - Brochures describing products
    - Letters of recommendation or endorsement
    - Historical financial data (at least three years)
    - Details of:
      a. Products and services
      b. Research and development
      c. Marketing
      d. Manufacturing
      e. Administration
      f. Finance

Growthink (www.growthink.com), an entrepreneurial consulting firm, has developed a methodology consisting of five steps they believe to be very helpful. These are

- *"Discovery*: conducting sessions to ensure that we understand our clients' precise vision;
- *Market Research*: performing market research to uncover and assess information;
- *Business Strategy:* conducting multiple business strategy sessions to refine and define our clients' business strategies;
- *Communications Strategy*: holding communications strategy sessions to determine how to best position and articulate the opportunity; and,
- *Communications Documentation*: developing the written business plan."

Cover Sheet

The cover sheet presents identifying information, such as the business name, address, and phone number. Also, readers should know at once who the principals are.

Executive Summary

The **executive summary** of your plan must be a real "grabber"; it must motivate the reader to go on to the other sections. Moreover, it must convey a sense of plausibility, credibility, and integrity. Your plan may be one of many evaluated by representatives of lending institutions. They tend to evaluate the worth of the plan on the basis of this summary; if it generates sufficient interest, the remainder of the document may be assigned to other persons for review. The executive summary outlines the entire business plan, its major objectives, how these objectives will be accomplished, and the expected results. Therefore, it is sometimes first sent to potential investors to see if they have any interest in the venture; if so, the entire plan will then be sent to them.

Remember, *the executive summary is just that—a summary—so keep it short!* It may be difficult to get so much information on one or two pages, but try to do so. Also, even though the summary is the initial component of the plan, *it should be written only after the rest of the plan has been developed.*

Figure 6.9 presents a sample outline of the executive summary required of individuals and firms seeking equity capital from the Venture Capital Exchange of the University of Tulsa (www.utulsa.edu). We recommend that your summary also contain sections on the ownership and legal form of the business.

> The **executive summary** is a brief overview of the most important information in a business plan.

Table of Contents

Because the table of contents provides an overview of what's in the plan, it should be written concisely, in outline form, using alphabetical and numerical headings and subheads.

History of the (Proposed) Business

Background information on the person(s) organizing the business, as well as a description of each person's contributions, should be discussed at this point. Explanations of how the idea for the product or firm originated and what has been done to develop the idea should also be included. If the owner or owners have been in business before, that should be discussed, and any failures should be explained.

Description of the Business

It is now time for you to describe your business! More information is needed than just a statement of what the firm does—or plans to do—and a listing of its functions, products, or services. This definition should tell what customer needs the business intends to meet.

FIGURE 6.9 |

Sample Outline of an
Executive Summary

A. Company
   1. Who and what it is
   2. Status of project/firm
   3. Key goals and objectives
B. Product/service
   1. What it is
   2. How it works
   3. What it is for
   4. Proprietary advantages
C. Market
   1. Prospective customers
   2. How many there are
   3. Market growth rate
   4. Competition (list three to six competi-
       tors by name and describe)
   5. Industry trends
   6. How the firm will compete
   7. Estimated market share
       a. In one year
       b. In five years

D. Operations
   1. How product/service will be
       manufactured/provided
   2. Facilities/equipment
   3. Special processes
   4. Labor skills needed
E. Channels of distribution: how
    product/service will get to end
    users
F. Management team
   1. Who will do what
   2. Their qualifications
   3. Availability
G. Sources and application of funds
   1. Present needs
   2. Future needs

One-page profit and loss statement showing annual totals for first three years, including detailed
costs of goods sold and overhead (general and administrative) breakdowns.

Source: Dr. Robert D. Hisrich, "Entrepreneur Application Profile of the Venture Capital Exchange" in working paper,
Weatherhead School of Management, Case Western Reserve University. Used by permission.

In writing this component, it might be helpful to distinguish between how you perceive
the business and what potential customers might think of it. Think about questions such as
these, from the *owner's* perspective:

• What do you think will sell?

• What is your largest line of inventory?

• Where is your greatest profit made?

and from the *customer's* perspective:

• What do you think they need or want to buy?

• What is the best-selling item?

• On what product or service is most personnel time spent?

Ask yourself whether the answers to these questions are closely aligned and
compatible or divergent. If they are divergent, the business may be in trouble. If they
are compatible—or can be made compatible—there is a good chance of success, as the
following example illustrates.

Real-World Example 6.7

The sales manager of an FM radio station evaluated the results of efforts to sell
advertising and found that advertising customers obtained 45 percent or more of their
business volume from the black community. Yet that group made up only a small
portion of the station's listening audience, and the station had never attracted the desired
volume of advertising. A shift to black disk jockeys and a program format attuned to
the black community produced a substantial increase in advertising revenues.

Definition of the Market

While the definition of the market is one of the most important—and most difficult—parts of the plan to develop, it should at least indicate the target of your marketing efforts (see Chapter 8), as well as the trading area served. It must answer questions such as these: Who buys what and why? What are your customers like? Does the competition have any weaknesses you can exploit?

Description of the Product(s)

This section should describe the firm's existing or planned product(s). The status of all research done and developments under way should be described, along with discussions of any legal aspects, such as patents, copyrights, trademarks, pending lawsuits, and legal claims against the firm. Are any government approvals or clearances needed? Catalog sheets, blueprints, photographs, and other visuals—if available—are helpful and should be included.

Management Structure

This is the place to describe your management structure, especially the expertise of your management team. Explain how its members will help carry out the plan. You could also discuss employee policies and procedures. To repeat: It is important to demonstrate the proven ability and dedication of the owner and staff.

Objectives and Goals

This part outlines what your business plans to accomplish, as well as how and when it will be done and who will do it. Sales forecasts as well as production, service, quality assurance, and financial plans should be discussed. Other items of interest to potential investors include pricing and anticipated profits, advertising and promotion strategies and budgets, a description of how the product(s) will be distributed and sold, and which categories of customers will be targeted for initial heavy sales effort, and which ones for later sales efforts.

Financial Data

One important purpose of the business plan is to indicate the expected financial results from operations. The plan should show prospective investors or lenders why they should provide funds, when they can expect a return, and what the expected rate of return on their money is. At this point in the new business's development, assumptions—or educated guesses—concerning many issues may have to be made. For example, assumptions must be made about expected revenues, competitors' actions, and future market conditions. Assumptions, while necessary, should be designated as such, and financial projections should be realistically based on how increased personnel, expanded facilities, or equipment needs will affect the projections. The budgetary process to be used is an important part of the business plan. And prices should reflect actual cost figures, as the following example illustrates.

Real-World Example 6.8

In a college town a restaurant owner who was in financial difficulty sought aid from the SBA (www.sba.gov). The first question asked by the SCORE (www.score.org) volunteer assigned as a consultant was: "What's the most popular item on your menu?" The owner replied, "Our $6.25 steak dinner." The consultant asked for a scale and a raw steak. He showed the restaurant owner that the raw steak alone cost $5.10. Obviously, the reason for the steak dinner's popularity was the markup of less than 23 percent on the cost of the steak alone. It was also the underlying cause of the business's financial troubles.

Appendixes

Other components needed in the plan are the firm's organizational structure, including organization charts. This part should include résumés of the officers, directors, key personnel, and any outside board members. If any of these have any special expertise that increases the chances of success, this should be mentioned. Historical financial information, with relevant documents, should also be included. Brochures, news items, letters of recommendation or endorsements, photographs, and similar items should be included as well.

Presenting the Plan

We know a SCORE adviser who tells his clients, "Investors decide during the first five minutes of studying the executive summary whether to reject a proposal or consider it further." Therefore, *presenting the business plan is almost as important as preparing it.* All the work is in vain if potential investors are not interested in it. Presentation involves both writing the plan and presenting it to the targeted audience.

This point was strongly reinforced by Joseph Mancuso, author of a leading book on how to prepare and present business plans. The director of the Center for Entrepreneurial Management in New York asserts that "a good business plan takes a minimum of five months to write, but you've got to convince your readers in five minutes not to throw [it] away."[20]

Writing the Plan

John G. Burch, a writer on entrepreneurship, made the following classic suggestions for writing an effective plan:[21]

- *Be honest,* not only by avoiding outright lies, but also by revealing what you actually feel about the significant and relevant aspects of the plan.
- *Use the third person,* not the first person ("I" or "we"). This practice forces you to think clearly and logically from the other person's perspective.
- *Use transitional words,* such as *but, still,* and *therefore,* and active, dynamic verbs as a means of leading the reader from one thought to another.
- *Avoid redundancies,* such as "*future* plans"; repetition adds nothing to the presentation.
- *Use short, simple words,* where feasible, so the plan will be easy to understand and follow.
- *Use visuals,* such as tables, charts, photos, and computer graphics to present your ideas effectively.

The plan should be prepared in an 8½-by-11-inch format, typed, and photocopied with copies for outsiders attractively bound. Most business plans can—and should—be presented effectively in 25 to 30 pages—or less. Of course, the plan should be grammatically correct, so have someone proofread it for spelling and grammar before you present it.

The plan should be reviewed by people outside the firm, such as accounting and business consultants, other business people, and attorneys, before it is sent to potential investors or lenders. Other helpful reviewers might include a professional writer, editor, or English teacher.

When pertinent, the cover and title page should indicate that the information is proprietary and confidential. However, there is always the chance that this practice might offend a potential investor.

The Written/Oral Presentation

In an oral presentation, you should present the plan in person to investors or lenders. Presenting your plan involves creative skills on your part to give the impression that you have (or plan to have) a profitable and stable business, and that its chances of continuing that way are good. Your listeners will be looking very carefully at *you,* to see what kind of person *you* are, for *you are the business*—and vice versa. Both written and oral presentations should be very positive and quite upbeat.

The plan should be delivered from the listener's perspective, not yours. Both oral and written presentations should demonstrate that you have a marketable product and that the business has a feasible plan for aggressively marketing it—at a profit. You should provide visual aids for key segments of the plan and be prepared for specific questions concerning the following:

- The adequacy of the research and development behind the product.
- The validity of the market research.
- Your understanding of the business.
- Financial projections and why they will work.
- Relative priority of the objectives.
- Your ability to "make it happen."

The amount of detail in the market data and financial projections will vary according to the plan's purpose. If it is to raise equity or debt financing, more detail is needed; if it is to improve operations and motivate employees, less detail is needed.

You must remember that you are probably the best expert on your product or service and may have only one brief opportunity to present your plan. So be prepared!

Even the best-prepared plan, though, may not be accepted by potential investors. The following example is one of the classic blunders in the history of computers.

Real-World Example 6.9

In 1946, J. Presper Eckert, Jr., one of the inventors of the ENIAC, the first digital computer, fired off a business plan to IBM (www.ibm.com), hoping it would yield an investment to produce and distribute the UNIVAC, the first giant electronic computer. IBM President Thomas J. Watson, Sr., after careful review, responded that it was the company's opinion that the world would ultimately need only about 5 or 10 such large computers, and Eckert's machine was therefore of no interest to IBM.

Implementing the Plan

Now you are ready to take the plunge! It is time to get a charter, obtain facilities and supplies, hire and train people, and start operating. Using the capital structure plan and the sources of funds you have developed, obtain the funds and put them in a checking account ready for use. Obtain the services of an attorney to help acquire the charter (if the business is to be incorporated), obtain occupational licenses and permits, and take care of other legal requirements.

Once the funds, charter, and permits are in hand refer to the timetable and start negotiating contracts; purchasing equipment, materials, and supplies; selecting, hiring, and training employees; establishing a marketing program; setting the legal structure in place; and developing an information system to maintain the records needed to run the business.

You are now a small business owner! You are operating your own business, you have all the risks, and you hope to receive the benefits and rewards of being on your own. Be ready for unforeseen problems, however, that may occur during the startup period.

Sample Business Plan

A sample business plan is presented as an appendix at the end of this chapter. It is a proposal for a new business center. Notice that it closely follows the form as presented in Figure 6.8.

What You Should Have Learned

1. Planning, one of the key managerial functions, is usually done first, since everything else depends on it. While planning establishes directions and goals for any business, it is especially difficult in small firms, where management is often fully engaged in day-to-day operation and "can't see the forest for the trees." Some barriers to planning in small firms are the fear of learning things you would rather not know, the unpredictability of plans, the uncertainty of plans, and especially the lack of adequate time to plan.

2. Strategic planning—from which other plans are derived—determines the very nature of the business. Next comes operational planning, which sets policies, methods and procedures, budgets and standards, and other operating plans.

3. Financial planning involves estimating income and expenses, estimating investment required, and locating sources of funds. Income and expenses should be estimated to ensure that the proposed business will be feasible. Estimates should be based on the firm's first year of operation, as well as a typical "good" year, because investors may be willing to assume some risk of loss at the beginning to achieve greater gains later. Also, estimates should be made of personal needs during the transition period. These projections permit the prospective new owner to estimate the initial investment needed. Finally, sources of funds must be determined. The two sources are the business owner(s) and others, either private individuals or lending institutions.

4. A business plan is important for obtaining funds and as a blueprint for operating success. The research and analysis required to write an effective plan help you focus on the company's goals, markets, expected performance, and problems that might be encountered. The plan keeps you from jumping into an enterprise without adequate thought and planning, and then serves as a yardstick against which to measure performance.

5. The plan should include at least the following: (a) cover sheet, (b) executive summary, (c) table of contents, (d) history of the (proposed) business, (e) description of the business, (f) definition of the market, (g) description of the product(s), (h) management structure, (i) objectives and goals, (j) financial data, and (k) appendixes. When used to raise funds, detailed financial projections of expected sales, profits, and rates of return should be emphasized. From discussions in this and the previous chapter, you should be able to prepare an effective business plan.

Key Terms

budgets 135	human resource	objectives 132
business plan 142	planning 136	operational planning 135
cash flow 140	human resources 133	physical resources 133
competitive edge 134	lenders 142	planning 128
equity investors 140	methods and	policies 135
executive summary 146	procedures 135	strategic planning 130
financial planning 138	microloan 142	strategies 134
financial resources 133	mission 132	variable expenses 138
fixed expenses 139	net profit 138	

Questions for Discussion

1. Explain why planning is so badly needed by small businesses. Why is it so often neglected?

2. Explain the two overall categories of planning. What are the essential differences between the two?

3. Explain each of the following: policies, methods and procedures, budgets, and standards.

4. In planning to operate the business, what are the factors that must be planned for? Explain each.

5. What is involved in financial planning?

6. What is the purpose of a business plan? Explain.

7. How can a business plan be useful even to a prospective business owner who does not need outside capital?

8. What should the business plan include?

9. Who should prepare the plan? Why? Why should the writer get help from outside professionals and businesspeople?

In lieu of cases, the authors suggest that students design their own business plan.

Experientials

1. Visit your local family owned restaurant. Ask the principal manager if they prepare an annual budget. Why or why not? If not, ask how they measure financial success.

2. This chapter gives you direction for a hands-on experience with a business plan and makes a great class project. Choose an industry that will have readily available information and give a presentation of your opening day.

3. In teams of three, research microloans to find sponsors of microloans for several different industries. Explain the SBA's role in the process.

Appendix

A Sample Business Plan: The Business Center*

Executive Summary

The Company

The Business Center will provide traveling businesspeople and vacationers with onsite access to office services such as photocopying, Internet access, secretarial services, and other related office needs.

Marketing Strategy

The Business Center will serve hotel clientele and local businesses. The major focus will be on hotel guests traveling in the area with business-related needs. As part of the hotel's informational literature, The Business Center will be featured as a convenient service for the guests. Other advertising will be achieved through placement of The Business Center's brochures inside adjacent hotels and other strategic locations.

Operations

The facility will be housed in the lobby area of the Marriott Courtyard. Using the services of an employment leasing service, one full-time employee will be on site during working hours.

Management Team

The three partners will maintain their current jobs. Management responsibilities will be divided according to their experience in their primary professions. Suzanne Hagan will be responsible for operations; Joseph Payne will be responsible for financial management; and Darrell Waldrup will be responsible for marketing procedures.

The goal of the management team will be to operate near breakeven for the first year, expand services to guests at neighboring hotels, and eventually service the needs of local businesses.

Financial Considerations

As shown in Appendix I, the expected profit for the first year is $6,159, with an anticipated 10 percent increase annually.

Table of Contents

---

*Prepared by Suzanne Hagan, Joseph Payne, and Darrell Waldrup of the University of Mobile.

III.   Objectives and Goals
    A.   Profit Plans
    B.   Marketing Plans
    C.   Quality Control Plans
    D.   Financial Plans

IV.   Definition of the Market
    A.   Customers
    B.   Competition
        1.   Competitors' Strengths
        2.   Competitors' Weaknesses
    C.   Substitutes
    D.   Barriers to Entry
    E.   Powers of Suppliers
    F.   Growth Strategy
    G.   Marketing Strategy

V.   Description of the Product
    A.   Office Services
    B.   Secretarial Services
    C.   Computer Workstation Rentals
    D.   Pickup and Delivery

VI.   Management Structure

VII.   Environmental Factors
    A.   Demographic
    B.   Economic
    C.   Technological

VIII.   Financial Data
    A.   Pricing Strategy
    B.   Cash Flow Projections
    C.   Income Projections

IX.   Appendixes
    A.   Résumés of Principals
    B.   Hotel Locations
    C.   Location of Competitors
    D.   Demographics of the Area
    E.   Economic Indicators
    F.   Pricing Flyer
    G.   Loan Payment Schedule
    H.   Three-Year Projected Cash Flow
    I.   Three-Year Projected Income Statement
    J.   Three-Year Projected Balance Sheet with Projected Ratios
    K.   Product Layout

I. History and Background of the Business

The Business Center will be a limited-liability corporation run by Suzanne Hagan, Joseph Payne, and Darrell Waldrup. The individuals are students at a local university working toward master's degrees in business administration. Their individual professional experiences will be utilized in the operation of the business. (Refer to Appendix A for each principal's professional experience.)

The concept of opening a business center came from the need for office services for businesspeople traveling and staying at hotels and motels in the vicinity. The area of concentration for this facility is proposed as an area along Interstate 65 near Airport Boulevard.

The facility will be housed in the lobby area of the Marriott Courtyard which is part of a complex of Marriott holdings including the Fairfield Inn and the Residence Inn located on three adjacent properties on the Beltline Highway facing the Interstate. In addition, there are 19 other motels located within a two-mile radius of the facility. (Refer to Appendix B for a map of hotel markets in this area.)

The income received from operations will not be the primary source of revenue for the principals. Each partner is currently employed in various business industries that will contribute to the success of this venture.

II. Definition of the Business

Every day, people are reinventing the way they do business. The Business Center will support this revolution by providing innovative ways to get the job done in a convenient and timely manner. It will offer a variety of services including photocopies, laser prints, facsimiles, secretarial services, computer workstation rentals, shipping, and office supplies. It will also offer Internet access with an emphasis on offering e-mail access for the businessperson.

III. Objectives and Goals

The company will be committed to doing whatever is needed to guarantee customer satisfaction with the organization's products and customer services.

A. Profit Plans

The company's goals will be to maximize profits through efficiency of operations. Through the use of minimum square footage they will provide minimum overhead and maximum service output; this will provide high return on investment.

B. Marketing Plans

The company will use service advertising and promotional programs to increase exposure to the target market.

C. Quality Control Plans

Through streamlining operations and responding to customers' concerns, the company hopes to narrow any gap seen by the client between their office and the services being provided.

D. Financial Plans

The principals will obtain an unsecured loan in the amount of $10,000, with the first payment not due for 90 days. The first $1,500 of the loan will be used to purchase supplies and equipment. The rest of the loan will be used as working capital. Each of the principals will supply personal funds of $1,000 toward startup costs for The Business Center. Future capital will be obtained through a line of credit from the bank for working capital.

IV. Definition of the Market

The area is currently experiencing rapid growth in the hotel and motel market. Lodging facilities are currently operating at 70 percent occupancy. The industry standard for minimum profit is 60 percent capacity. As long as capacity is above 60 percent, there is room for growth. The result is an expanding need of business services for guests staying in these facilities.

A. Customers

The target market is businesspeople visiting the area, either for business purposes such as company business or conventions, or for leisure activities. These are people who cannot afford to be away from the office and the services their office provides to them. The Business Center will become an office away from home, thereby filling this void in services.

The Business Center would also serve the general public, but recognizes that this is not its primary target market.

B. Competition

Direct competitors are three major franchises—Kinko's; Mail Boxes, Etc.; and Printing One—as well as small individually owned operations.

1. Competitors' Strengths

- The major franchises offer name recognition to the customer.
- Franchises also have corporate support in operations, management, accounting, and technological systems.
- The competitors have been in business long enough to target the most profitable services.

2. Competitors' Weaknesses

- The competitors are positioned away from where the customers are located; their location requires driving along major thoroughfares in unfamiliar territories. (Refer to Appendix C for a map showing competitors' locations.)
- Cost of operation of the competitors' facilities is high.
- The competitors, being located away from the hotels, would not be able to offer such personal services.

C. Substitutes

Substitutes for The Business Center include such things as personally owned fax machines and portable computers. Other substitutes could be making copies by hand.

D. Barriers to Entry

Some barriers to entry for The Business Center include the capital required to purchase the necessary business machines and securing a good location for the facility.

E. Power of Suppliers

The power of suppliers to affect The Business Center is relatively low, except in the circumstances of repair of a malfunctioning copier or computer.

F. Growth Strategy

Exhibits 1 and 2 show indicators of potential business for The Business Center. The Mobile Convention Center—located on the Mobile River in downtown Mobile—alone drew 195,000 guests in 1995/1996, with an anticipated annual growth of 10 percent. There are only two major hotels downtown near the convention center. Many guests are required to stay in one of the hotels located on the strip along Interstate 65 near Airport Boulevard.

EXHIBIT 1 | Selected Indicators of Visitors to Mobile County

Year	Enplaned Passengers	I-10 Westbound Welcome Center	I-10 Eastbound Welcome Center	Total
1992	365,777	335,589	492,651	1,194,017
1993	357,289	283,181	426,049	1,066,519
1994	353,626	332,888	423,313	1,109,827
1995	304,859	390,537	390,974	1,086,370
1996	378,706	335,015	392,017	1,105,738

EXHIBIT 2 | Hotels and Motels in Mobile County

Year/ Month	Occupancy Rate					
	Downtown	Beltline	I-10 West	City Average	State Average	U.S. Average
1995	N.A.	N.A.	N.A.	62.20	63.70	65.10
1996	N.A.	N.A.	N.A.	60.60	62.03	65.70
1997/1	43.23	57.48	51.70	54.67	51.50	53.70
1997/2	60.93	66.50	68.49	66.04	61.70	62.40
1997/3	52.75	69.87	78.88	67.16	65.00	65.30
1997/4	56.93	71.93	70.44	68.83	67.70	67.00
1997/5	49.40	64.58	74.73	62.54	N.A.	N.A.

According to these indicators, the county, in 1996, had a growth rate of 2 percent from 1995, indicating a small increase in the number of visitors. An increase in the number of visitors indicates an increase in the number of business travelers as well as vacationers. This would indicate an increase in the need of services provided by The Business Center.

G. Marketing Strategy

As mentioned earlier, the company will use service advertising and promotional programs to increase exposure to the targeted market.

Being part of the hotel complex shown in Appendix B, The Business Center will receive direct advertising from all of the corporate affiliates. As part of the hotel's informational literature, The Business Center will be featured as a convenient service for the guests.

Other advertising will be achieved through placement of The Business Center's brochures inside adjacent hotels and other strategic locations.

The Business Center will conduct periodic mailings to companies located in the two-county area. Corporations will be targeted for business services needed by their visiting associates. These mailings, also, could generate additional revenues from local businesses, helping to offset seasonal variations in volume.

V. Description of the Product

The Business Center plans to offer all the convenient services of a conventional office. These services would encompass everything from office supplies to Internet access.

A. Office Services

Customers will have access to basic office supplies, such as pens, paper supplies, folders, report covers, etc. Facsimile services will be available. Photocopying services will include plain-paper copies, color copies, and copying onto transparencies.

B. Secretarial Services

Customers will have access to services of a professional familiar with word processing, dictation, and spreadsheet applications. All work will be printed on laser printers using quality paper or transparencies for presentation. The availability of a service to develop professional presentations using Microsoft *PowerPoint* presentation software will also be available. The presentations could be printed or could be stored on floppy disks for the customers to use in their own computers.

C. Computer Workstation Rentals

Customers will have access to a computer workstation, complete with a laser printer, for their own personal use. The computer will be equipped with a modem to allow customers access to the Internet. A feature that The Business Center intends to offer is e-mail service for the customer. Currently, approximately half of all e-mail service providers offer access availability from remote locations, so customers would be able to access their own personal e-mail, receive and send messages, and continue to stay in touch while they are away from home.

D. Pickup and Delivery

Shipping via United Parcel Service and Federal Express will be available for customers. The company plans to establish the location as a drop-off/pickup point for both these services, therefore increasing business traffic.

The company will contract with a local delivery service for offsite pickup and delivery for customers staying at hotels other than the Marriott Courtyard and for local businesses.

VI. Management Structure

The three partners will maintain their current jobs. Using an employment leasing service, one full-time employee will be on site during working hours. During initial startup, the principals will meet weekly to discuss matters such as operational issues, client concerns, and financial analysis. Management responsibilities will be divided according to their experience in their primary professions.

Suzanne Hagan will be responsible for operations. Her many years of experience in the business sector make her well aware of the needs of the customers. Having managed office staff and worked with office facilities, she will utilize her contacts for purchasing of equipment and supplies, training office personnel, and working with personnel regarding operational problems and procedures.

Joseph Payne will be responsible for financial management. His years of experience in banking will prove to be an asset for the purpose of obtaining initial capital for this venture. Furthermore, his analytical skills in evaluating current trends and future outlooks of the company's financial position will be a valuable tool.

Darrell Waldrup will be responsible for marketing procedures. His understanding of the demands of customers and how to meet those demands will allow him to evaluate the performance of the business and keep operations running smoothly. He will also be responsible for developing new accounts and soliciting new business to continue the growth of the organization.

VII. Environmental Factors

A. Demographic

Although The Business Center's primary market is traveling businesspeople, the market that exists for permanent residents of the area cannot be overlooked. The location of The Business Center will allow for quick recognition among some of the city's most business-minded people. The Business Center is within close proximity to the residences of people who tend to be the highest spenders on such services as auto loans, home loans, investments, retirement plans, travel, and health insurance. (Refer to Appendix D.) These people have been targeted as the segment most likely to use these services other than traveling people. The Business Center will focus on maintaining and developing positive and supportive customer relationships with this group of people, especially in the initial introduction and growth stages of the businesses.

B. Economic

Over the past three years, several new corporations and businesses have come into the area. Existing corporations and businesses have been growing tremendously as well. The three largest areas of employment are in the following industries: Services, Retail and Wholesale Trade, and Government. With these new and expanding businesses come needs for business services. The Business Center recognizes the needs of these industries and is willing to serve them. (Refer to Appendix E.)

C. Technological

In today's business world, technology has a strong presence. The ability to use technology efficiently can be a tremendous asset to an organization. Information can be transferred, stored, and presented very quickly and efficiently by electronic means currently available. The Business Center recognizes this fact and uses some of the latest equipment and means to better serve the customer in an accurate, timely, and professional manner.

VIII. Financial Data

A. Pricing Strategy

Pricing will be competitive as it relates to the convenience of services provided to customers. (Refer to Appendix F for proposed pricing flyer.)

B. Cash Flow Projections

Refer to Appendix G: Loan Payment Schedule.
Refer to Appendix H: Three-Year Projected Cash Flow.

C. Income Projections

Refer to Appendix I: Three-Year Projected Income Statement.
Refer to Appendix J: Three-Year Projected Balance Sheet with Projected Ratios.

IX. Appendixes

A.   Résumés of Principals.

B.   Hotel Locations.

C.   Location of Competitors.

D.   Demographics of the Area.

E.   Economic Indicators.

F.   Pricing Flyer.

G.   Loan Payment Schedule.

H.   Three-Year Projected Cash Flow.

I.   Three-Year Projected Income Statement.

J.   Three-Year Projected Balance Sheet with Projected Ratios.

K.   Product Layout.

Appendix A: Résumés of Principals

Suzanne C. Hagan

Professional Experience

Vice President of Information Systems

♦ Directly responsible for operation of the corporation's mainframe computer system which includes accounting, parts and inventory and service operations.

♦ Coordinate all data communications between the mainframe and 35 personal computers throughout the company's four branch locations as well as satellite communications with a major vendor.

♦ Manage the telephone communication systems at all locations.

♦ Install software and train staff in usage.

♦ Monitor hardware and manage a network of PCs.

♦ Provide technical support to PC and laptop users in sales, repair diagnosis, parts, service, accounting, and general word processing.

♦ Coordinate the installation of, train staff, and maintain a contract management system used for direct mail and telecommunications.

♦ Work on the advertising team producing bimonthly direct mail brochures and periodic mail-outs. Publications include in-house and outsourced printing projects. Publish the monthly newsletter.

♦ Experienced in the procurement of hardware and software.

Vice President of Accounting and Data Processing

♦ Supervised all accounting and computer operations for corporate office and three branches.

♦ Directed the completion of monthly financial statements and led accountants during annual audits to prepare year end reports.

Office Manager

♦ Managed office and accounting operations including monthly financial statements.

♦ Hired and trained office personnel.

♦ Supervised the installation of the company's first computer as well as three subsequent computer upgrades.

Computer Operator

♦ Operated IBM keypunch machine, card sorter, and IBM computer to prepare life insurance policies as well as reissue policies after changes from field sales personnel.

Suzanne C. Hagan

Page Two

Technical Skills and Professional Development

Computer/software experience:

WordPerfect	Lotus 1-2-3
Alpha 4 Database	Windows 3.1/95
Desktop Publishing	Windows for Workgroups
Telemagic & Sidekick Contact Management Software	

Seminars in:

Performance Appraisals	How to be a Winner at Work
Understanding a Financial Statement	Job Skills for Success
Developing Productive Communications	Reward of Teamwork
Implementation of Inventory	Dealer's User Conference

Education

Master of Business Administration

Bachelor of Science (Organizational Management), Summa cum laude

Professional Affiliations

National Association of Women Business Owners
Executive Women's Forum
Career Women of Mobile
National Association of Women in Construction
    Chapter Treasurer, Secretary, Vice President, and President

References Available on Request

Joseph Payne

Professional Experience

Financial Sales Manager, Assistant Vice President

- Progressively promoted to Branch Manager and Bank Officer following first year accomplishments.
- Achieved top 1% company sales ranking—first year.
- Consistently ranked top 10% in sales performance.
- Lead area in Business Banking relational developments.
- Regional sales training officer for branch management.
- Supervise internal operational cash management.
- Perform daily financial and investment counseling.
- Responsible for motivational staff management.
- Personal Banker for a 4,500 customer base.
- Conduct Prospect and Client sales calls—increased deposit base by 11%.
- Selected as corporate CRA representative.
- Headed system update of a computerized financial program.

Buyer/Senior Merchandiser, Major Retail Store

- Managed a $1.33mm department at the district headquarters.
- Chosen to implement company pilot programs.
- Designed, developed, and initiated time/cost reduction program saving more than $1mm.
- Motivational training of 27 associates into a leading sales force.
- Responsibilities included:

Buying	Inventory Management
Sales and Profit Analysis	Merchandising Layout
Forecasting	Strategic Management
Advertising	Quality Control
Competitive Shopping Analysis	Prospecting
Personnel Training and Development	Marketing Research
Expanding Customer Base	Queuing
Promotional Management	

System Sales/Installation Manager—Radio Shack

- Systemized coordination of damaged inventory.
- Implemented introductory computer classes.

Technical Skills and Professional Development

Computer/software experience:

PC/Laptop/Mainframe	Database Design
WordPerfect	Lotus 1-2-3
Microsoft Word/Works	Microsoft Excel

Joseph Payne

Page Two

Education

Master of Business Administration

Bachelor of Science (Operations & Systems Management)

Professional Affiliations

University Alumni Board
Junior Achievement
    Board Member
    Economics Instructor, Project Business
Mentor/year-round Volunteer Teacher
Sickle Cell Disease Association
    Executive Board Member
Stone Street Baptist Church
    Sunday School Junior Superintendent/Teacher
    Laymen Organization Treasurer
Alabama Institute of Banking
    Education Committee Chairman
Midtown Optimist Club
United Way
    Corporate Chairman
American Diabetes Association
    Chairman
DECA Regional Competition
    Competition Judge
    Speaker

References Available on Request

Darrell E. Waldrup

Professional Experience

Graduate Assistant, School of Business, local university

♦   Assist key faculty in research and lecture tasks.

Lead Person, Sport Supply Group

♦   Implemented graphic art and developed managerial abilities.
♦   Met screen printing production demands.
♦   Produced quality merchandise within deadlines.
♦   Trained other employees in the production process.

Partner/Consultant, Southern Merchandise Liquidators

♦   Assisted in developing a successful small business.

Technical Skills and Professional Development

Computer/software experience:
Microsoft Office   Internet; Netscape

Major courses in:
Small Business Management   Managerial Marketing
Human Resource Management   Organizational Behavior

Education

Master of Business Administration

Bachelor of Science, Business Management

Honors and Activities

Summer Honors Program   Business Management Club
Presidential Leadership Scholarship   Accounting Club
J.L. Bedsole Academic Scholarship   Student Government Association
Mallory-Hand Academic Scholarship   Students in Free Enterprise (SIFE)
Graduate Assistant   Future Business Leaders of America

References Available on Request

Appendix B: Hotel Locations

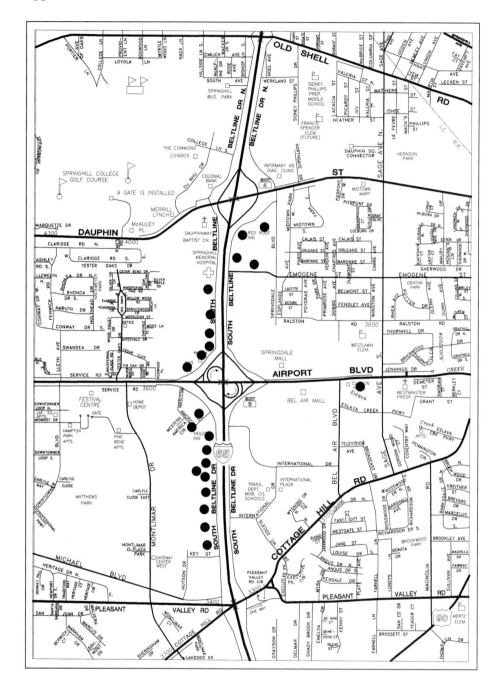

Appendix C: Location of Competitors

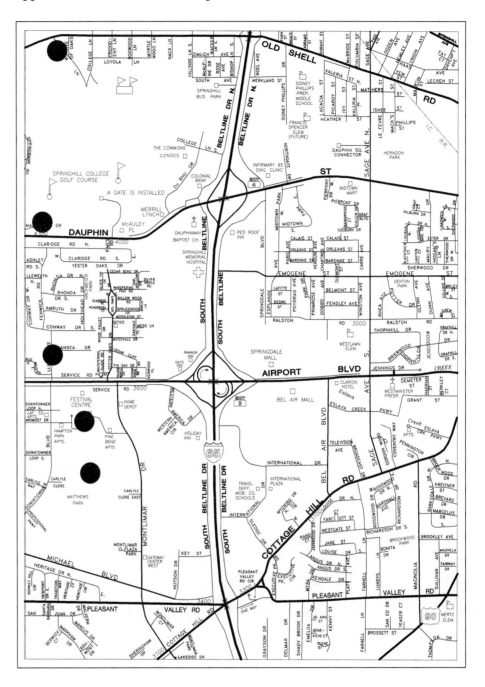

Appendix D: Demographics of the Area

Population Change				
Zip Code	1980	1990	1996	2001
36606	19,985	18,247	18,507	18,921
36607	9,944	8,610	8,607	8,706
36608	34,622	37,600	39,470	40,952
36609	19,913	23,667	25,518	26,898
36693	14,311	17,704	19,103	20,109
36695	13,898	21,467	25,772	28,485
Total	114,653	129,285	138,973	146,072

1996 Household Income Distribution (%)						
Zip Code	Less than $15,000	$15,000 to $24,999	$25,000 to $49,999	$50,000 to $99,999	$100,000 to $149,999	$150,000 or More
36606	25.8	20.4	35.5	16.3	1.5	0.06
36607	37.2	19.2	29.8	11.2	1.2	1.5
36608	18.1	17.0	33.8	21.4	5.5	4.3
36609	16.0	16.9	36.9	22.4	4.4	1.5
36693	12.7	13.0	33.7	31.5	6.3	2.7
36695	9.0	11.8	32.7	35.7	7.4	3.4

1996 Household Income Distribution (%)				
Zip Code	Auto Loan	Home Loan	Investments	Retirement Plans
36606	95	89	108	85
36607	92	79	100	76
36608	100	102	110	103
36609	98	99	89	91
36693	104	104	108	106
36695	103	105	81	98

Appendix E: Economic Indicators

Employment Composition				
	2005	**2006**	**Net Change**	
Construction and Mining	15,100	15,900	+	800
Manufacturing	27,000	27,100	+	100
Transportation and Public Utilities	12,900	13,000	+	100
Retail and Wholesale Trade	56,000	57,000	+	1,000
Finance, Insurance, and Real Estate	9,000	9,500	+	500
Services	55,900	57,400	+	1,500
Government	33,800	33,800		0
Total	**209,700**	**213,700**	**+**	**4,000**

Area Economic Indicators			
	Sept. 2007	**Sept. 2006**	**Year to Date 2007**
Business Activity			
Number of new businesses (city)	261	− 4.1%	2,377
Number of homes sold (county)	302	− 8.0%	2,820
Average price of homes sold		$103,411	+ 11.2%
Construction			
Number of building permits	372	+ 5.1%	3,281
Value of building permits	$10,926,805	− 49.0%	$138,141,846
Number of residential permits	18	− 33.4%	223
Value of residential permits	$1,540,943	− 35.2%	$18,627,691
Employment			
Labor force	264,510	− 0.1%	
Employed	252,160	− 0.2%	
Unemployment Rate (2007) (2006)			
City 4.7% 4.6%			
State 4.9% 4.7%			
U.S. 4.9% 5.2%			
Trade			
Sales tax revenue (city)	$5,704,449	+ 9.0%	$66,484,127
Sales tax revenue (county)	$3,446,865	+ 2.8%	$35,695,810
Lodging tax receipts (city)	$184,209	− 0.4%	$1,970,067
Transportation			
Enplaned air passengers	33,508	+ 12.3%	311,443

Appendix F: Pricing Flyer

THE BUSINESS CENTER
Marriott Courtyard
Phone: 555-675-5990 / Fax: 555-675-5991

PHOTOCOPIES		Per Copy
Black and White Copies		
20 lb., letter and legal	$	.15
Over 100 . . . . add	$	.10
Special paper . . . . add	$	.05
Transparencies	$	2.00
Color Copies		
Letter and legal	$	1.49
Over 100	$	.99
Transparencies	$	2.49

LASER PRINTS		
Letter and legal, per copy	$	.50

FACSIMILE		
Transmission—Domestic		
Per page	$	2.00
Transmission—International		
Per page	$	8.00
Reception		
Per page	$	1.00

SECRETARIAL SERVICES		
Per hour	$	35.00

COMPUTER WORKSTATION		
IBM workstations with modems and laser printers		
Per hour	$	35.00

SHIPPING
We will gladly ship your overnight letters or small parcels via Federal Express or UPS. Please inquire at **The Business Center** for current rates.

OFFICE SUPPLIES
We maintain an inventory of the most often needed office supplies. Please inquire at **The Business Center.**

Pickup and delivery service is available.
Call **The Business Center** *at 555-675-5990 for this service.*

THE BUSINESS CENTER
You're never too far from "the office."

Appendix G: Loan Payment Schedule

Amount financed	10,000
Annual interest	9.860
Duration of loan	3.6 years
Monthly payments	277.00
Total number of payments	43
Yearly principal + interest	3,324.00
Principal amount	10,000.00
Finance charges	1,966.40
Total cost	11,966.40

Payment Number	Payment Date	Beginning Balance	Interest	Principal	Balance	Accumulated Interest	Accumulated Principal
1		10,000.00	82.17	194.83	9,805.17	82.17	194.83
2		9,805.17	80.57	196.43	9,608.73	162.74	391.26
3		9,608.74	78.95	198.05	9,410.68	241.69	589.31
4		9,410.69	77.32	199.68	9,211.01	319.01	788.99
5		9,211.01	75.68	201.32	9,009.69	394.69	990.31
6		9,009.69	74.03	202.97	8,806.72	468.72	1,193.28
7		8,806.72	72.36	204.64	8,602.08	541.08	1,397.92
8		8,602.08	70.68	206.32	8,395.76	611.76	1,604.24
9		8,395.76	68.99	208.01	8,187.75	680.75	1,812.25
10		8,187.75	67.28	209.72	7,978.03	748.03	2,021.97
11		7,978.03	65.55	211.45	7,766.58	813.58	2,233.42
12		7,766.58	63.82	213.18	7,553.39	877.39	2,446.60

Appendix H: Three-Year Projected Cash Flow

THE BUSINESS CENTER
Projected Cash Flow
First Year of Operation

Summary	Quarter 1	Quarter 2	Quarter 3	Quarter 4	Year End
Opening balance	$3,000	$14,325	$15,214	$17,168	$3,000
Total receipts	$17,000	$7,300	$8,300	$6,600	$39,200
Total disbursements	5,675	6,411	6,346	6,421	24,853
Total cash flow	$11,325	$889	$1,954	$179	$14,347
Ending balance	$14,325	$15,214	$17,168	$17,347	$17,347

Receipts

	Quarter 1	Quarter 2	Quarter 3	Quarter 4	Year End
Cash revenues	$7,000	$7,300	$8,300	$6,600	$29,200
Loans	$10,000				$10,000

Disbursements

	Quarter 1	Quarter 2	Quarter 3	Quarter 4	Year End
Wages	$3,840	$3,840	$3,840	$3,840	$15,360
Leased equipment	$200	$380	$340	$340	$1,260
Advertising	$375	$175	$150	$225	$925
Supplies	$75	$75	$75	$75	$300
Rent	$525	$525	$525	$525	$2,100
Insurance	$150	$150	$150	$150	$600
Telephone	$285	$285	$285	$285	$1,140
Utilities	$225	$150	$150	$150	$675
Loan payments		$831	$831	$831	$2,493

THE BUSINESS CENTER
Projected Cash Flow
Second Year of Operation

Summary	Quarter 1	Quarter 2	Quarter 3	Quarter 4	Year End
Opening balance	$17,347	$17,979	$19,038	$21,269	$17,347
Total receipts	$7,700	$8,030	$9,130	$7,260	$32,120
Total disbursements	7,068	6,971	6,899	6,982	27,920
Total cash flow	$632	$1,059	$2,231	$278	$4,200
Ending balance	$19,979	$19,038	$21,269	$21,547	$21,547

Receipts

	Quarter 1	Quarter 2	Quarter 3	Quarter 4	Year End
Cash revenues	$7,700	$8,030	$9,130	$7,260	$32,120
Loans					

Disbursements

	Quarter 1	Quarter 2	Quarter 3	Quarter 4	Year End
Wages	$4,224	$4,224	$4,224	$4,224	$16,896
Leased equipment	$220	$418	$374	$374	$1,386
Advertising	$412	$193	$165	$248	$1,018
Supplies	$81	$83	$83	$83	$330
Rent	$576	$578	$578	$578	$2,310
Insurance	$165	$165	$165	$165	$660
Telephone	$312	$314	$314	$314	$1,254
Utilities	$247	$165	$165	$165	$742
Loan payments	$831	$831	$831	$831	$3,324

THE BUSINESS CENTER
Projected Cash Flow
Third Year of Operation

Summary	Quarter 1	Quarter 2	Quarter 3	Quarter 4	Year End
Opening balance	$21,547	$22,321	$23,570	$26,108	$21,547
Total receipts	$8,470	$8,833	$10,043	$7,986	$35,332
Total disbursements	7,696	7,584	7,505	7,595	30,380
Total cash flow	$774	$1,249	$2,538	$391	$4,952
Ending balance	$22,321	$23,570	$26,108	$26,499	$26,499

Receipts

	Quarter 1	Quarter 2	Quarter 3	Quarter 4	Year End
Cash revenues	$8,470	$8,833	$10,043	$7,986	$35,332
Loans					

Disbursements

	Quarter 1	Quarter 2	Quarter 3	Quarter 4	Year End
Wages	$4,646	$4,646	$4,646	$4,646	$18,584
Leased equipment	$241	$460	$411	$411	$1,523
Advertising	$454	$212	$182	$272	$1,120
Supplies	$91	$91	$91	$91	$364
Rent	$635	$635	$635	$635	$2,540
Insurance	$182	$182	$182	$182	$728
Telephone	$345	$345	$345	$345	$1,380
Utilities	$271	$182	$182	$182	$817
Loan payments	$831	$831	$831	$831	$3,324

Appendix I: Three-Year Projected Income Statement

THE BUSINESS CENTER
Projected Income Statement
First Year of Operation

	Quarter 1	Quarter 2	Quarter 3	Quarter 4	Year End
Product Sales					
Office services	$3,000	$3,100	$3,500	$2,800	$12,400
Secretarial services	$2,500	$2,500	$2,700	$2,200	$9,900
Computer rentals	$1,000	$1,200	$1,500	$1,200	$4,900
Pickup and delivery	$500	$500	$600	$400	$2,000
Total sales	**$7,000**	**$7,300**	**$8,300**	**$6,600**	**$29,200**
Operating Expense					
Wages	$3,840	$3,840	$3,840	$3,840	$15,360
Leased equipment	$200	$380	$340	$340	$1,260
Advertising	$375	$175	$150	$225	$925
Supplies	$75	$75	$75	$75	$300
Rent	$525	$525	$525	$525	$2,100
Insurance	$150	$150	$150	$150	$600
Telephone	$285	$285	$285	$285	$1,140
Utilities	$225	$150	$150	$150	$675
Interest		$242	$227	$212	$681
Total operating expense	**$5,675**	**$5,822**	**$5,742**	**$5,802**	**$23,041**
Net Income	**$1,325**	**$1,478**	**$2,558**	**$798**	**$6,159**

THE BUSINESS CENTER
Projected Income Statement
Second Year of Operation

	Quarter 1	Quarter 2	Quarter 3	Quarter 4	Year End
Product Sales					
Office services	$3,300	$3,410	$3,850	$3,080	$13,640
Secretarial services	$2,750	$2,750	$2,970	$2,420	$10,890
Computer rentals	$1,100	$1,320	$1,650	$1,320	$5,390
Pickup and delivery	$550	$550	$660	$440	$2,200
Total sales	**$7,700**	**$8,030**	**$9,130**	**$7,260**	**$32,120**
Operating Expense					
Wages	$4,224	$4,224	$4,224	$4,224	$16,896
Leased equipment	$220	$418	$374	$374	$1,386
Advertising	$412	$193	$165	$248	$1,018
Supplies	$81	$83	$83	$83	$330
Rent	$576	$578	$578	$578	$2,310
Insurance	$165	$165	$165	$165	$660
Telephone	$312	$314	$314	$314	$1,254
Utilities	$247	$165	$165	$165	$742
Interest	$196	$181	$165	$148	$690
Total operating expense	**$6,433**	**$6,321**	**$6,233**	**$6,299**	**$25,286**
Net Income	**$1,267**	**$1,709**	**$2,897**	**$961**	**$6,834**

THE BUSINESS CENTER
Projected Income Statement
Third Year of Operation

	Quarter 1	Quarter 2	Quarter 3	Quarter 4	Year End
Product Sales					
Office services	$3,630	$3,751	$4,235	$3,388	$15,004
Secretarial services	$3,025	$3,025	$3,267	$2,662	$11,979
Computer rentals	$1,210	$1,452	$1,815	$1,452	$5,929
Pickup and delivery	$605	$605	$726	$484	$2,420
Total sales	**$8,470**	**$8,833**	**$10,043**	**$7,986**	**$35,332**
Operating Expense					
Wages	$4,646	$4,646	$4,646	$4,646	$18,584
Leased equipment	$241	$460	$411	$411	$1,523
Advertising	$454	$212	$182	$272	$1,120
Supplies	$91	$91	$91	$91	$364
Rent	$635	$635	$635	$635	$2,540
Insurance	$182	$182	$182	$182	$728
Telephone	$345	$345	$345	$345	$1,380
Utilities	$271	$182	$182	$182	$817
Interest	$131	$114	$96	$78	$419
Total operating expense	**$6,996**	**$6,867**	**$6,770**	**$6,842**	**$27,475**
Net Income	**$1,474**	**$1,966**	**$3,273**	**$1,144**	**$7,857**

Appendix J: Three-Year Projected Balance Sheet with Projected Ratios

THE BUSINESS CENTER
Projected Balance Sheet
Three Years Ending December 31, 20__

	First Year	Second Year	Third Year
Current Assets			
Cash	$17,347	$21,547	$26,499
Total current assets	$17,347	$21,547	$26,499
Current Liabilities			
Notes payable, current	$2,634	$2,905	$2,649
Total current liabilities	$2,634	$2,905	$2,649
Long-Term Liabilities			
Notes payable, long-term	$5,554	$2,649	$00
Total long-term liabilities	$5,554	$2,649	$00
Total liabilities	$8,188	$5,554	$2,649
Net worth	$9,159	$15,993	$23,850
Total Liabilities & Net Worth	**$17,347**	**$21,547**	**$26,499**

THE BUSINESS CENTER
Projected Ratios

	First Year	Second Year	Third Year
Current ratio	6.6:1	7.4:1	10:1
Operating profit margin	21.1%	21.3%	22.2%
Return on equity	67.2%	54.3%	32.7%
Debt to owners' equity	89.4%	34.7%	11.1%
Current liabilities to owners' equity	28.8%	18.2%	11.1%

Appendix K: Product Layout

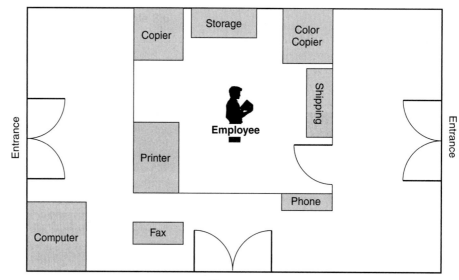

CHAPTER 7

How to Obtain the Right Financing for Your Business

Money makes money, and the money money makes, makes more money.
    —Benjamin Franklin

Many of the financial problems plaguing small businesses are avoidable, provided entrepreneurs analyze their own funding needs objectively and with sufficient lead time to act decisively.
    —Small Business Administration

Learning Objectives

After studying the material in this chapter, you should be able to:

1. Explain the importance of proper financing for a small business.

2. Tell how to estimate financial needs, and explain some principles to follow in obtaining financing.

3. Explain why equity and debt financing are used, and describe the role each plays in the capital structure of a small firm.

4. Distinguish the types of equity and debt securities.

5. Describe some sources of equity financing.

6. Describe some sources of debt financing.

7. Explain what a lender looks for in a borrower.

Photo courtesy of Sarah Coxwell

Meet Sarah Coxwell of Davis Coxwell & Co LLC

My husband, Cary worked part time for a health food store while he was in college and after my graduation I went to work for the same company as a manager of one of two local franchise stores that the current owners were interested in selling. I had been interviewing at local banks and investment brokerage firms, but took a chance at the lesser preferred manager position for the possibility of ownership in the near future. It took one year to finalize the deal and acquire the stores. We had no money starting out, but we were lucky enough to get the owner to finance a portion of both stores and took over the remaining notes on the two stores from financing through the franchisor. We still needed money for utility deposits, business licenses, and miscellaneous other items, so we borrowed against my used car to get $10,000 for start-up expenses. We literally started with nothing, using only borrowed money and loans.

In the beginning I managed both stores, while my husband worked at another job to provide enough income to live on while we were paying the notes. After about six months, my husband quit his other job and we each managed one store with two part-time employees. For a while we divided our time between the stores, both working about 20 hours a week so that one of us would always be off to stay home with our children. We decided that Cary would stay home full time while I continued to work at the stores and run the business.

Later, we added a third store, a corporate conversion. Corporate conversion means it was previously a corporate store and had been offered up for sale. We used franchisor financing, which is very easy to get but carries a higher rate than a bank, and used some money from the company profits for the down payment. We chose to buy the store when it became available because it is difficult to get stores in the exact geographic areas we desired.

In 2010 we opened two more stores. These were brand new so there was no history or existing customers. New stores are not profitable from the beginning but have the advantages of better locations, new fixtures, and creative layouts. Originally we had two stores and four employees. Now we have six stores and 25 employees.

The Numbers

In 2000 when we started, annual sales were just over $500,000. Today annual sales are $4 million. In our business we track what we call BLY or "Beat Last Year" (measurement of increase/decrease from previous year). Some stores have seen BLYs increase as much as 40 percent from the year 2000. Typically, a store's BLY may only go up 3–5 percent year to year but some years show increases of as much as 30 percent in a single year.

Margin is one of the most important aspects that we can control in our business. Every margin percent is

179

equivalent to dollars in our pocket, so it is very tightly controlled and sharply scrutinized. We bring in and focus on selling the highest margin products in any given category. We use PMs or Promotional Money which is employee commission on high margin items. We have about 30 to 40 PM items throughout the store ranging from 50 cents to 20 dollars on any given item. We do not sell bad products just because they may carry a high margin. We sell the highest quality and strongest products that at the same time carry a high margin. We will not sacrifice quality for margin. If we did, we would not expect the customer to come back for a weak poor product. Instead, we sell the strongest best product with the highest possible margin so that everyone is satisfied.

When we analyze a potential new store, one of the first things we do is check its margin because if it is low, we know we can expect to increase it and change its income perspective. At one store we purchased, we increased the margin 11 percent within two months.

Financing

We have tried to get financing for several stores over the years as an alternative to franchisor higher rate financing and owner financing. We have tried many different banks and brokers using SBA financing and all have been fruitless. We believe the SBA is a myth . . . as we have seen no real proof that it even exists! We have used home equity, family, signature car loans, and owner financing to fund our businesses. I think it's because the bank doesn't have any real usable collateral in a business loan. The only collateral is the business's inventory and a bank would have a tough time selling vitamins. In fact, the reason we were able to acquire a high-volume store was because the other buyers the former owner had for that store tried to get bank financing and were told that they would have to secure the store with their house for collateral, but they refused. So, the owner let us buy the store and use owner financing because we already had a good track record of repayment.

Eight years into our ownership we were able to get bank financing. It was with a small bank and with no SBA backing. It is now our primary bank for all the stores and with whom we have a long-term relationship. Even still, we were only able to get half of what we asked for and

the reason we were able to get that much was only because we had that same amount sitting in other accounts at the bank. So, in fact, we had the collateral in cash. Later we were able to get two more small bank loans—again without SBA backing—which were secured with cash on hand.

Optimal inventories in individual stores run between $45,000 and $100,000, depending on annual sales figures. One of the major success factors for our stores is inventory level. Often mismanagement of inventory spending sends the organization into a downward spiral that forces the franchisor to take over or force the franchisee to sell the operation. In our experience we have witnessed two major reason why franchisees must sell: mismanagement and retirement. Mismanagement of funds is often the result of inexperience rather than malicious intent.

Family

Our involvement now includes my younger brother, who upon graduation from college expanded the franchise by purchasing his first store. We mentored him throughout the entire process, helped him find an existing store, funds (both family and owner financing), and negotiate the deal. After an eight-month process he was ready to begin. His particular store had a manager in place and he was able to successfully operate it from our location. One of the benefits of our franchise system is the ability to operate multiple sites in various geographic locations from a home base.

As a family, we now own and operate nine separate businesses. Each maintains separate and exclusive control; however, we consult on all major decisions and work together as a team. Strength in numbers enhances our business family of family businesses.

Sarah Davis Coxwell has a Bachelor's of Science in marketing and finance. She has been the primary manager of three of the five company-owned stores for eight years. All stores have reported exceptional growth and profitability with inventory levels exceeding industry standards and recommendations.

Source: Various correspondence and interviews with Sarah Coxwell.

The Profile shows the importance of a truth that has been shown repeatedly throughout this text: *Sufficient capital is essential not only for small business startups but also for their continued operation.* One main reason for the high failure rate of small businesses is inadequate or improper financing. Too often, insufficient attention has been paid to planning for financial needs, leaving the new business open to sudden but predictable financial crises. Even firms that are sound financially can be destroyed by financial problems, for one difficulty most commonly experienced by rapidly growing firms is that they are unable to finance the investment needed to support sales growth.

Estimating Financial Needs

The degree of uncertainty surrounding a small firm's long-term financial needs primarily depends on whether the business is already operating or is just starting, as mentioned in the Profile. If a business has an operating history, its future needs can be estimated with relative accuracy, even with substantial growth.

If you seek the help of a financial planner, you need to make sure the one you choose is appropriate for your needs. When choosing a financial advisor, there is an "alphabet soup" of credentials for you to sift through. Some designations represent certifications and some require passing one or more Regulatory Board tests. Table 7.1 presents a few.

Even for an existing business, however, an in-depth analysis of its *permanent* financial requirements can be valuable. It may show the current method of financing the business to be unsound or unnecessarily risky. As a general rule, small businesses' long-lived assets, such as buildings and other facilities, should be financed with long-term loans, while short-lived assets, such as inventory or accounts receivable, should be financed with short-term loans.

However, if the business is just starting, it can be very difficult since there is no universal method for estimating startup costs. The Small Business Administration (sba.gov) suggests that you consider the following:

- Determine seed money needed to start up.
- Determine which costs are onetime costs.
- Determine ongoing costs.
- Separate your costs into fixed (does not change) or variable with sales.

TABLE 7.1 |

CFA	Certified financial planner
NAPFA	Fee-only financial advisor
CFA	Chartered financial analyst
CPA/PFS	Certified public accountant / personal financial specialist
ChFC	Chartered financial consultant
CRPS	Chartered retirement plans specialist
RIA	Registered investment advisor
CMFC	Chartered mutual fund counselor
CRC	Certified retirement counselor
CDFA	Certified divorce financial analyst
AEP	Accredited estate planner

Source: Christine Dugas, "Deciphering Financial Advisors' Credentials," *USA Today,* April 29, 2011, p. 4B.

- Do you need to renovate the facility?
- Identify which costs are essential or optional.

It is also very important to have funds set aside or available for emergencies, unexpected expenses, and personal support for at least 18 months. You should know by then if you can succeed.

Principles to Follow

Fixed assets are those that are of a relatively permanent nature and are necessary for the functioning of the business.

A new business, or a major expansion of an existing business, should be evaluated with great care, paying particular attention to its capital requirements. For example, the firm's **fixed assets** should be financed with equity funds, or with debt funds having a maturity approximately equal to the productive life of the asset.

Working capital is current assets, less current liabilities, that a firm uses to produce goods and services, and to finance the extension of credit to customers.

No business, however, can be financed entirely with debt funding, nor would such a capitalization be desirable—even if creditors were willing to lend all the funds required. Such a capital structure would be extremely risky, both for the creditors and for the business. This is especially true of **working capital,** which includes the current assets, less current liabilities, that a firm uses to produce goods and services and to finance the extension of credit to customers. These assets include items such as cash, accounts receivable, and inventories. Management of working capital is always a central concern for managers of small firms because they are often undercapitalized and overdependent on uninterrupted cash receipts to pay for recurring expenses. Therefore, small business managers must accurately estimate their working capital needs in advance and obtain sufficient financial resources to cover these needs, plus a buffer for unexpected emergencies.

Using Cash Budgets

Cash budgets project working capital needs by estimating what out-of-pocket expenses will be incurred and when revenues from these sales are to be collected.

An important tool small business managers can use to project working capital needs is a **cash budget.** Such a budget estimates what the out-of-pocket expenses will be during the next year to produce a product(s) for sale and when revenues from these sales are to be collected. In most businesses, sales are not constant over the year, so revenues vary a great deal from one period to another, while the costs of producing a product tend to be relatively constant. For example, most retailers have their greatest sales period from Thanksgiving to Christmas. Yet, if they extend their own credit, payments are not received until the following January or February—or even later. Also, small producers may have produced the goods during the previous summer and had to bear the out-of-pocket costs of production for up to six months before actually receiving cash payments.

In general, therefore, when sales are made on credit, *the firm must carry the costs of production itself for an extended period.* A cash budget can help the manager predict when these financing needs will be the greatest and plan the firm's funding accordingly. An accurate assessment of seasonal financing needs is especially important if commercial bank loans are used, since bankers usually require a borrower to be free of bank debt at least once a year.

Reasons for Using Equity and Debt Financing

Equity is an owner's share of the assets of a company. In a corporation, it is represented by shares of common or preferred stock.

Regardless of the type or size of the business, there are really only two sources of financing: equity financing and debt financing. While **equity** is the owner's share of the firm's assets, the nature of this claim depends on the legal form of ownership. For proprietorships and partnerships the claim on the assets of the firm is that they are the same as the owner's personal assets. Equity financing in a corporation is evidenced by shares of either common or preferred **stock.**

Stock represents ownership in a corporation.

Common stockholders
are the owners of a
corporation with claim to
a share of its profits and
the right to vote on certain
corporate decisions.

Preferred stockholders
are owners with a superior
claim to a share of the
firm's profits, but they often
have no voting rights.

Debt financing comes
from lenders who will
be repaid at a specified
interest rate within a
specified time span.

Common stockholders are the real owners of a corporation, and their financial claim is to the profit left after all other claims against the business have been met. Because they almost always retain the right to vote for company directors and/or on other important issues, common stockholders exercise effective control over the management of the firm.

Preferred stockholders, on the other hand, have a claim to the firm's profits that must be paid before any dividends can be distributed to the common stockholders; but they often pay for this superior claim by giving up their voting rights.

The other kind of capital, or funding, that a firm uses is **debt financing,** which comes from lenders, who will be repaid at a specified interest rate within an agreed-on time span. The lenders' income does not vary with the success of the business—unless the business defaults on its debts—while the stockholders' does.

As discussed in Chapter 3, capital can also be raised by using a limited partnership, which combines the benefits of both debt and equity financing.

Role of Equity Financing

The role of equity financing is to serve as a buffer that protects creditors from loss in case of financial difficulty. In the event of default on a contractual obligation (such as an interest payment), creditors have a legally enforceable claim on the assets of the firm. It takes preference over claims of the common and preferred stockholders. From an investor's point of view, common stock investments should have a higher financial return than debt investments because equity securities are riskier.

Role of Debt Financing

With debt financing principal and interest payments are legally enforceable claims against the business. Therefore they entail substantial risk for the firm (or for the entrepreneur if the debt is guaranteed by personal wealth). Despite the risks involved however, small firms use debt financing for several reasons. First, the cost of interest paid on debt capital is usually lower than the cost of outside equity, and interest payments are tax-deductible expenses. Second, an entrepreneur may be able to raise more total capital with debt funding than from equity sources alone. Finally, because debt payments are fixed costs, any remaining profits belong solely to the owners. This last strategy, employing a fixed charge to increase the residual return to common stockholders, is referred to as employing **financial leverage.**

Financial leverage
is using fixed-charge
financing, usually debt,
to fund a business's
operations.

A **lease** is a contract that
permits use of someone
else's property for a
specified time period.

One type of debt financing that is becoming more popular is leasing facilities and equipment from someone outside the business instead of buying them. A **lease** is a contract that permits you to use someone else's property, such as real estate, equipment, or other facilities, for a specified time period. While a lease is not usually classified as debt, it is in many respects financially very similar.

From the small business owner's point of view, the benefits of a lease are that (1) the payments are tax deductible, and (2) it may be possible for the business to lease equipment when it would be unable to secure debt financing to purchase it. A growing number of small firms are signing up for the extra services leasing can provide.

Real-World Example 7.1

For example, Ryder Commercial Leasing & Services (www.ryder.com) frees a small company of the paperwork of buying and operating vehicles. It handles the equipment, drivers, routing, and warehousing of trucks—that is, it performs the entire distribution function globally.[1]

Types of Debt and Equity Securities

Small companies use many types of securities, some of which are described in this section. This listing is incomplete but sufficient to illustrate the variety of financial sources that are a hallmark of the American financial system. Potential small business owners should remember that if they have a viable project, financing can be obtained from some source!

Equity Securities

Common stock,
representing the owners'
interest, usually consists
of many identical shares,
each of which gives the
holder one vote in all
corporate elections.

Preferred stock
has a fixed par value
and a fixed dividend
payment, expressed as a
percentage of par value.

To start operating, all firms must have some equity capital. In corporations, **common stock,** which represents the owners' interest, usually consists of many identical shares, each of which gives the holder one vote in all corporate elections. (See Figure 7.1 for an example of a share of stock in a new small business.) Common stockholders have no enforceable claim to dividends, and the liquidity of the investment will depend largely on whether there is a public market for the firm's stock.

A corporation may also issue **preferred stock,** with a fixed par value (the value assigned in the corporation's charter, usually $100 per share). It entitles the holder to a fixed dividend payment, usually expressed as a percentage of par value, such as 8 percent (equal to $8 per year). This dividend is not automatic; it must be declared by the firm's board of directors before it can be paid. Nor is it a legally enforceable claim against the business. However, no dividends can be paid to the common stockholders until preferred stock dividends have been paid. Moreover, preferred dividends that have been missed typically cumulate and must be paid in full before payments can be made to common stockholders. Preferred stock usually conveys no voting rights to its holder.

FIGURE 7.1 |
A Share of Stock in
a Small Business

Small company offering registration (SCOR) is the sale of common stock to the public through a regulated board such as Nasdaq or AMEX without the hassle of an initial public offering.

Short-term securities mature in one year or less.

Intermediate-term securities mature in one to five years.

Long-term securities mature after five years or longer.

Bonds are a form of debt security with a standard denomination, method of interest payment, and method of principal repayment.

A **mortgage loan** is long-term debt that is secured by real property.

A **chattel mortgage loan** is debt backed by some physical asset other than land, such as machinery, equipment, or inventory.

Asset-based financing accepts as collateral the assets of a firm in exchange for the loan.

Small company offering registration (SCOR) is equity financing that is permitted in most states. SCOR (www.nasaa.org) is a uniform registration allowing the company to raise up to $1 million by selling common stock directly to the public. These stocks in most instances can be traded on AMEX or Nasdaq's electronic over-the-counter (OTC) bulletin board (www.nasdaq.com). This type of financing is very helpful to small businesses allowing efficiencies in trading.

Debt Securities

Debt securities are usually in the form of bonds or loans. In general, publicly issued debt (such as bonds or commercial paper) is more commonly used by larger firms, whereas small companies rely more on private loans from financial institutions such as commercial banks, insurance companies, or finance companies.

A distinction is usually made among **short-term securities** (those with maturities of one year or less), **intermediate-term securities** (those with maturities of one to five years), and **long-term securities** (those with maturities of more than five years). As we will discuss more thoroughly in the next section, commercial banks prefer to make short- and intermediate-term loans; other financial institutions, such as insurance companies, prefer to make long-term loans.

If a small business manager negotiates a loan from a bank or other single lender, the amount of the loan is simply the amount borrowed. However, if securities are sold to the public or are privately placed with several lenders, most companies will issue the debt in the form of **bonds.** These have a standard denomination, method of interest payment, and method of principal repayment.

Long-term debt secured by real estate property is a **mortgage loan,** whereas a **chattel mortgage loan** is debt backed by some physical asset other than land, such as machinery, transportation equipment, or inventory. When companies are growing faster than they can make money, many prefer **asset-based financing.** Most asset-based loans are financed against accounts receivable and less often against inventory. Of all assets, accounts receivable is considered the most liquid of a service company's assets. If the company deals with inventory, it is usually considered the next in line for liquidity. Furthermore, many of the "unsecured" loans that banks extend to small businesses require personal guarantees by the manager or directors of the firm. Such loans are implicitly secured by the personal assets of these individuals.

Sources of Equity Financing

Obtaining sufficient equity funding is a constant challenge for most small businesses, particularly for proprietorships and partnerships. The only way to increase the equity of these two types of firms is either to retain earnings or to accept outsiders as co-owners.

Real-World Example 7.2

This is what David Getson did when he wanted to start *Icon Thoughtstyle* magazine, a bimonthly magazine focusing on "ideas" for young men. He brought in a fellow Princeton graduate who invested $25,000 as a partner. After seven issues the magazine had a circulation of 150,000.[2]

For corporations, the choices may be more varied. Some of the more frequently used sources of equity funding are discussed here.

"I run a small investment firm. Unfortunately, it used to be a large investment firm!"

(Source: © 1989 Doug Blackwell, Blackwell Cartoon Service. Used by permission.)

Small business investment companies (SBICs) are private firms licensed and regulated by the SBA to make "venture" investments in small firms.

Venture capital (VC) firms make investments based on projected future income and generally require a substantial return as either equity or profit.

Self

Overall, owners of small firms rely more on their own capital and less on external debt capital than owners of larger firms. Also, small firms are more dependent on short-term debt than on long-term debt. In fact, most small companies use external financing only occasionally. However, those few firms that experience rapid growth, or those that must maintain a high level of accounts receivable, use external financing frequently.

People who start a small business must therefore invest a substantial amount of their own funds in it before seeking outside funding. For example, Sarah Coxwell (Profile this chapter) borrowed money on her used car to help fund the purchase of her first business. Outside investors want to see some of the owner's own money committed to the business as some assurance that she or he will not simply give up operating the business and walk away from it. Many owners also prefer using their own funds because they feel uncomfortable risking other people's money or because they do not want to share control of the firm. In summary, for the smallest firms, owner capital is the most important source of financing.

Small Business Investment Companies (SBICs)

Small business investment companies (SBICs) are private firms licensed and regulated by the SBA to make "venture" or "risk" investments to small firms. SBICs supply equity capital and extend unsecured loans to small enterprises that meet their investment criteria. Because they are privately capitalized themselves (although backed by the SBA), SBICs are intended to be profit-making institutions, so they tend not to make very small investments.

SBICs finance small firms by making straight loans and by making equity-type investments that give the SBIC actual or potential ownership of the small firm's equity securities. SBICs also provide management assistance to the businesses they help finance.

SBICs prefer to make loans to small firms rather than equity investments, so we will discuss them further under the heading "Sources of Debt Financing" later in this chapter.

Venture Capitalists

Entrepreneurs often complain that it is "lonely at the top." If so, a venture capitalist can serve as a form of security blanket when needed. According to VentureOne, U.S. venture fund raising exceeded $24.4 billion in 2006.[3] Traditionally, **venture capital firms** have been partnerships composed of wealthy individuals who make equity investments in small firms with opportunities for fast growth, such as Federal Express (www.fedex.com), Apple Computers (www.apple.com), and Microsoft (www.microsoft.com) once were. In general, they have preferred to back fast-growth industries (usually high-tech ones), since the ultimate payoff from backing a successful new business with a new high-tech product can be astronomical.

A new generation of corporate venture capitalists, with a $50 billion-plus capital pie, is jumping in to fill the gap left by the departure of the traditional financiers. These new firms are returning to the more traditional relationship with small businesses. They are acting as business incubators and hands-on advisers.[4] Some of these corporate venture capitalists include such household names as Intel, Microsoft, Coca-Cola, and Procter & Gamble.

Another interesting trend is the entry of famous athletes into the venture capital field. For example, a $200 million New York venture fund called IMG Chase Sports Capital

Partners, had tennis great Andre Agassi and John McEnroe as investors. They and their fellow investors enjoyed a 400 percent return in 1999.[5]

Many venture capitalists rely more heavily on the executive summary of a business plan (see Chapter 6) than on the plan itself in making investment decisions. So many long and complex plans are presented to them that they need a quick way to evaluate proposals in order to quickly discard those they do not want to consider further. The percentage of business plans accepted by venture capitalists for investment purposes is very low. Yet in addition to money, the capitalists provide management skills and business contacts.

You should be aware when approaching either a venture capitalist or an SBIC for possible funding that neither will view your business the same way you do. While you may be content to remain relatively small in order to retain personal control, this is the last thing a professional investor will want. An SBIC or a venture capitalist will invest in a firm with the expectation of ultimately selling the company either to the investing public (through an initial public stock offering) or to a larger company. This potential conflict of goals can be very damaging to the new business owner unless the differences are explicitly addressed before external financing is accepted. We alluded to this danger earlier in the book in our discussion of the problems arising from "poorly planned growth." According to the Center for Venture Research (www.wsbe.unh.edu/cvr) angels and venture capitalists poured about $46 billion a year into young companies between 2006 and 2010.

Angel Capitalists

Angel capitalists or **business angels** are wealthy local businesspeople and other investors who may be external sources of equity funding.

Entrepreneurs have always tapped financial patrons, such as friends, relatives, and wealthy individuals, for beginning capital. These **angel capitalists** or **business angels** are a diverse group of high-net-worth individuals who will invest part of their assets in high-risk, high-return entrepreneurial ventures. The University of New Hampshire's Center for Venture concluded that in 2010, total investment by angel capitalists was $20.1 billion, which benefited 61,900 entrepreneurial ventures. These investments in turn led to the creation of 370,000 jobs. The number of angel investors has reached 265,400.[6] It has also been estimated that angel capitalists provide up to four times as much total investment capital for small businesses as the professional venture capital firms. While angels have always been around, fortunes made in the high-tech industries have spawned more angels than ever before.

Other Sources

In some cases, small business entrepreneurs may be able to acquire financial assistance from business incubators, employee stock ownership plans, their own customers, bartering, and others. It is interesting to note that some current business owners are willing to help others get started, for example:

Real-World Example 7.3

Lucy Valena's SBA advisor suggested that she seek funds from the Samuel Adams Brewing American Dream program, which provides microloans to food, beverage, and hospitality entrepreneurs. The loan she received amounted to $4,000 and allowed her to fund her espresso catering service, Voltage Coffee.

Non Profit Kiva.com distributes loans through microfinance institutions and has raised funds amounting to $211 million for worldwide projects. They have assisted nearly 550,000 entrepreneurs and the repayment rate is 99 percent.[7]

With many sources of creative financing out there you must be careful that you do not get burned by excessive interest rates. Be aware, too, of the many scam artists after your money and your business.

Business Incubators According to the National Business Incubation Association (NBIA) (www.nbia.org), a private, not-for-profit organization in Athens, Ohio, business incubation is "a dynamic process of business enterprise development."[8] Business incubators nurture young firms and help them to survive and grow during the startup period when they are most vulnerable. Hands-on management assistance, access to financing, and orchestrated exposure to critical business or technical support services are provided. Incubators offer entrepreneurial firms shared office services, access to equipment, flexible leases, and expandable space—all under one roof. As of May 2009, there are 1,900 incubators in North America. Incubators help clients to secure necessary capital in several ways:

- Managing in-house and revolving loan funds;
- Networking it to locate and connect venture capitalists;
- Connections with angel investors; and
- Assisting with loan applications. (www.nbia.org)

In addition, The National Business Incubation Association (NIBA) statistics indicate an 80 percent success rate for their clients as opposed to the approximately eight out of ten start-ups which normally fail in the first three years of operation.[9]

Employee Stock Ownership Plans (ESOPs) For existing small businesses, another source of financing is **employee stock ownership plans (ESOPs).** The company reaps tax advantages and cash flow advantages from selling shares to workers. The plan also makes employees think like owners, tending to make them more productive.

Your Customers Your customers are another source of financing. It happens often, and in many ways. For example, mail-order vendors, especially those who use TV commercials, require the customer to pay when ordering; they then have that money for operations, while the customer waits several weeks for delivery of the goods. Also, it is customary for artisans and contractors to require a substantial down payment before beginning to produce the product.

> **Employee stock ownership plans (ESOPs)** allow small businesses to reap tax advantages and cash flow advantages by selling stock shares to workers.

Real-World Example 7.4

For example, Diane Allen, a portrait artist, requires a down payment of one-third of the total price before she will begin a portrait. This money not only ensures that the contract will be honored but also can be used to buy supplies and cover other expenses.

> **Barter** consists of two or more companies exchanging items of roughly equal value.

Bartering **Barter** is an increasingly popular method of financing small businesses. In its simplest form, bartering consists of two companies swapping items of roughly equal value. But as this age-old business practice has become more popular—partly because of the competitive global business environment—bartering has become more creative. Now business owners trade everything from employee perquisites to corporate airfare with barter credits.

Bartering lends itself to many uses, such as (1) business travel, (2) debt collection, (3) closing a sale, (4) employee perks and bonuses, and (5) a line of credit. As bartering has become more popular—and complex—corporate barter networks, or regional trade exchanges, have developed to provide the needed exchange mechanism.

Bartering exchanges were largely considered disreputable in the 1970s and early 1980s because some would brag about "skirting income-tax reporting laws."[10] But a 1982 law required barter exchange, for the first time, to report the value of their transactions to the IRS (see IRS pub. 525), where they are subject to the same tax treatment as a cash transaction.

The International Reciprocal Trade Association (IRTA), an industry group located in Chicago (www.irta.com), reported that in 2010 there were as many as 700 barter groups, serving more than 400,000 business clients, in 31 countries, by brokering products and services valued at an estimated 12 billion.

Bartering can be an accounting nightmare that must be carefully documented, and you must follow the rules:

1. If the items are dissimilar—a truck for a desk, for example—record the new asset at its documented fair market value and remove the swapped asset at its book value and recognize the difference as either a gain or a loss.

2. If the items are alike, record the new one at the book value of the old one and *do not* recognize any gain or loss.

Remember never to discount the value of your services. The major challenge in bartering is to assign a price tag to a product or service that is difficult to value.[11]

For example, Chris DeMassa estimates that 10 percent of his annual million dollar sales are generated by barter. These sales would be lost without the barter system.[12]

Aaron Usher is a photographer who belongs to a barter club. He exchanges his services for trade dollars (credits) that can be used within his club for products and services of others.[13]

Sources of Debt Financing

Although, as stated earlier, most small business owners rely more on owner funding than on debt financing, research by the SBA and Federal Reserve Board found that a majority of them had used such funding in the past.[14] This is true at least in part because there are so many sources for such financing, several of which are described here.

Trade Credit

Trade credit is extended by vendors on purchases of inventory, equipment, and/or supplies.

With **consignment selling,** payments to suppliers are made only when the products are sold, rather than when they are received in stock.

Trade credit refers to purchases of inventory, equipment, and/or supplies on an open account in accordance with customary terms for retail and wholesale trade. In general, trade credit is one of the most important sources of debt financing for small business because it arises spontaneously in the normal course of operating the business. Firms seeking new and expanded wholesale and retail markets for goods have the option of using **consignment selling.** Small auto, major appliance, and farm equipment dealers consider consignments a form of trade credit because payments to suppliers are made only when the products are sold rather than when they are received in stock.

Commercial and Other Financial Institutions

Traditional financial institutions may provide the small business owner with borrowed funds. The proportion of funds such institutions make available ranges from 25 to 60 percent of the value of the total assets. Usually, the cost of such financing is higher than that of other alternatives, but such funds may be the most accessible.

Commercial Banks   Commercial banks are the dominant supplier of external financing to small firms. In fact, a few years ago, an exhaustive study found that 90 percent of small and midsized businesses identified their local bank as their primary financial institution for banking and other financial services. While commercial banks are still a good source for small borrowers who have funds of their own and proven successful financial experience, rarely will they make conventional loans to a startup business. However, according to Belinda Shoub, vice president/marketing at SouthTrust Bank, commercial banks do provide many services for small businesses. Her bank has a separate department to service small businesses. These services include, but are not limited to, loans, checking, business and personal priority management, online banking, insurance, international services, wealth management, and corporate cash management. It is also interesting to note that SouthTrust Bank requires a well-prepared business plan (see Chapter 6).

Banking institutions charge a higher rate of interest—usually two or three percentage points above the prime rate* —to small companies to offset the greater risk; the result is a greater return. Additionally, some financial institutions specializing in small business loans become more knowledgeable and therefore more efficient.

A **line of credit** permits a business to borrow up to a set amount without red tape.

If your business is successful, you may want to open a **line of credit** with your bank. This is an arrangement whereby the bank permits an ongoing business to borrow up to a set amount—say, $50,000—at any time during the year without further red tape. The business writes checks against its account, and the bank honors them up to the maximum amount. Usually, except for firms with an exceptionally high credit rating, the business is required to pay up all unsecured debts for a short period—say, 10 to 15 days—each year to prove its creditworthiness. This is usually done when the firm's cash level is at its highest in order not to inconvenience the borrower too much.

A well-prepared business plan, as described in Chapter 6, should help lower a firm's interest rate and possibly even extend the term of the loan. Even then, however, you may find it more advantageous to finance the business with a personal loan.

Credit Cards   Another form of credit line is the use of credit cards to finance your business. In fact, for companies with fewer than 500 employees, the use of credit cards to finance operations has increased.

Insurance Companies   Insurance companies may be a good source of funds for a small firm, especially real estate ventures. The business owner can go directly to the company or contact its agent or a mortgage banker. While insurance companies have traditionally engaged in debt financing, they have more recently demanded that they be permitted to buy an equity share in the business as part of the total package.

Small Business Administration (SBA)

One primary purpose of the SBA is to help small firms find financing, including those having trouble securing conventional financing, especially at reasonable rates. Many small firms need term loans of up to 25 years, but most lenders limit their lending to short-term loans.

Many entrepreneurs find that SBA loans are very hard—if not impossible—to obtain as stated by Sarah Coxwell in the Profile at the beginning of this chapter. According to Marshall Eckblad there are three major myths regarding SBA loans.[15]

---

*The prime rate (the rate banks charge their best commercial customers) is published periodically in *The Wall Street Journal.*

TABLE 7.2 | Eligibility for SBA-Guaranteed Business Loans by Industry Type

Type of Industry	Restrictions
Manufacturing	Maximum number of employees may range from 500 to 1,500, depending on the industry in which the applicant is primarily engaged.
Wholesaling	Maximum number of employees not to exceed 100.
Services	Annual receipts not exceeding $3.5 million to $13.5 million, depending on the industry in which the applicant is primarily engaged.
Retailing	Annual sales or receipts not exceeding $3.5 million to $13.5 million, depending on the industry.
Agriculture	Annual receipts not exceeding $0.5 million to $3.5 million, depending on the industry.

Source: U.S. Small Business Administration website (www.sba.gov/financing/7aloan.html).

- *It only lends to hard cases.* In 2008 in the height of the financial crisis, the SBA facilitated loans to nearly 70,000 businesses.

- *Lenders face no risks.* Loans issued through the 7a program carry a guarantee of between 75–85 percent, so the bank swallows 25 percent of any losses.

- *You'll get buried in paperwork.* The paperwork is very much consistent with what the bank requires for a conventional loan.

The SBA helps these small firms in several ways, including offering guarantees on loans made by private lenders and offering direct specialized financing.[16] As indicated earlier, it also provides some venture capital through SBICs. The SBA-licensed SBICs also include some **specialized SBICs** (called **SSBICs**) to assist socially or economically disadvantaged enterprises, which, in turn, provide future capital through equity-purchased long-term loans or loan guarantees. Much attention is currently being given to SBICs by Congress and the President.

Specialized small business investment companies (SSBICs) assist socially and economically disadvantaged businesses with venture capital.

Guaranteed Loans   The SBA guarantees 30 to 40 percent of all long-term loans to small businesses under its 7(a) program. The loans can be used to (1) purchase land, buildings, or equipment; (2) provide working capital; (3) refinance existing debt (under certain conditions); or (4) provide seasonal lines of credit. To qualify, a business must be unable to obtain private financing on reasonable terms but must have a good chance of success. Also, the borrower must meet the size standards shown in Table 7.2.

With the SBA's guarantee program, a bank actually extends a loan to a small firm, with the SBA guaranteeing repayment for a certain percentage of the loan. The amount guaranteed is usually 75 to 80 percent. The maximum rate the bank can charge is the prime rate plus 2.25 percent on loans for less than seven years or prime plus 2.75 percent on loans for seven years or more.

The procedure to be followed is for the business owner to contact a bank (preferably one with experience in SBA lending) to request an SBA loan. The following documents should already be prepared to expedite the process:[17]

- A narrative business plan with profit/loss projections for three years.

- Résumés for key managers and owners.

- An outline showing how the loan will be used, including an itemized list of assets to be purchased.

- At least three years of historical financial statements on the company and personal financial statements for all owners.
- A proposed collateral structure.

The bank then submits the application directly to the SBA for approval. The SBA also has a few other basic financial requirements. For existing businesses, the SBA generally looks for a debt-to-net worth ratio (that is, total liabilities divided by total assets) of not more than 3:1 (three to one) after the loan is granted. A startup business must have at least 30 percent equity invested by the owners. The SBA looks for (1) management ability and experience in the field of operations, (2) at least a simple, but feasible business plan, and (3) the ability to repay the loan. Also, all owners of 20 percent or more of a business must personally guarantee SBA loans.

Specialized Programs   The SBA also has several specialized programs. First, there are special government contracts to be awarded to small, disadvantaged business subcontractors, along with counseling and bonding assistance. The small business must be at least 51 percent owned by a "socially or economically disadvantaged individual." Included in this group are African Americans, Native Americans, Hispanic Americans, Asian Pacific Americans, and Subcontinent Asian Americans.

A second special program is the SBA Low Documentation (LowDoc) Loan Program (www.sba.gov/financing/lowdoc). It can be used for loans of less than $100,000. While the borrower must still work with a bank, the documentation is much less stringent. The LowDoc puts more emphasis on the borrower's credit history, projected cash flow, and character, and less on collateral and equity.

The SBA also has a CAPLine Revolving Line of Credit initiative (called CAPLine for short). Its purpose is to help small companies obtain short-term working capital through an established line of credit (www.sba.gov/financing/frcaplines.html).

Finally, the "Women's Prequalification Loan Program" (www.onlinewbc.gov) allows women business owners to receive prequalification from the SBA for a loan guarantee of up to $250,000 *before* going to a bank. Going directly to the SBA is a great advantage in saved time and effort. As with the LowDoc program, the primary focus is on character, credit history, and experience. The SBA guarantees the bank up to 80 percent in loans up to $100,000 and up to 75 percent on loans from $100,000 to $250,000. To be eligible, the business must be at least 51 percent owned, operated, and managed by women, have sales of less than $5 million, and employ fewer than 100 people.

Small Business Investment Companies (SBICs)

In addition to indirect equity financing, as previously discussed, SBICs also make qualified SBA loans. The SBA matches each dollar an SBIC puts into a loan. Loans are usually made for a period of 5 to 10 years. An SBIC may stipulate that it be given a certain portion of stock purchase warrants or stock options, or it may make a combination of a loan and a stock purchase. The latter combination has been preferred.

Recent changes in SBICs have created a surge in their popularity. They are no longer limited to the sale of debentures but are now permitted to sell securities similar to preferred stock. One must remember, however, that SBA funds are federal government monies and may dry up as attitudes in Washington change.[18]

U.S. Department of Agriculture (USDA)

The U.S. Department of Agriculture (USDA) (www.usda.gov) has also started investing in small business. With its novel programs to develop nonfood, nonfeed uses of farm products, the department has spent millions of dollars on large and small businesses to induce them to come up with innovative products.

> **Real-World Example 7.5**
>
> One example was an enterprising 11-year-old in Mankato, Minnesota, who developed a product—which felt like wood and looked like granite—from shredded newspapers, blended with glue in her mother's blender (which didn't survive the experiment). A local group of investors, which was looking for a **green product** to commercialize, adopted the girl's idea. But financing was a problem, so the USDA offered a $1 million loan if the company could raise the same amount, which it easily did.

A **green product** is an environmentally friendly product offered for sale commercially.

What Lenders Look For

What do lenders look for when considering a loan to a small business? In essence the basics apply today as they did in the past. First, if the loan is for a new business, the lender wants to see if you can live within the income of the business. Given your expected revenues and expenses, will you be able to repay the loan? How much collateral can you put up to insure the lender against your inability to repay?

Second, if the money is for an existing business, the lender will look at its track record. If there are problems, you will be expected to explain what's going to happen to make a difference in the future. Do you have a new business plan? Are you going to buy new equipment or technology? Is there a new marketing plan?

To a large extent, your ability to attract money will depend on the lender's perception of your character as well as your ability to return the money. First, *income* is important. Second, the lender will also look at your *stability,* to see how long you've lived in a given residence or neighborhood, as well as how long you've worked at a particular job or run a business.

In summary, your request for financing will almost certainly be checked by some major credit company, using computerized reference services. Therefore, knowing that your credit record will be checked immediately by the computer, you should ask for a credit printout (which can be obtained for free or for a few dollars) before you apply for funds. This will give you an opportunity to correct any errors or misunderstandings in your credit record.

Figure 7.3 provides some steps to use in developing a better relationship with investors, along with some questions the investor should ask you. Remember, while lenders should have an interest in how financially sound your business is, *they should not have a voice in managing it.* If you permit them to, they in reality become partners and must share responsibility for any failures.

FIGURE 7.3 |
How to Improve the
Entrepreneur-Investor
Relationship

There are at least five steps you should take in order to assure a good working relationship with the investor:

1. Establish the range of funds you will need.
2. Identify the investor's skills and abilities that could help advance your venture.
3. Find an investor with interests and personality traits similar to yours.
4. Find a long-term investor, not one who wants to "make a quick buck" and get out.
5. Find an investor with more to offer you than just money so that you may avoid having to hire outside consultants.

There are certain things the investor should find out about you:

1. Can you and the investor work together as a team?
2. Do you appear to be flexible and willing to accept new management if the project is highly successful?
3. Are you truly committed to this endeavor, and are you willing to expend the energy and resources to make it a success?
4. Can you accept constructive criticism, feedback, and assistance?
5. Do you have definite, fixed, realistic goals, and where do you plan to be in, say, one year? Five years? Ten years?

Source: International Reciprocal Trade Association.

What You Should Have Learned

1. Providing for financial needs is crucial to the success of a small business, which may be undercapitalized and living hand to mouth. Sufficient short- and long-term financing is needed to provide for fluctuations in sales or an unexpected business slump.

2. For a startup venture, the assets of a business should be financed with equity or with debt funds having a maturity about equal to the productive life of the asset. A useful tool for estimating financial needs is the cash budget, which projects the amounts and timing of expenses and revenue for the year.

3. The two major sources of funds are equity and debt financing. Equity financing never has to be repaid and provides an interest in the business, including a share of the profits and a voice in decision making. Debt financing, which must be repaid whether the company is profitable or not, is less expensive than equity financing (since interest payments are tax deductible), and it does not require as high a rate of return.

4. The most frequently used types of equity securities are common and preferred stock. Common stock conveys voting rights but has no enforceable claim to dividends. Preferred stock entitles the shareholder to a fixed rate of dividend whenever profits are sufficient, but

preferred stockholders usually have no voting rights. Debt securities include short-, intermediate-, and long-term loans and bonds. Loans made by a lender in standard denominations are called bonds. Long-term debt secured by real property is a mortgage loan, whereas a chattel mortgage loan is backed by some other physical asset. A lease can also be a form of debt financing.

5. Sources of equity financing include funds from the owner, family and friends, small business investment companies (SBICs), venture capitalists, angel capitalists, business incubators, employees, customers, and bartering.

6. Sources of debt financing include trade credit, commercial and other financial institutions—including commercial banks and insurance companies—the SBA, SBICs, the U.S. Department of Agriculture, and the Economic Development Administration (EDA). The SBA finances business ventures through guaranteed loans.

7. When deciding whether or not to finance a small business, lenders look for factors such as ability to repay the debt, the owner's and the business's financial and business track record, and the owner's income, stability, and debt management.

Key Terms

angel capitalists or
    business angels   187
asset-based financing   185
barter   188
bonds   185
cash budgets   182
chattel mortgage loan   185
common stock   184
common
    stockholders   183
consignment selling   189
debt financing   183
employee stock ownership
    plans (ESOP)   188

equity   182
financial leverage   183
fixed assets   182
green product   193
intermediate-term
    securities   185
lease   183
line of credit   190
long-term securities   185
mortgage loan   185
preferred stock   184
preferred
    stockholders   182
short-term securities   185

small business
    investment companies
    (SBICs)   186
small company
    offering registration
    (SCOR)   185
specialized small business
    investment companies
    (SSBICs)   191
stock   182
trade credit   189
venture capital (VC)
    firms   186
working capital   182

Questions for Discussion

1. Discuss the basic rules to follow in financing a business venture.
2. Why should small business managers assess working capital needs in advance?
3. What are some reasons small business entrepreneurs use equity financing? Debt financing?
4. What are the factors that determine the classification of debt securities?
5. List and discuss the primary sources of equity financing.
6. List and discuss the primary sources of debt financing.
7. Compare equity financing to debt financing.
8. Evaluate the role of the SBA in providing operating and venture capital.

Case 7.1

Ella Williams: Making It on Her Own

After working for 13 years in various departments at Hughes Aircraft Corporation, Ella Williams, believing in herself, decided to form a small business of her own. With the help of the SBA's Section 8(a), she took out a $65,000 second mortgage on her house and founded Aegir Systems in Oxnard, California, to provide engineering, environmental, multimedia, and computer services to the aircraft industry.

She struggled for three years—often scrounging aluminum cans from dumpsters to earn money to support herself and her two children. Her daughter was mortified, she said. "But she sure was interested in the money when I cashed them in."

It was an uphill battle to convince white-male–dominated firms that a black-woman–owned company could deliver the technical services she offered. Although she eventually proved to them that she could, it took three years to get her first client. The turning point came when she went back to her kitchen and baked cheesecake, breads, and muffins for her prospects. Shortly thereafter she got her first contract.

By 1998 she had 70 employees working in the Oxnard headquarters and regional offices in Los Angeles. Her talent and achievements have been recognized in numerous ways. In 1993, Northrop named Aegir its "Small Business Supplier of the Year." Williams was named one of "The Nation's Ten Most Admired Women Managers of 1993" by *Working Woman* magazine, and AT&T designated her "The 1993 Entrepreneur of the Year." In 1996, she was presented with the "Woman of the Year" award by the Women's Transportation Seminar, and in 1997 she was voted "Business Person of the Year" by *Business Digest* readers.

Questions

1. What kind of financing did Williams use to start her business?

2. How could SCORE have helped?

3. Do you think that this cycle of "uphill battle" is typical for minority-owned businesses?

Source: Andrew Tobias, "You Can Still Make a Million Dollars," *Parade* magazine, October 29, 1995, pp. 14–15; Kathy A. Price, "'Business Person of the Year'—Ella Williams," *Business Digest* 38 (Winter 1997) at www.bdigest.com/win38.html; and correspondence with Ella Williams.

Case 7.2

Karen & Co.

Karen Mitchell-Raptakis, a book-publishing assistant by day, loves creating greeting cards and has channeled that love into a profitable business—Karen & Co. Greeting Cards (www.sistathingcards.com). Humorous and sentimental, her ethnic greeting cards are carried by more than 80 retailers. Karen comes up with the words to her idea, and her illustrator develops it.

However, the business side has been tough. Creating the cards, she states, is the easy part, but gaining a toehold in the market is extremely hard for a small business such as hers. Before starting her business, Karen worked for a greeting card company to learn the basics of the business. Even though the pay was not much, she learned a great deal. She even took her cards to show women in places such as beauty salons and on subways. If their reaction was positive, she went with the card. If negative, she would discard it. To make the business stronger, she takes courses in marketing, licensing, financial strategy, and more.

Her efforts were rewarded, though, when one of her cards beat 1,100 other cards from 160 companies for the prestigious Louie award, the industry's equivalent of the Oscar. The message for the award-winning card, "Your Spirit Will Not Be Broken," mirrored her personal endeavors in starting her own business.

As with most small businesses, there are ongoing hurdles. While Karen's business is self-funded, she intends to enlist the help of her husband, an accountant, with the financial aspects before thinking about a small-business loan. She is also considering part-time help to manage the administrative work. Her sales have been concentrated along the East Coast, but Raptakis is now focusing on the South—which has a rich spiritual base—where she feels her cards would do very well.

Her tips for entrepreneurs: (1) Absolutely love what you do, or it won't work; (2) be comfortable with rejection; (3) know the industry you're getting into; and (4) get objective opinions about your product. Raptakis is encouraged by statistics showing that of the 5.8 million small companies with fewer than 500 employees in the United States, those owned by minority women are growing four times faster than all other companies, according to the Small Business Administration. Her love of creating meaningful cards keeps her going. The cover of one of her cards shows a runner wearing "No. 1" and crossing a finish line, reading, "The achievements of a people are based on the persistence and the perseverance of the individual." The inside message reads: "I say, You go girl!"

Questions

1. What is the first thing Karen needs to prepare before she applies for a loan?
2. What are other financing options?
3. Should Karen consider an incubator? Why or why not?

Source: Lorrie Grant, "Card Crafter Uses Creativity to Carve out Niche," *USA Today,* March 19, 2003, p. 7B. Reprinted by permission.

Experientials

1. In order to locate the right kind of financing for your need, you should find out your own credit worthiness. Determine your credit score.
2. Visit several lending institutions in your area and write a summary of loan requirements.

PART 3

How to Market Goods and Services

To succeed, a small business must effectively perform a number of essential business functions: marketing, organizing and managing, operations, and financing. The last three functions will be covered in Parts 4 and 5; this Part concentrates on the marketing function.

Marketing involves determining customers' needs, developing goods and services to satisfy those needs, and distributing those products to customers through various channels of distribution. It is an essential function because, unless the firm has—or can develop—a market for its product, performing the other business functions is futile.

Chapter 8, "Developing Marketing Strategies," covers the marketing concept; marketing research; strategy development, including marketing objectives, targets, and mix; types of products and their life cycles; marketing strategies for services; packaging; and pricing strategies.

In Chapter 9, "Promoting and Distributing," we discuss channels of distribution, global opportunities, using intermediaries or one's own sales force, supporting and controlling sales personnel, promoting the product, credit management, and physical distribution. ●

Developing Marketing Strategies

There are really only two important functions in business: marketing and innovations.
   —Peter Drucker

It's unwise to pay too much, but it's also unwise to pay too little. When you pay too much, you lose money, that is all. When you pay too little, you sometimes lose everything because the thing you bought was incapable of doing the thing it was bought to do. The common law of business balance prohibits paying a little and getting a lot—it can't be done. If you deal with the lowest bidder, it is well to add something for the risk you run. And, if you do that, you will have enough to pay for something better.
   —John Ruskin

There are thousands of manufacturers who make the most fantastic widget in the world. Yet, many of them are driven out of business because only half of the business is making widgets. The other half is getting people to buy them.
   —Deputy Postmaster General John Nolan

Learning Objectives

After studying the material in this chapter, you should be able to:

1. Describe the marketing concept and explain how it can be used by a small business.

2. Show how marketing research can be used to implement the marketing concept.

3. Explain how to develop and implement a marketing strategy.

4. Explain how the product life cycle affects marketing strategies.

5. Explain how packaging affects marketing.

6. Describe how prices are set and administered.

7. Show how marketing services differs from marketing goods.

Advanced Control Solutions

Advanced Control Solutions (ACS) (www.advanced controlinc.com) was started by David Pilliod in 1997. David Pilliod was a BSME graduate out of Wisconsin when he got his start in the industry with the industrial controls group of Westinghouse. After working there for a while, he went to work for a distribution company that specialized in industrial controls. Pilliod worked for this company for several years, but in 1997 decided to start his own company. In the previous 10 years, he had started up two companies offices in Atlanta, and now was ready to do it for himself. He financed the company from his own personal savings, and also through a second mortgage on his home. Today, ACS operates in Marietta, Georgia, with satellite offices in Knoxville and Nashville, Tennessee, and Greenville, South Carolina, and serves clients throughout the southeast in Alabama, Tennessee, South Carolina and Georgia. The company offers a wide variety of highly technical automation products and services. These offerings range from machine vision to sensing technologies, robotics and machine guarding mechanisms; they also offer in-house engineering services. Its customers range from well known companies such as Johnson & Johnson, Kimberly Clark, Coca-Cola, and Nissan to hundreds of other lesser known companies such as Kliklok and Chase Scientific. ACS provides innovative hardware and software solutions implemented by superior engineers and technical specialists and design

solutions specifically tailored to the needs of its customers to help them stay competitive.

Advanced Control Solutions's main goal is "to make our customers more competitive in their marketplace through technology." It strives to bridge the gap between the factory floor and the boardroom by using highly progressive technologies such as wireless, PC-based control solutions with ethernet connectivity for machine vision, motion control, and robotics applications. Additionally, ACS attempts to maintain ongoing relationships with its customers by offering free training classes on emerging technologies as well as free technical support and constant engineering services. It aims to be a one-stop solution house for automation manufacturing parts, services, and total solution packages. It carries out this goal by continuing to represent a wide variety of reputable product lines.

Advanced Control Solutions targets a small niche market within the automation manufacturing industry. It is a supplier to original equipment manufacturers—end users as well as certified integrators. These customers are generally large companies, but those making the decisions on behalf of the company are typically blue-collar factory workers who report their needs to engineering managers, safety managers, or quality control managers. Even these managers are often out on the factory floor in the midst of the operation. They directly feel the benefit from the products offered by ACS. The corporations themselves range from the automotive industry to packaging and the food and drug industry. Virtually any factory that produces any object could benefit from the products and services that ACS offers. Few realize that every consumer eventually benefits from the technology supplied by ACS.

Whether it is a simple bottle of water or a brand-new car, the technologies offered by ACS were, at some point, used to make sure that the product was suitable to sell. Through quality inspections of the product to labeling and bar coding the packaging, these technologies ensure that the product is 100 percent accurate and can be implemented in every aspect along the manufacturing process. They can be used in moving the product along a production conveyer, robotically assembling them, inspecting them for error, and using "pick and place" applications to put them into containers to ship. These technologies help companies automate processes that are prone to human error, thus reducing costs, increasing productivity, and increasing quality. This, in turn, keeps the selling prices low for the final consumer. When a consumer is in the grocery store purchasing a box of Cheerio's, he or she may never think about how those little O's are made or what keeps them from being burnt or misshaped. The technology provided by ACS and their skilled engineering department work together to make sure that these details are worked out before the O's ever make it into a box and are distributed to the stores for sale.

The overall benefits of ACS products and services are immeasurable, and the cost of the system can be well worth the money. The benefits from an effective and efficient quality control system can often mean the difference between signing or losing a major contract, while the benefits from an effective and efficient safety system can mean saving an employee's life. Proper safety systems can also prevent fines from Occupational Safety and Health Act (OSHA) and increases in workman's compensation insurance premiums. The benefits have been felt and noted by some of Advanced Control Solutions's most valuable customers, who have published testimonials regarding the value in comparison to the cost.

With only seven salesmen, seven engineers, and six inside operation employees, ACS must work extremely hard to develop and maintain a strong customer base. The ongoing relationship that ACS has with its customers is second to none. It offers ongoing, monthly training classes that are free to existing and potential customers. High-volume customers receive the benefit of an extra percentage off of specific purchases or in some cases, special pricing on all orders. ACS also offers ongoing, free technical support from in-house technical specialists. In the event a technical specialist cannot troubleshoot the problem over the phone, ACS takes the equipment in-house and reprograms it or does what is necessary to alleviate the problem. In addition, ACS makes a noticeable effort to remain in close contact with customers by phone calls, e-mails, and factory visits to ensure that customers have everything they need and to answer any questions. In most cases, ACS is willing to provide onsite demonstrations in order to prove that the system under consideration will do what the customer needs.

Technology is a growing part of today's businesses. Advanced Control Solutions is dedicated to researching emerging technologies to help its customers stay ahead of the curve and remain competitive in their markets. Close relationships with its customers, built and developed over time, have allowed ACS to become a trusted automation solutions provider and a source for all things technical. Customers turn to ACS first to inform them of new technologies that could benefit their organization in the long term. After only seven years of being in business, ACS has become a $4 million company and is the No. 2 distributor in the world for one of its major product lines.

To market its wide range of products and services, ACS uses one main tag line: "More than a supplier, we are your solutions provider." This phrase lets customers know that they are not simply walking into a distributor and buying piece parts—they can receive a total solution. Advanced Control Solutions markets through multiple media types; however, it must be extremely selective because marketing to the manufacturing industry is much different from marketing to the average consumer. Radio and television ads are not beneficial to companies such as Advanced Control Solutions because the general public is not the target market. ACS has to select publications such as *Southeastern Machinery and Industrial News* and *Vision Systems Design*. These publications are distributed to specific companies who are involved in manufacturing and automation. For example, *Southeastern Machinery and Industrial News* has a monthly circulation of approximately 17,300 and serves Alabama, Georgia,

Florida, Mississippi, North and South Carolina, Tennessee, and Virginia. Other mediums Advanced Control Solutions takes advantage of are publications such as the *Thomas Regional Directory*. The TRD specifically operates as a directory of Industrial Buying Resources. Through advertising in the TRD, Advanced Control Solutions is able to be a part of a publication with a circulation of more than 53,000, as well as being listed on its Web site. These types of very specific, regional, targeted publications allow for the largest spread of coverage through highly selective mediums.

Advanced Control Solutions markets its products and services mainly through direct mail. It keeps in close contact with its customers because of its active database of more than 5,000 customers. These contacts enable ACS to target specific people for specific products and services. It uses hand-addressed, direct-mail campaigns to distribute cut sheets of new products available and invitations to upcoming workshops, trade shows, and seminars, keep customers aware of what is new at ACS through its periodical newsletter. These direct-mail efforts make ACS's advertising more personal and offer a feeling of camaraderie between the company and the customer. Advanced Control Solutions takes great pride in its marketing efforts and is not afraid to spend money to make money. It has repeatedly won the Marketer of the Year award at global marketing summits for the industry and has gained as well as retained customers over the years due to these efforts.

The Profile illustrates an important aspect of the marketing function—marketing a service. It also gives an overview of marketing, including the importance of the marketing concept, product development, and customer service. This chapter is about those and other marketing strategies, including developing a favorable marketing mix of the Four Ps: product, place, promotion, and price.

Companies with a reputation for superior marketing tend to share some basic strategies for successful marketing. These include the following:[1]

- Moving quickly to satisfy customer needs.
- Using pricing to differentiate the product/service.
- Paying attention to packaging.
- Building customer loyalty.
- Offering samples and demonstrations.
- Educating customers.

The Marketing Concept

The **marketing concept** involves giving special consideration to the needs, desires, and wishes of present and prospective customers.

The **marketing concept** helps a business focus its efforts on satisfying customer needs in such a way as to make a satisfactory profit. The concept comprises three basic elements: a customer orientation, a goal orientation, and use of the systems approach. This concept emphasizes the truth that the survival of any business depends on providing service. With such a customer orientation, small firms will try to identify the group of people or firms most likely to buy their product (the target market) and to produce goods or services that will meet the needs of that market. Being consumer oriented often involves exploring consumer needs and then trying to satisfy them.

In focusing on customer orientation, however, the small firm must not lose sight of its own goals. Goals in profit-seeking firms typically center on financial criteria such as profit, return on investment, or market share, as well as service.

In a **system** all parts of the business work in unison.

The third component of the marketing concept is the systems approach. In a **system** all parts of the business work together. Thus, consumer needs are identified, and internal procedures are set up to ensure that the right goods and services are produced, distributed, and sold to meet those needs.

Meeting Customers' Needs

Your understanding of customers' needs starts with the realization that when people buy something, they purchase satisfaction as well as goods or services. Consumers do not simply choose a toothpaste, for example. Instead, some want a decay preventive, some seek pleasant taste, others desire tooth brighteners, and still others will accept any formula at a bargain price. Thus, understanding customers' needs means being aware of the timing of the purchase, what customers like and dislike, or what "turns them on."

Real-World Example 8.1

For example, the owner of a ladies' dress shop in a small town has a good business. Many of her customers live as far as 50 miles away. She knows her customers by name, understands their needs, and buys with them as individuals in mind. When she goes to market, she thinks, "This style is perfect for Mrs. Adams," or "Jane would love this." Then she calls Mrs. Adams or Jane when that style arrives.

The marketing concept should guide the attitudes of the firm's salespeople, who should be encouraged to build personal relationships with customers. A good example is Yoshihiro Shibata, a floor manager in an eye care supermarket in Tokyo, who wears as many as 27 different pairs of eyeglasses to get a handle on customer needs. Everyone in the store wears eyeglasses; many wear a different pair everyday.[2]

Small firms should add something extra in the way of customer service. Customers want a business to be helpful, and outstanding service will often generate good word-of-mouth advertising.

Real-World Example 8.2

For example, Avon Products Inc. (www.avon.com) reports that in 2002 its 4.4 million independent representatives handled over 1 billion customer transactions in 58 markets. The corporation serves its independent sales representatives by being the world's largest direct seller, the sixth largest global beauty company, and unusually broad in its geographic diversity. Avon was founded in 1886 by David H. McConnell, and the first sales representative was Mrs. P. F. E Albee. The first catalog was published November 2, 1896.

Keeping customers satisfied is more difficult than it seems, because it involves all aspects of the business. Customer satisfaction involves not just employees and customers but other factors as well, such as store design and upkeep, method of employee payment, and methods for providing feedback to and from customers. Unfortunately, as Yankelovich Partners (www.yankelovich.com) found in a recent survey, the vast majority of consumers feel they are not being served properly.

Implementing the Marketing Concept

In implementing the marketing concept, you should use the systems approach. As mentioned earlier, all parts of the business must be coordinated and marketing policies must be understood by all personnel in order to avoid problems such as that in the following example.

Real-World Example 8.3

A store sent its customers a flyer urging them to use its credit plan. Yet one customer received the flyer in the same mail with a harsh letter threatening repossession of earlier purchases if the customer's account wasn't paid within 24 hours.

You should try to apply the marketing concept by using one or more of the following ideas:

- Be conscious of image.
- Practice consumerism.
- Look for danger signals.

Be Conscious of Image   You should evaluate the business frequently to see what kind of image it projects—from the customers' point of view. You should ask: Can my customers find what they want, when they want it, and where they want it, at a competitive price? When looking for media attention, you should use a rapport-building technique. For example, Pam Lontos, a former Disney/Shamrock vice president, suggests you follow six steps to image-enhancing public relations:

- Show what is unique about your product—its positive benefits.
- Find future stories and explain how your company "fits."
- Be helpful, offer your research.
- Be unique and to the point; present your expertise.
- Don't be pushy.
- Speak with integrity, explain as if explaining for the first time and use current examples.[3]

Practice Consumerism   The major concerns of the consumer movement during the last three decades have been the rights of consumers to buy safe products, to be informed, to be able to choose, and to be heard. **Consumerism** recognizes that consumers are at a disadvantage and works to force businesses to be responsive in giving them a square deal. You can practice consumerism by doing such things as performing product tests, making clear the terms of sales and warranties, and being truthful in advertising.

Consumerism involves prodding businesses to improve the quality of their products and to expand consumer knowledge.

TABLE 8.1 | Danger Signals Indicating Marketing Problems

Indicator	Indication
Sales	Down from previous period
Customers	Walking out without buying
	No longer visiting store
	Returning more merchandise
	Expressing more complaints
Employees and salespeople	Being slow to greet customers
	Being indifferent to or delaying customer
	Not urging added or upgraded sales
	Having poor personal appearance
	Lacking knowledge of store
	Making more errors
	Good ones leaving the company
Store image	Of greed through unreasonable prices
	Inappropriate for market area
	Unclear, sending mixed signals

Look for Danger Signals   There are many danger signals that can indicate when the marketing concept is not being followed. Your business is in trouble if, over time, it exhibits one or more of the signs listed in Table 8.1. An uninterested employee—or manager—turns customers off, as the following classic example shows.

Real-World Example 8.4

Thomas Shoemaker was hunting for some Con-Tact paper in a Peoples Drug store in Washington, D.C. He finally gave up the search and was walking out when he saw a man with a Peoples ID badge adjusting some stock on a shelf. When Shoemaker asked him if the store carried Con-Tact paper, the man replied, "I don't know. I don't work here. I'm the manager."[4]

Seeking a Competitive Edge

There is a close relationship between key success factors and the competitive edge that a small business should seek. Some of these key factors, based on industry analysis, were discussed in Chapter 6. Your **competitive edge** (sometimes called *competitive advantage*) is something that customers want and only you can supply, which gives you an advantage over your competitors. George Anders relates, that in a service economy, "transform what you do into a sweeping solution to your customer's problem—and suddenly you're raking in big dollars from grateful clients."[5]

Some factors that might provide such an advantage are quality, reliability, integrity, and service, as well as lower prices. In some industries, such as electronics or toys, novelty and innovation provide the most important competitive edge.

In many small businesses, however, the competitive edge can be something as simple as courtesy, friendliness, and helpfulness. It may also involve a database program that

A **competitive edge** (competitive advantage) is a particular characteristic that makes one firm more attractive to customers than its competitors.

provides timely information indicating *who* should be contacted, *when* they should be contacted, and *how* to contact them.

In looking for a competitive edge or advantage, keep in mind that it is based on providing one or more of three forms of value to customers. Customers prefer goods and services that are better, cheaper, and faster. These forms of value can be summed up as follows:[6]

Better	Quality differentiation
Cheaper	Cost leadership
Faster	Quick response to consumer needs

These forms of competitive advantage create value for the customer, which can, in turn, increase the value of the firm. Be aware, though, that it is seldom possible for a small company to compete in all three areas, but you must find one area in which to compete. If your product costs more or your service takes longer than your competitors', then it must be of recognizably better quality. Or a product or service of moderate quality and average cost may be acceptable if it is available immediately.

In today's economy digital technology is key to success and consumers have shifted in a great part to **e-commerce.** E-commerce is technology-mediated exchanges between parties as well as the electronically based intra- or interorganizational activities that facilitate such exchanges. E-commerce is characterized by the exchange of digitized information between parties, is technology enabled and technology mediated, and supports intra- and interorganizational activities that support exchange. There are four direct categories: business to business, business to consumer, peer to peer, and consumer to business.[7]

Using Marketing Research to Implement the Marketing Concept

Market research is the systematic gathering, recording, and analyzing of data relating to the marketing of goods and services. It is an orderly, objective way of learning about customers or potential customers and their needs and desires. By studying customers' actions and reactions and drawing conclusions from them, you can use marketing research to improve your marketing activities. But bear in mind that marketing research does not solve all problems, as the following example illustrates.

> ### Real-World Example 8.5
>
> When the Ford Edsel was introduced in 1959, it was the most highly researched car in history, and it had innovations galore. It also had problems—from defective power steering to sticking hoods. The estimated loss was $250 million, or almost $1,117 per car.[8] According to Economic History Services (EH.net), this loss would be equal to about $1.8 billion in 2011 dollars, and the loss per auto would be about $8,327.

Marketing research is helpful at several points in the life of your business. Before starting the business, you can use marketing research to find out whether the location and surrounding population are right for your proposed product. After you open the business, marketing research can help you decide (1) whether to develop new or different products, (2) whether to expand at the original location or open additional locations, and (3) when and where to change emphasis on activities such as channels of distribution and advertising and promotion strategy.

E-commerce is technology-mediated exchanges between parties as well as the electronically based intra- or interorganizational activities that facilitate such exchanges.

Market research is the systematic gathering, recording, and analyzing of data relating to the marketing of goods and services.

How Does Marketing Research Aid Marketing?

Marketing research is part of a company's overall marketing system. By analyzing marketplace data such as attitudinal, demographic, and lifestyle changes, marketing research can help you plan your strategic efforts. The following are some areas in which marketing research is effective:

- Identifying customers for the firm's products.
- Determining their needs.
- Evaluating sales potential for both the firm and its industry.
- Selecting the most appropriate channel of distribution.
- Evaluating advertising and promotional effectiveness.

Real-World Example 8.6

For example, marketing research techniques are available to correlate data from actual customer purchases, using universal product code scanners in supermarkets and drugstores, with advertising information. The business owner can see how the amount and type of advertising and sales promotion lead to actual purchases.[9]

How to Do Marketing Research

Marketing research does not have to be fancy or expensive to meet your needs. It deals with people and their constantly changing likes and dislikes, which can be affected by many influences. Marketing research tries to find out how things really are (not how you think they are or should be) and what people are really buying or want to buy (not what you want to sell them).

Real-World Example 8.7

For example, during the early 1900s J. C. Hall conducted an early form of market research. His grandson, Don, says he would "watch people shopping, take notes and ask people, 'I noticed you didn't buy anything there,' or 'Why did you buy that?'" He then correlated this information with sales patterns and became convinced people were wanting a more expressive outlet than postcards could provide. He and his brother began producing greeting cards in 1915. Each card held a special insignia indicating purity—a "Hall mark." "Hallmark" first began appearing on Hall Brothers cards in 1928 and became the official company name in 1954.[10] Hallmark (www.hallmark.com) is based in Kansas City, is still privately owned, and produces about $4.2 billion in annual revenue created in more than 100 countries.

In its simplest form, marketing research involves (1) defining the problem and then (2) gathering and evaluating information. Many small business managers unknowingly do some form of marketing research nearly every day. For example, they check returned items to see if there is some pattern. They ask old customers on the street why they have not been in recently. They look at competitors' ads to find out what the competition is selling and at what prices.

> ### Real-World Example 8.8
> At a university small business seminar, the owner of a wholesaling firm that sold farm equipment and supplies stated that market research was not relevant in a small business. Later, he told the participants he visited dealers to learn their needs for shovels and other items before ordering these items for his stock. Without realizing it, he was doing marketing research.

Defining the Problem   Proper identification of the problem is the most important step in the process, since the right answer to the wrong question is useless. Thus, you should look beyond the symptoms of a problem to get at the real cause. For example, a sales decline is not a *cause* but rather a *symptom* of a marketing problem. In defining the problem, you should look at influences that may have caused it, such as changes in customers' home areas or in their tastes.

Gathering and Evaluating Information   Marketing research can use existing (secondary) data or generate new information (primary data) through research. So you must make a subjective judgment and weigh the cost of gathering more information against its usefulness. The cost of making a wrong decision should be balanced against the cost of gathering more data to make a better-informed decision.

Using Existing Information   You should "think cheap" and stay as close to home as possible when doing marketing research. Looking at your records and files, such as sales records, complaints, and receipts, can show you where customers live or work or how and what they buy, as the following example illustrates.

> ### Real-World Example 8.9
> The owner of a fabric shop used addresses on checks and cash receipts to pinpoint where her customers lived. She then cross-referenced the addresses with products purchased, which permitted her to check the effectiveness of advertising and sales promotion activities.

Credit records can also yield valuable information about your market, as customers' jobs, income levels, and marital status can be gleaned from them. Employees are a good source of information about customer likes and dislikes because they hear customers' gripes about the firm's products as well as about its competitors. They are also aware of the items customers request that are not stocked. Outside sources of information include publications such as *Survey of Current Business* and *Statistical Abstract of the United States,* trade association reports, chamber of commerce studies, university research publications, trade journals, newspapers, and marketing journals.

Doing Primary Research   Primary research can range from simply asking customers or suppliers how they feel about your business to more complex studies such as direct-mail questionnaires, telephone or "on the street" surveys, and test marketing. **Test marketing** simulates the conditions under which a product will eventually be sold. However, even a small market test is costly.

Primary research, which includes studies such as surveys, interviews, and questionnaires, should usually be left to experts. You might use this type of research, but take care to ask the right questions and obtain unbiased answers.

According to Grewel and Levy[11] developing a questionnaire is part art and part science, and in order to produce meaningful results it must be carefully worded. The questions should:

- Not be misleading.
- Address only one issue at a time.
- Use familiar vocabulary.
- Be appropriately sequenced.

The appearance should be professional and easy to follow and include appropriate instructions in suitable places.

Using Specialized Research Techniques   Other techniques include license plate analysis, telephone number analysis, coded coupons, and "tell them Joe sent you" broadcast ads, not to mention just plain people-watching.

In many states, license plates give information about where a car's owner lives—what city or county, for instance. By recording the origin of cars parked at the firm's location, the trade area can be estimated. Similarly, telephone numbers and zip codes can tell where people live. This type of data can be found on sales slips, prospect cards, and contest blanks, as well as on personalized checks used for payment.

Coded coupons and "tell them Joe sent you" broadcast ads can be effective, too. The relative effectiveness of your advertising media can be checked by coding coupons and by including in broadcast ads some phrase customers must use to get a discount on a given sale item. If neighborhood newspapers are involved, you can also get some idea of the area from which customers are drawn. Where they read or heard about the discount offered in the ads may also give information about their tastes.

Gathering Information on the Web

Companies of all sizes use information from their websites to segment their markets and target campaigns for maximum effect. Typically, customers voluntarily use the web for information or to submit information. Websites then track the number of total "hits" and follow the web surfer to the individual pages for different products or services.

There are several strategies for collecting customer/visitor information:[12]

- Piggyback questions on an online transaction such as addresses.
- Use an online form rather than an e-mail link to contact customers for use in your database.
- Use registration to play games or to take advantage of special offers as a way to gather information. Remember to include questions about all the demographic information you will need.

There are some basic guidelines that are helpful in deciding whether to use Internet-based research. Figure 8.1 should be of some help.

FIGURE 8.1 | Guidelines on Using the Internet for Marketing Research

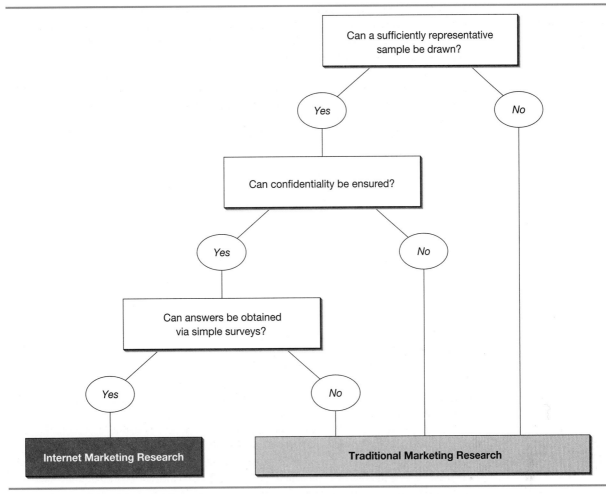

Using Computerized Databases

A wide variety of information is available at public libraries or online; many such sources also offer, for a fee, access to computerized databases, such as Standard & Poor's Daily News and Cumulative News (Corporation Records). By gathering data on selected kinds of companies (such as electronics firms producing home DVD's) or specific geographic areas (such as firms moving into a particular state or city), you can learn about companies that are expanding operations. Such information may be valuable to small retailers, service businesses, wholesalers, and manufacturers in selecting their target markets and marketing strategy.

Database marketing (See Chapter 16) is a tool that is used by many firms. Lands End (www.landsend.com) is a good example. Database marketing is a quick and efficient process for acquiring customers that involves obtaining meaningful consumer information; analyzing this information; and making marketing decisions. Business owners choosing this technique must have someone either on staff or available with the technology know-how to keep the system up and running.

Database marketing is a marketing process for acquiring customers that involves obtaining meaningful, individual-level, consumer information; respecting consumers' privacy; analyzing this information to estimate consumer response to various offers; and making marketing decisions based on this expected response.

FIGURE 8.2 |
No Cashiers?

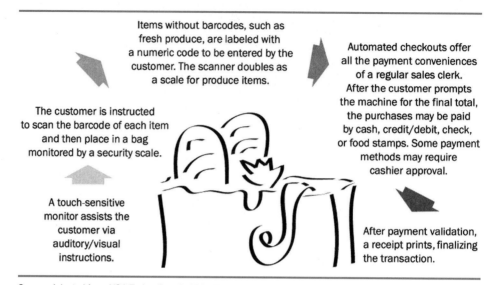

Items without barcodes, such as fresh produce, are labeled with a numeric code to be entered by the customer. The scanner doubles as a scale for produce items.

Automated checkouts offer all the payment conveniences of a regular sales clerk. After the customer prompts the machine for the final total, the purchases may be paid by cash, credit/debit, check, or food stamps. Some payment methods may require cashier approval.

The customer is instructed to scan the barcode of each item and then place in a bag monitored by a security scale.

A touch-sensitive monitor assists the customer via auditory/visual instructions.

After payment validation, a receipt prints, finalizing the transaction.

Source: Adapted from *USA Today,* June 7, 2001, P1A.

A variation of computerized databases is now being used by big and small businesses alike—from Federal Express to fast-food franchises to independent cabbies and pharmacists. Computer programs hooked to a phone with Caller ID can create a database that can increase efficiency, enhance security, control inventory, improve marketing, and simplify contacts with customers.

Real-World Example 8.10

For instance, if you call your favorite Domino's pizzeria (www.dominos.com), the person who answers the phone may say something like "Do you want another large deep-dish pepperoni with pineapples and anchovies?" How does the clerk know this much about your tastes? By looking into a convenient high-tech file: a computer that used Caller ID to tell who you are and then called up its records of where you live and what you like.[13]

Another form of computerized data systems is now being used by leading grocers around the country, such as Kroger, Safeway, Albertson's, A & P, and Pathmark. As shown in Figure 8.2, it computes the customer's total purchase and prints out a receipt when the customer pays with cash or a credit/debit card.[14]

Developing a Marketing Strategy

As a small business owner, you should develop a marketing strategy early in your business operations. Such a strategy consists of (1) setting objectives, (2) choosing target market(s), and (3) developing an effective marketing mix.

Setting Objectives

Marketing objectives should be tied in with your competitive edge and flow from your mission statement. For example, an image of higher quality than competitors' products at comparable prices may be an objective. To achieve this objective and still make planned

Does express checkout really exist? The new automated checkout stations sometimes cause more of a traffic jam than the express lane.

profits requires aligning all operations, including the added costs of improved quality, adequate capital, and so forth. Objectives must consider customers' needs as well as the survival of the business. To attain objectives, a target market must be identified and served.

Choosing Target Markets

A **target market** is the part of the total market toward which promotional efforts are concentrated.

The **target market** of a business should be the customers most likely to buy or use its product(s). Only when a clear, precise target market has been identified can an effective marketing mix be developed.

Real-World Example 8.11

For example, recent surveys of teens indicated that they felt discount stores such as Target provided better clothing at less expensive prices. K-Mart continually updates its line of Joe Boxer to remain hip enough for young shoppers.

Pacific Sunwear, "PacSun," has succeeded with its new urban clothing stores called d.e.m.o. These stores appeal to teens' love of hip-hop culture and have increased to 110 stores with double-digit sales increases. Torrid, a plus-size outgrowth of Hot Topic, is successful as an early responder or first mover.[15]

Market segmentation is identifying and evaluating various layers of a market.

Use Market Segmentation   To define a target market requires **market segmentation,** which is identifying and evaluating various layers of a market. Effective market segmentation requires the following steps:

1. Identify the characteristics of two or more segments of the total market. Then, distinguish among the customers in each segment on the basis of such factors as their age, sex, buying patterns, or income level. For example, adults desire a

table-service restaurant more than do teenagers and young children, who generally prefer a fast-food format.

2. Determine whether any of those market segments is large enough and has sufficient buying power to generate profit for your business.

3. Align your marketing effort to reach the selected segment of the market profitably.

Real-World Example 8.12

For example, when Bob Dylan did an ad for Victoria's Secret, a Google search got 7,760 hits for "Bob Dylan Victoria's Secret." This is powerful exposure for any vendor. Dylan's music is now selling in stores as a $10 custom CD compilation of his "most seductive songs." According to a *USA Today* survey, 21 percent of respondents thought the ads were very effective and liked the ads a lot.[16]

Shifting Target Markets   Choosing and maintaining a target market is becoming more difficult because of changing consumer characteristics. Therefore, small business owners should study the external environment for shifts in such factors as population patterns, age groups, and income levels, as well as regional patterns of consumption.

Real-World Example 8.13

Pizza Patron accepts Mexican pesos and dollars at 63 locations in 5 western states. Peso sales account for about 10 percent of total sales, which are up about 30 percent. It costs the stores about $60 each for new signage. The downside was about 3,000 e-mail protests at the franchise home office in Dallas.[17]

Population and Age Shifts   The underlying market factor determining consumer demand is the number and type of people with the purchasing power to buy a given product. In general, the U.S. population is shifting from the East and North to the West and South. Other important population factors are household size and formations, education, and the number of married couples, singles, single-parent families, unmarried couples, and children. According to the U.S. Census Bureau, the average size of U.S. households declined from 3.5 persons in 1940 to 3.14 in 1970, 2.63 in 1990, 2.62 in 2000, and 2.57 in 2009.[18]

Age groups also change. The average age of Americans has been rising and is expected to continue to rise in the foreseeable future. From 1990 to 2009 the average age increased from 32.8 to 36.8[19] years according to the U.S. Census Bureau (census.gov).

Also, the age distribution is shifting. As you can see from Figure 8.3, the number of young people and young adults is declining, while the 35-and-over group—especially the 45-to-64-year-old group—is currently increasing rapidly. Because people in each age group differ in their consumption patterns, different marketing strategies are needed.

Real-World Example 8.14

For example, the demographic group that is eligible for senior citizen discounts is exploding. The travel industry has recognized this shift and offers special discounts on airline, car rental, and hotel costs to those 50 years and older. There are now more than 75 million Americans who qualify.

FIGURE 8.3 |
Selling to Older
Consumers

*The growing ranks of
older consumers and
a decline in the size of
the youth market are
leading companies to
redesign products and
sales appeals to cap-
ture the increasingly
influential senior citi-
zen and aging baby-
boomer markets.*

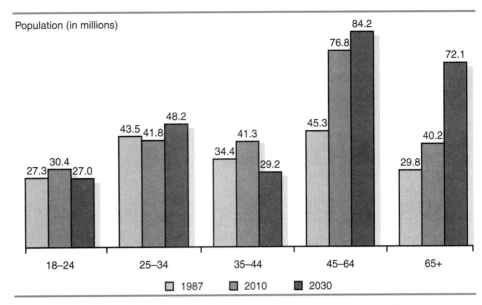

*Estimated

Source: U.S. Census Bureau, *Statistical Abstract of the United States: 2011* 130th ed., Washington, DC, 2010,
p. 12, table 8.

The 55-plus market is expected to grow almost 40 percent in the next 30 years, according to the U.S. Census Bureau. Figure 8.4 illustrates how the explosion is expected to
occur. A different set of data and projections from the U.S. Census Bureau forecast that the
segment of the U.S. population aged 65 and over is expected to increase 27 percent from
2010 to the year 2020.

The second trend—the need to use and conserve the skills of older workers—is forc-
ing employers to find productive ways to use those who want to keep on working. During
the coming decade, employers will have to choose from an aging workforce, as shown in
Figure 8.3, since there will be a crunch for younger workers with both basic and technical

FIGURE 8.4 |
Senior Spenders—
Percentage of U.S.
Population Age 55
and Over

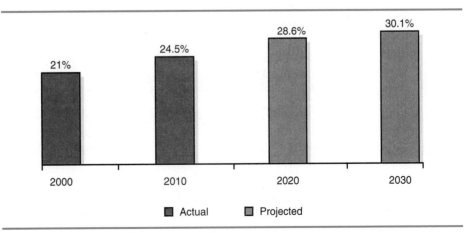

Source: U.S. Census Bureau, *Statistical Abstract of the United States: 2011* 130th ed., Washington, DC, 2010,
pp. 11 and 12, tables 7 and 8.

skills. In fact, *the number of 18-to-35-year-olds actually declined* until the year 2000, at which time it began to increase, but not as rapidly as the 45-and-over group. These shifts in age groupings will probably require redesigning jobs; rehiring retirees as consultants, advisers, or temporaries; using phased-in retirement programs; and aggressively recruiting older workers.

Regional Differences in Purchases   Purchasing habits and patterns also vary by region. These variations are significant, for where people live is one of the best clues as to what they buy.

Real-World Example 8.15

Cracker Barrel Old Country Store Inc. (www.crackerbarrel.com) is well known in the South for home-style cooking at modest prices. In a calculated gamble, it is now opening 70 percent of its new restaurants outside its core Southern market.

Because many of the new restaurants are in the North and West, the menu is being changed from Southern staples such as grits and fried okra to local specialties. For example, when Cracker Barrel opened its first store in Wisconsin, sales were only about 60 percent of those in the Southeast. After closing three restaurants, the company began to change its menu and now offers dishes such as thick-sliced bratwurst and fried cheese curds in areas such as Germantown, Wisconsin. It has also added a Friday-night fish fry. These changes turned the Wisconsin stores around.[20]

In the mid-1990s, demographic forces dramatically changed the nation's geographic economic balance. In addition to the flood of immigrants into New York, Florida, California, and the Southwest, there was an internal mass migration. People were drawn from California and the northern states to the southern and southwestern states.

Real-World Example 8.16

José Badia, for example, has nearly doubled his revenues since 1999. Badia Spices, a Miami-based company, expanded beyond its Cuban-only offering to generate current earnings of $30 million for 2003. When José noticed Miami's ethnic makeup was changing, he added new seasonings to their line of products. He added spices and flavorings such as chimichurri, Mexican chili, and a Spanish olive oil. The line includes 350 marinades, spices, and teas, which you can now find in Sam's Club and Costco.[21]

Developing an Effective Marketing Mix

A **marketing mix** is the proper blending of the basic elements of product, price, promotion, and place into an integrated marketing program.

A **marketing mix** consists of controllable variables that the firm combines to satisfy the target market. Those variables are the Four Ps: product, place, promotion, and price. The right *product* for the target market must be developed. *Place* refers to the channels of distribution. *Promotion* refers to any method that communicates to the target market. The right *price* should be set to attract customers and make a profit.

The Product Life Cycle

You may find that your most effective strategy is to concentrate on a narrow product line, develop a highly specialized product or service, or provide a product-service "package" containing an unusual amount of service. In setting strategy, competitors' products, prices, and services should be carefully analyzed. This is not easy to do because of the large number of new products introduced each year.

Stages of the Product Life Cycle

Products are much like living organisms: They are brought into the world, they live, and they die. When a new product is successfully introduced into the firm's market mix, it grows; when it loses appeal, it is discontinued. A new product may have a striking effect on the life cycle of other products as well.

> **Real-World Example 8.17**
>
> How do you get your music? Phonograph records are a good illustration of the product life cycle. Although 78 RPM records coexisted with the 45s, they gave way to the long-playing vinyl 33s. Then the compact disc (CD) began to dominate the market, threatening all records, even the 45s. Jukeboxes that play CDs offer vastly superior quality, along with lower maintenance costs. In 1998, although CDs themselves seemed secure, CD *players* were threatened by new technologies. Most CD-ROM and DVD players also play audio discs. Do you use MP3 or your smartphone?

The **product life cycle** consists of four stages: introduction, growth, maturity, and decline.

As shown in Figure 8.5, the **product life cycle** has four major stages: introduction, growth, maturity, and decline. As a product moves through its cycle, the strategies relating to competition, promotion, distribution, pricing, and market information should be evaluated and possibly changed. You can use the life-cycle concept to time the introduction and improvement of profitable products and the dropping or recycling of unprofitable ones.

Introduction Stage   The introduction stage begins when a product first appears on the market. Prices are usually high, sales are low, and profits are negative because of

FIGURE 8.5 |

Sales and Profits during the Product Life Cycle*

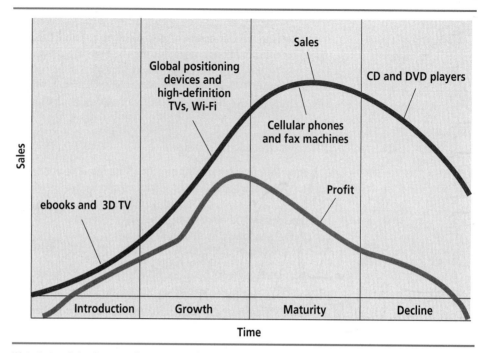

*Note that profit levels start to fall *before* sales reach their peak. When profits and sales start to decline, it's time to come out with a new product or remodel the old one to maintain interest and profits.

Source: William G. Nickels, James M. McHugh, and Susan M. McHugh, *Understanding Business,* 4th ed. (Burr Ridge, IL: Irwin, 1996), p. 449. Reprinted by permission of The McGraw-Hill Companies.

high development, promotion, and distribution costs. In this stage, it is vital to communicate the product's features, uses, and advantages to potential buyers. Only a few new products—such as telephones, microwave ovens, and home computers—represent major innovations. More often, a "new" product is an old one in a new form. Many products never get beyond the introduction stage because of insufficient or poor marketing research, design or production problems, or errors in timing the product's introduction.

Growth Stage   During the growth stage, sales rise rapidly and profits peak. As competitors enter the market, they attempt to develop the best product design. During this stage, marketing strategy typically encourages strong brand loyalty. The product's benefits are identified and emphasized to develop a competitive niche.

Maturity Stage   Competition becomes more aggressive during the maturity stage, with declining prices and profits. Promotion costs climb; competitors cut prices to attract business; new firms enter, further increasing competition; and weaker competitors are squeezed out. Those that remain make fresh promotional and distribution efforts.

Decline Stage   Sales fall rapidly during the decline stage, especially if a new technology or a social trend is involved. Management considers pruning items from the product line to eliminate unprofitable ones. Promotion efforts may be cut and plans may be made to phase out the product, though sometimes it can be saved by repackaging or other changes.

> ### Real-World Example 8.18
>
> For example, the Swanson TV Dinner, developed in 1955, had food to be cooked in an oven on an aluminum tray and eaten while watching TV. It flourished at the height of television's Golden Age but has now been relegated to the Smithsonian Institution (www.si.edu) for possible display at the National Museum of American History.

Need for a Wide Product Mix

The life-cycle concept indicates that many, if not most, products will eventually become unprofitable. Hence, small firms should investigate and evaluate market opportunities to launch new products or extend the life of existing ones. You should have a composite of life-cycle patterns, with various products in the mix at different life-cycle stages; as one product declines, other products are in the introduction, growth, or maturity stages. Some fads may last only a few weeks or months (such as a new video game or doll), while other products (refrigerators, for example) may be essentially unchanged for years.

Still other products will decline in popularity for a period and then reemerge. This trend provides great opportunities for small business entrepreneurs.

Packaging

Packaging, because it both protects and promotes the product, is important to you as well as to your customers. Packaging can make a product more convenient to use or store and can reduce spoiling or damage. Good packaging makes products easier to identify, promotes the brand at the store, and influences customers in making buying decisions.

> ### Real-World Example 8.19
>
> Many top-selling global brands have a common thread—*and it's not money.* Products such as Coca-Cola, Campbell's soup, and Colgate toothpaste all have one very important thing in common—*they're all packaged in red!* Others with red logos or names are Kellogg's, Nabisco, Dole, Del Monte, Lipton, Dentyne, and many other best sellers. Packaging experts and color psychologists say that a product's color and consumer buying preferences are closely linked. Red is considered to be warm and bright.[22]

A better box, wrapper, can, or bottle can help create a "new" product or market. For example, a small manufacturer introduced a liquid hand soap in a pump container, and it was an instant success. Sometimes, a new package improves a product by making it easier to use, such as reclosable plastic containers for motor oil, stand-up tubes and flip-open caps for toothpaste, or zipper-closure bags for cheese or sliced meat. Packaging can also improve product safety, as when drugs and food are sold in child-proof bottles and tamper-resistant packages. Sometimes variations in packaging are a last resort when everything else has been tried. How many times have you seen a "New, Improved" product and suspected that all that has changed is the label?

Pricing Your Product

Pricing can make the difference between success and failure for any business, but it is especially crucial for small businesses. Professor Anne B. Lowery, a marketing scholar, has concluded that owners of small businesses may not be able to consider all the many and complex economic variables involved in price setting. She has summarized demand, supply, and other variables into four categories, which she calls "the four Cs of pricing:"[23]

- Customer.
- Company.
- Competition.
- Constraints.

The customer and company categories are internal and therefore largely within the control of the owner or manager. Competition and constraints, on the other hand, are generally considered external to the business and therefore largely beyond the control of the small business.

In considering these four categories, there are three practical aspects of pricing that you must consider. First, regardless of the desirability of the product, the price must be such that customers are willing—and able—to pay it. Second, you must set your price to maintain or expand your market share and/or profit. If the new product is successful, competitors will introduce either a better product or a cheaper one. Third, if you want to make a profit on the new product, the price must be sufficiently greater than cost to cover development, introduction, and operating costs.

Establishing Pricing Policies

As shown in Table 8.2, there's a large variety of pricing policies you can adopt, but the first three deserve particular attention: product life cycle, meet the competition, and cost-oriented pricing.

Effect of Product Life Cycle   Notice the role played by the product life cycle, as discussed earlier. When you introduce a new product, you have two alternatives: (1) to set a **skimming price,** which will be high enough to obtain the "cream" of the target market before competitors enter, or (2) to set a **penetration price,** which will be low enough to obtain an adequate and sustainable market. Small producers sometimes use a combination approach, setting a realistic price but making an initial purchase more attractive by issuing discount coupons.

A **skimming price** is one set relatively high initially in order to rapidly skim off the "cream" of profits.
A **penetration price** is one set relatively low to secure market acceptance.

Meeting the Competition   You can also set prices by meeting the competition, that is, following the pricing practices of competitors. But this practice can lead to severe losses if cost and volume of sales are not taken into account. Small firms with an attractive, possibly unique product should not be afraid to charge what the product is worth, considering not only what it costs to provide the product but also what the market will bear.

Cost-Oriented Pricing   Cost is basic to all pricing policies. Total costs provide a floor below which prices should not be permitted to go, especially for long periods. Cost-oriented pricing involves adding a markup to the cost of the item.

TABLE 8.2 | Potential Pricing Policies for a Small Business

Policy Area	Description
Product life cycle:	
Skimming price	Aimed at obtaining the "cream" of the target market at a high price before dealing with other market segments.
Penetration price	Intended to try to sell to the entire market at a low price.
Meet the competition	Below the market price.
	At the competitors' price level.
	Above the market price.
Cost-oriented pricing	Costs are accumulated for each unit of product, and a markup is added to obtain a base price.
Price flexibility:	
One price	Offering the same price to all customers who purchase goods under the same conditions and in the same quantities.
Flexible price	Offering the same products and quantities to different customers at different prices.
Suggested retail price	Manufactures often print a suggested price on the product or invoice or in their catalog.
List prices	Published prices that remain the same for a long time.
Prestige pricing	Setting of high prices used, say, by fur retailers.
Leader pricing	Certain products are chosen for their promotional value and are priced low to entice customers into retail stores.
Bait pricing	An item is priced extremely low by a dealer, but the salesperson points out the disadvantages of the item and switches customers to items of higher quality and price. (This practice is illegal.)
Odd pricing	Prices end in certain numbers, usually odd, such as $0.95—e.g., $7.95, $8.95.
Psychological pricing	Certain prices for some products are psychologically appealing; there can be a range of prices that customers perceive as being equal to each other.
Price lining	Policy of setting a few price levels for given lines of merchandise—-e.g., ties at three levels: $8, $16, and $25.
Demand-oriented pricing	Potential customer demand is recognized, and prospective revenues are considered in pricing.

Markup is the amount added to the product's cost to determine the selling price.

Markup   **Markup** is the amount added to the cost of the product to determine the selling price. Usually, the amount of the markup is determined by the type of product sold, the amount of service performed by the retailer, how rapidly the product sells, and the amount of planned profit. Markup may be expressed in terms of dollars and/or cents, or as a percentage.

The way to figure markup percentage on cost is

$$\text{Markup as percentage of cost} = \frac{\text{Dollar amount of markup}}{\text{Cost of the item}}$$

For example, assume a retailer is pricing a new product that costs $6. The selling price is set at $9. Therefore, the total amount of markup is $3: selling price ($9) less cost ($6) equals markup ($3). The markup percentage, then, is

$$\text{Markup percentage (cost)} = \frac{\$3}{\$6} = 50 \text{ percent}$$

TABLE 8.3 | Discounts and Allowances Provided by Small Businesses

Reduction	Description
Cash discounts	Given as a reduction in price to buyers who pay their bill within a specified time period (e.g., 2/10, net 30 days).
Functional or trade discounts	List price reductions given to channel members for performance of their functions.
Quantity discounts	Reduction in the unit price granted for buying in certain quantities.
Noncumulative	Apply to individual shipments or orders only.
Cumulative	Apply to purchases over a given period (e.g., a year).
Seasonal discounts	Induce buyers to stock earlier than immediate demand would dictate.
Promotional allowances	Provided by manufacturers and wholesalers to retailers for promotion (e.g., point-of-purchase display materials, per case discounts, and cooperative advertisements).
Trade-ins	Allowance provided to customer by retailer in the purchase of, say, a major electric appliance.
Push money or prize money	Allowances provided retailers by manufacturers or wholesalers to be given to salespersons for aggressively selling particular products.

A **discount** is a reduction from the list price given to customers as an inducement to buy more of a product.

Allowances are given to customers for accepting quality or quantity reduction.

Discounts and Allowances   Sellers often use discounts and allowances to increase sales. **Discounts,** which are reductions from a product's normal list price, are given to customers as an inducement to buy the item. **Allowances** are given to customers for accepting less of something or as an adjustment for variations in quality. Some of the more popular discounts and allowances are shown in Table 8.3.

An example of discounts is the "Grandkid deal." As our population ages with better health, we have an entire target market of seniors (Generation G) who are healthy and wealthy enough to travel with their grandchildren. Hilton targets this market with "children 18 and under stay free." As more grandparents travel with children (15 percent of all child travel in 2002 was with grandparents), they seek out senior discounts. In 2003, one in three grandparents had traveled with grandchildren. Destinations range from the Grand Canyon to Paris. Many discount offers for this group require advance reservations and multi-night stays. The grandparent package may include goodies such as a disposable camera, popcorn, bubble bath, videos, and games.[24]

How Prices Are Set by Small Businesses

Prices are set differently by small service firms, retailers, wholesalers, producers, and building contractors. Some of the more popular methods are described here.

By Service Firms   Service firms either charge the "going rate" (that is, the usual rate for a given job) or they may set prices according to those prevalent in their industry. They try to set a price based on the cost of labor and materials used to provide the service, as well as direct charges, such as transportation costs, and a profit margin. Many firms charge customers an hourly rate, based on the time required to perform the services, plus any travel expenses. Others incorporate the labor, materials, and transportation costs into an hourly rate, or a rate based on some other variable.

By Retailers   Different types of products are priced differently. Staple convenience goods, such as candy, gum, newspapers, and magazines, usually have customary prices or

A customary price is what customers expect to pay because of custom, tradition, or social habits.

use the manufacturer's suggested retail price. **Customary prices** are the prices customers expect to pay as a result of custom, tradition, or social habits.

Real-World Example 8.20

For example, Hershey Chocolate Company (www.hersheys.com) sold candy bars for 5 cents in 1940. As cocoa and sugar became scarce and more expensive because of World War II, the price did not rise for a while. Instead, the size of the bars was cut in half by the end of 1942.

Some discount and food stores discount prepriced items such as candy, gum, magazines, and greeting cards by a set percentage—say, 10 or even 20 percent. Food World discounts all prepriced items 10 percent, and Wal-Mart discounts greeting cards 20 percent and sewing patterns nearly 50 percent.

Fashion goods, by contrast, have high markups but are drastically marked down if they do not sell well. High markups are also used on novelty, specialty, and seasonal goods. When the novelty wears off, or the selling season ends, the price goes down.

Real-World Example 8.21

Early-bird shoppers after holidays expect to find markdowns up to 50 or even 75 percent on Christmas wraps and toys or on Easter candy and stuffed rabbits. Customers also expect discounts on novelty items marketed as "stocking stuffers," holiday party clothes, and extravagantly priced items intended as gifts.

Unit pricing is listing the product's price in terms of some unit, such as a pound, pint, or yard.

Most grocery stores use **unit pricing** for products such as meats, produce, and deli items, charging so much per ounce or pound for each item. Information about unit prices of other items facilitates comparison shopping by customers.

Although influenced by competitors', vendors', and customary prices, retailers still must determine their own prices for the products they sell. The retailer's selling price should cover the cost of goods, selling and other operating costs, and a profit margin. In some cases, however, a store might use **loss leaders,** or items sold below cost, to attract customers who may also buy more profitable items.

A loss leader is an item priced at or below cost to attract customers into the store to buy more profitable items.

By Wholesalers   Wholesalers' prices are usually based on a markup set for each product line. Since wholesalers purchase in large quantities and cannot always immediately pass along price increases, price drops can cause heavy losses. Therefore, they may sometimes quote different prices to different buyers for the same products.

By Producers   While meeting competitors' prices is common among small producers, many set their prices relative to the cost of production, using a breakeven analysis. As shown in Chapter 14, their costs include purchasing, inventory, production, distribution, selling, and administrative costs, as well as a profit margin. Those figures are totaled to arrive at a final price.

Cost-plus pricing is basing the price on all costs, plus a markup for profit.

By Building Contractors   Most building contractors use **cost-plus pricing.** They start with the cost of the land; add expected construction costs for items such as labor, materials, and supplies; add overhead costs; add financing and closing costs and legal fees; and add the real estate broker's fee. They then total the costs and add on a markup for profit.

Other Aspects of Pricing

Product, delivery, service, and fulfillment of psychological needs make up the total package that the customer buys. A price should be consistent with the image the business wants to project. Because customers often equate the quality of unknown products with their prices, raising prices may actually increase sales.

However, the reverse might also be true: Selling at a low price might lead customers to think the product is of low quality. Sometimes, "cheap" can be too cheap, especially when compared with nationally advertised products.

In summary, small business owners commonly make two errors in setting prices for their products. First, they charge less than larger businesses and consider themselves price leaders. Because of their relatively small sales, costs per unit tend to be higher for a smaller business than for a larger one. Therefore, *small firms generally should not attempt to be price leaders.* Second, many firms offering services performed personally by the owner undercharge during the early period of operation. The owner mistakenly believes prices can be raised later as more customers are secured. However, it is easier to lower prices than to raise them, and raising them usually creates customer dissatisfaction.

Strategy for Marketing Services

Because the service sector of our economy is so important and has certain unique features, we will cover strategies for marketing services separately from marketing goods.

Nature of Service Businesses

Personal services are performed by a business for consumers.

Business services are provided to another business or professional.

There are two categories of services: personal and business. **Personal services** include activities such as financial services, transportation, health and beauty, lodging, advising and counseling, amusement, plumbing, maid services, real estate, and insurance. **Business services** may include some of these, plus others that are strictly business oriented, such as advertising agencies, market research firms, economic counselors, and certified public accountants (CPAs). Some services include aspects of both, as the following examples illustrate.

Real-World Example 8.22

Accident and Crime Scene Clean-Up Inc. does not do windows, but it does specialize in housework most homeowners would prefer not to contemplate. Many times, after a messy or violent crime, property owners or their maids or maintenance workers lack either the expertise or the willingness to clean up what the police or ambulance crew refuses to remove. Todd Menzies, owner and sole employee of the company, dons space-suit-like protective clothing and respiratory protection and goes to work, leaving the scene scrubbed, disinfected, and germ and odor free. Menzies says that in many cases insurance picks up at least part of the tab.[25]

Leo Rivera is the founder of Bishops Barbershop. He differentiated an old-school service—barbering—by opening a rock 'n' roll theme barbershop. In 2001, he invested $40,000 and added a DJ and beer. Sales for 2004 are projected at $1.6 million for four locations, with each store attracting 90 to 130 customers per day and polishing off 190 cases of beer per month.[26]

Personal services can be performed by individuals or by automated equipment. Two examples of the latter are automatic car washes and computer time-sharing bureaus.

There are many opportunities in service industries because the demand for services is expected to grow faster than for most other types of businesses. Some reasons for increased spending on services include rising discretionary income, services as status symbols, more women working outside the home (and earning more), and a shorter workweek and more leisure time.

On the other hand, service businesses have severe competition, not only from other firms, but also from potential customers who perform the services themselves and from manufacturers of do-it-yourself products.

How Services Differ

Because service firms must be chosen on the basis of their perceived reputation, a good image is of utmost importance. There are few objective standards for measuring the quality of services, so they are often judged subjectively. Not only is a service usually complete before a buyer can evaluate its quality, but also defective services cannot be returned.

Services cannot be stored in inventory, especially by firms providing amusements, transportation services, and room accommodations. Special features or extra thoughtfulness that create a memorable experience will encourage repeat business for service firms.

The level of customer contact required to provide and receive the service also varies. That is, the longer a customer remains in the service system, the greater the interaction between the server and customer. Generally, economies of scale are more difficult to achieve in high-contact services than in low-contact ones. For example, a beauty salon is a high-contact system, with the receptionist, shampoo person, and stylist all interacting with the customer. On the other hand, an automated car wash may have little contact with a customer.

Developing Service Marketing Strategies

Strategies for marketing services differ according to the level of customer contact. For example, in low-contact services the business does not have to be located near the customer. But a high-contact service, such as a plumbing firm, must be close enough to quickly meet the customer's needs. Quality control in high-contact services consists basically of doing a good job and maintaining an image and good public relations. Thus, if employees have a poor attitude, the firm may lose customers. Sometimes a company can gain a competitive edge by turning a low-contact service into a high-contact one, departing from the service approach taken by competitors.

Primacy of the Marketing Concept   The marketing concept is more important for service businesses than for other types of businesses, since customers often can perform the service themselves. The business must demonstrate why it is to the customer's advantage to let the service firm do the job.

Pricing Services   The price for a service should reflect the quality, degree of expertise and specialization, and value of its performance to the buyer. As shown earlier, a high price tends to connote quality in the mind of the customer, so lower prices and price reductions may even have a negative effect on sales, particularly in people-based businesses.

The pricing of services in small firms often depends on value provided rather than on cost. Customers will pay whatever they think the service is worth, so pricing depends on what the market will bear. Pricing decisions often consider labor, materials, and transportation costs, as the following example illustrates.

Real-World Example 8.23

Lynn Brown's Mini-Maid franchise team takes from 30 to 90 minutes to clean a house: make beds, scour sinks, clean glass doors, sweep and mop or wax floors, vacuum carpets, clean bathrooms, polish furniture, load the dishwasher, wipe cabinets, shine counters, change bed linens, remove garbage, freshen the air, and do general pickup.

Supplies and labor are furnished by Brown, and cleaning prices depend on the size of the house and the amount of work involved. When estimating the price, Brown considers the frequency with which customers use her services. The more often they use Mini-Maid, the better their rate.

Although Brown has an office in her home (with a 24-hour-a-day answering service), she spends most of the workweek in her minivan. She says her success results from doing specific activities, in a specific way, for a specific price—which, as she says, is the Mini-Maid way.[27]

Promoting Services   Word-of-mouth advertising, personal selling, and publicity are usually used by small firms to promote their business. Often, the message will have a consistent theme, which is related to the uniqueness of the service, key personnel, or the benefits gained by satisfied customers. Small service firms typically also use the Yellow Pages, direct mail, and local newspapers, and may use specialty advertising, such as calendars with the firm's name, to promote themselves. Referrals, that is, asking satisfied customers to recommend the service to friends, can be quite effective. Belonging to professional and civic organizations and sponsoring public events are also important in building a firm's revenues and profitability.

Implementing Your Marketing Strategy

Now that you have developed your marketing strategy, how do you implement it? Implementation involves two stages: the introductory stage and the growth stage.

The Introductory Stage

When introducing a new product, you should (1) analyze present and future market situations, (2) fit the product to the market, and (3) evaluate your company's resources.

Analyze Market Situations   This step determines the opportunities that lie in present and future market situations, as well as problems and adverse environmental trends that will affect your company. Because market size and growth are vital, potential growth rate should be forecast as accurately as possible.

Fit Product to Market   You should design your products to fit the market and then find other markets that fit those products. A market niche too small to interest large companies may be available.

> **Real-World Example 8.24**
>
> For example, a small firm manufacturing truck springs found that its product was a standard item produced by larger competitors that benefited from economies of scale. Because price competition was so severe, management decided to specialize in springs for swimming pool diving boards. This change in product strategy proved to be highly profitable.

Evaluate Company Resources   Your company's strengths, as well as its limitations, should be determined at each stage of the marketing process. Financial, cost, competitive, and timing pressures must be viewed realistically, and successes and failures need to be understood and regarded as important learning experiences.

The Growth Stage

Once you begin to grow, you can adopt one of three strategies: (1) expand products to reach new classes of customers, (2) increase penetration in the existing target market, or (3) make no marketing innovations but try instead to hold your present market share by product design and manufacturing innovations.

Expand Products to Reach New Markets   To reach new markets, you may add related products within the present product line, add products unrelated to the present line, find new applications in new markets for the firm's product, or add customized products, perhaps upgrading from low-quality to medium- or high-quality goods. This is **diversification,** or product line expansion, which tends to increase profits; contribute to long-range growth; stabilize production, employment, and payrolls; fill out a product line; and lower administrative overhead cost per unit.

Diversification involves adding products that are unrelated to the present product line.

    The major pitfall of diversification is that the firm may not have the resources to compete effectively outside its established market niche. But the advantages seem to outweigh the pitfalls in most cases.

Increase Penetration of Present Market   You may want to increase the sales of existing products to existing customers. If so, you might reduce the number and variety of products and models to produce substantial operating economies.

> **Real-World Example 8.25**
>
> David Neeleman, CEO of JetBlue, works to increase market penetration by flying on at least one flight per month to talk to travelers and listen for ideas. At the beginning of a flight he will stand and say, "Hi, my name is Dave Neeleman, and I'm CEO of JetBlue. I'm here to serve you this evening, and I'm looking forward to meeting each of you before we land." Dave says he gets most of his ideas from the customers on the flights: "The customers tell me what they want."[28]

Make No Marketing Innovations   The strategy of retaining current marketing practices without trying to innovate may suit your company if its strength lies in its technical competence. It is often advisable for retail store owners to follow this strategy.

Over the long term, a firm may follow one strategy for several years with the intent to change after certain marketing goals have been reached. But the change should occur if progress is desired.

What You Should Have Learned

1. You use the marketing concept when you focus your efforts on satisfying customers' needs—at a profit. Consumer needs and market opportunities should be identified, and the target market(s) most likely to buy your products should be determined. You should seek a competitive edge that sets your firm apart from, and gives it an advantage over, competitors.

2. Market research involves the systematic gathering, recording, and analyzing of data relating to the marketing of goods and services. It is part of the company's overall marketing system. By analyzing marketplace data, such as attitudinal, demographic, and lifestyle changes, marketing research can help small business owners plan their strategic efforts.

3. A marketing strategy involves setting marketing objectives and selecting target market(s) based on market segmentation. It means knowing consumers' needs, attitudes, and buying behavior, as well as studying population patterns, age groups, income levels, and regional patterns. Finally, the marketing mix, which consists of the controllable variables product, place, promotion, and price, should weigh heavily in decision making.

   The marketing strategies you can adopt are to expand products to reach new classes of customers, increase penetration in the existing target market, or make no marketing innovation but copy new marketing techniques instead.

4. A product life cycle has four major stages: introduction, growth, maturity, and decline. Strategies related to competition, promotion, distribution, and prices differ depending on the product's stage of the cycle.

5. Packaging both protects and promotes the product. It not only makes products more convenient and reduces spoiling or damage, but also makes products easier to identify, promotes the brand, and makes the purchase decision easier.

6. Pricing objectives should be set to achieve your firm's overall objectives. The "best" selling price should be cost and market oriented. Some pricing concerns for small businesses are product life cycle, meeting the competition, and cost orientation. Most small businesses employ cost-oriented pricing methods, using markups, discounts, and allowances. Different types of small firms use varying pricing practices.

7. The marketing of services differs from the marketing of goods. There are few objective standards for measuring service quality, but quality should be emphasized because customers measure services subjectively. Price competition in standardized services is quite severe; however, output of service firms is often difficult to standardize, and services cannot be stored, making thoughtfulness and special features important sources of a competitive edge for service businesses.

Key Terms

allowances   220
business services   222
competitive edge   204
consumerism   203
cost-plus pricing   221
customary price   221
database marketing   209
discount   220

diversification   225
e-commerce   205
loss leader   221
market research   205
market segmentation   211
marketing concept   201
marketing mix   215
markup   219

penetration price   218
personal services   222
product life cycle   215
skimming price   218
system   202
target market   211
test marketing   208
unit pricing   221

Questions for Discussion

1. What is the marketing concept, and why is it so important to small firms?

2. How are the key success factors for a firm related to its competitive edge?

3. Why is marketing research so important to a small business—especially a new one?

4. What is market segmentation, and how can it be made more effective?

5. Discuss some characteristics that should be considered in selecting a target market.

6. What controllable variables are combined into a marketing mix to satisfy the target market?

7. What are the major stages of the product life cycle, and how do marketing strategies differ at each stage?

8. In what ways is packaging important to small firms and their customers?

9. What are the three basic considerations in pricing products? Explain cost-oriented pricing. What is markup?

10. Explain how service firms, retailers, wholesalers, manufacturers, and building contractors actually set prices.

11. How does the marketing of services differ from the marketing of goods?

Case 8.1

Parkview Drug Store: Adding the "Personal Touch"

For 36 years, Bert and Barbara English have owned and operated Parkview Drug Store in Tuscaloosa, Alabama. Although not as high profile as Tuscaloosa's two main institutions—University of Alabama football and Dreamland Ribs—Parkview Drug Store is an institution.

The Englishes believe it is the "personal touch" that keeps customers coming back. "Big business has its place, but this is still the place for the personal touch," says Bert.

"We really thrive on the people and the relationships with families we've made throughout the years. Most people who come here know us on a first-name basis," adds Barbara.

Their "personal touch" philosophy definitely does not ring hollow like the marketing ploys and ad campaigns of many big businesses. Bert and Barbara truly foster a family atmosphere, and the effects of this approach are readily evident in their long-term relationship with customers. For example, the great-grandchildren of some of their original customers still patronize the store. Remarkably, five generations of one family have been—and still are—customers of the Englishes.

The bond between the owners and their customers is so strong, in fact, that over the years many customers have joined the Parkview family as employees. "Several of our customers' children have come back to work for us," says Barbara. "One time we had a grandmother and her three grandchildren working here at the same time."

One aspect of the Englishes' business and personal philosophy of establishing relationships with customers is their policy of never turning away a college student who needs medicine. "There's nothing worse than being in an unfamiliar place, sick, and alone," says Bert. "We decided a long time ago that we would not turn away any student who needed medicine. If a student can't pay for a prescription or over-the-counter medicine, we set up an account and bill the parents. We've been doing that for 35 years, and we've never been burned."

The Englishes were recently awarded a Community Service Award by the family pharmacy division of Amerisource Health Corporation.

Fittingly, Bert and Barbara met at Brown's Drug Store in Selma, Alabama, in 1959, when Bert was the young pharmacist, and Barbara was a college student who worked on weekends and during the summers. Bert says it was a whirlwind courtship. "We met that winter, I gave her a ring on Mother's Day, and married her in July. She didn't get a chance to think about it."

In September of that year, J. W. Brown, the store owner, made Bert an offer he couldn't refuse: Brown would buy Parkview Drug Store in Tuscaloosa if Bert would operate it. "I didn't have any money," Bert explains, "but I had the sweat. He had a lot of faith in me; I was so young and inexperienced." So the young couple was off, and the rest is history.

No success story, though, is complete without a recounting of "the hard times." Those came for the Englishes only two years after they moved to Tuscaloosa. For an entire year, the street facing Parkview Drug was closed to widen it to four lanes. "It was very difficult for anyone to get to us," Bert recalls. "We'd sit here a couple of hours and no one would come in the store." Things got so bad that friends began encouraging the young couple to declare bankruptcy and cut their losses. But Bert says they enjoyed what they were doing. "I figured we were young, our life was before us, and we had a great future mapped out for ourselves. We didn't want to give it up. We just tightened our belts and did a lot of praying and refinancing." Soon "the hard times" were over—they had made it through.

At 59, Bert says he is more than up to the challenges that face a small pharmacy in today's market, namely, insurance policies that require participants to purchase medicine by mail and large chain stores with in-house pharmacies. Because Bert and Barbara are not ready to retire just yet, their son recently suggested that they hire another pharmacist to help out. True to his "personal touch" business approach, Bert responded, "I don't want another pharmacist. I want to deal with my customers myself."

Bert sums up their success: "You treat people the way you want to be treated, and they'll remember you."

Questions

1. Do you think the "personal touch" is still feasible in today's mass-merchandising climate? Explain.

2. What are your thoughts on hiring customers? What are the strengths and weaknesses of this practice?

3. Is the policy of letting students without funds have medicine a practical one?

4. How do you explain the owners' success in using the Golden Rule as an operating philosophy?

Source: Prepared by William Jay Megginson from Gilbert Nicholson, "Down-Home Atmosphere," *Tuscaloosa* (Alabama) *News,* January 7, 1996, pp. 1E–2E.

Case 8.2

Buying Diamonds Online

Mark Vadon, looking for an engagement ring for his fiancé, was completely turned off when a jeweler advised him to pick a ring that "spoke" to him. At home, he went to his computer looking for Web sites dealing with diamond rings and found a site run by Doug Williams, an independent Seattle diamond wholesaler. Williams had discovered that by listing basic information about purchasing diamonds, he attracted men like Vadon.

After buying a diamond ring from Williams, Vadon flew to Seattle to talk to him about his business. Both men were impressed with the other: Williams was "blown away" by Vadon's research and knowledge of the subject. Vadon was impressed that Williams—even with two helpers—couldn't answer all the calls they were getting. Vadon surmised that if there are a lot of guys out there like him, this could be a winner. Over dinner he struck a deal with Williams to buy his business, went back to California, raised $57 million from venture capitalists, and closed the deal in May 1999.

Raising the money was not all that remarkable, as in the spring of 1999 venture capitalists were more than eager to back young entrepreneurs selling anything online. What was remarkable, however, was that Vadon's venture not only survived the dot-com implosion, it has thrived ever since.

Vadon used the money he raised to build a full-service e-commerce Web site (bluenile.com) and to assemble teams to handle various business activities. Within the first six months, Blue Nile generated $14 million in sales. Vadon's focus is on marketing to men rather than women. He feels that educated men making good incomes would be drawn to a Web site offering more insight into selecting fine jewelry. Helping customers make choices plus offering them online tutorials, are added incentives. His aim is to educate the customer, make him feel comfortable, and sell as cheaply as possible.

If Blue Nile were a traditional bricks-and-mortar jeweler, Vadon says, it would take 150 stores and 1,000 employees to sell $125 million worth of goods. "Our overhead is low, and we pass that savings on to our customers. We don't understand why anybody would trade anywhere but with us." His approach appears to be working. In January 2004, *Forbes* magazine named Blue Nile the Favorite Online Jeweler for the fifth consecutive year.

Questions

1. Personal selling seemed to fail. Why?
2. Why do you think the Blue Nile Web site is successful?
3. Explain the market segmentation used in the case.

Source: Byron Scohido, "He Turned Web Site in the Rough into Online Jewel," *USA Today,* Copyright October 20, 2003, p. 5B; and bluenile.com. Reprinted by permission.

Experiential

1. Choose your favorite snack food and design a new package for it. Explain your design.
2. Call several companies who provide professional services and ask if their trade certification organization has specific limits or requirements for advertising.

9

Promoting and Distributing

Don't sell the steak; sell the "sizzle."
 —Dale Carnegie sales slogan

Sales-management skills are very different from selling skills, and talent in one area does not necessarily indicate talent in the other.
 —Jack Falvey, management consultant, speaker, and writer

Much of what is included in the phrase "globalization" begins with changing our thinking. The first order of business for decision-makers is to think beyond our native borders and to adopt a mind-set that believes all world markets constitute one economy.
 —Fred Smith, Federal Express CEO

Learning Objectives

After studying the material in this chapter, you should be able to:

1. Describe the use of advertising to promote the sale of a product.

2. Discuss some opportunities and problems involved in selling to ethnic groups.

3. Describe the opportunities for small firms in global marketing.

4. Explain how physical distribution affects marketing strategy.

5. Describe different channels of distribution used for marketing products and discuss factors to consider in choosing an appropriate channel.

6. Describe the functions of intermediaries used in selling a product.

7. Describe the creative selling process used in personal selling.

Springdale Travel Inc.

In the late 1970's, Murray E. Cape recognized the profitable opportunities represented by the global travel industry. Recognizing the imperfection in the marketing niche, he responded on May 22, 1978, by opening Springdale Travel, Inc. In 1996 he decided to semiretire and his son Steve, and Bob Bender purchased the agency. March 2010 saw a major change in ownership when Bob Bender bought out his former partner of 14 years and became the sole owner of Springdale Travel, Inc. (www.springdaletravel.com). Springdale Travel represents all major airlines, tour companies, hotels, and cruise lines—both domestically and globally.

The travel agency accounts for many products and services. Air, cruise, and tour continue to be the primary products offered; however, group and incentive travel is growing every year. Airline ticket sales provide at least 60 percent of net profit. Corporations continue to utilize travel agencies to help them manage their travel, which is often one of their largest controllable expenses. But Springdale pursues all areas of the leisure travel business. With a ship operating out of the local port cruise sales have grown significantly in recent years. The group department has also begun offering charter packages to bowl games. For example, in 2010 the Auburn National Championship Game was one of the most successful groups in Springdale history. They are also managing fan alumni travel to regular football games for a local university. Springdale now operates a student travel department which accounts for several million dollars in sales each year. It consists mostly of band and performance art groups.

Springdale Travel continues its relationship with American Express as the only American Express Representative office in the area. This relationship brings many benefits in the way of discounts to their customers. The biggest change in the last year was the ability to redeem American Express Card points for travel. Springdale Travel has received the American Express Rep office in North America. Springdale Travel is one of the only three companies to receive the Readers choice award from the *Press Register* for each of the nine consecutive years it has been offered.

The company continues to stay on the cutting edge of technology. In August 2010, for example, the office upgraded its connectivity to fiber optic cable from traditional T-1 digital circuits, and they now have 100 megabits of bandwidth with no ceiling on adding bandwidth for the future. Then, in January 2011, Springdale Travel invested in 45 new PC's

FIGURE 9.1 |

Where Do You Begin
Planning Travel?

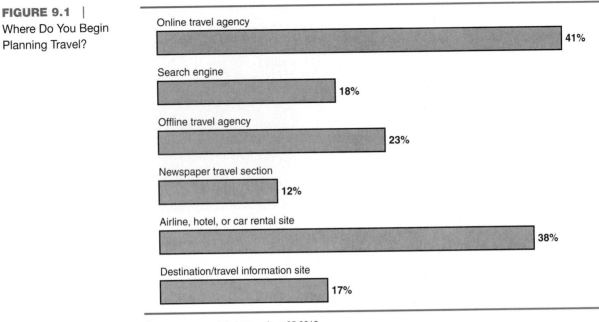

Source: www.myglobal.com., June 25,2012.

allowing them to take full advantage of the download speeds available via the new fiber connection. The results were huge in terms of speed. They now use a mix of digital analog telephones and IP telephones which allows them to place an employee on an IP telephone anywhere in the world with Internet access and connect them to call groups at Springdale Travel. This allows the movement of calls between branch offices and home-based agents. For example, they had several employees move to other cities in the last year and all were able to retain their positions with Springdale Travel using IP telephones. They have also upgraded their call management software to distribute calls to employees based on their skill base. For example, a call into the cruise department would look first at the agent extensions with the highest skill ranking for selling cruises. This allows for the greatest opportunity to place every call with the person best suited to assist the caller at the moment.

The global distribution systems or airline reservation systems distribute the majority of their inventory via global distribution systems. Both online agencies and brick-and-mortar agencies utilize these systems. In recent years airlines have begun to push back against the cost associated with this business model. They have used access to their inventory and fares as leverage. Their goal is for agencies to directly connect with their databases for access to their inventory. Unfortunately this segregates information making it more difficult to compare schedules and pricing. This battle continues to rage at this time.

Springdale Travel now offers an online booking tool that is customized for each individual corporation. This allows employees to manage their own reservations, while the corporation is still able to enforce policy and manage information. *Note:* The majority of reservations at Springdale are booked by email request, followed by telephone, but the number of online bookings are growing.

The company now utilizes client base (CRM software), which builds a personal history file on every customer. This software allows them to customize their online marketing offers. It also allows every agent to manage any booking in process.

Because Springdale Travel is located in a hurricane-prone area, the company added a 45 K generator in September 2010. Plagued by power outages particularly during hurricane season, the generator will allow for them to continue providing service during blackouts. Many of their customers are scattered across North America, and they expect Springdale Travel to maintain office hours regardless of any local power outages.

Bender and others in the travel agency industry are unclear about how the business model will look in a few years (see Figure 9.1). For certain it will change and continue to be affected by online distribution and continuously improving technology. As much as any industry, travel agents are going to have to react quickly to change and develop value-added services for which their customers are willing to pay.

The Profile illustrates much of the material covered in this chapter. The people at Springdale Travel use creativity in their advertising, sales promotion, and personal selling. This chapter deals with those subjects and also covers the channels of distribution to be used, the use of intermediaries for selling your product, other forms of promotion, the importance of considering ethnic groups in marketing products, opportunities in global marketing, physical distribution, and credit management.

Advertising

Advertising informs customers of the availability, desirability, and uses of products. It also tries to convince customers that the products are superior to those of competitors. Advertising is paid for by the marketer, who also controls the content, appearance, and/or sound of the message. The advertiser also has considerable authority over when, where, and how often advertising messages reach the target market.

Types of Advertising

Advertising can be either product or institutional. **Product advertising** is self-explanatory; **institutional advertising** is selling an idea about the company. Most advertising by small firms is a combination of the two. Institutional advertising tries to keep the public conscious of the company and its good reputation while also trying to sell specific products, as the following example illustrates.

Real-World Example 9.1

Many restaurants have jumped on the low-carb bandwagon, and Subway is no exception. They have a sandwich actually approved specifically by the Atkins diet plan. Subway has followed up the original advertisement for this product with a survey, which resulted in 34 percent of all respondents thinking the ad was "very effective."[1]

Holly Piturro, a nutrition therapist from Denver, said, "It may be smart marketing, but I don't agree that it's OK to eat so many protein-excessive products."[2]

Developing the Advertising Program

To be most effective, an advertising program should be used over an extended time period. The advertising should include preparing customers to accept a new product, suggesting new uses for established products, and calling attention to special sales. Such a program requires five basic decisions: (1) how much money to budget and spend for advertising, (2) what media to use, (3) what to say and how to say it, (4) what advertising agency to use (if any), and (5) what results are expected.

Setting the Budget

Advertising costs should be controlled by an *advertising budget.* The most popular bases for establishing such a budget are (1) a percentage of sales or profits, (2) units of sales, (3) objective (task), and (4) executive decision.

With the *percentage of sales or profits method,* advertising costs have a consistent relationship to the firm's sales volume and/or profit level. Thus, as sales/profits go up/down, advertising expenditures go up/down by the same percentage. One disadvantage of using this method is that advertising may be needed most when sales and profits fall.

Using the *units of sales method,* the firm sets aside a fixed sum for each unit of product to be sold. It is difficult to use this method when advertising many different kinds of products, for sporadic or irregular markets, and for style merchandise. But the method is useful for specialty goods and in situations where outside factors limit the amount of product available.

While the *objective (task) method* is most accurate, it is also the most difficult and least used method for estimating an advertising budget. Specific objectives are set, such as "to sell 25 percent more of Product X by attracting the business of teenagers." Then the medium that best reaches this target market is chosen, and estimates are made concerning costs.

With the most popular method of all, the *executive decision method,* the marketing manager decides how much to spend. This method's effectiveness depends on the manager's experience and/or intuition.

Selecting Advertising Media

The most popular advertising media used by small businesses are display ads in newspapers, store signs, direct mail, circulars and handbills, Yellow Pages ads, outdoor signs, radio, television, and the Internet. Probably the best medium for a small business, though, is word-of-mouth advertising from satisfied customers.

Some Popular Media Used by Small Firms   *Display ads* in the local newspaper are effective for most retail and service businesses. *Store signs* are useful in announcing sales or special events and for recruiting personnel. High postage rates are making the use of *direct mail* more expensive. Offset and instant printing have simplified the preparation of small quantities of *circulars* and *handbills;* however, printing and distribution costs are increasing, and local ordinances limit use of this medium. *Yellow Pages ads* are effective for special products, services, and repair shops. *Outdoor signs* are useful in announcing the opening or relocation of a business.

Radio advertising is helpful for small businesses in thinly populated areas. *Television* has generally been too costly and wasteful for many small firms to use. Now, however, local cable systems and low-power TV stations, have rates low enough to permit small firms to use them. QVC (QVC.com) is a good example of an entire television network dedicated to retail sales. With a format of demonstration, the products can be viewed at home and ordered by telephone or Internet. QVC is an intermediary for many companies, reaching more than 98 million U.S. households and about 195 million cable and satellite homes worldwide.

Real-World Example 9.2

For example, Kim and Scott's Gourmet Pretzels of Chicago (KimandScotts.com) employs 60 people with annual revenues in excess of $5 million. Kimberly and Scott Holstein invested $500,000 in labor and ingredients when they prepared their offering for QVC. This allowed the small manufacturer to compete with huge retailers and eventually gain enough name recognition to gain shelf space in places such as WalMart and Target. The Holsteins have appeared on QVC 24 times and sold more than 625,000 pretzels on air.[3]

Infomercials
(paid programming, teleshopping) are long, usually half-hour TV ads hosted by a hyper "sellevangelist" selling a relatively new product or service.

By no means a new advertising medium, the **infomercial** is an effective strategy for a small business in a fast-changing, or young, industry to emphasize its competitive advantages. These half-hour TV ads can be effective in helping small firms keep growing and enter markets once dominated by giant competitors. However, if they are to be effective in sales, infomercials must be produced professionally, by experts.

Real-World Example 9.3

Guthy-Renker (www.guthy-renker.com), based in Palm Desert, California, is such a professional organization, founded by Bill Guthy and Greg Renker. Their first infomercial, an instant hit that grossed nearly $10 million by 1988, featured ex-football great Fran Tarkenton endorsing a success program based on Napoleon Hill's book *Think and Grow Rich*. The partners bought time on six small-market TV stations and gradually expanded.

By 2007, Guthy-Renker was one of the world's largest direct response television companies with $1.3 billion in sales and annual average growth of 25 percent. They now focus into all areas of electronic retailing, worldwide, through broadcast television, cable and satellite, Internet, telemarketing, direct mail, and retail channels.

The Internet is an advertising medium that is exploding in use as companies are lured by the speed, the cost savings, and the possibility of more personalized pitches. Many search engines such as Google and Yahoo are going after local advertisers by testing local search marketing programs. These giants can identify the street where the searcher lives from data collected from users. In turn, the search engine can send local data in pop-up ads.

Real-World Example 9.4

For example, Brett Finkelstein handles marketing for a dating service dependent on local customers in the San Francisco area. When he switched advertising to the Google local program, he began getting about a dozen hits per month—up from five or six. This service costs about a nickel every time the ad is clicked.

Citysearch, a unit of InterActiveCorp, switched to pay-per-click in 2003 and has since increased from 5,000 to 25,000. One client, Lawrence Moore says his business is up 20 percent.[4]

Online shopping has greatly increased consumers ability to research and compare products and services. The increase in web shopping is due partly to consumers' feeling more comfortable using credit cards over the Internet. Online sales grew from about $5 billion in 1999 to $95 billion in 2006 for holiday gifts alone. The Census Bureau predicts that travel spending online will exceed $119 billion by 2010.[5] QVC.com attracts more than 6 million visitors each month.

Real-World Example 9.5

Some booksellers have completely abandoned traditional bookselling and turned instead to the Internet. For example, Karen Weyant, of Newport, Rhode Island, closed her store—Scribe's Perch—for good in 1996 after finding that her Internet sales were three times greater than her storefront sales. Now, using the Advanced Book Exchange site (www.abebooks.com), she sells only via the Net. Today Abebooks.com represents over 13,500 bookseller members worldwide and offers over 100 million selections. They employ 125 people and grossed over $21 million in 2010.[6]

How to Select the Appropriate Medium   The medium (or media) you choose will depend on several factors, including the target market, cost, and availability. The media of choice are those that your *target market* pays most attention to.

Real-World Example 9.6

For example, Lane Guest Ranch in the Colorado Rockies, a small mountain resort for 80 guests, has been advertising in *The Wall Street Journal* for 48 years. This type of advertising is appropriate to reach its target market for vacationers. The ad tells all about the resort and an extensive list of activities for both the lodge and the surrounding area.[7]

When considering media costs, you must look at both absolute cost and relative cost. *Absolute cost* is the actual expenditure for running an ad. *Relative cost* is the relationship between the actual cost and the number of consumers the message reaches (typically, the cost per 1,000 consumers reached). Finding the lower relative cost should be your objective. You should consider not only monetary costs but also public relations costs.

Developing the Message

The ideas or information you want to convey should be translated into words and symbols relevant to the target market. You must decide what is to be said, then how it is to be said, what form it will take, and what its style and design will be. Skilled employees of the chosen medium can help you develop the ads once you have decided on the central idea. For example, the new spokesman for Aflac is David McKeague, who was carefully chosen from a pool of 12,500 contestants to be the new voice of the Aflac duck. According to McKeague, he was known for making silly voices and he would imitate the commercial for his children ages 5, 8, and 11, who loved it.[8] Businesses can also get help from an advertising agency or a graphic arts firm.

When and How to Use an Advertising Agency

Most small business managers plan their own ad programs, particularly when they consider the rather high costs of retaining the services of an advertising agency. This practice may be false economy, however, because advertising agencies with experienced specialists can help you by (1) performing preliminary studies and analyses; (2) developing, implementing, and evaluating an advertising plan; and (3) following up on the advertising. Most small agencies tend to specialize in one area.

Measuring the Results of Advertising

Immediate-response advertising tries to get customers to buy a product within a short period of time so that response can be easily measured.

Measuring the results of advertising is important. Assume you want to determine whether your advertising is doing the job it was intended to do. You could do so by using some form of immediate-response advertising. **Immediate-response advertising** attempts to entice potential customers to buy a particular product from the business within a short time, such as a day, weekend, or week. The advertising should then be checked for results shortly after its appearance. Some ways of measuring results of these ads are coupons (especially for food and drug items) brought to the store, letters or phone requests referring to the ads, the amount of sales of a particular item, and checks on store traffic. Comparing sales during an offer period to normal sales, tallying mail and phone orders, and switching offers among different media can help determine which medium was more effective.

Merchandising, Sales Promotion, and Publicity

Many businesses use other means and go beyond advertising or support their advertising through merchandising, sales promotion, and publicity.

Merchandising

Merchandising is promoting the sale of a product at the point of purchase.

Merchandising is the promotional effort made for a product in retailing firms, especially at the point of purchase. It is the way the product is presented to customers, including window displays, store banners, product label and packaging, and product demonstrations. Window and counter displays are especially effective if they are attractively done and changed frequently. Some manufacturers and wholesalers provide retailers with advice on how to design better store displays and layouts.

Some retailers, however, use their own initiative in developing an effective merchandising strategy. The following example shows what one entrepreneur did to merchandise his stores.

Real-World Example 9.7

A classic example: Richard Ost owned three of the smallest drugstores you probably ever saw, located in one of Philadelphia's "most bombed-out and burned-up" neighborhoods. Yet he was doing $5 million of business a year in the mid-1990s, more than twice the rate of average drugstores.

How did he do it? He has succeeded by weaving himself into the fabric of the community. In retail health care, nothing succeeds like sensitivity. Ost instructed his employees to "be culturally competent." He enforced this idea by labeling prescriptions in Spanish for his Hispanic customers. He has loaded into his computer some 1,000 common regimens in Spanish. With a single keystroke, any one of these could be printed in Spanish rather than English. The program was so popular that he was the first Anglo in the community named "Hispanic Citizen of the Year." Business took off!

After he bought his second location, he found he had an Asian clientele, so he started labeling prescriptions in Vietnamese as well. Soon he was filling over 400 prescriptions a day at just the second location—half in English, 30 percent in Spanish, and 20 percent in Vietnamese.[9] The 2009 Census indicated that Hispanics are the largest U.S. minority group at 16 percent. Others included in the survey were African Americans, 13 percent; Asians, 5 percent; Native Americans, one percent; and Hawaiian-Pacific Islanders, 0.1 percent.[10]

Sales Promotion

Sales promotion includes marketing activities (other than advertising and personal selling) that stimulate consumer purchasing and dealer effectiveness.

Sales promotion, or activities that try to make other sales efforts (such as advertising) more effective, includes consumer promotions, trade promotions, and sales force promotions. *Consumer promotions* use coupons, discounts, contests, trading stamps, samples, rebates, and so forth. Rebates appeal to many manufacturers because few consumers actually redeem them, but they can also provide a competitive edge for retailers.

Real-World Example 9.8

For example, Office Max, an office superstore chain based in Cleveland, handles rebate submissions for customers as an added service. This attracts customers to both the product and the retailer.[11]

Trade promotions include advertising specialties, free goods, buying allowances, merchandise allowances, cooperative advertising, and free items given as premiums. *Sales force promotions* consist of benefits such as contests, bonuses, extra commissions, and sales rallies that encourage salespeople to increase their selling effectiveness.

There are many examples of such promotions. Retailers usually promote the opening of their business. A premium (or bonus item) may be given with the purchase of a product. During out-of-season periods, coupons offering a discount may be given to stimulate sales by attracting new customers. Holidays, store remodeling or expansion, store anniversaries, special purchases, fashion shows, or the presence in the store of a celebrity are other events suitable for promotions.

Trade show (trade fair) is an exhibition of products or services by companies in the same industry.

A **trade show** is a venue for your company to showcase goods or services to your target market. A fee for participating is paid for by the use of booth space. Usually vendors provide samples or demonstrations for the visitors. Exhibitors should plan well in advance and heed these six tips:

- Be sure to choose the appropriate trade show.
- Use teaser gifts to draw crowds.
- Pay attention to signage.
- Confer frequently with your staff and stay flexible.
- Follow-up on leads.
- Track sales resulting from your exhibit to see if it was all worth it.

Information regarding trade shows can be found at www.ceir.org and www.tsea.org.[12]

Real-World Example 9.9

In the 1800s William Wrigley, Jr., left Philadelphia for Chicago to sell soap. He offered baking soda to customers as an incentive to buy soap. Then he tried giving away chewing gum to get people to buy baking soda. Because gum sold best, he concentrated on selling it. When Wrigley first offered Spearmint in 1893, his marketing message was: "Tell'em quick and tell'em often." As a promotional gimmick, he sent a stick of gum to every person listed in the U.S. phone book in 1915.[13] Publicly owned since 1919, the Wm. Wrigley Jr. Company (www.wrigley.com) is still innovating. Wrigley brands are now produced in 19 factories around the world and sold in over 180 countries. Global sales for Wrigley are now up to $30 billion.

Publicity

Publicity is information about a business that is published or broadcast without charge.

Publicity can be considered free advertising. When your product, your business, or you as the owner become newsworthy, publicity may enhance sales. Many local newspapers are interested in publicizing the opening of a new store or business in their area. Take the initiative by sending a well-written publicity release to a news editor for possible use. Also, information about a new product or employees who perform various community services may be interesting to the editor.

Considering Ethnic Differences

There are growing opportunities for small businesses to increase the sales of their products to various ethnic groups, for they are growing much faster than traditional markets.

However, ethnic groups may require special attention in promoting your product. Language differences are an obvious example; more than 19 percent of U.S. families speak a language other than English in their homes. Some areas of the country have an even higher percentage. For example, about four out of 10 households in Los Angeles speak Spanish.[14] On the other hand, you should be careful not to regard all members of an ethnic group as a single target market. Some members of minority groups strive for what they perceive as white middle-income features or standards in material goods, while other sectors in ethnic markets disregard these objectives in favor of their traditional values.

The demographics for ethnic groups may vary, too. The median age of most such groups is much lower than that of whites. Because more minorities are in the earlier stages of the family life cycle, they constitute a better market for certain goods, especially durable goods. Separate marketing strategies may be needed for these ethnically or racially defined markets, as the following example illustrates.

Real-World Example 9.10

Longo Toyota (www.longotoyota.com) in El Monte, California—near Los Angeles—is the world's largest Toyota dealership. It has reached this distinction by blending cultures, races, and languages. The 550 employees represent 21 countries and speak 30 languages and dialects.[15] This culturally attained business is so large it has its own Subway and Starbucks.[16]

Ethnic media often produces better ad response rates from readers, viewers, or listeners who appreciate language specific communications. Here are four tips to help evaluate ethnic media:

1. Focus on media that are vital sources of information.
2. Look beyond circulation to "pass-along" values of print.
3. Look for frequency-of-use affordability.
4. Advertise in media that reach your target audience with little waste.[17]

Opportunities for Small Firms in Global Marketing

The author Heywood Broun stated: "Time and space cannot be discarded. Nor can we ignore the fact that we are citizens of the world." This is so for us as individuals and as small business owners. Think of the products you use every day. Notice how many of them originated outside the United States. Where does your coffee, tea, or cola drink come from? What type of music system do you use? Where was your television set produced? Look at the remote control to your electronic system and see if it was "Assembled in Mexico" or "Made in Malaysia." If you own a personal computer, chances are good that some of its components were designed, manufactured, or assembled in Japan, South Korea, or Taiwan.

Do you get the point? As students, teachers, consumers, and small business people, we're surrounded by the overwhelming evidence of **global marketing,** which involves buying and selling goods or services that are produced, bought, or sold throughout the world. Because of the growing importance of these activities, we estimate that *more than half of you will work in some aspect of international activities during your working life.*

Global marketing has two faces. One is **importing,** which is purchasing and marketing the products of other nations. The other, **exporting,** consists of marketing our products

Global marketing involves products that are produced, bought, sold, or used almost anywhere in the world.

Importing involves purchasing and marketing other nations' products.

Exporting involves marketing our products to other nations.

to other nations. According to the U.S. Department of Commerce in January 2010 both imports and exports were growing. We now explore both of these facets.

Importing by Small Firms

There are essentially two types of small business importers. First, there are those who engage in actual import activities by importing products and selling them to intermediaries or directly to customers. Second—and much more prevalent—are the millions of small retailers and service businesses that sell international products. Both types are interested in imports for a number of reasons.

Reasons for Importing   There are various significant reasons for importing. First, imported goods may be the product the company sells to customers or the raw material for the goods it produces. The small company must decide whether to purchase U.S. products, if available, or to import foreign products. If the items are imported, does the company purchase them from a U.S. wholesaler or from firms outside the country?

Second, companies from other countries are just as interested in selling to U.S. markets as our producers are in selling to international markets. Thus, imported goods may form the main source of revenue—or competition—for a small business in all stages of buying, producing, and/or selling a product.

Third, small business owners capitalize on the fact that some Americans have a preference for foreign goods or services. Goods such as English china, Japanese sports cars, Italian leather goods, Oriental carpets, Russian caviar, and French crystal are eagerly sought by American consumers. Also, small U.S. producers should understand that the increasing flow of new and improved products into the country can improve their output or increase their competitive level.

Some Problems with Importing   The benefits of importing must be weighed against the disadvantages. At present, for example, we see foreign goods flooding U.S. markets at the same time that some of our producers are suffering a lack of customers, or even going out of business.

Exporting by Small Firms

Along with the fascination we have with foreign business, there are many misconceptions concerning it, including the following:

1. *Only large firms can export successfully.* Small size is no barrier to international marketing.

2. *Payment for goods sold to foreign buyers is uncertain.* Not true with today's technology payment can be collected at the time of sale.

3. *Overseas markets represent only limited sales opportunities.* Our world is now a global village and the United States is just a very small part of it.

4. *Foreign consumers will not buy American products.* Although some goods may not travel or translate well, most American products are well received by others—movies, music, and blue jeans to name a few.

5. *Export start-up costs are high.* Not really, try intermediaries to begin.

Some Opportunities and Risks   Many opportunities are available for small firms interested in international or global operations. However, there are also many risks involved, as you can see from Figure 9.2. In general, the *opportunities* are to expand markets, use excess resources, and increase profits from higher rates of return and possible tax advantages.

FIGURE 9.2 |

Some Opportunities
and Risks in
International
Operations

Opportunities and challenges for small firms:

Expansion of markets and product diversification

More effective use of labor force and facilities

Lower labor costs in most countries

Availability, and lower cost, of certain desired natural resources

Potential for higher rates of return on investment

Tax advantages

Strong demand for U.S. goods in many countries

Benefits provided to receiving country, such as needed capital, technology, and/or resources

Problems and risks:

Possibility of loss of assets and of earnings due to nationalization, war, terrorism, and other disturbances

Rapid change in political systems, often by violent overthrow

Fluctuating foreign exchange rates

High potential for loss, or difficulty or impossibility of retrieving earnings from investment

Unfair competition, particularly from state-subsidized firms

Lower skill levels of many workers in underdeveloped countries

Difficulties in communication and coordination with the home office

Attitudinal, cultural, and language barriers, which may lead to cultural differences and/or misunderstandings

The *risks* overseas derive from the difficulty of getting earnings out of many countries and the changing political, economic, and cultural conditions there. Among other problems encountered in global operations is the temptation of entrepreneurs to enter international markets because they see ". . . dollar-dominated opportunities." However, when dealing with currency exchanges, fast and radical fluctuations are a constant possibility.

Also, cultural risks and pitfalls do abound. International business etiquette in the context of potential intercultural misunderstandings must be considered. Many books and journal articles warn Americans of the dire consequences of ambiguous or improper gestures, language, dress, gift giving, and business operations.

Another risk, which is beyond the control of the entrepreneur, is economic fluctuation. Exports largely depend on the ability of importers to sell products to local customers, using local currency. But when the importing company's economy "crashes," U.S. exporters must reduce their exports or find other markets.

Next, there is a growing problem with copyright and patent violations. This trend is particularly rampant in the electronics and music fields.

Finally, there are language and cultural problems. For example, when Chevrolet introduced the new auto "Nova" into Spanish speaking countries, sales were very slow. It was soon realized that the Spanish words "no" and "va" meant "no go."

Deciding Whether or Not to Export   If you expect to export, you must be willing to commit the resources necessary to make the effort profitable. Thus, you should make sure you (1) have a product suitable for export, (2) can reliably fill the needs of foreign countries while still satisfying domestic demand, (3) can offer foreign buyers competitive prices and satisfactory credit terms, and (4) are willing to devote the time and skills needed to make export activities a significant part of your business.

The U.S. Department of Commerce (www.doc.gov) is a good source for identifying countries that have been predicted to be the best partners for potential trading with the

United States. The best selections are countries that are trying to attract trading partners by rebuilding infrastructure and privatizing selected industries. These efforts enhance the countries' attractiveness for small businesses seeking international targets.

Help with Exporting Is Available Despite the barriers facing small firms, help with exporting is available from many sources. This help takes two forms: (1) providing information and guidance and (2) providing financial assistance. The latter is particularly important to small firms.

Both government and private groups provide practically unlimited information and guidance, including technical expertise. Ten different government agencies and some 63 Small Business Development Centers (see Chapter 4) funded by the SBA (www.sbaonline.sba.gov), offer export counseling. An SBA pamphlet, *Market Overseas with U.S. Government Help,* provides excellent information on overseas marketing. Other SBA help comes from members of SCORE (www.score.org) who have many years of practical experience in international trade. Small business institutes also provide export counseling and assistance.

Finally, the U.S. Department of Commerce offers assistance through its Trade Information Center and its Global Export Market Information Service. The department's computerized market data system has information on nearly 200 nations, and the department has contacts in around 75 countries.[18]

Small companies needing export-related electronic data processing services can get help from the Commerce Department's Census Bureau. You can obtain financial assistance for your export program from the Foreign Credit Insurance Association (FCIA) and the Export-Import Bank of the United States (www.exim.gov).

Distribution

Because of its many cost-saving potentials, distribution should be important to small companies. **Distribution** includes the whole range of activities concerned with the effective movement of a product from the production line into the hands of the final customer. To perform the complex operation of distribution effectively, you must make decisions in such important areas as protective packaging, materials handling, inventory control, storing, transportation (internally and externally), order processing, and various aspects of customer service. Because of space limitations we will discuss only storing, order processing, and transportation.

Distribution involves the effective physical movement of a product from the production line to the final consumer.

Storing

Until sold or used, goods must be stored by manufacturers, wholesalers, and retailers. While some small manufacturers and wholesalers have their own private warehouses, more of them use public warehouses, which are independently owned facilities that often specialize in handling certain products, such as furniture or refrigerated products. Public warehouses are particularly useful to small firms wanting to place goods close to customers for quick delivery, since the firms then avoid investing in new facilities.

Order Processing

Effective order processing improves customer satisfaction by reducing slow shipment and incorrectly or incompletely filled orders. Order processing begins the moment a customer places an order with a salesperson. The order goes to the office, often on a standardized order form. After the order is filled, the goods are sent to the customer.

Transportation

Transportation modes are the methods used to transfer products from place to place.

Transportation involves the physical movement of a product from the seller to the purchaser. Because transportation costs are the largest item in distribution, there are many opportunities for savings and improved efficiency. The two most important aspects in terms of cost savings are choosing the transportation mode to be used and understanding delivery terms. **Transportation modes** are the methods used to take products from one place to another. A small producer has many choices of ways to move goods to and from its plant and/or warehouse, and each mode has advantages and disadvantages. Which mode you choose to use will depend on questions of speed, frequency, and dependability required, points served, capability (capacity, flexibility, and adaptability) to handle the particular product, and cost. Whether containers are used affects the choice of transportation system. Shipping can be an extremely burdensome task for small businesses, particularly if it is not a big part of operations. There are two ways to deal with this: do it yourself or outsource to someone else. The following example of outsourcing is an easy way to deal with your shipping problems.

Real-World Example 9.11

The UPS Store (www.theupsstore.com) now handles all of the transportation issues that most small businesses encounter. They provide services such as printing, copying and duplicating, and shipping. Shipping services include United Parcel Service, U.S. Postal Service, custom packing, mailing, and pickup and delivery to and from you. Each UPS Store is independently owned and operated by licensed franchisees of Mail Boxes Etc. Inc., an indirect subsidiary of United Parcel Service Inc.[19]

Railroads, trucks, pipelines, and waterways are popular means of transporting bulky and heavy materials. Although the modes of transportation for heavy materials are changing, these still tend to be the primary systems used by producers.

Railroads continue to be important movers of goods, carrying around 17 percent of all tonnage moved each year. Their primary advantage is the capacity to carry large volumes of goods, fairly quickly, at a low cost. The main disadvantage is that they operate only on fixed routes, often on fixed schedules.

Trucks play an important role in shipping because of their flexibility and because of improved highway systems. Trucks carry about 71 percent of all tonnage. However, changing traffic configurations and government rules and regulations may affect the efficiency of truck use, as the following example suggests.

Real-World Example 9.12

A Nebraska feed-and-seed store owner spent much time, money, and effort to get his city to rescind a recent ordinance prohibiting tractor-trailers from unloading in front of his store. The extra cost of unloading on the edge of town and transporting sacks of feed and seed to the store would have forced him out of business.

Oil pipelines carry about 6 percent of all tonnage moved; waterways carry 6 percent. The use of air transport is increasing, particularly for products that must be delivered in a hurry, as well as for products with a high unit value and low weight and bulk. In such cases, a site for the firm near an airport should be considered if the costs are not too high.

Intermodal shipping is the use of a combination of truck, rail, or ship to transport goods.

The shipment of freight by a combination of truck, rail, or ship—called **intermodal shipping**—is now used extensively by small firms. One percent of all transport is intermodal. Many companies use a combination of trucks and air to expedite service. For example, Gateway (www.gateway.com) and many other mail-order computer vendors work with Federal Express (www.fedex.com). UPS (www.ups.com) is used by many small businesses. These carriers use a system of airplanes and trucks.

Some "products" can be delivered in ways that might not immediately spring to mind in a discussion of modes of transportation. The Internet has revolutionized the sale and distribution of digital products; think about Kindle and nook. Most downloadable software is free—Microsoft's Internet Explorer and updates and "patches" to other applications are good examples—but many software vendors have their products for sale in downloadable form. Data transmission (whether of products or of sensitive business documents) has offered a new niche market.

There are sites that will compare shipping costs for you. www.iship.com and www.intershipper.com gather your information, such as size, weight, and location, and then calculate the least expensive way to ship your product.[20]

Choosing a Distribution Channel

One of the first things a small business producer of goods or services must do to promote sales of its product is to choose a distribution channel. A **distribution channel** consists of the various marketing organizations involved in moving the flow of goods and services from producer to user. The distribution channel acts as the pipeline through which a product flows. While the choice of distribution channels is quite important, it is not a simple one because of the many variables involved. Also, the channels for distributing consumer and industrial goods differ.

A **distribution channel** consists of the marketing organizations responsible for the flow of goods and services from the producer to the consumer.

"ANYWHERE OUT OF CELL PHONE RANGE."

(Source: © 2005 Reprinted courtesy of Bunny Hoest and PARADE Magazine.)

Factors to Consider in Choosing a Distribution Channel

Small business producers should design their own distribution channels, if feasible, to attain the optimum income from their good or service. In doing so, they need to seek a *balance between maintaining control over the flow of the product and minimizing the cost involved.* The primary factors to consider include the following:

- Geographical markets and consumer types arranged in order of importance.
- Whether the product will be distributed through many outlets, selected outlets, or exclusive distributors.
- Kind and amount of marketing effort the producer intends to exert.
- Need for receiving feedback about the product.
- Adequate incentives to motivate resellers.

New products commonly require distribution channels different from those used for well-established and widely accepted products. Thus, you may introduce a new product using one channel and then switch to another if the product does not sell well. Also, a new channel may be required if you seek new markets for your products.

Finally, multiple distribution channels can create conflicts, and distribution can be hampered unless these conflicts are resolved. Producers should anticipate and provide for this problem. Choosing the right channel also permits a difference in pricing.

Real-World Example 9.13

For example, Hill's Science Diet dog and cat foods are so expensive that they could never compete with other pet foods in grocery stores, so they are sold in pet stores and by veterinarians to people who are evidently willing, on the vet's recommendation, to pay the premium price.

Distribution Channels for Consumer Goods

Figure 9.3 shows the traditional channels for distributing consumer goods. As you can see, a small business has essentially two choices: (1) sell directly to the consumer or (2) sell through one or more intermediaries. This decision is usually made (at least initially) when choosing what type of business to enter. The first channel (direct from producer to consumer) is the most frequently used by small firms, probably because it is the simplest.

FIGURE 9.3 |
Distribution Channels
for Consumer Goods

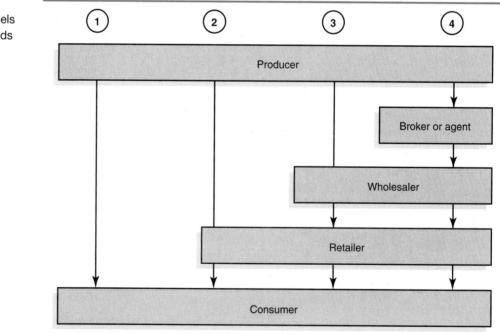

FIGURE 9.4 |
Distribution Channels
for Industrial Goods

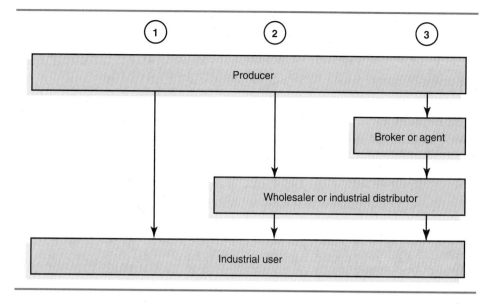

As discussed in Chapter 8, small firms performing services and selling goods at retail usually deal directly with consumers. Most of our discussion in this chapter will concentrate on the remaining channels, which use intermediaries.

Real-World Example 9.14

Louisiana strawberries are an interesting example of using channel 4 depicted in Figure 9.4. Because strawberries are so perishable, they must be sold quickly. So they are picked, placed in refrigerated railroad cars, and shipped before they are sold. As they travel north, agents or brokers contact wholesalers in cities along the line to Chicago. As the berries are sold, the cars carrying them are diverted to the appropriate city, where the wholesaler picks them up and sells them through the remainder of the channel.*

Distribution Channels for Industrial Goods

Distribution channels for industrial goods are shown in Figure 9.4. Channel 1 (direct from producer to industrial user) is the most frequently used. In general, items produced in large quantities, but sold in relatively small amounts, move through channel 2. Large, bulky items that have relatively few buyers, or whose demand varies, flow through channel 3.

---

*Sometimes they are not sold by the time they reach Chicago, the train's destination, and must be sold at distressed prices or allowed to rot. Then the farmers not only lose the value of their crop but must pay transportation costs as well.

Selling through Intermediaries

Intermediaries are those units or institutions in the channel of distribution that either take title to or negotiate the sale of the product. The usual intermediaries are (1) brokers, (2) agents, (3) wholesalers, and (4) retailers.

Brokers

A **broker,** for a fee, brings the buyer and seller together to negotiate purchases or sales but does not take title to, or possession of, the goods. The broker has only limited authority to set prices and terms of sale. Firms using brokers usually buy and/or sell highly specialized goods and seasonal products not requiring constant distribution, such as strawberries or crude oil. Canned goods, frozen-food items, petroleum products, and household specialty products are also often distributed through brokers.

Agents

Because brokers operate on a one-time basis to bring buyers and sellers together, a small business that wants a more permanent distribution channel may use an agent to perform the marketing function. These **agents,** who market a product to others for a fee, are variously called *manufacturers' agents, selling agents,* or *sales representatives (reps),* depending on the industry.

Wholesalers

Wholesalers take actual physical possession of goods and then market them to retailers, other channel members, or industrial users. They maintain a sales force and provide services such as storage, delivery, credit to the buyer, product servicing, and sales promotion.

Retailers

Retailers sell goods and services directly to ultimate consumers. They may sell through store outlets, by mail order, or by means of home sales. Included in this category are services rendered in the home, such as installing draperies and repairing appliances.

Services Performed by Retailers   Retailers must essentially determine and satisfy consumer needs. They deal with many customers, each making relatively small purchases. Some major decisions of retailers are what goods and services to offer to customers, what quality of goods and services to provide, whom to buy from and sell to, what type of promotion to use and how much, what price to charge, and what credit policy to follow.

Current Trends in Retailing   The more traditional retail outlets are department stores, mass-merchandising shopping chains, specialty stores, discount stores, factory outlets, supermarkets, and mail-order selling.

A newer version of the discount house is **off-price retailers,** such as T. J. Maxx and Hit or Miss. They buy designer labels and well-known brands of clothing at less than wholesale prices and pass the savings along to the customers, using mass-merchandising techniques and providing reduced services.

Another recent development is self-service fast-food restaurants. Many of these are now following the gasoline companies' move to cheap, self-help "refueling stops."

Even supermarkets now use this approach. First came self-service, with the customers selecting their own items, taking them to the checkout counter, and paying the

---

Intermediaries are those units or institutions in the channel of distribution that either take title to or negotiate the sale of the product.

Brokers bring buyers and sellers of goods together to negotiate purchases or sales.

Agents are marketing intermediaries who market a product to others for a fee.

Wholesalers are intermediaries who take title to the goods handled and then sell them to retailers or other intermediaries.

Retailers sell goods or services directly to the ultimate consumers.

Off-price retailers are those who buy designer labels and well-known brands of clothing at low prices and sell them at less than typical retail prices.

"THEY'RE CRICKETS, NOT BEEPERS."

(Source: © 2005 Reprinted courtesy of Bunny Hoest and PARADE Magazine.)

checker-cashier. Now customers in some stores can select, ring up, and pay for their groceries using handheld scanners.

Another innovation is similar to automated teller machines (ATMs), namely, computerized video kiosks in shopping malls that replace salespersons. Many retailers are now installing these devices, which utilize existing technologies, such as computer science, video display, laser disks, voice recognition, and sophisticated graphics.

Another emerging marketing channel is the Internet (discussed earlier in the chapter). People are now using it to swap items and information. And some people are using it to sell information, products, and services.

Selling with Your Own Sales Force

Selling expertise is needed in all business activities. While advertising may entice customers to desire a product, it alone is not usually sufficient to complete a sale. Customers appreciate good selling and dislike poor service. They believe salespeople should show an interest in them and assist them in their buying. Often, when competing businesses carry the same merchandise, the caliber of the salespeople is the principal reason one outsells the other. The following letter, which came from a homemaker in the Washington, D.C., area, illustrates this point.

Real-World Example 9.15

I went to the cosmetic counter at Lord & Taylor (www.lordandtaylor.com), intending to get one or—at the most—two items. Instead, the Estée Lauder area sales rep who was there gave me such an overwhelming sales pitch that I ended up buying a horrifying amount of stuff. In addition, they signed me up for the free workshop next week, where they will make me over to show what I should be wearing. After trying *three* Lauder counters in *three* different stores *with no satisfaction,* it was nice to have someone take *a personal interest in me.*[21]

Need for Personal Selling

In self-service operations, the burden of selling merchandise is placed on the producer's packaging and the retailer's display of the merchandise. Some retailers have found that 80 percent of the shoppers who made unplanned purchases bought products because they saw them effectively displayed. Self-service reduces retail costs by having smaller sales salaries and more effective use of store space. However, risks from pilferage and breakage increase.

Some items are packaged differently for self-service. For example, where film is kept behind the counter, the boxes are stacked in bins; but for self-service, the box has a large extra flap with a hole, permitting it to hang on an arm, which increases its visibility and also cuts down on shoplifting. Similarly, the same pens that stand en masse in a bin display in a small office supplies store are packaged in hanging blister packs in drug, grocery, and variety stores.

A quiet revolution is sweeping department store retailing in an effort to counter such factors as apathy, lack of training, and lack of initiative, which have kept salespeople's productivity (and pay) low. Now many retailers are using straight commission, rather than salary or salary plus commission, to pay their salespeople. They hope that the promise of potentially higher pay will motivate existing staff and attract better salespeople (and encourage them to train and develop themselves to be better producers). It seems to be working, as the following example shows.

Real-World Example 9.16

John L. Palmerio, a veteran salesman in the men's shoe department at the Manhattan Bloomingdale's store (www.bloomingdales.com), increased his earnings by 25 percent after switching from a straight hourly scale to a 10 percent commission on sales. Similar experiences are being reported at other stores, including the Burdines chain in Florida.[22]

The largest promotional expenditure for small businesses is almost always for personal selling. Effective sales personnel are especially important to small businesses, which have difficulty competing with large ones in such areas as variety, price, and promotion. Personal selling is one activity where small firms, particularly retailers, can compete with larger competitors—and win! But effective selling does not just happen. Rather, small business managers must work hard to attain a high level of sales effectiveness.

Steps in the Creative Selling Process

The creative selling process, as shown in Figure 9.5, may be divided into eight steps. You should inform your people that these steps are needed for effective selling—therefore, they should know the steps and use them.

Preparation   Before any customer contact is made, the salesperson should know the company's policies, procedures, and rules; how to operate equipment, such as the cash register; and a great deal about the product, including how and when to use it, its features in comparison with those of other models or brands, and available options (such as color, size, and price).

FIGURE 9.5 |
Steps in the Sales
Process

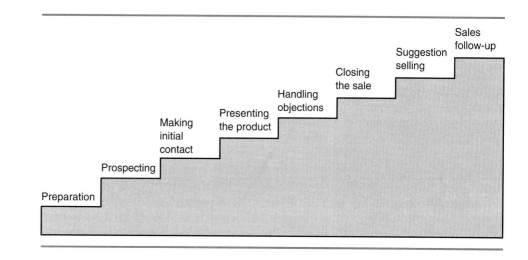

Prospecting is taking
the initiative in seeking
out customers with a new
product.

Prospecting **Prospecting** consists of taking the initiative in dealing with new and regular customers by going to them with a new product or service idea. An example of new customer prospecting is when a salesperson contacts a bride-to-be or new mother and tells her about goods or services that might be appropriate. Regular customer prospecting is effective because a firm's best prospects are its current customers. A salesperson should periodically call regular customers to tell them about products and services, but not so often that they lose the sense of being special, or feel they are being badgered. Prospecting for new customers may require a more creative approach.

Prospecting has become much easier with the introduction of address and phone information databases on CD-ROM. Many small businesses are beginning to use them to find potential customers. They can gain telemarketing and direct-mail opportunities without using—and paying for—directory assistance calls. Telemarketing, however, is now regulated and prospectors must honor the "do not call" list. A fine of $11,000 can be imposed on one errant call. Legal telemarketing does work with a response rate of between 2 and 20 percent, according to the American Teleservices Association. To remain legit, telemarketers should upgrade their technology to keep current of do-not-call lists and look to wider areas that are untouched by regulations.[23]

Making Initial Contact Whenever possible, serving customers should be given top priority. Nothing is more annoying to a customer than waiting while a clerk straightens stock, counts money, finishes a discussion with another clerk, or continues a phone conversation.

In the initial contact with a customer, the salesperson should begin on a positive note. The salesclerk might ask, "May I help you?" The customer replies, "No, thank you. I'm just looking." This common, automatic greeting shows no creativity on the part of the clerk. Instead, salespeople should treat each customer as an individual, reacting differently to each one. Initial contact also includes acknowledging customers when they enter the sales area, even if they cannot be waited on immediately. For example, you could say, "I'll be with you in a moment." When free, you should be sure to say, "Thank you for waiting." These actions will result in fewer customers leaving without being served and produce a higher sales volume.

Presenting the Product   In presenting the product to a customer, you should stress its benefits to the buyer. Get the customer involved in the presentation by demonstrating several features and then have the customer handle it. At this stage, you should limit the choices the customer has. For example, you could use the "rule of two"—do not show more than two choices at one time. If more than two items are placed before the customer, the chance of a sale lessens, and the possibility of shoplifting increases. For this reason, many stores limit the number of clothing items that may be taken to a dressing room.

"Canned" sales presentations are generally ineffective. You should therefore try to find out how much the customer already knows about the product in order to adapt the presentation to his or her level of expertise. A sale can be lost both by boring the customer with known facts and by using bewildering technical jargon.

Real-World Example 9.17

For example, Jerry Fisher suggests that when you need to capture your prospects' attention, remember: less is more. Your ad or presentation must pass the billboard test and make its point to a set of eyes traveling 60 plus mph. To do this, you can divide your offerings' benefits into a set of three descriptors or icons that will register quickly with prospects.[24]

Handling Objections   Objections are a natural part of the selling process. Thus, if the customer presents objections, you should recognize that as a sign of progress, because a customer who does not plan to buy will seldom seek more information in this way. In many cases, an objection opens the way for you to do more selling. For example, if the customer says a dress looks out of date, you could answer, "Yes, it does look old-fashioned, but that style is back in fashion." This is more diplomatic than a flat contradiction, such as, "That dress was first shown at the market this season. It's the latest thing."

Closing the Sale   Some closing techniques you can use to help the customer make the buying decision are offering a service ("May we deliver it to you this afternoon?"), giving a choice ("Do you want the five-piece or the eight-piece cooking set?"), or offering an incentive ("If you buy now, you get 10 percent off the already low price.").

Suggestion Selling   You should make a definite suggestion for a possible additional sale. Statements such as "Will that be all?" or "Can I get you anything else?" are not positive suggestions. When a customer buys fabric, you should offer matching thread, buttons, and the appropriate interfacing. A supply of bags is a natural suggestion to a vacuum cleaner buyer. And customers' attention should always be drawn to other items in the product line. Many customers like to receive valid suggestions that keep them from having to come back later for needed accessories.

Sales Follow-Up   Follow-up should be a part of every sale. The close, "Thank you for shopping with us," is a form of sales follow-up if said with enthusiasm and sincerity. Follow-up may also consist of checking on anything that was promised the customer after

FIGURE 9.6 |
How to Lose a Sale

1. *Speak more than your potential client*. If you do all the talking, you won't be able to ascertain the needs of the buyer. The most successful sales reps spend 70 to 80 percent of the time listening.

2. *Wing it*. Don't call without first finding out as much as you can about your potential customer. Research the company's size, history, products, and challenges using *Hoover's Handbook, Dun & Bradstreet, Value Line*, or other such resources, which can be found at the library.

3. *Forget to ask questions*. Most people drift off after five or six minutes of a presentation, so be sure to interject questions to keep clients alert and involved. Focus on your buyer's criteria by asking, "What does the next vendor need to do to earn your business?" "What is your business's biggest challenge?" "What differentiates your company from your competition?"

4. *Rely on your memory*. You can't afford to miss important points, and nobody's memory is perfect. Ask the customer if it's okay to take notes, and use key points the customer made in a follow-up letter after the sales call. Start it with, "Just to make sure we're on the right track, the following is a list of your key needs . . ."

5. *Go off on tangents*. Instead of expounding on every passing thought, stay focused to make a strong case. Before you start your presentation, give your customers an overview of what you'll be telling them, and highlight key points at the end. Don't forget to follow up.

the sale. If delivery is scheduled for a given day or time, you could check to make sure the promise is met and, if not, notify the customer of the problem.

Attributes of a Creative Salesperson

Many efforts have been made to identify and isolate those personal characteristics that can predict a knack for selling. So far, however, evidence indicates there is no perfect way to determine who will be successful, for salespeople just do not fit a neat pattern.[25] Still, there are some mental and physical attributes that seem to make some people more effective than others at selling. Barry J. Farber, author of the book *State of the Art Selling*[26] and an audio training program of the same name,[27] emphasizes the attributes of a good salesperson by telling salespeople what *not* to do. Figure 9.6 provides his advice.

Mental Attributes   Judgment—often called common sense, maturity, or intelligence—is essential for effective selling. For example, good salespeople do not argue with customers, nor do they criticize the business in front of customers. Tact is also needed. Good salespeople have a positive attitude toward customers, products, services, and the firm. Occasionally your salespeople may feel inadequate to handle the sale to the consumer. When that happens, Barry Farber claims that there are three ways to get ready to deal with the issues:

1. Look to the history books for those who overcame great odds to be successful.
2. Learn to fall the right way and do not make the same mistake twice. Try again!
3. Don't be afraid to try something new. Insights are only as good as the level of implementation. Don't give up![28]

Physical Attributes   As Figure 9.7 indicates, personal appearance is important for success. For example, a slim salesperson would be more appropriate than a larger person for a

FIGURE 9.7 |
First Impressions

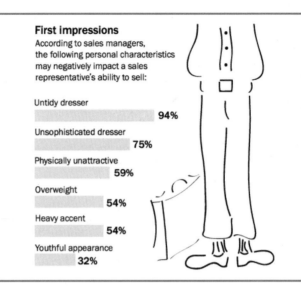

First impressions

According to sales managers, the following personal characteristics may negatively impact a sales representative's ability to sell:

Untidy dresser
94%

Unsophisticated dresser
75%

Physically unattractive
59%

Overweight
54%

Heavy accent
54%

Youthful appearance
32%

Source: Survey results reported within "Does Image Matter." *Sales and Marketing Management,* March 2001, © 2004 VNU Business Media, Inc. Used with permission.

health spa. Poor personal hygiene may lead to lost business. An observant manager should watch out for hygiene problems among the staff and, when necessary, counsel offending employees in private.

What You Should Have Learned

1. Advertising should be continuous and governed by an advertising budget based on (*a*) a percentage of sales or profits, (*b*) a given amount per unit of desired sales, (*c*) the actual amount required to accomplish the sales objective, or (*d*) an executive decision. Advertising media include newspapers, store signs, direct mail, circulars and handbills, Yellow Pages ads, outdoor signs, radio, television, and the Internet. Infomercials are now extensively used to advertise specialty products.

 Some factors affecting a company's choice of media are target market, cost, and availability. Using an advertising agency to develop and place advertisements may be desirable. The results of advertising should be measured to determine its effectiveness by some form of immediate-response advertising.

2. Ethnic groups in the United States may require special attention in the promotion of goods and services, but you should not lump all members of an ethnic group together into one target market, since many members of new groups adopt the values and tastes of middle America while others cherish the traditional preferences of their culture.

3. The opportunities in global marketing are growing rapidly. All of us—students, teachers, consumers, and members and owners of large and small businesses—are already involved. Millions of small businesses are importing and selling foreign products. While these imports provide many opportunities for some small firms, they may force some others out of business.

 Some opportunities provided by exporting are (*a*) expansion of markets, (*b*) more effective use of resources, particularly personnel, (*c*) potentially higher rates of return on investment, and (*d*) tax advantages. Some problems are (*a*) the difficulty of getting earnings out of the host country, (*b*) political or economic conditions in the form of unfair competition from state-subsidized firms and favorable treatment given to local firms and products, (*c*) unstable political climates, and (*d*) fluctuations in currency exchange rates and in economic conditions in general.

Small firms can become involved in international marketing at one of five levels, namely, (*a*) casual, or accidental, exporting; (*b*) active exporting; (*c*) foreign licensing; (*d*) overseas marketing; and (*e*) foreign production and marketing.

4. Distribution, which is moving the product from the seller to the buyer, includes the vital functions of storing, order processing, and transporting the product.

5. Marketing a product begins with deciding how to get it into the users' hands through a distribution channel. A small business essentially has the choice of selling directly to the customer or selling through intermediaries. In making the choice, you should be guided by the nature of the product, traditional practices in the industry, and the size of the business and of its market.

6. The usual intermediaries are brokers, independent agents, wholesalers, and retailers. A broker receives a commission for sales of merchandise without physically handling the goods. Independent agents, such as selling agents and manufacturers' agents (manufacturers' representatives), also represent clients for a commission, but they may do more actual selling than brokers.

Wholesalers take physical possession of the goods they sell and provide storage, delivery, credit to the buyer, product servicing, and sales promotion. Retailers buy goods from manufacturers or wholesalers and sell them to the ultimate consumer. Retailers determine customer needs and satisfy them with choice of location, goods, promotion, prices, and credit policy. The current trends in retailing are toward more self-service, more automation or computerization, and using TV and the Internet.

7. Personal selling is required at all levels of the marketing process. All sales personnel should know the steps in the creative selling process, namely, preparation, prospecting, making initial contact, presenting the product, handling objections, closing the sale, suggestion selling, and following up on the sale. A creative salesperson should possess judgment, tact, and a good attitude toward customers, products, services, and the firm.

Key Terms

advertising   236
agents   250
brokers   250
distribution   245
distribution channel   247
exporting   242
global marketing   242
immediate-response
   advertising   239

importing   242
infomercials   237
institutional
   advertising   236
intermediaries   250
intermodal shipping   247
merchandising   240
off-price retailers   250
product advertising   236

prospecting   253
publicity   241
retailers   250
sales promotion   240
trade show   241
transportation
   modes   246
wholesalers   250

Questions for Discussion

1. What basic decisions should be made about an advertising program?
2. Describe some opportunities and problems in catering to ethnic differences.
3. Do you believe international marketing is as important as stated? Explain.
4. What are some reasons for importing? What are some problems?
5. List the opportunities available in exporting.
6. Describe some risks and problems involved in exporting.

7. What factors should be considered in choosing a channel of distribution?

8. Describe the traditional channels of distribution for consumer goods.

9. Describe the traditional channels of distribution for industrial goods.

10. Name two types of independent agents. What are the advantages and disadvantages of using them?

11. Describe the eight steps in the creative selling process.

Case 9.1

Taking Your Store to Your Customers

There are several channels that producers can use to get their products to the market. Sometimes these distribution channels may be long and complicated, using several intermediaries between the producer and consumer. However, as Sarah Hammet, owner of Feeling Special Fashions, has shown, it does not have to be that complicated.

Hammet sells clothing specially designed for senior citizens. It is called "adaptive" clothing—dresses and separates for seniors whose mobility and dexterity are restricted. Hammet bypasses the usual intermediaries, such as retail stores, and takes her product directly to the customers. She sells clothing at 50 nursing homes and retirement communities in two states and the District of Columbia.

Four days out of the week, every spring and fall, Hammet and an assistant load half a dozen racks of clothes into the back of a van and hit the road. She conducts fashion shows and offers individual consultations at every facility they visit. This type of personal selling has been effective for Hammet, who thought up the idea in the early 1980s while visiting her elderly father in a Kentucky nursing home. She was appalled by the careless and drab manner in which patients were dressed. Hammet perceived a need and stepped in to fill it.

The clothing she sells is manufactured by Comfort Clothing Inc., which is located in Canada. The items are stylishly designed and come in various colors and prints. The clothing is different in that armholes are bigger, buttons often hide Velcro fastenings, and waists are uncinched and come with optional belts. The garments can be stepped into rather than pulled on over the head. They are washable and cost between $40 and $60. Through a combination of creative merchandising and personal selling, Hammet has established a growing business.

Questions

1. What type of distribution channels does Feeling Special Fashions use?

2. Should Sarah Hammet consider selling through intermediaries, such as retailers? Discuss the advantages and disadvantages.

3. How would you rate Hammet's selling strategy? Recommend ways she could increase sales.

4. Should Feeling Special Fashions advertise? Discuss the advantages and disadvantages.

5. How do you rate Hammet's chances for success? Why?

Case 9.2

Clark Copy International Corporation's China Experience

In the early 1980s, China's powerful State Economic Commission launched a major effort to attract small Western enterprises. It was dissatisfied with large firms that sell expensive consumer items such as VCRs that do little to aid China's economy.

This policy helped Clark Copy International Corporation, a small company making plain-paper copiers in a cramped plant in Melrose Park, Illinois, beat out the industry's world leaders to sign a lucrative contract with China. At that time, it had only 14 employees and had earned only $58,000 on $1.5 million of sales for 1982. Clark agreed to sell 1,000 CMC 2000 copiers assembled and ready to use, as well as to provide parts and instructions for the Chinese to assemble into another 5,000 machines. Also, Clark would train 1,600 Chinese technicians to manufacture the copiers and other Clark products for domestic and export sales in a new plant in Kweilin in the south of China.

How did Clark do it? According to Clark's founder and president, Otto A. Clark, a Slovak who emigrated to the United States in 1950, "You can't do business in China on a simple buy-and-sell basis, like most multinationals do. Instead, you have to establish a close human relationship and a commitment to stay." That relationship was established with the help of David Yao, Clark's Far East representative, who was born in Shanghai and speaks fluent Chinese.

Yao and Clark went to China eight times to negotiate before closing with China's National Bureau of Instrumentation Industries in April 1982. In the mid- to late 1980s, the Chinese attitude toward private enterprise and foreign investments changed, and Clark wasn't permitted to complete the agreement. By 1991, it was out of business.

Questions

1. Evaluate the procedure followed by Otto Clark in his effort to enter global operations.
2. What went wrong? Explain.
3. What—if anything—would you have done differently?

Source: Correspondence with Clark Copy International; the Melrose Park, Illinois, Chamber of Commerce; and others.

Experientials

1. Call your local Chamber of Commerce and inquire about trade shows in your area. Do they require admission? Are they limited to the public? Contact the trade association and inquire about the cost to display, size of display area, and days/hours of operation.
2. Visit a culturally diverse retail store and ask if the manager has a feel for the ethnic mix of patrons that consume the goods or services offered. What is the target market? Are the employees multilingual?

PART 4

How to Organize, Manage, and Operate the Business

Many management texts begin with a statement such as "Management is getting things done through people." And the annual reports of most companies include statements such as "Our people are our most important asset." Both of these statements are correct: Whether the business is large or small, its success or failure depends on having a capable, well-trained, and motivated workforce to operate and manage your physical resources.

In essence, all owners of small businesses are human resource managers. They must decide what work is to be done, determine the type and number of employees needed to do it, recruit and employ those employees, train and develop them, reward them with adequate pay and benefits, and lead and motivate them to perform effectively. The activities to actually operate your business include determining what product to sell, planning, acquiring, configuring, and maintaining your operational facilities.

Chapter 10 looks at the overall problem of managing human resources in small firms while Chapter 11 deals with maintaining relationships with employees and their representatives.

Chapter 12 discusses developing systems, choosing the right location—especially for retails stores and manufacturing plants—planning physical facilities, and improving operations. Chapter 13 examines purchasing and inventory control, as well as planning and controlling operations and quality. ●

CHAPTER 10

How to Obtain and Manage Human Resources and Diversity in Small Companies

Small businesses must make wooing and keeping employees as high a priority as attracting and retaining customers.
    —**John L. Ward,** Loyola University of Chicago

A moment's insight is sometimes worth a life's experience.
    —**Oliver Wendell Holmes**

The key to ... success is superior customer service, continuing internal entrepreneurship, and a deep belief in the dignity, worth, and potential of every person in the organization.
    —**Tom Peters,** coauthor of *In Search of Excellence*

Learning Objectives

After studying the material in this chapter, you should be able to:

1. Explain how small business managers plan human resource needs and develop sources from which to recruit employees.

2. Name some methods used for recruiting human resources, and describe the steps in the employee selection process.

3. Explain the importance of employee development, and discuss some development methods.

4. Tell how selection of managers differs from selection of nonmanagerial employees, and describe some methods of manager development.

5. Discuss the laws that affect recruiting, selection, and development.

6. Describe how to compensate employees with money and employee benefits.

7. List some factors influencing employee health and safety, and tell how to safeguard employees in small firms.

PROFILE

Mary H. Partridge and Michael Levy: Even Small Companies Merge!

Michael Levy and Mary H. Partridge, a married couple in Austin, Texas, operated separate businesses for more than 12 years. He was owner and president of Michael Levy & Associates, consultants in training and organization development; she was owner and president of Impact Consulting, consultants in human resource administration and development.

When they moved to Austin from Houston in 1994, they set a goal of developing a clientele in Austin, a fast-growing, high-tech environment. Having relied on repeat business and word-of-mouth referrals for years, they realized they would have to have a more aggressive marketing plan in the new environment. To maximize the return on advertising and promotional dollars, they decided to focus their efforts on marketing one company—Impact Consulting. So, after 18 years of marriage and more than a decade of operating two separate companies, they decided to "merge."

As they planned the "merger," they asked themselves what they would advise a client to do in a similar situation. Following their own advice, they arranged for their college intern to facilitate a "planning meeting" to define the goals and strategies of the new, consolidated company. In addition, they identified the concerns that each of them had about "merging" and their core competencies. Using that approach, they divided functional responsibilities such as marketing and technology planning.

One benefit of the two companies had been autonomy of operation and their ability to make decisions without delay or consultation with a second decision maker. But many of the services they offered were of equal interest to both Partridge and Levy. The solution they found was to divide clients between themselves in such a way that each client had a designated "Account Executive" who had primary responsibility for all decisions, planning, coordination, and account management.

Much of their time is spent on executive coaching and 360-degree feedback. The latter involves individual consultations with managers to help them improve their management approach, communication abilities, and leadership style.

Practicing what they preach, the two consultants avoid hiring staff and incurring burdensome overhead. Instead, they use a network of familiar independent contractors, as needed, to supplement the owners' efforts. Levy and Partridge have developed workable relationships with their own personnel—each other and hired freelancers—and are able to translate their knowledge and experience to benefit the companies they serve.

By 1999, they had established a strong client base in Austin and a comfortable, successful partnership in business, which reflected and enriched their partnership in life.

Source: Author's correspondence and discussions with Mary H. Partridge and Michael Levy.

The Profile emphasizes the importance of managing human resources in a small firm. You must have a sufficient supply of adequately trained and motivated employees if you are to succeed as the owner or manager of a small business. In the late 1800s, a young entrepreneur, Andrew Carnegie, expressed this thought when he said, "Take away all our factories, our trade, our avenues of transportation, and our money, but leave our organization, and in four years, I will have reestablished myself." In other words, while physical and financial resources are *important* to any business, large or small, *human resources are vital.*[1] While larger firms have professional human resource managers to perform these activities, owners of small businesses must do it themselves—in addition to their many other duties. The trend continues that small companies create the most jobs. In the United States, 5.8 million small employers have nearly half of all workers.[2]

Being able to identify and hire good employees can mean the difference between having a successful and an unsuccessful business. This basic management function of **staffing** involves (1) planning for, (2) recruiting, (3) selecting, and (4) training and developing employees, as well as compensating them and providing for their health and safety. That is what is discussed in this chapter.

Planning for Human Resource Needs

You cannot wait until you need a new employee to think about your human resource needs. Like larger competitors, small businesses must (1) determine which human resources are needed and (2) develop sources from which to recruit future employees, especially people from diverse ethnic groups.

Small businesses find it difficult to plan for human resource needs, since many are facing absolute labor shortages because of the declining workforce. To a large extent, this shortage has been brought on by the aging of the U.S. population. According to the U.S. Bureau of the Census (www.census.gov), the average age of Americans is expected to rise to over 37 by the year 2020.

The shortage of skilled workers has created a paradox for many small employers. Thousands of prospective employees are being rejected because of inadequate skills. This trend leaves many unhappy employers (because jobs remain unfilled), not to mention frustrated job seekers. A 2007 survey of nearly 37,000 employers in 27 countries worldwide indicated that 41 percent were having problems filling skilled positions. The 2,407 respondents in the U.S. also had a 41 percent talent void. Australia and Japan reported 61 percent while Mexico reported 82 percent.[3]

To meet this declining supply of potential employees, many small businesses are changing the way they operate. They are spending more on technology, using new methods to attract more applicants, making their workplaces more attractive, and using employee benefits and other incentives to retain valued employees. Finally, small companies are also stepping up automation and even subcontracting out part of their work to reduce the number of employees needed.

Determining Types of Employees Needed

When business owners want to construct a building, they obtain a set of blueprints and specifications. When they buy merchandise, materials, and supplies, they develop specifications for those items. In the same way, even the smallest businesses should have some type of **job specifications,** which are statements of the mental, physical, and other qualifications required of a person to do the job. Drawing up job specifications begins with a **job description,** which is a list of the job's duties, responsibilities, and working conditions, as well as relationships between it and other jobs in the organization. When

---

Staffing involves planning for, recruiting, selecting, and training and developing employees, as well as compensating them and providing for their health and safety.

Job specifications are detailed written statements of work assignments and the qualifications needed to do the job acceptably.

A **Job description** lists the duties and responsibilities of a given job.

FIGURE 10.1 |

Components of a Simplified Job Description and Job Specification

---

- *Identification of job:* Job title, department, code, salary range, supervisor, etc.
- *Job description:*
  a. Physical demands of the job and the minimum physical requirements needed to fill it.
  b. Working conditions, including psychological conditions such as relationships with others and responsibilities for other people, money, and equipment.
  c. Summary of the duties and responsibilities of the job.
  d. Days and hours of work.
  e. Machines, tools, formulas, and equipment used.
- *Job specifications:*
  a. Educational background and knowledge, skills and techniques, and training and experience required to perform the job, as well as special training and development needed.
  b. Personal characteristics such as sociability, articulateness, or aggressiveness.

---

the personal qualities, education, training, and experience needed to perform the job are added, the result is a set of job specifications that forms the basis for recruiting and selecting new employees, as shown in Figure 10.1.

Just a word of caution: *Job descriptions should be flexible in very small firms to give the owner more freedom in assigning work to available employees, whether the work fits their job description or not.*

Do not ask for more than is needed to do the job properly! Ask yourself, "Is a college education really needed, or can a high school graduate do the job?" Or again, "Are three years' experience required, or can an inexperienced person be trained to do the work?" "If an inexperienced person can be trained, is there someone to do the training?" Increasing education and experience levels raises the starting pay expected, and you may actually be better off training someone to do things your own way.

It is interesting to note that 82 percent of job seekers are willing to change industries, while 66 percent will accept a low salary, and 65 percent will accept a lesser job title. Only 34 percent are willing to relocate.[4]

Developing Sources from Which to Recruit Potential Employees

As with purchasing supplies for building and running the business, you need sources from which to seek new workers. Some of these sources are shown in Figure 10.2. Not all of them will be appropriate for all small businesses.

"Welcome aboard. You're just what we're looking for—not too bright, no ambition, and content to stay on the bottom of the ladder and not louse things up!"

(Source: Cartoon courtesy of J. Nebesky.)

Internal Sources   Filling job openings with present employees rather than going outside the business makes good sense. This method raises morale and improves employees' motivation, since they know they can move up in your firm. It also saves time, effort, and money, since outside recruiting is time-consuming and costly.

Filling jobs from within is also effective because the worker's performance has been observed and evaluated. Further, this method leads to stability. Employees can be upgraded, transferred, or promoted to fill job openings.

FIGURE 10.2 | Where to Find Needed Employees

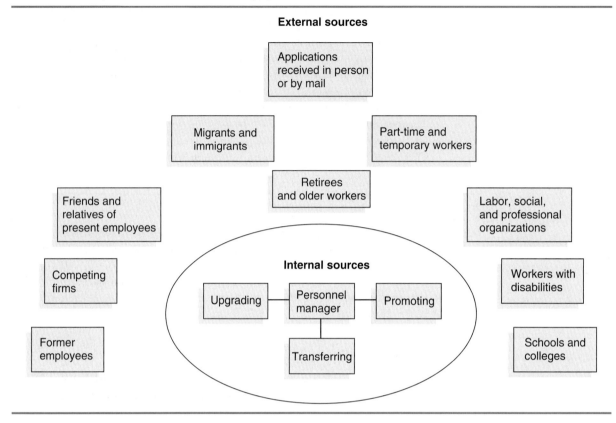

Upgrading occurs when an employee who is presently not capable of doing a job that has become more difficult receives training to enable him or her to do the work successfully.

Transferring is moving an employee from one location or department to another, without necessarily changing job title or pay. **Promoting** is moving a person to a higher position, frequently with increased responsibilities, greater status or prestige, a new title, and a higher salary. If the company is family owned, the owners' children can be "promoted" as they become capable of assuming more responsibility.

External Sources   You may need to use external sources as the business grows, especially to fill lower-level jobs. External sources may also be used to provide new ideas and perspectives and to obtain needed skills when necessary, especially for scientific, technical, and professional positions.

Many small firms keep a list of *former employees* as a potential source of trained workers. If a worker left voluntarily and for good reason, is in good standing, and seeks reemployment, rehiring may be a good idea.

Upgrading involves retraining workers so they can do increasingly complex work.

Transferring is moving an employee from one job to another, without necessarily changing title or pay.

Promoting is moving an employee to a higher position, usually with increased responsibilities, title, and pay.

Real-World Example 10.1

Diane Allen worked for an art supply store. When her husband started teaching at a college 40 miles away, she resigned. Later, when the store moved to a new location and its business increased, Diane was asked to come back, and she agreed.

As will be shown later, *friends and relatives* of present employees may also be a good source of dependable people. But remember, if a friend or relative is hired but does not work out and must be terminated, you have lost a friend as well as an employee.

You should make it a habit to keep *applications that come in either through the mail or in person*. Also, in some areas (especially in shopping centers), workers change jobs frequently, so attracting workers from *other businesses*—even competitors—is another good source.

Managers and technical and professional personnel may be found in various *social and professional organizations*. Also, *schools and colleges* can be a good source for skilled personnel and part-time employees.

With the unprecedented increase in corporate consolidations, downsizing, and outsourcing, there is a large pool of *retirees and older workers* now available. The mandatory retirement age has been outlawed, and a shift toward more favorable retirement programs now rewards workers who stay in the workforce longer. The number of workers over age 55 who were planning to reenter the workforce in 2009 was about 1.5 million.[5] This number was five times that of 2005. One survey indicated that 16 percent of all retirees will return to the workforce[6] providing small firms with the opportunity to hire experienced workers who are well seasoned and ready to return to work. These workers generally are working because they want to work, and they make loyal employees.

Real-World Example 10.2

John Kerr, age 65, moved from a 40-year career in fundraising for a public radio station in Boston to working as a summertime park ranger in Yellowstone Park.[7]

Part-time and temporary workers (temps), who provide scheduling flexibility, as well as a way of reducing hiring (and benefit) costs, will become even more important in the future. No longer is part-time employment only for students seeking summer jobs or homemakers supplementing the family income. Instead, recent college grads, retirees, corporate dropouts (or those pushed out), and others are taking temporary jobs. There are over 37 million people in the workforce that work less than 35 hours per week. More than 28 million are doing so for noneconomic reasons. The average hours worked by part-time employees was 23 in 2009.[8] Small business owners must be able to clearly define the job and be able to deal with temporary-staffing agencies before going this route. Using temporary help is like dating, you try each other out before making a commitment. However, you must remember that temporary workers are best for temporary assignments. If the job is expected to last more than a few months, you are better off with part- or full-time employees. Justify this by hiring on a probationary time period.[9]

Leased manpower
refers to employees obtained from an outside firm that specializes in performing a particular service.

Leased manpower is another source of part-time employees. These workers may work full time for the leasing firm and only part time for the small employer. This is an especially useful source of employees for clerical, maintenance, janitorial, and food service tasks. It permits greater flexibility to cut back on staff when business is slack. This group is also fast becoming a permanent part of the American workforce.

Economic conditions have reshaped our workforce in recent years, establishing a smaller "core" of permanent employees surrounded by a flexible border of temporary and part-time workers.

Recruiting and Selecting Employees

Once the number, types, and sources of employees needed are known, the small business manager starts looking for the people. Do not limit applications to people who drop in and ask for a job; instead, *go out and recruit them!*

No matter what you cover in a standard interview, you must remember that it is not until the employee is actually doing the job that his or her talents are revealed. You need a "good fit." Try a few of these tips at the recruiting stage to help:

1. Ask your current employees and offer a finding fee for leads to new hires.
2. Search for seniors—people over 55 have proven to be very dependable employees.
3. Consider internships—most universities can help here.
4. Try local church bulletins—this is excellent for part-time help.
5. Ask the right questions—be specific about job-related talents.[10]

Methods of Recruiting Employees

Recruitment is reaching out to attract applicants from which to choose one to fill a job vacancy.

Recruitment, as shown in Figure 10.3, is reaching out to attract a supply of potential employees. It is generally done by advertising but may also be accomplished using

FIGURE 10.3 |
Methods Used to
Recruit Employees

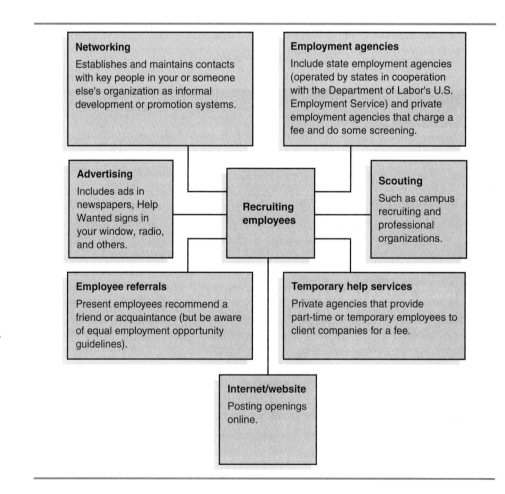

Networking is the process of establishing and maintaining contacts with key persons in one's own or another organization as informal development or promotion systems.

employee referrals, temporary help services, **networking,** state and private employment agencies, and scouting: One study found that while "networking" was the fastest-growing method used, Help Wanted ads were the most frequently used. Employee referrals were second, followed by temporary help services, networking, and employment firms.

Another rapidly growing recruitment vehicle is the Internet. An employer's job announcement on the Net can gain "an instant audience that can run into the thousands."[11] Some company websites even match job openings with the qualifications of candidates who have previously visited the company's site and notify them by e-mail of the opportunities. Using a website can considerably speed up the recruitment process.

Real-World Example 10.3

There are several online testing companies that help in the recruiting process so that the prospective employees can be evaluated before a lengthy and expensive selection procedure. True Star Solutions specializes in recruiting on the Web. Profiles International offers a psychometric profile that looks for competitiveness, persistence, self-reliance, and energy. This 75-question profile is given over the Internet, takes 15 to 20 minutes, and is available in 12 languages.[12]

Methods of Selecting the Right Person for the Job

Selection involves choosing the applicant who has the qualifications to perform the job.

Selection is the process of determining whether an applicant has personal qualities that match the job specifications for a given position. Some of the qualities that working men and women say helped them get ahead are hard work, ability, and high standards.

No potential employee is perfect! So do not expect to find someone with all the qualities you ideally want. Instead, find people who have the qualities you need, and be willing to accept qualities you do not need or want, so long as those qualities do not harm the business. The selection procedure involves (1) gathering information about the applicant, (2) making a job offer, and (3) orienting the new employee.

Validity is making sure that the test given actually relates or corresponds to job performance.

Validity   You must be very careful when you perform any preemployment or employee testing, to make sure that the procedures and instruments used are valid. In other words you must make sure that what you are testing relates or corresponds to actual performance on the job. **Validity** is not only important in the selection procedure but also can become a very important measure in defense of discrimination allegations in court.

Gathering Information about the Applicant   Many people applying for a job will not be qualified, so try to find out all you can about what they can—and cannot—do. *In general, what a person has done in the past best indicates future performance.* You should therefore use the most appropriate techniques to help discover a person's past performance and future possibilities.

The amount of information you need to know about an applicant depends on the type of employee being recruited. Figure 10.4 shows some selection techniques that are frequently used to gather the information, but not all are needed for every job. Also, these techniques are based on having several applicants for each job, which is not always true of most small businesses.

FIGURE 10.4 | Techniques for Gathering Information about Potential Employees

Techniques used to gather data	Characteristics to look for	Applicants who are available as potential employees
Preliminary screening or interview	Obvious misfit from outward appearance and conduct	
Biographical inventory from application blank, résumé, or other document	Lacks adequate educational and performance record	
Testing Intelligence test(s)	Fails to meet minimum standards of mental alertness	
Aptitude test(s)	Lacks specific capacities for acquiring particular knowledge or skills	
Proficiency or achievement test(s)	Unable to demonstrate ability to do job	
In-depth interview	Lacks necessary innate ability, ambition, or other qualities	
Verifying biographical data from references	Unfavorable or negative reports on past performance	
Physical examination	Physically unfit for job	
Personal judgment	Overall competence and ability to fit into the firm	

Using Employee Input   When selecting human resources, it helps to bring present employees into the process—in an advisory capacity. The consequences of hiring an incompatible worker in a small company can be very disruptive.

Preliminary Screening   You should do some form of preliminary screening of applicants early in the selection procedure. This can be done in a formal interview or informally through reviewing a candidate's application form, letter, résumé, or other submitted material. Most firms use some form of interviewing at this point. You should look for such obvious factors as voice, physical appearance, personal grooming, educational qualifications, training, and experience. Many applicants are eliminated at this stage for reasons such as inappropriate dress, attitude, education, or experience.

It is at this stage of selection that many small business owners or managers inadvertently—or intentionally—run afoul of equal employment opportunity (EEO) laws (to be discussed in detail later). Table 10.1 presents some questions to avoid asking applicants at this stage—or at any other time before a job offer is made.

TABLE 10.1 | General Topics to Avoid When Interviewing Applicants

Here is an up-to-date summary of 10 of the most dangerous questions or topics you might raise during an interview.

1. *Children.* Do not ask applicants whether they have children, plan to have children, or have child care.

2. *Age.* Do not ask an applicant's age unless job specific.

3. *Disabilities.* Do not ask whether the candidate has a physical or mental disability that would interfere with doing the job.

4. *Physical characteristics.* Do not ask for such identifying characteristics as height or weight on an application.

5. *Citizenship.* Do not ask applicants about their citizenship. However, the Immigration Reform and Control Act does require business operators to determine that their employees have a legal right to work in the United States.

6. *Name.* Do not ask a female candidate for her maiden name.

7. *Lawsuits.* Do not ask a job candidate whether he or she has ever filed a suit or a claim against a former employer.

8. *Arrest record.* Do not ask applicants about their arrest records.

9. *Smoking.* Do not ask whether a candidate smokes. While smokers are not protected under the Americans with Disabilities Act (ADA), asking applicants whether they smoke might lead to legal difficulties if an applicant is turned down because of fear that smoking would drive up the employer's health care costs.

10. *AIDS and HIV.* Never ask job candidates whether they have AIDS or are HIV-positive, as these questions violate the ADA and could violate state and federal civil rights laws.

Gathering Biographical Information   Biographical information comes from application forms, résumés, school records, military records, credit references, and so forth. You should look for solid evidence of past performance, concrete information on which to base the decision instead of depending on opinions or assumptions. Having applicants fill out an application form in your presence—in longhand—serves as a simple performance test of their neatness and communications ability, or even simple literacy. No matter how good an applicant's record appears, do not base a decision on her or his unconfirmed statements. Unfortunately, there is a trend toward inflating résumés, so you should make it a point to verify education and employment history and check references. Depending on the sensitivity of the job a complete background check may be needed.

Several "red flags" may indicate a phony résumé: gaps in dates or sequences that do not add up, such as the time between getting a degree and a job; degrees from unknown schools; vagueness; and accomplishments that do not make sense, such as years of education and experience that are greater than possible for the applicant's age.

Giving Preemployment Tests   Since 1971, when the U.S. Supreme Court ruled that preemployment tests must be job related, most small firms have minimized their use because of the cost involved and the possible legal hassles. Also, some experts in the field warn that testing may be based on the false assumption that a test can determine whether an applicant fits a given "profile." A recent survey by the Society for Human Resource Management indicated that 40 percent of the Fortune 100 use some form of psychological testing in their employee selection.[13]

The **polygraph** is an instrument for simultaneously recording variations in several different physiological variables.

A word of caution is needed about the use of a special test, the **polygraph,** or "lie detector." Before 1989, many companies used the polygraph. Because of conflicting results, Congress has since passed a law barring most private employers from using polygraph tests. Now, written and computerized tests for assessing employee honesty are increasingly being produced and sold.

Interviewing Applicants in Depth   Applicants who have survived the procedure this far are often subjected to an **in-depth interview** at this time. Sometimes called a **preemployment** or **diagnostic interview,** its purpose is to probe the applicant's character, motivation, and other aspects of personality. Some suggestions for improving the interview process are

In-depth, preemployment, or **diagnostic interviews** are detailed, probing, and penetrating interviews seeking to determine the applicant's character and other aspects of personality.

- Do not ask the obvious questions.
- Do not ask legally indefensible questions.
- Do ask the right questions, but be sure to know how to evaluate the answers.
- Do try not to focus too much attention on the candidate's self-evaluation.
- Do not be overly influenced by first impressions.
- Do not miss important clues.
- Do not rely too much on past credentials.

Many times the selection process fails because the wrong questions are asked at the interview stage. Four good strategies to consider are

1. Stick to predetermined questions. The more thought that goes into an interview, the less time and expense needed to correct a bad decision.
2. Do not make an emotional hiring decision. This is the number one cause of hiring errors.
3. Dig deep. History is by far the key to the future, it often repeats itself.
4. Be very clear about job performance expectations. This will scare off the mediocre and challenge the best.[14]

Checking References   References play an important role in gathering information about an applicant. The three most frequently used types of references are personal, academic, and past employment. For applicants with any work history, the most valued references are from former employers. Using a personal visit, a telephone call, or a personal letter, you can verify work history, educational attainments, and other information the applicant has presented. By law, former employers may, if they choose, limit their responses to information about dates and title of the most recent job and total period of employment. Be sure to get the applicant's permission before contacting the present employer, who may not know the employee is job hunting.

Just as some applicants are not honest with their prospective employer, neither are the persons giving them a reference always entirely candid.

Giving Physical Examinations   In the past, the final step in selecting employees was some type of physical exam. Now, however (as you can see in Table 10.2 in the section "Laws Providing for Equal Opportunity"), the Americans with Disabilities Act (ADA) limits the use of such exams in hiring by employers with 15 or more employees. To prevent possible discrimination against the disabled, the law prohibits asking questions about an applicant's medical history or requiring an exam *before* a preliminary job offer is made.

Making a Job Offer   When you have decided to hire an applicant, you should make him or her a firm job offer. It should include details of working conditions, such as pay, work hours, holidays, vacations, and other employee benefits, as well as the new employee's duties and responsibilities. Given the increasing tendency for workers to sue their employers, you should put job offers in writing and get the applicant to sign, indicating his or her understanding and agreement.

Orienting the New Employee   Selection also should include orienting new employees to the job. Starting a new job is usually a difficult and frustrating experience, even for the best-qualified people. Thus, orientation should include, at a minimum, an introduction to co-workers; an explanation of the business's history, policies, procedures, and benefits; and working closely with the new employee during at least the first pay period. More employees leave a firm during that period than at any other time during their employment, as the following example shows.

Real-World Example 10.4

After more than 20 years as a full-time wife and mother, Elaine Reeves* accepted her first job outside the home. When she reported for work on Monday morning, Elaine was greeted by the business's owner and shown the word processor, other office machines, and the supply cabinet. Then she was left on her own while the owner went to call on several contractors. In these unfamiliar surroundings and with the other employees wrapped up in their own work, which made them seem unfriendly and unhelpful, she felt shaken and discouraged and was thinking of turning around and going home. The owner walked in just in time to stop her.

Training and Developing Employees

The effectiveness of a small business results not only from the ability of the owner but also from (1) the inherent abilities of its employees; (2) their development through training, education, and experience; and (3) their motivation. The first of these depends on effective recruiting and selection. The second results from personnel development. The third, motivation, which will be covered in Chapter 11, results from the manager's leadership abilities.

Not only must new employees be trained, but the current ones also must be retrained and upgraded if they are to adjust to rapidly changing job requirements. Some of the results of training and developing workers include (1) increased productivity, (2) reduced turnover, (3) increased earnings for employees, (4) decreased costs of materials and equipment due to errors, (5) less supervision required, and (6) improved employee satisfaction.

---

*Name disguised at her request.

Ways of Training Nonmanagerial Employees

You can use many methods to train nonmanagerial employees including (1) on-the-job training (OJT), (2) apprenticeship training, (3) internship training (4) cross-training, and (5) E-training.

On-the-job training (OJT) or **on-the-job learning (OJL)** has the worker actually performing the work, under the supervision of a competent trainer.

On-the-Job Training   The most universal form of employee development, **on-the-job training (OJT),** which is in reality **on-the-job learning (OJL),** occurs when workers perform their regular job under the supervision and guidance of the owner, a manager, or a trained worker or instructor. Thus, while learning to do the job, the worker acts as a regular employee, producing the good or service the business sells. Whether consciously planned or not, this form of training always occurs. While the methods used vary with the trainer, OJT usually involves

- Telling workers what needs to be done.
- Telling them how to do the job.
- Showing them how it must be done.
- Letting them do the job under the trainer's guidance.
- Telling—and showing—them what they did right, what they did wrong, and how to correct the wrong activity.
- Repeating the process until the learners have mastered the job.

The main *advantages* of OJT are that it results in low out-of-pocket costs and production continues during the training. Also, there is no transition from classroom learning to actual production. Research and experience have repeatedly shown that OJT is a cost-effective and proven alternative to formal training programs, as it both educates *and* motivates employees.[15]

On the other hand, the *disadvantages* of OJT are excessive waste caused by mistakes and the poor learning environment provided by the production area. While most OJT is done by owners and managers, they are not necessarily the best ones to do it, since their primary focus is on running the business. For this reason, another capable employee or even an outside trainer should be assigned this responsibility, if possible.

Apprenticeship training blends OJT with learning of theory in the classroom.

Apprenticeship Training   For workers performing skilled, craft-type jobs, **apprenticeship training** blends the learning of theory with practice in the techniques of the job. If the job can best be learned by combining classroom instruction and actual learning experience on the job, this training method should be used. It usually lasts from two to seven years of both classroom learning and on-the-job training. For young people who cannot—or will not—finish a high school program, an effective apprentice program can put a good job within their reach.

Internship training combines OJT with learning at a cooperating school or college.

Internship Training   **Internship training** combines education at a school or college with on-the-job training at a cooperating business. It is usually used for students who are prospective employees for marketing, clerical, technical, and managerial positions. Co-op programs prepare students for technical positions, provide income to meet the cost of their education, and give them a chance to see if they would like to go to work for the company. This method also gives the small business owner a chance to evaluate the student as a prospective full-time employee.

Real-World Example 10.5

For example, auto shop students at 12 high schools in the Kansas City, Missouri, area can participate in an internship program called "Jump on Life." Sponsored by local Jiffy Lube (www.jiflube.com) franchises, it gives the students technical and management training. After graduation, all 15 of its first graduates were hired by local Jiffy Lube franchises.[16]

Cross-training involves workers learning many job skills so they are more versatile.

Cross-Training   With the shortage of skilled job applicants, some small businesses are turning to **cross-training** to make their employees more versatile—and keep them more satisfied. While specialized training tends to improve performance, it may also result in boredom and fatigue. Cross-training, which has employees learn many kinds of jobs, may reduce turnover by keeping workers more interested in their jobs.

Real-World Example 10.6

For example, Kirk's Suede-Life in Willowbrook, Illinois, hosts classes at their cleaning school to cross-train laundry/dry-cleaning workers. Students participate in hands-on instruction for many areas of their profession. Cross-training topics include wet processing, safe prespotting, and spray recoloring procedures.[17]

E-training involves computer interaction with either specific software packages or specific online sites for employee training.

E-training   Electronic learning and online training involves computer interaction with either specific software packages or specific online sites for employee training.

Online training has been adopted by several companies due to its competitive advantage, its ability, and its long-term cost savings. For example, Borders Group Inc. normally receives 15,000 calls per week just from customers, and many employees have little time for one-on-one instruction for new software and such. To eliminate the time it takes to personally train employees, Borders adopted a program called Click2Coach Trainer. This system teaches the call center employees how to record their calls, so screening and review of the calls do not have to be done immediately.[18]

In the education world, many professors are not only teaching online, but recently educators can now earn some of their required credits and continuing education requirements online. Also, in relation to insurance companies, e-training is becoming popular. Insurance agents and brokers often attend insurance classes or take self-study courses to fulfill their continuing education requirements. Now, online training has given them alternative ways to acquire those hours.[19]

Online training does not only apply to continuing education. The Social Security Administration employees are now learning everything they need to know about sexual harassment due to online training. Originally, the SSA provided satellite broadcast technology to train; however, training will now be delivered right to their desktops.[20]

Also, the U.S. Veteran's Benefits Administration is using online training to improve productivity because 40 percent of its workforce will soon retire. Fast learning is needed, and E-training will bring new and reassigned employees up to speed.[21]

Real-World Example 10.7

Online training has many benefits for a company. Brandon Hall, the CEO of a large California consultancy, predicts that the cost benefit is a 50 percent reduction for delivering a training course online versus instructor-led classroom training. Human resource managers and other employee development departments dealing with entry-level employees can now spend more time on internal organizational responsibilities, rather than the teaching and setting up of training classes. Due to its efficiency, online training is currently being implemented in many organizations.[22]

Outside Help with Training

Many outside programs are available to help you train your employees. For example, the National Apprenticeship Act of 1937, administered by the U.S. Labor Department's Bureau of Apprenticeship and Training (www.doleta.gov/oa), sets policies and standards for apprenticeship programs. Write to this bureau for help in conducting such a program. Vocational-technical schools, business schools, junior colleges, and small private firms help small companies by conducting regular or special classes. Through such programs, potential employees can become qualified for skilled jobs such as machinist, lathe operator, computer operator, and legal assistant.

Selecting and Developing Managers

Determining the job requirements for someone to be a manager is more difficult than filling other positions because managerial jobs differ so greatly. But one generalization usually applies: *The employee who is a good performer at the nonmanagerial level does not necessarily make a good manager, because the skills needed at the two levels differ drastically.* Adding to this difficulty is the constant change in managerial methods and terms. Many small businesses cannot always be abreast of these changes. Therefore, such concepts as total quality management (TQM), reengineering, benchmarking, and rightsizing might be desirable goals, but are often unattainable.

Managers generally are paid at a higher rate than most employees, and this sometimes places a serious burden on the successful small business owner. At times of growth, most monies need to be funneled back into the company. However, the entrepreneur may need to hire a competent manager to assist in the daily operations. An MBA is usually a good choice since they have a very well-rounded business education and usually have work experience.

Selecting Managers

In small firms, managers are usually promoted from within, but many businesses hire college graduates for management trainee programs. We have found in directing and teaching in management development programs that the characteristics to be developed to produce good managers are creativity, productivity, innovativeness, communication skills (including oral, written, nonverbal, and telephone), self-motivation, and the drive and energy to motivate and energize others to achieve consistently large amounts of high-quality work. You can see that these tend to be the same qualities that lead to success as an entrepreneur, as shown in Chapter 1.

FIGURE 10.5 |
Methods Used to
Develop Managers

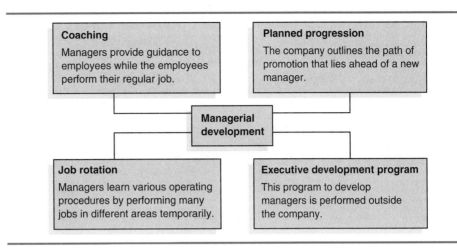

FIGURE 10.5 |
Methods Used to
Develop Managers

Developing Managers

In addition to the usual methods used to develop all employees, some special techniques are used to develop managerial personnel. These include (1) coaching, (2) planned progression, (3) job rotation, and (4) executive development programs, as shown in Figure 10.5. Also, many franchisers, such as McDonald's and Holiday Inn (www.holidayinn.com), have their own schools at which their franchise owners and managers learn the desired system and how to make it work.[23]

The small company owner's need for ways to train a person to become a supervisor or manager is often overlooked. Yet the move up from being an employee to being "an overseer is one of the most difficult in people's careers."[24]

Complying with Equal Employment Opportunity (EEO) Laws

Federal and state laws and regulations affect almost all aspects of personnel relations. Because state laws vary so widely, only the most significant federal laws affecting recruiting and selecting employees are discussed here.

Laws Providing for Equal Employment Opportunity

Since 1963, Congress has passed various acts to create equal employment opportunity and affirmative action. Table 10.2 summarizes the most significant legislation in this area.

Special mention should be made of the **Americans with Disabilities Act (ADA)** of 1990, because it changed the way employers must deal with the 20 million U.S. citizens in the workforce who have physical or mental disabilities.[25] This law has probably had a greater impact on small business management than any other law: It requires positive actions on the part of employers.

The act mandates the removal of social and physical barriers against the disabled, two-thirds of whom are unemployed. It covers disabilities such as cancer, blindness, arthritis, chemical dependency, speech and hearing impairment, learning disabilities, and mental illness, and also protects employees infected with the HIV virus. The act specifically excludes sexual behavior disorders, gambling, kleptomania, and others. This act, which targets employers with 15 or more workers, is particularly hard on small business owners because it assumes that they can comprehend and act on the needs of the mentally ill. Yet employers have enough difficulty just understanding the intent of the law.

The **Americans with Disabilities Act (ADA)** requires the removal of many social and physical barriers to employing the disabled.

TABLE 10.2 | Primary Legal Influences on Equal Employment Opportunity (EEO) and Affirmative Action

Laws	Coverage	Basic Requirements	Agencies Involved
Title VII of Civil Rights Act of 1964, as amended	Employers with 15 or more employees and engaged in interstate commerce; federal service workers; and state and local government workers	Prohibits employment decisions based on race, color, religion, sex, or national origin.	Equal Employment Opportunity Commission (EEOC)
Executive Order 11246, as amended	Employers with federal contracts and subcontracts	Requires contractors who underutilize women and minorities to develop affirmative action plans (AAPs), including setting goals and timetables; and to recruit, select, train, utilize, and promote more minorities and women when contracts exceed $50,000 a year.	Office of Federal Contract Compliance Programs (OFCCP) in the Labor Department
Age Discrimination in Employment Act of 1967	Employers with 20 or more employees	Prohibits employment discrimination against employees aged 40 and over, including mandatory retirement before 70, with certain exceptions.	EEOC
Vocational Rehabilitation Act of 1973	Employers with federal contracts or subcontracts	Prohibits discrimination and requires contractor to develop affirmative action programs to recruit and employ handicapped persons. Requires development of an AAP.	OFCCP
Vietnam-Era Veterans Readjustment Act of 1974	Employers with federal contracts or subcontracts	Requires contractors to develop AAPs to recruit and employ Vietnam-era veterans and to list job openings with state employment services, for priority in referrals.	OFCCP
Americans with Disabilities Act of 1990 (ADA)	Employers with 15 or more employees	Prohibits discrimination based on physical or mental handicap, including HIV infection (affirmative action required).	EEOC
Civil Rights Act of 1991	Same as Title VII	Amends Title VII and ADA to allow punitive and compensatory damages in cases of intentional discrimination and permits more extensive use of jury trials.	EEOC
The Genetic Information Nondiscrimination Act of 2008 (GINA)	Same as Title VII	This law makes it illegal to discriminate against employees or applicants because of genetic information. Genetic information includes information about an individual's genetic tests and the genetic tests of an individual's family members, as well as information about any disease, disorder, or condition of an individual's family members (i.e., an individual's family medical history). The law also makes it illegal to retaliate against a person because the person complained about discrimination, filed a charge of discrimination, or participated in an employment discrimination investigation or lawsuit.	EEOC

Source: Various government and private publications.

Enforcing EEO Laws

You must remember that *all employees—temporary as well as permanent—are entitled to equality in all conditions of employment.* Hiring, training, promotions and transfers, wages and benefits, and all other employment factors are covered. Posting available job openings on a bulletin board to give present employees a chance to bid on them has been found to be a good method of complying with EEO laws. There must be no discrimination in rates of pay, including pensions or other deferred payments. Recreational activities—company sports teams, holiday parties, and the like—should be open to all employees on a nondiscriminatory basis.

As shown in Table 10.2, the **Equal Employment Opportunity Commission (EEOC)** (www.eeoc.gov) is the primary enforcing agency for most EEO laws. Figure 10.6 shows some regulations it has issued to prevent discrimination such as age discrimination.

Another difficult issue for small—and large—businesses is how to cope with sexual harassment. According to the EEOC, this is the fastest-growing employee complaint. The term is difficult to define because the nature of the act lies as much in the reaction of the victim as in the intentions or actions of the offender; that is, what makes a gesture, remark, or pinup photo "harassment" is that it is "unwelcome." Small employers should therefore install an effective prevention program, for the U.S. Supreme Court ruled in June 1998 that if the harassment results in a job loss, such as firing or demotion, the employer is legally responsible, even if unaware of the behavior. If the employee's job was not threatened, the employer can still be held liable unless the company can show it had effective anti-harassment policies in place and complaint procedures that the employee did not invoke.[26]

Religious discrimination is another employee issue that must be scrupulously dealt with by small business owners. In essence, employers (or potential employers) must cope with two essential questions. First, can a business force an employee, while in the workplace, to remove clothing with religious significance, or can it refuse to hire an employee who will not make such concessions? Second, if a business honors the request of a client or consultant to exclude employees of certain religious persuasions from certain positions, can the employer be held liable? In answering these and related questions, the employer should consider how it treats employees of religious persuasions different from that of the employee alleging discrimination.

The Labor Department's Office of Federal Contract Compliance Programs (OFCCP) (www.oalj.dol.gov) requires employers with government contracts or subcontracts to have

The **Equal Employment Opportunity Commission (EEOC)** is the federal agency primarily responsible for enforcing EEO laws.

FIGURE 10.6 |
Principal EEOC
Regulations

- Sex discrimination guidelines
- Questions and answers on pregnancy disability and reproductive hazards
- Religious discrimination guidelines
- National origin discrimination guidelines
- Interpretations of the Age Discrimination in Employment Act
- Employee selection guidelines
- Record keeping and reports
- Affirmative action guidelines
- EEO in the federal government
- Equal Pay Act interpretations
- Policy statement on maternal benefits
- Policy statement on relationship of Title VII to 1986
- Immigration Reform and Control Act
- Policy statement on reproductive and fetal hazards
- Policy statement on religious accommodation under Title VII
- Policy guidance on sexual harassment
- Disabilities discrimination guidelines

Affirmative action programs (AAPs) provide guidelines to help firms eliminate discrimination against women and minorities.

affirmative action programs (AAPs) to put the principle of equal employment opportunity into practice. The OFCCP can cancel a guilty firm's contract or prohibit it from getting future contracts if a violation is blatant.

Compensating Employees

Another aspect of managing human resources and diversity is providing what employees consider fair pay for their activities. Their earnings should be high enough to motivate them to be good producers, yet low enough for you to maintain satisfactory profits. Some employers are coming up with new ways to distribute earnings.

Legal Influences

There are many federal and state laws that affect how much small business owners pay their employees (see Table 10.3 for the primary federal laws involved). According to the

TABLE 10.3 | Legal Influences on Compensation and Hours of Work

Law	Coverage	Basic Requirements	Agencies Involved
Public Construction Act of 1931 (Davis-Bacon Act)	Employers with federal construction contracts or subcontracts of $2,000 or more	Employers must pay at least the prevailing wages in the area, as determined by the Secretary of Labor; overtime is to be paid at 1½ times the basic wage for all work over 8 hours per day or 40 hours per week.	Wage and Hour Division of the Labor Department
Public Contracts Act of 1936 (Walsh-Healy Act)	Employers with federal contracts of $1,000 or more	Same as above.	Same as above
Fair Labor Standards Act of 1938 (wage and hour law)	Private employers engaged in interstate commerce; retailers having annual sales of $325,000 (many groups exempted from overtime requirements)	Employers must pay a minimum of $5.15 per hour and 1½ times the basic rate for work over 40 hours per week and are limited (by jobs and school status) in employing persons under 18.	Same as above
Equal Pay Act of 1963	All employers	Men and women must receive equal pay for jobs requiring substantially the same skill, working conditions, effort, and responsibility.	Equal Employment Opportunity Commission
Service Contracts Act of 1965	Employers with contracts to provide services worth $2,500 or more per year to the federal government	Same as Davis-Bacon.	Same as Davis-Bacon
Family and Medical Leave Act of 1993	Employers with 50 or more employees within a 75-mile radius; certain employees are exempted	Employers must provide workers up to 12 weeks of unpaid leave during a 12-month period for (1) birth of a child; (2) placement of a child for adoption or foster care; (3) caring for a spouse, child, or parent with a serious health condition; and (4) a serious condition of the employee. Health coverage must be continued during the leave period and same or comparable job be available upon return.	Department of Labor

Source: Various government and private publications.

Wage and Hour Law, 14 is the minimum working age for most nonfarm jobs. Thus, you can hire workers aged 14 and 15 for nonhazardous jobs for up to three hours on a school day and eight hours on any other day, but no more than 18 hours per week from 7:00 AM to 7:00 PM during the school term. Those aged 16 and 17 can work an unlimited time on non-hazardous jobs.

Because state laws vary so much from each other and from the federal law, we suggest you check the laws for the state in which you operate.

As of this writing there are 18 states plus Washington D.C. with a higher minimum wage than required by federal law. Table 10.4 reflects these states and their requirements. For current data, refer to www.dol.gov.

Setting Rates of Pay

In addition to legal factors, many variables influence what employees consider a *fair wage*. First, they think they should be paid in proportion to their physical and mental efforts on the job. The standard of living and cost of living in the area also matter. And unions help set wages in a geographic area through collective bargaining, whether the company itself is unionized or not. The economic factors of supply and demand for workers help set wages, but the employer's ability to pay must ultimately be the deciding factor.

In actual practice, most small businesses pay either the minimum wage of $7.25 per hour, or the same wages that similar businesses in the area pay. If you pay less than the prevailing wage, you will have difficulty finding employees. Conversely, you cannot afford to pay much more unless your employees are more productive. In the final analysis, you pay whatever you must to attract the people you really need—and can afford.

TABLE 10.4 | States with Higher Minimum Wage

State	State Minimum Wage ($), January 1, 2011
Arkansas	$7.75
Arizona	7.35
California	8.00
Colorado	7.36
Connecticut	8.25
District of Columbia	8.25
Florida	7.31
Illinois	8.25
Maine	7.50
Massachusetts	8.00
Michigan	7.40
Montana	7.35
Nevada	8.25
New Mexico	7.50
Ohio	7.40
Oregon	8.50
Rhode Island	7.40
Vermont	8.15
Washington	8.67

Source: www.dol.gov

Using Money to Motivate

Many small businesses use some form of financial incentive to motivate their employees to use their initiative and to perform better. Some of the more popular financial incentives are (1) merit increases, (2) incentive payments, and (3) profit sharing. A few years ago, a Conference Board survey of 382 companies found that around three-quarters of them provided some type of incentive pay, including bonuses for cost-saving suggestions or for learning new skills.

Real-World Example 10.8

For example, ArchivesOne provides an unusual incentive for their employees. Every year they select two of the company's 140 employees and award to them a low-interest home loan. They believe this has reduced employee turnover from 20 percent to 14 percent. To qualify, employees must have been with the company a year, have a household income of $75,000 or less, and be buying a primary residence costing no more than $225,000. "It's not for the executives. It's for the laborers making 10 bucks an hour."[27]

Merit increases are based on the employee's ability and performance.

Merit Increases   **Merit increases,** which base a person's wage or salary on ability and merit rather than on seniority or some other factor, tend to be effective motivators. Merit programs identify, appraise, and reward employees for outstanding contributions toward your company's profits. Thus, an employee's wage or salary relates directly to that person's efforts to achieve your objectives. Many companies—large as well as small—are basing employee pay on observed competence.

Incentive Payments   Incentive payments can be paid in the form of incentive wages, bonuses, commissions, and push money.

An **incentive wage** is the extra compensation paid for all production over a specified standard amount.

An **incentive wage,** which is the extra compensation paid for all production over a specified amount, is effective in situations in which a worker can control the volume of sales or production. Piece rates, commissions, and bonuses are forms of incentive payments. Under a *piece-rate system,* an employee's earnings are based on a rate per unit times the number of units produced. But you should give some form of guaranteed base rate to ensure that the employee earns at least a minimum amount. Piece-rate systems, which are usually used in production- or operations-type activities, can be quite effective, as the following example illustrates.

Real-World Example 10.9

A pilot study of the use of piece rates in the corrugated shipping container industry found that 16 of 18 operations showed significantly increased productivity after use of such incentives. On the average, productivity per employee increased about 75 percent.

A **commission** is incentive compensation directly related to the sales or profits achieved by a salesperson.

Commissions, which consist of a given amount per sale or a percentage of sales, are used extensively to reward salespeople, especially in retailing. They are particularly useful in rewarding door-to-door selling of items such as encyclopedias and magazine subscriptions, but they are also used by most department stores and similar retail outlets and are the only form of compensation for real estate agents.

A **bonus** is a reward—not specified in advance—given to employees for special efforts and accomplishments.

Bonuses are amounts given to employees either for exceeding their production quotas or as a reward on special occasions. Many production or sales personnel have work quotas and receive bonuses if they exceed that amount.

Another form of incentive payment is called **push money (PM),** or **spiff,** which is a reward given to employees for selling an item the business is making a special effort to sell—in other words, pushing.

Push money (PM), or **spiff,** is a commission paid to a salesperson to push a specific item or line of goods.

Profit Sharing

In **profit sharing,** employees receive a prearranged share of the company's profits. Profit sharing can be effective in motivating employees by tying rewards to company performance. Not only does it reward good performance, but a good plan can also reduce turnover, increase productivity, improve communication, and reduce the amount of supervision needed. The oldest, best-known, and most successful profit-sharing plan is that of the Lincoln Electric Company of Cleveland, Ohio (www.lincolnelectric.com).

Profit sharing is an arrangement—announced in advance—whereby employees receive a prescribed share of the company's profits.

If you can afford to do so, you might want to use an **employee stock ownership plan (ESOP),** which is a modification of profit sharing. In general, an ESOP borrows money, purchases a block of the company's stock, and allocates it to the employees on the basis of salaries and/or longevity. These plans are particularly attractive to small companies because they provide a source of needed capital, boost the company's cash flow, raise employee morale and productivity, and provide a very beneficial new employee benefit.

An **employee stock ownership plan (ESOP),** a form of profit sharing, borrows money, purchases some of the company's stock, and allocates it to the employees on the basis of salaries and/or longevity.

Compensating Managerial and Professional Personnel

In general, managers of small businesses are paid on a merit basis, with their income based on the firm's earnings. Many small companies also use profit sharing, bonuses, or some other method of stimulating the interest of managerial and professional personnel.

Providing Employee Benefits

Employee benefits, or **fringe benefits,** are the rewards and services provided to workers in addition to their regular earnings.

Employee benefits (sometimes called **fringe benefits**) are the rewards and services provided to employees in addition to their regular earnings. Some of them are required by law, while others are offered voluntarily by the employer. Figure 10.7 lists some of the most popular of these benefits.

In general, these benefits increase in importance as employees' lifestyles expand and it takes more than just wages to satisfy them. But benefits are costly. And once given, they are difficult—if not impossible—to take back. In addition to the actual cost of the benefits, the cost of administering them is tremendous. Still, employees want and expect them, almost as much as they do their salary! Employee health benefits seem to top the list.

Real-World Example 10.10

For example, one restaurateur found that health care benefit costs rose 20 percent in 2003 and now eat a big chunk from his profit. In addition, the California law is expected to require an additional push that could require him to sell one of his four eateries in order to accommodate the additional expense.[28]

FIGURE 10.7 |

Some of the Most Popular Employee Benefits

Legally required

Social Security/Medicare
Unemployment insurance
Workers' compensation
Family and medical leave

Voluntary, private

a. Health and accident insurance
    Eye care and eyeglasses
    Chiropractic care
    Dental and orthodontic care
    Health maintenance—diagnostic visits/physical exams
    Major medical/hospitalization
    Psychiatric and mental care
    Accident and sickness insurance

b. Life and disability insurance
    Accidental death and dismemberment
    Group term life insurance
    Long-term disability

c. Sick leave, including maternity leave

d. Income maintenance
    Severance pay
    Supplemental unemployment benefits (SUBs)
    Pensions

e. Pay for time off
    Holidays
    Personal time
    Sabbatical leaves
    Union activities
    Vacations

f. Employee services and others
    Alcohol and drug rehabilitation
    Auto insurance
    Child care and day care centers for other family members
    Christmas bonuses
    Clothing and uniforms
    Company car
    Credit unions
    Discount privileges on organization's products or services
    Loans and financial assistance
    Food services and cafeteria
    Group tours and charter flights
    Gymnasium and physical training center
    Legal assistance
    Liability coverage
    Matching gifts to charitable organizations or schools
    Matching payroll deductions and savings plans
    Moving and transfer allowances
    Personal counseling and financial advice
    Recreation center
    Service awards
    Stock purchase and profit-sharing plans
    Transportation and parking
    Tuition for employee and/or family members

Source: Various government and private publications.

Legally Required Benefits

Small employers are legally required by the Social Security Act to provide retirement, disability, survivors, and medical benefits; unemployment insurance; and workers' compensation. Also, according to the Consolidated Omnibus Budget Reconciliation Act of 1986 (COBRA), employers with 20 or more employees must continue offering health insurance for up to 18 months for employees when they leave—either voluntarily or otherwise—and up to 36 months for widows, divorced or separated spouses, and employee dependents. While the former employee pays the cost of the insurance, employers must establish procedures for collecting premiums and keep track of former employees. Employers with 50 or more employees within a radius of 75 miles of their home office must provide for family and medical leave.

Social Security is a federal program that provides support for the retired, widowed, disabled, and their dependents.

Social Security   Under the **Social Security** system, you act as both taxpayer and tax collector, as you must pay a tax on employees' earnings and deduct an equal amount from their paychecks. In 2011, the tax rate was 7.65 percent per employee (6.2 percent for Social

Security and 1.45 percent for Medicare and the employees' rate was 5.65 percent), and the taxable wage base was $106,800 for Social Security and unlimited for Medicare. Self-employed people must pay the entire cost themselves.

Unemployment insurance provides some financial support to employees laid off for reasons beyond their control.

Unemployment Insurance   State governments receive most of the **unemployment insurance** tax. If the business can lower its unemployment rate, the tax is reduced under a merit rating system. Using funds from the tax, the state pays unemployed workers a predetermined amount each week. This amount varies from state to state.

The federal government also requires a deduction for unemployment insurance. The employer is required to pay 6.2 percent of each employee's wages up to $7,000 per year. Each state also collects unemployment insurance. The state rates vary from 1 to 4 percent and affect the first $7,000 through $36,000, depending on the state. Employers may receive an offset credit up to 5.4 percent of the federal rate, which means that in 2011 the average net federal requirement is about 0.8 percent.

Workers' compensation involves payments made to employees for losses from industrial accidents and occupational diseases.

Workers' Compensation   Employee losses from accidents and occupational diseases are paid for under state **workers' compensation** laws. Each employer is required to pay insurance premiums to either a state fund or a private insurance company. The accumulated funds are used to compensate victims of industrial accidents or work-related illnesses. A firm's premiums depend on the hazards involved and the effectiveness of its safety programs. The amount paid to an employee or to his or her estate is fixed according to the type and extent of injury. According to the U.S. Census Bureau, the costs of these programs was $58 billion in 2008. *This trend threatens small firms, which may not be able to bear the increasing costs.* It is interesting to note, however, that overall incident rates are decreasing.

The **Family and Medical Leave Act** requires employers with 50 or more employees to provide up to 12 weeks of unpaid leave for births or adoptions, and to care for sick children, spouses, or parents.

Family and Medical Leave   Employers with 50 or more workers who live within 75 miles of the plant must guarantee workers up to 12 weeks of unpaid leave a year for births, adoptions, or the care of sick children, spouses, or parents. The **Family and Medical Leave Act** covers employees who have been on the job at least one year, but the employer can exclude the top-paid 10 percent of employees. Employees are required to give 30 days' notice when practical, such as for births and adoptions, and may be required to use vacation or other leave time first. Couples employed at the same place may be restricted to 12 weeks total leave each year. Employers must continue to provide health insurance during leave and guarantee workers the same or an equivalent job on return. In spite of the protection provided by the law, many workers find it too costly to use—both financially and professionally. Some do not use it because of the burden it places on fellow employees who must cover for them. Others cannot afford to miss their paychecks. A recent study by Coopers & Lybrand found that the average number of employees per company using this leave was 5 percent.

"Our pension plan is simple and portable. However, it does not involve much in the way of actual money."

(Source: From *AARP Bulletin,* November 1995, p. 2.)

Some Other Popular Benefits

As shown in Figure 10.7, there are many voluntary benefits in addition to the legally required ones. Health, accident, life, and disability insurance are especially popular with small businesses and their employees. Most small firms find it very hard to provide health care insurance because of skyrocketing costs. However, according to the Health Research Educational Trust (www.hret.org), very small firms with only three to nine employees increased health care benefits from 46 percent participation in 2009 to 59 percent in 2010. One of the best ways for small companies to provide these benefits is through membership in a professional association. For example, for a $149 annual membership fee, a small business owner who joins the Independent Business Alliance has access to affordable insurance and other financial services not available elsewhere.

Other voluntary benefits are as varied as small businesses themselves. In trade and service businesses, discounts on the firm's goods or services are well received by employees. Some conscientious employers go much further.

Pension programs were common in small firms until the passage of the Employee Retirement Income Security Act (ERISA) in 1974. Because the law proved too complex and difficult for small businesses to conform to, many of them gave up their voluntary pension programs, especially after the law was amended in 1989.

Real-World Example 10.11

Ronald Turner, of Clarksburg, West Virginia, dropped his employee pension plan and gave his employees the cash due them from the fund, saying that he had tried to obey the law, but quit after the required paperwork grew from 35 to 77 pages and the IRS (www.irs.gov) disqualified the plan "on a technicality."[29]

A **defined-contribution plan** is a pension plan that establishes the basis on which an employer will contribute to the pension fund.

A **defined-benefit plan** is a pension plan whereby the amount an employee is to receive at retirement is specifically set forth.

401(k) retirement plans permit workers to place up to a certain amount of their wages each year in tax-deferred retirement savings plans.

A **cafeteria-style benefit plan,** or **flexcomp,** allows the employer to provide all employees with the legally required benefits, plus an extra dollar amount that each employee can choose how to use.

Many small firms have decided to let their employees establish private pension programs. Most of them are now encouraging their workers to use a **defined-contribution plan,** which establishes the basis on which the employer will contribute to the pension fund. The contributions may be made through profit sharing, thrift plans, employer-sponsored Individual Retirement Accounts (IRAs), and various other means. The amount an employee receives at retirement is determined by the funds accumulated in his or her account at the time of retirement and what retirement benefits these funds will buy. **Defined-benefit plans** have a fixed amount of payout at retirement.

Currently the most popular retirement plan in America is the **401(k).** This plan permits workers to place a certain amount of their wages in a tax-deferred retirement savings plan.

Flexible Approach to Benefits

A **cafeteria-style benefit plan,** also known as **flexcomp,** can help you reduce your annual increase in benefit costs. Under this system, you tell your employees the dollar value of benefits they are entitled to receive. Each employee then tells you how to allocate the money among a variety of available programs. This system increases employee awareness of the value of the benefits and offers freedom of choice and a personalized approach. These plans are now a viable option for small firms because third-party administrators can take care of the paperwork.

Protecting Employees' Health and Safety

Totally safe working conditions are impossible to provide, so employee safety is a condition involving *relative* freedom from danger or injury. In this section we look at how small business owners can maintain working conditions in which employees not only *are* safe but also *feel* safe. *In other words, employees need to know that you care about their safety.*

Unlike large firms, which employ specialists to be responsible for health and safety activities, small businesses must rely on employees with various job responsibilities to cover this area as well as most of the other areas of human resource management we have discussed. There are, however, consulting firms that specialize in helping small businesses provide healthy and safe work environments.

Factors Influencing Workers' Health and Safety

There are many and varied factors bearing on the maintenance of healthy, safe working conditions. We cover only the most significant ones: (1) type of industry, (2) type of occupation, and (3) human variables.

Type of Industry   Although the safety records of industries vary periodically, the type of industry does have a correlation with safety. For example, the least safe industries usually include wood product and primary metal manufacturing.[30]

(Source: © 1996 by Margaret P. Megginson. Used with permission.)

Repetitive stress injuries (RSIs), or **cumulative trauma disorders (CTDs),** are muscular or skeletal injuries to the hand, wrist, or other areas that bear the brunt of repeated motions. Among the most common is **carpal tunnel syndrome.**

Type of Occupation   The type of occupation also affects safety. Workplace dangers and injuries that once were considered likely—or were reported—only in construction and factories have now spread to a variety of operations. For example, back injuries are quite prevalent among health care workers, who must frequently lift patients or heavy bedding. According to the Bureau of Labor Statistics, nursing health services, curriers, and messengers have higher rates of illness and injury than the average for the private sector.[31]

A growing health problem for small firms, especially in offices, is **repetitive-stress injuries (RSIs),** also known as **cumulative trauma disorders (CTDs)** (one of the best known is **carpal tunnel syndrome**). Aetna Life & Casualty (www.aetna.com) estimates that workers' compensation claims from employees such as reporters, telephone operators, data processors, and checkout clerks using scanners may soon cost as much as $20 billion a year. And the Americans with Disabilities Act may make it easier for victims of RSIs to sue their employers.

The most common work-related problem for both men and women is back injuries—38 percent for women and 34 percent for men. The second most common for women is wrist injuries, 20 percent (as opposed to 12 percent for men, making it the third most common for them). Burns, cuts, and bruises are second for men (16 percent) and third for women (6 percent).

Human Variables   The most important human variables influencing safety are job satisfaction, personal characteristics, and management attitudes. Studies indicate a close relationship between safety and employees' satisfaction with their work.

The Role of the Occupational Safety and Health Act

The **Occupational Safety and Health Administration (OSHA)** establishes specific safety standards to ensure, to the extent feasible, the safety and health of workers.

The Occupational Safety and Health Act created the **Occupational Safety and Health Administration (OSHA)** (www.osha.gov) to ensure—to the extent feasible—safe and healthful working conditions for U.S. employees. In Europe this is called the European Agency for Safety and Health at work (http://osha.europa.eu). The law covers businesses that are engaged in interstate commerce and have one or more employees, except those covered by the Atomic Energy Act (www.em.doe.gov) or the Federal Mine Safety Act.

Employee Rights   OSHA encourages increased examination and questioning of management's staffing decisions and equipment selection. If workers believe their employer's violation of job safety or health standards threatens them with physical harm, they may request an OSHA inspection without being discharged or discriminated against for doing so. They can participate in any resulting hearings and can protest if they think the penalty is too light. And they can request that the Department of Health and Human Services (www.dhhs.gov) check to see if there is any potentially toxic substance in the workplace and have safe exposure levels set for that substance.

Employer Obligations and Rights   Even though many accidents result from employees' own lack of safety consciousness, employees usually do not receive citations. Instead, OSHA holds employers responsible for making employees wear safety equipment (for an example, see Case 10.1 "The Case of Sam Sawyer," at the end of the chapter).

Employers are subject to fines for unsafe practices regardless of whether any accidents occur.

Real-World Example 10.12

OSHA fined Millard Refrigerated Services in the amount of $52,500 in penalties for 16 violations. Millard failed to implement "a safe and timely shutdown" after an ammonia leak in one of their plants. This plant prepares chicken for worldwide distribution, and ammonia is the key to their refrigeration process. About 150 area workers and many nearby residents were exposed to the leak, which could have been fatal. More than 120 people were transported to local hospitals.[32]

Therefore, you should provide safety training for your employees, encourage and follow up on employee compliance with safety regulations and precautions, and discipline employees for noncompliance. Assistance may be obtained from OSHA and National Safety Council (www.nsc.org) chapters. Also, your workers' compensation carrier may suggest ways to improve safety and employees' health. You may obtain useful information from equipment manufacturers, other employers who have had an inspection, trade associations, and the local fire department.

Thousands of small business owners call OSHA each year requesting a visit from one of the OSHA consultants. These inspections are free for organizations that have fewer than 250 employees and are classified as "high hazard" under the government's Standard Industrial Classification (SIC) code, but may not always be possible to schedule.

Some Generalizations about OSHA Enforcement   Firms with fewer than eight employees do not have to maintain injury and illness records, except when a fatality occurs or an accident hospitalizes five or more persons. Also, OSHA does not inspect firms with 10 or fewer employees in "relatively safe" industries, which exempts nearly 80 percent of firms from inspections. Finally, inspectors concentrate on workplaces with unsatisfactory records.

Since 1988, small businesses have found that the paperwork burden makes it especially difficult for them to comply with OSHA's Hazard Communications Standard, which requires every employer in the country to identify hazardous substances in the workplace, list them, and train employees to use them safely. At first, the law applied only to manufacturers, but now the rule applies to nearly all employers. Dry-cleaning establishments, especially, find the rules onerous.

Because the inspection program and its technical nature constantly change, you are advised to use the resources suggested previously, as well as local chambers of commerce, area planning and development commissions, and local offices of the SBA and OSHA.

Environmental Protection

The Environmental Protection Agency (EPA) (www.epa.gov) was created to help protect and improve the quality of the nation's environment. Its mandate includes solid-waste disposal, clean air, water resources, noise, pesticides, and atomic radiation. Environmental protection, though beneficial to society, can be hard on small firms. Many marginal plants have closed because of EPA requirements that pollution control equipment be installed. You owe it to your employees, for humanitarian reasons as well as financial ones, to protect their environment. Environmental protection efforts may also give your company a competitive edge.

What You Should Have Learned

1. The most important resource for any business is its people. Therefore, you must determine the needed number and skills of employees and the sources from which to recruit them. This process begins with a job description and job specifications.

   Employees can be recruited from either internal or external sources. When feasible, it is best to upgrade, transfer, or promote from inside the business, all of which increase employee morale and save time and money; also, employees' past performance is known. External sources include former employees, applications, friends and relatives of present employees, competing firms, social and professional organizations, schools and colleges, retirees and older workers, those with disabilities, and part-time and temporary workers.

2. Employees can be recruited through advertising, employment agencies, temporary help services, networking, employee referrals, scouting, Internet, and temporary help services. Newspaper want ads are the most common method of recruiting.

   You can evaluate prospective employees by (a) a preliminary screening interview or review of the candidate's application or résumé; (b) biographical information from the application or résumé and from school, military, and other records; (c) some form of testing; (d) verifying references; and (e) giving a physical examination after a preliminary job offer is made.

   Ultimately, the decision regarding whom to employ involves your personal judgment. Once the decision has been made, a clear—preferably written—job offer should be extended. Orientation can range from a simple introduction to co-workers to a lengthy training process.

3. After employees are hired, they should be retrained and developed periodically. Training methods include (*a*) on-the-job training (OJT), (*b*) apprenticeship training, (*c*) internship training, and (*d*) cross-training.

4. In selecting managers, you should look for *managerial qualities*, which are not the same as an individual's *nonmanagerial competencies*. Techniques used for developing managers include (*a*) coaching, (*b*) planned progression, (*c*) job rotation, and (*d*) executive development programs—especially these developed by universities.

5. You must conform to federal and state laws in your dealings with current and prospective employees. The equal employment opportunity (EEO) provisions of the Civil Rights Act and the requirements of the Americans with Disabilities Act are especially important. Legislation has been passed to prevent discrimination on the basis of race, creed, color, sex, age, religion, disabilities, or national origin. The Equal Employment Opportunity Commission (EEOC) and the Office of Federal Contract Compliance Programs (OFCCP) enforce these laws. Age, sex, and language discrimination charges are particularly troubling to small firms.

6. Money is an important motivator, so you must pay your employees not just the minimum wage, but also enough to attract and keep them. You can use merit increases, incentive payments, and profit sharing to motivate your employees.

Employee benefits, which are increasingly significant to both employees and employers, are quite costly. While Social Security, Medicare, unemployment insurance, workers' compensation, and family and medical leave are legally required, pension plans—especially 401(k) savings plans—and various kinds of insurance are also popular voluntary benefits. Cafeteria-style benefit plans (sometimes called flexcomp) are now feasible for small companies.

7. Employee health and safety varies with the size of the organization, the type of industry, the type of occupation involved, and personal and human variables. Repetitive stress injuries are becoming a serious health problem for small firms, especially in their offices. OSHA, the government agency responsible for promoting safe and healthful working conditions, concentrates its enforcement activities on the businesses most likely to be unsafe or unhealthy.

While environmental protection is undoubtedly beneficial for everyone, the costs of required equipment and/or procedures can be a hardship for small businesses.

Key Terms

affirmative action programs (AAPs)   280
Americans with Disabilities Act (ADA)   277
apprenticeship training   274
bonus   283
cafeteria-style benefit plan or flexcomp   286
carpal tunnel syndrome   287
commission   283
cross-training   275
define-benefit plan   285
defined-contribution plan   285
E-training   275
employee benefits or fringe benefits   283
employee stock ownership plan (ESOP)   283
Equal Employment Opportunity Commission (EEOC)   279
Family and Medical Leave Act   285
401(k) retirement plans   286
incentive wage   282
in-depth, preemployment, or diagnostic interviews   272
internship training   274
job description   264
job specifications   264
leased manpower   267
merit increases   282
networking   269
Occupational Safety and Health Administration (OSHA)   288
on-the-job training (OJT) or on-the-job learning (OJL)   274
polygraph   272
profit sharing   283
promoting   266
push money (PM) or spiff   283
recruitment   268

Questions for Discussion

1. Which external sources are usually used by small businesses for finding new employees?

2. What are some advantages and disadvantages of filling job openings from within the company?

3. Distinguish among upgrading, promoting, and transferring employees.

4. What does the personnel selection procedure involve?

5. Describe the methods used to gather information about prospective employees.

6. What are the primary methods used to train employees? Explain each.

7. What should you look for in a potential manager?

8. How do EEO laws affect recruiting and selecting employees?

9. Which agencies enforce EEO laws? How do they enforce them?

10. What are some factors that affect the amount and form of compensation paid to employees?

Case 10.1

The Case of Sam Sawyer

Sam Sawyer was a top-rated operator in a building where a material with caustic soda was processed. The five stages of the process were located on five separate floors. Operators moved the material in open buggies from the first stage to a chute in the floor and dumped it onto equipment on the floor below, where the next stage began.

Because of the corrosive nature of the material, close-fitting goggles were provided. Until a year earlier, safety rules had required that goggles be worn only when removing material from equipment, because that was when the greatest possibility of injury existed. Their use at other times was up to the discretion of each operator.

At two stages in the process, though, the material was light and fluffy, and occasional backdrafts through the chutes caused it to fly. After this had resulted in three cases of eye irritations, the rules were changed, and operators were required to wear goggles whenever they were near exposed material.

Dave Watts, supervisor of operations for two years, had worked on all stages of the operation his first year out of engineering school. He had gotten along well with the men, was grateful to them for teaching him the "tricks of the trade," and might have been tempted to be lenient with them. Watts's boss, however, was very safety minded and insisted that safety rules be followed to the letter.

Sam Sawyer, who had worked on the operation for 20 years, was an outstanding operator and was looked up to by his fellow workers. His safety record was one of the best in the plant, as he had had only one minor injury in all his years of service.

When the new safety rule went into effect, Dave was bothered because everyone went along with it except Sam, who contended that it was unnecessary to wear goggles except when unloading equipment. This caused problems for Dave, because the others followed Sam's example. After much discussion, however, Sam agreed to go along with the rule.

Dave had a strong feeling that Sam was complying with the rule only while he was around. On half a dozen occasions he thought Sam had put on the goggles just as he came on the floor. Before the rule change, Sam had worn the goggles around his neck when they were not needed, but he had recently started wearing them pushed up on his forehead.

Dave's doubts were confirmed today when he came on Sam unexpectedly and saw him bob his head to shift the goggles from his forehead to his eyes.

Questions

1. What does the case show about the need for management emphasis on safety?
2. How can you explain the workers' lack of interest in their own safety?
3. What would you do if you were the supervisor?
4. How would you explain it to an OSHA inspector?
5. What does this case illustrate about the role of informal leaders?

Source: Prepared by Bruce Gunn, Florida State University. Used with permission.

Experientials

1. In groups, select a favorite cartoon character and design a valid job description for the character's purpose. (Refer to Figure 10.1.)
2. Poll your fellow students and determine what percentage of their jobs (current and previous) had documented job descriptions.

CHAPTER 11

How to Maintain Relationships with Your Employees and Their Representatives

The only difference between chaos and a smoothly functioning operation is leadership.
   —**David P. Campbell**
You can't manage people—you can only work with them. For your business to succeed, you must work closely with them and take exceedingly good care of them.
   —**Paul Hawken, Growing a Business**
The good boss selects people with demonstrated capabilities, tells them what results are expected, largely leaves them alone to decide the means by which they can be obtained, and then monitors the results.
   —**Sanford Jacobs, entrepreneur**

Learning Objectives

After studying the material in this chapter, you should be able to:

1. Explain how managerial assumptions affect human relationships with workers.

2. Explain why exercising effective leadership is so important in small business.

3. List some barriers to effective communication, and show some ways to improve communication.

4. Explain how to improve employee motivation.

5. Tell why employee appraisals are used and how they are done.

6. Define counseling, and discuss areas in which it may be needed in small firms.

7. Outline procedures for handling employee complaints and imposing discipline.

8. Discuss some complexities of dealing with unions.

9. Understand the difficulty in terminating employees.

10. Discuss basic organizational concepts, and show how small firms can use them.

PROFILE

Cathy Anderson-Giles: Master Motivator

Good leadership, whether in the military, in sports, or in business, is not a one-way street in terms of communication and motivation. Effective leaders know not only how and when to speak, but how and when to listen.

Judging from the success of her small business, Equity Technologies Inc., and the feedback from her employees, Cathy Anderson-Giles, the company's CEO, is a tremendous leader and motivator who employs a progressive management style. Equity Technologies specializes in removing, repairing, and cleaning telecommunications equipment.

An important aspect of Anderson-Giles's leadership is having a very informal, friendly working atmosphere. Employees wear jeans and enjoy an open-door policy. One employee noted that it was Anderson-Giles's extra touches—such as using fine china at the company Christmas party, putting fresh flowers in the office, and letting employees choose the colors in their offices—that made work and the working atmosphere pleasant. "I call it employee-friendly. We're sort of a family here," remarked Reginald Croshon, repair technician coordinator. "We try not to look at it as 'I'm the boss, you're the employee.'"

Anderson-Giles's background in Vicksburg and Jackson, Mississippi, is just as nontraditional as her management style. Because her son had a disability, she originally decided to pursue a career in physical education for the handicapped. She went back to school at Jackson State University (www.jsums.edu).

After a brief teaching stint, however, she realized this was not the profession for her. So she worked in the insurance industry while she attended law school at night. After receiving her law degree, she set up in private practice in her hometown of Jackson.

In 1984, her husband, who worked for AT&T (www.att.com), was transferred to Mobile, Alabama. It was then that she and her husband started their own company, Business Communication Distributors, which he continues to run. Six years later, they and two other investors started Equity Technologies Inc. with Anderson-Giles at the helm. "It was the logical step for me," she said. "I enjoy the process of creating businesses."

Anderson-Giles's employees seem to enjoy working for her. Perhaps her most important key to success is that she listens to and actively seeks the advice of her employees. Chip McNeill, manager of information services, states: "We have a lot of input in the day-to-day operation of the company." This style of leadership not only motivates employees but also makes them feel valued.

Anderson-Giles seeks advice from her employees because she believes in them, and they believe in—and perform for—her. Another motivating factor is that the employees know performance means advancement in the company. "We know the growth's here and there are opportunities for advancement," says Darrell Coxwell, assistant manager in the auditing department.

LaKeshia Joiner was one of the original employees hired by Anderson-Giles. Although LaKeshia had no work experience and only a high school diploma, Anderson-Giles saw considerable potential in her and continues to encourage her. Now LaKeshia has completed a degree at Southeast College of Technology, is the supervisor of the company's auditing division, and is working on a business degree. Enthusiastically, LaKeshia declares, "I haven't reached my peak yet."

Neither has Equity Technologies Inc., which had to move four times in five years in order to expand. The company grew from 10 to 48 employees in the 1990s. Because of the company's excellent growth at that time, Equity Technologies won the Small Business Technology Award given by the Business Council of Alabama.

Anderson-Giles says that the key to her leadership and motivational skills is that she realizes "there's so much undiscovered talent in everybody." Apparently, she is adept at finding it, as evidenced by the fact that in 1999 she was appointed to serve on the board of directors of the Business Council of Alabama. She now serves on the Governor's Commission on Education Spending, specifically on the Committee on K–12 Education Spending. For more information, you may access her Web site (equitytechcorp.com) or e-mail her at (cagiles@equitytechcorp.com).

Source: Prepared by William Jay Megginson from various sources.

In previous chapters you have seen how to recruit, select, train, and compensate employees, as well as maintain their health and safety. You will now find out how to organize them, communicate with and motivate them, counsel them, discipline them, and deal with the labor unions that serve as their representatives.

Good Human Relations Is Needed in Small Firms

The opening quotations and Profile illustrate the importance of good human relations in small firms.

Defining the term *human relations* is difficult, for it means different things to different people. Dr. Alfred Haake, lecturer for General Motors, would begin his lectures on human relations by saying, "Some people say that good human relations is treating people as if it were your last day on earth. Ah, no!" he would continue. "Good human relations is treating people as if it were *their* last day on earth." This thought is also expressed in the Golden Rule, which states: "So in everything, do to others what you would have them do to you (Bible)."

Human relations *involves the interaction among people in an organization.*

Human relations involves the cooperative and friendly interaction of people in an organization, especially in the areas of leadership, communication, and motivation. Regardless of the definition used, your success as a small business owner is based on practicing good human relations, according to the late Douglas McGregor.[1]

Good human relations occurs when both the employees and the small business owner develop a form of social contract, which outlines their rights and duties to each other. There are five topics to address with employees, namely,

- Reasons for being in business.
- Growth goals.
- Product goals.
- People involvement.
- Ethics statement.

Leading *is the management function of getting employees to do what you want them to do, by communicating with, motivating, and disciplining them.*

Exercising Effective Leadership

Leading, one of the basic management functions, is getting employees to do the things you want them to do, by means of communicating with, motivating, and disciplining them.

While management and leadership are similar, there are some significant differences. Leading is an important part of managing—but not the whole of it. **Leadership** is the ability of one person to influence others to strive to attain goals or objectives. Management, while requiring the use of leadership, also includes the other functions of planning, organizing, staffing, and controlling. Leadership is especially important for small business owners. Without it they cannot get workers to strive to achieve their goals or the business's objectives.

> **Leadership** is the ability of one person to influence others to attain objectives.

Today, effective small business owners are recognizing the role played by diversity in exercising effective leadership. In our competitive global environment, managers must realize that how humans behave and interact with others at work is governed by their beliefs, thought patterns, and values. While these may be largely subconscious, they are often so ingrained into our brains that they generate almost reflexive behavior. There is a growing sense among progressive owners and managers that this diversity can be successfully managed.

Communicating with Employees and Others

Communication, the process of transferring *meaning*—that is, ideas and information—from one person to another, is your number one job. Classic studies have shown that verbal communication takes up about 80 percent of a manager's time.[2]

> **Communication** is the transfer of meaning from one person to another.

Communication is so important because people need and want to know what is going on so they can do their jobs properly. Owners, employees, customers, vendors, and others need to coordinate their work, so communication must be clear and complete. In addition, speaking pleasantly and persuasively makes people want to do good work; as a Japanese proverb says, "One kind word can warm three winter months."

What Happens When You Communicate?

While explaining a process as complex as communication is difficult, Figure 11.1 shows that the process involves: (1) someone (the source) having an idea, thought, or impression that

FIGURE 11.1 |
The Communication Process

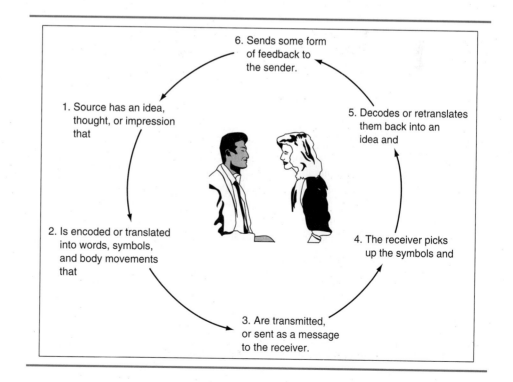

1. Source has an idea, thought, or impression that
2. Is encoded or translated into words, symbols, and body movements that
3. Are transmitted, or sent as a message to the receiver.
4. The receiver picks up the symbols and
5. Decodes or retranslates them back into an idea and
6. Sends some form of feedback to the sender.

(2) is encoded or translated into words or symbols that (3) are transmitted, or sent as a message, to another person (the receiver), who (4) picks up the symbols and (5) decodes, or retranslates, them back into an idea and (6) sends some form of feedback to the sender. Feedback completes the process, because communication cannot be assumed to have occurred until the receiver demonstrates understanding of the message. *Because communication is an exchange of meaning (rather than words or symbols), many forms of nonverbal communication convey meaning through signals, signs, sounds (other than words), and facial expressions.*

Barriers to Effective Communication

Despite the importance of communication and the amount of time we spend communicating, the transfer of meaning is not always effective. There are many causes of this ineffectiveness, especially some barriers erected by the business itself or by the people involved.

First, because of the owner's position of authority, employees tend to believe what the owner says, regardless of whether it is true or not, when they might be better off thinking through a problem on their own. The status of the communicator either lends credibility to what is being said or detracts from it; messages of higher-status people automatically tend to carry greater credibility than those of lower-status people. The individuals in authority may get carried away by this tendency and not listen to their people, who may be closer to a problem.

The imprecise use of language also serves as a barrier. Have you noticed how frequently people use the expression "you know" in daily communications, lazily hoping their listener really does know, or adopt buzzwords (especially those from high-tech fields) without caring what they mean? For example, an employee being dismissed is sometimes said to be "outplaced" or "re-placed," often as a result of a "downsizing" (or "rightsizing") effort in the company, whether or not such jargon is applicable in the particular case.

Perhaps the greatest barriers to effective communication are simply inattention and poor listening. Small business owners, as well as managers of bigger companies, are often so preoccupied with running their businesses that they may not pay attention to employee feedback.

How to Improve Communication

You can become a more effective communicator by clarifying your ideas, considering the environment in which the communication occurs, considering emotional overtones as well as the message, following up on communication, and being a good listener. As we have emphasized, communication is a two-way street. Even more important than getting your meaning across is listening to and understanding what the other person says. If you will pay attention to the communication process, then you will be in a position to take advantage of new technology.

First there was interpersonal, face-to-face communication. Then came the telephone, followed by cable, cellular, and satellite communications. New technology provides small business owners with cost savings, access to new markets, and the ability to respond more rapidly to changing customer and supplier demand.

Real-World Example 11.1

For example, "At Shell, everyone's the answer man." In 1998 Shell installed a private Web bulletin board that allowed employees to swap advice. One of the problems they incurred was encouraging users. This $1 million installation saves the company about

$200 million a year. They follow five rules in this communication system:

1. Keep it simple.

2. Recruit the initial users.

3. Encourage diversity (different job types).

4. Enlist cheerleaders.

5. Archive the best advice.[3]

Shell archives discussions and creates a database of answers that is both informal and popular.

Motivating Employees

Before reading the following material, complete the exercise in Figure 11.2. This exercise helps explain why motivation is so complex and why it is so difficult to motivate some employees. You must use different incentives to motivate different people at different times

FIGURE 11.2 |
What Do You Want
from a Job?

Rank the employment factors shown below in their order of importance to you at three points in your career. In the first column, assume that you are about to graduate and are looking for your first full-time job. In the second column, assume that you have been gainfully employed for 5 to 10 years and that you are presently employed by a reputable firm at the prevailing salary for the type of job and industry you are in. In the third column, try to assume that 25 to 30 years from now you have "found your niche in life" and have been working for a reputable employer for several years. (Rank your first choice as 1, second as 2, and so forth through 9.)

	Ranking of Selected Employment Factors		
Employment Factor	**As You Seek Your First Full-Time Job**	**Your Ranking 5–10 Years Later**	**Your Ranking 25–30 Years Later**
Fair adjustment of grievances			
Good job instruction and training			
Effective job supervision by your supervisor			
Promotion possibilities			
Recognition (praise, rewards, and so on)			
Job safety			
Job security (no threat of being dismissed or laid off)			
Good salary			
Good working conditions (nice office surroundings, good hours, and so on)			

in their working lives. Yet it is difficult for us to always know what a given employee wants at a given time. Understanding those needs and understanding how to use the appropriate motivation are the secrets of successful small business ownership and management.

What Is Motivation?

Motivation is the inner state that activates a person, including drives, desires, and/or motives.

You can use **motivation** to bring out the best in your employees by giving them reasons to perform better, but it's not easy. *You are always motivating employees—either positively (to perform) or negatively (to withhold performance)—even when you are not conscious of doing so.* When you give employees a reason to perform better, you create positive motivation; on the other hand, if you say or do something that annoys, frustrates, or antagonizes employees, they will react negatively and either withhold production or actually sabotage operations.

Real-World Example 11.2

For example, a customer went into an ice cream shop in a college town and ordered a banana split. When it came, something was obviously wrong. There were five scoops of ice cream, double portions of fruit and nuts, and a huge serving of whipped cream, with several cherries on top. The customer, who was a management professor at a local university, asked the young employee, "What's wrong?" The young man didn't even pretend not to understand. "I'm mad at the boss," he promptly replied. A few months later, the shop went out of business.

The best way for you to succeed in business is to increase employee productivity and efficiency. While there is a limit to improvements in employee productivity, effective motivation can have a positive effect. However, *because many factors affect productivity, motivation alone is not enough.*

In general, employee performance is a product of the employee's ability to do the job and the application of positive motivation; that is,

$$\text{Performance} = \text{Ability} \times \text{Motivation}$$

or

$$P = A \times M$$

Most employees go to work for a company expecting to do a good job, receive a satisfactory income, and gain satisfaction from doing a good job. However, performance and satisfaction are dependent on the *ability* to do the job. If your employees are not performing as you would like them to, they may be unsuited for the job, inadequately trained, or unmotivated. If they are unsuited, move them to a more suitable job, and if untrained, train them. If they are both suited and trained, try harder to motivate them.

Why Motivate Employees?

One reason managerial motivation is so difficult to use is that there are different purposes for motivating people, each of which requires different incentives. Usually managers use motivation to (1) attract potential employees, (2) improve performance, and (3) retain good employees.

Attracting Potential Employees   If you want to encourage potential employees to work for you, you must find and use incentives that appeal to a person needing a job. These incentives usually include a good income, pleasant working conditions, promotional possibilities, and sometimes a signing bonus.

The exercise in Figure 11.2 has been used with junior- and senior-level business students since 1957. With very few exceptions, "good salary" has been the primary consideration in looking for a first job in over 200 surveys reviewed, while "promotion possibilities" and "good working conditions" are a close second and third. How did you rate these factors?

Improving Performance   You can also use motivation to improve performance and efficiency on the part of present employees. You can do this by praising good work, giving employees more responsibility, publicly recognizing a job well done, and awarding merit salary increases.

Real-World Example 11.3

Notice in the Profile at the beginning of the chapter that Cathy Anderson-Giles treats her people well to bring out the best in them. She gives them personal at-tention, helps them with their problems, and gives them challenging work to do.

Retaining Good Employees   Motivation can also be used to retain your present employees. This is accomplished primarily through the use of employee benefits, most of which are designed to reward employees who stay with the company. However, many other incentives can help explain today's work force retention, many of them individual and personal.

Real-World Example 11.4

For example, Cal Ripken, the shortstop for the Baltimore Orioles baseball team (www.theorioles.com), had not missed playing in a scheduled game from 1982 until June 28, 2001 with a record of 2,632 consecutive games played.

There is also Elena Griffing, at Bates Medical Center, who took her last sick day in 1952. She explained her feat by saying: "Watching the healing process makes it worth going to work."

Another reason to retain good employees is the high cost of employee turnover. These costs are about 400 percent of annual salary for top level employees and about 50 percent for entry level.[4]

How to Motivate Employees

The theory of motivation is relatively simple, as shown in Figure 11.3. An employee has a need or needs, and you apply some kind of incentive (or stimulus) that promises to satisfy that need. Your main problem in motivating employees is to know them well enough to know what they need and what incentives will stimulate them to perform such as the following example.

FIGURE 11.3 |

The Motivational
Process

Quality circles (QCs)
are small employee groups
that meet periodically to
improve quality and output.

A **zero-defects
approach** uses pride in
workmanship to get
workers to do their work
"right the first time."

Job enrichment is
granting workers greater
responsibility and authority
in their jobs.

A **variable work
schedule** (also called
a **flexible work
arrangement**) permits
employees to work at
times other than the
standard five 8-hour days.

Flextime is an
arrangement under which
employees may schedule
their own hours, around a
core time.

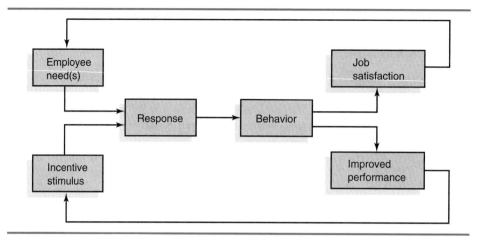

Employee need(s) → Response → Behavior → Job satisfaction
Incentive stimulus → Response → Behavior → Improved performance

Real-World Example 11.5

Beryl Companies strive to deliver value to their employees by constantly reminding them of their importance to the company. They send handwritten notes for personal occasions and accomplishments, earn trust by sharing financial performance, invest in employee's futures, prioritize fun activities (e.g., pajama day and dress-like-the-70s day), and by focusing on what matters most to each employee. Treating employees like stakeholders has not only increased the bottom line but also reduced employee turnover.[5]

Some Practical Ways to Improve Motivation

While we cannot give you a "cookbook" answer as to how to motivate your people, we do know that the old ways of motivating people through "command and control" are no longer viable options. Instead, we must turn to the "real world" to see how the more progressive managers motivate their employees.

Some of the progressive methods that have shown good results in motivating employees, especially in small businesses, are: (1) quality circles, (2) zero-defects programs, (3) job enrichment, (4) variable work schedules, and (5) job splitting and sharing.

Quality circles (QCs) are small, organized work groups that meet periodically to find ways to improve quality and output. They motivate by getting employees involved and taking advantage of their creativity and innovativeness.

The **zero-defects approach** is based on getting workers to do their work "right the first time," thus generating pride in workmanship. It assumes that employees want to do a good job—and will do so if permitted to.

Job enrichment emphasizes giving employees greater responsibility and authority over their jobs as the best way to motivate them. Employees are encouraged to learn new and related skills or even to trade jobs with each other as ways of making jobs more interesting and therefore more productive.

Variable work schedules (also called **flexible work arrangements**) permit employees to work at times other than the standard work week of five eight-hour days. Such schedules are being extensively used by small firms to motivate employees. **Flextime** allows

The company's new Whip-Matic Productivity System helped boost profits by 21 percent.

employees to schedule their own hours as long as they are present during certain required hours, called *core time.* This gives employees greater control over their time and activities.

Job splitting is dividing a single full-time job into distinct parts and letting two (or more) employees do the different parts. In **job sharing,** a single full-time job is shared by two (or more) employees, with one worker performing all aspects of the job at one time and the other worker doing it at another time.

Small business owners are faced with a dilemma when considering such motivational programs. They may believe that using one or more of the new methods will improve employee performance and hence increase profits. But they may not have the knowledge, time, money, or personnel to implement the method or methods.

Job splitting occurs when employees divide a single job into two or more different parts, each one doing one of the parts.

Job sharing occurs when a single full-time job is retained, but its performance is shared by two or more employees working at different times.

Motivation Is More than Mere Technique

Successful motivation of employees is based more on a managerial philosophy than on using a given technique. Thus, you should try to create an environment in your firm in which employees can apply themselves willingly and wholeheartedly to the task of increasing productivity and quality.

Real-World Example 11.6

This thought was expressed soon after World War II (1940s) by Clarence Francis, chairman of General Foods, when he said, "You can buy a man's time; you can buy a man's physical presence at a given place; you can even buy a measured number of skilled muscular motions per hour or day; but you cannot buy enthusiasm; you cannot buy initiative; you cannot buy loyalty; you cannot buy devotion of hearts, minds, and souls. You have to earn these things."[6]

Performance appraisal is the process of evaluating workers to see how well they are performing.

Appraising and Evaluating Employees' Performance

If your employees' actual output cannot be measured, you need an effective system of **performance appraisal** (also called *employee evaluation* or *merit rating*) to help you answer the question "How well are my people performing?" Under such a system, each employee's performance and progress are evaluated, and rewards are given for above-average performance. Appraisals should be based on the employee's job description. You cannot measure performance unless you have requirements. For example, Figure 11.4 is a spoof of Scooby Doo's gang; notice the specifics of the job. This job description gives us enough information to measure employee performance by simply checking off the requirements one by one as either accomplished or not. There are probably hundreds of ways to quantify your evaluation, but you should now have a good idea of how the process works.

Often, this technique is used in determining merit salary increases, special merit raises, training decisions, layoffs, or promotions or transfers. Appraisals can also be used for disciplinary actions such as reprimands, suspensions, demotions, or discharges. Finally, the results of formal appraisals can be used to support or refute disciplinary documentation in proceedings before such bodies as the EEOC (www.eeoc.gov) and in Unemployment Compensation Appeals hearings.

Employee appraisals are usually based on such factors as quantity and quality of work performed, cooperativeness,

"In the interests of a fair and equitable gratuity, your service is being evaluated."

Source: Cartoon by Fred Maes. Copyright 1996 by Fred Maes.

FIGURE 11.4 |

Job Description

Position Title:	**Job Code:**
Member of Scooby gang	911
Department:	**EEOC Class:**
Mystery solving	Field work
Reports to:	**FLSA Status:**
Other members of team	Nonexempt
Prepared by:	
(Supervisor)	

General Summary

Working with a team consisting of four other members, one of which is a dog, to solve mysteries in a clever and humorous manner.

Essential Job Function

1. Traveling to various locations, under the pretense of just a relaxing vacation or visiting a relative.
2. Recognizing mysteries where there might not seem to be a mystery at all.
3. Collaborating with other team members to gather clues that will ultimately lead to the solving of the mystery.
4. Forming a plan with your teammates to trap the wrongdoers in the middle of the crime.
5. Expose the wrongdoers and hand them over to the police.
6. Relax and party for a job well done.
7. Do all of these things in a humorous and entertaining way.

Knowledge, Skills, and Abilities

1. Knowledge of laws, so you can tell when they are being broken.
2. Knowledge of various monsters.
3. Knowledge of the criminal mind.
4. Skills in quick deduction.
5. Skills in analytical thinking.
6. Skills at spontaneous problem solving.
7. Ability to operate a variety of motor vehicles.
8. Ability to work well with other team members.
9. Ability not to be frightened when face to face with monsters and ghosts.
10. Ability to quickly evaluate clues to form conclusions.
11. Ability to constantly remain entertaining.

Education and Experience

High school diploma or GED and at least one year experience working in a group effort.

Physical Requirements

	0–24%	25–49%	50–74%	75–100%
Seeing Although glasses or contacts may be worn, perfect sight is required for seeing far off villains as well as clues.				X
Hearing Must be optimal to be able to hear suspicious sounds and communicating with teammates.				X
Running Must be able to outrun bad guys.				X
Climbing, Stooping, Kneeling				X
Lifting, Pulling, Pushing				X
Swimming, Scuba Diving				X

Working Conditions

Working conditions are very physically demanding and constantly changing.

Note

The statements herein are intended to describe the general nature and level of work being performed by employees and are not to be construed as an exhaustive list of responsibilities, duties, and skills required of personnel so classified.

FIGURE 11.5 | How Performance Appraisals Operate

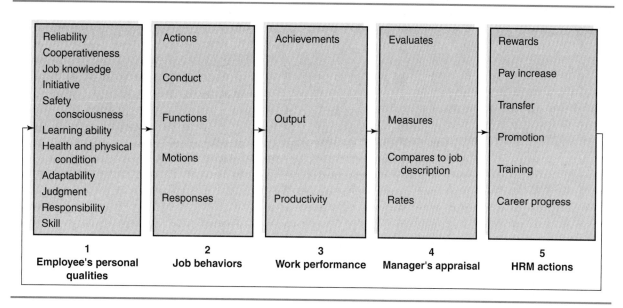

1	2	3	4	5
Reliability	Actions	Achievements	Evaluates	Rewards
Cooperativeness				
Job knowledge	Conduct			Pay increase
Initiative				
Safety				Transfer
consciousness	Functions	Output	Measures	
Learning ability				Promotion
Health and physical	Motions		Compares to job	
condition			description	Training
Adaptability				
Judgment	Responses	Productivity	Rates	Career progress
Responsibility				
Skill				
Employee's personal qualities	**Job behaviors**	**Work performance**	**Manager's appraisal**	**HRM actions**

initiative, dependability (including attendance), job knowledge, safety, and personal habits. While appraisals are usually done by the employee's direct supervisor, they may also be done by the affected employee, his or her peers, or subordinates, or by the use of electronic devices.

Employee evaluations should be related to promotions and salary increases in addition to identifying marginal workers and designing training activities for them. They can also be used to motivate employees, if the evaluations are adequately translated into rewards.

Performance appraisals are based on the assumption that employees have (1) personal abilities and qualities that lead to (2) job behaviors that (3) result in work performance that (4) can be identified and measured. Therefore, as shown in Figure 11.5, you need to (1) determine which personal qualities an employee has that result in (2) his or her behaving in a certain way on the job that (3) results in a certain level or quality of work being performed. You must evaluate, measure, or rate work performance in order to take some type of human resource management action involving that worker.

Although employee appraisals themselves are important, it is the feedback from them that really leads to improved performance. An early research study found that those who took some form of constructive action as a result of performance appraisals "did so because of the way their superiors had conducted the appraisal feedback interview and discussion."[7]

Counseling Troubled Employees

Counseling helps to provide people with an understanding of their relationships with their supervisors, fellow workers, and customers.

Counseling is designed to help employees do a better job by helping them understand their relationships with supervisors, fellow workers, and customers. While most small firms do not have formal counseling programs, they counsel employees on a day-to-day basis. The points for discussion with a troubled employee in Figure 11.6 may help you do informal counseling. If you do not feel qualified to perform this counseling activity, specialized employees may be used. Or free one-on-one counseling may be obtained from SCORE executives, who have had hands-on experience.

FIGURE 11.6 |

How to Approach a
Troubled Employee

1. Establish the standards of job performance you expect.
2. Be specific about behavioral criteria, such as absenteeism and poor job performance.
3. Restrict criticism to job performance.
4. Be firm and consistent.
5. Be prepared to deal with resistance, defensiveness, or even hostility.
6. Point out the availability of internal or external counseling services.
7. Explain that only the employee can decide whether or not to seek assistance.
8. Discuss drinking only if it occurs on the job or the employee is obviously intoxicated.
9. Emphasize the confidentiality of the program.
10. Get a commitment from the employee to meet specific work criteria and monitor this with a plan for improvement based on work performance.

While counseling may benefit all areas of employee relations, most counseling needs fall into the categories of (1) job-related activities, (2) personal problems, and (3) employee complaints.

Job-Related Areas Needing Counseling

The areas that may most need counseling are (1) health and safety, (2) retirement or termination, (3) stress, and finally, (4) discipline, which will be treated separately in the next section.

Health and Safety   As shown in Chapter 10, the whole complex area of health and safety requires considerable counseling and guidance. Because safety is largely a matter of attitude, your role is to counsel employees on the need for safe operations and to actively support all safety efforts.

Retirement or Termination   Employees need considerable preparation for retirement, especially with regard to the benefits coming to them. But counseling is even more urgently needed when an employee must be terminated—with or without cause. Now that U.S. businesses are more concerned with cost saving, primarily because of foreign competition, terminations are more frequent.

When employees just cannot produce or when the business cannot afford to keep them, termination, often called *outplacement,* is sometimes the only option. But, as will be shown later, you might want to help the worker find other employment. Even with such help, though, termination is still traumatic for the worker, and counseling is needed.

Stress   Stress is a nasty buzzword in workplaces. Nearly everyone feels the presence of stress, and few can fully escape it. Stress can arise suddenly or gradually and can last for a short time or can persist for years. Whatever its nature, job-related stress often begins when individuals are placed in a work environment that is incompatible with their professional work style and/or temperament. And stress becomes aggravated when individuals find that they can exercise little control over their work environment.

Contrary to popular belief, a fast-paced, chronically pressured work environment alone is not the primary cause of stress; instead, stress begins when individuals and environments are mismatched. Some people thrive on a fast-paced, even frenzied work atmosphere, while others prefer a slow-paced environment.

Stress can be a killer for a small business. When stress becomes great enough, it can result in **job burnout,** which is physical or mental depletion to a level significantly below one's capable level of performance. Stress of such intensity is a major cause of absenteeism and work site antagonisms.

Job burnout is a physical or mental depletion to a level significantly below a person's capable level of performance.

Personal Problems Needing Counseling

Many employees suffer personal problems, which reduce productivity. Two-thirds of those problems are controlled substance related, while the others tend to be emotional problems. Some problems that can result from substance abuse are absenteeism, accidents, increases in medical expenses, insubordination, thefts, and product or service quality problems. Employers are coping with these problems through counseling, referral to trained professionals, and employee-assistance programs (EAPs).

Since 1989, small businesses with federal contracts and grants have been required to have a substance abuse policy that conforms to the Department of Defense's "Drug-Free Workforce Rules." These rules impose sweeping new obligations on contractors and grantees.* While the cost of such a drug-free environment is unknown, many small firms may be unable to bear the cost.

Handling Employee Complaints

Because complaints will inevitably occur, you should encourage employees to inform you when they think something is wrong and needs to be corrected. An effective procedure to do this should provide (1) assurance to employees that expressing their complaints will not jeopardize their employment, (2) a simple procedure for presenting their complaints, and (3) a minimum of red tape and time in processing complaints and determining solutions.

Unresolved complaints can lead to more problems, so you should listen patiently and deal with them promptly even if they seem to be without foundation. You should analyze the complaint carefully, gather pertinent facts, make a decision, inform the employee of it, and follow up to determine whether the cause of the problem has been corrected. Detailed, written records of all complaints (and disciplinary actions), as well as how they were resolved, should be maintained in employees' files as a defense against legal charges that may be brought against you.

Imposing Discipline

Discipline involves fairly enforcing a system of rules and regulations to obtain order.

Employees like to work in an environment where there is **discipline**—in the sense of having a system of rules and procedures and having them enforced fairly. You can achieve such an orderly, disciplined environment by either (1) motivating employees to exercise self-discipline or (2) imposing discipline on them.

Encouraging Self-Discipline

To be effective, your employees should have confidence in their ability to perform their jobs, see good performance as compatible with their own interests, and know you will provide support if they run into difficulties. Therefore, you should encourage self-discipline among employees rather than rely on direct control. In this respect, the personal example of the owner is important in influencing employee discipline, as the following example illustrates.

---

*Contact your nearest SBA office for more information on these laws.

> ### Real-World Example 11.7
> The owner of a small firm selling and installing metal buildings had a problem with employees taking long lunch breaks. When he asked his supervisors to correct this practice, one of them had the courage to say, "That would be easier to do if you didn't take two-hour lunches yourself."

Using Positive Discipline

Positive discipline deals with an employee's breach of conduct by issuing an oral "reminder" (not a reprimand), then a written reminder, followed by a paid day off so the employee can decide if he or she really wants to keep the job. If the answer is "yes," the employee agrees in writing to be on his/her best behavior for a given period of time.

We have heard managers of small firms say that traditional discipline does not work for them. Instead, some are using **positive discipline** to improve morale and lower turnover. Under this approach, employees who commit some breach of conduct receive an oral "reminder," not a reprimand. Then there is a written reminder, followed by a paid day off so they can decide whether they really want to keep their job. If the answer is yes, the employee agrees in writing to be on his or her best behavior for a given period. The employee who does not perform satisfactorily after that is fired. Because the cases are fully documented, employees usually have little recourse.

How to Discipline Employees Legally

Most employees rarely cause problems. Yet if you do not deal effectively with the few who violate rules and regulations, employees' respect for you will decline. Therefore, *an effective disciplinary system that meets union and legal guidelines involves*

- Setting definite rules and seeing that employees know them.
- Acting promptly on violations.
- Gathering pertinent facts about violations.
- Allowing employees an opportunity to explain their behavior.
- Setting up tentative courses of action and evaluating them.
- Deciding what action to take.
- Taking disciplinary action while observing labor contract and EEO procedures.
- Setting up and maintaining a record of actions taken and following up on the outcome.

The **judicial due process** of discipline involves (1) establishing rules of behavior, (2) setting prescribed penalties for violating each rule, and (3) imposing the penalty(ies) only after determining the extent of guilt.

This type of discipline system follows the pattern established for **judicial due process.** The procedure should distinguish between major and minor offenses and consider extenuating circumstances, such as the employee's length of service, prior performance record, and the amount of time since the last offense.

Dealing with Unions

The percentage of the U.S. workforce represented by unions is declining. It has dropped from 23 percent in 1983 and is now only 12 percent.[8]

While union organizers have tended to concentrate their organizing efforts on larger firms, because they are easier to unionize, they are now also trying to organize smaller firms, because that is where potential new members are. Also, small business owners are more active

TABLE 11.1 | Some Laws Governing Union–Management Relations

Law	Coverage	Basic Requirements	Enforcement Agencies
Railway Labor Act of 1926	Nonmanagerial employees of private railroads and airlines	Provides that employees are free to choose their own representatives for collective bargaining, and to settle disputes by mediation, arbitration, and emergency boards.	National Mediation Board; National Railroad Adjustment Board
Norris-LaGuardia Act of 1932	Union employees	Restricted the power of federal courts to issue injunctions against unions engaged in peaceful strikes and declared a national policy permitting employees to organize.	
National Labor Relations Act of 1935, as amended (also called the Wagner Act)	Nonmanagrial employees in nonagricultural private firms not covered by the Railway Labor Act, and postal employees	Employees have the right to form or join labor organizations (or to refuse to), to bargain collectively through their representatives, and to engage in other concerted activities such as strikes, picketing, and boycotts. There are unfair labor practices in which the employer and the union cannot engage.	National Labor Relations Board (NLRB)
Labor–Management Relations Act of 1947, as amended (also called the Taft-Hartley Act)	Same as above	Amended NLRA; permits states to pass laws prohibiting compulsory union membership; sets up methods to deal with strikes affecting national health and safety.	NLRB; Federal Mediation and Conciliation Service
Labor–Management Reporting and Discourse Act of 1959, as amended (also called the Landrum-Griffin Act)	Same as above	Amended NLRA and LMRA; guarantees individual rights of union members in dealing with their union; requires financial disclosures by unions.	U.S. Department of Labor

Source: Various government and private publications.

in lobbying Congress and state legislatures, through groups such as the National Federation of Independent Business (NFIB) (www.nfibonline.com), for laws and regulations unions oppose. Therefore, you need to know something about unions and how to deal with them.

Laws Governing Union–Management Relations

The *National Labor Relations Act (NLRA)* (also called the *Wagner Act*), as amended, requires management to bargain with the union if a majority of its employees desire unionization. (See Table 11.1 for the provisions of this and related laws.) Managers are forbidden to discriminate against employees in any way because of union activity. The *National Labor Relations Board (NLRB)* serves as the labor court. Its general counsel investigates charges of unfair labor practices, issues complaints, and prosecutes cases. The union or management can appeal a ruling of the board through a U.S. circuit court all the way up to the U.S. Supreme Court.

In some states a *union shop clause* provides that employees must join the recognized union within 30 days after being hired. But under **right-to-work laws** in effect in 22 states, the union shop is not legally permitted. Figure 11.7 shows the states with those laws in effect in 2011.

Right-to-work laws permit states to prohibit unions from requiring workers to join a union.

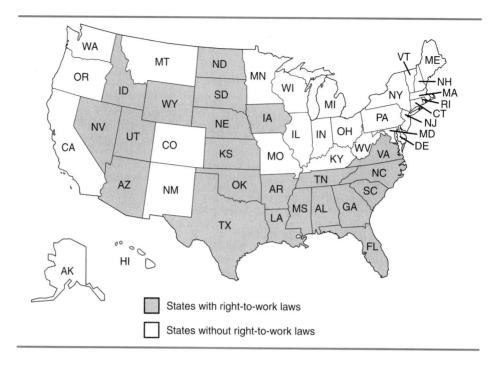

☐ (gray) States with right-to-work laws

☐ (white) States without right-to-work laws

What Happens When the Union Enters

Unions exist to bargain with the employer on behalf of their members for higher wages, fringe benefits, better working conditions, security, and other terms and conditions of employment. To do this, the union must first organize the company's employees.

The first thing you should do if your employees want to form a union is to recognize that it is because they believe they need the protection the union offers. You should therefore ask yourself such questions as: Why do my employees feel that it is necessary to have a union to represent them? Is it a lack of communication, or have I failed to respond to their needs? Am I treating them arbitrarily or unfairly? Studies of successful nonunionized companies find that management and employees participate in the business process as a team rather than as adversaries.

The second thing you should do is call in a competent consultant or labor lawyer. Small firms are increasingly turning to advisers to deal with unions.

If your company is unionized, you should be prepared for certain changes. Your actions and statements may be reported to union officials, and the union may file unfair labor practice charges with the NLRB. Your best defense is to know your rights under the prevailing laws—and to maintain favorable relationships with employees.

Negotiating the Agreement

Negotiating an agreement with the union requires much preparation, as well as the actual bargaining, and these require patience and understanding, so again it is advisable to consult your labor lawyer.

Preparing for the Bargaining   Preparation may well be the most important step in negotiating the agreement. Obtaining facts about the issues before sitting down at the bargaining table should improve your position. You should collect information on other contracts in the industry and in the local area. Disciplinary actions, complaints, and other key matters that arose before the union's entry should be studied. Current business literature concerning business in general and the status of union–management relations in the industry can be useful. A carefully researched proposal should be developed well in advance of the first bargaining session.

Bargaining with the Union   If you have prepared properly, you should be in a positive negotiating position instead of a defensive stance against the union's proposals. The "I do not want to give away any more than I have to" attitude generally leads to poor bargaining. All too frequently, however, fear seems to overcome the owner's willingness to develop in advance a proposal with attractive features that will appeal to employees, while protecting the company's position.

You should recognize the negotiation step as critical: It must be handled properly, preferably with outside assistance. Also remember that anything given away will be difficult to take back.

Be prepared to bargain over at least the following:

- Union recognition.
- Wages.
- Vacations and holidays.
- Working conditions.
- Layoffs and rehiring.
- Hours of work.
- Management prerogatives.
- Seniority.
- Arbitration.
- Renewal of the agreement.

The **management prerogatives clause** defines the areas in which you have the right to act freely as an employer, without interference from the union.

Specific agreements must be reached in each of these areas, and rules established that should be obeyed by the company and the union. The **management prerogatives clause** is very important because it defines the areas in which you have the right to act freely as an employer without interference from the union.

Living with the Agreement

Because the agreement becomes a legal document when it is signed, you must learn to live with its provisions until time for renegotiation. Your managers should be thoroughly briefed on its contents and implications. The meaning and interpretation of each clause should be reviewed and the wording clearly understood. Supervisors' questions should be answered to better prepare them to deal with labor matters.

Real-World Example 11.8

For example, the Associations of Flight Attendants has asked a federal judge to appoint an examiner to investigate their allegations that United Airlines duped more than 2,000 attendants into early retirement by suggesting they could lock in inexpensive medical benefits. United was attempting to cut medical benefits for retirees.[9]

Information and advice can be obtained from government sources, such as federal and state mediators, NLRB regional offices, state industrial relations departments, and members of SCORE. Private sources include employer groups, trade associations, labor relations attorneys, and labor relations consultants.

Terminating Employees

Employment at will
means that employers may hire or fire workers with or without cause.

Although you still have the right to terminate employees for cause, the concept of "employment at will" is losing acceptance in courts and legislatures. **Employment at will** essentially means employers may fire employees with or without cause at any time they choose. Courts and legislators are now applying the "good faith and fair dealing" concept, whereby termination must be "reasonable" and not "arbitrarily" or "indiscriminately" applied. Violating this concept may lead to punitive damages in addition to actual damages that have been sustained by one of the protected employees.

Setting up the Organizational Structure

Organizing is determining those activities that are necessary to achieve a firm's objectives and assigning them to responsible persons.

The organizational structure of a business governs relationships between the owner, managers, and employees. **Organizing** involves determining the activities needed to achieve the firm's objectives, dividing these activities into small groups, and assigning each group to a manager with the necessary authority and expertise to see that they are done. A major problem for many small business owners is that they do not organize their activities properly. The following discussion should help you understand how best to organize a business.

Many problems within the organization can be addressed with the publication and use of an employee handbook. Some companies refer to this as a standard practices manual or standard operating procedures (SOP) manual. This type of company publication will quite often contain an organization chart, job descriptions, company policies, and all procedures generally used. Large organizations may have volumes of very detailed company procedures. Small business owners should document as many policies and procedures as possible. This serves two purposes: (1) clarify employee/employer role and (2) serve as basis for defense in many employment-related court actions.

Some Basic Organizational Concepts

There are at least three basic organizational concepts that apply to growing small businesses: (1) delegation, (2) span of management, and (3) specialization. It must be added that *while these concepts should be applied to businesses as they grow larger, they must often be adjusted when applied to mom-and-pop businesses.*

Delegation is assigning responsibility to subordinates for certain activities and giving them the authority to perform those activities.

Delegation   **Delegation** means assigning responsibility to subordinates for doing certain activities, giving them the authority to carry out the duties, and letting them take care of the details of how the job is done. Many owners and managers of small firms find it difficult to delegate authority. Yet you need to learn to delegate if you answer yes to most of the questions in Figure 11.8. When you delegate work to subordinates, try to delegate sufficient authority to them to carry out their responsibilities. Otherwise, they lack the means of performing their duties.

Except in very small mom-and-pop shops, you should give employees a *job description,* which is a written statement of duties, responsibilities, authority, and relationships (see Chapter 10 for details). When you delegate authority to employees to do certain duties, you must be willing to let them do it; yet you cannot relinquish your responsibility for seeing that those duties are performed.

FIGURE 11.8 |
How Well Do You
Delegate?

- Do you do work an employee could do just as well?
- Do you think you are the only one who actually knows how the job should be done?
- Do you leave work each day loaded down with details to take care of at home?
- Do you frequently stay after hours catching up?
- Are you a perfectionist?
- Do you tell your employees how to solve problems?
- Do you seem never to be able to complete the work assigned to you?

Specialization is using
employees to do the work
that they are best
suited for.

Specialization

You should try to use **specialization,** whereby employees do the work they are best suited for. This concept is hard to apply in very small businesses, where rigid specialization can result in some employees being idle while others are overworked. You must exercise judgment in assigning job responsibilities according to employees' talents and desires without neglecting an equitable distribution of work.

Some Organizational Problems in Small Firms

A common problem in small firms is the owner's reluctance to delegate authority. This practice prevents the owner from devoting time to more pressing needs while also preventing others from developing into well-rounded workers.

> **Real-World Example 11.9**
>
> For example, the owner of a small wholesale company was chairman of the board, president, and treasurer. He handled all financial affairs; supervised accounting operations, wages, salaries, and sales commissions; and made recommendations to the board on the payment of dividends. Yet the company also had a vice president, sales manager, and operations manager.

This example describes an owner who does not delegate authority. Another kind of problem is an owner who is afraid to make decisions, so the business becomes paralyzed. Then there is the owner who reverses decisions made by others. Perhaps he has not developed policies to cover the major repetitive situations and business functions.

The following are other indications of organizational trouble:

- The owner holds too many meetings attended by too many people, resulting in wasted hours and excessive costs.

- Administrative expenses grow more rapidly than sales.

- The owner spends too much time following proper procedures or resolving conflicts rather than "getting production out."

- The attention of key people is not directed toward key activities of the firm and their performance.

Failure to delegate places an immense burden on you, making it difficult for you ever to be absent from the business. Also, it virtually guarantees the failure of the business if you become incapacitated for a long time, because no one else has been trained to perform management tasks. Another issue with delegation is one of avoiding three common first-timer mistakes. In delegating, you need to make sure that the person you choose is able to carry out your needs. They must be able to

1. Learn from other people's mistakes.

2. They must follow the formula (plan).

3. They must be teachable.[9]

Also, remember, with each delegation, the authority needed to carry out the task must be awarded.

Some Ways of Organizing a Small Business

You can organize your business in many ways, but the most frequent ways are (1) by types of authority granted and (2) by activities to be performed. As we discussed earlier in the book, there is now a movement in small businesses toward using teamwork to bolster effectiveness, as larger companies have been doing for some time.

Organizing by Types of Authority   The organizational forms based on types of authority are (1) the line organization and (2) the line-and-staff organization. Within these types of organization is found another type—the informal organization.

As was shown in Figure 1.6, a business may start with the owner doing all the work and then hiring a few people who do a variety of duties in producing, financing, and selling the firm's product. The owner is directly responsible for seeing that the employees do these things. This is called a **line organization,** as shown in Figure 11.9.

As the firm grows and becomes more complex, specialized workers—called staff—are hired to advise and perform services for those doing the operations, financing, and selling. Some examples are accountants (or controllers), personnel officers, and legal staff. This type of organization is called a **line-and-staff organization** (see Figure 11.10).

If the business is small and unincorporated, a tight, formal organization structure could stifle creativity and reduce initiative. Instead, you might have a structure similar to that shown in Figure 11.11.

An **informal organization** always exists within the formal structure of a business. It involves the many interpersonal relationships that arise on and off the job. Two examples are the *informal-leader* and *grapevine-communication* systems. *You cannot fight it, so if you are wise, you will determine who the informal leaders are and get their support for your activities.*

In a **line organization,** the owner has a direct line of command over employees.

A **line-and-staff organization** is one that has specialists to advise and perform services for other employees.

The **informal organization** is the set of interpersonal relationships that come about as a result of friendships that develop on and off the job.

FIGURE 11.9 |
A Simplified Line
Organization

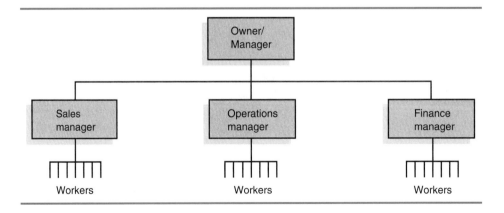

FIGURE 11.10 |
A Simplified Line-and-Staff Organization

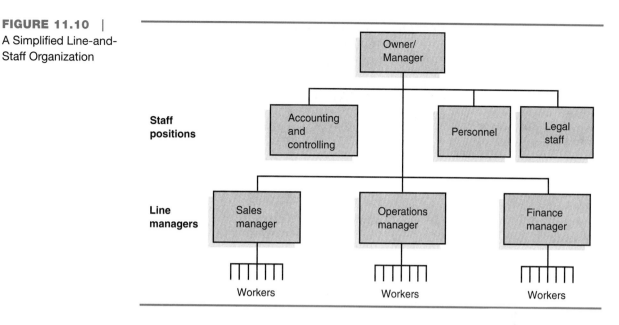

Real-World Example 11.10

What informal organizations do you belong to? A morning coffee group? A study group? A social get-together once a week?

Organizing by Activities to Be Performed   When you set up your formal organization structure, you can group the activities into small, workable groups according to

1. *Function performed,* such as production, sales, or finance, as shown in Figure 11.9.

2. *Product sold,* such as menswear, ladies' wear, and so forth.

3. *Process used,* such as X-rays, operating room, and food service in a hospital.

4. *Area served,* such as urban, suburban, or rural.

5. *Types of customers served,* such as industrial, commercial, institutional, or governmental.

6. *Project being managed,* such as constructing a store or an apartment complex.

FIGURE 11.11 |
Organization of a Small, Unincorporated Mom-and-Pop Business

Preparing an Organization Chart

There is no one structure that is best for all businesses, either large or small. However, the following discussion may help you organize your business to achieve its objectives.

An **organization chart** shows the authority and responsibility relationships that exist in a business.

Begin by setting up a series of authority and responsibility relationships expressed in a formal **organization chart,** as shown in Figures 11.9 and 11.10. Even in a small business, a chart can be useful in establishing present relationships, planning future developments, and projecting personnel requirements (Figure 11.11).

Using Team Management to Improve Performance

The use of team management has become an important stepping-stone in the growth of many small businesses. Of all the methods used, quality improvement and teamwork may be the ones best suited to small firms. The goal of teamwork is to improve performance by involving employees in meeting customers' needs. When each member of each team fully understands the business's products, services, and culture,[10] team members then have a better grasp of the contribution their work makes to fulfilling the company's mission. And by doing more of the work formerly done by managers, they broaden their scope in the business by acquiring new skills.

Problem-solving teams meet on a regular basis to discuss ways to improve quality, efficiency, and the work environment.

Self-managing work teams take over managerial duties and produce an entire product.

Cross-functional teams cut across different parts of the organization to monitor, standardize, and improve work processes.

While teamwork may not be feasible for small mom-and-pop operations, several types of teams are found in larger, entrepreneurial-type small businesses. It appears as if the most successful teams have lots of links and that information flows in many directions.[11] It is also important that new team members do not have to face the "clique syndrome." While it is true that a strong relationship among employees is good for teamwork you must remember that new hires are often left out and may even resign.[12] The more important types of teams are

- **Problem-solving teams,** which meet for an hour or two a week to discuss ways to improve quality, efficiency, and the work environment.
- **Self-managing work teams,** which take over some managerial duties, such as work and vacation scheduling, hiring new members, and ordering materials.
- **Cross-functional teams,** which are formed to monitor, standardize, and improve work processes that cut across different parts of the organization, to develop products, or to otherwise address issues calling for broad representation and expertise.

What You Should Have Learned

1. Good human relations implies the cooperative and friendly interaction of people in an organization, resulting from good leadership, communication, and motivation.

2. Leadership is the ability of one person to influence others to attain organizational objectives. There is no one ideal leadership style; the most effective one depends on the situation and the characteristics of the people involved.

3. Managers spend 80 percent of their time communicating, that is, attempting exchanges of significant

meaning, but not always succeeding. Barriers to effective communication include, among others, imprecise use of language and poor listening skills. You can become a better communicator by identifying your audience and the environment of the communication so as to frame your message clearly and by practicing being a good listener.

4. You can increase employee productivity and improve employee satisfaction through effective motivation. Your challenge is to know your employees well enough to know what incentives will stimulate

them to perform. Different incentives must be used according to the purpose of the motivation.

Some currently popular motivational techniques include quality circles, zero-defects programs, job enrichment, variable work schedules, and job splitting and sharing. Motivation is more than mere technique, however, and the best motivators recognize the worth of employees and expect the best from them.

5. Performance appraisals—also called *employee evaluations* or *merit ratings*—are used to answer the question "How well are my people performing?" Essentially, appraisals look at employees' personal qualities that lead to their job behaviors which affect work performance. Evaluating all these, the manager can not only estimate how well the employee is doing but also give feedback and prescribe improvement.

6. Counseling may involve listening to an employee gripe about some petty grievance, or it may be needed to correct a serious work problem. Counseling is needed in the job-related areas of health and safety, retirement or termination, and job stress, as well as the personal areas of illness, mental and emotional problems, and substance abuse. Counseling assistance can be obtained from SCORE.

7. While some complaints from employees are inevitable, they can often be handled informally. To discipline unsatisfactory employees, however, an established procedure is needed. In the ideal work situation, employees discipline themselves, but for those who do not, a procedure should be set up to take into account the severity of the offense and the number of times it has been committed, as well as other factors and extenuating circumstances. Positive discipline, which challenges employees to discipline themselves, is being used in many small firms.

8. Dealing with a union is a challenge most owners and managers of small businesses do not want to face, and most will try to keep the union out. However, when a union does enter, many things change. Many laws govern labor–management relations, so hire a good consultant to help you. Negotiating an agreement with the union requires much preparation. After agreement is reached, supervisors should be briefed on the terms of the contract and instructed on how to deal with labor matters. Managers can get help in dealing with a union from many government and private sources.

9. Because of civil rights legislation and court decisions, it is becoming increasingly difficult to terminate even the most ineffective employees. This trend is costing small businesses much in lost time and money.

10. Some important organizational concepts that apply to small firms as they grow are delegation, span of management, and specialization. Following these principles helps you delegate authority so as to get the best from employees, tends to eliminate tensions, and eases employee frustrations.

You can organize your business by (*a*) type of authority used or (*b*) activities performed. The simplest structure is the line organization, where orders are handed down from the top to the bottom. With growth, specialized people are needed to perform tasks not strictly related to operations, selling, or finance, resulting in a line-and-staff structure. Informal organizations found in all businesses, should not be ignored because their informal leaders and grapevine communications can affect your bottom line. Team management can also be used to improve performance.

Key Terms

performance
 appraisal   303
positive discipline   308
problem-solving
 teams   316

quality circles (QCs)   302
right-to-work laws   309
self-managing work
 teams   316
specialization   313

variable work schedule
 or flexible work
 arrangement   302
zero-defects
 approach   302

Questions for Discussion

1. How would you define (or explain) *good human relations?*
2. What is leadership? Why is it so important in small business?
3. Why is communication so important in a small business? What are some barriers to effective communication? How can these barriers be overcome?
4. What is motivation? Why is it so important to a small business manager?
5. What are some practical ways to improve employee motivation?
6. What is the purpose of performance appraisals? Why are they so important?
7. Discuss the areas requiring counseling. What, if anything, can a small business manager do to improve counseling in those areas?
8. Explain the differences between self-discipline and externally imposed discipline.
9. Explain how national labor laws affect small businesses. Should you, as a small business owner, favor or oppose your employees' unionizing? Defend your answer.
10. Explain why it is becoming so difficult to terminate employees.
11. Explain some of the basic organizational concepts used in organizing a small business.

Case 11.1

Personnel Policies Help Intermatic Grow

Intermatic Inc., is a Spring Grove, Illinois, producer of timing devices and low-voltage lighting. Jim Miller, CEO, claims his company's personnel policies and programs have been the key to its growth, profitability, and survival, and thinks they saved it from disaster.

Several years ago, when Intermatic was on the verge of bankruptcy, Miller, a former employee, was asked to return as president. To save the company, he reduced the work force by 50 percent, closed one division, restructured the staff, consolidated positions, and instituted the employee relations policies and programs that have since assured the firm's success.

An incentive system for production workers earns them about 135 percent of their base pay, and some of the unusual employee benefits are (1) programs that pay workers to shed pounds; (2) free eye examinations and glasses; (3) aerobics classes; (4) goslf lessons; (5) an outside exercise course; (6) an indoor track; (7) tennis courts; (8) membership in arts-and-culture clubs; (9) shopping at company-subsidized stores for items such as jeans, T-shirts, and baseball caps; and (10) reimbursement of tuition for college courses.

In addition, Miller is quite open in his communications with employees, telling them what has to be done and why it must be done. He also is available to help people with personal problems, knows them by name, and knows their family situations. The payoff? Turnover is only 3 percent, compared with more than 5 percent for similar firms, and it has become such a popular place to work that there's a waiting list of people seeking employment with Intermatic.

Questions

1. How do you explain the improved performance at Intermatic?
2. Would Jim Miller's methods work at all companies? Explain.
3. Would you like to work at Intermatic? Why or why not?

Source: Author's correspondence with Intermatic Inc.

Case 11.2

Visiting Angels

Connie Hill, whose father was at home sick, became sensitive to the needs and struggles of senior citizens who wish to remain at home. After losing her hospital job a few years after her father's death, she purchased the franchise of Visiting Angels, a national network of nonmedical, senior home care agencies providing service to help elderly and older adults who continue to live in their homes.

Hill reasoned that, from a business standpoint, a well-developed strategy focused on improving the welfare of senior citizens has a good opportunity to succeed. As people are living longer, there are more seniors who wish to remain in their own homes while needing assistance in daily living. She felt that starting her own business created a greater potential for good income while controlling her own fate.

"Management experience is the essential skill that individuals interested in my job field need," states Hill. The experience she gained managing staff at the hospital in her previous job proved to be invaluable in coaching employees and building effective teams.

"I personally meet with every client before their care begins. It makes them feel comfortable. I want people to say 'Call Connie' when they need care for a loved one. I want my name to be synonymous with Visiting Angels."

When screening potential employees to administer this care, Hill states that it's vital to establish the right fit between caregivers and clients. When she hires, even if the person's credentials and skills are top-notch, she asks herself, "Is this someone I would want to take care of my mother?"

She feels that the most important thing to fulfill the needs of seniors is finding individuals with a "heart for serving." Hill says they are available 24 hours a day. "We want to make Visiting Angels available whenever our clients need us. My first priority is meeting the needs of my clients."

She states that even after 12 to 13 hours of work, this kind of business makes you feel good because you know you've helped someone. As her business continues to grow, she says she never wants to stop her hands-on involvement with the seniors they care for, their families, and her team. "To be in this field and to succeed in it you should have both the heart and the passion for assisting in and easing the life of senior citizens."

Questions

1. Do you think that Hill's method of screening potential employees has a positive effect on her relationship with them?

2. Do you agree with her hiring techniques?

3. Do you think she should have a different approach hiring potential employees to work with the elderly?

4. Does Hill's hands-on approach to her business help to break some of the barriers to effective communication?

Source: Written by Jo Claire Megginson, abstracted from ladieswholaunch.com.

Experientials

1. Investigate several industries and search for jargon used. Identify words or phrases that are the same but have different meanings in various industries.

2. Classrooms work like businesses in their discipline procedures. Compare your school's discipline policies with those of a local business.

CHAPTER 12

Obtaining and Laying Out Operating Facilities

A terrible business owner in a great location can do okay, but a great business owner in a poor location will struggle to succeed.
—**Unknown**

You know your company is ready for robots when you recognize that automating is cheaper than relocating in South Korea or Taiwan.
—**Bruce H. Kleiner, management professor**

Learning Objectives

After studying the material in this chapter, you should be able to:

1. Explain what an operating system is and how it functions.

2. Discuss how to determine the right location for a small business.

3. Describe the important factors involved in choosing a retail location.

4. Describe the most important factors involved in choosing a manufacturing site.

5. Identify the steps in planning the layout of physical facilities, and show how to implement them.

6. Explain the emerging role of telecommuting in small firms.

7. Discuss some ways of improving operations.

8. Explain how to set and use performance standards.

PROFILE

Koi and Lilies

Ten years ago Kathy Barnard found a new hobby, raising koi and goldfish. The hobby became a passion, and she realized she wanted to do more than just raise fish. She wanted to start a business so she could share her passion with others. In doing so, she would also be able to educate the public on the proper maintenance for their fish and ponds.

Barnard did not become an expert on fish overnight. She learned many lessons through years of experience. One very important lesson she learned was that infections can kill the fish. If fish live in a stressful environment, they will not be able to survive. Keeping the fish at optimum health requires checking many things: pH balance of water, ammonia nitrates, parasites, and ich, among others. Being knowledgeable of pathogenic bacteria is one of the most important steps in maintaining a healthy pond, with healthy fish. There are numerous types of pathogenic bacteria that can infect your pond. The most common of these are aeromonas and pseudomonas. More koi are killed annually by these two bacteria than all other pathogens together. A thorough knowledge of these pathogens is a necessity in controlling them.

Ulcers (hole-in-the-side disease), fin rot, mouth rot, and tail rot are all effects of aeromonas and pseudomonas. The damage these bacteria impose on the fish will eventually lead to their death, if left unattended. Many hobbyists believe that if none of these signs are visible, their pond is free of these

bacteria. They are seriously mistaken. Aermonas and pseudomonas are present in almost every single koi pond in the world. The secret is that it is possible for fish to be around these bacteria and not become infected. Koi have a natural defense mechanism that helps them to protect themselves from the bacteria. This defense mechanism consists of their slime coat and immune system. Never allow yourself to be tricked into thinking your fish are perfectly fine just because they look healthy. Their health can change rapidly. The question for you to ask yourself is: How well do you care for your pond to prevent aeromonas and pseudomonas from multiplying before infecting your Koi?

A little over three years ago, when realizing her dream of wanting to open up a business, she began to implement the steps to expedite the process. Kathy found 10 acres of land for sale, five minutes from the interstate and one mile from a major intersection. Realizing what an amazing location it was, and the amount of space it would provide; she knew she could not pass. She had been saving money for five years to start up this business. When this land came up for sale, she took a loan out from the bank and from there it is history. However, time was an obstacle Barnard could not overcome by herself. Working as a nurse consultant for insurance companies, she was already very busy. She hired Connie Borg and Kathy Huffmaster as full-time employees. They also found their passion through a hobby. Much like Barnard,

323

they discovered their love and enjoyment of koi and gold-fish through backyard ponds of their own.

Koi and Lilies breed and sell koi; they also sell pond, filtration, and nursery supplies. They make house calls and carry medical supplies to assist owners in extending the life of their fish. Today the operation is still owned and operated by Kathy Barnard with the assistance of a manager and three additional full-time employees.

Koi and Lilies almost closed in November 2011 due to the economic downturn of the U.S. economy, but held on and had the best year ever in 2011. Barnard credits the recession. People were staying home and focusing on their backyards rather than spending money on expensive vacations. With the focus on customer service Koi and Lilies can help purchasers create a relaxing, comfortable atmosphere at home. With a unique structure of house calls and allowing an "enjoy first and buy later" approach, they have found a niche market that reduces the tough competition of big box retailers.

Koi and Lilies has many types of koi and goldfish and several varieties of lilies. Barnard has her fish transported in from out of state. They have kohaku koi during the summer. These fish are identified by their white bodies with red accent marks on their backs. They also have oranda and comet gold-fish. The oranda's distinct traits are colorful bodies with hooded heads. The comets are a small goldfish only growing to one or two inches in length. Koi and Lilies keeps the fish in large, filtered tanks. There is a great variance in price. The rarer the members of the species are, the more expensive. They have a greenhouse with four large troughs where they raise numerous types of water lilies. The two main categories of water lilies are hardy and tropical. "The hardy varieties can survive the Mobile winters; they are tougher," says Huff-master. She goes on to say, "The tropical lilies are not as comfortable here during the winter months."

Source: Conversations with Kathy Barnard.

As the Profile illustrates, all businesses—large or small—produce some product, either selling a good or providing a service. A retailer forecasts demand and then purchases merchandise and displays, sells, and delivers it to customers. A producer forecasts demand and then purchases material, processes it into products, and sells and delivers the products to customers. A service business tries to satisfy the needs of customers by providing a service.

This chapter examines what you must do to produce your product, how to choose the right location to produce it, how to plan and lay out physical facilities, and how to constantly improve operations. It also explores the new trend toward telecommuting.

Developing Operating Systems

The steps required to start a business, as indicated in Chapter 5, are (1) searching for a product, (2) studying the market for the product, (3) deciding how to get into business, (4) making strategic plans, and (5) making operational plans, including planning the many aspects of operating the business once it is started. This last step involves setting up your operating systems and providing building(s), materials, equipment, and people to produce the product.

Operating systems in different businesses are really quite similar, although the sequence of events and activities may vary as each business adjusts the system to fit its own needs. Also, support systems, such as accounting, personnel, and cash flow systems, must be integrated into the overall producing system.

Operating systems have the following productive elements: (1) a system for changing form, place, or time; (2) a sequence of steps to change the inputs into outputs; (3) special skills, tools, and/or machines to make the change; (4) instructions and goods identification; and (5) a time frame within which the work is to be done.

What Are Operating Systems?

An **operating system** consists of inputs, processes, and outputs. The **inputs** include materials, people, money, information, machines, and other factors. The **processes** involve converting these inputs into the goods or services the customers want, using the employees, machines, materials, and other factors. The **outputs** consist of the goods and services required by the customers; desired outputs also include satisfying the needs of employees and the public.

Figure 12.1 shows some examples of how inputs are processed into outputs. The processes shown are for the major operations of the company: Cloth, thread, and buttons are sewn into shirts; or a computer program is derived from customer information through design, installation, and testing. In addition, each company has processes such as accounting, maintenance, and quality control that support its main activities. All processes are designed to result in proper operating systems.

How Operating Systems Work

Operations, or **production,** includes all the activities from obtaining raw materials through delivering the product to the customers. Thus, the word *operations* refers to those activities necessary to produce and deliver a service or good.

Operating systems consist of the inputs, processes, and outputs of a business.

Inputs are materials, people, money, information, machines, and other productive factors.

Processes convert these inputs into products customers want.

Outputs are the products produced and the satisfactions to employees and the public.

Operations, or **production,** is converting inputs into outputs for customers.

FIGURE 12.1 | Examples of Operating Systems

The following activities, or processes, must be performed by all businesses, regardless of their nature. These procedures include (1) marketing, (2) finance, and (3) operations. In manufacturing and similar plants, operations is called production, but in retail and service-type firms the activity is often called operations.

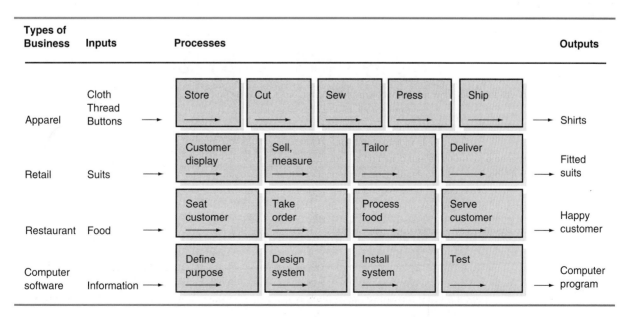

All businesses usually have systems in addition to the production system, and as the following example shows, these systems must be coordinated for the best production.

Real-World Example 12.1

The objective of fast-food operations is to supply food quickly and with little customer effort. At Burger King, for example, there are three systems:

1. *A marketing system.* The order for a Whopper is taken from the customer and money received to pay for it.
2. *A production system.* The order is given to someone to prepare the hamburger and package it, while someone else prepares drinks.
3. *A delivery system.* The completed order is handed to the customer.

   These three systems are coordinated to provide quick service and to keep the line moving. Figure 12.2 shows how Burger King's production system operates. Notice how the inputs—such as rolls, meat patties, mayonnaise, lettuce, onions, and pickles—are processed by cooking, assembling, and wrapping into the output— a Whopper—which is then delivered to the customer.

How to Begin Operations

After identifying the product (output), inputs, and processes, you are ready to begin operations, which involves: (1) choosing the right location, (2) planning physical facilities, (3) deciding on a layout, and (4) implementing your plans.

Choosing the Right Location

As shown in Chapters 5 and 6, you must define the character of your business and decide on your objectives and strategies before you begin to investigate available locations for it. Because company location is a major factor in success or failure, you must ask yourself

FIGURE 12.2 |
Operations Involved in
Producing a Whopper

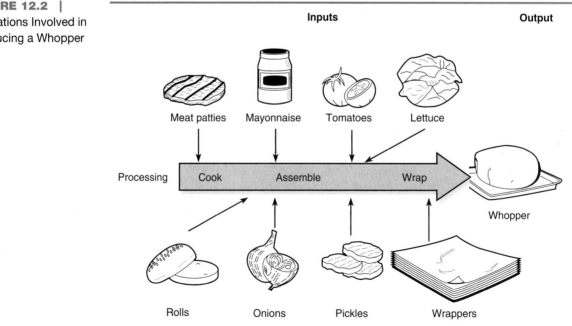

such questions as this: Do I plan to have just one location or to grow regionally or nationwide? Do I intend to concentrate on one product area or expand into several? The answers to these questions will focus your search.

Why Choosing the Right Location Is So Important

Location is one factor that can make the difference between success and failure for a small business. Sales come from customers who find it advantageous to buy from you rather than someone else. Have you, as a customer, patronized a business because it is near you? Or driven miles to obtain a special product? What factors caused you to live where you do now? Companies must consider similar factors to find suitable locations for their operations. Factors influencing the customer's choice of a business include variables such as convenience, time, cost, reliability, quality, and good service. These factors must be evaluated for each potential location before selecting the most suitable one.

When you choose a location, you usually expect to stay there for some time. Not only is it expensive to move to another location, but also customers, who follow established patterns of activity and do not like changes, may not follow you to a new location. Employees are affected in much the same way.

Some Important Factors Affecting Location Choice

Information on which to base a location decision can come from a variety of sources, as discussed in Chapters 5 and 9. However, you should consider at least two sets of factors when choosing a location for your business: (1) general factors that affect all types of businesses and (2) specific factors that pertain to specific types of businesses.

General Factors Affecting All Businesses

The more important general factors include the following:[1]

1. Access to a capable, well-trained, stable workforce.
2. Availability of adequate and affordable supplies and services.
3. Availability, type, use, and cost of transportation.
4. Taxes and government regulations.
5. Availability and cost of electricity, gas, water, sewerage, and other utilities.

Flexibility in office space has become a problem in today's businesses. With rental usually locked into long-term leases, only about 40 percent of all office space is in use. A new trend is to outsource your office space on a short-term basis.

Real-World Example 12.2

Regus Group PLC, is a company where you can order up offices in 950 locations in 400 cities worldwide. These offices can be up and running in 24 to 48 hours and can have a phone, an address, and a native-speaking employee on site. The client never has to waste time searching for space in an appropriate location. For example: Genny Forster needed to set up an office in Milwaukee to test the market demand for her business. She called Regus Group to find her space and was in operation in two days.[2]

Specific Factors to Consider for Various Businesses

The type of business—retailing, producing, or service—influences most location decisions because it determines the relative importance of the general factors mentioned above. For example, location of customers may

TABLE 12.1 | Some Important Location Factors

Factors Affecting Selection of		
City	**Area in City**	**Specific Site**
Retailer		
Size of trade area	Attraction power	Traffic passing site
Population trends	Competitive nature	Ability to intercept traffic
Purchasing power	Access routes	Compatibility of adjacent stores
Trade potential	Zoning regulations	Adequacy of parking
Competition	Area expansion	Unfriendly competition
Shopping centers	General appearance	Cost of site
Producer		
Market location	Zoning	Zoning
Vendor location	Industrial park	Sewer, effluent control
Labor availability	Transportation	Transportation
Transportation		Terrain
Utilities		Utilities
Government, taxes		Labor availability
Schools, recreation		

Source: U.S. Small Business Administration, *Choosing a Retailing Location,* Management Aid No. 2.021 (Washington, DC: U.S. Government Printing Office), p. 2. Used by permission.

be more important to a large department store, while location of employees will be more important to a manufacturing plant. Table 12.1 shows some specific factors to be considered in making location decisions. Although the factors have been separated into retailer and producer, many of them apply equally to retailing, producing, and service organizations.

Retailers sell goods to the ultimate consumer.

Retailers are concerned with people who come to, or are drawn into, the store to make a purchase. Therefore, location is concerned with people's movement, attention, attitudes, convenience, needs, and ability to buy. In other words, which location will provide sales at a reasonable profit?

Real-World Example 12.3

This problem was faced by Dana Brigham, co-owner of Brookline Booksmith, a long-time independent bookstore in Brookline, Massachusetts. Several years ago, a big Barnes & Noble store opened down the street from her. Six other big chain bookstores opened nearby. She and the other owners took a hard look at their mission to see what was important to them. They got busy and upgraded their customer services from . . . 'somewhat indifferent' to 'every customer leaves with a better experience.' This strategy paid off in increased sales.[3]

Producers convert materials into products in considerable volume for others to sell to ultimate consumers.

Producers are concerned with converting, usually in considerable volume, materials, parts, and other items into products. They emphasize selling those products through intermediaries to the ultimate consumer, as discussed in Chapter 9. Compared with the merchandise of retailers, producing units are often larger and fewer and sold to a smaller number of customers. The plant and customer can be located some distance apart, so other factors become more important. Still, nearness to customers and suppliers helps to keep costs

With the growth of large book retailers like Barnes & Noble, the smaller, family-owned bookstores have had to develop new ways to retain customers.

down and permits more satisfactory service. Primary emphasis on locating, though, is placed on cost and service.

Service companies have some characteristics of both retailers and producers. The performance of some services—such as those provided by hair stylists, dentists and doctors, and auto service stations—usually requires customers to come to the business's location, where the service is performed. The locations of service companies, therefore, depend on convenient and economical travel.

Some other services—such as home nursing care, landscaping and gardening, and plumbing and electrical repairs—require going to the client's home. But even those who perform these services should try to locate near where customers are clustered. However, some businesses that cannot attract enough customers to a central location may take all, or a part, of their activities "on the road" to obtain more income.

Service companies, which provide a service for customers, have some characteristics of both retailers and producers.

Real-World Example 12.4

For example, Sue Ley, the owner of CleanDrum Inc., a company that straightens and cleans metal oil drums, tried using a mobile unit to clean drums at customers' locations. Although she found that this was too heavy a load for her limited work force at the time, she hopes to resume the service later.

Many small service businesses start and continue to operate out of the owner's home. This is a logical arrangement since the owner may be tentative about going into business and may not want to have the fixed expense of an office. Also, these owners tend to go to the clients to perform their service. Finally, as will be shown in Chapter 15, there are tax benefits.

At some point, the data collected must be analyzed to provide the information necessary for a decision. A score sheet like that in Figure 12.3 can be valuable in comparing possible locations. Evaluations can sometimes be quantitative, such as number of households times median income times percentage of income spent on store items times some special factor for this store. Others are ratings, grading factors from 1 for the lowest to 10 for the highest.

Some factors are very important and should be given more weight than others. One factor in a given site might be so intolerable that the site must be eliminated from consideration. When you seek to operate a franchise you may receive a lot of help from the franchisor. Many franchise contracts require location approvals from the franchisor. The success of the franchisor is dependent on the franchisee and the appropriate location can be a success or failure decision. In fact, some locations will have to be evaluated, selected, and demanded by the franchisor.

Locating Retail Stores

In choosing a site for a retail store, two interrelated factors are important: the type of store (i.e., the type of goods sold) and the type of location. There is a perception that market forces and the economies of scale enjoyed by big chains are relentlessly consuming small stores. A study by consultant Gary A. Wright, however, found this conclusion only partially valid. Instead, Wright found that "many small retailers who find a [specialized] niche and provide strong personal service to customers will survive. In other words, *service, expertise, and location* are the dominion of small specialty retailers, as the following example illustrates.

FIGURE 12.3 |
Rating Sheet for Sites

Grade each factor: 1 (lowest) to 10 (highest)
Weight each factor: 1 (least important) to 5 (most important)

Factors	Grade	Weight
1. Centrally located to reach my market.	—	—
2. Raw materials readily available.	—	—
3. Quantity of available labor.	—	—
4. Transportation availability and rates.	—	—
5. Labor rates of pay/estimated productivity.	—	—
6. Adequacy of utilities (sewer, water, power, gas).	—	—
7. Local business climate.	—	—
8. Provision for future expansion.	—	—
9. Tax burden.	—	—
10. Topography of the site (slope and foundation).	—	—
11. Quality of police and fire protection.	—	—
12. Housing availability for workers and managers.	—	—
13. Environmental factors (schools, cultural, community atmosphere).	—	—
14. Estimate of quality of this site in five years.	—	—
15. Location of this site in relation to my major competitor.	—	—

Source: U.S. Small Business Administration, *Locating or Relocating Your Business, Management* Aid No. 2.002 (Washington, DC: U.S. Government Printing Office), p. 6. Used by permission. Copies of this and other publications are available from the SBA for a small processing fee.

Real-World Example 12.5

The 17th Street Surf Shop targets males ages 8 to 28 with specialized surf gear. The store has expanded to a nine-store operation by selling surfing gear at a ratio of 90 percent soft goods to 10 percent hard goods.

Types of Stores

Customers view products in different ways when selecting the store from which to buy. Therefore, stores can be grouped into (1) convenience, (2) shopping, (3) specialty stores, and (4) seasonal according to the type of goods they sell.

Convenience goods
are products that customers buy often, routinely, quickly, and in any store that carries them.

Convenience Goods Stores   **Convenience goods** are usually low-priced items that are purchased often, are sold in many stores, are bought by habit, and lend themselves to self-service. Examples are candy bars, milk, bread, cigarettes, and detergents. Although the term *convenience goods* may make you think of *convenience stores* (small markets with gas pumps), convenience goods stores are better typified by the grocery and variety stores where we regularly shop for consumable items. Convenience goods stores are interested in having a high flow of customer traffic, so they try to get people to want to satisfy their needs and come in to purchase the items currently on display. The quantity of customer flow seems more important than its quality. These stores are built where the traffic flow is already heavy.

For instance, our research has shown that nearly 70 percent of women patronize stores within five blocks of their residence. Convenient store hours were also found to be very important for this type of store.

Shopping goods
are goods that customers buy infrequently, after shopping at only a few stores.

Shopping Goods Stores   **Shopping goods** are usually higher-priced items, which are bought infrequently, and for which the customer compares prices. People spend much time looking for these items and talking to sales personnel about them. Therefore, capable salespeople with selling ability are required (see Chapter 9 for more detail). Examples of these goods are suits, automobiles, and furniture.

Specialty goods
are bought infrequently, often at exclusive outlets, after special effort by the customer to drive to the store.

Specialty Goods Stores   **Specialty goods** are usually high-priced shopping goods with trade names that are recognized for the exclusive nature of their clientele. By their very nature, specialty goods stores often generate their own traffic, but customer flow can be helped by similar stores in the vicinity. Some examples of specialty goods are quality dresses, precious jewelry, and expensive video and sound equipment. In essence, people do not comparison shop for specialty goods, but just buy the name on the item.

Seasonal stores
are those that target customers for specific seasons or events. Some are open year-round and some are only open seasonally.

Seasonal Stores   **Seasonal stores** are those that target customers for specific seasons or events. Some are open year-round and some are only open during the "season." Christmas stores are the most prevalent and can be found in freestanding facilities, shopping malls, and in kiosks operated seasonally. Sporting goods stores will frequently target many sports so they can remain open year-round. Many communities celebrate events that are so popular that the seasonal stores can be open year-round. For example, many Mardi Gras stores are open throughout the year in New Orleans; however, in Mobile, Alabama, where the holiday was first celebrated in the United States, a few gift shops carry the products all year and the large outlets open for about three months.

Real-World Example 12.6

Toomey's is a company that is located in a 70,000-square-foot building housing inventories of Mardi Gras throws and supplies that have been directly imported in bulk with a retail space cordoned off at the front. In addition, they operate Mobile Carnival Museum Gift Shoppe by Toomey's and Mardi Gras–Seasonal Eastern Shore. The warehouse allows the company to build up inventories that will be sold before the parades. This community presents dozens of parades each season, and each organization spends about $150,000 on throws for each parade. The location of the warehouse allows easy access to the products for the individual maskers.

Types of Locations

In general, the types of locations for retail businesses are (1) downtown business districts, (2) freestanding stores, and (3) community shopping centers or malls.

Downtown Business District   Changes in retail locations have occurred as discounters have located their stores outside the downtown area. Now, governments, financial businesses, and the head offices of large firms provide most of the business for retail stores in **downtown locations.**

Downtown locations
attract business-oriented activities, as government, financial businesses, and head offices of large firms are usually located in the downtown area.

A downtown location has many advantages, such as lower rents, better public transportation, and proximity to where people work. But the disadvantages often include limited shopping hours, higher crime rates, poor or inadequate traffic and parking, and deterioration of downtown areas. In some cases, one or a few downtown areas are preferred to the exclusion of others.

Freestanding stores,
found in various locations are usually best for customers who have brand or company loyalty.

Freestanding Stores   **Freestanding stores,** found in many locations, may be the best for customers who have brand or company loyalty, or for those who identify with a given shop, where a business has a competitive edge over its competitors, where the character of customers and growth objectives blend well. Low costs, good parking, independent hours and operations, and restricted competition in these locations tend to fit the more entrepreneurial types of businesspeople. However, to attract customers, especially new ones, you may have to do considerable advertising. Moreover, acquiring a suitable building and land may be difficult.

Innovative entrepreneurs may find a lucrative location in neighborhoods formerly avoided by other businesses. *But the market niche—product and clientele—must conform to the needs of the customers in the area.* Because we lead such busy lives, a trip to the mall can require more time than we really have to spare. This has led to a revival of freestanding stores, where shoppers can gain quicker access.

Shopping centers vary in size and are designed to draw traffic according to the planned nature of the stores to be included in them.

Shopping Centers   **Shopping centers** are planned and built only after lengthy and involved studies. These centers vary in size from small neighborhood and strip centers, to community centers, to the large regional malls. One of the largest of these in the United States is the Mall of America in Bloomington, Minnesota (www.mallofamerica.com). It occupies 4.2 million square feet, has four anchor stores, and 520 specialty stores.

Why Shopping Centers Are So Popular   Shopping centers are designed to draw traffic according to the planned nature of the stores to be included in them. The design of the centers ranges from small, neighborhood convenience goods stores to giant regional centers with a wide range of goods and services, which may or may not be specialized. Shopping centers offer many services, such as specialized activities to bring in traffic, merchant association activities, parking, utilities, and combined advertising. A current trend is for large "power centers" to compete with one another to be the largest.

Another reason for the popularity of shopping centers is the growing interest in shopping. According to Tourism Works for America, a tourist trade group, "Shopping has become the most popular pastime of vacationers, surpassing outdoor activities such as hiking, swimming, or fishing."[4] This trend is especially noticeable in New England. For example, an ad in the local *New England Brochure* features "The Best Hiking in Vermont," but the description is of the crowded outlet malls, not the region's spectacular trails.

Enclosed malls have eliminated weather problems for customers. Indeed, older people are encouraged to use the mall for exercise in a controlled climate.

Anchor stores are those that generate heavy traffic in a shopping center.

The typical shopping center has two **anchor stores.** These stores, often large department stores, are usually located at the ends of the arms of the mall, where they are not only easily accessible from the parking lot but also generate heavy traffic for the small stores between them.

Within the malls, kiosks and carts often serve as magnets, occupying potentially prime selling spots. These small "stores" are fast growing in importance as malls increase in popularity. Carts and kiosks are also found in freestanding locations such as in parks, outside office buildings, and on street corners. They can provide a quick, easy, and inexpensive way to start a small business, as the following example illustrates.

Real-World Example 12.7

In 1995, Wally Rizza, age 21, spent $25,000 to launch Shades 2000 Inc., a sunglasses cart in the Irvine Spectrum Entertainment Center in Irvine, California. Within a year he had sales of $184,000. Soon he had three sunglasses carts, a jewelry cart, and a watch cart and expected to gross $500,000 for the year.

Some malls may have a theme that stores are expected to conform to. The purpose of the theme is to pull the stores together and have them handle products of similar quality. For example, the center may have regulations on shopping hours, how to use the space in front of the store (what to display and how), and so on.

Drawbacks of Shopping Centers   In addition to these advantages, which are considerable, there are also disadvantages to locating in a center. Some of the most significant of these are cost, restrictions imposed by the center's theme, operating regulations, and possible changes in the center's owners and managers, which could bring policy changes.

There is now a "total rent" concept for costs that must be considered in evaluating the costs of renting space in a shopping center. These costs may include dues to the merchants' association, maintenance fees for the common areas, and the cost of special events or combined advertising. The most common rental is a basic rent, usually based on square footage, plus a percentage of gross sales (usually 5 to 7 percent). In total, these costs tend to be high and often discourage tenants, as you can see from the following.

For example, if your mall space is 30 feet wide and 75 feet deep, you would have 30×75 or 2,250 square feet. If the entire mall space was 500,000 square feet, your store would occupy 2,250/500,000 or 0.45 percent of the entire mall. You could then project rent and related expenses as follows:

Annual Expenses		
Common area maintenance	$100,000 × 0.0045 =	$ 450
Real estate taxes	$20,000 × 0.0045 =	90
Rent @ $10 per square foot	$2,250 × $10 =	22,500
Merchants association fees @ 10%	$1 × 2,250 × 0.10 =	225
Total		$23,265

The average monthly amount would be $23,265 \div 12$ months = approximately $1,939. However, many landlords require additional "percentage" rent after a certain level of gross retail sales has been met. For example, in the above analysis, gross or annual rent equals 5 percent of $450,000 annually or $37,500 per month ($450,000/12). So when gross sales exceed $37,500 per month, you must pay an additional 5 percent on the excess!

Locating Manufacturing Plants

Manufacturing, or production, usually involves making or processing materials into finished goods.

Manufacturing (or **production**) usually involves making or processing raw materials into a finished product. The materials may be extracted from the ground or harvested from the earth, or they may be outputs of other companies (such as metal plates, silicon chips, or ground meat for hamburgers), that are changed in form or shape, or assembled into a different type of product. The location of a manufacturing plant is usually selected with the aim of serving customers properly at the lowest practical cost. Of the factors to consider in locating a manufacturing plant (see Table 12.1), the most important are nearness to customers and vendors and availability and cost of transportation.

Of considerable importance to producers are the time and cost of transporting finished goods to the customers and acquiring raw materials from vendors. The success of a given location can hinge on the availability and cost of the proper mode of transportation, as discussed in Chapter 9. Unfortunately today, with all the laws on zoning, wages, taxes, pollution, and so on, many manufacturing plants are moving off shore where costs are lower. A good example is eGo (see Profile in Chapter 15). EGo originally built their product in a small village in the southeastern United States. The high costs forced a major change for the company, and they are now producing in mainland China.[5]

Planning Physical Facilities

Facilities are the buildings, machines and other equipment, and furniture and fixtures needed to produce and distribute a product.

Once you've selected your location, you must begin planning, acquiring, and installing facilities. These **facilities,** which include the building, machines and other equipment, and furniture and fixtures, must be designed or selected to produce the desired product at the lowest practical cost.

There are five steps involved in this process: (1) Determine the product to be sold and the volume in which it is to be produced, (2) identify the operations and activities required to get the product to the customer, (3) determine space requirements, (4) determine the most effective layout of the facilities, and (5) implement your plans.

Determine Product to Be Produced

Facilities should be planned not only for products to be produced now, but also for changes anticipated in the foreseeable future. Projections for five years are normal, and industry standards for the space required for planned sales or production volume can be a good start in planning.

Identify Operations and Activities to Be Performed

You will remember that operations include all the activities from buying the materials through delivering the finished product to the customer. These activities include (1) purchasing materials and parts for production or goods to sell, (2) performing operations needed to produce the product, and (3) carrying out support activities.

Sequences of operations may be fixed (e.g., producing the hamburger in Figure 12.2) or may change from order to order, as happens in retail stores or service businesses.

Determine Space Requirements

Space is required for materials, equipment, and machines, as well as the movement of customers and employees. Space is also needed for carts and trucks, inventory, displays, waiting areas, personal facilities, maintenance and cleaning, and many other services. The number and size of all these areas depend on the volume of output planned.

Real-World Example 12.8

Chad Summerlin and his partner started an Internet company distributing air filters from a small storage building that has turned into a large facility that now manufactures its own products. They purchased a large parcel of real estate near a rural interstate exchange and built their 55,000-square-foot production facility and office space. They are now planning to build another 55,000-square-foot building and can do so because they bought enough property to allow for growth.

How Telecommuting Affects Physical Facility Needs

Determining space requirements is becoming easier—or more complicated, according to your point of view. The changing nature of production, operations, and service activities is also changing *where* people work, and therefore the amount of space needed. **Telecommuting,** which is using modern communication media—such as telephones, fax machines, computers with modems or fax/modems, and scanners—to work anywhere, has changed the concept of work.

According to one estimate, nearly 22 million (16 percent of the adult workforce) Americans telecommuted during the year 2005.[6] According to JALA International, an industry consultant, this practice saved employees an average of $8,634 per employee.[7]

Telecommuting is the use of modern communication media, such as telephones, fax machines, computers, modems and fax/modems, and scanners, to work from an office, home, or any location.

Real-World Example 12.9

Rita Seeley is a classical example of a telecommuter. She operates a travel agency out of her Colorado Springs, Colorado, home. Every weekday morning, she gets up, eats breakfast, dresses in a professional suit, and goes to work—by walking through the door of her living room into the adjoining room—her home office.[8]

However, there is a downside to this practice. In a recent survey, only 46 percent of such workers said they were "satisfied" or "very satisfied" with their lives compared with 60 percent of all office workers studied. The dissatisfied workers felt ". . . disadvantaged for raises and promotions." Also, stress increased as workplace and home became one.[9] One stress comes from remote locations lacking DSL service or even efficient shipping carriers. Jane Applegate, small

The increase of telecommuters in the United States has allowed for positive financial advantages for both employers and employees.

business consultant and author of "The Entrepreneur's Desk Reference," recommends before going rural to escape crowds, traffic, and frenzied lifestyle you consider the following:

1. Access to phone systems, services, and availability of high-speed Internet service.
2. Order the best computer and telecommunications technology you can afford.
3. If UPS, FedEx, and USPS do not pick up and deliver to your doorstep, locate the closest shipping outlet, invest in a postage meter, and explore online postage printing.
4. Locate the nearest store to purchase your supplies, or consider shopping online.
5. Check year-round weather in your area, especially the duration of winter, average snowfall, and how inclement weather affects doing business (i.e., power outages).
6. Consider a gas-efficient car for road travel, with four-wheel drive for inclement weather.
7. Have contingency plans.[10]

Decide on the Best Layout

The objective in layout planning is to obtain the best placement of furniture and fixtures; tools, machines, and equipment; storage and materials handling; service activities such as cleaning and maintenance; and places for employees and customers to sit, stand, or move about.

Figure 12.4 shows the layout of the previously mentioned CleanDrum Inc., which cleans 50-gallon oil drums. Notice the movement of drums from one end of the plant to the other, the use of roller conveyors (even through machines), movement in a vat, and space for inventory, employees, and an office. Before installation, a model of the planned layout had been constructed and tested to iron out any kinks.

Types of Layout   The two general types of layout are *product* and *process*. In practice, however, layouts often combine the two types.

A **product layout** has the facilities laid out according to the sequence of operations to be performed.

Product Layout   In a **product layout,** facilities are arranged so materials, workers, and/or customers move from one operation to another with little backtracking. This type is used in the school cafeteria shown in Figure 12.5A. The advantages of the product layout plan include specialization of workers and machines, less inventory, fewer instructions and controls, faster movement, and less space needed for aisles and storage. This arrangement tends to improve efficiency and maximize sales, especially in the automobile and fast-food industries.

> **Real-World Example 12.10**
> Notice in the earlier Figure 12.2 that if you order a Whopper, its production moves forward from cooking the meat to assembling, wrapping, and delivering the Whopper to you.

A **process layout** groups the facilities doing the same type of work.

Process Layout   The **process layout** groups machines performing the same type of work and workers with similar skills such as the cafeteria shown in Figure 12.5B.

The process layout requires more movement of material or people, as is shown by the figure, and requires a larger inventory. But it also provides flexibility to take care of change and variety, often can use the same general-purpose machines and equipment for several steps in the operation, and permits more efficient scheduling of equipment and workers.

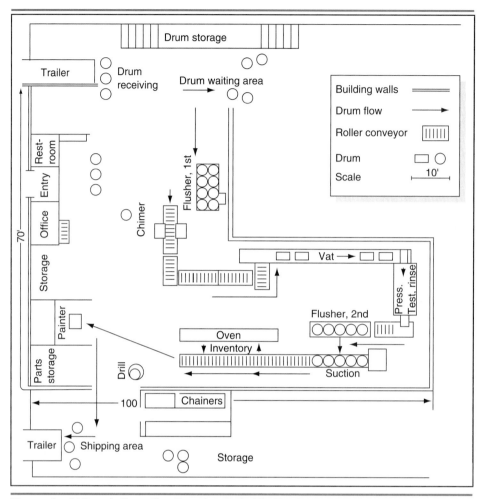

See section IV, Sample Case: CleanDrum Inc., in the Workbook at the end of the book.

Few layout plans are totally product or process layouts. Instead, most layout plans combine the two to obtain the advantages of both.

Determining the General Layout   The next step in the design process is determining the general layout by grouping machines, products, or departments. This helps to establish the general arrangement of the plant, store, or office before spending much time on details. Using similar layouts as an example, you can estimate the space needed. Space should also be provided, where appropriate, for maintenance, planning, and food and other needed services. Each service should be placed conveniently near the units that use it.

Entrance locations are important in the layout of retail and service establishments. Customers usually enter downtown stores from the street, parking lot, or corridors, and goods usually enter from the back. External factors to consider include entrances for employees, parking for customers, connections to utilities, governmental restrictions, and weather factors.

In manufacturing and large retail and wholesale warehouses, materials-handling devices such as conveyors, carts, hand trucks, and cranes are used to move materials. The objective is to move the items as quickly as possible, with a minimum of handling, and without increasing other costs (see Figure 12.4).

FIGURE 12.5 |
Product and Process
Layout Comparison of
Cafeterias

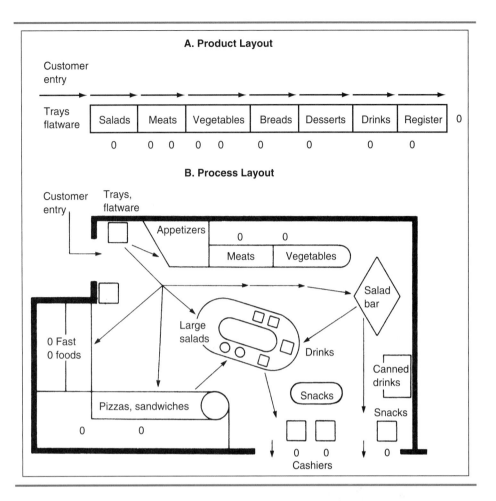

Determining the Final Layout   If your performance is to be efficient, the final layout must be planned in detail, so examine each operation to ensure easy performance of the work. If workers spend too much time in walking, turning, twisting, or other wasted motion, the work will take longer and be more tiring. Tools and other items to be used should be located close at hand for quick service. Some specific factors to consider when doing your final layout are shown in Figure 12.6. Since the first of these, space for movement, is particularly important, you should ask questions such as these: Is there enough room if a line forms? Can shelves be restocked conveniently? Are aisles wide enough for one- or two-way traffic?

Real-World Example 12.11

For example, grocery store aisles are designed to allow passage of two carts, but they often become blocked by special displays of new or sale items. Similarly, it may be difficult to squeeze between the display racks in department stores, and office planners often fail to allow enough space for storage of accumulated files.

The last consideration in the list in Figure 12.6, aesthetics, is also important, so ask yourself: Are the layout and surroundings attractive to workers and customers?

FIGURE 12.6 |
Questions to Ask
about a Production
Layout

1. *Space for movement.* Are aisles wide enough for cart and truck movement? Is there enough room for lines that form at machines and checkout stations? Can material be obtained easily and shelves restocked conveniently?

2. *Utilities.* Have adequate wiring and plumbing, and provision for changes, been planned? Has provision been made for proper temperature? Does the area meet Environmental Protection Agency (EPA) standards?

3. *Safety.* Is proper fire protection provided, and are Occupational Safety and Health Administration (OSHA) standards being met? Are there proper guards on machines, in aisles, and around dangerous areas?

4. *Working conditions.* Do workers have enough working space and light? Is there provision for low noise levels, proper temperature, and elimination of objectionable odors? Are workers safe? Can they socialize and take care of personal needs?

5. *Cleanliness and maintenance.* Is the layout designed for effective housekeeping and waste disposal at low cost? Can machinery, equipment, and the building be maintained easily?

6. *Product quality.* Has provision been made to ensure proper quality and to protect the product as it moves through the plant or stays in storage?

7. *Aesthetics.* Is the layout attractive to customers and employees?

Real-World Example 12.12

The Gloucester, Virginia, ServiStar Hardware Store, which once was patronized primarily by men, was dank, dark, and ugly. With more women becoming do-it-yourselfers and buyers of more hardware store items, ServiStar decided to change its image. It installed bright lights, chrome gridwork, and even murals. "Some of the old guys come in and kid us about being a disco," says Robert Fitchett, whose family owns the store, "but our sales are up 33 percent from last year."

Layout is also important for those working at home. One successful interior designer offers these suggestions: (1) Design your workplace with you at the center; (2) use furniture with flexible spaces and cubbyholes; (3) keep a few supplies close at hand, and store the rest out of the way; (4) build shelves up to the ceiling; and (5) use the top of filing cabinets to hold peripherals, not as a place for paper collection.

Implement Your Plans

Finally, you should test your layout plans to see if they are sound. One way to do this is to have employees, customers, or other knowledgeable people review the plans and make suggestions.

An important point to remember is that, although the layout of the interior of your facility is important, the walls and what is outside them can be equally vital to your success. Construction of a new building requires consideration of the type and method of construction, arrangements for vehicular movement and parking, provision for public transportation, if available, and landscaping.

How to Improve Operations

Products and methods of operation are constantly changing as competition pushes out obsolete or inefficient businesses. Some tools are available in the disciplines of work simplification and industrial engineering to help you keep up to date and constantly improve your operations.

The steps used in designing and improving work are (1) state the problem; (2) collect and record information; (3) develop and analyze alternatives; and (4) select, install, and follow up on new work methods. Computers are now used to help improve operations, particularly through the use of software that simulates operations. Be sure to record your analysis on paper, tape, or disk for review.

State the Problem

As usual, it is best to begin by clearly stating *the problem—not a symptom of the problem.* Ask questions such as, Is the cost of the work too high? Is the quality of the service low? Is the service to customers delayed?

Collect and Record Information

This step consists of collecting information for the *what, how, where, who, why,* and *when* of the work being done. Observing the work being performed, talking with knowledgeable people, and studying available data are methods of obtaining information.[11]

Develop and Analyze Alternatives

Listing the available alternatives is basic to any type of analysis and a critical step in decision making. All work and services can be performed in many ways, and products can be made from many different materials.

Some questions that might be used in improving work performance include

- Who performs the activity, what is it, and where is it being done?
- Why is the activity being performed?
- Can the activity be performed in a better way?
- Can it be combined with another activity (or activities)?
- Can the work sequence be changed to reduce the volume of work?
- Can it be simplified?

Real-World Example 12.13

An example of improving work performance may now be seen in the food service industry. Many restaurants are turning to prepackaged frozen food instead of making menu items from scratch. Blaming price increases and the need for quality consistency, these restaurants are looking to others to prepare and freeze those items that are time-consuming to prepare.[12]

Select, Install, and Follow Up on New Methods

Using your objectives, such as lower costs or better service, as a guide, pick the method that best suits your goals. Installing this new method includes setting up the physical equipment, gaining acceptance, and training workers. Test the method to see that it works and follow up to see that workers are familiar with it and are following procedures.

Setting and Using Performance Standards

One of the most difficult problems you will face in your business is measuring the performance of employees, since there are few precise tools for establishing standards against which to measure performance. Instead, you must rely heavily on people's judgment. Physical work can be measured more precisely than mental work, but doing so still requires judgment.

Performance standards can be set by (1) estimates by people experienced in the work; (2) time studies, using a watch or other timing device; and (3) synthesis of the elemental times obtained from published tables. Most small business owners use the first method, using estimates of experienced people. These estimates should be recorded and given to workers for their guidance. The standards should allow for the time needed to do the work at normal speed, plus time for unavoidable delays and personal requirements. A good set of standards can be determined this way at a minimal cost.

What You Should Have Learned

1. All businesses have operating systems, which process (or transform) inputs of people, money, machines, methods, and materials into outputs of goods, services, and satisfactions.

2. Some general factors to be considered in locating any business are access to: (*a*) the work force, (*b*) utilities, (*c*) vendors, and (*d*) transportation, as well as (*e*) the effect of taxes and government regulations.

3. The most important factors to consider in choosing a retail location are the type of business and the type of location. The type of business largely determines the location. Convenience goods stores are usually located where the traffic flow is high, shopping goods stores where comparison shopping can be done. Specialty goods stores often generate their own traffic but are helped by having similar stores in the vicinity.

   The types of retail locations are downtown in the business district, in freestanding stores, and in shopping centers.

4. Among the most important factors in choosing a manufacturing site are nearness to customers and vendors and the availability and cost of transportation.

5. In planning physical facilities you (*a*) determine the product to be sold and the volume to produce, (*b*) identify the operations and activities required to process it and get it to the customer, (*c*) estimate the space needed, and (*d*) determine the best physical arrangement and layout of those facilities. The types of layout are product and process, or a combination of both.

   Physical facilities must be laid out to provide for a smooth flow of work and activities, space for movement, adequate utilities, safe operations, favorable working conditions, cleanliness and ease of maintenance, product quality, and a favorable impression.

6. Telecommuting is becoming more important to small business because of the convenience and flexibility it provides employees—and even owners—of small businesses.

7. The methods used to improve operations include (*a*) stating the problem; (*b*) collecting and recording information; (*c*) developing and analyzing alternatives; and (*d*) selecting, installing, and following up on the new methods.

8. Standards for measuring performance are needed. Standards can be set by (*a*) estimates by people experienced in the work; (*b*) time studies, using a watch or other timing device; and (*c*) using a synthesis of elemental times from published tables. Small businesses usually use estimates of experienced people.

Key Terms

anchor stores   332
convenience goods   330
downtown locations   331
facilities   333
freestanding stores   331
inputs   325
manufacturing or
    production   333

operating systems   325
operations or
    production   325
outputs   325
process layout   335
processes   325
producers   328
product layout   335

retailers   328
seasonal stores   331
service companies   329
shopping centers   332
shopping goods   330
specialty goods   331
telecommuting   334

Questions for Discussion

1. What are some characteristics of an operating system? What are some inputs into an operating system? What are some outputs resulting from the operating processes?
2. Explain some of the more important general factors affecting location choice.
3. Explain the two most important factors in choosing a retail location.
4. Explain the two most important factors in locating a manufacturing plant.
5. Explain the steps involved in planning facilities.
6. Explain the three different types of layout.
7. What are some objectives of layout planning?
8. Explain the four steps involved in improving operations.
9. Which of the two cafeteria layouts in Figure 12.5 do you think would be more effective? Why?
10. Do you remember your movements during course registration at college the last time? What improvements could you make in the process?
11. What is telecommuting, and why is it growing in importance for small firms?

Case 12.1

Telecommuting in the Rockies

In today's world of notebook computers, tiny printers, cell phones, and fax machines, many of us work at home, on the road, and at the beach. There is even a town in Colorado that bills itself as a "telecommuting town."

Located in the southwest quadrant of Colorado, Telluride has only 1,500 residents, but one-third of them now have access to the Internet. One of the advantages of having the town wired for high tech is the relief of not having to leave home to go to work (the town's average annual snowfall is 300 inches). Another advantage is the savings to one's employer—$4,000 to $6,000 a year in reduced office space alone. These advantages are the result of $130,000 provided by the State of Colorado in 1993 to bring 21st century communications into the area.

Bernie Zurbriggen of Frisco, Colorado, is an example of how telecommuting works. After a brush with death, he resigned a highly stressful job and relocated in the Rocky Mountains. There he created U.S. Trans Comm (bernie@colo.com), the ultimate transportable company, through which he supplies customers, nationwide, with up-to-the-minute used car prices. In fiscal 1995, U.S. Trans Comm received 35,000 calls. As he adds new services, he predicts that call volume will rise significantly during the twenty-first century. His office (home) has 10 phones—and a breathtaking view of Buffalo Mountain and the Continental Divide.

Zurbriggen uses technology (both old and new) to provide the information services needed to keep in contact with customers—and he stays at home to do it.

Questions

1. Do you think this type of arrangement and location would be beneficial to a small business? Explain.

2. Do you think your productivity—in this situation and location—would be increased, be reduced, or stay the same? Explain.

Source: *Telluride Visitors Guide,* Telluride Publishing Co., Winter 1995–1996; Kerry Hannon, "A Long Way from the Rat Race," *U.S. News & World Report,* October 30, 1995, pp. 86–87; Andrew Feinberg, "Frisco System," *Forbes ASAP,* October 9, 1995, p. 21; and author's communication and conversations with Telluride Visitor Services, November 1995.

Case 12.2

Nell Hill's: An Adventure in Shopping

Mary Carol Garrity opened a gourmet food and gift shop in Atchison, Kansas, in an old bank building. Because of her canny purchasing and creative displays, the shop soon evolved into a home furnishings store, Nell Hill's, named after her grandmother. While her goal was to serve the few residents of Atchison, her store soon began to attract customers from as far away as Kansas City, 60 miles distant.

For seven years the store made no profit, and Garrity took home a salary of only $12,000 a year. But then customers began to arrive from all over the state. For a store that does not advertise, is not listed in any Kansas City phone directory, and has received hardly any media attention, the influx of thousands of women driving long distances to shop is amazing. Nearly 95 percent of Nell Hill's sales are to shoppers who live more than 50 miles away, mostly in greater Kansas City. The number of shoppers is rapidly increasing, as evidenced by the fact that, in the last decade, sales have risen between 20 and 30 percent annually, reaching $1.7 million.

Garrity's success largely derives from her energy and dedication to not only finding unusual products but displaying them in creative ways. Because of her unique ability, Hallmark Cards Inc. of Kansas City, Missouri, has added Atchison to its itinerary—along with New York and Paris—as a place for their artists to seek inspiration.

While Nell Hill's is not a discounter, it is able to keep prices low because its expenses are so low. The store itself and the warehouse where the merchandise is stored are in space that was abandoned when Garrity rented it.

Another attraction of Nell Hill's is the appeal of purchasing items directly from the store's owner and buyer. She greets most of her customers by name, will go to their homes to help them decorate, and has her customers send her photographs of their homes, which she then uses to help them remodel.

The success of Nell Hill's is part of a trend among upmarket shoppers. Convenience, value, and selection are no longer enough for many of these discriminating shoppers. Instead, they are looking for adventure. According to Nancy Ornce, creative director of gift wrapping and other specialty products at Hallmark Cards, "People are looking for shopping experiences that are off the beaten path." Apparently this trend is working in Garrity's favor. According to her, Nell Hill's has succeeded not in spite of its distance from customers, but because of it. "It's the romance of a small town," she says.

Like many other successful small business owners, Garrity has expanded to an additional location in Atchison, one in Kansas City, and now operates an online store at www.nellhills.com.

Mary Carol has been dubbed "one of the hottest little retailers" by *Forbes* magazine, been featured on the CBS *Early Show,* NBC *Today Show, The Wall Street Journal, Fortune, Midwest Living, Country Living,* and more. She has her own series of books, a syndicated column, and a line of home accent products carried in 750 stores.[i]

---

[i]Source: Correspondence with Mary Carol Garrity, September 2011.

Questions

1. Evaluate the approach used by Mary Carol Garrity in developing and opening her store.

2. Do you agree with the statement that "The success of Nell Hill's is part of a trend among upmarket shoppers"? Explain.

3. Go to the Nell Hill's website and evaluate the choice made to open the new locations. Do you think Mary Carol Garrity should open more stores?

Experientials

1. Commercial lodging has two basic layouts, interior or exterior hallways. Locate one of each in your area and find out why the owners picked the specific layout style.

2. Again, you can relate your classroom to business. Compare three local businesses' performance standards to those of your professor.

CHAPTER 13

Purchasing, Inventory, and Quality Control

It's unwise to pay too much, but it's also unwise to pay too little. When you pay too much you lose a little money, that is all. When you pay too little, you sometimes lose everything, because the thing you bought was incapable of doing the thing it was bought to do. The common law of business balance prohibits paying a little and getting a lot—it can't be done. If you deal with the lowest bidder, it is well to add something for the risk you run. And if you do that, you will have enough to pay for something better.
    —John Ruskin

Nothing can be produced out of nothing, any more than a thing can go back to nothing.
    —Marcus Aurelius

Resources must be employed productively and their productivity has to grow if the business is to survive.
    —Peter F. Drucker

Learning Objectives

After studying the material in this chapter, you should be able to:

1. Discuss the importance of purchasing.

2. Explain the need to choose suppliers carefully.

3. Describe how to establish an effective purchasing procedure.

4. Discuss how to establish and maintain effective inventory control.

5. Explain what is involved in operations planning and control.

6. Describe how to maintain quality control.

Anders Book Stores: Dealing with Hundreds of Suppliers

Bob and Kathy Summer find owning and managing Anders Book Stores (ABS) www.andersbookstore.com "frustrating—but fun!" They purchased the store from Jim Anders in 1982 after spending several years working for him, during which time they learned some of the ins and outs of running a high-quality operation.

The Summers have divided the responsibilities so Bob specializes in college-level books and Kathy handles everything associated with textbooks and supplies for 14 private schools. After ordering and receiving the books she groups them by grade, sells them, and returns unsold copies to publishers. In handling these activities, as well as being responsible for materials and supplies, she deals with nearly 1,000 suppliers each year.

Bob handles sales to students from the University of South Alabama (www.usouthal.edu), which has its own bookstore across the street, and from other colleges in the area. Bob receives the book orders from campus bookstores in the area; buys, receives, sells, and now rents the books; reorders if necessary; and returns unsold books to publishers. Anders also provides Internet sales and ships from "California to Texas to Maine—and just about every state."

A new market has opened up to them since they went online with sales. They have discovered a market for "no value" books. These are old or no longer used editions of texts that, under normal conditions, would simply be put in the garbage. Now many of these books are actually in demand from online customers, and this new market segment is showing a profit.

A major problem Anders faces is estimating how many copies of each text to order. Each book order Bob receives has the estimated number of students in the class; so taking into consideration that some students will share a book and some will not buy a text, Bob estimates how many copies of each text to order.

Bob buys used books from students and used-book wholesalers; new textbooks come from the publishers. ABS has 500 publishers listed in its computer, although it regularly buys from "only" about 200 in any one year. When you consider that Kathy also buys from more than 1,000 suppliers, you can understand why they say "buying and bookkeeping problems are horrendous."

About six weeks before classes start, orders are sent to publishers via computer modem. Publishers then ship the

345

books, via UPS (www.ups.com), FedEx Corporation (www.fedex.com) or freight, sometimes as much as four weeks before they are needed.

Another problem is not having enough textbooks to meet student needs. When this happens, Bob reorders and books are shipped by UPS or FedEx. The supplier usually ships the books one to seven days after the order is received. If needed immediately, a book can be shipped second-day express—at an additional charge. One year enrollment increased so rapidly that Bob had to place more than 50 reorders, for about 25 percent of the books sold.

Even worse is the problem of unsold books. Even when publishers allow returns for a refund, there is usually a restocking fee. And in the present economic climate of rapid mergers, sometimes the publisher that sold the books has been acquired by another house, so where should the books be returned? Given the already low gross profit margin of only 15 to 20 percent, returns put a severe financial strain on the business. When asked about how online sales affected ABS sales, Summers stated that it was an issue; however, he not only sells books and supplies but also provides services of buy/sell, returns, refunds, and special

services for his customers that they cannot get online. Brick-and-mortar stores are always going to be around, especially those that provide good customer relations.

Poor-quality books pose another problem. In one order, some books had the first 78 pages glued together. In another, some sections came unglued and fell apart. Although the publisher replaces books, replacement is inconvenient and time-consuming.

Most of the large publishers send out an annual evaluation form for their dealers to complete. Since they have been doing this, Bob and Kathy have noticed an improvement in service from the publishers.

Like other small businesses, ABS has many personnel problems. For instance, increases in the minimum wage rate make a strong impact on operations. Such increases reduce the number of people who can be hired, with the result that there is more work to be done by fewer workers. The Summers used to employ many college students but now hire only a few. Also, they say, "the loss or death of a key employee can cripple a small business such as ours for an extended period of time. Therefore, we need to plan ahead and try to have a certain degree of depth to cover these employees. And usually these employees must be paid more in order to retain them."

Bob and Kathy's daughter is proving to be a budding entrepreneur. She now works for the company and has introduced a newer upscale shopping experience. With the addition of a new monogramming machine, she is able to provide onsite products for the new University of South Alabama football program. She also has brought in many boutique items such as handbags, baskets, and baby items. These items can also be personally monogrammed.

Finally, taxes pose a problem for ABS. Not only are the taxes themselves a burden, but the amount of time and effort involved cut into core business activities.

And when you pour a recession on top of the issues discussed, problems just magnify.

Source: Author's discussions with Kathy and Bob Summer.

The Profile shows that the profitability of a small business depends largely on effective purchasing, operations, inventory, and quality control. Most small firms have many potential sources of supply for goods and services, each of which requires close study to secure the proper quality, quantity, timing, price, and service needed. This chapter emphasizes the strategies and procedures needed for effective purchasing, as well as inventory, operations, and quality control.

The Importance of Purchasing

Your business will need products provided by someone else, and the wide variety of items available requires careful study to ensure proper selection. Some items, such as electricity, come from only one supplier, but even they require a careful analysis to obtain them at a favorable cost. Others, such as insurance (see Chapter 17), machines, and equipment, also require special attention because they are often expensive and are purchased infrequently. Still other items, such as paper clips and welding rods, are relatively cheap, and they are purchased routinely. Finally, materials that are part of the company's main product and have a high cost relative to revenue will take up a large amount of your time. This chapter is primarily concerned with this last group, those that are an important part of your main product.

What Purchasing Involves

Purchasing determines the company's needs and then finds, orders, and assures delivery of those items.

Obtaining all items, including goods and services, in the proper form, quantity, and quality, and at the proper place, time, and cost, is the main objective of **purchasing.** Purchasing identifies the needs of the company and then finds, negotiates for, orders, and assures delivery of those items. Thus, you should coordinate your needs with the operations of suppliers, establish standardized procedures, and set up and maintain controls to ensure proper performance. As you probably noticed, Bob and Kathy Summer do all these things for Anders Book Stores.

In retail stores, buying requires coordinating the level of stock of many items with consumer demands, which change as styles, colors, technology, and personal identification change. (And many customers may expect to buy year-round certain "standard" items that do not reflect fashion changes.) Each type of item may be handled differently, so those doing the buying must work closely with those doing the selling to satisfy these differing needs.

Purchasing for a manufacturing plant involves getting the proper materials and processing them into finished goods while maintaining proper control of inventory and quality. Thus, those doing the purchasing must work closely with those doing the production and selling.

Purchasing by the federal government has become so complex and costly that it discourages small businesses from trying to sell to it. At the urging of the SBA (www.sbaonline .sba.gov), though, the Federal Acquisition Streamlining Act was passed. It urges government agencies to buy off-the-shelf goods rather than items made to its own detailed specifications. The law also permits the government to communicate with vendors on-line rather than with paperwork. These changes make it easier for small companies to bid on federal contracts.

Why Purchasing Is So Important

The cost of materials and other goods and services needed to produce a product is about half the revenue received for it. This means all other costs, plus profit, almost equal the cost of purchases. In many cases, the cost of purchases is as much as two-thirds of sales revenues.

Just-in-time (JIT) delivery is having materials delivered to the user at the time needed for production.

While the price of purchases is important, other aspects can be just as critical. For example, obtaining **just-in-time (JIT)** delivery—where the materials are delivered to the user just at the time they are needed for production—can save on inventory costs. Recent statistics suggest that JIT inventory management has helped keep warehouses from overflowing. The U.S. Department of Commerce reports that the inventory-to-sales ratio for manufacturing has steadily declined since the early 1980s. Close coordination between you and your supplier can greatly improve efficiency by shifting inventory costs and management to the distributors. The distributor, in turn, usually discounts the price to the purchaser as a result of lower costs from increased production. These arrangements take on aspects of a partnership (as discussed in Chapter 3).

Supplier-base downsizing means reducing the number of suppliers to concentrate purchasing.

Two current trends in purchasing that are causing considerable problems for small firms are supplier-base downsizing and fully integrated production networks. **Supplier-base downsizing,** which means reducing the number of suppliers to concentrate purchasing, is a result of corporate downsizing.

Fully integrated production networks are entire geographic regions where a fully integrated supply chain, from raw materials to finished products, is built up.

The second problem, **fully integrated production networks,** is a primary problem for U.S. companies in global operations. If small U.S. suppliers are to survive, they must ensure that all suppliers in a supply chain achieve—and operate at—similar high standards and collectively market their skills to global competitors.

Finally, not having the appropriate stock—the right style, at the right price, at the right time, and of the proper quality—properly displayed for customers can result in added costs, lower profits, and unhappy customers.

Assign Responsibility for Purchasing to One Person

While capable subordinates, such as specialty buyers, may be delegated the authority to order in their areas of expertise, in general *one person should be given the overall purchasing responsibility.* But that person should ask for—and get—the help of people knowledgeable in areas such as engineering and planning.

Stockouts are sales lost because an item is not in stock.

Those doing the purchasing should be aware of trends and special situations that can affect operations and should call situations such as the following to your attention:

1. *Expected changes in price.* Buying later for expected decreases in price or buying increased quantities for expected inflation in price can result in savings. However, **stockouts,** which are sales lost because an item is not in stock when customers want it, and inventory costs that are too heavy should be guarded against.

2. *Expected changes in demand.* Seasonal products and high-fashion items fall into this category.

3. *Orders for specialty goods.* The quantity ordered should match expected demand, so no material is left over. Because demand for these items is usually unknown, forecasts should include estimates of losses that may occur from stockouts or old and stale inventory.

4. *Short supply of materials,* as the following classic example illustrates.

"Sorry, girls! We just didn't order enough UltraToys. Can you come back next week?"

(Source: © 1996 by Margaret P. Megginson. Reprinted with permission.)

Urban Cowboy caused the demand for Western wear to skyrocket. Salaminder was swamped with orders and expanded its work force to 60 employees. But sales plummeted when the fad died just as suddenly as it had begun.[1]

Selecting the Right Supplier

You will be more successful in purchasing if you can find several acceptable sources of goods and services. Because reliability in delivery and quality affects nearly all operations, suppliers can be valuable sources of information for various aspects of operations, and suppliers can provide valuable service.

You can find many good sources by consulting the Yellow Pages (www.yellowpages .com), the *Thomas Register of American Manufacturers* (www.thomasnet.com), the *McRae Bluebook,* newspapers, trade journals, and publications of research organizations. In addition, visits to trade shows and merchandise marts give you an opportunity to view exhibits and talk with salespeople. Internet and World Wide Web networks (to be discussed in Chapter 16) can be used to obtain information on possible sources. Many small firms are now hiring expert consultants when purchasing becomes complex.

The **supply chain** is an integrated-coordinated system of activities to transform raw materials into finished products delivered to the end consumer.

Small businesses often appear as a small link in the **supply chain.** For some products there are many stages of movement from raw material to end product. For example: if you want to go out for a gourmet dinner, consider everything that happens to your food before it is set in front of you—from planting seeds to raising meat, processing, cooking, and final server service. Or perhaps diamonds that are mined, transported, graded, cut, sold to jeweler, mounted into a setting, and finally sold to the consumer.

Supply chain management (SCM) is the process of planning, organizing, directing, and controlling a supply chain from origin to consumption.

Supply chain management (SCM), or logistics, is the process of coordinating the movement, storage, and all processes, from beginning to end. SCM integrates supply and demand between many companies and within some.

According to Jacobs and Chase, the largest hurdle in the supply chain relationship is trust. This creates a strain on the small business owner if he has any doubts about receiving future inventory needs.

Selection of suppliers should be carefully investigated by the small business owner. The local Better Business Bureau is a good start and communication with existing users can be very helpful.[2]

Types of Suppliers

As discussed in Chapter 9, you can purchase from brokers, jobbers, wholesalers, producers, or others. Each provides a particular type of service. Notice that Anders Book Stores buys new books from the producers (the publishers) but buys used ones from wholesalers (used-book companies) and students. Also, supplies and other items are ordered from a variety of sources.

Use Few or Many Suppliers?

Should you buy from one, a few, or many suppliers? A single source of supply can result in a closer and more personalized relationship. So, if you use one source, when shortages occur you should receive better service than when many sources are used. Also, discounts may be obtained with larger-volume buying. If one seller can supply a wide assortment of the items needed the cost of ordering is reduced. On the other hand, multiple sources provide a greater variety of goods and often better terms. Most small firms use several sources.

Sometimes it is desirable—or even necessary—to use a single source for specialized items. The following example illustrates how this happened in one interesting development.

Real-World Example 13.3

Several years ago Wynton M. and Carolyn Blount donated the land and money to build the Wynton M. Blount Cultural Park in Montgomery, Alabama, where the Alabama Shakespeare Festival is located (www.mainstreetusa.com/clients/al). Because they were great admirers of Queen Elizabeth II's beautiful black swans, they inquired as to where she had found them. The answer came back from England that they had been bought at a farm just a few miles from Montgomery—the only known source of supply of the beautiful birds.

Investigating Potential Suppliers

Potential supply sources should be checked for factors such as quality of output, price, desire to serve, reliability, transportation, terms of payment, and guarantees and warranties. Because all these factors affect your company's performance, a minimum standard must be set for each of these.

Suppliers should not be chosen on the basis of price alone, for quality and/or service may suffer if the supplier has to lower prices to obtain your order. Instead, suppliers should be chosen to meet carefully set quality and service standards. These standards can be used to ensure acceptable quality without paying for quality higher than needed.

Evaluating Supplier Performance

Just as you investigate potential suppliers, you should also evaluate their performance. Some services publish ratings of products. Also, while it requires some time and effort, you could develop a rating system of your own to use in selecting, evaluating, and retaining suppliers. Rating systems pick out important factors such as quality, service, and reliability, as well as price, and then use those to evaluate each supplier.

Real-World Example 13.4

Sharp Corporation (www.sharp-usa.com) uses a rating system of this kind in its Memphis plant to evaluate its many suppliers, most of which are small firms. A copy of its creed, "Practice Sincerity and Creativity," is given to each potential supplier with a statement that Sharp "expects 100% quality parts," delivered precisely on schedule. Suppliers who agree to this stipulation become Sharp's suppliers and receive a periodic report card showing how they rate on satisfying quality, price, prompt delivery, and other standards.[3]

Establishing an Effective Purchasing Procedure

In addition to deciding on the suppliers to use, you must establish a purchasing procedure to ensure effective ordering and receiving of materials. While there is no one best way, Figure 13.1 presents a computer flowchart of a well-designed purchase order system. The procedure should accomplish several major objectives concerned with purchasing. The proper materials, parts, goods, and so forth needed to produce the goods or services must be obtained. The total price paid for the items purchased must be satisfactory for sale of the finished product. Moreover, the amount of resulting inventory should be in balance with customer demand to minimize total costs. Finally, a simple—yet effective—inventory control system should be established.

Requisitioning Goods or Services

Effective small companies establish standards for various aspects of the quality of their products and/or services. These standards are usually developed with the help of professional/technical people who are knowledgeable in technical, marketing, and production areas. The derived standards are then converted into specifications to be sent with orders to suppliers. See item 1 in Figure 13.1.

The request to purchase materials or services (called a purchase requisition) can originate from many sources. If a service is needed, the request usually comes from the user of that service, as when the accounting manager requests an outside audit, the personnel

FIGURE 13.1 |
Purchase Order
Process Flowchart

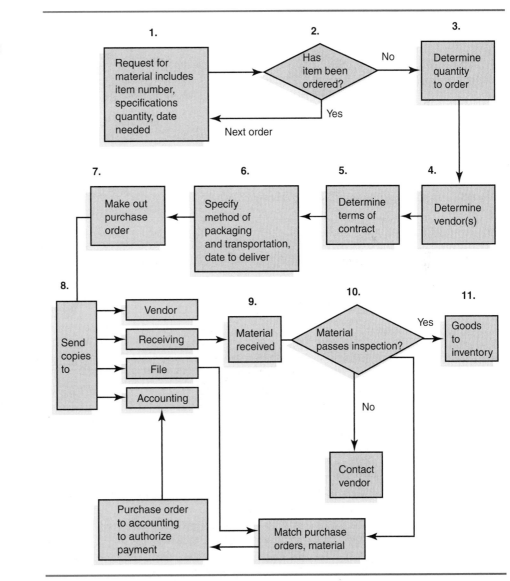

manager needs to install or change an insurance program, or the marketing manager needs to place an ad with an agency. But when materials are needed, the request can originate in any of several ways, such as when (1) someone observes that inventory is low, (2) the system automatically identifies the need for an item, (3) an operating manager requests it, (4) a customer requests a given item, or (5) the purchasing manager observes some special conditions that indicate the need to purchase an item.

Purchasing by retailers poses different problems from purchasing by a producer. Figure 13.2 shows a suggested schedule for a retailer to buy and sell style goods. The procedure operates as the following discussion illustrates.

In the spring or summer, a retailer visits a trade show—or consults suppliers—and places orders based on evaluation of styles and plans. Between August—when the goods are received—and February goods are sold, more goods are produced, and plans for the spring and summer are completed. Goods are received in time for the selling seasons; inventory and sales are checked to consider reordering. End-of-season sales late in the winter and summer can help reduce inventory. The cycle is repeated for each selling season.

Making and Placing the Purchase Order

A **purchase order** tells the supplier to ship you a given amount of an item at a given quality and price.

Standing orders set predetermined times to ship given quantities of needed items, at a set price.

There are many ways of placing orders for needed goods (see items 7 and 8 in Figure 13.1) depending on your needs and the supplier's demands. Issuing **purchase orders** is very common since they become legal records for the buyer and seller. Establishing **standing orders** with the supplier simplifies the purchasing procedure and allows for long-range planning. It involves setting schedules for delivery of goods in predetermined quantities and times and at agreed-to terms.

Technology enters the picture at this point. As indicated earlier, many big purchasers are reducing the number of vendors they deal with. In other words, if a vendor does not have the appropriate technology to adequately serve a purchaser, the purchaser will look elsewhere.

Paying a Satisfactory Price

The importance of the price of goods and services has been mentioned earlier in this chapter. *However, quality and price must be balanced against each other.*

FIGURE 13.2 | Schedule of Semiannual Production and Retail of Style Goods

Activity	Summer 2013	Fall 2013	Winter 2013–2014	Spring 2014	Summer 2014
Retailer plans and orders		**Plans S&S 2014 Sales**			
		Selects styles and orders	Plans sales and promotion (*Reorders F&W 2013–2014*)	**Plans F&W 2014–2015 Sales**	
				Select styles and orders	Plans sales and promotion (*Recorders S&S 2014*)
Retailer receives and sells goods	Receives F&W 2013–2014 goods	**Sells F&W 2013–2014 Goods**			
		Regular sales	Markdown sales Receives S&S 2014 goods	**Sells S&S 2014 Goods**	
				Regular sales	Markdown sales
Producer receives orders and produces goods		Produces S&S 2014 goods		Produces F&W 2014–2015 goods	

Note: F&W = fall and winter; S&S = spring and summer.

> ### Real-World Example 13.5
>
> Fresh Direct (www.freshdirect.com) is an online distributor of fresh foods. They buy direct from the farms in order to be able to sell for lower prices. So in addition to low prices they provide fresh food delivery from online orders eliminating intermediaries and saving time for the consumer.

Customers naturally want high quality, but high quality tends to result in high production costs and a resulting high price. A low price is also attractive but generally reflects lower quality. Therefore, selection should not be made on the basis of price alone.

Prices set by suppliers are only one element of cost to be considered. There are added costs such as transportation, paperwork, reliability of the supplier, processing, and payment. Selection of a supplier should be based on total cost. Also, as discussed in Chapter 8, the possibility of discounts and allowances should be investigated.

Receiving the Items

Receiving the ordered goods and placing them in inventory (items 9, 10, and 11 in Figure 13.1) are the last steps in the purchasing procedure. A copy of the purchase order, including the desired specifications, is sent to those receiving the goods. On arrival, the condition of the goods is checked, and they are checked against the order to make sure they are the desired items, in the correct color, material, size, quantity, and so on. Computers and proper receiving procedures help detect deviations from these standards and speed up the process. As discussed in Chapter 9, transportation systems are constantly improving their service.

Using Computers to Aid Purchasing and Inventory Control

The recent great advances in electronic processing of all sorts of information and the drop in costs (as will be discussed in Chapter 16) have revolutionized the purchasing and inventory operations. Small companies are increasingly using technology to keep track of inventory items, spot replenishment needs, identify sources of supply, and provide information needed for ordering and checking the accuracy of receipts. Computers now largely provide the information needed by the buyer to use in the purchasing process. For example, the use of a fax (in item 8 in Figure 13.1) would speed up the transfer of information. Steps 1 through 7 can also be performed automatically with a computer and selected programs.

Controlling Inventory

An **inventory** is a formal list of all the property of a business, or the property so listed.

An **inventory** is a formal list of property of a business, or—the way we will use the term—the property so listed. No business can operate without some kind of inventory, if only office supplies. Therefore, there is by definition no way to avoid carrying inventory—no matter how hard you may try—and *the best you can do is manage its movement and control its cost.*

> ### Real-World Example 13.6
>
> For example, second-generation Web grocery FreshDirect's CEO, Joe Fedele, is finding his way through the $1.6 billion industry by concentrating on developing a goal plan. He buys direct from farmers, fishermen, and slaughter houses and uses a superefficient distribution center to hold down costs. The key to success he states is, "Don't hold onto inventory." With a capital investment of $140 million,

> Fedele has a built-to-order model that cuts out the middleman and focuses on more lucrative perishables. With his superefficient distribution center, the action begins at midnight, where online orders are cut off, input into an Oracle database, processed, and placed in refrigerated trucks for delivery.[4]

Bar codes are derived from a language called symbologies and used for specific identification of the objects.

Bar codes can be used to track your inventory from purchase to sale. **Bar codes** are derived from a language called symbologies and are used for specific identification of the objects.

Real-World Example 13.7

For example, the bar code on the back of your textbook specifically identifies this book and may be used for pricing and inventory control.

The first Universal Product Code (UPC) said to have been scanned in retail was on Wrigley's Chewing Gum in 1966.

Radio-frequency identification (RFID) is a method of specific identification transponders that contain information and can be read from several meters distance.

Another specific inventory control method is Radio-Frequency Identification Tags (RFID). **Radio-frequency identification** (**RFID**) is a method of specific identification transponders that contain information and can be read from several meters distance. Current uses for RFID include passports, supply chain management, libraries, auto keys, and for imbedding into pets for identification.

Real-World Example 13.8

For example, Airlines are considering the use of RFID tags on a global level to assist in the problem of lost luggage. It reduces the need for manual sorting to one percent as compared to the usual 20 percent. RFID tags will enhance tracking delayed luggage and greatly reduce the number of lost bags.[5]

Some companies are using this technology for employee identification. The RFID can also be used to keep track of workers and of hours worked at different sites. Would you want to be "chipped" by your employer?

The Role Played by Inventory

Inventory is carried to disconnect one segment of the operating process from another so each part can operate at its optimum level. A crude example is in your home. If you did not have a supply of food, you would have to go out, find some, buy it, bring it home, and prepare it every time you were hungry. Having surplus food in your pantry or refrigerator, however, you can buy more food at your convenience, keep it as inventory, and then process it when you get hungry.

The same holds true in a producing plant as shown in Figure 13.3. The figure shows what happens from the receipt of raw materials, through each of three operations, to final sale to customers. Inventories are shown at different levels at different stages of the operation, and the inventory level at a given stage depends on what activities have occurred in the operations process.

FIGURE 13.3 | Diagram of Material Flow and Inventory

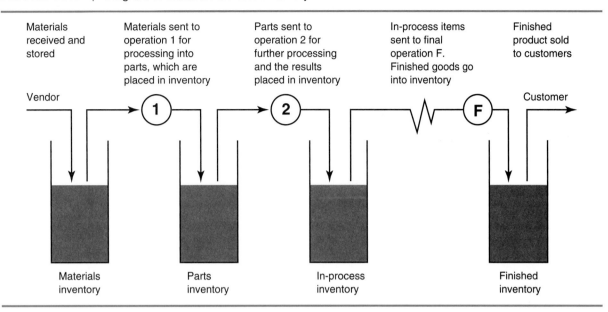

A similar situation occurs in retail stores. Retailers receive goods, store them, put them on display for sale, sell them to customers, and then order more of the goods. The level of inventory at any given time depends on the amount of goods bought—and stored in inventory—relative to the quantity sold. Thus, a retailer must have enough goods in inventory after an order is received to last until the next order is placed and received. Figure 13.4 illustrates this process. When the goods on the left are received they are stored with similar goods as inventory. Then, after being put on display and gradually sold, they are replaced by other goods.

Types of Inventory

Inventories exist in small firms at all times in one or more of the following forms: (1) finished items on display for sale to customers; (2) batches of goods, such as materials, parts, and subassemblies, awaiting processing or delivery; (3) repair parts awaiting use; (4) supplies for use in offices, stores, or shops, or for use in processing other goods; and (5) miscellaneous items, such as tools placed in a toolroom.

These inventories, especially the first two kinds, represent a major investment by all businesses—large ones as well as small. Many companies have failed because their inventory tied up too much money or the items in inventory became obsolete, damaged, or lost.

Inventory Mix

According to the **80–20 rule,** approximately 80 percent of a company's income usually comes from 20 percent of its products.

According to the **80–20 rule,** approximately 80 percent of a company's income usually comes from 20 percent of its products. Companies having multiple products, parts, and services should therefore concentrate their attention on those items that have the greatest impact on costs and income. Similarly, 20 percent of the items in inventory represent 80 percent of the cost. Companies should be sure that these items are truly needed.

Costs of Carrying Inventory

Having inventory on hand costs a small business much more than most people realize. The costs of carrying inventory consist of: (1) the cost of providing and maintaining storage

FIGURE 13.4 |
Goods Flow and
Inventory in a Retail
Firm

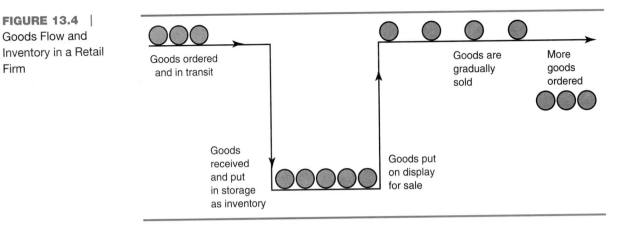

space, such as rent or depreciation, heating, lighting, and security; (2) insurance and taxes; (3) profits lost because money is tied up in inventory (called *opportunity cost*); (4) theft and destruction; and (5) obsolescence and deterioration of the items. Estimates of the sum of these costs range from 15 percent to more than 100 percent of their value; 20 to 25 percent is the amount most frequently mentioned.

Determining When to Place an Order

Figure 13.3 shows the changing inventory levels as materials are ordered, processed, stored, and sold. Figure 13.4 shows how levels change as a retailer orders goods, stores them, and then sells them. The real problem in both these instances is knowing when is the most appropriate time to order needed items. Costs associated with ordering inventory may include clerical and labor costs of processing orders, inspection and return of poor-quality products, handling and transporting.

The optimum inventory level can be maintained by having items arrive just in time for sale to customers. The actual system tries to approach zero inventory but normally balances inventory carrying costs and stockout costs. This calculation is not easy, and you will make mistakes, but with rational analysis, practice, and a certain amount of intuition—and luck—you will make it. Remember, stockout occurs when there is insufficient stock to supply customers. This usually happens during the order lead time between placing and receiving the product(s).

Determining How Much to Order

The order quantity is determined by the level of inventory and the order interval. When orders are placed at *certain, regular intervals,* the order quantity should be set to bring the inventory level up to a predetermined amount. When *inventory level* determines the time to order, the order quantity is a fixed amount called the **economic order quantity (EOQ).**

The **economic order quantity (EOQ)** is the quantity to purchase that balances the cost of placing the order with the cost of carrying the inventory.

The EOQ model identifies the inventory order size that will minimize the annual costs of ordering and carrying inventories. In practice, there are many variations of the basic EOQ model. For example, the basic model assumes that the price of the inventory items will remain fixed. On the other hand, some EOQ formulas can take into consideration varying prices resulting from quantity discounts. Still other formulas can be used to determine the optimum lot size for items the company produces for itself. However, the basic EOQ model is useful in practice because it helps small business owners understand the role of the cost of ordering and carrying inventory.

In summary, *the EOQ is determined by balancing (1) the cost of placing an order for items to be placed in inventory with (2) the costs involved in carrying that inventory in stock.* Refer again to Figure 13.2 which shows a situation in which the order size is determined by how much the company can sell during a season. There are several very good and inexpensive software packages to help you address your inventory issues.

Inventory turnover is a key ratio (see Chapter 14) in inventory control and indicates how many times per year your products flow through the system.

$$\text{Inventory turnover rate} = \frac{\text{Cost of Goods Sold}}{\text{Average Inventory}}$$

While weeks supply calculations measure how many weeks of Inventory is on hand.

$$\text{Weeks supply} = \frac{\text{Average Inventory}}{\text{Cost of Goods Sold}} \times 52$$

Operations Planning and Control

As shown in Chapter 6, operations planning and control begins when you determine what business you are going into, what product(s) you will sell, and what resources are needed to produce the quantity you expect. If you are to have products available when demanded by customers, you must carefully forecast and plan for sales. Predicting the sales of a small company with any degree of accuracy is difficult, but even crude estimates are better than none, because considerable cost is involved in trying to serve customers if the items they seek are not in stock.

Handling Variations in Demand

Demand for products varies from one period to another for such reasons as changing lifestyles, economic conditions, and seasons. Most sales of goods and services have seasonal variations. Therefore, you may be constantly hiring, training, and laying off employees; not using facilities efficiently; changing levels of inventory; and facing cash flow problems and product shortages.

Several operating plans may be used to cope at least partially with seasonal variations. The most popular such plans are these:

- Allow operations to rise and fall according to changing sales demands. This requires periodically hiring and laying off workers.
- Use self-service to reduce the number of employees and hire temporary or part-time workers during peak periods.
- Use inventory buildups (or drawdowns) to smooth out operations.
- Carry complementary products, such as winter and summer items.
- Subcontract production during maximum demand periods.
- Lose sales by not expanding operations to meet increased demand.
- Use special inducements to stimulate sales during periods of low demand.

Scheduling Operations

Scheduling is setting the times and sequences required to do work.

Scheduling involves setting the times and sequences needed to perform specialized activities, including when and how long it takes to do them. You are often faced with this problem of scheduling. For example, you try to schedule your classes to minimize inconvenience and for your greatest benefit. Then you have to schedule appointments with the doctor or dentist around them. Computers are now being used effectively by many firms to perform scheduling operations. Look again at Figure 13.2 which shows a schedule of the steps involved in selling style items.

Controlling Operations

Even if you make the best of plans, communicate them effectively, and use the best workers and materials to perform the work effectively, controls are still needed. Without adequate control over the operations the process will fail.

In simple systems, the comparison of planned performance with actual performance can be made informally by personal observation. Usually, though, a system of formal checks is needed. Standards are set, data on actual performance are collected, standards and actual data are compared, and exceptions are reported.

Quality and Its Control

In recent years, American consumers have shown increasing concern about the quality of U.S. goods and services, since so often foreign companies produce and sell products of superior quality. Now, though, many U.S. companies are taking steps to improve their products. This is particularly true of small companies, as discussed in Chapter 9.

While small businesses must compete in the market with large companies, many are finding that emphasizing quality and reliability and designing output to match customer needs are better tactics than lowering prices. The service a customer receives may determine which product he or she will buy.

Real-World Example 13.9

For example, if at any time a customer or client gets hung up in an endless loop of holding on an automated response system, the product brand involved is likely to move to the bottom of the list. Do customers really care if their calls are being monitored when they only desire a quick answer about a product or service? In this case, how do you measure your standards of customer service?[6]

What Is Quality?

Quality refers to product characteristics and/or the probability of meeting established standards.

The term **quality** can have many meanings, two of which are significant to small business owners. First, it refers to characteristics of products being judged. Second, it means the probability that products will meet established standards. In the discussion that follows, we will use the meanings interchangeably.

Assessment of the quality of a product is relative; it depends on the expectations of the evaluator—the customer. Customers who are used to high-quality goods and services tend to be much more critical of purchases than those accustomed to lower standards. Because small companies usually cannot cater to all quality levels, they must set their sights on the level demanded by their customers and try to reach some level of total quality.

For example, Kathy Barnard (see PROFILE in Chapter 12) at Koi and Lilies provides house calls and medical expertise to assist her customers with the quality of life for their fish and reliablity of service.

The idea of Total Quality (TQ) has not evolved as a theory but has developed from actual practice in manufacturing settings and has validated itself through the economic successes of adopting companies. In order for TQ to work, the principles and practices involved must be part of the entire organization. The application of TQ is most commonly known as Total Quality Management (TQM) (www.tqmnet.com). TQM is used not only in manufacturing, but also in services. One of the best-known organizations practicing quality service is Disney (www.disney.com).

Real-World Example 13.10

The Disney Institute (www.disneyseminars.com) periodically offers three-and-a-half–day behind-the-scenes seminars at the Walt Disney World Resort to give participants ". . . new insights into customers, business, and operating systems." Disney's seminars, "The Disney Approach to Quality Service," are designed to show how Disney's best management practices can be applied to many service and retail organizations.[7]

Quality involves many characteristics of a product: strength, color, taste, smell, content, weight, tone, look, capacity, accomplishment, creativity, and reliability, among others. Part of the quality of a *service* are such factors as salespersons' smiles, attentiveness, friendly greetings, and willing assistance. Standards to meet the desires of customers must be established for each characteristic.

Customers tend to want high quality, but often they want to pay only a limited price for the product. Still, some qualities, such as a friendly greeting, cost little; others, such as precision jewelry settings, cost much. Quality-level analysis is thus based on the value of quality to the customer and the cost of producing that level of quality. To make the decision you must ask the following questions: Who are my customers? What quality do they want? What quality of product can I provide, and at what cost? Will customers pay that cost?

How do you determine where to set the quality level? Market research, questionnaires, talking to customers, comparison with competitors' products, and trial and error are a few of the methods. Recent advances in technology have helped raise the level of quality attainable—while keeping costs low.

Improving and Controlling Quality

There are many ways a small business can improve quality, but we will discuss only three: (1) setting up quality circles, (2) designing quality into the product and operations, and (3) installing a good quality control process.

Establishing Quality Circles   Many progressive companies report good results from using quality circle programs. As you can see from Figure 13.5, in **quality circles,** small groups

Quality circles (QCs) are small work groups meeting periodically to find ways to improve quality and performance.

of workers meet regularly to identify and develop ways to solve company problems, especially quality. The members, who are usually not supervisors, receive training in areas such as problem identification, communications, and problem solving. Also, as they meet, they may have access to resource people who can provide further expertise. Quality circles seem to be more successful when top management gives them unrestricted support.

Designing Quality into the Process   If quality is to be achieved during the production of a product, the processes must be designed to produce the desired quality. Machines must be capable of turning out the product within set tolerances, workers must be trained to produce

FIGURE 13.5 |

How Quality Circles
Operate

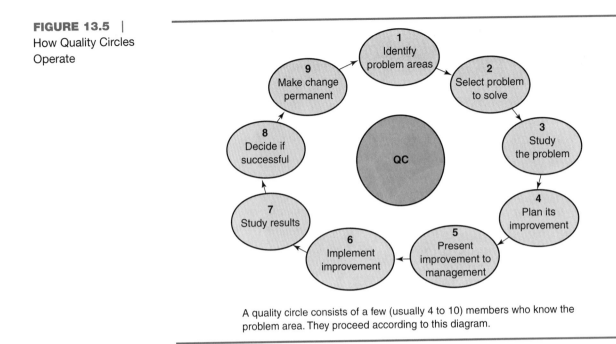

A quality circle consists of a few (usually 4 to 10) members who know the problem area. They proceed according to this diagram.

that level of quality, and materials and goods must be purchased that meet the stated standards. In service companies employees must be trained to understand a customer's needs and to perform the work to the customer's satisfaction. If the process or employees cannot produce the proper quality of output, no type of control can correct the situation.

Installing a Quality Control System   Quality control, or quality assurance, is a system used by a producer to ensure that the finished goods or services meet the expectations of customers, as advocated by the late W. Edwards Deming, the "Quality Guru."* Deming condensed his management philosophy and techniques into his famous "14 Points," as shown in Figure 13.6. These points stress the necessity for owners and top managers to become involved in continuous improvement processes, as the following example illustrates.

Real-World Example 13.11

Four brothers from Taiwan decided to open an instant-noodle factory in Lianjin, China, several years ago. At first they made very little profit because of the low profit margin—one-tenth of a cent per packet. The brothers then changed their tactics to answer one of the deepest anxieties of Chinese life: "When do I eat, and will it be clean?" They put their instant noodles in a shrink-wrapped Styrofoam bowl and sold it for 24 cents, which compared favorably to the 60-cent price of their only competitor, imported from Japan and Taiwan. The product was so successful that the factory had immediate shortages. To ensure continued high quality, eldest brother Wei Ying-chan taste-tests his company's noodles every morning for breakfast.[8]

---

*Deming died in 1993 at the age of 93, having achieved considerable fame as a quality expert in Japan, where the country's top quality award is the Deming Medal.

FIGURE 13.6 |
Deming's 14 Points

W. Edwards Deming distilled his self-developed methods of management into 14 points. Though they have been described and elaborated on in hundreds of books, videos, and seminars, in their original form they still provide the bedrock of most Deming processes.

1. Create constancy of purpose toward improvement of product and service.
2. Adopt the new philosophy.
3. Cease dependence on mass inspection.
4. End the practice of awarding business on the basis of a price tag.
5. Improve constantly and forever the system of production and service.
6. Institute training.
7. Institute leadership.
8. Drive out fear.
9. Break down barriers between departments.
10. Eliminate slogans, exhortations, and targets for the work force.
11. Eliminate quotas.
12. Remove barriers to pride of workmanship.
13. Institute a vigorous program of education and self-improvement.
14. Take action to accomplish the transformation. It's everybody's job.

Regardless of what methods or techniques are used to achieve it, effective quality control involves at least the following steps:

- Setting standards for the desired quality range.
- Measuring actual performance.
- Comparing that performance with established standards.
- Making corrections when needed.

Some standards may be measured by instruments, such as rulers or gauges for length; but color, taste, and other standards must be evaluated by skilled individuals. Measurement may be made by selected people at selected spots in the process, usually on receipt of material and always before the product goes to the customer. Quality can also be controlled by feedback from customers, as shown in Figure 13.7.

Craftspeople are a key example of excellent quality. Often the market niche is so narrow for a specific craft that the loss of quality in production is created by the lack of demand and talent. For example, a leading pointe-shoe (ballet) manufacturer is losing quality as many experienced cobblers are now retiring and creating backlogs of at least seven months for custom-made shoes. Some dancers require as many as two pair every day at a cost of about $80 a pair. With cobbler art dying, quality is lost, and soon assembly line pointe-shoes, not custom-made, will be the norm for principal dancers.[9] According to some, craft is becoming a heritage industry. For more than two generations we have become a disposable, instant gratification society.

The International Organization for Standardization (ISO) is a nongovernmental bridging organization of 146 countries establishing global standards for quality. They include health, safety, specifications for materials, testing and many others, particularly a common technical language. Standardized symbols for danger are a good example of ISO benefits. ISO standards are developed by committees with input from any interested stakeholder. More information may be found on the ISO Web site (iso.org).

FIGURE 13.7 |
Example of Feedback
Quality Control in a
Restaurant

Management Encourages Your Comments

Date _5/19/2013_

Waiter or waitress _Phyllis_

Please circle meal   Breakfast   (Lunch)   Dinner

	Yes	No
1. Were you greeted by host or hostess promptly and courteously?	✓	—
2. Was your server prompt, courteous, and attractive in appearance?	✓	—
3. Was the quality of food to your expectations?	—	✓
4. Was the table setting and condition of overall restaurant appearance pleasing and in good taste?	✓	—
5. Will you return to our restaurant?	—	✓
6. Will you recommend our restaurant to your friends and associates?	—	✓

Comments:

Food was overcooked. Potatoes were left-overs. Meat was tough. This was my second visit and I brought a friend with me. We were both very disappointed.

Please drop this in our quality improvement box provided as you exit room.

Thank you and have a good day.

What You Should Have Learned

1. Purchases are a small company's largest single type of cost. Goods and services must be obtained at the proper price, quality, and time and in the proper quantity. One person should be made responsible for the purchasing function.

2. Sources of supply must be found and investigated and one or more suppliers selected. Reliability in delivery and quality affect nearly all operations. You must also decide whether to use one or multiple suppliers.

3. An effective purchasing procedure consists of (*a*) determining the items needed, in what quantity, from whom to purchase, and the terms of the contract; (*b*) sending the purchase order; (*c*) receiving the goods; (*d*) inspecting them; and (*e*) paying for them.

4. Inventory is carried to disconnect one part of the operating process from another so each part can operate effectively. Inventory takes many forms, from raw materials to finished products. The cost of carrying inventory consists of providing and maintaining storage space, insurance and taxes, profits lost from money tied up in it, obsolescence and deterioration, and theft and destruction. The cost of inadequate inventory is dissatisfied customers from stockouts.

5. Operations planning and control start with a forecast of sales from which operating plans are developed. Alternative plans for seasonal sales include (a) producing to demand, (b) using self-service and part-time workers to help meet peak demand, (c) producing at a constant rate and inventorying for future demand, (d) carrying complementary products, (e) subcontracting high demand, (f) not meeting high demand, and (g) using off-season sales inducements.

Scheduling is setting the times and sequences required to do work. Control of operations is obtained by reacting to exceptions to plans.

6. In small firms, the emphasis should be on quality of goods and services rather than on low price. The term quality refers both to acceptable characteristics and to reliability of the product. Quality circles have been used by small companies to improve performance.

Quality control involves (a) setting standards, (b) measuring performance, (c) comparing actual performance with standards, and (d) making corrections. Sampling inspections and customer feedback are used to check performance or quality.

Key Terms

bar codes 354	purchase order 352	standing orders 352
economic order	purchasing 346	stockouts 348
quantity (EOQ) 356	quality 358	supplier-base
80–20 rule 355	quality circles 359	downsizing 348
fully integrated production	radio-frequency	supply chain 349
networks 348	identification	supply chain
inventory 353	(RFID) 354	management
just-in-time (JIT) 347	scheduling 357	(SCM) 349

Questions for Discussion

1. Discuss the advantages and disadvantages of buying locally versus buying from a distant seller.

2. What are the advantages and disadvantages of shopping at a single store rather than at several?

3. A company orders widgets in batches such as 1,000 units. The company uses a constant number each month (say 2,000) in production. Show how the inventory level changes over time between orders. What factors would cause you to change the order size up or down?

4. How would you make an economic study to determine the quantity of a food item to buy for your family on each trip to the store? How often should purchases be made?

5. In some parts of the country, building construction varies seasonally. Is this a problem for company management? What decisions must management make concerning these variations?

6. Many times, sales personnel do not practice good selling relations. How would you control the quality of this type of service?

7. What is quality? How can it be measured? How can it be controlled?

8. Outline instructions for installing a new quality circle.

9. In Figure 13.2, styles are changed twice a year. What changes would be required with seasonal changes of four or more styles?

10. What would you do if you received a large number of customer response forms with comments similar to those in Figure 13.7?

11. What effect on your company would the delivery of an increased percentage of defective parts have? What would you do about this?

Case 13.1

Eddie & Company: Exceeding the Relevant Range

Eddie & Company is a small manufacturer located in the North Central part of the United States. The company manufactures auto and truck axles for automobile producers. Most of its output is sold to one of the larger auto companies. Because its sales have recently increased beyond all expectation, that company now wants Eddie & Company to increase its production level to satisfy the increased demand.

This request poses a serious dilemma for the owners of Eddie & Company. It would have to considerably increase production in order to ship more axles to the automaker. However, it has already been operating at full capacity just to meet the demands of its customers, including the automaker, when sales were low. The only ways to satisfy the increased demand would be (1) to buy the needed new products from its competitors and resell them to the automaker—at no profit—or (2) to increase its own production capacity in order to satisfy the demand.

The first alternative would satisfy the short-run increase in demand, but not the long-range one. But the second alternative of increasing production capacity would pose different problems. First, there is no assurance that the increased demand from the automaker will be permanent, and Eddie & Company could find itself with unused capacity. Second, this alternative would mean increased fixed expenses, which would raise the company's break-even point. And this increase would continue even if the automaker cut back its orders to the original level.

Questions

1. What options are available to the company?

2. What would you do if you faced the same situation?

3. Would you buy the product from your competitor to meet the contract? Explain.

4. Would you add the additional capacity? Explain.

Experientials

1. Inventory control is a must for all businesses. Visit several local retailers and inquire about the use of bar codes (UPCs) and PFID tags on merchandise. Ask the manager or owner how new inventory is entered into their system.

2. Also, inquire about their turnover rate and compare it to the industry average for their type of business.

PART 5

Basic Financial Planning and Control

As we have shown throughout this text, the requirements for success in small business include an understanding of the importance of financial management; knowledge of how financial relationships affect profit or loss; and the devotion of time, energy, and initiative to planning and controlling financial activities. We discuss in this part how such planning and control ensure that the business will not only survive but also grow and develop.

Chapter 14 explains the need for, and methods of, planning for a profit and guides you through the steps of planning the profit for a hypothetical company. It also covers the basic financial structure of a business.

Chapter 15 explores the basic structure of control and shows how to collect information and compare actual performance with standard performance. The design and use of budgets and budgetary control are also covered, along with the use of ratio analysis. The chapter focuses on the taxes that a small business must pay and how to collect, handle, and report those taxes and credit management.

Chapter 16 deals with information technology. It emphasizes the importance of gathering and maintaining information, and explains how to record it. It also emphasizes the need for, and explains how to use, computers in small firms, including e-commerce.

Chapter 17 discusses your need to minimize the risks incurred in owning and operating a small business. Most losses can be minimized by establishing insurance and reserves. With properly planned operations and crime prevention, including security measures, the chances—or magnitude—of other losses can be reduced. ●

CHAPTER 14

Basic Financial Planning

Earning a profit—staying in business—is still the No. 1 thing. Unless you can make money, you cannot do any of the other things.

—Irving Shapiro, on his retirement as chairman of Du Pont

Accounting is a tool and, like most tools, cannot be of much direct help to those who are unable or unwilling to use it or who misuse it.

—Financial Accounting Standards Board

Learning Objectives

After studying the material in this chapter, you should be able to:

1. Explain the need for profit planning for a small business.

2. Discuss what causes changes in the financial position of a company.

3. Understand the financial structure of a business.

4. Apply the theory of cost of goods sold.

5. Learn how to plan to make a profit in a small business.

6. Plan for a profit for an actual small business.

Carpe Diem

"I knew from the beginning we were going to be successful! We had a good business plan and were exceeding our profit projections." Tomi Sue Rusling did her homework and has operated her popular specialty coffee shop, Carpe Diem, since 1995.

The vision began when Rusling wanted to semiretire from her position in retailing that required constant travel in multiple states. She and her late husband Van had a deep love for specialty coffees. Rusling had years of experience in management and Van was an entrepreneur at heart—he always had great creative visions and ideas. With both sets of skills and a great mentor and role model from their favorite coffee shop, Carpe Diem was created.

Carpe Diem was first created on paper and was the result of one year of in-depth study and preparation. Rusling began a methodical A–Z game plan. She talked to coffee shop owners in several cities and thoroughly researched the industry. After a trip to northern California, she convinced herself she also needed to include a "microroaster" in her business. According to Prime Roasting (prices for equipment microroasters range anywhere from $8,000 to $28,000), industry demographics indicated a need for a location that included an upper income highly mobile neighborhood (those would demand upscale coffee), colleges (students need a place to "nest"), private college preparatory schools, churches (attract from other areas), and with a high traffic count.

Rusling based her financial plan on how many cups of coffee were needed for breakeven. In her one year study she had accumulated all costs for equipment and supplies. Her mentor, Clark Cadzow, allowed her to work in his store for one month to learn the ropes and meet the vendors who traveled the globe looking for green coffee beans.

The next step was to combine her demographic study with her physical plant needs and find the ideal location. In 1995 the Ruslings opened Carpe Diem (a subchapter S corporation), which was the metropolitan area's first specialty coffee shop, in Springhill Village. This location was in an old established upper-class neighborhood within walking distance of one college, one private college prep school, and three churches. Also near were grocery, banking, and boutique shopping. This gentrified location also had open sidewalks with lots of foot traffic.

Rusling knew that she needed to stay focused in the narrow niche for specialty coffee and not be distracted or tempted to branch out. The microroaster and concentration on specialty coffee shop services made Carpe Diem

unique. She never had any intention to grow beyond these boundaries.

This theory was reinforced in 1997 when the Gulf Coast Exploreum Museum of Science convinced her to provide her services on site. As it turned out, the market of waiting parents was overrun by very active and huge bus groups of children. She also verified that multiple locations dilute management skills. At around the same time a very successful bagel bakery convinced her to provide specialty coffee with them in a retail bakery store—this one was a great marriage until the bagels caught on so fast and were in such high demand that the owner tried to grow too quickly and lost the entire business. Back to square one, the specialty coffee niche.

In 2000, Rusling decided to enlarge her business to include the sale of her "market knowledge" of coffee beans, coffee roasting, and retail.

With the addition of Alan Tolson, who is a professional master roaster, Carpe Diem began a limited wholesale distribution of roasted beans. Carpe Diem roasts beans from more than 10 countries around the world and serves more than 28 coffeehouses and retailers in the southeast United States.

In 2005 she lost the visionary side of the business with the death of her husband Van. She reflects that he had done everything possible to ensure that her business flourished. Because of very close relationships with employees, they rallied around her and made sure the business carried on through the emotional turmoil.

Rusling says she empowers her employees by making sure they are well trained and have purpose within the company. For the right employee fit, future growth within the company is expected—"Employees are family."

In fact, Carpe Diem's manager, Ginger Jesser, and baker, Melinda Young, have both been with the company for more than 12 years.

Carpe Diem, Inc., was started with $100,000, 100 percent totally financed. Resources used for the business plan were various books, www.sba.gov, Service Corps of Retired Executives (www.score.org), and the local office of the women's business center (www.sba.gov/womeninbusiness). $30,000 of the original loan was used for operations and the business opened four months after the loan was granted.

Rusling says the loan was rejected at first, then the SBA was consulted, the plan tweaked, and the loan successful. To this day, she credits her success to the original and ongoing business plan. She had a mission—"To deliver to our customers the finest quality products and service available, to offer to the community a comfortable and enjoyable gathering place for all to share and, above all, to give back through our community service and support"—and stuck to it. She has a practices and policies manual that has been updated and is kept current.

Today Carpe Diem coffee can be found at the local regional airport; however, it is used with a contractual agreement for the name. Recipes and roasted beans are purchased from the original and only Carpe Diem in Springhill Village.

Rusling's advice to new small businesses is to pay your bills on time, watch your cash flow, and keep a close relationship with your bank. She goes on to suggest that you purchase your site and building if possible. There are many site issues for new businesses. These include parking, drainage, and landscape issues, plus zoning and variance, and health department approvals. Also, pay attention to maintenance that could create liability, such as steps and potholes.

Public relations and marketing are mainly supported by ads in school yearbooks, donated gift baskets, gift cards, and their own 5K Christmas Eve Santa Run. Carpe Diem also donates to various local charities and public events, as well as supporting the local arts. Through their efforts Carpe Diem's leadership has been able to pull together a very active merchants association for Springhill Village and allow for "the local community to refer to Carpe Diem as their public living room." Rusling says that all of her efforts allow for her to give back and support the community.

(Source: CATHY © 1997 Cathy Guisewite. Reprinted with permission of UNIVERSAL PRESS SYNDICATE. All rights reserved.)

Profit cannot be left to chance in small firms. Yet all too frequently it is, because small business owners tend to know little about financial planning and control. Even when efforts *are* made to plan for profit, they are often inadequate, for owners tend to assume that history will repeat itself—that past profits will be repeated in the future. Instead, small business managers must learn to identify—and prepare for—all income and costs if they are to make a profit.

The type of business you are entering, for example, is critical in determining the amount of startup funds you will require. While a retail business can generate income immediately, a service business may require a wait of 30 to 90 days. So you must factor this information into your estimate of the working capital you will need.

Profit planning is particularly difficult for new entrepreneurs who have given up well-paying jobs in order to go out on their own. They realize they have given up their pension plan and insurance program(s), but they often fail to realize they have also given up such amenities as the former employer's copy and fax machines; subscriptions to professional literature; and seemingly insignificant incidentals such as stamps, memo pads, and pens, all of which may result in hundreds or even thousands of dollars in expenses.[1] These items must be included in your profit planning.

Eventually many corporate dropouts find it more attractive to start anew in the corporate world, and many of them succeed in the reverse transition. So if you are sure that you never want to work for "the man" again, you must be realistic about what you are giving up in exchange for your freedom and you must do some careful profit planning.

What Is Profit Planning?

Profit planning is a series of prescribed steps to be taken to ensure that a profit will be made.

The definition of **profit planning** may seem obvious: planning for profit. To make a profit, however, your prices must cover all direct and indirect costs and include a markup for planned profit. This chapter will help you (1) determine how much profit you want and how to achieve it; (2) learn how to set up an accounting system for your firm and how to read, evaluate, and interpret its accounting and financial figures; and (3) evaluate, or estimate, your firm's financial position.

Later in the chapter, we will outline a step-by-step process to follow in order to ensure that a profit results. The important thing to realize at this point is that, because it establishes targets, *profit planning must precede other activities.* This is what Ms. Rusling (Profile) did in her preparation before opening Carpe Diem.

A lack of accurate cost information, a recurring problem among small business owners, usually results in profits of unknown quantity—or even a loss. Also, it can foster the illusion of making a greater profit than is really earned, if any is earned.

Real-World Example 14.1

The owner of Children's Party Caterer* illustrates this point. During the first interview with a SCORE counselor, she said she had . . . "around $800 worth of party materials . . ." in her pantry at home. But when asked the cost of materials used and the time involved in preparing for each party, she could not answer. The counselor gave her a homework assignment to determine the time she spent preparing for and giving each party, as well as the cost of materials.

She was surprised to find she spent 18 to 20 hours per party, and the cost of materials ranged from $40 to $50. Also, she had not included the cost of transportation or the $10 to $12 baby-sitting cost for her two children. Yet she charged only about $40 to $50 for each party. To the suggestion that she raise her prices to cover these costs, plus a markup for profit, she responded, "People won't pay it." When the counselor replied, "You aren't in the charity business," her exuberant reply was, "Oh, but I enjoy doing it!"

How a Business's Financial Position Changes

The operations of any business . . . especially a small one . . . result from decisions made by its owner and managers and the many activities they perform. As decisions are made and operations occur, the firm's financial position constantly changes. For example, cash received from sales increases the bank balance; credit sales increase accounts receivable; and purchases of material—while increasing inventory—also increase accounts payable or decrease the bank balance. At the same time, machines decrease in value, materials are processed into inventory, and utilities are used. These constant changes in the financial position of the business must be recorded and their causes and effects analyzed.

Tracing Changes in a Company's Financial Position

During all operations, the important question for small business owners is whether their business is improving its chances of reaching its primary objective—to make a profit. *However, some small firms make a profit and still fail, since profits are not necessarily in the form of cash.* Accounts receivable may reflect profits, but many of those accounts may not be collectible. Too much money may be tied up in other assets and not available to pay bills as they come due. The "bottom line" is not an end in itself, but it is the beginning of the more difficult process of tracking cash flow. (See Chapter 15 for more on budgeting and controlling operations.)

First, we should trace the changes in our own small companies. Next, we should carefully monitor—or **benchmark**—those companies on which we depend. Benchmarking is setting up standards (for reference), and then measuring performance against them.

The importance of cash flow may be illustrated with a personal example—your own finances. Your allowance, earnings, and/or other income may be adequate to pay for food, clothing, and other operating expenses, but you may have an unexpected expense, such as replacing a broken-down or worn-out car, for which you must make a cash down payment.

Benchmarking is setting up standards (for reference) and then measuring performance against them.

* Name disguised.

Real-World Example 14.2

Say, for example, that your parents send you $750 per month for living expenses while at school, and you have the following expenses:

Cash allowance	$750
Food @ $10/day × 30 days	300
Gas for automobile	60
School supplies	75
Left to save or spend	$165

Now ask yourself if your car breaks down and repairs will cost $248, do you walk or cut down on food?

If your funds are invested in a fixed asset, such as a loan on your car, they are not available for paying bills. The same is true of a small business. In fact, you can use the same computer programs to handle both your business and your personal finances.

Importance of Accounting

Accounting records are records of a firm's financial position that reflect any changes in that position.

Accounting is quite important in achieving success in any business, especially a small one. In fact, accounting is so tied to your financial well-being that, without it, you would not know what the bottom line is—or even whether it is a positive or negative amount. Therefore, your **accounting records** must accurately reflect the changes occurring in your firm's assets, liabilities, income, expenses, and equity. The continued operation of your business also depends—as Irving Shapiro points out in one of the chapter's opening quotations—on maintaining the proper balance among its investments, revenues, expenses, and profit. Because profit margins are so critical to the success of a business, any decline in them should trigger an immediate search for the cause.

Many small business owners do not realize their business is in trouble until it is too late. Also, many fail without knowing what their problem is—or even that they have a problem. All they know is that they end up with no money and cannot pay their bills. These owners fail to monitor all aspects of their businesses. They often consider financial statements ". . . a necessary evil . . ." and think everything is fine as long as sales are increasing and there is ". . . money in the bank." They do not realize that what they do in their day-to-day business activities is reflected in the financial statements. They tend to pay little attention to the information accountants give them. One young entrepreneur found this out the hard way.

Real-World Example 14.3

For Richard Huttner, the hardest problem in running New York's Parenting Unlimited Inc. was doing the accounting necessary to run its new acquisition, *Baby Talk* magazine. Although *Baby Talk* had revenues of several million dollars a year, it had no financial management, accounting system, general ledger, or bank account when it was acquired. Consequently, while trying to master an ongoing business, Huttner had to spend nearly a third of his time the first three months paying bills and doing accounting. He lamented, "Stanford didn't teach me how long it takes out-of-state checks to clear. At first, that caused us constant cash flow problems."[2]

In the discussion of financial management to come in this chapter, we have used an actual small business, which we have disguised as The Model Company Inc., to illustrate the basic concepts. Assume throughout the following discussion that, while the company is owned by Mr. Model, you manage it for him. Therefore, you must make the required management decisions.

What Is the Financial Structure of a Business?

Financial structure describes the relative proportions of a firm's assets, liabilities, and owners' equity.

A **balance sheet** is a statement of a firm's assets, liabilities, and owners' equity at a given time.

The assets, liabilities, and equity accounts of a business, which are interrelated and interact with each other, represent the **financial structure** of a firm, which changes constantly as business activities occur. Always keep in mind the most basic accounting truth: *The total of liabilities plus owners' equity always equals the total assets of the firm.*

At regular intervals, a **balance sheet** is prepared to show the assets, liabilities, and owners' equity of the business. See Figure 14.1 for the arrangement and amounts of the accounts for our hypothetical business, The Model Company.

Remember, you can use the balance sheet as a gauge of the financial health of your company. It not only shows how assets are being used but also provides a snapshot of the company at a given moment. To get a realistic look at your company, you should go over the balance sheet with your accountant instead of leaving everything up to her or him.

FIGURE 14.1

THE MODEL COMPANY, INC.
Balance Sheet
December 31, 20____

Assets

Current assets:			
Cash		$ 7,054	
Accounts receivable		60,484	
Inventory.		80,042	
Prepaid expenses		1,046	
Total current assets			$148,626
Fixed assets:			
Equipment	$100,500		
Building	40,950		
Gross fixed assets.		141,450	
Less: accumulated depreciation.		16,900	
Net fixed assets			124,550
Total assets			$273,176

Liabilities and Owners' Equity

Current liabilities:			
Accounts payable	51,348		
Accrued payable.	3,060		
Total current liabilities		$ 54,408	
Long-term liabilities:			
Mortgage payable		20,708	
Total liabilities.			$ 75,116
Owners' equity:			
Capital stock.		160,000	
Retained earnings		38,060	
Total equity			198,060
Total liabilities and owners' equity.			$273,176

Another good source of financial support would be a trusted banker. For more information, see the appendix at the end of this chapter.

Assets

Assets are the things a business owns.

Assets are the things a business owns. They include land, cash, accounts receivable, inventory, equipment, building and other things of value to the company.

Current Assets   Current assets are expected to turn over—that is, to change from one form to another—within a year. Cash includes the bills and coins in the cash register, deposits in a checking account, and other deposits that can be converted into cash immediately. A certain level of cash is necessary to operate a business; however, holding too much cash reduces your income because it produces no revenue.

Accounts receivable are current assets resulting from selling a product on credit.

Accounts receivable result from giving credit to customers for less than a year, as shown in Chapter 15. While selling on credit helps maintain a higher level of sales, care must be taken to select customers who can be expected to pay within a reasonable time.

Liabilities

Liabilities are the financial obligations of a business.

As discussed in Chapter 7, a business can obtain funds by owner investment and by borrowing, which is creating an obligation to pay. The first, which is necessary, increases *owners' equity,* or the *owners' interest* in the business. The second results in a **liability** of the business to pay back the funds—plus interest. Borrowing from creditors is divided into current and long-term liabilities.

Accounts payable are obligations to pay, resulting from purchasing goods or services.

Accounts payable are obligations to pay for goods and services purchased and are usually due within 30 or 60 days, depending on the credit terms. Because any business should maintain current assets sufficient to pay these accounts, maintaining a high level of accounts payable requires a high level of current assets. Thus, you should determine whether or not early payment is beneficial; some sellers offer a discount for early payment, such as 1 or 2 percent if bills are paid within 10 days. This is a good return on your money!

Owners' Equity

Owners' equity is the owners' share of (or net worth in) the business, after liabilities are subtracted from assets.

Owners' equity is the owners' share of (or *net worth* in) the business, after liabilities are subtracted from assets. The owners receive income from profits in the form of dividends or an increase in their share of the company through an increase in retained earnings. Owners also absorb losses, which decrease their equity. (See Chapters 7 and 15 for further details.)

Profit-Making Activities of a Business

The profit-making activities of a business influence its financial structure. These activities are reflected in the revenue and expense accounts, as shown by the following example:*

$$\text{Net income (profit)} = \text{Revenue (income)} - \text{Expenses (costs)}$$
$$\$46,700 = \$530,000 - 483,300$$

An **income statement (profit and loss statement)** periodically shows revenues, expenses, and profits from a firm's operations.

During a given period, the business performs services for which it receives revenues. It also incurs expenses for goods and services provided to it by others. These revenues and expenses are shown in the **income statement,** also known as the **profit and loss statement** (see Figure 14.2).

---

* Figures are from Figure 14.5.

FIGURE 14.2

THE MODEL COMPANY, INC.
Income Statement
January 1 through December 31, 20__

Net sales.	$463,148	
Less: Cost of goods sold.	291,262	
Gross income		$171,886
Operating expenses:		
Salaries	$ 83,138	
Utilities.	6,950	
Depreciation	10,050	
Rent	2,000	
Building services	4,920	
Insurance	4,000	
Interest	2,646	
Office and supplies	6,550	
Sales promotion.	11,000	
Taxes and licenses.	6,480	
Maintenance	1,610	
Delivery	5,848	
Miscellaneous	1,750	
Total expenses.		146,942
Net income before taxes		24,944
Less: Income taxes		5,484
Net income after taxes.		$19,460

Revenue and Expenses

Revenue (also called **sales income**) is the value received by a business in return for services performed or goods sold. The business receives revenue in the form of cash or accounts receivable.

Expenses, such as the costs of paying people to work for you (or for goods or services provided to you), include such items as materials, wages, insurance, utilities, transportation, depreciation, taxes, supplies, and advertising. As these costs are incurred, they are deducted from revenue.

Cost of goods sold is the total cost in terms of raw materials, labor, and overhead of the business that can be allocated to production. It is a broad term that encompasses many things depending on the nature of the operation. Imagine that you are in charge of a company that manufactures and sells widgets. If you are trying to figure out what your cost of goods sold is you will want to segregate production costs from all other operational costs of the business. Obviously the materials and labor that go into producing widgets would be included, but you would also have to factor in overhead that you can attribute to production. This could be something as simple as determining how much of your company's utility bills can be allocated to the production floor's machinery, lighting, and phone service.

Including all costs of production, both direct and indirect, will help a small business owner gain greater insight into the true costs of the product he or she is selling. This, in turn, will help the entrepreneur decide which costs can be managed and which costs can only be monitored.

> ### Real-World Example 14.4
>
> Smith Inc. manufactures widgets by utilizing both raw materials and manual labor in their production. Production takes place on a factory floor that is overlooked by the company's offices. Supervisors who do not directly participate in the manufacturing process are on the production floor at all times to make sure the operation is running smoothly.
>
> To determine Smith Inc.'s cost of goods sold, the owner must not only look at the obvious, the raw materials and the direct labor. He or she will also have to take the supervisors' salaries into account, as well as the electric and water usage for the factory floor. However, the overhead for the offices as well as the salaries of the office personnel will not affect cost of goods sold.

Profit

Profit (income) is the difference between revenue earned and expenses incurred.

Profit, also called **income,** is the difference between revenues earned and expenses incurred. Depending on the type of expenses deducted, profit may be called *gross income, operating profit, net income before taxes,* or *net income.*

Your profit margin indicates the relationship between revenues and expenses; therefore, a decline in profit margin should trigger a search for the cause. The problem could be a rise in expenses, a per unit sales revenue decline caused by discounting or pricing errors, or changing the basic operations of the business.

How to Plan for Profit in a Small Business

According to a Dun & Bradstreet report, a well-managed small business has at least the following characteristics:

- It is more liquid than a badly managed company.
- The balance sheet is as important to the owner as the income statement.
- Stability is emphasized, instead of rapid growth.
- Long-range planning is important.

Need for Profit Planning

As you study the income statement in Figure 14.2, you may interpret it as saying, "The Model Company received $463,148 in net sales, expended $291,262 for costs of goods sold, paid out $146,942 in total operating expenses, and had $24,944 left as net income (or profits) before income taxes." Under this interpretation, *profit is a "leftover," not a planned amount.* While neither you nor Mr. Model can do anything about the past, you can do something about future operations. Because one of your goals is to make a profit, you should plan the operations now to achieve your desired profit goal later. So let's see how you can do it!

Steps in Profit Planning

To achieve your goal during the coming year, you need to take the following profit-planning steps:

1. Establish a profit goal.
2. Determine the volume of sales revenue needed to make that profit.

3. Estimate the expenses you will incur in reaching that volume of sales.

4. Determine estimated profit, based on plans resulting from steps 2 and 3.

5. Compare the estimated profit with the profit goal.

If you are satisfied with the plans, you can stop at this point. However, you may want to check further to determine whether improvements can be made, particularly if you are not happy with the results of step 5. Doing steps 6 through 10 may help you to understand better how changing some of your operations can affect profit.

6. List possible alternatives that can be used to improve profits.

7. Determine how expenses vary with changes in sales volume.

8. Determine how profits vary with changes in sales volume.

9. Analyze your alternatives from a profit standpoint.

10. Select an alternative and implement the plan.

Need for Realism in Profit Planning

Be realistic when going through these steps, or you may be unable to reach the desired profit goal. You may feel the future is too uncertain to make such plans, but *the greater the uncertainty, the greater the need for planning.*

Real-World Example 14.5

For example, the president of a small firm said his forecasts were too inaccurate to be of any help in planning operations, so he had stopped forecasting. His business became so unsuccessful he eventually had to sell out.

The owner of another small business recently stated she cannot forecast the next year's revenue within 20 percent of actual sales. However, she continues to forecast and plan, for she says she needs plans from which to deviate as conditions change.

Profit Planning Applied in a Typical Small Business

This section uses the preceding steps to plan profits for The Model Company. As manager, you must start planning for the coming year several months in advance so you can put your plans into effect at the proper time. To present a systematic analysis, assume you are planning for the company for the first time.*

Step 1: Establish the Profit Goal

A **profit goal** is the specific amount of profit one expects to achieve.

Your **profit goal** must be a specific target value. For example, Ms. Rusling at Carpe Diem set her target at breakeven and did not expect any profit in the beginning. So her profit goal was $0. To begin with, as you manage the business, pay yourself a reasonable salary. Also, Mr. Model should receive a return on his investment—not only his initial investment but also any earnings left in the business—for taking the risks of ownership. To do this, compare what you would receive as salary for working for someone else and the income

---

* Actually, you should be planning for each month at least six months or a year ahead. This can be done by dropping the past month, adjusting the rest of the months in your prior plans, and adding the plans for another month. Such planning gives you time to anticipate needed changes and do something about them.

Mr. Model would receive if the same amount of money were placed in a relatively safe investment, such as U.S. government bonds or high-grade stocks. Each of these investments provides a return with a certain degree of risk—and pleasure. If Mr. Model could invest the same amount of money at an 8 percent return, with little risk, what do you think the return on his investment in The Model Company should be?

Mr. Model originally invested $160,000 in the company and has since left about $40,000 of his profits in the business. He has made approximately 10 percent on his investment this past year, which he thinks is too low for the risk he is taking. Instead, he believes about a 20 percent return is reasonable. So, as step 1 in Figure 14.3, you enter his investment, desired profit, and estimate of income taxes (from the past and after consultation with his accountant). You determine that he must make $52,000 before taxes, which would be a 26 percent return on his investment, if he is to reach his desired profit. After you and Mr. Model have set this goal, you should determine what the profit before taxes will be from your forecast of next year's plans.

Step 2: Determine the Planned Sales Volume

A **sales forecast** is an estimate of the amount of revenue expected from sales for a given period in the future.

A **sales forecast** is an estimate of the amount a firm expects to sell during a given period in the future. In preparing operating and sales budgets, these forecasts are used to estimate revenues for the next quarter, for the year, or perhaps even for three to five years. Learning how to forecast accurately can spell the difference between growth and stagnation for your business.

Different parts of the business use these forecasts for planning and controlling their areas of operations. Then, scheduling production, securing financial resources, purchasing plant or equipment, hiring and paying personnel, scheduling vacations, and planning inventory levels must be done.

In our example, you would probably forecast sales for the coming year on estimates of several factors, such as market conditions, level of sales promotion, estimate of competitors' activities, and inflation. Or you could use forecasts appearing in specialized business and government publications. Also, your trade associations, banker, customers, vendors, and others can provide valuable information. Using all this information—and assuming 6 percent inflation for the coming year—you would probably estimate that sales would increase about 8 percent, to $530,000 ($1,000 per unit × 530 units), which you enter as step 2 in Figure 14.3.

Step 3: Estimate Expenses for Planned Sales Volume

To estimate expenses for the coming year, first track your expenses closely for a month or two,[3] then record last year's figures as part of step 3. You should then adjust them for changes in economic conditions (including inflation), changes in expenses needed to attain the planned sales, improved methods of production, and a reasonable salary for your services as the owner.

You then compute that about 63 percent of your revenue is to pay for materials and labor used directly to produce the goods you will sell. Using this figure—adjusted 6 percent for inflation—you enter the result, $333,900, as ". . . cost of goods." You then estimate the amount of each of the other expenses, recognizing that some expenses vary directly with volume changes, while others change little, if at all. Enter each expense figure in the appropriate place. The total of all expected expenses is $490,000.

Step 4: Determine the Estimated Profit

In determining your estimated profit, you first deduct the figure for estimated expenses from the estimated sales income. Then add the total of any other income, such as interest. After you calculate this amount you find that profit before taxes is estimated to be $40,000 ($530,000 − $490,000), which is higher than the $24,944 made last year.

FIGURE 14.3

THE MODEL COMPANY, INC.
Planning for Profit for the Year 20__

Step Description	Analysis	Comments
1. *Establish your profit goals.*		
Equity invested in company	$160,000	
Retained earnings	40,000	
Owners' equity	200,000	
Return desired, after income taxes	40,000	20% × $200,000
Estimated tax on profit	12,000	
Profit needed before income taxes	$ 52,000	
2. *Determine your planned volume of sales.*		
Estimate of sales income	$530,000	530 units × $1,000 / unit
3. *Estimate your expenses for planned volume of sales.*	Estimated, 20__	Actual, last year
Cost of goods	$333,900	$291,262
Salaries	88,300	88,138
Utilities	7,100	6,950
Depreciation	10,000	10,050
Rent	2,500	2,000
Building services	5,100	4,920
Insurance	5,000	4,000
Interest	3,000	2,646
Office expenses	6,000	5,550
Sales promotion	11,800	11,000
Taxes and licenses	6,900	6,480
Maintenance	1,900	1,610
Delivery	6,500	5,848
Miscellaneous	2,000	1,740
Total	$490,000	$442,194
4. *Determine your estimated profit, based on steps 2 and 3.*		
Estimated sales income	$530,000	
Estimated expenses	490,000	
Estimated net profit before taxes	$ 40,000	
5. *Compare estimated profit with profit goal.*		
Estimated profit before taxes	$ 40,000	
Desired profit before taxes	52,000	
Difference	−$ 12,000	
6. *List possible alternatives to improve profits.*		
A. Change the planned sales income:		
(1) Increase planned volume of units sold.		
(2) Increase or decrease planned price of units.		
(3) Combine (1) and (2).		
B. Decrease planned expenses.		
C. Add other products or services.		
D. Subcontract work.		

FIGURE 14.3 | *concluded*

Expense Item	Sales Volume of 364 Fixed Expenses	Sales Volume of 364 Variable Expenses	Sales Volume of 364 Total Expenses	Sales Volume of 530 Variable Expenses	Sales Volume of 530 Total Expenses	Sales Volume of 700 Variable Expenses	Sales Volume of 700 Total Expenses
7. *Determine how expenses vary with changes in sales volume.*							
Goods sold		$229,200	$229,200	$333,900	$333,900	$440,789	$440,789
Salaries	$50,000	26,304	76,304	38,300	88,300	50,585	100,585
Utilities	6,000	755	6,755	1,100	7,100	1,453	7,453
Depreciation	10,000		10,000		10,000		10,000
Rent	2,500		2,500		2,500		2,500
Building services	4,000	755	4,755	1,100	5,100	1,453	5,453
Insurance	5,000		5,000		5,000		5,000
Interest		2,060	2,060	3,000	3,000	3,962	3,962
Office expenses	2,800	2,198	4,998	3,200	6,000	4,226	7,026
Sales promotion		8,104	8,104	11,800	11,800	15,585	15,585
Taxes and licenses	5,000	1,305	6,305	1,900	6,900	2,509	7,509
Maintenance	800	755	1,555	1,100	1,900	1,453	2,253
Delivery		4,464	4,464	6,500	6,500	8,585	8,585
Miscellaneous	2,000		2,000		2,000		2,000
Total	$88,100	$275,900	$364,000	$401,900	$490,000	$530,600	$618,700

8. *Determine how profits vary with changes in sales volume.*

	Sales Volume of 364		Sales Volume of 530		Sales Volume of 700	
Revenue @ $1,000 per unit	$364,000		$530,000		$700,000	
Expenses						
Fixed		$ 88,100		$ 88,100		$ 88,100
Variable		275,900		401,900		530,600
Total	364,000		490,000		618,700	
Estimated profit before income tax	$000,000	(Break-even)	$ 40,000		$ 81,300	

9. *Analyze alternatives from a profit standpoint.*
   Increase income by increasing price? Decreasing price?
   Increase income by increasing advertising?
   Decrease variable costs?

10. *Select and implement the plan.*

Step 5: Compare Estimated Profit with Profit Goal

Next, you compare the estimated profit ($40,000) with your profit goal ($52,000). Because estimated profit is $12,000 less than you would wish, you decide to continue with steps 6 through 10.

Step 6: List Possible Alternatives to Improve Profits

As shown in step 6 of Figure 14.3, you may have many alternatives for improving profits. Some of these are as follows:

A. Change the planned sales income by
    1. Increasing planned volume of units sold by increasing sales promotion, improving the quality of the product, making it more available, or finding new uses for it.

2. Increasing or decreasing the planned price of the units. The best price may not be the one you are currently using.

3. Combining (1) and (2). On occasion, some small business owners become too concerned with selling on the basis of price alone. Instead, price for profit and sell quality, better service, reliability, and integrity.

Real-World Example 14.6

For example, several years ago Bert Olson stopped using pesticides on his 450-acre farm for two reasons. One was concern for the environment. The other consideration was cost: he was going broke as a conventional farmer. After the change, he started showing considerable profit as consumers' demand for organically grown foods increased.[4]

B.   Decrease planned expenses by

1. Establishing a better control system. Spotting areas where losses occur and establishing controls may reduce expenses.

2. Increasing productivity of people and machines through improving methods, developing proper motivators, and improving the types and use of machinery.

3. Redesigning the product by developing new materials, machines, and/or methods for improving products and reducing costs.

C.   Reduce costs per unit or add other products or services by

1. Adding a summer product to a winter line of products.

2. Using idle capacity innovatively.

3. Making some parts that are customarily purchased from the outside.

Kaizen costing sets cost targets for all phases of design, development, and production of a product for each accounting period.

4. Using the concept of **kaizen costing,** which sets in advance cost targets in all aspects of product design, development, and production. Kaizen costing requires each department—or cost center—to set specific cost reduction plans for each accounting period.

D.   Subcontract work.

Having listed possible alternatives, you must evaluate each of them and concentrate on the best one or ones.

Step 7: Determine How Expenses Vary with Changes in Sales Volume

Although you have estimated your planned sales volume at 530 units (at $1,000 per unit), you will probably want to see what happens to expenses if you sell fewer or more units. This can be done by reviewing your expected expenses in step 3 and varying them up and down, remembering that some are fixed and some vary with level of sales. We have shown this in step 7 at three levels: 364, 530, and 700 units. Notice that total expenses increase from $364,000 at 364 units, to $490,000 at 530 units, and to $618,700 at 700 units. Some expenses, however, are hard to plan.

Real-World Example 14.7

Remember from the Profile on Springdale Travel (Chapter 9) that sales were almost recovered from September 11, 2001? Well, the airlines have recovered passenger numbers but the mix of leisure/business has altered, this means more lower fare tickets are sold. Also the price of oil has skyrocketed as of this writing and has made the fuel costs very hard to budget or plan.[5] In fact most airline profit plans have taken a big hit with increased fuel prices and many believe fuel costs will not decline.[6]

While an analysis of past costs is helpful in projecting future expenses, be aware that

1. The relationships exist only within limited changes in sales volume. Very high sales volumes may be obtained by extraordinary and costly efforts; low volumes result in extra costs from idle capacity, lost volume discounts, and so forth.

2. Past relationships may not continue in the future. Inflation or deflation, changing location of customers, new products, and other factors can cause changes in the unit costs.

Step 8: Determine How Profits Vary with Changes in Sales Volume

As you notice in step 8 of Figure 14.3, profit (or loss) can be estimated for different levels of sales. We have done that for the three levels—364, 530, and 700 units—using fixed expenses, variable expenses, and the resulting profit before income taxes.

These figures were then incorporated into a chart (Figure 14.4) to show what sales volume would result in The Model Company's neither making nor losing money on its operations. This figure, called the **breakeven point,** was 364 units, where sales revenues and total expenses were $364,000.

The **breakeven point** is that volume of sales where total revenue and expenses are equal, so there is neither profit nor loss.

Real-World Example 14.8

An example is the "Angus beef-burger bandwagon." Hardees, Krystal, and Burger King faced new challenges when they added Angus beef. Not only did demand grow by about 5 percent, but the prices also increased. Think about how the breakeven will change with both of these factors included. The increase for the price of the upscale Angus beef must also be considered.[7]

Real-World Example 14.9

For example, Carpe Diem planned a volume that would achieve breakeven, or how many cups of coffee must be sold for expenses and revenues to equal. Sometimes the price may need to be either increased (or decreased) to meet your goal; however, you must be careful not to price yourself out of the market!

Step 9: Analyze Alternatives from a Profit Standpoint

Using the information you have generated so far, especially from steps 6, 7, and 8, can lead you to consider alternatives such as the following to increase profits:

- Change sales price.
- Change media—and/or amount budgeted—for advertising.

FIGURE 14.4 |

Breakeven Chart for
The Model Company

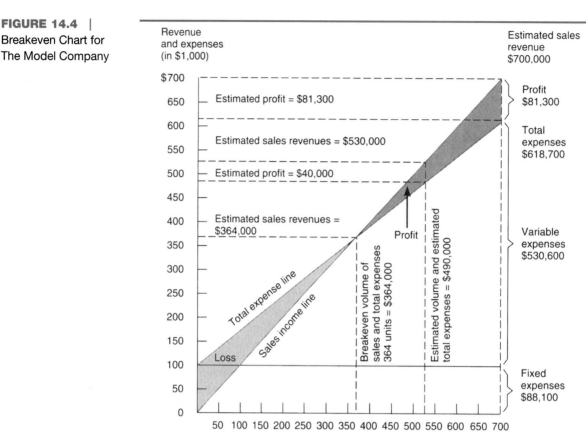

Estimated sales
revenue
$700,000

Revenue
and expenses
(in $1,000)

FIGURE 14.5

THE MODEL COMPANY, INC.
Income Statement for the Year 20__

Sales income		$530,000
Less:		
Cost of goods sold	$327,200	
Other expenses	156,100	
Total expenses		483,300
Net profit before taxes		$46,700
Pretax return on equity		23.4%
Pretax profit margin		8.8%

- Reduce variable costs.
- Change quality of products.
- Stop producing and selling low-margin products.

Other alternatives can be evaluated in much the same manner. Then, having made these economic analyses, you will be ready to make your final plan for action.

Step 10: Select and Implement the Plan

The selection of the plan for action depends on your judgment as to what will most benefit the business. The results of the analyses made in the prior steps provide the economic inputs. These must be evaluated along with other goals. Cost reduction may result in laying off employees or in reducing service to customers.

Mr. Model has just read this text and has been studying other management literature. After hearing you present the above analyses to him, he believes the company can reduce the cost of goods sold by about 2 percent. Figure 14.5 shows a simplified statement of the planned income and outgo for the next year, based on the work you and he have done. How does it look to you?

What You Should Have Learned

1. Not only do small business owners often fail to plan for a profit, but they also sometimes do not even know whether or not they are making a profit. Because healthy sales income does not guarantee a profit, it is important to determine the true cost of a product in order to set a fair price and budget and plan accordingly.

2. A business's financial position is not static. Assets and liabilities fluctuate every time a product is sold, money comes in, inventory is bought, or credit is given. Rapid growth and "paper profits" can be the downfall of small business owners who do not keep accurate records and do not listen to the conclusions accountants draw from the figures.

3. A company's financial structure consists of its assets, liabilities, and owners' equity. Assets are the things a company owns. Current assets, which turn over within a year, include cash, accounts receivable, and inventory, as well as short-term investments and prepaid expenses. Fixed assets—such as buildings, machinery, store fixtures, trucks, and land—are things the company expects to own for a longer time. Part of their cost is written off each year as depreciation expense.

   Liabilities are obligations created by borrowing or buying something on credit. Current liabilities, payable within one year, include accounts payable, notes payable, and accrued expenses. Long-term liabilities, with terms of a year or longer, should be used to pay for fixed assets and to acquire working capital.

   Owners' equity is the owners' share of a business after liabilities are subtracted from assets. Profits may be distributed to owners as cash or dividends, or accumulated in the business in the form of retained earnings.

4. A company's cost of goods sold includes all costs of production, both direct and indirect, and will help a small business owner gain greater insight into the true costs of the product he or she is selling. This, in turn, will help the entrepreneur decide which costs can be managed and which costs can only be monitored.

5. A company's profit (net income) is what is retained after expenses—the costs of doing business—are subtracted from revenues—the proceeds from sales. When sales increase, not only does sales income rise, but variable costs change as well, and it may sometimes be necessary to increase fixed costs.

   To plan for a profit, you must have a profit target, which is your reason for being in business. Detailed profit planning includes at least the first 5 of the following 10 steps: (1) establish the profit goal, (2) determine the planned volume of sales, (3) estimate the expenses for the planned sales volume, (4) determine estimated profit for the planned sales volume, and (5) compare the estimated profit with the profit goal. If the results of (5) are unsatisfactory, (6) list possible alternatives that can be used to improve the profit position, (7) determine how expenses vary with changes in sales volume, (8) determine how profits vary with changes in sales volume, (9) analyze alternatives from a profit standpoint, and (10) select one of the alternative plans and implement it.

6. The chapter concluded by illustrating these steps for a hypothetical company.

Key Terms

accounting records 371	cost of goods sold 374	owners' equity 373
accounts payable 373	expenses 374	profit (income) 375
accounts receivable 373	financial structure 372	profit goal 376
assets 373	income statement (profit and	profit planning 369
balance sheet 372	loss statement) 373	revenue (sales
benchmarking 370	kaizen costing 380	income) 374
breakeven point 381	liabilities 373	sales forecast 377

Questions for Discussion

1. Why is planning for profit so important to a small business?
2. In analyzing the changing financial position of a small business, what things should you look for?
3. "If a small firm is making a profit, there's no danger of its failing." Do you agree? Why or why not?
4. What is a firm's financial structure? What are the components of this structure?
5. Explain each of the following: (*a*) assets, (*b*) current assets, (*c*) fixed assets, (*d*) liabilities, (*e*) current liabilities, (*f*) long-term liabilities, (*g*) owners' equity, (*h*) retained earnings, (*i*) income (profit and loss) statement, (*j*) balance sheet, (*k*) profit, and (*l*) cost of goods sold.
6. What steps are needed in profit planning?
7. How do you establish a profit goal?
8. How do you determine planned volume of sales? How does profit change with volume of product sold?
9. How do you determine planned expenses? Variable expenses? Fixed expenses?
10. What are some alternatives that could improve planned profits? Explain each.

Case 14.1

Eillen Dorsey and Walter Hill, Jr., Use Financial Planning

Eillen Dorsey and Walter Hill, Jr., are successful entrepreneurs today because they learned early in life the importance of personal financial planning. Eillen, the youngest of eight children, was reared in Harford County, Maryland. Her parents taught her that if she dreamed long enough—and hard enough—and was committed to a dream, she would make it become real. But that meant saving her money for college and then for investment.

Dorsey attended Catonsville and Essex Community Colleges, where she began building a network of people who worked in corporate America and in local government agencies. She developed a particularly strong relationship with Walter Hill, Jr., who had attended Morgan State University and the University of Maryland—and also knew the value of savings.

Dorsey and Hill decided to use their savings to start a business in the Baltimore, Maryland, area when they noted that almost every corporation producing machinery had to buy some type of electrical components. They also knew that many of those companies were interested in doing business with a minority firm, so they saw an opportunity to become entrepreneurs.

Dorsey had been a salesperson for Technico, an electrical component company, and was familiar with firms that wanted electrical components. Hill, who was working at Westinghouse, also knew people in the industry. So they quit their respective companies to form ECS Technologies.

Each partner contributed $5,000 to get the business started, and they secured a $35,000 loan by using their homes as equity. Their homes thus became an important investment vehicle as well. The partners had already won a contract before they applied for the loan, making it easier for the lender to grant their request. Because the partners had invested their own money and assets, the banks were willing to give them a line of credit totaling $200,000.

Questions

1. Evaluate the way Dorsey and Hill did their financial planning.
2. Do you think their early personal financial planning influenced their professional financial planning? Explain.
3. To what extent do you think the two entrepreneurs will succeed in their venture? Explain.

Source: Reprinted from William G. Nickels, James M. McHugh, and Susan M. McHugh, *Understanding Business,* 4th ed. (Burr Ridge, IL: Richard D. Irwin, Inc., 1996), p. 667. Reprinted by permission of the McGraw-Hill Companies.

Case 14.2

The Need for a Cash Budget

A small firm in Wichita, Kansas, specialized in the sale and installation of swimming pools. The company was profitable, but the owners devoted very little attention to the management of working capital. The company had never prepared a cash budget.

To be sure that money was available for payments as needed, the owner of the firm kept a minimum of $25,000 in a checking account. At times, this account grew larger, until at one time it totaled $43,000. The owner felt that this practice of cash management worked well for a small company because it eliminated all the paperwork associated with cash budgeting. Moreover, it had enabled the firm to always pay its bills in a timely manner.

Questions

1. What are the advantages and weaknesses of the minimum-cash-balance practice?
2. There is a saying, "If it ain't broke, don't fix it." In view of the firm's present success in paying bills promptly, should it be encouraged to use a cash budget? Defend your answer.

Experientials

1. Take a trip to your local coffeehouse. Estimate how many cups of coffee are sold in an hour. Pretend there is a three-cent increase in the price and figure the total increase in income for one year.

2. Now figure a ten-cent increase. Would you pay ten cents more for your coffee? Three cents?

CHAPTER 15

Budgeting and Controlling Operations and Taxes

If you think your business can fly without a budget, you may be in for a crash landing.
—Bob Weinstein

Noah must have taken two taxes into the ark—and they have been multiplying ever since!
—Will Rogers

Learning Objectives

After studying the material in this chapter, you should be able to:

1. Explain how managers exercise control in a small business.

2. Tell what a budget is, explain the different types, and tell how they are prepared and used.

3. Discuss how information on actual performance can be obtained and used.

4. Explain how ratios can be used to evaluate a firm's financial condition.

5. Explain how the U.S. tax system operates.

6. Name and describe the taxes imposed on the small business itself.

7. Explain how the ownership of the business results in direct taxation of the owner.

8. Understand the importance of record keeping and tax reporting.

9. Discuss some factors and problems involved in granting credit.

Allen Smith: eGo

Electric bikes! Allen Smith and his partners, Andrew Kallfelz, Jim Hamann, and Tad Borek, are giving new meaning to bicycles. These battery-powered wonders plug into a regular AC outlet and after six hours can provide speeds up to 20 miles per hour with a 25-mile range. The designer of the bikes, Smith, decided to leave a steady, well-paying job and follow his dream of producing the electric vehicle.

The company was incorporated in the fall of 2000 and 5 percent was sold to private investors raising $100,000 for the organization. The original four partners are committed to keeping the company under their own control. A loan of $150,000 through the U.S. Department of Agriculture represents their debt financing.

The eGo is sold primarily off their Web site, www. egovehicles.com; however, President Andrew Kallfelz is establishing a network of bicycle and surf shops as on-premises dealers. The bikes sell for about $1,600 and are street legal in all 50 states. Standard features include twin halogen headlights, extra bright tail/brake lights, rear rack, mirror, bell, and kickstand. Optional features include removable wire basket, suspension seat post, rain cover, hitch mounted auto rack, custom colors, and for those of us with a poor sense of direction—a global positioning unit (GPS)!

Mass production began in April 2001, after refinement and a 25,000-mile testing of prototypes since 1998. eGo can produce 200 units per month at full capacity. Mr. Smith said that producing any product in the United States is a learning experience in itself. Problems with zoning and compliance with the many laws and ordinances are just the beginning of production headaches. Offshore manufacturing was much less expensive, but eGos were American made.

In January 2002 production moved to Providence, Rhode Island, and in February eGO went international when the first bikes were assembled and shipped from a factory in Taiwan and the Providence factory site was closed. The home office was moved to Providence in January 2003, and the following March saw the first shipment of bikes to England.[1] This user-friendly product is looking to fill two types of target markets. Urbanites in densely populated areas can enjoy their trek to work, play, or shop without the hassle of auto upkeep and parking. Vacationers can "play with a new toy," and utilize the alternative means of transportation for fun. Secondary markets will include college campuses, industrial plants, boat and recreation vehicle owners, and rental companies in resort towns. Allen Smith has now relocated to Hood River, Oregon, and is working with a team to develop long-range, unmanned airplanes. After a bitter parting of the original operations, he still owns about a half million shares in eGO Vehicles Inc., but he is no longer directly involved with the daily operations. "Maybe someday it'll [eGO stock] be worth something."[2]

The Profile illustrates what this text has stressed throughout, namely, the importance of controlling your firm's operations. In this chapter, we emphasize the nature, objectives, and methods of control; the design and use of budgets; the importance of budgetary control; and the role of taxes.

What Is Involved in Control?

Profit planning alone—as discussed in the previous chapter—is not enough! After developing plans for making a profit, you must design an operating system to implement those plans. As you will see, that system, in turn, must be controlled in order to ensure that plans are carried out and objectives, such as profit and customer satisfaction, are reached.

The Role of Control

Control is the process of ensuring that organizational goals are achieved.

We continually exercise **control** over our activities and are, in turn, subject to controls. We control the speed of the car we drive; signal lights control the traffic flow. We control our homes' thermostats, which keep the temperature within an acceptable range. Ropes in an airport terminal guide passengers to the next available clerk. Controls that have been established to help accomplish certain objectives are found everywhere.

As shown in Chapter 6, planning provides the guides and standards used in performing the activities necessary to achieve company goals. Then, a system of controls is installed to ensure that performance conforms to the organization's plans. Any deviation from these plans should point to a need for change—usually in performance, but sometimes in the plans themselves.

Steps in Control

The control process consists of five steps:

1. Setting up standards of performance.
2. Measuring actual performance.
3. Comparing actual performance with planned performance standards.
4. Deciding whether any deviations are excessive.
5. Determining the appropriate corrective action needed to bring actual performance into conformity with planned performance.

These steps are performed in all control systems, even though the systems used may be quite different. Later in this chapter, these five steps are covered in detail, but the first step should be strongly emphasized at this point.

Setting Performance Standards

Performance standards set—in advance— acceptable levels to which employee achievement should conform.

Performance standards tell employees—in advance—what level of performance is expected of them. They also measure how well employees meet expectations. Performance standards are usually stated in terms of (1) units consumed or produced or (2) price paid or charged. Some examples are *standard hours per unit* to produce a good or service, *miles per gallon* of gasoline used, and *price per unit* for purchased goods. There are many ways of developing these standards, such as intuition, past performance, careful measurement of activities, and comparison with other standards or averages.

Once standards of performance are set, they should be communicated by means of written policies, rules, procedures, and/or statements of standards to the people responsible for performance. Standards are valuable for stimulating good performance, and locating sources of inefficiencies.

Characteristics of Effective Control Systems

Effective control systems should be (1) timely, (2) cost effective, (3) accurate, and (4) quantifiable and measurable. They should also (5) indicate cause-and-effect relationships, (6) be the responsibility of one individual, and (7) be generally acceptable to those involved with implementing them.

Using Budgets to Communicate Standards

A **budget** is a detailed statement of financial results expected for a given future period.

Performance standards serve as building blocks for the preparation of a **budget,** *which is a detailed statement of financial results expected for a given future period.* The time period may be a month, a quarter, or a year. The budget is expressed in monetary terms but may also include other measurements, such as number of units expected to be sold, units of inventory used, and labor hours worked (see Chapter 6). The budget should be based on realistic and attainable goals and should be applied to all items needing control. In essence, *budgets are the communication devices used to tell people responsible for performing tasks what is expected of them.*

Types of Budgets

The three most important types of budgets are (1) capital budgets, (2) operating budgets, and (3) cash flow budgets.

A **capital budget** plans expenditures for obtaining, expanding, and replacing physical facilities.

The **capital budget** reflects a business's plans for obtaining, expanding, and replacing physical facilities. It requires that management preplan the use of its limited financial resources for needed buildings, tools, equipment, and other facilities.

An **operating budget** forecasts sales and allocates expenses for achieving them.

The **operating budget** is based on profit plans for the budget period (as shown in Chapter 14). It contains a forecast of the amounts and sources of sales income and the materials, labor, and other expenses that will be needed to achieve the sales forecast.

A **cash flow budget** forecasts the amount of cash receipts and cash needed to pay expenses and make other purchases.

The **cash flow budget** is a forecast of expected cash receipts and expected cash payments. It shows whether sufficient cash will be available for timely payment of budgeted expenses, capital equipment purchases, and other cash requirements. It also tells whether arrangements need to be made for external sources of cash, such as borrowing or owner investments.

Preparing the Operating Budget

The purpose of the operating budget is to plan and control revenue and expenses in order to obtain desired profits. Therefore, the *sales budget* is planned first, giving consideration to the production and personnel functions. If you or your sales employees are frequent flyers for your company, you can plan in your budget for carriers that provide special fares and mileage credits. Even one frequent flyer award per year could save about $1,100.[3]

The *production budget* is then set so that the sales budget plans can be achieved. This budget includes production, purchasing, and personnel schedules as well as inventory levels. It includes units such as amount of materials and personnel time, as well as their costs.

Next, a *personnel budget* is developed for the number of people needed to produce the product, any costs of training them, their pay and benefits, and other factors involved. The amount of detail in each of these budgets depends on its value to the company.

The *sales budget* is the most basic plan to consider. As you saw in Figure 14.3, step 2, the sales budget must be prepared before you can plan your production and personnel budgets. Because it was discussed in detail there, we will not discuss it further in this chapter.

Preparing the Cash Flow Budget

It surprises some small business owners that their businesses may be making profits and yet fail because they do not have the cash to pay current expenses. But a cash flow crisis can be triggered by many and varied factors, such as a major equipment breakdown, seasonal business fluctuations, or customers who pay late—or not at all. Therefore, *provision must be made to have adequate cash on hand to pay bills when they are due and payable.* This cash planning takes two forms: (1) the daily and weekly cash requirements for the normal operation of the business and (2) the maintenance of the proper balance for longer-term requirements.

Planning Daily and Weekly Cash Needs   The first type of planning tends to be routine and is done on a daily or weekly basis. For example, you may have a fairly constant income and outgo, which you are able to predict with fair accuracy. Thus, you can establish policies for the amount of cash to maintain and set up procedures to control that level of cash. These routine demands represent a small part of the needed cash on hand, and they tend to remain fairly constant.

Planning Monthly Cash Needs   The second type of planning requires a budget for each month of the year. Payments for rent, payroll, purchases, and services require a regular outflow of cash. Insurance and taxes may require large payments a number of times each year. A special purchase, such as a truck, may place a heavy demand on cash. So, it takes planning to have the *right* amount of cash available when needed. Robert Hackley, executive vice president of Hotsy, a Central Florida dealership that sells industrial pressure cleaning equipment and detergents, offers the following advice on how to prepare for cash flow crises:[4]

- Establish and maintain a good credit rating.
- Set aside some funds in an interest-bearing account that you can draw on in an emergency.
- Schedule your payments to your maximum advantage; that is, don't pay anything before you have to, but also watch for early-payment discounts.
- Keep your fixed costs low and your variable expenses tied to revenue so that, if income drops, so do expenses.

According to Missy Mastel, president of Mass Communications Inc. (a telecom outsourcing audit company), you can save money in your budget by rightsizing your network and communications system. Most companies are paying for services they do not need or never use. It is important to determine a rational number of lines and services based on your number of employees.[5]

Procedure for Planning Cash Needs

Figure 15.1 shows the form used by The Model Company to budget its cash for three months in advance. Each month is completed and recorded before the next month is shown. Items 1 through 4 give estimates of cash to be received. For example, The Model Company expects to receive 20 percent of its monthly sales in cash (item 1). A check of its accounts receivable budget can provide an estimate of the cash to be received in January (item 2). Other income (item 3) might come from sources such as interest on investments or the sale of surplus equipment. Item 4 shows the expected total cash to be received.

Expected cash payments—items 5 through 18—show the items The Model Company might list in its planned budget (see step 3 in Figure 14.3). Cash is often paid in the month

FIGURE 15.1

THE MODEL COMPANY Cash Budget For Three Months Ending March 31, 20__						
	January		February		March	
Items that change cash level	Budget	Actual	Budget	Actual	Budget	Actual
Expected cash receipts						
1. Cash sales						
2. Collections—accounts receivable						
3. Other income						
4. Total cash receipts						
Expected cash payments						
5. Goods purchases						
6. Salaries						
7. Utilities						
8. Depreciation						
9. Rent						
10. Building services						
11. Insurance						
12. Interest						
13. Office expenses						
14. Sales promotion						
15. Taxes and licenses						
16. Maintenance						
17. Delivery						
18. Miscellaneous						
19. Total cash payments						
Cash balance						
20. Cash balance—beginning of month						
21. Change—item 4 minus item 19						
22. Cash balance—end of month						
23. Desired cash balance						
24. Short-term loans needed						
25. Cash available—end of month						
Cash for capital investments						
26. Cash available—line 25						
27. Desired capital cash						
28. Long-term loans needed						

during or after which the goods are received or the service is performed. Examples include payments for electricity and for material purchases. Some cash payments can be made at any one of several times. For example, payments on a new insurance policy can be set up to come due when other cash demands are low.

As shown in Figure 15.1, the cash budget shows when payments are to be made. For example, the cash balance on the first of January (item 20), plus the month's receipts (item 4), less the month's total cash payments (item 19), provide an expected cash balance at the end of January as follows:

$$\text{Balance at} \atop \text{beginning of month} \quad + \quad {\text{Total cash} \atop \text{receipts}} \quad - \quad {\text{Total cash} \atop \text{payments}} \quad = \quad {\text{Balance at} \atop \text{end of month}}$$

A negative balance will require an increase in cash receipts, a decrease in payments, or the necessity of a short-term loan. A company should have a certain amount of cash on hand to take care of contingencies. Item 23 in Figure 15.1 shows the desired amount of cash needed as a minimum balance.

A three-month projection is probably the optimum time estimate for a cash budget. If sales are seasonal, or you expect heavy demands on the cash balance, longer periods may be necessary.

Using Budgetary Control

Budgetary control is the system of budgets used to control a company's financial activities.

By itself, a budget is only a collection of figures or estimates that indicate plans. But when a system of budgets is used for control purposes, it becomes **budgetary control.** This process involves careful planning and control of all the company's financial activities. It includes frequent and close controls in the areas where poor performance affects a company most severely. Other areas may be controlled less often. For example, the cost of goods sold by The Model Company is planned for 63 percent of the sales dollar, and utilities are 1.34 percent of sales (see steps 2 and 3 in Figure 14.3). Cost of goods sold may be divided into material and labor and checked weekly, while utilities might be checked monthly.

Controlling Credit, Collections, and Accounts Receivable

As shown in this Chapter, extending credit increases the potential for sales—and losses from bad debts. You may have found that the amount of accounts receivable for The Model Company was large relative to its credit sales (see Figures 14.1 and 14.2). Waiting until the end of the year to find this out is potentially dangerous, since the average retailer loses more from slow accounts than from bad debts. Checks should be made often enough to identify customers who are slow in paying and to determine the reason for it. In general, the longer an account goes unpaid, the less the chance of collection.

The best control of bad-debt losses starts with investigating the customer's ability and willingness to pay and by providing clear statements of the credit terms. Then, you should monitor past-due accounts each month so that each slow account is followed up promptly.

You may decide to write off some accounts as a bad-debt expense, while providing some incentive for earlier payment by slow-paying customers. Uncollectable accounts receivable create a misstatement of income and therefore an unjustified increase in business income tax liability.

Other Types of Budgetary Control

Many other types of budgetary control can be used to restrain a company's activities and investments. Any expense item can increase gradually without the change being recognized.

Have you noticed how fast the cash in your pockets disappears? A small business has similar problems. Contributing to this creeping increase in the firm's costs may be such diverse situations as a clerk added to process increased paperwork, a solicitor asking for donations, a big customer requesting special delivery, an employee or union demand for additional services, rising energy costs, and inflation-increased costs. These costs must be controlled if the firm is to survive.

Real-World Example 15.1

For example, many areas offer free trade zones. The Argentine government has developed a network of free trade zones in each of its 23 provinces. These areas provide generous tax breaks to zone users so that they may store goods to be reexported without having to pay the required 21 percent value added tax or any other charges. Utilities are much cheaper because they are tax free.[6]

Using Audits to Control the Budget

An **audit** is a formalized examination and/or review of a company's financial records.

An **audit** of a company consists of a formalized, methodical study, examination, and/or review of its financial records, with the intent of verifying, analyzing, informing, and/or discovering opportunities for improvement. There are three main types of audits: (1) financial, (2) internal, and (3) operations audits.

In *financial auditing,* an outside certified public accountant (CPA) verifies the records and financial statements of a company—usually once a year. This audit furnishes the owner(s), creditors, potential and current investors, and regulatory agencies with information on the company's financial status and operations.

Internal auditing is an appraisal of accounting, financial, and/or operations activities by someone in the firm, with the intention of measuring and evaluating the effectiveness of controls. Such audits function primarily as a service to management for the improvement of its financial controls.

An *operations audit* studies the basic operations of a company in order to identify problem areas. It may include studies of functional areas (such as marketing, finance, production, organization structure, personnel, and planning). Closely related to internal auditing, operations auditing emphasizes operations more than financial activities.

In summary, a company should be audited annually to ensure continued proper financial reporting. Bankers often require financial statements audited by a CPA before they will grant a loan. If any questions arise as to proper controls, inefficient operations, or lost opportunities, some form of internal or operations audit should also be considered.

Obtaining and Using Performance Information for Control Purposes

Feedback is the response a receiver gives through further communication with the sender of the message or some other person.

Information on actual operational performance comes through some form of **feedback.** This feedback takes the form of observation, oral reports, written memos or reports, and/or other methods.

Obtaining the Information

Observation will probably be most satisfying because you are at the scene of action and have direct control over the situation. However, this method is time consuming, and you cannot be in all places at one time. But you can justify using this method if your knowledge is needed, your presence may improve the work, or you are present for other purposes.

Oral reports, the most prevalent type of control used in small firms, are also time consuming, but they provide two-way communication. Rumors are an informal form of feedback and can be useful so long as one can "separate the wheat from the chaff."

Written memos or reports are prepared when a record is needed or when many facts must be assembled. This type of feedback is costly unless the reports are the original records. A good record system, as will be discussed later, is a valuable aid, and it should be designed to be a ready source of reports.

(Source: CATHY © 2001 Cathy Guisewite. Reprinted with permission of UNIVERSAL PRESS SYNDICATE. All rights reserved.)

Comparing Actual Performance with Performance Standards

The ability to keep costs low is a primary advantage of small businesses. To do this, an effective record-keeping system and cost-sensitive controls are vital. Information about actual performance, obtained through feedback, can be compared with predetermined standards to see if any changes are needed.

Simple, informal controls can usually be used by small firms. By this method comparisons are made as feedback is received, and decisions are made accordingly. Examples of the use of standards were discussed in Chapter 13 and follow the same pattern as control through the use of budgets.

Determining Causes of Poor Performance

Poor performance can result from many factors, both internal and external, including the following:

*   Having the wrong objectives.
*   Customers not buying the company's product.
*   Poor scheduling of production or purchases.
*   Theft and/or spoilage of products.
*   Too many employees for the work being performed.
*   Opportunities lost.
*   Too many free services or donations.

Once management isolates the true causes of the firm's poor performance, remedies can probably be found.

Evaluating the Firm's Financial Condition

Having considered the financial structure and operations of a company, we now consider the methods of evaluating its financial condition. Look at Figures 14.1 and 14.2, which show the financial statements of The Model Company. Is the company in a good financial position? How can you tell? You can do so by establishing and analyzing **ratios,** which are relationships between two or more variables. For example, the amount of current assets needed depends on other conditions of a company, such as the size of its current liabilities. So the **current ratio**—current assets divided by current liabilities—shows how easily a company can pay its current obligations.

Unfortunately, no standard figures have been determined for successes or failures, but reasonable evaluations are possible. Two sets of values can be used for evaluation purposes: (1) a comparison of the current value of your firm's operations with those of the past and (2) a comparison of your operations with those of similar businesses and the industry.

Some Important Ratios and Their Meanings

Some of the more important ratios, and the ways to compute them, are shown in Table 15.1. Spaces are provided for computing the ratios for The Model Company, using the data provided in Figures 14.1 and 14.2. Comparable figures for the industry are provided for comparative purposes.

These ratios will help you answer such questions as the following: (1) Are profits satisfactory? (2) Are assets productive? (3) Can the business pay its debts? (4) How good are the business's assets? and (5) Is your equity in the business satisfactory?

Are Profits Satisfactory?

Is the owner of The Model Company getting an adequate or reasonable return on investment? The ratio of *net profit (income) to owners' equity* (ratio 1 in Table 15.1)—often called **return on equity (ROE)**—is used to evaluate this, but several other ratios should be considered in profit planning and decision making.

How much return does your company make on its sales dollar? The ratio of *net profit (income) to net sales* (ratio 2) provides this information. Suppose The Model Company now makes 4.3 cents profit (after taxes) per dollar of sales. Is the trend up or down? How does it compare with the experience of similar companies? If it is dropping, why? Costs may be increasing without an increase in price; competitors may be keeping their prices lower than The Model Company; it may be trying to obtain a large sales volume at the expense of profit. An increase in sales volume with the same investment and net profit per dollar of sales will increase ROE; a decrease will reduce ROE.

Are Assets Productive?

Does your company obtain enough sales from its producing assets? The answer is reflected in the ratio of *net sales to fixed assets* (ratio 3)—fixed assets representing the producing units of the company. So many variables exist (such as leasing instead of owning fixed assets) that this ratio can change rapidly with changes in policy.

Does your company have enough sales for the amount of investment? The ratio of *net sales to owners' equity* (ratio 4) provides an answer. This ratio can be combined with the *net profit to net sales* ratio (ratio 2) to obtain the *return on equity (ROE)* ratio (ratio 1).

Ratios are relationships between two or more variables.

The **current ratio** is the amount of current assets divided by the amount of current liabilities.

Return on equity (ROE) is the percentage of net profit your equity earns, before taxes.

TABLE 15.1 | Financial Ratios

Ratio	Formula	The Model Company	Industry Average*
1. Net profit to owners' equity	$\dfrac{\text{Net profit before taxes}}{\text{Owners' equity}}$	= _____	18.4%
2. Net profit to net sales	$\dfrac{\text{Net profit before taxes}}{\text{Net sales}}$	= _____	3.1
3. Net sales to fixed assets	$\dfrac{\text{Net sales}}{\text{Fixed assets}}$	= _____	5.8
4. Net sales to owners' equity	$\dfrac{\text{Net sales}}{\text{Owners' equity}}$	= _____	7.5
5. Current ratio	$\dfrac{\text{Current assets}}{\text{Current liabilities}}$	= _____	1.3
6. Acid test (quick ratio)	$\dfrac{\text{Current assets} - \text{Inventory}}{\text{Current liabilities}}$	= _____	1.0
7. Receivables to working capital†	$\dfrac{\text{Accounts receivable}}{\text{Working capital}}$	= _____	1.2
8. Inventory to working capital	$\dfrac{\text{Inventory}}{\text{Working capital}}$	= _____	0.4
9. Collection period	$\dfrac{\text{Accounts receivable}}{\text{Average daily credit sales‡}}$	= _____	43.0 days
10. Net sales to inventory	$\dfrac{\text{Net sales}}{\text{Inventory}}$	= _____	22.0
Inventory Turnover Rate $= \dfrac{\text{Cost of Goods Sold}}{\text{Average Inventory}}$		= _____	6 times
11. Net sales to working capital	$\dfrac{\text{Net sales}}{\text{Working capital}}$	= _____	10.0
12. Long-term liabilities to working capital	$\dfrac{\text{Long-term liabilities}}{\text{Working capital}}$	= _____	0.7
13. Debt to owners' equity	$\dfrac{\text{Total liabilities}}{\text{Owners' equity}}$	= _____	1.6
14. Current liabilities to owners' equity	$\dfrac{\text{Current liabilities}}{\text{Owners' equity}}$	= _____	1.1
15. Fixed assets to owners' equity	$\dfrac{\text{Fixed assets}}{\text{Owners' equity}}$	= _____	1.2

*Times unless otherwise specified.

†Working capital = Current assets − Current liabilities.

‡If 80 percent of sales are on credit, average daily credit sales are: Annual sales ÷ 365 × 0.80 = _____.

Can the Business Pay Its Debts?

Can your business pay its current obligations? A number of ratios can help answer this question. As mentioned earlier, the best known is the *current ratio* (ratio 5), which is the ratio of current assets to current liabilities. You may be making a good profit but not be able to pay your debts, for cash does not necessarily increase when you make a profit. The **acid test (quick) ratio** (ratio 6), which is the ratio of current assets minus inventory to current liabilities, is an even more rigorous test of the ability to pay debts quickly.

The **acid test (quick) ratio** is the ratio of current assets, less inventory, to current liabilities.

Working capital is the amount of current assets less current liabilities.

Another check is obtained by using the concept of **working capital,** which is current assets less current liabilities, as a basis. Working capital indicates the ability a company has to pay its current liabilities. The ratios of *accounts receivable to working capital* (ratio 7) and *inventory to working capital* (ratio 8) provide an insight into the riskiness of the company's ability to make current payments.

How Good Are the Business's Assets?

How good are your assets? Cash on hand is the best asset, but it does not produce any revenue. *Accounts receivable* represent what you should receive in cash from customers sometime in the future. However, as indicated earlier, the older an account, the greater the chance of loss. So the *collection period* ratio (ratio 9), which consists of accounts receivable divided by average daily credit sales, provides a guide to their quality.

Inventories can be evaluated in about the same way as accounts receivable. Because goods in inventory become obsolete if not sold within a reasonable period of time, they should generally be turned over as many times as necessary during the year to keep the product either fresh (as in milk and eggs) or desirable (such as changing technology). The *turnover rate* is expressed by the ratio of *net sales to inventory* (ratio 10). If your company turns its inventory over too slowly, you may be keeping obsolete or deteriorating goods. Too high a ratio may result from an inventory so low that it hurts production. It can also result from not providing satisfactory service to customers.

To get an idea of the support that you receive from your current assets, compute the ratio of *net sales to working capital* (ratio 11). Accounts receivable and inventory should increase with an increase in sales, but not out of proportion. Increases in payroll and other expenses require a higher level of cash outflow. On the other hand, too low a ratio indicates available surplus working capital to service sales.

Is Your Equity in the Business Satisfactory?

How much equity should you have in your company? Assets are financed either by equity investments or by the creation of debt—which is a liability. Thus, any retained earnings, which are part of your equity, can be used to increase your assets or decrease your liabilities. You can maintain a high level of equity, with a relatively low level of risk, or a relatively high level of liabilities with a higher expected return on equity—but greater risk.

Most small companies do not like to maintain a large amount of long-term debt because the risk is too great. The ratios commonly used to check the company's source-of-funds relationships are *long-term liabilities to working capital* (ratio 12), *debt to owners' equity* (ratio 13), *current liabilities to owners' equity* (ratio 14), and *fixed assets to owners' equity* (ratio 15). An extremely high value for any of these ratios puts your company in a risky situation. While a bad year will probably decrease your income, the obligation to pay continues. On the other hand, a very good year results in large returns to you.

Ratios Are Interrelated

While each individual ratio indicates only part of the firm's position, the ratios overlap one another because a company is a complex total system. Thus, a change in the size of one of the accounts, such as cash, affects other values.

The financial ratios for the items on the profit and loss statement can be expressed in percentages of sales. This information is usually hard to obtain from competing small firms. High cost of goods sold as a percentage of sales income may indicate a poor choice of vendors, inefficient use of material or labor, or too low a sales price. A high percentage of salaries may indicate overstaffing of the company.

The U.S. Tax System

The U.S. tax system includes all the federal, state, and local tax systems, each of which has at least two parts. *The first part is the system for determining what the taxes will be and who will pay them. The second part is the system for collecting the taxes.* Information about federal taxes can be found on the Internet at www.irs.ustreas.gov.

Who Pays the Taxes?

Indirect taxes are not paid by a person or firm, but by someone else.

Direct taxes are those paid directly to a taxing authority by the person or business against which they are levied.

Taxes can be either indirect or direct. **Indirect taxes** are paid not by the person or firm against which they are levied but by someone else. Because indirect taxes are part of the cost of doing business, they must either be added to the price of the firm's product or shifted backward to the persons who produced the product.

Direct taxes are paid directly to the taxing authority by the person or business against which they are levied.

Real-World Example 15.2

For example, the owner of a building containing a retail shop pays the property tax (direct) to the tax collector, but the amount of the tax is included in the rent paid by the retailer to the owner (indirect). In turn, the retailer includes this tax in the price a customer pays for the goods or services being sold (indirect).

Also, as will be shown later, you pay tax on your income (direct) even though your employer may withhold it and send it to the tax collector for you.

Table 15.2 gives an overview of some selected taxes on small businesses. It shows the kind of tax, who is the taxpayer, the point at which the tax is collected, and the governmental unit collecting the tax.

How Taxes Affect Small Businesses

Taxes affect almost every aspect of operating a small business. First, there is the direct taxation of business income as an income tax on corporate profits.

Second, employers must withhold—and often match—a variety of employment-related taxes levied on their employees, such as federal and state taxes on personal wage and salary incomes, and federal taxes levied to fund the Social Security and Medicare systems.

Third, owners must pay personal taxes on their salaries and other ownership-related income they withdraw from the business. And if part of their wealth is invested outside the business, they face taxes on the investment income they receive.

Fourth, taxes are levied on the transfer of ownership of the business. Therefore, the owner must do careful estate planning to minimize the tax bite on an inheritance. This concept was discussed in Chapter 2.

Fifth, taxes also affect business decisions on other levels as well. For example, as shown in Chapter 3, the choice of the best form of business entity largely depends on the profitability of the business and the tax status of the owner(s).

Finally, the administrative cost of being a tax collector for the government is becoming burdensome. As shown in Table 15.2, it is the responsibility of the business owner to collect several taxes for the government by withholding sums from employees' paychecks or by adding the tax (such as sales or use taxes) to the price of products sold to

TABLE 15.2 | Selected Direct Taxes Paid by Small Firms

Kind of Tax	Taxpayer	Point of Collection	Collecting Agency
Corporate income tax	Corporations	Tax collectors	Internal Revenue Service State revenue departments City tax collectors
Corporate franchise tax (on capital stock)	Corporations	Tax collectors	States
Undistributed profits tax	Corporations	District IRS office	Internal Revenue Service
Customs duties	Corporations	Customs agents	U.S. Customs Service
Excise taxes	Businesses Customers	Utility companies Wholesale distributors Tax collectors	Internal Revenue Service State revenue departments
Motor fuel taxes	Businesses	Wholesale distributors	Internal Revenue Service State revenue departments
Highway use tax	Motor transport businesses	Interstate Commerce Commission	Interstate Commerce Commission
Unemployment compensation	Employers	Internal Revenue Service	Internal Revenue Service
Licenses, permits	Businesses	Tax collectors	City tax collectors State revenue departments CAB, ICC, FCC, etc.
Old Age, Survivors, Disability, and Hospital Insurance (OASDHI)	Employers Employees	Businesses	Internal Revenue Service
Sales and use taxes	Customers	Businesses	City and state revenue departments
Property tax	Businesses	Local tax collectors	City and county tax collectors
Inventory or floor tax	Businesses	Local and state tax collectors	City and county tax collectors
Public utility taxes	Utility companies	City, county, and state tax collectors	City, county, and state tax collectors

Note: This table applies to direct taxes only; the shifting of taxes from the point of collection backward or forward is not considered.

customers. These administrative costs become very expensive in terms of personnel, time, and money.

Get Professional Help!

One of the purposes of this chapter is to make you aware of the current tax environment in which you will operate and to raise some basic tax issues important to every business owner. *It is very important for someone in every small firm to understand the tax system in order to take advantage of the opportunities available for deductions, credits, and tax savings.* Therefore, it is wise to hire a competent adviser on tax and other important financial matters. The IRS has many programs to educate and assist the owners of small businesses such as the Small Business Tax Education Program, which includes *Your Business Tax Kit* (www.irs.ustreas.gov).[7]

While the U.S. Internal Revenue Service, as well as state and local agencies, will willingly help you determine whether you owe additional taxes, *they accept no responsibility for the accuracy of their advice. The responsibility is yours, so get professional help!* Also, you should familiarize yourself with the *Tax Guide for Small Business,* which covers income, excise, and employment taxes for individuals, partnerships, and corporations. Remember, *the final responsibility for determining and paying your taxes rests with you.*

Types of Taxes

Because it is impossible to discuss all of the taxes you will have to pay, we have grouped them into four categories: (1) taxes imposed on the business itself, (2) employment-related taxes, (3) personal taxes that owners pay, and (4) estate taxes, which were discussed in Chapter 2.

Taxes Imposed on the Business

Numerous taxes are imposed on the small firm as a condition of its doing business. We have grouped these together as (1) taxes and fees paid for the "right" to operate the business; (2) excise and intangible property taxes; (3) state and local taxes on business receipts; and (4) federal, state, and local income taxes.

Taxes and Fees Paid to Operate the Business

Some license fees, incorporation taxes, and the cost of permits must be paid before the business begins operating. Figure 15.2 lists some of the most important of these. These fees and permits are often intertwined with taxes, insurance, capital requirements, and the nature and scope of the business itself.

Excise and Intangible Property Taxes

An **excise tax** is an additional tax on certain items imposed by the federal government.

The federal government places an **excise tax** on many items such as tires for automobiles and other moving vehicles, cigars and cigarettes, and alcoholic beverages. Many states also apply such taxes. Taxes on intangibles such as copyrights, patents, and trademarks are another source of income for many states. Some states even have a tax on inventories in stock.

FIGURE 15.2 |
Selected Licenses, Permits, and Registrations Required of Small Firms

- *Business license (city, county, state).* Generally, you must apply for one or more business licenses. Often a tax identification number will be printed on your business license, and you will need to use the number when filing various tax returns. Your state department of revenue can assist you in defining your reporting requirements.
- *Employer's federal ID number (SS-4) (federal).* A federal ID number is needed to identify an employer on all federal tax filings and correspondence. Some local jurisdictions also require the federal ID number on various filings. The SS-4 form is available from the IRS.
- *Incorporation or partnership registration (state).* You should plan on using an attorney to assist with registering your company as a corporation or partnership. If it is a corporation, you'll also need articles of incorporation, bylaws, stock certificates, a corporate seal, and other legal items.
- *Trade name registration (state).* You will need to register any trade names used in your business (e.g., if your legal incorporated name is Superior Semiconductors of California Ltd., but you generally go by the name "Superior," you will need to register your alternative name).
- *Zoning permits (city or county).* If your business constitutes an "alternative use" or other special case, you will need appropriate zoning permits.
- *Building permits (city or county).* If you are doing any remodeling, construction, or related work, be sure you have the appropriate permits.
- *Mailing permits (federal).* Check with your post office about any bulk, presorted first class, business reply mail, or other mailing permits.
- *Professional registrations (state).* Generally, these are employee specific, such as registered engineer, notary public, and other professionals.

State and Local Sales and Use Taxes

A **use tax** is a tax on the use, consumption, or storage of goods within a taxing jurisdiction.

Many states and localities have sales and use taxes, which generate large amounts of revenue. **Use taxes** are usually imposed on the use, consumption, or storage of goods within the taxing jurisdiction. This type of tax is often applied to automobiles and other moving vehicles that are purchased outside the jurisdiction and brought in for future use, or for inventory items that are removed and used by the company itself instead of being sold.

A **sales tax** is a tax added to the gross amount of the sale for goods sold within the taxing jurisdiction.

Sales taxes are usually based on the gross amount of the sale for goods sold within the taxing jurisdiction and are the responsibility of the merchant. Separate municipalities may also have additional sales taxes, so be sure to check in your sales area. Table 15.3 is a composite of basic state sales taxes. A new trend is to tax sales in other locations as well, so you will need to check for your liability for sales taxes in those locations. Exemptions from sales taxes are often provided for goods to be resold and for machinery or equipment used exclusively in processing or assembling other goods. Service businesses are often exempt, as are drugs, unprepared foods, and agricultural products in certain states. *The application of sales taxes can be extremely complex,* so hire a competent financial person.

TABLE 15.3 | State Sales Taxes

State	%	State	%
Alabama	4	Montana	0
Alaska	0	Nebraska	5.5
Arizona	6.6	Nevada	6.85
Arkansas	6	New Hampshire	0
California	8.25	New Jersey	7
Colorado	2.9	New Mexico	5.125
Connecticut	6	New York	5.75
District of Columbia	6	North Carolina	4.25
Delaware	0	North Dakota	5
Florida	6	Ohio	5.5
Georgia	4	Oklahoma	4.5
Hawaii	4	Oregon	0
Idaho	6	Pennsylvania	6
Illinois	6.25	Puerto Rico	5.5
Indiana	7	Rhode Island	7
Iowa	6	South Carolina	6
Kansas	6.3	South Dakota	4
Kentucky	6	Tennessee	7
Louisiana	4	Texas	6.25
Maine	5	Utah	5.95
Maryland	6	Vermont	6
Massachusetts	5.25	Virginia	5
Michigan	6	Washington	6.5
Minnesota	6.875	West Virginia	6
Mississippi	7	Wisconsin	5
Missouri	4.225	Wyoming	4

Cite: Various Sources

Real-World Example 15.3

For example, in the state of Maryland, services, prescription drugs, and food items in grocery stores are exempt from the state's 6 percent sales tax. However, in 1992 the General Assembly imposed a sales tax on "snacks" such as potato chips, pretzels, popcorn, and the like. In 1997, this tax was repealed for sales by grocery and convenience stores for off-premises consumption and for vending machine sales. Other food items, such as soft drinks, alcoholic beverages, and candy, as well as single servings of ice cream and frozen yogurt, continued to be taxed. The Maryland State Comptroller's Office reported getting 300 to 400 phone calls a day during the first week after the tax was repealed. In Seattle a 10-cent tax was proposed on espresso drinks (latte tax). This proposal was to help fund early childhood programs. The reasoning for the tax was, if someone was "willing to pay $3 for a triple grand mocha, they're willing to pay an extra ten cents for a good cause."[8]

One word of caution: Even if you do not collect these taxes from your customers or clients, you will probably be held liable for the full amount of the uncollected taxes. It is very important for small businesses to know what taxes they are responsible for and what taxes are proposed by the governing bodies that could directly affect their company.

Federal, State, and Local Income Taxes

Almost everyone, businesses and individuals alike, is concerned about income taxes, those taxes presently in effect and those that may result from proposed changes. Because of the variation and complexities of the state and local laws, we will discuss only the federal law.

From the very beginning of your business, you should have a qualified accountant to provide you with information and help you make important decisions, compile facts for accurate tax returns, and protect you from costly errors. There are three major decisions involving these taxes that you must make at the start, namely, (1) the method of handling your income and expenses, (2) the time period for paying taxes, and (3) the form of business to use.

How the Form of a Business Affects Its Taxes

As discussed in Chapter 3, the amount and methods of handling income taxes affect the choice of business form you choose to use. Thus, you may choose a partnership or proprietorship rather than pay higher taxes on corporate income and then pay additional individual taxes on dividends.

U.S. tax laws permit some corporations to seek S corporation status. S corporation shareholders (individuals, estates, and certain trusts) are taxed at individual rates, which are lower than corporate rates; yet they still enjoy the legal protection that comes with corporate status. But remember: S corporations do have disadvantages, such as restrictions on benefit plans and a limit of 100 shareholders.

Another relatively new type of organization that may be helpful to a small business owner is the limited-liability company (LLC). As discussed in Chapter 3, it combines the benefits of a partnership and a corporation.

Finally, as shown in Chapter 10, the use of employee stock ownership plans (ESOPs) can lead to tax advantages as well as cash flow advantages.

Treatment of Federal Corporate Income Taxes

There are three questions small corporations need to answer when handling their federal income taxes: What tax rate applies to the business? What is taxable income? What are deductible expenses?

A corporation's tax rate is based on its income, with progressively higher rates at increasing income levels. Since these rates are subject to frequent revision, you should consult your tax accountant or IRS literature for the current rates.

Taxable income is total revenues minus deductible expenses.

For income tax purposes, **taxable income** is defined as total taxable revenues minus deductible expenses. While this definition sounds simple, problems arise in measuring both income and expenses. While the government has set the rules for calculating income for tax purposes, the firm may have discretion in reporting income to its stockholders.

Many not-for-profit businesses generally pay little or no tax. The growing trend toward nontaxpaying competitors has become a source of concern, frustration, and anger on the part of some small business owners.

Normally, deductions from income are classified as *cost of goods sold, selling expenses,* and *administrative expenses.* Administrative expenses are those needed to run a business office, such as rent, accounting and legal expenses, telephone and other utilities, dues and subscriptions to business publications, and professional services.

Inventory Valuation   Another accounting decision you must make is how to value inventory that is used during the year (and included in cost of goods sold). The problem is particularly acute when prices are changing rapidly and/or when a firm holds inventory for long periods. The three methods of computing inventory used in production are (1) the *first-in, first-out (FIFO) method,* (2) the *last-in, first-out (LIFO) method,* and (3) the *average-cost method.* In general, when prices are rising, small firms tend to use the LIFO method to save taxes.

Interest Payments   The U.S. Revenue Code favors the use of debt by small firms, because interest on debt is deductible while dividends paid to stockholders are not. The total amount of interest paid is deducted from revenue to find taxable income.

Business Lunches, Entertainment, and Travel   Allowances for meals and entertainment are subject to frequent changes by the Internal Revenue Service. According to IRS Code Sec. 274(K)(1)(B), "Any business meal is deductible only if the following conditions are met: (1) The meal is directly related to or associated with the active conduct of business. (2) The expense is not lavish or extravagant. (3) The taxpayer is present at the meal."

Real-World Example 15.4

For example, Robert Bennington says he writes off the cost of taking his mother out to lunch every week to talk about business; in addition she talks about his business to others and passes out his business cards.[9]

In recent years, many businesses have tried to reduce travel expenses by using electronic conferencing. They use such techniques as the Internet, telephone, and video. Many companies are now using e-conference for sales and staff meetings, employee training, and job candidate interviews.

Automobile, Home, and Computer Expenses Many small business owners operate out of their homes, and certain expenses—such as automobile, utilities, repairs and maintenance, computer operations and maintenance, and home insurance and taxes—can be deducted from income taxes if they are business related. The deductions are quite beneficial to the owner, but there are restrictions, which are enforced. For an automobile, you can either deduct the actual cost of running your car or truck, or take a standard mileage rate. You must use actual costs if you use more than one vehicle in your business. In 2011, the standard mileage rate was 55.5 cents (www.irs.gov) in addition to parking fees and tolls.

When you work out of your home, you can claim *actual business-related expenses,* such as telephone charges, business equipment and supplies, postage, photocopying, computer paper and magnetic media, and clerical and professional costs. A deduction is also allowable for any portion of your home used "exclusively" and "regularly" as your principal place of business.

Real-World Example 15.5

For example, you can deduct expenses for taxes, insurance, and depreciation on that portion of your home that is used exclusively as your office. The IRS rule is this: The home must be the principal place of business for your trade or business, or a place of business used by clients, patients, or customers.

The Deficit Reduction Act of 1984 limits the conditions under which computers used in the home can be deducted as business expenses. The simple test is this: If you use a home computer for business purposes over 50 percent of the time, it qualifies for the appropriate credits or deductions.

You have to be very careful when writing off anything that can lend itself to personal use. Even though the IRS can be fairly intimidating, everything that you legitimately use while conducting business is acceptable as a deduction. The key is careful documentation and good common sense.[10]

Employment-Related Taxes

As shown in Chapter 10, employers are legally required to provide their employees with Social Security and Medicare, unemployment compensation insurance, and industrial insurance (commonly called workers' compensation). In addition, the employer must withhold taxes from employees for city, county, state, and federal income taxes. Also, since 1986, the Employee Retirement Income Security Act (ERISA) has required employers with 20 or more employees to continue health insurance programs for limited periods for employees who are terminated and for widows, divorced spouses, and dependents of employees.

FIGURE 15.3 |
Selected Employee-
Related Tax Forms
Needed by Small
Firms

Federal tax forms

For companies with paid employees:

- Form SS–4, Application for Employer Identification Number
- Form W–2, Wage and Tax Statement
- Form W–2P, Statement for Recipients of Periodic Annuities, Pensions, Retired Pay, or IRA Payments
- Form W–3, Transmittal of Income and Tax Statements
- Form W–4, Employee's Withholding Allowance Certificate, for each employee
- Form 940, Employer's Annual Federal Unemployment (FUTA) Tax Return
- Form 941, Employer's Quarterly Federal Tax Return
- Form 1099–MISC, Statement for Recipients of Nonemployee Compensation

Income tax forms and schedules, which vary depending on your organizational status, type of income/losses, selection of various elections, etc.

ERISA Form 5500 series, depending on your status under the Employee Retirement Income Security Act

State and local forms

Income and/or business and occupation taxes

Industrial insurance ("workers' compensation")

Unemployment compensation insurance

Income Tax Withholding

The IRS and certain states, counties, and localities require you to withhold the appropriate amount of income tax from each employee's earnings during each pay period. The amount of this pay-as-you-go tax depends on each employee's total wages, number of exemptions claimed on his or her withholding exemption certificate, marital status, and length of pay period. Each employee must complete and sign a W–4 form for your files. See Figure 15.3 for the important employee-related forms needed by small firms.

The amount withheld from all employees must be submitted to the IRS, along with Form 941, on a quarterly basis. However, if $2,500 or more has been withheld from employees during the month, that deposit must be made within three banking days following the end of the month.

Form W–2, "Wage and Tax Statement," must be completed and mailed to each employee by January 31 immediately following each taxable year. Employers submitting an annual amount of $50,000 or more must transmit to the IRS by electronic media transfer.

Real-World Example 15.6

Illegal workers are paying their taxes to the tune of over one million filers. Many say that by being a good citizen and following the rules, they will have a better chance of becoming legal. Tax preparer Petra Castillo helps these workers collect IRS refunds and charges a flat rate of $40, and many are prepared from mail requests.[11]

Social Security/Medicare Taxes

As shown in Chapter 10, the Social Security program requires employers to act as both tax collectors and taxpayers. Therefore, not only do you have to withhold a certain percentage of each employee's income, but you must also match it with a payment of your own. These taxes are technically for the Federal Insurance Contributions Act (FICA) but are usually referred to as "Social Security and Medicare" taxes. For example, in 2010, the employer had to collect 6.2 percent of an employee's total earnings—*up to a maximum of $106,800*—and then match that amount out of business revenues. Another 1.45 percent of the employee's total earnings must be collected for Medicare. These taxes are sent to the IRS each quarter, along with Federal Form 941, Employer's Quarterly Federal Tax Return. Self-employed people must pay the combined employee's and employer's amount of taxes, which amounted to 15.3 percent in 2001.

Unemployment Compensation Insurance

The **federal unemployment tax** is a tax paid to the federal government to administer the unemployment insurance program.

Unemployment compensation insurance has two parts. First, a small basic amount is paid to the U.S. government as a **federal unemployment tax** to administer the program. In 2010 the rate was 6.2 percent on the base wage of $7,000. A second part, which is determined by the states, builds up a fund from which employees are paid in case they are laid off. Federal Form 940, Employer's Annual Federal Unemployment (FUTA) Tax Return, must be filed annually. However, you may be liable for periodic tax deposits during the year.

Workers' Compensation

Employers are required to provide industrial insurance for employees who are harmed or killed on the job. These payments are usually funded through an insurance program, with higher rates for higher-risk employees.

Personal Taxes Paid by Owners

There are several ways of withdrawing cash from the business for your own use. Some of these are taxable to you, and some are taxable to the firm.

Taxes on Amounts Withdrawn from the Business

First, salaries and bonuses received from the business corporation are expenses to the business. But individual income taxes are also paid on those sums. You can also withdraw cash from a proprietorship or partnership, and these sums are also taxable to you as an individual.

When owners receive a dividend from a corporation, it is taxed twice. The corporation pays taxes on it but gets no tax deduction, and owners must pay taxes at their individual rates.

Employees can also receive tax-free benefits from the business, which are deductible by the firm. These include such noncash items as medical and legal reimbursements, tuition assistance, and other employee benefits, as well as travel and entertainment expense reimbursements.

Finally, there are many pension and profit-sharing plans, the payment of which is deductible by the business. Payments from the plans are not taxable to the recipients until they are received.

Taxes on Amounts Received from Sale of the Business

Usually, when entrepreneurs sell their companies, the contracts contain the following important provisions: (1) a noncompeting clause from the seller, (2) warranties and representations by the seller about the debt and liabilities of the company being sold, and (3) the purchase price—whether it is paid in cash, with a promissory note, in stock in the acquiring company, or with some combination of the two provisions.

Under the Tax Reform Act of 1986, most sales of assets are subject to double taxation, both corporate and personal, as shown earlier, so many such transactions now involve the exchange of stock. Therefore, the form in which the proceeds are to be received can be as critical as the price and should be included in negotiations between buyer and seller, as the following example illustrates.

Real-World Example 15.7

Jan and Al Williams started Bio Clinic Co. in their garage in Southern California in the early 1960s. By 1985, the business was so successful that Sunrise Medical Inc. (www.sunrisemedical.com), a Torrance, California, company, offered $7.2 million for it. The Williamses, who were in the process of divorcing at the time, wanted different things when they negotiated the terms of sale. Jan wanted stock because she expected the stock of Sunrise to grow in value. Al, on the other hand, wanted as much cash as possible. The parties worked out a compromise—$2 million in stock, and $5.2 million in cash.[12]

In summary, the tax consequences from the sale of a business are that either (1) you pay an immediate capital gains tax on cash payments from the sale or (2) if you receive part of the payment in stock, you may be able to defer some taxes to a later period.

Recordkeeping and Tax Reporting

The importance of recordkeeping has been emphasized throughout this text. There are essentially two reasons for keeping business records. First, tax and other records are required by law; second, they help you manage your business better. While the IRS allows some flexibility in records systems, it does require that records be kept, be complete, and be separate for each individual business.

Maintaining Tax Records

When you start your business, as shown in Chapter 5, you should set up the kind of records system most suitable for your particular operations. Also, keep in mind that the records should be readily available to compute, record, and pay taxes as they become due and payable. A variety of accounting software packages are available to help small businesses maintain the necessary records.

The IRS requires that tax records be retained for up to three years after a tax return is filed. If there is reason to suspect fraud, the IRS may look at your tax records for longer periods.

The Online Women's Business Center recommends basic types of business records to keep (See Table 15.4). Although there are no legal requirements, you need to have sufficient records to support your tax reporting. For example, invoices, deposit slips, cash

TABLE 15.4 | Guidelines for Keeping Many Business Records

Category	Time	Category	Time
Accident reports	10 years	Garnishments	10 years
Accounts payable ledgers and schedules	10 years	General ledger	Permanently
Accounts receivable ledgers and schedules	10 years	Group disability reports	
Articles of incorporation	Permanently	Insurance policies-expired	3 years
Attendance records	4 years	Insurance records	Permanently
Auditors' reports	Permanently	Internal audit reports	4 years
Bank reconciliations and statements	4 years	Inventory lists	4 years
Bills of lading	4 years	Invoices	4 years
Board of directors minutes	Permanently	Journals	Permanently
Budgets	2 years	Legal correspondence	Permanently
Bylaws	Permanently	Mortgages	6 years
Canceled checks	4 years	Notes Receivable	10 years
Capital stock and bond records	Permanently	OSHA logs	6 years
Cash books	Permanently	Patents	Permanently
Chart of accounts	10 years	Payroll records	10 years
Checks-canceled	10 years	Personnel accident report / injury claim	11 years
COBRA records	3 years		
Contracts and agreements	Permanently	Personnel files	6 years
Copyrights	Permanently	Property records	Permanently
Correspondence—general	2 years	Purchase orders	10 years
Correspondence—legal and important	Permanently	Retirement and pension records	Permanently
Credit memos	4 years	Safety records	
Deeds	6 years	Sales records	10 years
Depreciation records	4 years	Servicemarks	Permanently
Employee benefit plans	2 years	Settled insurance claims	Permanently
Employee expense reports	4 years	Stock and bond records	10 years
Employee payroll records	6 years	Subsidiary ledgers	10 years
Employment application forms	3 years	Tax returns	Permanently
Employment tax returns	4 years	Time cards and daily time reports	4 years
Financial statements-annual	Permanently	Trademarks	Permanently
Financial statements-interim	4 years	Union agreements	Permanently
Fire inspection reports		Withholding tax statements	10 years

register tapes or files, credit card charges, and receipt books help to support income. Purchases and direct expenses can include vendor invoices, canceled checks, cash register receipts, and credit card charges. Indirect expenses may include all these plus petty cash receipts. For assets you will need complete records to document depreciation and gain or loss on sale, invoices, closing statements, canceled checks, costs of improvements, and all depreciation schedules and records. There are five major tax-saving ideas for small business owners:

1. Contribute to a retirement plan.
2. Keep detailed business records.
3. Employ family members.
4. Examine your business structure.
5. Review special estate tax treatment for family owned businesses.[13]

While the IRS has up to three years to look at your records, you also have up to three years from the date of filing to straighten out tax matters as the circumstances demand. If changes are needed, you may file a one-page amended return on Form 1040X. Particularly check out IRS Publication 583, "Starting a Business and Keeping Records."

Reporting Your Taxes

All federal (www.irs.gov), state, and local governments having jurisdiction over your business require that you submit a written monthly, quarterly, or annual report on income. Because the requirements vary so much for state and local agencies, you must contact each agency for a current list.

Credit Management

Credit management
involves setting and administering credit policies and practices.

Credit management involves (1) deciding how customers will pay for purchases, (2) setting credit policies and practices, and (3) administering credit operations. The objectives of each of these activities are to increase profits, increase customer stability, and protect the firm's investment in accounts receivable, which is often the largest single asset on the firm's balance sheet.

Another aspect of credit management is foreign currency exchange rates. Small business owners who are buying or selling offshore need to be aware of the fluctuation of the dollar's worth. Timing is the key to successful transactions.

Methods of Payment

Customers can pay for purchases in a number of ways, and you must decide early in the life of your business which method(s) to accept. Payment methods include cash, checks, and various kinds of credit.

Cash   Given a choice, every business owner would probably prefer to make all sales for cash. Recordkeeping would be easier, and there would be no bad debts. But it is unrealistic to expect buyers to carry cash for every purchase, especially large purchases. Soon it may not be necessary to carry cash at all, however. Taking credit cards and debit cards one step further, companies such as Citibank (www.citibank.com) and Chase Manhattan (www.chase.com), after many trials and delays, created bank cards that let consumers buy small items such as coffee and newspapers without using coins and bills. These cards have a microprocessor in the plastic called a "smart card" chip that will be able to download funds as the ATM machines do. Smart plastic originated in Europe as the need arose to leapfrog antiquated telephone systems.

Checks   Because accepting checks for payment increases sales, most small business owners think the risks involved are worth it. With proper verification procedures, bad-debt losses can be minimized. Checks can be treated the same as cash in recordkeeping, and they are actually safer to have on hand than cash and easier to deal with in making bank deposits.

Credit   To stimulate sales, various forms of credit may be used, including installment payment plans and credit cards or a business's own credit plan. Granting your own credit allows you to choose your own customers and avoid fees to credit card issuers. Customer accounts can be paid off every month or can be *revolving charge accounts* such as those used by large department stores. For major purchases, you may give the buyer more time to pay before interest is charged or the account is turned over to a finance company. To extend credit even longer, you may offer an *installment payment plan* that gives the buyer up to a year or more to pay for the purchase. Buyers make a down payment, make regular weekly or monthly payments, and pay interest charges on the unpaid balance.

This practice, though, can be costly because whenever you extend credit, recordkeeping becomes more complex. Small firms can use manual or computer methods to maintain their charge accounts internally, or they can turn the accounts over to a service firm for handling. Either way, there are costs for billing and collections, as well as bad-debt losses.

Some of these responsibilities and costs can be avoided by accepting bank or corporate *credit cards,* so-called *plastic money.* Today's consumers have come to expect most firms of any size to accept the major cards, *which are, in effect, a line of credit granted to the customer by the card issuer.* Acceptance of credit cards is especially necessary in resort areas or other venues where customers are less likely to have large amounts of cash, local checking accounts, or a store charge account.

Although merchants pay a fee to join and a fee on sales, many find it worth the expense; provided they follow required authorization procedures, sellers are guaranteed payment, largely eliminating bad-debt losses. Authorization, once cumbersome, is now almost universally automated through the use of readers that scan the card's magnetic strip, dial the number of a database, get authorization for the charge, and record the sale, all in just a few seconds.

Again, if you deal with foreign currency, not only must you be aware of currency exchange rates, but also all foreign currency conversion fees that could be charged to you and cardholders by credit card companies. Most banks pass on the fees with additional fees of 1.5 percent to 2 percent to their customers14. Be sure you check on these fees with your banker.

Debit Cards   Once a business is set up to accept credit cards, it is generally simple to include debit cards as well. **Debit cards** are issued by banks, look like credit cards, and can be scanned in the same way. Instead of a line of credit, however, debit cards represent a plastic check, as the amount of purchase is immediately deducted from the user's checking account. Many banks now offer ATM cards that can be used in this way.

A **debit card** is usually plastic and enables the owner to withdraw money or to have the cost of purchases charged directly to the holder's bank account.

> **Real-World Example 15.8**
> Eighteen to 25 year olds are now called "Generation Plastic" and 76 percent of this age group uses some form of payment card. One-third "rarely carry cash."[15]

Setting Credit Policies

Small businesses need to be aware of the cost of accepting different types of cards. Processing fees vary from card company to banks. It is interesting to note that, at the time of this writing, debit machines requiring Personal Identification Numbers (PIN) are less expensive per transaction than the traditional signature method.[16]

While your credit department can contribute to increased sales and profit, several factors should be considered in formulating a credit policy; some factors are beyond your control. Any credit policy should be flexible enough to accommodate these internal and external factors.

Some credit policies you can use are (1) liberal extension of credit with a liberal collection policy, (2) liberal extension of credit with a strictly enforced collection policy, and (3) strict extension of credit with a collection policy adjusted to individual circumstances.

Real-World Example 15.9

Debit card ownership and use in the United States has surpassed that of credit cards. It was revealed in a survey conducted by the Federal Reserve Bank of Boston in 2009 and released in 2010 that 80 percent of consumers own a debit card compared with 78 percent who own a credit card. Clearly the average consumer sees the debit card as equal—and possibly superior—to the credit card.[17]

Generally, being liberal in extending credit or in collecting bad debts tends to stimulate sales but increase collection costs and bad-debt losses. Strict policies have the reverse effect. Whatever policy is chosen, you should extend a businesslike attitude toward credit customers.

Carrying Out Credit Policies

The person managing credit for you should have ready access to the accounts receivable records and be free from interruptions and confusion. Several tools this person can use in performing the function include the accounts receivable ledger or computer printout, invoices and other billing documents, credit files, account lists, credit manuals, reference material, and various automated aids.

Classifying Credit Risks

You should begin by classifying present and potential customers according to credit risk: good, fair, or weak. These risks can be determined from information in the customer's file, trade reports, financial reports, and previous credit experience.

Good credit risks may be placed on a preferred list for automatic approval within certain dollar limits. Periodic review of these accounts usually suffices. Fair credit risks will require close checking, particularly on large amounts or in case of slow payment. While weak credit risks may be acceptable, they should be closely watched. You ask for problems when you unwisely extend credit.

Investigating Customers' Creditworthiness

A major cause of bad-debt losses is making credit decisions without adequate investigation. Yet prompt delivery of orders is also important. Thus, your credit-checking method should be geared to need and efficiency to improve the sales and delivery of your product. For new accounts, a complete credit application may be desired. Direct credit inquiry can be effective in obtaining the name of the customer's bank and trade references. Outside sources of valuable credit information include local credit bureaus, which are linked nationally through Associated Credit Bureaus, Inc., and others who provide guidelines and mechanisms for obtaining credit information for almost any area in the United States.

Establishing Collection Procedures

The collection of unpaid accounts is an important part of credit management. The collection effort should include systematic and regular follow-up, which is vital to establish credibility with the customer concerning credit terms. The follow-up should be timely, which is now feasible since most businesses have computer capacity to show the age of a bill.

When an account is past due, prompt contact with the customer, made tactfully and courteously, generally produces results. If this does not work, holding customers' orders can be effective. But you should respond rapidly when the customer clears the account so that unnecessary delays in shipping are avoided.

What You Should Have Learned

1. After planning is done, a control system should be established to aid in carrying out the plans. The control process is composed of (*a*) setting standards, (*b*) measuring performance, (*c*) comparing actual performance with standards, (*d*) deciding whether corrections are needed, and (*e*) acting to make the corrections.

2. The budgetary control system is designed and used for control of financial affairs. Items in the financial statements should be checked frequently, with emphasis on where poor performance most affects the company.

3. Information on actual performance can be obtained by observation or from oral or written reports. Actual performance can be compared with standards to determine the causes of poor performance.

4. Various ratios can be used to compare the company's current and past performance, as well as its performance relative to competitors. They can help determine whether profits are satisfactory, whether assets are productive, how able the company is to pay its debts, how good its assets are, and how much equity the owners have.

5. The U.S. tax system is very complex. Federal, state, and local governments impose taxes directly on individuals and businesses and require them to collect taxes from others. The four types of business taxes are (*a*) those imposed on the business

itself, (*b*) employment-related taxes, (*c*) personal taxes paid by the owners, and (*d*) estate taxes.

6. You are required to provide Social Security, Medicare, unemployment insurance, and workers' compensation for your employees, and to withhold taxes from them. Each employee must complete a W–4 form. The withheld amounts must be submitted to the IRS periodically. A W–2 form must be mailed to each employee by January 31 of the following year. Unemployment insurance payments build up a fund from which a state can pay employees if they are laid off.

7. From the time you begin your business, you should maintain complete and accurate tax records. For tax purposes, records must be retained up to three years after the date of filing the return. If for any reason the IRS suspects fraud, there is no time limitation.

8. Credit management includes deciding on customer payment methods, establishing credit policies, and administering credit operations. A credit policy should be flexible and help increase revenues and profits. Customers should be classified according to their creditworthiness—good, fair, or weak. Credit investigations should be conducted, and the collection of outstanding receivables should be systematic and include regular follow-up. The overall results of the credit functions and collection efficiency should be evaluated to see that they are achieving their objectives.

Key Terms

acid test (quick) ratio 396	current ratio 395	performance standards 388
audit 393	debit card 410	ratios 395
budget 389	direct taxes 398	return on equity (ROE) 395
budgetary control 392	excise tax 400	
capital budget 389	federal unemployment tax 406	sales tax 401
cash flow budget 389	feedback 393	taxable income 402
control 388	indirect taxes 398	use tax 401
credit management 409	operating budget 389	working capital 397

Questions for Discussion

1. What is control? List the steps in an effective control process.
2. What are performance standards? Why are they used? List some examples.
3. What is budgetary control? How can it be used by a small business?
4. How can information about actual performance be obtained in a small firm?
5. Compute the ratios listed in Table 15.1 for The Model Company, using the data in Figures 14.1 and 14.2 (pages 389 and 398).
6. Evaluate the financial condition of The Model Company.
7. Evaluate your personal financial situation and operations, using material developed in this chapter.
8. Name the three main types of taxes a small firm must pay.
9. How does the form of a business affect its taxes?
10. Name and explain the three types of employment-related taxes.
11. Why are records so important for tax purposes?
12. What is credit management, and why is it so important to small business? Why is the acceptance of credit cards by small businesses increasing?

Case 15.1

Theme Restaurants

Theme restaurants were the biggest restaurant craze of the 90s, and they popped up everywhere from Boston to Bangkok to Berlin. The craze is believed to have started with the opening of the first Hard Rock Cafe in the site of a former Rolls-Royce showroom in London, England. There are now 105 cafes in 38 countries, hotels, a Las Vegas casino, concert halls, a music label, and a rock festival.[18] Hard Rock Cafes are now found in many of the major cities of the world, and the name is a much imitated and hotly defended trademark. Other theme restaurants include Planet Hollywood, the Harley-Davidson Cafe, Dive!, Fashion Cafe, and the Rainforest Cafe. By 1999 diners were getting pickier and theme restaurants' stock prices slumped, creating fierce competition.

The success of these restaurants can be attributed to a perfect balance between novelty and food. Many of the theme restaurants such as the Hard Rock Cafe and Planet Hollywood look to celebrities to bring in the crowds. Both of these restaurants feature artifacts from past and present celebrities. And celebrities often visit the restaurant, making a diner's experience even more enjoyable. Planet Hollywood restaurants are designed to fit the culture and customs of the region. The Harley-Davidson Cafe attracts customers with vintage motorcycles, while the Rainforest Cafe mimics a peaceful outdoor setting. The Fashion Cafe has models strolling a runway, and the Dive! is a faux submarine backed by director Steven Spielberg and others.[19]

But novelty alone is not enough. According to one restaurant owner, theme restaurants draw their initial crowd with the "wow," but if the food is not good, customers will not come back. To attract repeat customers, theme restaurants try to create attractive menus that follow the image suggested by the theme. The Rainforest Cafe, for example, offers food seasoned with spices from South America. The Harley-Davidson Cafe, on the other hand, has a general line of American fare with specialty drinks such as the Shock Absorber and Wheelie, while Planet Hollywood looks to its signature Chicken Crunch to bring people back.

To successfully provide the customer with the appropriate food, excellent service, and requested products, the manager must have specific guidelines for control. One area needing control is the budgeting process. Many operations use a food cost percentage (FCP) as a guideline for quality control. FCP is the comparison of the sales price to the cost of the materials necessary for production. For instance, if the FCP is too low, it could indicate unacceptable ingredients; on the other hand, if the FCP is too high it might indicate inventory shrinkage (employee theft), purchasing fraud, and lack of appropriations skills, or indicate a need to raise prices. The individual operations can also compare these data to the industry average or to competitors' data to establish a yardstick by which to measure and compare. For example, according to the American Restaurant Association's *Restaurant Industry Operations Report of 2001,* the average FCP was 28 percent for full-service restaurants and 32 percent for limited-service restaurants.

FCP is only one aspect of the budgeting process. Budgets should be realistic, flexible, and prepared for various time frames. For example, the capital budget that outlines major expansions and acquisitions may project five to seven years into the future, while the operating budget outlines the operating or fiscal cycle for one year.

How long will the theme restaurant craze last? No one can say, but Standard and Poor's Industry Surveys indicate that midscale sit-down restaurants are expected to benefit from increased demand. U.S. customers spent about $215 million in bars and restaurants in 1995—or more than $400,000 every day on eateries. For a restaurant chain there are basically three ways to grow: build sales at existing sites, open new units, and make acquisitions.

Can these restaurants be successful over a long time? That is still to be seen, but getting people to come back is what separates successful theme restaurants from the nice ideas that won't turn heads or profits.

Questions

1. Do you think theme restaurants are a permanent part of the restaurant industry? Why or why not?

2. What suggestions would you make to improve the attractiveness of these restaurants?

3. Would you like to own and operate a theme restaurant? Why or why not?

Case 15.2

How to Deal with Cash Flow Problems

Financial experts can suggest many ways to deal with cash flow problems. You, the small business owner, must remember to always make finances your number one priority. Constant monitoring is the best way to identify problems at the earliest possible stage. Many small business operators, and those who have at one time or another been involved with small business, will tell you that you can never spend too much effort or time on the financing aspect of operations.

Key areas to watch include:

- Cash balances.
- Accounts receivable turnover.
- Accounts payable balance.
- Interest payments and percentages.
- Worker productivity.
- Unnecessary expenses or excesses.
- Obsolete assets and inventory.
- Making sure that the people handling your cash are capable and honest.

Questions

1. Which of the above can you quantify?
2. Which of the above do you think is the most important point? Why?
3. Which of the above can be compared to a budget? Which budget?
4. What other suggestions do you have? Explain.

Experientials

1. After studying this chapter, you should be able to construct a budget for your educational expenses. Prepare a budget for your next term in good form. Do not forget incidentals like goodies from snack machines.
2. Present and discuss in class your budget prepared in Experiential number 1.

CHAPTER 16

Using Computer Technology in Small Businesses

Technology enables me to change, and technology forces me to change.
—**David H. Freedman**

Farms, factories, even tiny one-person businesses are reaping benefits—and surviving the frustrations—of computerization.
—**Jared Taylor, business consultant**

Learning Objectives

After studying the material in this chapter, you should be able to:

1. Explain the importance of information to a small business, and state which information is needed.

2. Discuss the need for—and how to choose—management information systems (MISs) for a small business.

3. Describe the growing role of technology in business.

4. Explain how the microcomputer (PC) has affected small business.

5. Explain some of the potential problems with computer technology in small business.

6. Understand the basics of e-commerce.

The Rose Bud Flowers and Gifts

The flower shop: a place that some people would not believe there would be much use for modern technology. This could not be farther from the truth. Services such as FTD and Teleflora connect flower shops all over the world through the Internet and telephone.

"Two years after opening in 1981, we realized we had a need for more automation of our accounts receivable," says Allen Kirksey, owner of The Rose Bud in Chickasaw, Alabama. Back in 1983, there were not as many software companies as there are today and the florist software industry was virtually nonexistent. Luckily for the Rose Bud, a florist in Tennessee wrote and produced Daisy, a software package for florists, for the Apple II computer. After several demonstrations, Allen purchased the software and hardware.

"We were one of the first florists in Mobile (Alabama) to use a computer. We were also the first florist in the area to install cell phones in our delivery vans. The old cell phones in our vans had to be physically bolted to the vehicle because they were so large. Despite their size, they really helped us and our drivers keep track of deliveries and cut down on confusion if a delivery change had to be made."

Over the years, many upgrades were made to the Daisy system. A few of those include adding a wire in/out service to shops who had compatible computer systems, instant local flower shop lookup based on the delivery address, and automatic credit card processing. "We actually used the Apple II-based Daisy system up until the late 1990s because it worked so well."

Daisy eventually discontinued the Apple II software, and The Rose Bud switched to a PC running a Linux version of Daisy. It was the same software they were used to, only now it ran on a more modern system. In 2005, The Rose Bud began searching for a replacement for the Daisy system. "We needed something that would automate deliveries, design, marketing, and accounting. Daisy is good at what it does, but it doesn't do everything."

Allen now faced the hard decision of finding another piece of software that could do what he wanted. In 2006 The Rose Bud purchased a new software package designed for flower shops. The software also required a new set of computers, so brand new PCs were purchased. Although transitioning from a familiar system to something new is always hard, it became apparent that this particular new software package was not going to work.

"After three days, we realized that this software just couldn't handle the demands of a large flower shop like ours. We ended up returning the entire package, computers and all, and went back to Daisy. At least with Daisy, we knew its limitations and could live with them while we started searching all over again. We bought an upgraded version of the Daisy system and computers to go with it and decided to wait it out."

Finally, in June 2007 Allen found a piece of software that did almost everything he wanted. The system, named RTI, is produced by Teleflora, a wire service for florists. RTI is a point-of-sale software specifically for flower

417

shops. RTI can do many things, such as cash register transactions, wire orders, instant credit card transactions, customized gift cards, design management, e-mail marketing, accounting through QuickBooks, employee time clocks, and delivery management.

"RTI is totally different from what we were used to with Daisy. It's not perfect, but we are able to do more with this system and are still learning new things every day."[1]

As of 2011 RTI is still the software of choice for the Rose Bud. This is in spite of the fact that the field for floral shop management software has grown since 2007. Allen visited trade shows and called software vendors to see if there were any new choices or improvements to RTI's competitors. "In June [2011], I had a chance to try and review all of the latest floral software from various vendors," he said. "Of them all, I found that RTI is still the best choice for what we do."

Sources: Adapted from an interview with Allen Kirksey, owner of the Rose Bud Flowers & Gifts.

Chances are that when you start your own business, you will have some sort of technology. It may be as simple as a phone system or as complex as an enterprise resource planning (ERP) package. Smaller firms actually spend faster on technology, and 60 percent of these expenditures goes for software. Part of this can be explained by a Congressional tax break for small firms.[2] However, you might find it interesting to note that tech firms lead the pack when it comes to failures.

This chapter is designed to show how computers and related technologies are used to help the small business owner-operator compete. We will also look at some of the basics of e-commerce, including Internet marketing and web design.

The Role of Information in Small Business

Have you ever considered how many records you keep or generate? You probably have in your possession at least a driver's license, credit card(s), debit card, student ID, Social Security card, and checkbook. Without these items, you would find it difficult to transact much of your daily business. Also, whenever you use one of these items, records (or entries in the records) are generated.

Real-World Example 16.1

For example, when you use a credit card, it generates a sales or credit slip, a monthly statement, and a record of payment. You use the statement to write a check and to deduct the amount from your bank balance. All the while, you keep some information (such as your Social Security number) in your head to save time in filling out forms.

As you can see, information is a most important resource for a small business, as well as for a person. It should help provide answers to such questions as: Is the product selling properly? Will the cash flow be adequate? Are the employees paid the correct amounts—and on time—and are the employment taxes handled properly?

Obviously, these questions cannot be answered without the appropriate data. Just as your personal records provide data for your personal decisions, your company must also collect data for its operations.

"It's called a phone booth, kids. Back in the days before cell phones ..."

A **management information system (MIS)** collects, records, processes, reports, and/or converts data into a usable form.

There are so many ways that your business can take advantage of technology, depending on what you do. Many different kinds of software are available to help with tasks such as accounting, inventory, payroll, invoicing, security, drafting and design, word processing, and many more. Some of us get just a little too dependent on our correcting technology and Figure 16.1 may be the result.

Our basic computer software needs usually include word processing, e-mail, and accounting packages. Retailers have several good inventory/point-of-sale products from which to choose. So many times we are tempted to "overbuy" our technology instead of concentrating on our basic needs at startup. Figure 16.2 gives examples of just a few available software packages for your personal computer (PC) or your small business network.

Efficient information systems are needed by small firms—as well as large ones—to convert data to information so management can use it to operate successfully. And as you will see, many of these information systems are now computerized—even in many small businesses.

Elements of a Management Information System (MIS)

As shown in Chapter 12, all types of systems involve the same basic elements: inputs, processes, and outputs. A **management information system (MIS)** is designed to collect, record, process, report, and/or convert data into a form suitable for management's use. For example, as will be shown later, an accounting system records and processes data and produces reports. A system may be entirely manual or, at the other extreme, almost entirely machine or computer operated.

All these systems start with inputs, process them, and furnish outputs. Whether or not computers are used, an organized MIS is necessary for the efficient operation of any business. Defining the needs of each part of a business for information and its processing and use is the first step in designing an information system.

What Information Is Needed?

Everyone in the small firm should consider the questions "What do I need to know in order to do my job better?" and "What information do I have that will help others do their jobs better?" The accumulation of these pieces of information, with analysis of what data are reasonably available, is the initial step in forming an information system. Emphasis should be on developing a system adapted to present needs—yet flexible enough to accommodate future changes. An obvious but often overlooked bit of advice: *Even the best information system is of no value if it is not used—and used properly.*

Purposes for Which Information Is Used   In determining what information is needed, you should ask yourself why you want it. The usual answers are as follows:

- *To plan a course of action,* such as deciding the number of items to purchase, the number of salespeople to hire, and/or the amount of accounts receivable to expect.
- *To meet obligations,* such as repaying borrowed money.
- *To control activities,* such as ensuring that ordered materials have arrived.

FIGURE 16.1 |
Spelling Technology!

The Spelling Chequer

Eye have a spelling chequer
It came with my pea sea
It plainly marques four my revue
Miss steaks eye can knot sea.

Eye strike a key and type a word
And weight four it to say
Weather eye am wrong oar write
It shows me strait a weigh.

As soon as a mist ache is maid
It nose bee fore two long
And eye can putt the error rite
Its rare lea ever wrong.

Eye have run this poem threw it
I am shore your pleased two no
Its letter perfect awl the weigh—
My chequer tolled me sew.

Source: *Mississippi Association of Professional Surveyors* 44, no. 1 (Spring 2004), p. 8.

- *To satisfy government regulations,* such as conforming to safety, employment, and ethical standards.
- *To evaluate performance.*

After determining the information needed, you must know how to use it. This involves classifying it into a usable form and establishing systems and procedures to ensure the availability of critical information.

Examples of Needed Information   The kinds of information you might need are too numerous to discuss, but the most important are (1) records of service provided to customers and (2) records of services performed for the business.

FIGURE 16.2 |
Some Examples of
Software

Type	Function	Price
AutoCAD	Mechanical drawing and design	$900
Ultimate Employer	Human resource management	$500
File Maker	Store, track, and archive	$300
Ultimate Financial Forecaster	Sales forecast, budgets, P&L, ratio analyses	$80
Retail Pro	Inventory management system with point-of-sale interface	N/A
ScreenNow	Check employee background	$175
Mydatabase	Organize and report information	$40
Creating a Successful Business Plan	Business plan	Free
Retail Ice	Inventory and point of sale	$65
Turbo Tax	Income tax	$40
Microsoft Office 2007 Small Business Edition	Office package that includes Word, Excel, PowerPoint, Publisher, Outlook, and Accounting Express	$400
QuickBooks Point of Sale Pro	Retail inventory sales management system	$1050
QuickBooks Premiere	Financial management and forecasting	$400
QuickBooks Accountant Premiere	Accounting package	$400
osCommerce	Open source point-of-sale system with inventory control and customer management	Free
phpPoS	Open source point-of-sale system with inventory control and customer management.	N/A

Services to customers provide revenue in the form of cash, checks, or promises to pay. Both real-time and delayed transactions occur in this system. When products are sold, sales slips are made out to give to customers. Later, the slips are used as daily summaries of sales, sales taxes, and so forth, which are then recorded in journals. Unlike direct sales, rental of items requires additional transactions.

Services performed for the business must also be recorded. Goods sold to, or services performed for, a firm are its expenses of doing business, and payments must be made for them. In addition, payments are made to increase assets and reduce obligations.

Even very small businesses need formal systems for keeping records. In the past, very simple recordkeeping systems such as manila folders, shoe boxes, and entries in a checkbook have been used for this purpose. These methods are simple and easy to understand but in many cases do not meet the demands of today's competitive marketplace.

Timing of Information Flow(s)

Data from activities may be needed (1) at the time of transaction (real-time processing) or (2) after transactions accumulate (batch processing). For example, a customer is given a sales slip on completion of the sale, which is *real-time processing.* An MIS can be designed to take care of such immediate feedback. For example, portable computers, modems, mobile phones, electronic wands or scanners, and radios can be used to collect and provide information quickly, as in the following example.

Real-World Example 16.2

Ernest Gore, an architect, visited Jean Soor, who was interested in building a house. During the discussion, Ernest opened his laptop computer and laid out the house plan as Jean described her ideas. Several times, they discussed "what ifs," and he made the changes to show their effects. He left with the plans well developed. Ernest attributes a great deal of his success in making the sale and satisfying the customer to this type of rapid feedback.

Job scheduling is done after more than one transaction has occurred, such as at the end of an hour or at the end of the day when the daily sales are summarized. Slower turnaround may meet the requirements of the system and be less expensive, so you should balance the speed and convenience of real-time processing with the economy of batch processing, as the following example illustrates.

Real-World Example 16.3

A chef in a restaurant is usually a highly skilled individual who schedules, cooks, and assembles meals. The server is a less-skilled person who uses an information system to transmit information from the customer to the chef. Many restaurants use turnstiles for placing orders. First, the orders are written. Then the slips are clipped to a turnstile that the chef can turn to read the order. The slips on the turnstile serve to schedule orders in sequence, and they may also become the customer's bill. The turnstile causes a brief delay in the MIS but is simple and effective. Also, being impersonal, it does not make the higher-status chef seem to be taking orders from the lower-status servers.

Now, many restaurants—especially fast-food chains—are using computers to convey orders from servers or front-counter order takers to the kitchen staff. In addition to eliminating bottlenecks in taking orders, computer systems can reduce waste and labor costs in food preparation and even serve as a marketing tool by tracking customers and their eating habits.

Companies that apply technology effectively stand a good chance of achieving a competitive edge. Unfortunately, there is no universal set of rules for bringing technology into a small business.[3]

Choosing an MIS

Figure 16.3 presents a checklist you can use to define your company and the types and volume of information it needs. Completion of this checklist should help you form a better idea of the system to install.

The Role of Technology in Business

Laptops and Other Electronic Devices

> **Hardware** consists of the CPU, monitor, keyboard, and other parts that you can see and touch.

As you may know, a computer consists of hardware and software. **Hardware** consists of the CPU (Central Processing Unit), the monitor, the keyboard, and other parts that you can see, feel, and touch. (For our purposes, the CPU is what we will call the unit that houses the processor, memory, hard drive, DVD drive, motherboard, and so on.)

FIGURE 16.3 | Defining What a Company Needs in an MIS

Type of business

Retail _____ Wholesale _____ Mfg. _____ Professional services _____
Real estate _____ Agriculture _____ Nonprofit _____ Other _____

Business size

Gross income _____ Net profit as percentage of gross income _____

Types of information needed

Numerical _____ Textual _____ Graphics _____ Communications _____

Location(s)

Single _____ Dispersed _____ Franchise _____ Subsidiary _____

Transaction volume

Invoices/month _____ Average accounts receivable _____ Average inventory _____
Inventory turnover _____ Number of inventory items _____
Number of customers _____ Number of employees _____

Current information system (Describe.)

_____

_____

Trouble areas (Rank each according to importance and number of people involved. Use more paper if needed. Be as complete as possible.)

_____

_____

_____

Potential future needs (Include all possible needs, as they may be economically feasible in any system designed.)

_____

_____

Applications

Business areas to be addressed (Number in order of priority.)

Accounting _____ Financial reporting _____ Inventory management _____
Cash flow planning _____ Market and sales analysis _____ Decision support _____
Billing _____ Scheduling _____ Quality control _____ Payroll _____
Employee benefits _____ Commissions _____ Customer tracking _____
Portfolio management _____ Legal defense _____ Long-term planning _____
Tax reporting _____ Word processing _____ Other (be specific) _____

Computer skills available in company

_____

Proposed budget for MIS

$_____ Maximum _____

Time Frame

Desired start _____ Latest allowed start _____

Software is the programs, manuals, and procedures that cause the hardware to operate in a desired manner.

The **technology S-curve** is the product life theory applied to technological devices.

Backward compatible hardware will run existing programs designed for older equipment.

A **laptop computer** is a small, battery-powered package that can be used anywhere.

Personal data assistant (PDA) is a handheld, pocket-sized computer that is often a completely wireless system.

A **smartphone** is a cellular phone with personal data assistant (PDA) capabilities.

Software includes the programs, manuals, and procedures that allow the hardware to function in a manner desired by the user. Examples of software range from operating systems such as Linux or Microsoft Windows to programs such as Adobe Photoshop and Firefox.

Sometimes advancements in technology move so swiftly that software cannot keep up. This can be shown graphically with the **Technology S-curve** (see Figure 16.4). On the left side of the S-curve, a product is introduced and there are very few adopters. On the right side, the product has reached maturity and is beginning to lose consumer interest; this is roughly the point in which a new product is introduced.

When new technology comes out, you hope that it is backward compatible with your old software. Saying something is **backward compatible** means that existing programs will run on the new hardware while still allowing newer software to take full advantage of the recent technological advancements. A simple example of something being backward compatible would be the Playstation 2 (PS2) game console. The PS2 allowed users to play older Playstation 1 software as well as the newer PS2 games.

Perhaps the most revolutionary development in technology is the **laptop computer**. In the past, laptops were pricey and usually required compromises in functionality when compared to their desktop counterparts. New developments in computer technology have driven prices down and allowed the laptop to easily match the capabilities of desktops. For sales representatives on the road, engineers in the field, soldiers on the battlefield, employees taking inventory, or even film editors on the go, laptops are ideal. Laptops have become standard carry-on luggage for "road warriors," who can use the hours spent on planes, airports, and hotel rooms to stay on top of their paperwork.

Lightweight laptops are also popular with students because they can be taken to the classroom or library to facilitate note taking. Further miniaturization has resulted in personal data assistant (PDA) computers and smart phones which can run "light" versions of popular word processing, spreadsheet, and communications and Web browsing software.

Most of us like electronic gadgets, and many of these can be very useful to the small business owner. **Personal data assistants (PDAs)** and **smartphones** are capable of doing just about anything. Originally used for scheduling and contacts, they now do all basic

FIGURE 16.4 |
The Technology
S-Curve

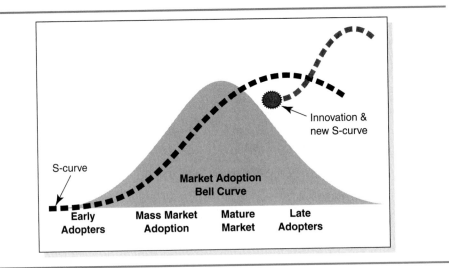

Source: Innovation Lifecycles, *www.innovation-point.com.*[4]

computer functions from word processing, Internet browsing, e-mail, and even online multiplayer games. These devices exchange data with partners such as laptops, PC workstations, websites, and other PDAs and smartphones. PDAs and smartphones are more affordable every day, currently starting around $100, with smartphones generally requiring a separate contract with a cellular company. Some of the pricier PDAs and smartphones even include Wi-Fi for web browsing on the go. The downside to these miniwonders is the tiny keyboard for input. However, this problem can easily be solved by PC input and synchronization between units by using an external keyboard.

Cell phones are practically a necessity now. In 2010 there were 325.6 million subscribers, up from 109 million in 2000. Some, as stated previously, contain PDA features and are called smartphones. Most cell phones contain digital cameras, USB and Bluetooth connection capabilities for data transfer and contact synchronization, and MP3 music playback. Of all cell-phone users in the United States, 16 percent, or 16.7 million, use their cell phones to access the Wed.[5]

You may even have a key chain that will beep when lost if you have a remote, or a chip in your wallet or luggage that will do the same thing. If so, you may be interested in a new pair of pants marketed by Dockers (www.dockers.com). These high-tech pants come with "a myriad of pockets."

Gadget explosion has opened a niche for consultants. These entrepreneurs answer the question, "Help, I plugged the thingie into the thing, but it still doesn't work."

Real-World Example 16.4

For example: Avi Rosenthal, a self-described "electronic architect," charges from $50 to $125 an hour to make house calls and to answer consumer questions. Demand for digital handymen has led to a nonprofit Internet Home Alliance and trade group to certify these electronic architects. In one year, more than 100 certificates were issued nationwide.[6]

There are hundreds if not thousands of small devices that can assist us in not only the operations of our businesses, but also, they can make our work more fun.

RFID and Inventory Control

RFID stands for Radio Frequency Identification and may be the replacement for bar codes.

RFID, which stands for Radio Frequency Identification, is the latest in inventory control. Similar to bar codes, RFID "tags" transmit data about a product when scanned. The difference is RFID tags can be scanned by just being near, them unlike bar codes where a device has to be pointed at the code.

RFID tags are in everything from labels on boxes to U.S. passports and even American Express credit cards. Frequent toll booth users in the Northeast even have RFID tagged cards in their cars so they can pass through without even stopping. This system is called "EZPass."

If you know someone who likes to make off with easy-to-miss items at hotels and restaurants (such as towels and silverware), you may want to tell him or her to think twice. The business may be watching. Some of the bigger hotels have begun purchasing towels and bathrobes with waterproof and heat-proof RFID tags embedded in them in order to keep customers from stealing them.[7]

There are many different types of RFID tags. Some are "passive," which means that they do not require a battery to transmit data. This means that they are cheaper to produce, but only have a range of a few feet. Passive tags cost anywhere from 20 to 50 cents each.

"Active" RFID tags require a battery, but increase the range in which they can be read to nearly 300 feet. The cons are that the battery will need to be replaced in three to seven years and the price is substantially higher. Active tags cost between $50 and $100 per tag.

There are security risks involved with RFID tags that were not there with bar codes. Because one does not have to physically have access to the RFID device like with a bar code, the data can be read from almost anywhere. For example, say that a criminal wants to find out your passport information. All the criminal has to do is have an RFID scanner and scan your RFID-enabled passport just by being near you.

RFID tags are also subject to viruses, just like computers. Students at Vrije University in Amsterdam created the first RFID virus in 2006. An RFID virus could be something as simple as changing prices on products to something that could destroy a business's product database.[8]

(Source: CATHY © 2002 Cathy Guisewite. Reprinted with permission of UNIVERSAL PRESS SYNDICATE. All rights reserved.)

Strengths and Weaknesses of Computers for Small Firms

The key to whether a computer is an asset or a liability in a small firm is the use made of it. The computer itself is not likely to be a limiting factor. The primary limitation is the availability of software that can economically accomplish the desired tasks. Figure 16.5 gives a list of the applications for which a computer is especially well suited and for which software is currently available (as well as a list of tasks not usefully delegated to computers).

Notice that the areas in which computer technology can be most useful are *repetitive, high-volume, quantitative tasks*. By contrast, the areas in which this technology is less useful are the *unstructured, open-ended activities in which human creativity or judgment is required*. While the latter are more innovative or people oriented, the former are the boring, detail-oriented jobs once performed by lower-paid employees. Smart business owners will delegate these activities to the computer, freeing competent staff to handle the more interesting, long-term problems.

The Internet

The Internet is a collection of computers and computer networks linked together to receive and distribute information around the world. Most colleges and universities, along with public schools, government agencies, businesses, and individuals, are connected to "the Net."

The Internet is like any other resource available to the entrepreneur. Those who use this tool in the most expedient and innovative way will reap the largest rewards from their efforts. Like all other tools, this one, used in the wrong way, will be of little or no value and may even

The **Internet** is a collection of computers and computer networks linked together to receive and distribute information around the world.

FIGURE 16.5 |

What Computers Do
Best—and Worst

The computer is most helpful in the following applications, for which software is readily available:

- Repetitive, data-oriented operations, such as accounting, record keeping, or mailing lists.
- Organizing data into information, such as financial reporting.
- Codifying and monitoring procedures, such as technical manuals and production control.
- Calculations, such as financial ratios and tax analyses.
- Forecasting, such as trend projection and materials requirements planning.

The computer is less valuable, and may even be a liability, in operations of the following types:

- Solving unstructured problems or those that are not clearly defined, as in invention or innovation.
- Defining and/or establishing true authority in a company, such as leadership roles.
- Identifying new markets or products. The computer can be a major asset here, but only as a tool to assist human workers.
- Interpersonal relations, such as contract negotiations or establishing corporate culture.
- Defining the corporate mission.

be detrimental to the business. It is best to enlist the help of professionals to design web pages and set up order-processing systems to be used on the Internet. A website that is difficult to navigate will be frustrating to the user and of little benefit to the firm. Likewise an automated system that is slow or inaccurate will be a liability to the firm rather than an asset.

Some Potential Problems with Computer Technology

There are many advantages and disadvantages to using computer technology. Therefore, careful planning is needed to ensure accuracy, acceptability, and adaptability. Errors or inadequacies that develop in the system are much easier to detect and correct if the system is carefully designed and if employees are supportive and motivated to make it work. But even when errors and malfunctions are detected, they may not be easy to correct.

Another problem caused by the introduction of computerized operations is the need to upgrade your and your employees' skills. If this seems overwhelming to you, please take note. Help is available through other small companies specially set up to help you revamp or even get started in the computer world. Many computer retailers, including franchises such as Entré Computer Centers, provide software instruction, and some local Internet service providers offer free classes to get subscribers started "surfing."

Computers Require Added Security

Computers are used for generating and storing important—often confidential—records, which makes controlling access an important issue. In addition, as more people have access to information, it becomes more important to set up procedures to ensure that data are accurately entered and protected from being accidentally (or intentionally) destroyed or altered. This suggests that an important part of a computerized MIS are the procedures set up for entry, updating, and control (to be discussed more fully in Chapter 17). Some steps that can be taken to provide security, however, include:

- Physical control of facilities, such as guards and emergency power.
- Access control, such as identification of users and specifying who has the authority to use the equipment.
- Backups, such as appropriate saving of data.

428 Part Five Basic Financial Planning and Control

Just as important as the security of the information you are storing is the integrity of that information. "Hackers" (computer programmers who experiment to see what mischief they can do) have created computer "viruses" that can destroy your data and programs without your being able to stop them. These are programs that "hide" in other programs and are transmitted from one computer to another through exchange of disks or by downloading files from a remote computer or network. Small businesses have long been the target of hackers and criminals, largely because small businesses typically do not have the security measures of larger companies. Many companies simply cannot afford the sophisticated security technology available to other companies, and others think their business is too small to attract such notice.

For those in the latter category the following statistics may be a surprise! In June of 2011 alone some 20,000 to 30,000 small company websites were attacked by hackers. A company is never too small to slip under the radar of criminals![9]

To protect your system, you need to get antiviral programs along with the system and minimize the use of programs and/or disks of unfamiliar origin. Your antiviral program should be of the type that can be updated frequently.

Antivirus Programs

Choosing the right antivirus ("AV") program for your small business can be a hassle. There are dozens of companies out there selling and giving away their own AV programs, but which one will best suit your company's needs?

Pay programs come with yearly subscriptions and, generally, are updated once or multiple times per day against new viruses. They may also have their own firewalls and defend against spyware too. Many companies offer small business discounts if you have more than one computer in your office.

Free AV programs are usually stripped down versions of their pay counterparts. While they still offer protection from viruses, updates may not come as often. These programs are best for home, home office, or student use. Table 16.1 breaks down some of the antivirus programs available for your PC.

A survey of 300 tech managers found that the average recovery costs from a virus attack in a major system is $100,000.[10] PC protection is an easy fix for small business owners and is often free; www.grisoft.com is one example.

The National Institute of Standards and Technology (NIST) reports that new software problems, or bugs, cost as much as $59.5 billion a year in fixes, downtime, and lost business.[11] There are various causes for bugs, such as defective code, partial testing, and rush to get the product to market before it becomes obsolete.

According to another recent survey, small business owners are willing to take extreme measures to stop spam or unwanted e-mail. Fifty-six percent would consider stricter e-mail systems, 55 percent would be willing to change the company e-mail address, and 42 percent would be willing to give up business e-mail altogether to avoid the problem. Spam happens when a virus-infected e-mail is opened. With almost 70 percent of small businesses having a presence online, the stakes are high.[12] Solutions for spam include not opening any e-mail from unknown vendors. There are several antispam filters and other security software available today. Most Internet providers do this for you; for example, Hotmail has a "junk" mail message page. This helps the user to eliminate unwanted e-mail. Spam makes up 31 percent of the e-mail small businesses receive.[13]

One recent survey of chief security officers indicates that electronic crime is on the increase. Forty-three percent of responders said cyber crime had increased within their company.[14] Security software is available for all system sizes. Small business technology spending in general is increasing, and security purchases are expected to increase by 28 percent.

TABLE 16.1 |

Antivirus Programs for Your PC or MAC

Name	Pay Service or Free	Operating Systems	Small Business Discount
NOD 32 eset.com	Pay (yearly)	Windows 2K/XP/Vista/7	Yes, sold under "Small Business Edition"
Kaspersky Anti-virus kaspersky.com	Pay (yearly)	Windows XP/ Vista/7	Yes, sold under "Business Security— Small and Medium Businesses"
Symantec Antivirus symantec.com	Pay (yearly)	XP/Vista/7	Yes, sold under "Business Pack"
AVG Anti-Virus www.avg.com	Pay (yearly) Free version available	XP/Vista/7	Yes, sold under "SBS Edition"
Avast! Antivirus avast.com	Pay (yearly) Free version available	XP/Vista/7	Yes, sold under "SBS Suite"
Avira Antivirus avira.com	Pay (yearly) Free version available	XP/Vista/7	Yes, sold under "Small Business Suite"
Microsoft Security Essentials microsoft.com	Free for individuals & small businesses up to 10 PCs Pay version available for larger businesses	XP/Vista/7	Free for Small Businesses under 10 PCs

Antivirus Programs That Run from a Web Browser

Name	Operating Systems Supported	Web Browsers Supported
Trend Micro Housecall housecall.trendmicro.com	XP/Vista/7	Internet Explorer 6 and above, Mozilla Firefox
Panda Security Activescan pandasecurity.com	Windows 98SE/ME/2K/ XP/Vista/7	Internet Explorer 6 and above, Mozilla Firefox

Reluctance of Some Owners to Use Computer Technology

In case we have led you to believe that most small businesses use computer technology, that is not necessarily so! Many middle-aged and older entrepreneurs have resisted computerizing their small businesses. In general, this reluctance derives from two sources. First, many small businesses use only the most basic forms of computerization because of the cost involved. Others, though, lack the self-confidence to venture far out into this new, and often bewildering, field, as the following classic example illustrates.

Real-World Example 16.5

Ben Satterfield, age 55, overcame his "fear of computers" when he realized he could no longer manage the bills and orders overwhelming his business, Mug-A-Bug Pest Control Inc. of Lawrenceville, Georgia. While the move was tough, it

continued

Choosing Software, Hardware, and Employee Training

The primary software applications likely to be needed by a small business include word processing, spreadsheet analysis, account processing, file management, and electronic mail/messaging. It is easy to assume that your business is unique and requires a specially designed system to match your needs. Be wary of this approach, however, because there are many "off-the-shelf" programs (already designed and available) that, while they may not satisfy all your needs, will likely provide a cost-effective solution to most of them.

Having defined your computer needs and the software desired, you must then choose the hardware. A wide range is available, from simple, inexpensive desktops to complicated, expensive servers. Most small companies need a system somewhere in the middle—one that is not too costly but does the work satisfactorily. The line between PCs and Macs have blurred in the last few years with the introduction of Intel-based Apple computers. If you need the simplicity and ease-of-use of an Apple computer, but still need to run Windows-based software, Apple computers can now run both Mac and PC programs with the help of software such as Boot Camp or Parallels. Figure 16.6 lists some selected sources of information to help you choose hardware, software, and employee training.

It may be more satisfactory for a small business owner to have a machine custom-built by one of the estimated 100,000 small PC makers who operate out of their homes, warehouses, and small shopping centers. These small producers have carved out a market niche by offering personalized service and in some cases even designing and custom-building machines for anyone who walks in the door. In fact, the "hand holding" that local PC builders and sellers can offer customers now gives them a special edge as home users and small businesses increasingly move into the PC world and the Internet.

FIGURE 16.6 |

Sources of Information about Computer Hardware, Software, and Training

The following sources can be used to obtain information to help in choosing hardware, software, and training.

- *Computer stores and consultants.* These can provide need-specific advice, packaged systems, and ongoing support, but they may be more oriented toward their sale than to your needs. The quality of advice may vary. Future availability of recommended systems is critical.

- *Friends or peers, user groups, bulletin boards, and seminars or workshops.* These can give more specialized advice, though it may not match your needs. Because hands-on experience is often possible, you may gain a better understanding of your needs, if not a specific answer. These are good sources of answers to technical questions, but beware of sales pitches.

- *Magazines, books, and libraries.* Although these are good sources of background information and comparative evaluations of hardware and software, the volume and technical nature of the information may create information overload, and the information is usually not tailored to your needs.

- *Computer company promotional material and mail order.* This is more oriented to specific hardware and software than to your needs, but it permits comparison of detailed technical specifications. Some mail-order firms offer ongoing support, but be sure to check, because this is important.

- *Industry associations.* These may have systems already fully designed to handle your specific problems and data that could be useful to you, but they may include a membership cost or licensing fee.

- *Government publications and SCORE/SBA.* These are inexpensive sources of information, data services, consultant referrals, and possibly even funding, but the quality may vary and may not include the most recent technology.

Small Business and E-Commerce

For those who shop at Amazon.com or other online retailers, you know it is common to receive an invoice in your e-mail as soon as the order is completed. It has been this way for years. Did you know that there are brick-and-mortar stores that are considering doing the same thing? Large retailers such as Gap and Nordstrom are touting just such an option to computer-savvy customers who cannot be bothered with more paperwork in their lives. Whether it is practical or not is yet to be seen, but it is clear that the Internet is creeping more and more into even traditional markets.[18]

Digital technology has changed the economy. The primary source of value creation for consumers has shifted from physical goods to service and information. In essence, **e-commerce** is characterized by several attributes:

- It is about the exchange of digitized information between parties.
- It is technology enabled.
- It is technology mediated.
- It includes intra- and interorganizational activities that support the exchange.

e-commerce
Technology-mediated exchanges between parties as well as the electronically based intra- or interorganizational activities that facilitate such exchanges.

Real-World Example 16.7

Ken Swerlick, owner of Restaurant Equipment Paradise Inc., generates 10 percent of his revenue from eBay. He says to attract bidders you need to "Write a descriptive title," include lots of pictures, and have a predetermined shipping cost in mind.[19]

Close to Home

"Steve! There's a bunch of our junk selling on eBay! The bid total is $2,700 and the seller is our garbage man!"

(Source: CLOSE TO HOME © 2004 John McPherson. Reprinted with permission of UNIVERSAL PRESS SYNDICATE. All rights reserved.)

Internet marketing is the process of building and maintaining customer relationships through online activities.

eBay is the world's largest online auction site and is used by about 430,000 entrepreneurs, who can reach buyers worldwide. The auctions usually last from 1 to 10 days.[20]

Internet Marketing

If traditional marketing (Chapter 8) is about creating exchanges that simultaneously satisfy the firm and customers, what is Internet marketing? **Internet marketing** is the process of building and maintaining customer relationships through online activities to facilitate the exchange of ideas, products, and services that satisfy the goals of both parties.[21] Many businesses are using this technique to aid in their marketing success. Internet marketing can be divided into the following five components:

1. *Process.* Like a traditional marketing program, an Internet marketing program involves a process. The seven stages of the Internet marketing program process (see Figure 16.7) are framing the market opportunity, formulating the marketing strategy, designing the customer experience, crafting the customer interface, designing the marketing program, leveraging customer information through technology, and evaluating the results of the marketing program as a whole. These seven stages must be coordinated and internally consistent. While the process can be described in a simple linear fashion, the marketing strategist often has to loop back and forth during the seven stages.

2. *Building and maintaining customer relationships.* Successful marketing programs move the target customer through three stages of relationship building: awareness, exploration, and commitment. It is important to stress that the goal of Internet marketing is not simply building relationships with online customers. Rather, the goal is to build offline as well as online relationships. The Internet marketing program may well be part of a broader campaign to satisfy customers who use both online and offline services.

3. *Online.* Internet marketing deals with levers that are available in the world of the Internet. The success of an Internet marketing program may rest with traditional, offline marketing vehicles.

4. *Exchange.* At the core of both online and offline marketing programs is the concept of exchange. Firms must be very sensitive to cross-channel exchanges; an online marketing program must be evaluated according to its overall exchange impact—not just the online exchange impact. Online marketing may produce exchanges in retail stores. Firms must be increasingly sensitive to these cross-channel effects if they are to measure the independent effects of online and offline marketing programs.

5. *Satisfaction of goals of both parties.* Customer satisfaction and company revenue must balance out. While the hype of Internet marketing has died down, it is clear that Internet marketing is here to stay and should be an important component of any marketer's arsenal.[22]

Web Design

When the decision is made to utilize the Internet, the design of a web page is a solid logical decision. This also may be the time to consult an experienced web page designer.

FIGURE 16.7 |
The Seven Stage
Cycle of Internet
Marketing

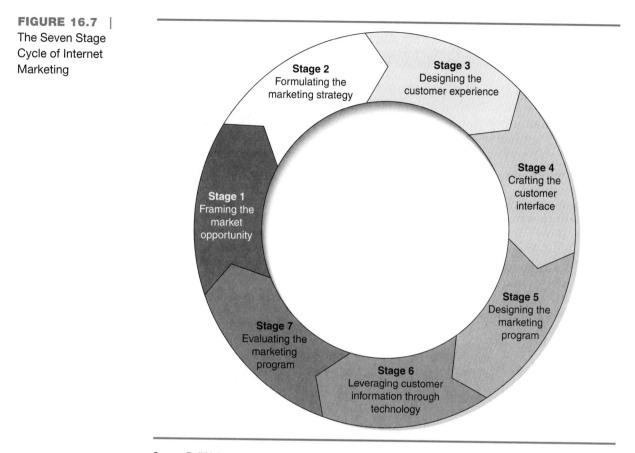

Source: Rafi Mohammed, *Internet Marketing,* 2nd ed. (Burr Ridge, IL: McGraw-Hill /Irwin, 2004), p. 9. Reprinted by permission of The McGraw-Hill Companies.

The Seven Design Elements of the Customer Interface

According to Jeffrey Rayport,[23] there are seven elements needed for a good web page. Figure 16.8 illustrates the 7Cs framework for customer interface or web page design. The interface is the virtual (and, to date, largely visual) representation of a firm's chosen value proposition. Like a retail storefront, it answers questions that prospective customers may have: Is this site worth visiting? What products or services does it sell? Does it include price? Is it easy to use? Consistent with a tightly constructed business model, an effectively designed website should both attract target segment customers and discourage others.

These seven elements are explained as follows:

1. A website's *context* captures its aesthetic and functional look-and-feel. Some sites focus on bold graphics, colors, and design features, while others emphasize utilitarian goals, such as ease of navigation. Figure 16.8 contains a page from RoseBudFlowers.com. The Rose Bud's website balances aesthetic elements (single red rose on a black background with a scripted logo) and functional ones (crisp, uncluttered design) to emphasize the flowers and products they sell.

FIGURE 16.8 |

2. While context focuses on how a site is designed, *content* refers to what is presented. All the digital subject matter—text, video, audio, and graphics—on a website is considered content and together all those forms present information about a company's products and services. Consider again the RoseBudFlowers.com page: it uses text, photographs, and graphics to convey information about its product categories, services, and offline support (through the toll-free phone number).

3. *Community* is interaction between site users. It can happen through one-on-one interactions (e-mail, instant or text messages, or game playing) or among many users such as chat rooms or community sites such as Facebook or MySpace. It does not refer to site-to-user interactions.

4. A website's ability to tailor itself to each user is called *customization*. When customization is initiated and managed by the firm, we call it tailoring. When it is initiated and managed by the user, we call it personalization. On RoseBudFlowers.com, users can choose from a list of premade arrangements and tell the designers what flowers or items to add or leave out of that arrangement.

5. *Communication* refers to dialogue between a website and its users. It can take three forms: site-to-user communication (such as e-mail notifications), user-to-site communication (such as a customer service request), or two-way communication (such as instant

messaging). RoseBudFlowers.com lets you e-mail your questions or attach them to an order and you can either receive an e-mail response or request a customer service representative to call you.

6. *Connection* refers to the degree to which a website links to other sites. RoseBudFlowers.com does not host connections to other sites. Instead, the site uses FTD and Teleflora's website services to connect users with flower shops in their area if they are out of The Rose Bud's delivery area.

7. A website's *commerce* capabilities allow it to sell goods, products, and services. RoseBudFlowers.com, as mentioned earlier, allows users to choose arrangements or goodie baskets and customize them to fit their desires and add them to their digital shopping cart. Information about items in the shopping cart—quantity, description, size, price, and availability—is always available, as is a summary feature that displays the total price, including taxes and delivery cost. Another commerce feature is a secure server for customers' billing information and credit card numbers.

> ### Real-World Example 16.8
>
> For example, chat rooms are a good way to get to know your market. You can collect both primary and secondary data by initiating a tightly focused discussion. Message boards and discussion lists on the Internet debate every imaginable topic, and chances are some will partially match your customer profile.[24]

Now that you understand what it takes to design a web page, it is interesting to note that many shoppers prefer brick-and-mortar stores. For example, electronics shoppers were surveyed and it was discovered that 35 percent believe that the prices are better in stores, 38 percent feel more comfortable returning items, 25 percent believe stores are more convenient, and 25 percent of those surveyed said that stores have special offers that are not available online.[25]

Text Marketing

According to a survey conducted by the CTIA in the last half of 2009 nearly 91 percent of the American population has a mobile phone of some sort. That's about 285 million people! And nearly all of these mobile units are "data capable." That means they are able to accept text messages and have Internet access, among other things.[26]

In recent years marketing companies and large corporations have embarked on text marketing. Text marketing, in its simplest terms, is advertising through the use of text messaging. Companies will pull up lists of customer phone numbers and send them advertisements from time to time via text.

While it can be compared to sending e-mail advertisements text marketing has the ability to reach the end user much more quickly. Even with cheap smartphone technology many people still do not have Internet access on their phones. But, nearly everyone has the ability to send and receive text messages. Since most people check their messages as soon as they receive them, an advertiser is getting its message out almost instantly.

Small businesses have started to see the benefit of such a marketing tool. For example, say a pizza place has been collecting customer cell-phone numbers on a voluntary basis. Early one day the owner decides he wants to do a daily special. To get the word out he can pull up the list of customers and send them a text ad. If he times this properly (preferably before the lunch hour or just before quitting time at the end of the day) he could find his restaurant packed with people clamoring for the special.

Text marketing can be a very powerful tool, if used correctly. It allows businesses to reach out to frequent and loyal customers in a quick and targeted manner. Best of all, it is quite inexpensive.

Real-World Example 16.9

Groupon is an online coupon-sharing site designed to give small businesses and restaurants an edge on the big box retailers and chain-style restaurants by providing a hub for interested parties to go and scan for discounts in their local area. While this sounds great it is not profitable for all small businesses as Groupon requires them to offer discounts that many simply cannot absorb. In fact, several small businesses in San Clemente, California, are currently participating in a study by Web Marketing Partners to determine if businesses can be just as successful by advertising through text messages as their counterparts are with Groupon and other hub sites. The expense is far less and each business has the ability to determine the type and length of a discount on their own terms. The results of the study should prove interesting.[27]

Facebook and Twitter

Many celebrities, political candidates, and small businesses have come to realize the benefit of social media in reaching out to fans, adherents, and customers. In an age where brand recognition is king any method of establishing oneself is to be utilized to its fullest.

Using online social media such as Facebook, Twitter, and MySpace can be as powerful as—if not more powerful than—having a well-made company website. If you can attract a customer to follow your Facebook comments or your Twitter feed you have the potential to reach out to them any time you wish. Individuals who use Facebook or Twitter will almost always be checking the status of the people they follow. A well-placed advertisement or comment has the potential to bring in lots of business.

As with text marketing the use of social media is relatively inexpensive and can yield great results. It also has the added bonus of showing potential customers and clients that your company is on the cutting edge. This has appeal to younger generations and can attract them to your business even if your business has very little to do with computer technology (a restaurant, for example).

DILBERT reprinted by permission of United Feature Syndicate, Inc.)

QR Codes

Originally created by Toyota to keep track of individual cars and trucks as they worked their way through the plant floor, the Quick Response (QR) code is a type of barcode that has since become extremely popular in the realm of mobile devices. Many businesses have begun placing them on ads, brochures, magazine covers, and business cards. Simply scanning them with a QR-equipped mobile device immediately downloads the information in the code, typically a hyperlink to a company website.

How accepted have QR codes become? They're being used in advertisements for companies both big and small. Churches and music groups have begun utilizing them to promote their own websites. One company in Seattle—Quiring Monuments—has even begun putting them onto tombstones.[28] The title of a July 2011 *USA Today* article by Laura Ruane says it all: "QR Codes Everywhere—Even on Grave Markers." That's pretty mainstream! Ruane goes on to write that companies big and small have begun using QR codes in advertisements.

Companies are realizing that for mobile device users it is far easier to scan a code and instantly be on a website than it is for them to type out an URL. If you can save a potential customer time to look at the product then you have already taken a big step toward ultimately selling them that product.

QR codes are very inexpensive for companies to set up and use. Websites exist that automatically generate the barcodes once you have provided the URL for the code you want to send. Then people simply scan it. In many cases this can be done absolutely free of charge. For many small businesses, this is a great way to tap into the mainstream.

What You Should Have Learned

1. Information is an important resource for small businesses as well as for people. Companies collect and process data, make decisions, act on those decisions, and start the cycle anew.

2. A management information system (MIS) collects, processes, records, reports, and/or converts data into a usable form for management. Data can be processed in *real time*, with instantaneous feedback, or *job scheduled* later at a lower cost.

3. Computers are increasingly important in business because they can process data so quickly. A computer—hardware—is physical equipment used for storing, processing, and presenting large quantities of data. Programs—software—direct the computer to process the data. Much of the value of a computer system comes from the software.

4. The microcomputer (PC) has made it feasible for a small business to process data related to such areas as accounting, employees, forecasting, and operations. Most systems involve both manual and computer operations, and the choice of the appropriate system depends on output, cost, and the situation in the business.

In choosing a computer system, analyze the present situation in terms of available software, hardware, and employee training.

5. A potential problem with computer technology is that the possibility of errors and inaccurate information being turned out is magnified. Also, the owner and employees need to continually upgrade their skills. Greater security of the equipment and information is required. Some middle-aged and older owners are reluctant to install the technology for various reasons. Finally, some older computers will have to be reprogrammed—at considerable expense—to enter the 21st century.

6. E-commerce can be formally defined as follows: technology-mediated exchanges between parties (individuals or organizations) as well as the electronically based intra- or interorganizational activities that facilitate such exchanges. Internet marketing is the process of building and maintaining customer relationships through online activities. There are seven elements of web design: context, content, community, customization, communication, connection, and commerce.

Key Terms

backward compatible   424
e-commerce   431
hardware   422
Internet   426
Internet marketing   432

laptop computer   424
management information
   system (MIS)   419
personal data assistant
   (PDA)   424

RFID   425
smartphone   424
software   424
technology S-curve   424

Questions for Discussion

1. What are some of the management decisions owners of small businesses must make?
2. What types of information do they need to make those decisions?
3. What are some of the sources of the needed information?
4. Explain how the use of computers by business has grown.
5. Explain how the microcomputer (PC) has affected small business.
6. What effect(s) do you think the Internet has had on small business?
7. What are some problems with computer technology for small firms?
8. Explain how e-commerce affects small businesses.

Case 16.1

Herman Valentine: Customizing Computers for Military Use

Herman Valentine, chairman and president of Systems Management American (SMA) Corporation, remembers the time years ago when he shined shoes on the corner of Monticello and Market streets in downtown Norfolk, Virginia. His best customers were executives working in the four-story department store and the 16-story Maritime Towers office building across the street. He now owns the entire block, including the store—which serves as headquarters for his company—and the office building.

SMA is a computer systems integrator serving the government and private industry. Its capabilities include manufacturing, installation, integrated logistics support, software/hardware development, configuration management, command and control, image processing, and data conversion services.

SMA has grown from a one-man operation in 1970 into a national corporation with a staff of 430. Not realizing how difficult it was going to be, Valentine "put in long hours, borrowed often from banks, and spent a lot of time on proposals for contracts he did not get." SMA is now one of the larger black-owned businesses in the United States.

An outstanding high school basketball player, Valentine wanted to play in college and the NBA, but he wanted a car more! So he took part-time jobs to buy one, finished high school, went into the army, married, and at age 23 returned to Norfolk. After earning a bachelor's degree from Norfolk State University in three years (paid for by more part-time jobs), he became an executive officer for the U.S. Department of Agriculture and later business manager for Norfolk State.

In 1970, he opened Systems Management Associates, a consulting firm for black businesses, with $5,000 he had saved. With an answering service, a post office box, and a part-time secretary, Valentine sold administrative and financial advice to black entrepreneurs and performed data processing and programming for them. Two years later, with 12 employees (mostly part-timers), he began bidding on—and winning—small government data processing jobs.

But his business really took off in 1981, when he snagged a contract to design, install, and maintain sophisticated recordkeeping computers aboard Navy ships. The Navy thought the job was too big for him, but he persuaded them to send an evaluation team, which found no reason why he could not do the job. Revenues skyrocketed for a while, and they have been as high as $60 million. Valentine has pared down his operations somewhat, but SMA continues to bid on—and be awarded—government contracts.

Valentine is concentrating on more contract diversification, which includes the government as well as the private sector, as military budget cuts begin to affect the computer industry. After closing three small offices around the country and cutting $4 million out of overhead, he and his staff are "lean and competitive."

He trains his employees—many of whom are unskilled workers—to be computer technicians and high-tech specialists. He also encourages other minority individuals to become entrepreneurs.

Questions

1. How do you explain Valentine's success?
2. To what extent do you think his diversification plan will work? Explain.
3. What suggestions would you make to him for adjusting to the changing economic environment?

Source: Author's correspondence with Systems Management American Corporation.

Case 16.2

Switchpod.com

Imagine having to balance running a successful web-based business with a customer base of over 6,000, having to answer around 100 tech support e-mails generated per day, and remembering to do your homework for your high-school physics class. One such enterprising 17 year old does this balancing act every single day, and makes a salary of $40,000 per year to boot.

Weina Scott, a senior at Krop Senior High School in North Miami Beach, Florida, runs a website named Switchpod.com where users can share video and audio as downloadable podcasts. Switchpod was founded by Weina and her 16-year-old friend Jake Fischer. Jake and Weina met on a message board dedicated to website hosting. They soon agreed to create Switchpod, and before they knew it, they were receiving 300,000 visitors per month.

Running a popular website, let alone a business, is tough stuff for anyone, let alone a teenager. Luckily for them, their success caught the eye of the owner of Wizzard Software Corp, Chris Spencer. Chris was looking for a popular podcasting website to help push Wizzard's text-to-speech software. After careful study, Chris chose Switchpod. Not long after this decision, Jake and Weina were selling their company to Wizzard for $200,000 in stock options.

Jake and Weina are now CEOs of Switchpod and both make $40,000 per year salaries. Chris was apprehensive at first when it came to hiring teenagers, but now says that he "would love to have a ton more workers just like them."

Both of the teens have learned important things from the buyout. Jake says he has "learned how to be more of a manager type," while Weina has learned how to overcome the technical hurdles, such as moving their server to London to increase download speeds. They also understand the need for more credibility: "Now it's not two teenagers running Switchpod or two people you don't know. It's a public company."

The teens haven't let the success get to their heads, however. Weina says that her friends haven't changed, "They're surprised, I guess. Maybe a bit jealous."

Questions

1. Why do you think their business has been such a success?

2. Do you think that their website would have been so successful without the buyout by Wizzard?

3. If you were Weina and Jake, what would you do next with Switchpod?

Adapted from Bridget Carey, "Tech Savvy Teen Is CEO of $200k Podcasting Website," *The Miami Herald*, September 22, 2006.

Experientials

1. Contact a local small business and ask the owner what kind of computer system (if any) the company uses in its day-to-day activities. Is it specialized to their industry or do they use off-the-shelf software?

2. Find a company's website and print out its homepage. Using the printout, identify the seven design elements.

3. List some software or hardware that is *backward compatible*.

CHAPTER 17

Risk Management, Insurance, and Crime Prevention

Everything is sweetened by risk.
  —AlexanderSmith

Assets are vital for companies to function to their maximum. The loss of an asset reduces the ability for companies to achieve this potential.
  —**Anonymous**

Carrying liability insurance these days is almost a liability in itself. . . . Premiums are rising at a fantastic rate . . . In fact, in some cases insurance coverage has become impossible to obtain—at any cost.
  —**Charles W. Patchen, CPA and writer**

Learning Objectives

After studying the material in this chapter, you should be able to:

1. Define risk and explain some ways of coping with it.

2. Explain what insurance is and show how it can be used to minimize loss due to risk.

3. Discuss some guides to be used in choosing an insurer.

4. Show how crime prevention can reduce risk and protect people and assets.

5. Discuss some techniques for safeguarding against theft.

6. Describe how to safeguard employees with preventive measures.

PROFILE

Dr. Jeffrey F. Van Petten: A Unique Entrepreneur

Jeff Van Petten's veterinary practice includes much more than traditional family pets and traditional pet care. When asked to describe his activities, he explains, "My practice is rapidly becoming an alternative medicine animal hospital that utilizes acupuncture, chiropractic, and homeopathy forms of treatment. As a professional, I like to look past the normal for better answers to problems."

Van Petten's interests and research have led to video productions, such as those dealing with "Barrel Horse Wellness." His films identify ways to diagnose musculoskeletal problems in horses and ways to prevent them.

Growing up in a rural environment gave Van Petten his love of animals and desire to keep them healthy. He is active in many associations that help him stay current on the latest discoveries and techniques in veterinary medicine. He is a member of the International Veterinary Acupuncture Society (www.IVAS.org), was certified by the society in 1991, and is now also a member of good standing in the American Academy of Veterinary Acupuncture (www.AAVA.org). Van Petten is also involved with the American Association of Equine Practitioners (www.aaep.org), the Kansas Veterinary Medical Association (in which he served on the Public Relations Committee and Chairperson Alternative Medical Providers Committee 2007), and the American Veterinary Medical Association (www.avma.org).

In addition to his many professional affiliations, Van Petten is very active in many local organizations. He is a member of the local school board, vice president High School Rodeo association, national director for Kansas, and was the First President of Meriden Chamber of Commerce. He is also on the Kansas State University Rodeo Development Council. Yet he still has time for hobbies such as hunting, fishing, roping, and riding horses.

When asked what motivates him to continue his practice, besides a love of animals, he will tell you that the pay is good. While there are approximately 66,000 veterinarians in the United States, most veterinary practices generate less than $500,000 in annual revenue.[1]

Van Petten's veterinary practice is an S corporation. Van Petten purchased his practice in 1987 with 100 percent borrowed capital. The previous owner held a contract on the building, and a local bank financed equipment and startup funds. The location on a highway, in a growing area, was very attractive, and near family and friends.

Being near family was important because, like many small businesses, Van Petten's practice is a family enterprise. Van Petten's wife, Jackie, daughter, Jolie, and son, Jarek, are supportive in many ways. Besides encouraging his involvement in professional activities and research—and tolerating the hours involved—they also pitch in as needed to help with client relations, clean cages, exercise animals, and perform any other needed support services.

The operation of veterinary medicine is affected by zoning laws and health department regulations on the size of and space available in the facilities, runoff animal waste, and handling of needles and prescription drugs. Regulations for prescription drugs for veterinary use are much the same as those for medical doctors and pharmacists.

Since there is an inherent danger in handling animals, the State of Kansas has passed the Kansas Livestock Liability Act, which was designed to create relief for both animal owners and handlers. Briefly described, it protects against liability for injury to people. This law has not been tested, so, to be on the safe side, veterinarians obtain a written release. Veterinarians also carry malpractice, professional liability, and errors and omissions insurance—in addition to the usual fire, theft, and similar coverage. Some of Van Petten's insurance is a form of self-insurance handled by the AVMA.

Source: Author's correspondence and conversations with Joyce Allen Baker and Jeffrey and Jackie Baker Van Petten.

In this chapter we will discuss some of the most prevalent risks facing you as a small business owner, such as the liability and omissions risks just mentioned in the Profile. Then we will show how you can cope with them.

The first section of the chapter deals with risk and its management; the second section, with using insurance to minimize loss due to risk; the third, with crime prevention; and the last, with how to safeguard employees with preventive measures.

Risk and Its Management

Small business losses of money and property often occur as a result of fire, severe weather, theft, lawsuits, bankruptcy, politics, and other misfortunes, as well as the death, disability, or defection of key personnel. A hurricane, fire, or tornado may destroy your property outright. Remodeling, street repairs, or flooding may temporarily close your business and reduce income. Goods may be stolen, damaged, destroyed, or spoiled in transit, for which the carrier is not liable. Banks may either call in, or refuse to renew, loans. Customers may be unable to pay accounts receivable. The government may cut back on military spending. A competitor may hire one of your key employees. Given this rogues' gallery of lurking perils, what is a small business owner or manager to do?

Risk management is the process of conserving earning power and assets by minimizing the shock from losses.

The answer is to use **risk management,** which is the process of conserving a firm's earning power and assets by minimizing the financial shocks of accidental losses. It lets a firm regain its financial balance and operating effectiveness after suffering an unexpected loss.

Types of Risk

Pure risk is the uncertainty that some unpredictable event will result in a loss.

There are two primary types of risk you will face as a small business owner. A **pure risk** is uncertainty as to whether some unpredictable event that can result in loss will occur. Pure risk always exists when the possibility of a loss is present but the possible extent of the loss is unknown. For example, the consequences of a fire, the death of a key employee, or a liability judgment against you cannot be predicted with any degree of certainty. Many of these risks, however, can be analyzed statistically and are therefore insurable.

Speculative risk is the uncertainty that a voluntarily undertaken risk will result in a loss.

On the other hand, a **speculative risk** is uncertainty as to whether a voluntarily undertaken activity will result in a gain or a loss. Production risks, such as building a plant that turns out to have the wrong capacity or keeping an inventory level that turns out to be too high or too low, are speculative risks. Speculative risk is the name of the game in business.

> **Real-World Example 17.1**
>
> For example, Levi Strauss (www.levistrauss.com) tried to sell its jeans through mass merchandisers such as Sears (www.sears.com) and Penney's (www.jcpenney.com), only to have department stores turn to Lee jeans (www.leejeans.com).

Some business risks are insurable and others uninsurable. As you know, the greatest risk facing any small business—the possibility that it will be unprofitable—is uninsurable. Other uninsurable risks are associated with the development of new products, changes in customers' preferences, price fluctuations, and changes in laws. In this chapter we deal only with insurable risks.

Ways of Coping with Risk

There are many ways you can cope with risk.* The most common of these are:

- Risk avoidance.
- Risk prevention, or loss control.
- Risk transfer.
- Risk assumption, or self-insurance.

Risk avoidance is refusing to undertake, or abandoning, an activity in which the risk seems too costly. The following classic example illustrates a case where this was necessary.

Risk avoidance is refusing to undertake an activity when the risk seems too costly.

> **Real-World Example 17.2**
>
> A New York bank experimented with having depositors of less than $5,000 either pay a fee to see a teller or use an automatic teller machine. When customers rebelled, the project was dropped as too risky.[2]

Risk prevention (loss control) is using various methods to reduce the possibility of a loss occurring.

Risk prevention, or **loss control,** consists of using various methods to reduce the probability that a given event will occur. The primary control technique is prevention, including safety and protective procedures. For example, if your business is large enough, you might try to control losses by providing first-aid offices, driver training, and work safety rules, not to mention security guards to prevent pilferage, shoplifting, and other forms of theft, as the following example illustrates.

> **Real-World Example 17.3**
>
> Many malls are now using uniformed security guards to replace plainclothes officers. For example, New Orleans' Plaza Mall has moved its security station to a glass-enclosed room in the center of the mall. Passersby can see the officers monitoring closed-circuit TV sets. Some shopping centers are even having uniformed officers patrol their parking lots on horses or bicycles.[3]

*These methods have been summed up mnemonically by Professor Charles N. Armstrong, Kansas City Community College, who points out that you can *TAME* risk: that is, you can *T*ransfer it, *A*ssume it, *M*inimize it, or *E*liminate it.

Risk transfer is shifting a risk to someone outside your company.

Risk transfer means shifting the consequences of a risk to persons or organizations outside your business. The best-known form of risk transfer is **insurance,** which is the process by which an insurance company agrees, for a fee (a premium), to pay an individual or organization an agreed-upon sum of money for a given loss. According to a recent survey, insurance was cited as the biggest problem for small businesses. Taxes are cited as the second most important issue. But because of escalating health care costs, many companies are shifting part of the risk to their employees, who must pay higher deductibles and a larger percentage of nonreimbursed expenses.

Insurance is provided by another company that agrees, for a fee, to reimburse your company for part of a loss.

Insurance for Your Business

The pathway from business startup to business success will often be filled with risks that will often mean the difference between triumph and failure. Luckily, there are ways to lessen one's vulnerability to these risks by sharing them with others. This sharing of risks among a large pool of people is the basic definition of the word *insurance*. The types of insurance and the number of insurance companies offering the products are almost too many to count.

Most new companies start up on a wing and a prayer as they are often very underfunded and have inadequate cash flow. Statistics say that most new businesses will not show a profit in the first two years. Life insurance will be needed to provide for the heirs and to pay off debts incurred for the business. If money is indeed in short supply, then the purchase of large-term insurance policies would be the short-term solution to the risk. This would also protect the insurability of the owner and provide coverage that could be converted to a permanent type of insurance when cash flow permits.

As a company grows and becomes successful, their need for life insurance for the principal often increases and these needs are usually of a permanent nature and require a permanent type of insurance. An example of that would be found in most partnerships. Suppose that Tom and Larry had started a company a few years back and now they are very successful. Tom is the outside salesman and Larry handles all the inside office work. Neither would be successful without the other. In this case, key man insurance is bought on both of them. This negates the risk caused by death as money would come into the company to enable the survivor to hire someone to do the work of the deceased partner.

Other risks that owners must be prepared for are those that pertain to health. Health insurance can be obtained to protect against catastrophic health claims, and disability insurance can be obtained to protect one from loss of income.

Most companies will have some broad form of legal risks for which some type of liability insurance will be needed. What that insurance is called is determined by the type of product or service one provides. It can range from professional liability insurance for insurance agents to medical malpractice insurance for doctors. It may be insurance to protect a company from lawsuits concerning environmental issues or insurance to protect against injury lawsuits of customers. A good insurance agent can become an invaluable asset to a business owner's team.[4]

Risk assumption (self-insurance) is setting aside funds to meet losses that are uncertain in size and frequency.

Risk assumption usually takes the form of **self-insurance,** whereby a business sets aside a certain amount of its own funds to meet losses that are uncertain in size and frequency. This method is usually impractical for very small firms because they do not have the large cash reserves needed to make it feasible.

Generally, more than one method of handling risks is used at the same time. For example, a firm may use self-insurance for automobile damage, which costs relatively little, while using commercial insurance against liability claims, which may be prohibitively high.

FIGURE 17.1 |
How to Determine
Whether You Need
Insurance

To determine how to handle business risks, ask yourself, What will happen if:

- I die or suddenly become incapacitated?
- A fire destroys my firm's building(s), machines, tools and equipment, and/or inventories?
- There is theft by an outsider, a customer, or an employee, or an employee embezzles company funds?
- My business is robbed?
- A customer is awarded a sizable settlement after bringing a product or accident liability suit against me?
- Someone, inside or outside the business, obtains unauthorized information from my computer?

Using Insurance to Minimize Loss Due to Risk

The principal value of insurance lies in its reduction of your risks from doing business. In buying insurance, you trade a potentially large but uncertain loss for a small but certain one (the cost of the premium). In other words, you trade uncertainty for certainty. But if the insurance premium is a substantial proportion of the value of the property, do not buy the insurance.

A well-designed insurance program not only compensates for losses but also provides other values, including reduction of worry, freeing funds for investment, suggestions for loss prevention techniques, and easing of credit.

In deciding what to do about business risks, you should ask yourself the questions about disasters shown in Figure 17.1. Often, when such disasters occur in small companies with inadequate or no insurance protection at all, either the owners are forced out of business or operations are severely restricted.

Types of Insurance Coverage

Because there are so many types of insurance, we will discuss only those you will need most as a small business owner.

The very minimum coverage you need is

- Fire,
- Liability, and
- Theft.

Before you actually purchase any insurance you should check out the company (www .ambest.com or www.weissratings.com) and make sure it is regulated by the insurance commissioner in your state.[5]

The basic *fire insurance policy* insures only for losses from fire and lightning and losses due to temporary removal of goods from the premises because of fire. In most instances, this policy should be supplemented by an *extended-coverage endorsement* that insures against loss from windstorm, hail, explosion, riot, aircraft, vehicle, and smoke damage. A fire can be devastating to a small business as the following example illustrates.

Real-World Example 17.4

A small formal wear company burned and accumulated about $1 million worth of damage to their clothing. An even larger problem surfaced when the owner could not contact the individuals who had contracted clothing for their weddings because the fire also eliminated all records.

Coinsurance is having the business buy insurance equal to a specific percentage of property value.

To ensure reimbursement for the full amount of covered losses, most property insurance contracts have a **coinsurance** provision. It requires policyholders to buy insurance in an amount equal to a specified percentage of the property value—say, 80 percent.

Business interruption coverage should also be provided through endorsement, because such indirect losses are frequently more severe in their eventual cost than are direct losses. For example, while rebuilding after a fire, the business must continue to pay fixed expenses such as salaries of key employees and such expenses as utilities, interest, and taxes. You also need this type of insurance for other types of business interruption.

Casualty insurance consists of automobile insurance (both collision and public liability) plus burglary, theft, robbery, plate glass, and health and accident insurance. Automobile liability and physical-damage insurance are necessary because firms may be legally liable for vehicles used on their behalf, even those they do not own. For example, when employees use their own cars on company business, the employer is liable in case of an accident.

A related type of insurance is known as *professional liability (malpractice) insurance*. This type of insurance protects the small business from suits resulting from mistakes made—or bad advice given—by someone in a professional context.

Product/service liability insurance protects a business from losses resulting from the use of its product.

Product/service liability insurance protects a business against losses resulting from the use of its product. It is particularly important for small firms because in conducting business, companies are subject to common and statutory laws governing negligence to customers, employees, and anyone else with whom they do business. One liability judgment, without adequate insurance, can easily result in the liquidation of a business. As a result, premiums for liability coverage are becoming almost prohibitive. In fact, the crisis has reached such proportions that some companies are dropping products rather than face the danger of bankruptcy. Toy manufacturers, for example, face very high rates because the statute of limitations for children continues until they are 21 or older. Product liability insurance for small toy companies average about $7,500 a year.[6]

Another growing problem for small firms is what to do about *liability when sponsoring athletic teams or some potentially dangerous activities.* Employers are facing the problem in two ways. Some are trying to get reasonably priced insurance coverage. When this is not feasible, many small firms are abandoning the practice.

As discussed in Chapter 10, *workers' compensation* policies typically provide for medical care, lump sums for death and dismemberment, and income payments for disabled workers or their dependents. There are some things owners and managers of small companies can do to improve safety. These actions, which should also help reduce premiums, include the following:

- Involve employees in safety matters.
- Establish an open, two-way communication system.
- Make participation companywide.
- Make a big deal of the safety awards that are given, and be sure awards have a reasonable value.
- Keep the program exciting.
- Be especially watchful during high-risk periods.

Group health and life insurance for employees are also important in small firms. Life insurance provides protection for an employee's estate when he or she dies while still in the income-producing years, or lives beyond that time but has little or no income. Health insurance provides protection against the risk of medical expenses, including doctor and hospital bills and prescription expenses.

Health insurance is one of the most important benefits offered by small firms, but it's also one of the less frequently used. A major cause of low coverage by small firms is the cost. Health insurance costs have increased at more than twice the inflation rate for over a decade, and some small firms have experienced 25 to 50 percent annual increases. Widely recognized as an acute problem for the entire country, this is critical for small businesses, which usually do not provide such coverage for part-time (temporary) employees. One of the toughest decisions for those who are trying to decide whether or not to open their own business is the issue of health care insurance. Not only is it very expensive, but it is also a huge part of employee expense if you choose to provide health care for your employees.

Real-World Example 17.5

Daniel Feldkamp and Randy Sowash work 14-hour days at their year-old photography studio because paying for employee health insurance would be too expensive. So rather than hire help, they opt to operate Visual Edge Imaging Studios in Beavercreek, Ohio, on their own.[7]

The Visual Edge Imaging Studios experience is not unique. In fact, it is not uncommon for proprietors of mom-and-pop businesses to be uninsured, as they cannot afford the high cost of coverage.

Small firms' average health insurance costs continue to rise. Now, like all companies, they face a "crisis in health insurance." Health care issues hit farmers particularly hard. Thirty-two percent of farmers nationwide have no health insurance and rate 28 fatalities per 100,000 workers and seven injuries or illnesses per 100 workers each year, making farming one of the 10 most dangerous professions.[8]

Finally, insurance companies treat large and small businesses differently. If a big company has a bad year, with a high total health bill, the insurer regards it as a natural occurrence and assumes that costs will decline the following year. But it is common for rates at a very small business—one with 10 to 20 people covered—to skyrocket if just one employee racks up huge health claims during the year.

Business insurance describes the use of life and disability insurance to solve financial issues of businesses and business owners.

Dan Feldkamp, left, and Randy Sowash, owners of Visual Edge Imaging Studios, work on a client's project in their studio.

Business owner's insurance is another important protection you need. **Business insurance** describes the use of life and disability insurance to solve financial issues of businesses and business owners. It consists of (1) protection of owner or dependents against loss from premature death, disability, or medical expenses and, (2) provision for the continuation of a business following the death of an owner, (3) economic loss to a business when a key employee dies, (4) disposition of a business owner's interest upon the death or separation from the business, (5) attraction and retention of valuable employees, and (6) rewarding faithful employees.[9] Also, business continuation life insurance is used in closely held corporations to provide cash on the death of an owner. The cash can be used to retire the interest of a partner or, in case of death, to repurchase the stock of a closely held corporation.

A variation of this type of insurance, called *key person insurance,* insures the life (or lives) of important employees. Key person insurance is used more often in small firms than in large ones, for a given individual can be more important to the well-being of a smaller company.

Insurers issue *fidelity and surety bonds* to guarantee that employees and others with whom the company transacts business are honest and will fulfill their contractual obligations. Fidelity bonds are purchased for employees occupying positions that involve the handling of company funds. Surety bonds provide protection against the failure of a contractor to fulfill contractual obligations. Problems with bonding restrict the growth of many small contractors.

In summary, as important as it is for small businesses to carry many types of insurance, the cost is oppressive. Still, no prudent small business owner will be without the key types of insurance discussed, for one devastating claim could ruin the business.

Guides to Choosing an Insurer

In choosing an insurer, consider the financial characteristics of the insurer, the insurer's flexibility in meeting your requirements, and the services rendered by the agent. While insurance companies have agents representing them, independent agents represent more than one company. These independent agents use the following logo:

Independent Insurance Agent

Some Red Flags to Look For   As in any industry, there are some black sheep or shady operators to look out for in choosing an insurer. To make sure you are being provided the coverage for which you have paid, be on the lookout for the following red flags:[10]

- An agent who delays giving answers, fails to hand over a policy, or neglects to provide proof of endorsements.
- Routine answers such as: "Don't worry about it, it's a computer glitch."
- A delayed premium refund.
- A hand-delivered policy instead of one sent directly from the company.
- An adjuster who says it will cost you more to process the claim than the amount of your deductible.
- Delay tactics to encourage you into a lower settlement.
- Attempts to minimize your damages to save the company from having to pay on the claim.
- Request by the adjuster to keep the claim or proposed settlement a secret.
- An offer of a new policy to replace one that is flawed.

Financial Characteristics and Flexibility of Insurer   The major types of insurers are stock companies, mutual companies, reciprocals, and Lloyd's groups. While mutuals and reciprocals are cooperatively organized and sell insurance "at cost," in practice their premiums may be no lower than those of profit-making companies. In comparing different types of insurers, you should use the following criteria:

- Financial stability and safety.
- Specialization in your type of business.
- Ability to tailor its policy to meet your needs.
- Cost of protection.

Valid comparisons of insurance coverage and its costs are difficult to make, but your insurance brokers, independent insurance advisers, or agents can assist you. In addition, the following are a few things you can do to ease the pain when your insurance comes up for renewal.

According to Amy Danise, senior managing editor for insure.com, there are five ways you can reduce the costs of insurance. They include buy policies from the same insurer, raise your deductible, check rates before you buy, look for discounts, and maintain good credit.[11]

Services Rendered by the Agent   Decide which qualifications of agents are most important, and then inquire about agents among business friends and others who have had experience with them. In comparing agents, look for contacts among insurers, professionalism, degree of individual attention, quality of service, and help in time of loss. Choose an agent who is willing and able to (1) devote enough time to your individual problems to justify the commission, (2) survey exposure to loss, (3) recommend adequate insurance and loss prevention programs, and (4) offer alternative methods of insurance.

Photo of Alfred Corina

According to Alfred Corina (<u>acorina@ft.newyorklife.com</u>), when choosing your agent, two very specific criteria come into play. The first is to understand which companies he or she can represent. Statistics seem to indicate that mutual companies are faring better in our depressed economy. Also, you should keep in mind that there are four major rating systems and they are all different. For example, an A+ rating by one company may be an excellent rating, while it may be a poor rating for another. The second is to look at the longevity of the agent you choose. With a failure rate of 85 percent, look for an agent with which you can build a longterm relationship. Chartered Life Underwriters (CLUs) are at the top of the learning curve and are a good choice. In searching out the investment arena look for the designations of Chartered Financial Consultant (ChFC), Certified Financial Planner (CFP),[12] or the even more proficient Registered Investment Advisor (RIA).

Crime Prevention to Protect People and Assets

Small business owners need to practice crime prevention to reduce risks and protect their assets. Not only do you need to prevent major crimes, such as armed robbery, theft, and white-collar crimes, but you also need protection from trespassing, vandalism, workplace violence (http://apps.opm.gov/publications), and harassment.

An awareness of the potential dangers helps to minimize the risks involved and reduces losses from crime. It is impossible to have a security program that will prevent all criminal acts, so you can only hope to minimize their occurrence and severity. In order to reduce workplace violence you must work at "keeping the peace." Steven and Jane Bahls recommend the following:

- Adopt a zero-tolerance policy.
- Screen carefully.
- Train supervisors to recognize personality changes and warning signs.
- Defuse disputes.
- Check and double-check security.
- Terminate with care—then change the locks.[13]

A study conducted by America's Research Group Inc. revealed that more than a third of American customers have changed their shopping habits because of safety concerns. The study found that 42 percent of shoppers no longer shop after dark, 25 percent keep car doors locked, 15 percent refuse to shop alone, and 60 percent are very uneasy about carrying large amounts of money. Businesses are suffering as a consequence.

Law enforcement agencies and the business community are learning to identify areas particularly susceptible to crime. Crimes appear to fall into patterns. Armed robbery may occur frequently in one type of neighborhood, theft in another, and both in a third. A prospective business owner needs to evaluate a potential site with this problem in mind. Examples of sites that appear to be particularly vulnerable to criminal acts are public housing projects, low-rent neighborhoods, areas of high unemployment, and areas with a high incidence of illiteracy.

Criminal acts have forced not only small but even large businesses into insolvency. Armed robbery, theft, and white-collar crimes are the major crimes affecting small firms.

Armed Robbery

In recent years, the number of armed robberies has increased significantly. The Bureau of Labor Statistics reports that "about 18,000 clerks are victims of nonlethal assaults annually." Around the turn of the twenty-first century, OSHA issued suggested safety guidelines specifically for convenience stores. Included were (1) adequate lighting, (2) video cameras, (3) increased night staff levels, (4) alarms, and (5) bulletproof glass. OSHA also suggested better training for managers and clerks and emergency procedures for dangerous situations.[14]

Armed robbers usually enter a business's premises with the intent of obtaining cash or valuable merchandise and leave as quickly as possible to minimize the risk of identification or apprehension. Since time is critical in such circumstances, locations that afford easy access and relatively secure escape routes seem most vulnerable. This type of criminal usually wants to be in and out of the location in three minutes or less, and the pressure of the situation tends to make the robber more dangerous.

Several measures can be taken to reduce the chances of being robbed. They include modifying the store's layout, securing entrances, using security dogs, controlling the handling of cash, and redesigning the surrounding area.

Modifying Store Layout   Location of the cash register and high visibility inside and from outside the store are important in preventing armed robbery. If robbers cannot dash in, scoop up the cash, and dash out again within a short time, they aren't as likely to attempt the robbery, as the following example shows.

Real-World Example 17.6

One convenience food chain removed from the windows all material that would obstruct the view into the store. In addition, it encouraged crowds at all hours with various gimmicks and attracted police officers by giving them free coffee. The average annual robbery rate dropped markedly.

Securing Entrances   The security of entrances and exits is extremely important in preventing robbery. Windows and rear doors should be kept locked and barred. In high-crime neighborhoods, many businesses use tough, shock-resistant transparent materials in their windows instead of glass.

Using Security Dogs   Security dogs are trained to be vicious on command. Business people have found these animals to be effective deterrents against armed robbers. When 589 convicted criminals were asked how best to foil burglars, the largest number—15.8 percent—said, "Have a dog." However, health and sanitation regulations in some jurisdictions may prevent the use of dogs.

Controlling the Handling of Cash   Making daily cash deposits and varying the deposit time from day to day are highly recommended. Some modern cash registers are designed to signal "too much cash" and will not operate until an employee has removed the excess to a safe and reset the register with a key. Banks and other businesses rigidly enforce maximum-cash-on-hand rules for cash drawers to reduce losses in the event of an armed robbery.

Many businesses hide safes in unobtrusive places and limit knowledge of their combinations to only one or two people. It is not uncommon for a sign to be posted on the safe, or near it, advising that the person on duty does not have access to the combination or saying, "Notice: Cash in drawer does not exceed $50." Other stores, such as gas stations, use locked cash boxes and accept only correct change, credit cards, and/or payment through secured windows during certain hours.

Redesigning the Surroundings   Well-lighted parking lots help deter robbers. If possible, try to keep vehicles from parking too near the entrance to your business. Armed robbery can be reduced by making access less convenient. For example, many convenience food store parking lots have precast concrete bumper blocks distributed so as to deter fast entry into and exit from the lot. Also, some businesses use silent alarms, video cameras to photograph crime in action, or video cameras tied to TV monitors in a security office.

The National Crime Prevention Council's Bureau of Justice Statistics has suggested a number of ways to make your workplace safer. In addition to those already mentioned, these include (1) requiring identification from delivery or repair people or strangers seeking confidential information, (2) calling police or security people if you notice anyone—or anything—suspicious, (3) asking a co-worker or security guard to escort you to your car or a cab, and (4) when working late, trying to arrange for someone else to work—or stay—with you.[15]

"The salesman said it was the most effective home security system on the market."

(Source: Reprinted from *The Wall Street Journal*, permission Cartoon Features Syndicate.)

Theft

Theft is always a serious problem for businesses. According to the Centre for Retail Research (www.retailresearch.org), in 2011, retail shrinkage in North America amounted to over $45 billion, globally $119 billion, or 1.45 percent of retail sales. Apparel tops the list at 1.87 percent followed by health/beauty/pharmacy at 1.79 percent. Because of the extent of the problem, many national merchandising businesses add 2 to 3 percent to their prices to cover the cost of theft, but even this may not be enough to compensate for the total loss. The two major types of theft are (1) theft by outsiders, usually known as shoplifting, and (2) theft by employees (see Figure 17.2). Retailers sometimes refer to losses from both kinds of theft as *shrinkage.*

Shoplifting   Shoplifting is a major hazard for retail establishments. Professional shoplifters, not amateurs and kleptomaniacs, cause the greatest prevention problems. The amateur may be a thrill seeker who takes an item or two to see whether or not he or she can get away with it. (This is often the case with children and teenagers.) The kleptomaniac has an uncontrollable urge to take things, whether needed or not. Kleptomaniacs and amateurs are more easily detected than professional shoplifters, who may wear specially equipped clothing or baggy garments, carry large handbags, or use an empty box to conceal stolen merchandise to be picked up by an accomplice. Business owners and managers are often shocked by the techniques people use to remove merchandise from their premises, and by the people who do it.

Real-World Example 17.7

A well-known Houston matron was at the checkout counter. Upon inspection, her large purse was found to contain several prepackaged steaks and packages of luncheon meat. The store owner observed, "I thought she was one of our best customers. She has been coming here for years. I wonder how much she has taken."

A new twist on shoplifting is high-tech. For example: Shoppers purchase inexpensive items and reproduce the bar code. While shopping at a later date, they pasted the copied bar code to expensive items and then paid the cheap price. These high-tech criminals then resell on the Web.

Retailers are now striking back at shoplifters by means of a new tactic called *civil recovery,* or *civil restitution,* demanding payment of shoplifters or their parents for the items taken. Some states permit not only recovery of the amount stolen but also damage awards for additional costs of crime prevention, damage to displays, or injuries resulting from the crime.

Employee Theft   According to John Warren, associate general counsel for the Association of Certified Fraud Examiners, "Employee theft is the single most expensive form of crime . . . there is in this country."[16] As shown in Figure 17.2, employee theft is the major source of inventory loss in the retail industry. It may range from the simple act of an individual who takes only small items (such as pens or paper clips) to raids by groups that remove truckloads of merchandise. According to the TV program *Justice Files,* one out of every 33 employees is accused of theft each year.[17] As you can see from Figure 17.3, Global retailers lost more than $45.5 billion in 2010 from shoplifting and theft.

Sometimes employees conspire with outsiders to steal from their employers—for example, by charging the outsiders a lower price or by placing additional merchandise in accomplices' packages.

FIGURE 17.2 |

Look Who's Stealing
(Sources of Inventory
Loss in the Global
Retail Industry)

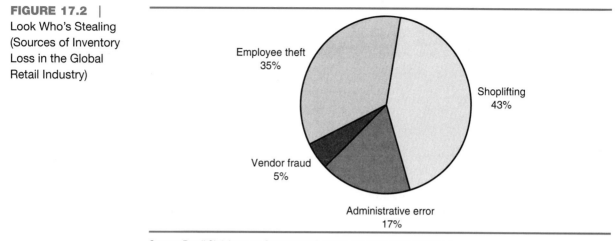

Source: Retail Shrinkage by Country 2010, by the Centre for Retail Research.

Who Steals?   Research has shown that employees who think their income is too low, or stagnating, steal more often and in greater amounts than other employees. A study showed that those who steal tend to be young, full-time employees operating alone, and that they steal merchandise more often than cash.[18] A classic study found that the high turnover rate among temporary employees can cause serious security problems.[19]

Techniques for Preventing Theft   Retail establishments have found the use of the following measures effective in reducing theft:

- Wide-angle and one-way mirrors to observe employee or customer behavior.

- TV cameras, tied to monitors, to observe a large area of the store. For example, there are many new types of monitors that are wireless and can be moved from time to time. These can also have audio capabilities.[20]

- Electronic noise activators—some visible to customers, some not—to warn of unprocessed merchandise leaving the store.

- Paper-and-pencil tests of a potential employee's honesty.

FIGURE 17.3 |

Source: Retail Shrinkage by Country 2010, by the Centre for Retail Research.

- Security guards, if economically feasible.
- Security audits, such as the following:

   Unannounced spot checks of critical activity areas, such as cash registers, employees' packages, car trunks, lunch pails, and waste disposal holding areas.

   Visible security surveillance of work activities.

   Weekly, monthly, or quarterly physical inventory checks.

In addition to using dogs and security guards, construction contractors have found the following measures effective:

- Scheduling operations and purchasing materials for just-in-time delivery.
- Scheduling lower inventory levels on weekends.
- Fencing and lighting storage yards and clearing the area adjacent to the fence.
- Using locking systems that are difficult to jimmy.
- Unannounced rotation of the person responsible for receiving materials.
- Assigning a trusted employee the responsibility for checking materials or equipment into the job site, to prevent problems such as that in the following example.

Real-World Example 17.8

A contractor purchased a mobile concrete mixer and sent it to the site of one of his jobs. Those responsible for the mixer left it outside the fenced-in area that night, and it was stolen. Later, the contractor found that a subordinate had failed to record it for insurance coverage.

White-Collar Crime

Another category of serious and rapidly rising abuse against small businesses is white-collar crime. Factors such as reduced company loyalty, global economic turmoil, faulty pension systems, lack of corporate exposure, and more sophisticated technology are causing such crimes to boom worldwide.

White-collar crimes
are those committed by managerial, professional, and technical employees.

Types of White-Collar Crimes   **White-collar crimes** are primarily committed by managerial, professional, and technical employees. They include the falsification of accounts; fraudulent accessing and manipulating of the computer; bribing of purchasing agents and other officials; collusion that results in unrecorded transactions; sale of proprietary information; and sabotage of new technology, new or old products, or customer relations. According to an earlier survey, white-collar crime adds 15 to 20 percent to the price of everything we buy.

The pirating of information and technology is particularly troubling, as it is mushrooming in scope and complexity. According to Kevin Reirson, president of the Minnesota branch of Ross Engineering, a company that evaluates businesses for vulnerability to information theft, "All types of businesses are targets of espionage: large and small—even the local pizza parlor."[21]

Computer security is becoming a real problem for small firms. Not only has the number of computer crimes increased, but so has their magnitude. The two main problems are intentional destruction of data and fraudulent use.

Ways to Minimize White-Collar Crime   The passage of the Economic Espionage Act in 1996 made the theft of business-related intellectual property a crime.[22] Still, special measures must be taken to minimize crimes by white-collar personnel. Some deterrents you can use include audits, being aware of employee work habits, identification, and bonding. Also, as mentioned above, small firms that use computers may need the services of a firm with computer security expertise. Audits of data such as past sales transactions, inventory levels, purchase prices, and accounts receivable may uncover undesirable activities. Ralph Nader suggests a dozen reforms for cracking down on corporate crime:

- Track the extent and cost of corporate crime.
- Increase corporate crime prosecution budgets.
- Ban corporate criminals from government contracts.
- Crack down on corporate tax avoidance.
- Restore the rights of defrauded investors.
- Democratize corporate governance.
- Rein in excessive executive pay.
- Regulate derivatives trading.
- Expand disclosure.
- End conflicts of interest on Wall Street.
- Fix the pension system.
- Foster a national discussion on corporate power.[23]

How can you protect yourself? You should be aware of your white-collar employees' work habits. They may all be open and aboveboard, but they should be checked. You should ask such questions as: Do they work nights regularly? Do they never take a day off? Do they forgo their usual vacation? Standards of living, dress, car, housing, entertainment, and travel that seem to cost more than an employee should be able to afford often signal economic misconduct.

Proper identification, along with a device that takes pictures of a check and the person cashing it, tends to discourage bad-check artists. Although this practice may be too expensive for your small firm, your bank may assist in developing effective identification procedures. Many states have passed bad-check laws, which permit a business that receives a bad check to collect not only its face value but also double or triple damages in small claims court. This financial penalty helps to reduce loss.

Because credit cards are frequently stolen, additional identification should be required. Be sure the signature corresponds to the one on the card. Also, you should be sure to ascertain the validity of trade documents, such as invoices and securities. Each year, millions of dollars are lost by businesspeople through carelessness that allows others to palm off bogus documents.

Fidelity bonding helps insure against employee fraud or theft. The employer pays a premium to an insurance company, which then assumes the risk and reimburses the company for any loss.

Document Security

Our personal experience working with small businesses, as well as press releases in recent years, has made us aware of the importance of document security. As shown in Chapter 16, *information is a vital factor in managing and controlling business activities, and its management and maintenance help to ensure the continuation of the business.* The life of your business depends on the appropriate recording of information, its transmission to the appropriate persons, and its security. Records with confidential information should be stored in bank lockboxes, safes, or restricted areas, and only authorized persons should have access to them. And all records should be protected by backups.

As previously mentioned, the proprietary nature of confidential business records and various documents makes it essential that you protect them from unauthorized eyes and hands. The trade secrets and competitive advantage of your business may be lost if this information passes into the wrong hands. Therefore, a list of authorized personnel should be prepared and provided to those responsible for document security. Also, even the smallest companies should have security policies to protect sensitive business information.[24]

An unbending rule should be that under no circumstance is it permissible to remove confidential material from the restricted area or from the business premises. Some business owners think they can save on personnel costs by permitting material to be carried to an employee's residence where the employee works on the firm's records after hours. The chance of loss, the opportunity for access by unauthorized persons, and the risk of a claim for adequate compensation make this practice inadvisable.

Safeguarding Employees with Preventive Measures

Within a business, various types of accidents and health problems occur, causing potential losses. The use of insurance to eliminate or minimize disastrous financial losses to a company was discussed earlier in this chapter. In addition, safeguards can be instituted to reduce human suffering as well as costs to a company and employees.

Employees are a valuable resource that you should protect through proper safety procedures as shown in Chapter 10. *These procedures should be preventive in nature.* Not only should you provide a safe workplace for workers, but, in addition, they must work safely, since most accidents occur because of human error such as driving an automobile carelessly or handling equipment improperly. Guards over moving tools, devices to keep hands away or stop machines, employee protective gear, warnings of unsafe conditions, and medical treatment are some safeguards used to protect employees from accidents and health problems and to prevent lawsuits.

On April 28, 1998, the Occupational Safety and Health Administration (OSHA) (www.osha.gov) released a set of federal guidelines for curbing late-night retail crime. As homicide is the second-leading cause of work-related fatalities (estimated to be about 15 percent of fatal work injuries), these guidelines are supposed to reduce that hazard. But Peter Eide, manager of labor law policy at the U.S. Chamber of Commerce (www.uschamber.com), said, "We see some problems with it [as] it could be cited as grounds for a lawsuit."[25] Lawyers said they were already getting calls from employers worried that they could be held liable if the "voluntary" guidelines were not followed.

Two of the guidelines, recommending bulletproof glass and surveillance cameras, were estimated to hit smaller employers especially hard. According to Mary Leon of the National Federation of Independent Business, "The costs are excessive for small convenience stores."[26]

What You Should Have Learned

1. One of the greatest challenges for small businesses is dealing with risk. Risk management minimizes financial shocks. Pure risk of losses is unpredictable and uncertain, but it is often measurable and insurable. Speculative risk is uncertainty about gain or loss from voluntary decisions and is not insurable. Risk may be avoided, prevented, assumed (self-insurance), or transferred through insurance.

2. Insurance can be used to minimize losses due to risks. Small businesses usually need the following types of insurance: (*a*) fire, (*b*) business interruption, (*c*) casualty, (*d*) professional liability, (*e*) product/service liability, (*f*) liability while sponsoring athletic teams and/or other dangerous activities, (*g*) workers' compensation, (*h*) health, (*i*) death or disability of owner, (*j*) key person insurance, and (*k*) fidelity and surety bonds.

3. In choosing an insurer, consider its financial characteristics, flexibility in meeting your requirements, and the services it renders. An insurance company can be judged on financial stability, specialization in types of coverage, ability to tailor policies to meet your needs, and cost of protection.

4. Although businesses should be insured against losses, they should also take steps to prevent crimes—armed robbery, theft, and white-collar crime, especially computer crimes. Measures that can reduce the chances of being robbed include modifying the store's layout, securing entrances, using security dogs, controlling the handling of cash, and redesigning the surrounding area.

5. Theft includes shoplifting by outsiders and employee theft. Security measures to reduce theft include wide-angle and one-way mirrors, bullet-resistant glass, TV cameras, electronic noise activators on merchandise, screening of prospective employees, security guards, and security audits.

   White-collar crime includes removal of cash; falsification of accounts; fraudulent computer access and manipulation; bribery; collusion resulting in unrecorded transactions; sale of proprietary information; and sabotage of new technology, products, or customer relations. Ways to minimize white-collar crime include auditing of records, observing employees' work habits, requiring proper identification with checks and credit cards, and fidelity bonding. Confidential documents should be stored in bank lockboxes, safes, or restricted areas.

6. A small firm has a special responsibility to protect employees, to provide a safe workplace, and to encourage employees to maintain safe work habits.

Key Terms

business insurance 449	pure risk 444	risk prevention
coinsurance 448	risk assumption (self-	(loss control) 445
insurance 446	insurance) 446	risk transfer 446
product/service liability	risk avoidance 445	speculative risk 444
insurance 448	risk management 444	white-collar crimes 456

Questions for Discussion

1. What is meant by risk management?
2. Distinguish between pure risk and speculative risk as they apply to small businesses.
3. Discuss four ways small firms can cope with risk.
4. What are some considerations in determining a small business's need for insurance?

5. What types of insurance are commonly carried by small businesses? Describe each type of coverage.

6. What criteria should you use in choosing an insurer?

7. Discuss some methods a small business can use to reduce the chances of being robbed.

8. What is meant by white-collar crime? What are some ways to minimize it?

9. What are some methods used to safeguard employees?

Case 17.1

Beware of "Softlifting"

These days, even the smallest of businesses are using computers. As mentioned in Chapter 16, the computer has replaced the file cabinet, resulting in a great need for computer security. When we think about computer security we generally think in terms of protecting the equipment or the data on the hard disk. However, there is another type of computer security that business owners must be aware of, namely, guarding against "softlifting." A business owner who has more than one computer may be tempted to buy one copy of the needed software and install it on all the computers to save money. DO NOT DO IT!

This is softlifting and it's a very common problem. According to the Software Publishers Association (SPA), one in five personal computer programs in use today is an illegal copy. Software bootlegging costs U.S. software publishers $1.2 billion each year, on sales of only $6 to $7 billion. This is why "Software Police" are cracking down hard and the penalties are harsh. Softlifting recently became a felony with penalties of up to $250,000 and five years in jail.

The University of Oregon Continuation Center in Eugene, Oregon, thought it would "save a few bucks" by softlifting. But it got caught and had to pay a $130,000 fine and hold a national conference on copyright laws and software use.

Parametrix Inc. of Seattle also learned the hard way. It was raided by the "Software Police," who had a search warrant and were accompanied by a U.S. marshal. The raid turned up dozens of bootlegged copies of software programs. Parametrix agreed to pay fines totaling $350,000. How does the SPA find out about these abuses? The tip-off usually comes from a call to the SPA's toll-free piracy hotline. Often the caller is an ex-employee or a disgruntled employee who is seeking revenge. More and more companies are getting caught. Obviously, thousands don't get caught, but since 1984 the SPA has conducted 75 raids and filed more than 300 lawsuits.

The best advice is: *Stay legal!* Do not risk losing the business you have worked so hard to build just to save a few bucks, because according to the SPA, if you're softlifting you are definitely living on borrowed time.

Questions

1. How severe do you perceive this problem to be? Why or why not?

2. Are you aware of any organizations that have participated in "softlifting"? If so, do they deserve to be caught and punished, in your opinion?

3. How can a small business owner prevent employees from making bootlegged copies of software programs for themselves?

4. You have a small business with five computers. Your old software is obsolete and must be replaced, but your business is struggling financially. Would you risk buying one copy of the software and installing it on all five machines? Explain why or why not.

Source: From "Companies, Beware of 'Software Police,'" Associated Press release, in *Mobile* (Alabama) *Press Register*, November 16, 1992, p. 5B. Used by permission of the Associated Press, via Valeo Intellectual Property.

Case 17.2

When Inventory and Sales Don't Balance

Jeff Thomas, manager of a clothing store in Dallas, Texas, observed that over the past several months, inventory and sales were not equal. When he began to compare evening and daytime sales, he noticed that sales were staying the same, but the inventory count was lower in the evening than in the morning. Most of his 20 employees are on alternate schedules from daytime to evening. In an effort to curb possible stealing, Jeff began taking inventory more frequently and keeping a tighter control over the employees he put in charge of inventory counting and control.

Questions

1. What are some ways Jeff can improve security?
2. How can Jeff detect whether an employee is stealing?

Experientials

1. Assess your risk. Canvass insurance providers in your area, and compare rates and coverage for both auto and renters insurance.
2. Examine the credentials of each agent contacted in Experiential 1. What did you learn?

Workbook for Developing a Successful Business Plan

I. Introduction

A. What Is a Business Plan?

The business plan is probably the most useful and important document you, as a current or prospective small business owner, will ever put together. It is a written statement setting forth the business's mission and objectives, its operational and financial details, its ownership and management structure, and how it hopes to achieve its objectives.

B. What Is the Purpose of a Business Plan?

A well-developed and well-presented business plan can provide you with a "road map to riches"—or at least a pathway to a satisfactory profit. There are at least five reasons for preparing a business plan, which include the following:

1. It provides a blueprint, or plan, to follow in developing and operating the business. It helps keep your creativity on target and helps you concentrate on taking the actions that are needed to achieve your goals and objectives.

2. It can serve as a powerful money-raising tool.

3. It can be an effective communication tool for attracting and dealing with personnel, suppliers, customers, providers of capital, and others. It helps them understand your goals and operations.

4. It can help you develop as a manager, because it provides practice in studying competitive conditions, promotional opportunities, and situations that can be advantageous to your business. Thus, it can help you operate your business more effectively.

5. It provides an effective basis for controlling operations so you can see if your actions are following your plans.

   In summary, the plan performs three important functions: (1) being an effective communication tool to convey ideas, research findings, and proposed plans to others, especially financiers; (2) serving as a blueprint for organizing and managing the new venture; and (3) providing a measuring device, or yardstick, by which to gauge progress and evaluate needed changes.

C. What Is Included in a Business Plan?

Regardless of the specific format used, an effective plan *should include at least* the following:

1. Cover sheet.
2. Executive summary.

3. Table of contents.

4. History of the (proposed) business.

5. Description of the business.

6. Description of the market.

7. Description of the product(s).

8. Ownership and management structure.

9. Objectives and goals.

10. Financial analysis.

11. Appendixes.

II. How to Prepare a Business Plan

You should start by considering your business's background, origins, philosophy, mission, and objectives. Then, you should determine the means for fulfilling the mission and obtaining the objectives. A sound approach is to (1) determine where the business is at present (if an ongoing business) or what is needed to get the business going, (2) decide where you would like the business to be at some point in the future, and (3) determine how to get there; in other words, determine the best strategies for accomplishing the objectives in order to achieve your mission.

The following is one feasible approach you can use in preparing a business plan:

1. Survey consumer demands for your product(s) and decide how to satisfy those demands.

2. Ask questions that cover everything from your firm's target market to its long-run competitive prospects.

3. Establish a long-range strategic plan for the entire business and its various parts.

4. Develop short-term detailed plans for every aspect of the business, involving the owner(s), managers, and key employees, if feasible.

5. Plan for every facet of the business's structure, including finances, operations, sales, distribution, personnel, and general and administrative activities.

6. Prepare a business plan that will use your time and that of your personnel most effectively.

III. How to Use This Business Plan Workbook

This workbook is a detailed, practical, how-to approach to researching and preparing an actual business plan. It is designed so that you can answer the questions that are asked or find the information that is called for, record it in the spaces provided, and prepare the final plan.

A. Sources of Information

There are several possible sources of information you can use in preparing this workbook. First, we have included a case study of an actual business (the name has been disguised at the request of the owner) that contains most of the information—except the location—that you will need to complete the workbook. A second source is a business with which you trade, the business of a friend or relative, or some other business that will be willing to provide the information.

Finally, you may want to come up with a possible business to start on your own. In that case, you would start from scratch, gathering the information you need to complete the workbook.

B. Completing the Workbook

The workbook should be completed essentially in two stages. The first stage is to gather the information beginning with Item 4, History of the (Proposed) Business, and going through Item 11, Appendixes.

After this information is gathered and recorded, come back and complete Item 1, Cover Sheet; Item 2, Executive Summary; and Item 3, Table of Contents.

Finally, type (or word process) the information from the worksheet into a final form (such as the example at the end of Chapter 6).

Item 1, Cover Sheet   On the cover sheet you should include identifying information so that readers will immediately know the business name, address, and phone number; the names and titles of the principals; and the date the plan was prepared.

1. Cover Sheet
Business name, address, and phone number:

_____

_____

_____

Principals: _____

_____

_____

Date: _____

Item 2, Executive Summary   The executive summary should be a succinct statement of the purpose of the plan. Thus, it should be designed to motivate the reader to go on to the other sections of the plan. It should convey a sense of excitement, challenge, plausibility, credibility, and integrity. Even though the summary is the second item in the plan, *it should be written last, after the rest of the plan has been developed.* Remember, *the executive summary is just that—a summary—so keep it short!*

2. Executive Summary
Brief summary of plan

_____

_____

_____

_____

_____

_____

_____

_____

Major objectives

_____

_____

_____

_____

_____

_____

_____

_____

Description of product(s)

_____

_____

_____

_____

_____

_____

Marketing strategy

_____

_____

_____

_____

_____

_____

_____

Financial projections

_____

_____

_____

_____

_____

_____

_____

_____

_____

Item 3, Table of Contents   Because the table of contents provides the reader an overview of what is contained in the plan itself, it should be written and presented concisely, in outline form, using numerical and alphabetical designations for headings and subheadings.

3. Table of Contents (each section listed, with subheads)

_____

_____

_____

_____

_____

_____

_____

_____

_____

_____

_____

_____

_____

_____

_____

_____

_____

_____

_____

_____

_____

_____

_____

_____

_____

_____

_____

_____

_____

_____

_____

_____

Item 4, History of the (Proposed) Business   The history of the (proposed) business should include a discussion of how the idea for the business, or product, originated and what has been done to develop the idea up to this point. If the owners or managers have been in business before, and their experience is pertinent to the success of the business, include that information. Other relevant background information on the persons, products, capitalization, source(s), funds, and anything else of potential interest to the readers should also be included.

    4. History of the Business
       Background of the principals, and/or company origins

_____

_____

_____

_____

_____

_____

_____

_____

       Background of the product(s)

_____

_____

_____

_____

_____

_____

_____

_____

Corporate structure

_____

_____

_____

_____

_____

_____

_____

_____

Capitalization, or source of funds

_____

_____

_____

_____

_____

_____

_____

_____

_____

Brief outline of company successes or experiences, if any

_____

_____

_____

_____

_____

_____

_____

_____

Item 5, Description of the Business   Item 5 is the place to define your business, as you see it. Therefore, you should essentially answer such questions as: What business am I in? What services do I provide? This item should include more than just a statement of plans and a listing of activities. It should tell readers what customer needs the business intends to meet. In writing this component, try to put yourself in the position of the reader and include information that potential investors, customers, employees, and community members in general might need to assess your plan.

  5. Description of the Business

_____

_____

_____

_____

_____

_____

_____

_____

_____

Item 6, Description of the Market   The description of the market is one of the most important—but most difficult—items of the plan for you to develop. In it, you should try to answer such questions as: Who will buy my product? Where is my market? What is my sales strategy? What marketing strategy(ies) will I use? Who buys what, when, where, and why? What are my customers like? Who constitutes my target market (or what special niche am I aiming for)? You should also look at your competition and appraise it carefully, showing any weaknesses it has that you are able to, and plan to, exploit.

6. Description of the Market
   Target market: Who? How many?

_____

_____

_____

_____

_____

_____

_____

_____

   Market pentetration projections and strategies

_____

_____

_____

_____

_____

_____

_____

_____

_____

Analysis of competition: How many? Strengths and weaknesses?

_____

_____

_____

_____

_____

_____

_____

_____

Item 7, Description of the Product(s)   Item 7 should describe all of your existing or planned products, including services to be performed as well as goods to be produced. You should also look at any research and development activities and new plans to improve or redevelop the product, along with any patents, trademarks, and copyrights you hold—or that are pending.

7. Description of the Product(s)
    What is to be developed or sold?

_____

_____

_____

_____

_____

_____

_____

_____

_____

Status of research and development

_____

_____

_____

_____

_____

_____

_____

Patents, trademarks, copyrights

_____

_____

_____

_____

_____

_____

Item 8, Ownership and Management Structure   Item 8 is the place to describe the owner(s), including those you identified by name and title in Item 1. Here you would want to give more detail about their experience and expertise. Also, you should describe your management team, along with their abilities, training and development, and experience. Then, designate who will carry out the plan once it is enacted. Finally, something should be included about organizational structure, including employee policies and procedures.

8. Ownership and Management Structure
    Owners and their expertise

_____

_____

_____

_____

_____

_____

_____

    Managers and their abilities, training and development, and experience

_____

_____

_____

_____

_____

_____

_____

Organizational structure

_____

_____

_____

_____

_____

_____

_____

_____

_____

Item 9, Objectives and Goals   In essence, your objectives and goals outline what you plan to accomplish in your business, as well as showing how it will be done. Include such items as sales and revenue forecasts; marketing plans, including how sales are to be made and what advertising, sales promotion, and publicity will be used; manufacturing plans, including provisions for quality assurance and control; and financial plans (but not the specific financial data, ratios, or analyses, which are in the next item).

9. Objectives and Goals
   Revenue forecasts

_____

_____

_____

_____

_____

_____

_____

_____

Marketing plans

_____

_____

_____

_____

_____

_____

_____

_____

How sales are to be made

_____

_____

_____

_____

_____

_____

_____

_____

Advertising and sales promotion

_____

_____

_____

_____

_____

_____

_____

_____

_____

Manufacturing plans

_____

_____

_____

_____

_____

_____

_____

_____

Quality assurance plans

_____

_____

_____

_____

_____

_____

_____

_____

_____

Financial plans

_____

_____

_____

_____

_____

_____

_____

_____

Item 10, Financial Analyses   Because one purpose of the plan is to attract prospective investors or lenders, Item 10 is the place in the plan where you can indicate the expected financial results of your operations. It should show prospective investors or lenders *why* they should provide funds, *when* they can realistically expect a return, and *what* the expected return on their money *should* be. While you must make assumptions—or educated guesses—at this point, you should at least try to include projected income statements and balance sheets for up to three years, as well as projected cash flow analyses for the first year by months. There should be an analysis of costs/volume/profits, where appropriate. Finally, you should provide projected statements of changes in financial position that you anticipate. If practical, you might want to provide some financial ratios.

10. Financial Data
   Projected income statements (three years)

_____

_____

_____

_____

_____

_____

_____

_____

Projected balance sheets (three years)

_____

_____

_____

_____

_____

_____

_____

_____

Projected cash flow analyses (first year, by months)

_____

_____

_____

_____

_____

_____

_____

_____

Cost/volume/profit analyses, where appropriate

_____

_____

_____

_____

_____

_____

_____

_____

_____

Projected statements of changes in financial position

_____

_____

_____

_____

_____

_____

_____

_____

Financial ratios, if practical

_____

_____

_____

_____

_____

_____

_____

_____

_____

Item 11, Appendixes   In the appendixes you can include pertinent information about yourself and your business that is not included elsewhere in the plan. Some possible details to include are (1) narrative history of firm; (2) organizational structure (if not done in Item 8), including management structure, organization chart(s), and résumés of key people; (3) major assumptions you have made in preparing the plan; (4) brochures or other published information describing the product(s) and services you provide; (5) letters of recommendation or endorsement; (6) historical financial information, for the past three years (if not done in Item 10); (7) details of objectives and goals; and (8) catalog sheets, photographs, or technical information.

11. Appendixes

Use separate sheet(s) of paper to write this information.

_____

_____

_____

_____

_____

_____

_____

_____

IV. Sample Case: CleanDrum Inc. (CDI)

For nine years, Sue Ley served as a forklift truck operator for a local oil company. Then she drove a tractor-trailer for the company for four more years. Tiring of this type of work, and thinking she would like to get into selling, she applied to participate in the company's education program, which paid tuition for employees taking college courses, and was accepted.

Sue enrolled in the marketing program at the local university. While continuing to drive the truck, she completed her marketing course work in three years and graduated with a bachelor's degree in business administration. But when she applied for a transfer to the marketing department, she was told that it would be "four or five years" before there would be an opening for her.

Sue's uncle, who had taken over her grandfather's steel oil drum cleaning business, suggested that she start a similar business. Assuring her that she could make about $100,000 per year ($300,000 by the third year) if she founded a business of this sort, he offered to help her get the business started. She could not see any future with the oil company in marketing and did not want to drive trucks the rest of her life. Having saved $25,000 that she could put into the business, she decided to take a chance and start her own company.

History of the Business

Sue approached the local Small Business Development Center (SBDC) to find out if there was a large enough market for such a company in her area. The center arranged for two members of the local chapter of SCORE (the Service Corps of Retired Executives) to work with Sue. The Center's survey of 200 firms confirmed that a sufficient market existed for a "quality operation." While other firms were performing a similar service, their quality was not high enough to be considered true competition.

In 1993, using information provided by her uncle, Sue had an accounting firm prepare projected balance sheets, income statements, and changes in cash for five years. Sales projections were for 31,000 units in 1993 and up to 50,000 in 1998. Sales were estimated to be $367,000 in 1993, up to $558,000 in 1998, and net income was estimated to increase from $9,000 to $62,000.

Armed with these projections, and at the request of her banker, Sue approached potential customers and obtained letters indicating their willingness to do business with her "if high quality, good service, and competitive prices were offered."

Sue then prepared a business plan. On the basis of the plan, the SBDC report, financial projections, the letters, a personal history, and interviews with the loan officer, the bank approved a $60,000 loan. Adding her $25,000 as equity, Sue had a lawyer draw up incorporation papers for CleanDrum Inc. (CDI). Sue was ready to enter the business of buying, straightening, cleaning, painting, and selling used 55-gallon steel drums; and buying, cleaning, and selling used plastic drums for transporting and storing oil, chemicals, and similar products.

She started by renting a building. Her uncle then arranged for purchase of the necessary machinery (at a "special" price of $59,000). (She later learned that he had bankrupted her grandfather's business and that the quality of the equipment he had purchased was "suspect.")

When the machinery arrived, her uncle failed to come to supervise its installation. It took Sue three months to hire mechanics, plumbers, and electricians to set up and connect the equipment, and to hire and train six laborers to operate the machinery. She studied her uncle's plant for two weeks to learn enough to enable her to run CDI. All these extra activities delayed her startup and drained much of her cash.

Sue sold only 500 drums during the first month of operation, which did not provide sufficient income to cover her direct labor costs. In the first four months, she drove a truck during the daytime hours four days a week, and ran the drum-cleaning operations until 11 P.M. each night. The rest of the time, she was on the road selling CDI's drum-cleaning services.

She concentrated her sales activities on the people that had responded positively to the SBDC survey. But she had only limited success.

CDI's losses continued. She had expected her uncle to help her sell, but he did not. Her banker insisted that she quit driving trucks and devote her full energies to her business or close it.

At the end of 1993, CDI had cleaned and sold about 18,000 drums, but it was still $30,000 in the hole. The bank loaned her another $12,000, and she mortgaged her home to obtain additional funds.

Management, Ownership, and Personnel

Early the next year, the financial situation was at its lowest point. At that time, a friend, Edie, invested $32,000 in CDI in return for 50 percent ownership.

Shortly thereafter, Edie expressed concern about the firm's losses and felt that labor costs should be reduced and a supervisor hired. Sue argued, however, that despite already low wages, the employees were efficiently producing a quality product. She said, "In the past, when I came to work, I often found a breakdown, a lack of materials, or that an employee hadn't shown up for work. Now, however, after their training, they have become productive."

By the eighth year, the number of workers had grown from six to eight, and the pay scale had grown from minimum wage to a range from minimum for recently hired employees to $8 per hour for the group leader. Social Security, workers' compensation, and unemployment insurance were the only employee benefits provided.

Sue had discussed with her SCORE advisers the possibility of giving the workers a bonus to recognize and encourage good work. "But," she added, "how do we pay for it?" She said that she was considering using temporary workers in order to avoid the problems of handling fringe benefits.

Product Line and Production Process

CDI performs two types of service. First, it buys steel and plastic drums with the intention of processing and selling them. This requires finding, pricing, purchasing, transporting, and selling drums. It then owns the drums until they are cleaned and sold.

Second, it has an ongoing drum exchange service, delivering processed drums and picking up old drums to be processed. CDI does not own those drums during processing. Sales are about evenly split between the two types of service, and steel drums make up about 85 percent of those handled.

The company rents a 5,000-square-foot building, where operations are conducted. (See Exhibit 1 on page 482 for its layout.) Sue estimated that the machinery could process about 5,000 drums a month and that current production averaged about 4,000 drums per month. Machines are not fastened to the floor, but have electrical and pipe connections. The operations and their sequence for processing steel drums are shown in Exhibit 2 on page 483.

The drums are brought to the plant in trailers, pulled by CDI's only tractor (267 drums make up a trailer load). The company has three trailers so that two can stay at the plant to be unloaded and loaded while the other is delivering clean drums to customers. CDI tries to move drums in full trailer loads which sometimes requires several stops. However, CDI has learned that orders for fewer than 50 drums are not profitable, so it does not accept them—unless the customer pays the transportation costs. The production process involves the following steps, in the order shown:

1. Drums are received and unloaded over a period of several days. The bungs (stoppers screwed in the tops of the drums) are removed and the drums checked for quality. The drums are stacked, moved to a waiting area, or moved to first flush. About 300 drums are in each of the receiving and shipping areas.

2. Each drum is upended on a pipe and flushed with steam and a chemical.

3. Each drum is righted, and a light is lowered into it so the drum can be inspected for rust. Rusty drums are rolled to a separate room where the rust is removed. They are then returned for further processing.

4. Drums needing straightening are run through the chimer.

5. Drums are placed on a conveyor, and rolled into a vat for cleaning. Six drums can be cleaned at the same time.

6. Drums are mechanically lifted, turned, and rolled into the outside rinser.

7. Drums are pressure tested. Those not meeting the pressure test are removed from the operation for further processing or discarding.

8. Drums roll down the conveyor where a worker lifts and upends each onto a steam pipe for final flushing.

9. Each drum is righted and placed on the floor where a suction pipe is inserted to dry the inside.

EXHIBIT 1 |
Layout of CleanDrum
Plant

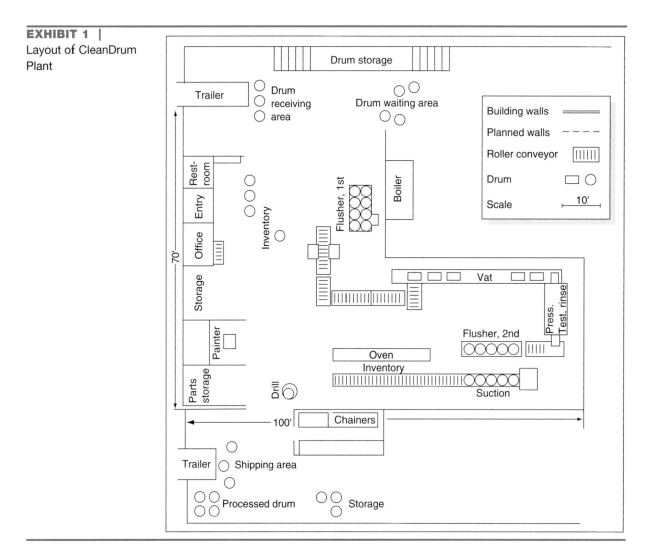

10. Final inspection for rust is made.

11. Drums are rolled to the paint booth for individual spray painting while being turned. A label is affixed to signify that the drum has gone through the entire cleaning process and conforms to established standards.

12. Drums are put into a waiting trailer for delivery or are moved to storage.

Freight can be a prime factor in the cost of some jobs. First, the distance that a tractor-trailer travels is a cost variable. And second, it is critical to keep empty or partial truckloads to a minimum. Therefore, *scheduling is very important.*

Plastic drums follow a separate path, which "causes some confusion." After the first flush, they are manually pressure tested, flushed again, and washed on a mobile cradle.

At times, space around the machines is crowded with drums (some stacked) awaiting the next operation. During the summer, the plant is extremely hot even with the draft through the open ends of the building. So, to help reduce the heat, a six-foot-diameter fan is placed in the wall by the vat. In rainy weather, workers in receiving and shipping wear raincoats or other protective wear.

EXHIBIT 2 | Sequence of Operations at CleanDrum

Steel Drums	Plastic Drums	Machines Used	Time in Drum
1. Receive	1. Receive	Trailer	
2. First flush	2. First flush	Flusher	3 minutes
3. Inspect for rust; if so, clean with chain		Visual	3 minutes
		Chainer*	15 minutes
4. Straighten		Chimer	1 minute
5. Clean		Vat	10 minutes
6. Outside rinse		Rinser	3 minutes
7. Pressure test; if not passed, cut out top		Forced air	20 seconds
		Hand cutter	10 minutes
	3. Pressure test	Hand tester	2 minutes
8. Last flush	4. Flush	Flusher	4 minutes
	5. Wash outside	Hand washer	3 minutes
9. Dry		Suction/Oven	2 minutes
10. Inspect for rust; if not passed, cut 9" hole		Visual	2 minutes
		Drill press	10 minutes
11. Paint (90%)		Paint booth	4 minutes
12. Ship	.	Truck	.

*About 5 percent.

Sue has considerably enlarged the production facilities since starting the company. She now feels that she needs to reduce the handling of the drums and, in the process, increase production capacity. She has found a larger first flusher, a larger chainer, a delivery trailer, and some roller conveyers at used-equipment prices that will give production the efficiency and capacity desired. Also, she needs a cutter-beader to get into the open top drum market. To rearrange the layout and reduce congestion, the plant needs to be enlarged.

Quality inspection of drums was recently combined with receiving drums to better tie the price to their condition. Sue feels that the changes are showing up in profits. They may also result in moving the chaining (rust removal) nearer the receiving area.

Recently, an outside firm made an environmental health and safety audit of the company. This audit included fire protection, human protection and movement, management policies, signs, and guards. Sue also explained that steps were being taken to make corrections that should avoid problems when OSHA inspectors come again. The $400 cost of the study should probably save from $1,500 to $2,000 in OSHA penalties.

Marketing and Sales Promotion

Since starting the company, Sue has spent part of her time on the road selling CDI's services. Currently, she spends two to three days each week on the road making contact with customers. Although she also makes many phone calls to her clients, Sue believes that these cannot replace face-to-face contacts. She plans her itinerary to stay within a 200-mile radius to minimize travel time and mileage costs.

The 200-mile radius is considered the extent of CDI's market. This area is served by five companies, and total market demand is estimated to be 13,000 drums a month. Currently, CDI's sales volume places it in the lower middle of the group.

Sue estimates that she has more than 100 customers, including about 50 percent of the companies that originally indicated a need for her services. About 75 percent of the sales have been drawn from competitors' customers.

Oil and chemical companies are CDI's major customers. Some call in to alert CDI to their need for its product. For example, one of the major customers recently called to tell her, "We have 100 drums ready to be cleaned, and will have 200 by the end of next week." Several companies order twice a month, while some order once every six months.

Sue has been selling about 3,500 to 4,000 drums a month, but her eye is set on sales of 5,000 per month. She explains that the goal is attainable for several reasons. First, the number of customers has steadily increased since CDI opened. Second, a competing company recently went bankrupt, and Sue picked up most of its customers. Finally, as will soon be discussed, several customers and sales reps from other noncompeting companies have "boosted" CDI to their customers.

Presently, Sue feels that quality and service should be her main selling emphasis. Even though CDI has chosen to compete on these points, however, it must also compete with price-cutting by some competitors. Pricing practices vary. Sue has heard reports that one competitor quotes a high price for the purchase of good drums and then finds enough wrong with them to drive the purchase price down so it can sell the processed drums for lower prices.

But Sue estimates the market for CDI drum cleaning is mainly among quality processors. She also believes that the market is restricted by freight costs, is expanding in the local market, and is stable, because several national companies need CDI's services.

Sue says she has seen delivered drums, processed by others, that have been carelessly processed, while others have not been pressure tested. Early on, CDI "almost lost a good customer because a part-time worker left some refuse in some drums."* Sue also cited a customer that was lost because somebody tampered with some of CDI's delivered drums. She hopes to convince potential customers who are currently buying substandard processing that it's in their best interest to obtain quality service.

CDI, which does only limited advertising and sales promotion, distributes magnetic calling cards and is the only company listed under "Barrels & Drums—Equipment & Supplies" in the Yellow Pages of the local telephone directory. Sue does not know of any other publication in which it would be worthwhile to advertise.

Some companies, having received poorly processed used drums, now use only new drums. Sue has approached some of these companies asking for a chance to demonstrate the quality of CDI's delivered drums. Although she has not had much success, she says she plans to continue trying this sales pitch. Also, her satisfied customers and others are referring other companies to CDI.

Financial Affairs

During the early years of the company, Sue used her checkbook to do the accounting. When cash was received, she entered it in the checkbook; when she paid a bill, she paid it by check. She used sales and shipping slips to keep track of sales and invoices received. At the end of the year, she took all the slips, invoices, and checks to the firm's accountant and received in return a financial package, plus completed tax forms.

Several years ago, however, a multicolumn income/expense form was introduced. Each column was designed for an item of income or expense and each sheet represented a month of activities. The form was summarized each month in order to obtain accounting information for management to use in decision making.

---

*Sue consistently emphasized to the authors how important the workers' performance was to the company.

EXHIBIT 3

CLEANDRUM INC.
Balance Sheet
December 31, 2015
($000s)

	2013	2014	2015
Assets			
Current assets:			
Cash in bank	$ 6.7	$ —	$ 4.0
Accounts receivable	12.8	19.8	21.4
Inventory	7.7	27.2	31.0
Prepaid items	—	—	23.0
Total current assets	27.2	47.0	79.4
Property and equipment			
Equipment	156.6	178.8	203.7
Leasehold improvements	5.5	—	53.0
Less: accumulated depreciation	−102.2	−123.0	−146.1
Net property and equipment	59.9	55.8	110.6
1 Total assets	$ 87.1	$ 102.8	$ 190.0
Liabilities and Stockholders' Equity			
Current liabilities:			
Accounts payable	$ 38.9	$ 50.5	$ 51.0
Current long-term debt	16.4	15.0	50.7
Notes payable	59.0	15.3	1.6
Accruals	11.8	6.9	14.4
Total current liabilities	126.1	87.7	117.7
Long-term debt	96.5	78.7	128.1
2 Total liabilities	**222.6**	**166.4**	**245.8**
Stockholders' equity			
Common stock	1.0	1.0	1.0
Added paid-in capital	16.7	108.3	108.3
Accumulated deficit	(153.2)	(172.9)	(165.1)
Total stockholders' equity	(135.5)	(63.6)	(55.8)
Total liabilities and stockholders' equity	$ 87.1	$ 102.8	$ 190.0

A computer has been installed and accounting programs are used for storage and processing data throughout the company. Costing and pricing have been simplified as has the printing of statements, such as those shown in Exhibits 3 and 4 on pages 485 and 486.

During the early years, when annual sales were below $350,000, CDI incurred losses which accumulated and are now shown as a negative value in the equity section of the balance sheet. This negative value has been of grave concern to Sue and she has discussed CDI's pricing policy many times with the SCORE counselors. Some counselors have suggested reducing the price to gain sales, while others have suggested raising prices to increase profit margins. Sue says, however, she cannot raise prices because of the competition.

CDI's pricing procedure is basically as follows: Used drums are purchased from various sources for about $4 each, depending on their condition. Those needing straightening and/or rust removal can be purchased at lower prices. After processing, a cleaned and painted drum is sold for about $12 to $13.

EXHIBIT 4

CLEANDRUM INC.
Profit and Loss Statements
($000s)

Item	2013	2014	2015
Sales	$320.4	$436.2	$490.1
Cost of sales:			
Materials	99.1	175.4	183.9
Labor	74.6	87.3	104.9
Freight	42.0	11.3	23.3
Total cost of sales	215.7	274.0	312.1
Gross profit	$104.7	162.2	$178.0
Operating, administrative, and selling costs:			
Depreciation	16.7	24.3	23.1
Repair and maintenance	14.5	19.0	17.2
Rent	7.2	11.9	13.6
Utilities	18.0	19.0	24.9
Salary	20.9	25.0	25.0
Insurance	14.5	17.0	10.7
Office expense	3.6	2.6	3.8
General tax, legal, accounting	.5	14.2	13.6
Selling, travel, auto	10.4	10.3	14.6
Telephone	7.6	9.3	6.0
Miscellaneous	0.5	0.2	0.0
Total operating, administrative, and selling costs	$114.4	$152.8	$152.5
Operating profit	(9.7)	9.4	25.5
Income—legal	10.1	—	—
Interest expense	(19.9)	(11.7)	(17.9)
Net Income	$(19.5)	$ (2.3)	$ 7.6

Customers' drums are processed and returned to them for about $7 a drum—again depending on the condition before processing. Drums sold for waste and parts storage are sold for about $5 each. Sue feels that CDI's pricing is in line with its competitors'. (One competitor sells drums at a lower price, but he does not pressure test them and appears to obtain dirty drums at lower prices than CDI.)

Recently, CDI obtained a contract to clean (only) a new type of drum that Sue feels will be profitable. Also, she sees a new market opening up for drums with removable tops, but this will require an investment in a cutter/beader. A year ago, CDI had a mobile cleaning unit made to service cleaning at drums' source. Sue feels there is a future in this business, but not now. The unit is used only as backup equipment.

While Sue has enlarged the production facilities in the past, she now feels they need to be expanded further—as noted earlier. Her plans would cost about $40,000, including machines and rearrangements. Rent would increase about $500 per month.

Sue has often spoken of CDI's difficulty with its cash flow. She is gathering information to use in a business plan to approach an investor or loan agent. As she has had difficulty in the past, Sue knows that she must present the most favorable impression of the company.

But Sue is optimistic, as she sees an expanding market, and 2015 shows that the company has a bright future. Also, she has found some sources of money where entrepreneurial women such as she are favored.

A

accounting records Records of a firm's financial position that reflect any changes in that position.

accounts payable Obligations to pay, resulting from purchasing goods or services.

accounts receivable Current assets resulting from selling a product on credit.

acid test (quick) ratio The ratio of current assets, less inventory, to current liabilities.

advertising Advertising informs customers of the availability, desirability, and uses of a product.

affirmative action programs (AAPs) These provide guidelines to help firms eliminate discrimination against women and minorities.

agents Marketing intermediaries who market a product to others for a fee.

allowances Allowances are given to customers for accepting quality or quantity reduction.

Americans with Disabilities Act (ADA) Law that requires the removal of many social and physical barriers to employing the disabled.

anchor stores Those that generate heavy traffic in a shopping center.

angel capitalists Wealthy local businesspeople and other investors who may be external sources of equity funding.

apprenticeship training Training that blends OJT with learning of theory in the classroom.

articles of copartnership These are drawn up during the preoperating period to show rights, duties, and responsibilities of each partner.

articles of incorporation The instrument by which a corporation is formed under the corporation laws of a given state.

asset-based financing Accepts as collateral the assets of a firm in exchange for the loan.

assets The things a business owns.

audit A formalized examination and/or review of a company's financial records.

B

backward compatible Hardware that will run existing programs designed for older equipment.

balance sheet A statement of a firm's assets, liabilities, and owners' equity at a given time.

bankruptcy A formal legal condition of being unable to repay debts. People or businesses can petition courts to be relieved of financial obligation.

bar codes Codes derived from a language called symbologies and used for specific identification of objects.

barter Barter consists of two or more companies exchanging items of roughly equal value.

benchmarking Setting up standards (for reference) and then measuring performance against them.

bonds Bonds are a form of debt security with a standard denomination, method of interest payment, and method of principal repayment.

bonus A reward—not specified in advance—given to employees for special efforts and accomplishments.

breakeven point That volume of sales where total revenue and expenses are equal, so there is neither profit nor loss.

brokers Brokers bring buyers and sellers of goods together to negotiate purchases or sales.

budgetary control System of budgets used to control a company's financial activities.

budgets Detailed plans, expressed in monetary terms, of the results expected from officially recognized programs for a given future period.

business angels See *angel capitalists.*

business ethics The standards used to judge the rightness or wrongness of a business's relations to others.

business format franchising This grants the franchisee the right to market the product and trademark and to use a complete operating system.

business incubators Facilities characterized by shared space, shared services, and shared equipment in an environment with controlled overhead and extensive consultation and training.

business incubators They nurture young firms and help them survive and grow during the startup period when they are most vulnerable.

business insurance Describes the use of life and disability insurance to solve financial issues of businesses and business owners.

business plan A formal plan prepared to serve as a tool for attracting the other components of the business formation package, including people and money.

business services Services provided to another business or professional.

buy-sell agreement Agreement that explains how stockholders can buy out each other's interest or how the corporation can buy back a shareholder's stock when he or she leaves the company.

C

C corporation   A regular corporation that provides the protection of limited liability for shareholders, but whose earnings are taxed at both the corporate and shareholder levels.

cafeteria-style benefit plan   Allows the employer to provide all employees with the legally required benefits, plus an extra dollar amount that each employee can choose how to use.

capital budget   Budget that plans expenditures for obtaining, expanding, and replacing physical facilities.

carpal tunnel syndrome   See *repetitive stress injuries.*

cash budgets   Cash budgets project working capital needs by estimating what out-of-pocket expenses will be incurred and when revenues from these sales are to be collected.

cash flow   The amount of cash available at a given time to pay expenses.

cash flow budget   Budget that forecasts the amount of cash receipts and cash needed to pay expenses and make other purchases.

Chapter 11   Provides for reorganizing a bankrupt business, whether the bankruptcy petition is filed voluntarily or involuntarily.

chattel mortgage loan   Debt backed by some physical asset other than land, such as machinery, equipment, or inventory.

coinsurance   Having the business buy insurance equal to a specific percentage of property value.

combination franchising   In combination franchising, big-name franchise operations offer both companies' products under the same roof.

commission   Incentive compensation directly related to the sales or profits achieved by a salesperson.

common stock   Common stock, representing the owners' interest, usually consists of many identical shares, each of which gives the holder one vote in all corporate elections.

common stockholders   The owners of a corporation, with claim to a share of its profits and the right to vote on certain corporate decisions.

communication   The transfer of meaning from one person to another.

competitive edge   A particular characteristic that makes a firm more attractive to customers than its competitors. Also called *competitive advantage.*

complementary branding   See *combination franchising.*

conservation   Practicing the most effective use of resources, while considering society's current and future needs.

consignment selling   With consignment selling, payments to suppliers are made only when the products are sold, rather than when they are received in stock.

consumerism   Consumerism involves prodding businesses to improve the quality of their products and to expand consumer knowledge. It is the organized efforts of government, private, or business groups to protect consumers from undesirable effects of poorly designed or produced products.

control   The process of ensuring that organizational goals are achieved.

convenience goods   Products that customers buy often, routinely, quickly, and in any store that carries them.

cooperative   A business owned by and operated for the benefit of patrons using its services.

corporate charter   States what the business can do and provides other organizational and financial information.

corporation   A business formed and owned by a group of people, called stockholders, given special rights, privileges, and limited liabilities by law.

cost of goods sold   The total cost, in terms of raw materials, labor, and overhead, of the business that can be allocated to production.

cost-plus pricing   Basing the price on all costs plus a markup for profit.

counseling   Helping to provide people with an understanding of their relationships with their supervisors, fellow workers, and customers.

credit management   Setting and administering credit policies and practices.

cross-functional teams   Teams that cut across different parts of the organization to monitor, standardize, and improve work processes.

cross-training   Training in which workers learn many job skills so they are more versatile.

cumulative trauma disorders (CTDs)   See *repetitive stress injuries.*

current ratio   The amount of current assets divided by the amount of current liabilities.

customary price   What customers expect to pay because of custom, tradition, or social habits.

D

database marketing   Marketing process for acquiring customers that involves obtaining meaningful, individual-level consumer information; respecting consumers' privacy; analyzing this information to estimate consumer response to various offers; and making marketing decisions based on this expected response.

debit card   Enables the owner to withdraw money or to have the costs of purchases charged directly to the holder's bank account; is usually plastic.

debt financing   Debt financing comes from lenders, who will be repaid at a specified interest rate within a specified time span.

defined-benefit plan   Pension plan whereby the amount an employee is to receive at retirement is specifically set forth.

defined-contribution plan   Pension plan that establishes the basis on which an employer will contribute to the pension fund.

delegation   Assigning responsibility to subordinates for certain activities and giving them the authority to perform those activities.

diagnostic interviews   See *in-depth preemployment, interviews.*

direct taxes   Those paid directly to a taxing authority by the person or business against which they are levied.

discipline   Fairly enforcing a system of rules and regulations to obtain order.

disclosure statement   See *prospectus.*

discontinuance   A voluntary decision to terminate a business.

discount   Reduction from the list price given to customers as an inducement to buy more of a product.

distribution   The physical movement of a product from the production line to the final consumer.

distribution channel   A distribution channel consists of the marketing organizations responsible for the flow of goods and services from the producer to the consumer.

diversification   Adding products that are unrelated to the present product line.

diversity   Diversity in the workforce is achieved by employing more members of minority groups, women, and older workers.

downsizing (rightsizing)   Reducing the number of employees to increase efficiency.

downtown locations   Downtown locations attract business-oriented activities, as government, financial businesses, and head offices of large firms are usually located in the downtown area.

dual branding   See *combination franchising.*

due diligence   The research and analysis of the company that is done before a business transaction.

E

e-commerce   Technology-mediated exchanges between parties as well as the electronically based intra- or interorganizational activities that facilitate such exchanges.

e-training   Computer interaction with either specific software packages or specific online sites for employee training.

economic order quantity (EOQ)   The quantity to purchase that balances the cost of placing the order with the cost of carrying the inventory.

80–20 rule   According to the 80–20 rule, approximately 80 percent of a company's income usually comes from 20 percent of its products.

employee benefits   The rewards and services provided to workers in addition to their regular earnings.

employee relations   Showing interest in and concern for employees' rights.

employee stock ownership plans (ESOPs)   ESOPs allow small businesses to reap tax advantages and cash flow advantages by selling stock shares to workers; a form of profit sharing, they borrow money, purchase some of the company's stock, and allocate it to employees on the basis of salaries and/or longevity.

employment at will   Employers may hire or fire workers with or without cause.

entrepreneur   The goals of an entrepreneur include achievement, profit, and growth, achieved through innovation and strategic management.

entrepreneurial venture   In an entrepreneurial venture, the principal objectives of the owner are profitability and growth.

environmental protection   Tries to maintain a healthy balance between people and their environment.

Equal Employment Opportunity Commission (EEOC)   Federal agency primarily responsible for enforcing EEO laws.

equity   Equity is an owner's share of the assets of a company. In a corporation, it is represented by shares of common or preferred stock.

equity investors   Equity investors are those who actually become part owners of the business.

estate planning   Preparing for the orderly transfer of the owner's equity in the business when death occurs.

excise tax   An additional tax on certain items imposed by the federal government.

executive summary   The executive summary is a brief overview of the most important information in a business plan.

expenses   The costs of labor, goods, and services.

exporting   Marketing our products to other nations.

F

facilities   The buildings, machines and other equipment, and furniture and fixtures needed to produce and distribute a product.

failure   A failure results from inability to succeed in running a business.

Family and Medical Leave Act   Law that requires employers with 50 or more employees to provide up to 12 weeks of unpaid leave for births or adoptions and to care for sick children, spouses, or parents.

family limited partnership   Allows business owners to pass assets to heirs with a minimum of income and estate tax costs while retaining control of assets during their lifetime.

family limited partnership (FLP)   FLP is the organizational type where the majority of the partners are related to each other as spouses, parents, grandparents, siblings, cousins, nieces, or nephews.

federal unemployment tax   A tax paid to the federal government to administer the unemployment insurance program.

feedback   The response a receiver gives through further communication with the sender of a message or some other person.

financial leverage   Financial leverage is using fixed-charge financing, usually debt, to fund a business's operations.

financial planning   Planning that involves determining what funds are needed, where they can be obtained, and how they can be controlled.

financial resources   Cash flow, debt capacity, and equity available to finance operations.

financial structure   This describes the relative proportions of a firm's assets, liabilities, and owners' equity.

flexcomp   See *cafeteria-style benefit plan.*

flexible work arrangement   See *variable work schedule.*

flextime   An arrangement under which employees may schedule their own hours, around a core time.

formal failures   Failures ending up in court with loss to creditors.

401(k) retirement plans   These permit workers to place up to a certain amount of their wages each year in tax-deferred retirement savings plans.

fractional ownership   A percentage share of an expensive asset.

franchise   An agreement whereby an independent businessperson is given exclusive rights to sell a specified good or service.

franchise fee   A one-time fee paid by the franchisee to the franchiser for the business concept, rights to use of trademarks, management assistance, and other related services from the franchiser.

franchisee   Independent businessperson who agrees to sell the product according to the franchiser's requirements.

franchiser   The franchiser owns the franchise's name and distinctive elements and licenses others to sell its products.

franchising   Marketing system whereby an individual owner conducts business according to the terms and conditions set by the franchiser.

freestanding stores   Found in various locations, they are usually best for customers that have brand or company loyalty.

fringe benefits   See *employee benefits.*

fully integrated production networks   Entire geographic regions where a fully integrated supply chain, from raw materials to finished products, is built up.

G

general partnership   In a general partnership, each partner actively participates as an equal in managing the business and being liable for the acts of other partners.

global marketing   Marketing of products that are produced, bought, sold, or used almost anywhere in the world.

green product   Environmentally friendly product offered for sale commercially.

H

hardware   The CPU, monitor, keyboard, and other parts of the computer that you can see and touch.

high-knowledge industries   Those in which 40 percent or more of the human resources are professionals, technicians, or other "knowledge workers."

human relations   The interaction among people in an organization.

human resource planning   The process of converting the business's plans and programs into an effective work force.

human resources   The personnel that make up the business's work force.

I

immediate-response advertising   Advertising that tries to get customers to buy a product within a short time period so that response can be easily measured.

importing   Purchasing and marketing other nations' products.

incentive wage   Extra compensation paid for all production over a specified standard amount.

income statement   Periodically shows revenues, expenses, and profits from a firm's operations.

in-depth, preemployment, or diagnostic interviews   Detailed, probing, and penetrating interviews seeking to determine the applicant's character and other aspects of personality.

indirect taxes   Taxes not paid by a firm or a person, but by someone else.

infomercials   Long, usually half-hour TV ads hosted by a hyper "sellevangelist" selling a relatively new product or service.

informal organization   The set of interpersonal relationships that come about as a result of friendships that develop on and off the job.

inputs   Materials, people, money, information, machines, and other productive factors.

institutional advertising   Selling an idea about the company.

insurance   Another company agrees, for a fee, to reimburse your company for part of a loss.

intermediaries   Those units or institutions in the channel of distribution that either take title to or negotiate the sale of the product.

intermediate-term securities   These mature in one to five years.

intermodal shipping   Use of a combination of truck, rail, or ship to transport goods.

internet   A collection of computers and computer networks linked together to receive and distribute information around the world.

internet marketing The process of building and maintaining customer relationships through online activities.

internship training Training that combines OJT with learning at a cooperating school or college.

inventory A formal list of all the property of a business, or the property so listed.

J

job burnout Physical or mental depletion to a level significantly below a person's capable level of performance.

job description Lists the duties and responsibilities of a given job.

job enrichment Granting workers greater responsibility and authority in their jobs.

job sharing When a single full-time job is retained, but its performance is shared by two or more employees working at different times.

job specifications Detailed written statements of work assignments and the qualifications needed to do the job acceptably.

job splitting When employees divide a single job into two or more different parts, each one doing one of the parts.

joint venture A form of temporary partnership whereby two or more firms join in a single endeavor to make a profit.

judicial due process The judicial due process of discipline involves (1) establishing rules of behavior, (2) setting prescribed penalties for violating each rule, and (3) imposing the penalty(ies) only after determining the extent of guilt.

just-in-time (JIT) Just-in-time delivery is having materials delivered to the user at the time needed for production.

K

kaizen costing This sets cost targets for all phases of design, development, and production of a product for each accounting period.

L

laptop computer A small, battery-powered device that can be used anywhere.

leadership The ability of one person to influence others to attain objectives.

leading The management function of getting employees to do what you want them to do, by communicating with, motivating, and disciplining them.

lease A contract that permits use of someone else's property for a specified time period.

leased manpower Employees obtained from an outside firm that specializes in performing a particular service.

lenders Lenders provide money for a limited time at a fixed rate of interest.

liabilities The financial obligations of a business.

limited-liability company (LLC) The LLC combines the advantages of a corporation, such as liability protection, with the benefits of a partnership, such as tax advantages.

limited liability partnership (LLP) A partnership organized to protect individual partners from personal liability for the negligent acts of other partners or employees.

limited partnership In a limited partnership, one or more general partners conduct the business, while one or more limited partners contribute capital but do not participate in management and are not held liable for debts of the general partners.

line-and-staff organization One that has specialists to advise and perform services for other employees.

line of credit This permits a business to borrow up to a set amount without red tape.

line organization In a line organization the owner has a direct line of command over employees.

living trust Resembles a will but, in addition to providing for distributing personal assets on the maker's death, it also contains instructions for managing those assets should the person become disabled.

long-term securities These mature after five years or longer.

loss control See *risk prevention.*

loss leader An item priced at or below cost to attract customers into the store to buy more profitable items.

M

management information system (MIS) Collects, records, processes, reports, and/or converts data into a usable form.

management prerogatives clause Defines the areas in which the employer has the right to act freely without interference from the union.

manufacturing Making or processing materials into finished goods.

market research The systematic gathering, recording, and analyzing of data related to the marketing of goods and services.

market segmentation Identifying and evaluating various layers of a market.

marketing concept The marketing concept involves giving special consideration to the needs, desires, and wishes of present and prospective customers.

marketing mix The proper blending of the basic elements of product, price, promotion, and place into an integrated marketing program.

markup The amount added to the product's cost to determine the selling price.

merchandising   Promoting the sale of a product at the point of purchase.

merit increases   Pay increases based on the employee's ability and performance.

methods   Methods provide standing instructions to employees on how to perform their jobs.

microloan   A small short-term loan provided by the SBA through intermediaries.

microprocessor   Miniaturized computer processor designed and based on a silicon chip.

mission   Defines the present business scope and broadly describes the organization's present capabilities, focus, and activities.

mortgage loan   Long-term debt that is secured by real property.

motivation   The inner state that activates a person, including drives, desires, and/or motives.

multiformat franchising   See *combination franchising.*

N

net profit   The amount of revenue (sales) over and above the total amount of expenses (costs) of doing business.

networking   The process of establishing and maintaining contacts with key persons in one's own or another organization as informal development or promotion systems.

niche marketing   The process of finding a small—but profitable—demand for something and producing a custom-made product for that market.

nonprofit corporation   Corporation formed for civic, educational, charitable, and religious purposes.

O

objectives   The purposes, goals, and desired results for the business and its parts; the goals toward which the activities of the business are directed.

Occupational Safety and Health Administration (OSHA)   Establishes specific safety standards to ensure, to the extent feasible, the safety and health of workers.

off-price retailers   Those who buy designer labels and well-known brands of clothing at low prices and sell them at less than typical retail prices.

on-the-job learning (OJL)   See *on-the-job training.*

on-the-job training (OJT)   Training in which the worker actually performs the work, under the supervision of a competent trainer.

operating budget   Budget that forecasts sales and allocates expenses for achieving them.

operating systems   Operating systems consist of the inputs, processes, and outputs of a business.

operational planning   Operational planning sets policies, procedures, and standards for achieving objectives.

operations or production   Converting inputs into outputs for customers.

organization chart   Chart that shows the authority and responsibility relationships that exist in a business.

organizing   Determining those activities that are necessary to achieve a firm's objectives and assigning them to responsible persons.

outputs   The products produced and the satisfactions to employees and the public.

owners' equity   The owners' share of (or net worth in) the business, after liabilities are subtracted from assets.

P

partnership   A business owned by two or more persons who have unlimited liability for its debts and obligations.

penetration price   Price set relatively low to secure market acceptance.

performance appraisal   The process of evaluating workers to see how well they are performing.

performance standards   Standards set—in advance—for acceptable levels to which employee achievement should conform.

personal data assistant (PDA)   A handheld, pocket-sized computer that is often a completely wireless system.

personal ethic   One's own belief system that tells one what to do if or when the laws and/or any pertinent codes of ethics are silent.

personal (informal) failures   In personal (informal) failures, the owner who cannot succeed voluntarily terminates the business.

personal services   Services performed by a business for consumers.

physical resources   The buildings, tools and equipment, and service and distribution facilities that are needed to carry on the business.

planning   The process of setting objectives and determining actions to reach them.

policies   General statements that serve as guides to managerial decision making and supervisory activities.

pollution control   The effort to prevent the contamination or destruction of the natural environment.

polygraph   An instrument for simultaneously recording variations in several different physiological variables.

positive discipline   Positive discipline deals with an employee's breach of conduct by issuing an oral "reminder" (not a reprimand), then a written reminder, followed by a paid day off so the employee can decide if he or she really wants to keep the job. If the answer is "yes," the employee agrees in writing to be on his/her best behavior for a given period of time.

preemployment interviews   See *in-depth interviews.*

preferred stock   Preferred stock has a fixed par value and a fixed dividend payout, expressed as a percentage of par value.

preferred stockholders   Owners with a superior claim to a share of a firm's profits, but they often have no voting rights.

problem-solving teams   Teams that meet on a regular basis to discuss ways to improve quality, efficiency, and the work environment.

procedures   See *methods.*

process layout   Where facilities doing the same kind of work are grouped together.

processes   Processes convert inputs into products customers want.

producers   Producers convert materials into products in considerable volume for others to sell to ultimate consumers.

product advertising   Product advertising calls attention to or explains a specific product.

product and trademark franchising   This grants the franchisee the right to sell a widely recognized product or brand.

product layout   Where the facilities are laid out according to the sequence of operations to be performed.

product life cycle   The product life cycle consists of four stages: introduction, growth, maturity, and decline.

product/service liability insurance   Protects a business from losses resulting from the use of its product.

production   See *operations* and also *manufacturing.*

professional service corporation (PSC)   PSC must be organized for the sole purpose of providing a professional service for which each shareholder is licensed.

profit   Revenue received by a business in excess of the expenses paid.

profit (income)   The difference between revenue earned and expenses incurred.

profit goal   The specific amount of profit one expects to achieve.

profit and loss statement   See *income statement.*

profit motive   Expecting to make a profit as the reward for taking the risk of starting and running a business.

profit planning   A series of prescribed steps to be taken to ensure that a profit will be made.

profit sharing   An arrangement—announced in advance—whereby employees receive a prescribed share of the company's profits.

promoting   Moving an employee to a higher position, usually with increased responsibilities, title, and pay.

proprietorship   A business that is owned by one person.

prospecting   Taking the initiative in seeking out customers with a new product.

prospectus (disclosure statement)   Provides background and financial information about the franchiser and the franchise offering. Sometimes called an offering circular, it is a document that provides information on 20 items required by the Federal Trade Commission.

publicity   Information about a business that is published or broadcast without charge.

purchase order   A purchase order tells the supplier to ship you a given amount of an item at a given quality and price.

purchasing   Purchasing determines the company's needs and finds, orders, and assures delivery of those items.

pure risk   The uncertainty that some unpredictable event will result in a loss.

push money (PM)   A commission paid to a salesperson to push a specific item or line of goods.

Q

quality   Quality refers to product characteristics and/or the probability of meeting established standards.

quality circles (QCs)   Small employee groups that meet periodically to improve quality and output.

R

radio-frequency identification (RFID)   A method of specific identification transponders that contain information and can be read from several meters distance. RFID may be the replacement for bar codes.

ratios   Relationships between two or more variables.

recruitment   Reaching out to attract applicants from which to choose one to fill a job vacancy.

recycling   Reprocessing used items for future use.

reengineering   The redesign of operations, starting from scratch.

reinvention   The fundamental redesign of a business, often resulting in reduction in size and markets.

repetitive stress injuries (RSIs)   Muscular or skeletal injuries to the hand, wrist, or other areas that bear the brunt of repeated motions. Among the most common is carpal tunnel syndrome.

retailers   Retailers sell goods or services directly to the ultimate consumers.

return on equity (ROE)   The percentage of net profit your equity earns, before taxes.

revenue (sales income)   The value received by a firm in return for a good or service.

right-to-work laws   Laws that permit states to prohibit unions from requiring workers to join a union.

risk assumption   Setting aside funds to meet losses that are uncertain in size and frequency.

risk avoidance   Refusing to undertake an activity when the risk seems too costly.

risk management   The process of conserving earning power and assets by minimizing the shock from losses.

risk prevention   Using various methods to reduce the possibility of a loss occurring.

risk transfer   Shifting a risk to someone outside your company.

royalty fee   Continuous fee paid by the franchisee to the franchiser usually based on a percentage of the franchisee's gross revenue.

S

S corporation   A corporation that is exempt from multiple taxation and excessive paperwork.

sales forecast   An estimate of the amount of revenue expected from sales for a given period in the future.

sales income   See *revenue.*

sales promotion   Marketing activities (other than advertising or personal selling) that stimulate consumer purchasing and dealer effectiveness.

sales tax   A tax added to the gross amount of the sale for goods sold within the taxing jurisdiction.

scheduling   Setting the times and sequences required to do work.

SCORE (Service Corps of Retired Executives)   A group of retired—but active—managers from all walks of life who help people develop their business ideas.

seasonal stores   Those that target customers for specific seasons or events. Some are open year round and some are only open during the season.

selection   Choosing the applicant who has the qualifications to perform the job.

self-insurance   See *risk assumption.*

self-managing work teams   Teams that take over managerial duties and produce an entire product.

service companies   Companies that provide a service to customers and have some characteristics of both retailers and producers.

shopping centers   Shopping centers vary in size and are designed to draw traffic according to the planned nature of the stores to be included in them.

shopping goods   Goods that customers buy infrequently, after shopping at only a few stores.

short-term securities   These mature in one year or less.

skimming price   Price set relatively high initially in order to rapidly skim off the "cream" of the profits.

small business   A business that is independently owned and operated, is not dominant in its field, and doesn't engage in new or innovative practices.

small business investment companies (SBICs)   Private firms licensed and regulated by the SBA to make "venture" investments in small firms.

small business owner   A small business owner establishes a business primarily to further personal goals, including making a profit.

small company offering registration (SCOR)   The sale of common stock to the public through a regulated board such as Nasdaq or Amex without the hassle of an initial public offering.

smart phone   A cellular phone with personal data assistant (PDA) capabilities.

social objectives   Goals regarding assisting groups in the community and protecting the environment.

social responsibility   A business's obligation to follow desirable courses of action in terms of society's values and objectives.

Social Security   Federal program that provides support for the retired, widowed, disabled, and their dependants.

software   The programs, manuals, and procedures that cause the hardware to operate in a desired manner.

specialization   Using employees to do the work that they are best suited for.

specialized small business investment companies (SSBICs)   These assist socially and economically disadvantaged businesses with venture capital.

specialty goods   Goods bought infrequently, often at exclusive outlets, after special effort by the customer to drive to the store.

speculative risk   The uncertainty that a voluntarily undertaken risk will result in a loss.

spiff   See *push money.*

staffing   Planning for recruiting, selecting, and training and developing employees, as well as compensating them and providing for their health and safety.

standing orders   These set predetermined times to ship given quantities of needed items, at a set price.

stock   Stock represents ownership in a corporation.

stockouts   Sales lost because an item is not in stock.

strategic planning   Strategic planning provides comprehensive long-term direction to help a business accomplish its mission.

strategies   The means by which a business achieves its objectives and fulfills its mission.

supplier-base downsizing   Reducing the number of suppliers to concentrate purchasing.

supply chain   An integrated-coordinated system of activities to transform your materials into finished products delivered to the end consumer.

supply chain management (SCM)   The process of planning, organizing, directing, and controlling a supply chain from origin to consumption.

synergy   The concept that two or more people, working together in a coordinated way, can accomplish more than the sum of their independent efforts.

system   In a system, all parts of the business work in unison.

T

target market   The part of the total market toward which promotional efforts are concentrated.

taxable income   Total revenues minus deductible expenses.

technology S-curve   The product life theory applied to technological devices.

telecommuting   The use of modern communication media, such as telephones, fax machines, computers, modems and fax/modems, and scanners to work from an office, home, or any location.

test marketing   Simulates the conditions under which a product is to be marketed.

tort   A wrongful act by one party, not covered by criminal law, that results in injury to a second party's person, property, or reputation, for which the first party is liable.

trade credit   Trade credit is extended by vendors on purchases of inventory, equipment, and/or supplies.

trade show (trade fair)   An exhibition of products or services by companies in the same industry.

transferring   Moving an employee from one job to another, without necessarily changing title or pay.

transportation modes   Methods used to transfer products from place to place.

U

unemployment insurance   Financial support to employees laid off for reasons beyond their control.

Uniform Commercial Code (UCC)   Set of uniform model statutes to govern business and commercial transactions in all states.

unit pricing   Listing the product's price in terms of some unit, such as a pound, pint, or yard.

upgrading   Retraining workers so they can do increasingly complex work.

use tax   A tax on the use, consumption, or storage of goods within a taxing jurisdiction.

V

validity   Making sure that the test given actually relates or corresponds to job performance.

variable work schedule   Work schedule that permits employees to work at times other than the standard five 8-hour days.

venture capital (VC) firms   Make investments based on projected future income and generally require a substantial return as either equity or profit.

W

white-collar crimes   Those committed by managerial, professional, and technical employees.

wholesalers   Intermediaries who take title to the goods handled and then sell them to retailers or other intermediaries.

workers' compensation   Payments made to employees for losses from accidents and occupational diseases.

working capital   Current assets, less current liabilities, that a firm uses to produce goods and services and to finance the extension of credit to customers.

Z

zero-defects approach   Approach that uses pride in workmanship to get workers to do their work "right the first time."

Endnotes

Chapter 1

1. *U.S. Small Business Administration,* April 2003.

2. T. K. Maloy, UPI Deputy Business Director, "Entrepreneurial Activity Bouncing Back," *Washington* (Washington, D.C.) *Times,* July 22, 2004.

3. Jim Hopkins, "Venture Capital 101: Entrepreneur Courses Increase," *USA Today,* January 5, 2004, p. 1B.

4. Darryl Haralson and Suzy Parker, "Few Teens See Business as Ideal Job," *USA Today,* March 17, 2004, p. 1B.

5. Laura Petrecca, "Fewer Choose Self-Employment," *USA Today,* September 8, 2011, p. 1B.

6. John Bussy, "Shrinking in a Bad Economy: America's Entrepreneur Class," *USA Today,* August 12, 2011, pp. B1, B2.

7. Richard A. Greenwald, "Solo Support," *The Wall Street Journal,* February 14, 2011, p. R8.

8. Ibid.

9. Stephen Ohlemacher, "Studies Say Baby Boomers Expecting to Work Longer," *Press-Register,* June 12, 2007.

10. Lynn Brenner, "If You're Starting a Business . . .," *Parade Magazine,* March 15, 1998, p. 22.

11. Sara Nathan, "Small-Business Start-Ups Drop," *USA Today,* February 16, 2000, p. 1B.

12. Patrick J. Sauer, "Because She's a Lot Like Other Kids—and Then Again . . .," *Inc.,* April 2004, pp. 133–34.

13. As told to Dr. M. Jane Byrd by Megan Crump.

14. Stephanie Armour, "Buiding a New Life After a Layoff," *USA Today,* March 27, 2001, p. 7B.

15. Barbara Haislip, "Laid Off and Launching," *The Wall Street Journal,* February 11, 2011, p. R5.

16. Laura Vanderkam, "The Sanity of Self-Employment," *USA Today,* July 12, 2004, p. 15A.

17. Darryl Haralson and Suzy Parker, "Small Businesses Are Not Worried About the Future," *USA Today,* September 3, 2004, p. 1B.

18. Frasas Verhees and Matthew Meulenberg, "Market Orientation, Innovativeness, Product Innovation, and Performance in Small Firms," *Journal of Small Business Management* 42, No. 2 (April 2004), pp. 134–54.

19. Jim Hopkins, "Micro-Businesses Targeted as a Source of Sales Revenue," *USA Today,* April 3, 2001, P. 1B.

20. Randall E. Stross, "In Praise of Start-Ups," *U.S. News and World Report,* June 12, 2000, p. 48.

21. Office of Advocacy, "Newsrelease," May 20, 2003.

22. U.S. Census Bureau, *Statistical Abstract of the United States: 2011* (130th ed.). Washington, DC, 2010, p. 510, table 772.

23. Anne R. Curry and Sam Ward, "Who Ranks Highest in Patent Applications," *USA Today,* March 7, 2011, p. 1A.

24. Jamie Roberts, "Sweet Victory," *MyBusiness,* December/January 2004, p. 12.

25. Darryl Haralson and Frank Pompa, "What Worries Small Business Owners," *USA Today,* September 4, 2003, p. 1B.

26. Office of Advocacy, U.S. Small Business Administration, "Website 101: newsrelease," May 29, 2003.

27. Ibid.

28. Victoria Neal, "Pass It On," *Entrepreneur,* June 2000, p. 105.

29. Laura Cummings, "A Guide to Start-Up Pitfalls," *BBC News Online,* August 13, 2003.

30. Thomas J. Stanley, "Inside the Millionaire Mind," *Mobile* (Alabama) *Register,* January 30, 2000, p. 1F.

31. Susan S. Clarke, "Serial Entrepreneus Learn from the Past," *Mobile* (Alabama) *Register,* October 29, 2000.

32. Reuters Limited, "Good Climate for Start-Ups in U.S.," CNBC and *The Wall Street Journal,* March 12, 2001, p. 1.

33. Geoff Lewis, "Who in the World Is Entrepreneurial?" FSB, June 2007.

34. Based on material provided by Levi Strauss & Co.

35. www.bls.gov/oco, accessed September 29, 2011.

36. James Aley, "Where the Jobs Are," *Fortune,* September 18, 1995, pp. 53–54, 56.

37. Todd Logan, "Trapped," Inc., January 1995, pp. 21–22.

38. Conversations with Tom Segwald, Center for Entrepreneurial Excellence.

Chapter 2

1. Jolene Mckenzie, "Coming to Terms with Life, May 1, 2011.

2. www.nfda.org/nfda/factsheets.php, accessed May 6, 2004.

3. Olan Hutcheson, "The End of a 1,400-year-old Business," BusinessWeek.com, accessed April 18, 2007.

4. Jim Hopkins, "Family Firms Confront Calamities of Transfers," *USA Today,* August 29, 2000, p. 1B.

5. James Lea, "People-Related Challenges Crop Up in Family Companies," *Jacksonville Business Journal,* www.amcity.com;80/jacksonville/stories/031698/smallb2.html, p.1.

6. Marco R. dellaCava, "Mission Statements Put Goals on Paper," *USA Today*, April 29, 2004, p. 1D.

7. "Home Business Motivation."

8. www.levyrestaurants.com, accessed August 9, 2011.

9. Darrl Haralson and Suzy Parker, "Women Gaining in Business Ownership," *USA Today*, June 8, 2004, p. 1B.

10. Colleen DeBaise, Sarah Needleman, and Emily Maltby, "Married to the Job," *The Wall Street Journal*, February 14, 2011, p. R1, 4.

11. Susan Gallagher, "Mom and Pop Trucking," *Press-Register*, May 13, 2007, p. 5F.

12. "Women's Family Firms Do as Well with Less," *USA Today*, August 27, 2003, p. 1B.

13. Darryl Haralson and Suzy Parker, "Women Gaining in Business Ownership," *USA Today*, June 8, 2004, p. 1B.

14. Patricia Schiff Estess, "The Daught Also Rises," *Entrepreneur*, March 2001, pp. 90–91.

15. Colleen DeBlaise, Emily Maltby, and Sarah E. Needleman, "He rocked her to sleep. She learned to ride a bike from him. Now they're starting a business together. Can they make it work?" *USA Today*, November 18, 2010, pp. R1, R8.

16. Randall Lane, "Let Asplundh Do It," *Forbes 400*, October 16, 1995, pp. 56–64.

17. Jeffrey Landers, "How to Divorce Proof Your Business: The Prenup," *Huffington Post*, January 25, 2011.

18. Stephanie Armour, "Some Moms Quit as Offices Scrap Family-Friendliness," *USA Today*, May 4, 2004, p. 1A.

19. Daisy Maxey, "Double Duty," *The Wall Street Journal*, November 13, 2006, p. R10.

20. "By the Numbers," *USA Today*, May 5, 2004, p. 2D.

21. Survey by Nancy Bowman-Upton, as reported in "Reasons Children Join Family Businesses," *The Wall Street Journal*, May 19, 1989, p. B1.

22. "Question of the Week: What Opportunities Are Out There?" *Home Business Resource Centre*, at www.describe.ca/yourbiz/htm, September 17, 1997.

23. Stan Roberts, "Paint the Town with Profits," *Get Rich at Home* 16 (2003), p. 86.

24. Conversation with Deanna Feuerborn Wolken, June 14, 2011.

25. John Ward, as reported in Buck Brown, "Succession Strategies for Family Firms," *The Wall Street Journal*, August 4, 1988, p. 23.

26. "Clothes Relationship," *National Clothesline*, April 2004, p. 6. Used by permission.

27. Walter Bryant, "Hat, Shoe Care Shops Becoming a Rarity," *Mobile* (Alabama) *Register*, May 29, 2001, p. 7B.

28. Jean K. Mason, "Selling Father's Painful Legacy," *Nation's Business*, September 1988, p. 30.

29. Tom Herman, "The Risk of Filing Your Taxes Early," *The Wall Street Journal*, January 24, 2007, pp. D1, D2.

Chapter 3

1. Thomas A. Stewart, "How Teradyne Solved the Innovator's Dilemma," *Fortune*, January 10, 2000.

2. Found at www.onlinebc.gov, June 23, 2004.

3. Nichole L. Torres, "Puttin' on the Glitz," *Entrepreneur*, April 2004, pp. 96, 98.

4. Found at www.onlinebc.gov/docs/finance/org_fprm.html, June 23, 2004.

5. Paul Leinberg, "Ten Entrepreneurial Mistakes That Can Kill Your Company," *Home Business Journal*, January 2001, pp. 52–53.

6. Nichole Torres, "Nice to Meet You," *Entrepreneur*, April 2004, pp. 104–5.

7. "Hands On: When Partnerships Go Bad," *Inc.*, April 2004, p. 64.

8. Joseph Nocera, "The Corporation Comes Home," *Fortune* 141, no. 5, Special 70th Anniversary Issue, p. F72.

9. U.S. Census Bureau, *Statistical Abstract of the United States: 2011*, 130th ed. (Washington, D.C. 2006), p. 496, Table 752.

10. From *West's Business Law with Online Research Guide*, 9th ed. Reprinted with permission of South-Western, a division of Thomson Learning: www.thomsonrights.com Fax (800) 730-2215.

11. Ibid.

12. Correspondence with Ben Hedrick, April 27, 2011.

13. U.S. Census Bureau, "Statistical Abstract of the United States," 2011 (130th edition) Washington, DC, 2010, Table 581.

14. "Venture Is Planned to Supply Iron Ore from Australia to China," *The Wall Street Journal*, March 2, 2004, p. A10.

Chapter 4

1. Janice Revell, "Martha Gets 5 to 20; Investors Get Life," *Fortune*, March 22, 2004, p. 40.

2. Author correspondence with Fred Ware, July 19, 2007.

3. Rodney Ho, "Small Businesses in Areas Hurt by NAFTA Can Apply to New Loan Guarantee Plan," *The Wall Street Journal*, August 7, 1997, p. B2.

4. "Let the Vans Roll," *The Wall Street Journal*, July 14, 1997; and "The Vans Roll," *The Wall Street Journal*, August 13, 1997, p. A14.

5. www.carservice11211.com, accessed June 29, 2007.

6. U.S. Department of Commerce, *Survey of Current Business* (Washington, D.C.: U.S. Government Printing Office, August 1983), p. 24.

7. Jeffrey A. Tannenbaum, "Government Red Tape Puts Entrepreneurs in the Black," *The Wall Street Journal*, June 12, 1992, p. B2.

8. Steve Forbes in a lecture at Hillsdale College, Hillsdale, Michigan, published as "The Moral Case for the Flat Tax, *Imprimis* 25, no. 2 (October 1996), p. 2.

9. John J. Fialka, "Finding Help: I'm from the Government . . . ," *The Wall Street Journal*, May 21, 1998, p. R18.

10. www.epa.gov, accessed June 29, 2007.

11. Kevin Murphy, "Report: IRS Doesn't Do Enough to Aid Smaller Firms," *Mobile* (Alabama) *Register*, January 24, 2001, p. 3F.

12. Jane Easter Bahls, "Law Talent," *Entrepreneur*, October 2004, p. 98.

13. *How to Choose and Use a Lawyer* (Chicago: American Bar Association, 1990). For information, contact the ABA at 750 N. Lake Shore Drive, Chicago, IL 60611.

14. Kimberly Weisul, "Gifts of Gab: A Start-Up's Social Conscience Pays Off," *Business Week On-Line*, February 5, 2001.

15. April Y. Pennington, "A World of Difference," *Entrepreneur*, October 2004, pp. 79–82.

16. Carol Hymowitz, "Drawing the Line on Budding Romances in Your Workplace," *The Wall Street Journal*, November 18, 1997, p. B1.

17. Traci Watson, "GE Might Get Bill for Hudson River Clean-Up," *USA Today*, August 2, 2001, p. 4A.

18. Anne B.Carey and Alejandro Gonzalez, USA TODAY Snapshots, *USA Today*, April 5, 2011, page 1A.

19. Geanne Rosenburg, "Truth and Consequences," *Working Woman*, July/August 1998, p. 79.

20. Darryl Haralson and Adrienne Lewis, "Teens Question Executives' Ethics," *USA Today*, November 11, 2003.

21. "McDonald's Announces Commitments to Offer Improved Nutrition Choices," www.aboutmcdonalds. com, July 26, 2011.

22. Steven Reinberg, "Almost 10 Percent of U.S. Medical Costs Tied to Obesity," abcnews.go.com, July 28, 2011.

23. Toddi Gutner, "Do the Right Thing—It Pays," *BusinessWeek*, August 28, 2000, p. 266.

24. Dave Anderson, "Close Every Sale," *Start Your Own Business*, March 2004, p. 10. Used by permission of the author.

25. Robin Liss, "The Ethical Edge," *Fortune Small Business*, March 2007, p. 73.

26. David Newton, "It's No Accident," *Entrepreneur*, November 2004, p. 30.

27. Thomas M. Goodsite, "The 'Golden-Rule' Rotarian," *The Rotarian*, October 1994, pp. 39–39.

28. Name withheld, personal interview by author, July 15, 2007.

29. Rebecca Barnett, "Honor and Values," *Get Rich at Home* 16 (2003), p. 14.

Chapter 5

1. Conversations with Brynn Albretsen, July 1, 2011.

2. This section is based on F. J. Roussel and Rose Epplin, *Thinking about Going into Business?* (U.S. Small Business Administration Management Aid No. 2.025). This and other publications are available from the SBA for a small processing fee.

3. An excellent guide to use is the SBA's *Checklist for Going into Business*, Management Aid No. 2.016. To obtain this aid, contact your nearest SBA office.

4. Mya Trazier, "Drink Up," *Entrepreneur*, September 2006, p. 93.

5. Stan Roberts, "Cash in Trash," *Get Rich at Home* 16 (2003), p. 76.

6. Shannon Scully, "Rain Man," *MyBusiness*, December/January 2004, p. 58.

7. Nicole Gull, "Taking a Niche Player Big Time," *Inc.*, January 2004, p. 34.

8. Francis Huffman, "Living Large," *Entrepreneur*, October 1997, pp. 156–59.

9. "SCORE and UPS Store Franchise," *Franchise*, Spring 2006, p. 55.

10. www.chick-fil-a.com.

11. Jeff Elgin, "Why do so many franchises fail," Entrepreneur, December 10, 2010. (www.entrepreneur .com).

12. Conversations with Katherine Tait, February 25, 2010

13. Michael Seid, "How Do You Spot a Franchise Scam?" *Franchise*, Summer 2006, p. 22.

14. Robert E. Bond and Stephanie Woo, *Bond's Franchise Guide 2004*, 15th ed. (place of 2pub: Source Book Publications, Oakland, California, 2004).

15. Donna Slipher, "Too Much Too Soon," *Inc.*, November 2003, p. 40.

16. "Latest Industry Trends," *Start Your Own Business*, May 2004, p. 12.

17. Matthew Shay, "Franchising Growth," *Franchise*, Spring 2006, p. 21.

18. Michael H. Seid, "Should You Buy a Franchise?" *Franchise*, Spring 2006, p. 18.

19. Gwendolyn Bounds and Raymond Flandez, "Why Running a Franchise Is Easier Than Ever," *The Wall Street Journal*, June 25, 2007, p. R1.

20. www.chick-fil-a.com.

21. "Latest Industry Trends," *Start Your Own Business*, May 2004, p. 12.

22. Jeffrey A. Tannenbaum, "Right to Retake Subway Shops Spurs Outcry," *The Wall Street Journal*, February 2, 1995, [[. B1. B2.

23. Richard Gibson, "Court Decides Franchisees Get Elbow Room," *The Wall Street Journal*, August 14, 1996, p. B1.

24. Nancy Rathburn Scott, "When Speed amd Convenience Count, Count on Fast Franchises," *USA Today,* July 25, 2001, p. 13B.

25. Theresa Howard, "Subway Sees Success with Low-Carb Campaign, Sandwiches," *USA Today*, February 9, 2004. p. 10B.

26. "Low-Carb Diets Take Bite out of Krispy Kreme's Earnings, *USA Today*, May 10, 2004, p. 7B.

27. Nancy Rathburn Scott, "Franchises for Techies," *USA Today,* February 28, 2001, p. 17B.

28. Ibid.

29. "In R2D2, Helen Greiner Saw Her Future," *Reader's Digest*, August 2002, pp. 152, 154.

30. "Lube Shops on Corner Statins," *Mobile* (Alabama) *Register*, October 4, 1992, p. 8E.

31. Jeffrey A. Tannenbaum, "Broiling Pace: Chicken and Burgers Create Hot New Class: Powerful Franchisees," *The Wall Street Journal*, May 21, 1996, p. A1.

Chapter 6

1. Ashley Wilborn, "SBDC Teaches Entrepreneurs the ABCs," *C & BA Executive* 7, no. 1 (Spring/Summer 2001), p. 30.

2. Ibid.

3. Terry Thomas, "Six Keys to Business Success," *Home Business Journal,* January 2001, pp. 62–63.

4. Stan Caplan, "On Drycleaning: Your Mission and Operation Plan," *National Clothesline*, April 2004, p. 32.

5. Ellen Paris, "Relief Wanted," *Entrepreneur*, March 2001, p. 33.

6. Cassandra Andrews, "Baldwin resident brings aloha spirit to south Alabama," *Mobile* (Alabama) *Register*, July 15, 2001, p. E1.

7. Tommy Sue Rusling, Interview, June 2007.

8. "An Exterior View May Be What Some Companies Need in Their Strategic Plans," *The Wall Street Journal*, December 14, 1995, p. A1.

9. Stephanie Armour, "More Firms Ask Retirees to Remain," *USA Today*, January 4, 2001, p. 1B.

10. Hal Lancaster, "Fear of Flying Solo? Some Takeoff Tips from Two Consultants," *The Wall Street Journal*, February 28, 1995, p. B1.

11. See "How to Start a Small Business: Focus on the Facts," AIG Library, WWW adaptation of SBA publication FF2 by Anjoch Investors Group, www.anjoch-investors.com, accessed September 1, 1998.

12. Thomas Fogerty, "Mall Owners Fill Gaps with Non-Retail Tenants," *USA Today*, February 9, 2001, p. 1B.

13. "Resources for Start-Up Capital: Pursuing Resources," *Home Business*, April 2000, p. 60.

14. Ibid.

15. Paul Davidson, "Creative Uses of Seed Money," *USA Today*, p. 1B, May 9, 2011.

16. Nicole Gull, "Plan B (and C and D and . . .)," *Inc.,* March 2004, p. 40.

17. The SBA has several free publications to help you in preparing a plan. For example, SBA Management Aid No. 2.007 is a Business Plan for Small Manufacturers.

18. Joyce M. Rosenburg, "The Biggest Investment," *Mobile* (Alabama) *Register*, July 9, 2000, p. 2F.

19. N.C. Tognazzini, "Man with a Plan," *MyBusiness*, December/January 2004, p. 56.

20. William G. Nickels, James M. McHugh, and Susan M. McHugh, *Understanding Business*, 5th ed. (New York: McGraw-Hill, 1996), p. 189.

21. John G. Burch, *Entrepreneurship* (New York: John Wiley & Sons, 1986), pp. 377–82.

Chapter 7

1. Julie Candler, "Leasing's Link to Efficiency," *Nation's Business*, May 1995, pp. 30–34. See also Dean D. Baker, "Lease vs. Buy: Avoid Excess Costs," *Management Accounting,* July 1995, pp. 38–39, for some pitfalls to avoid when leasing.

2. Tom Post, "Impossible Dream," *Forbes*, May 4, 1998, pp. 80, 82.

3. Pui-Wing Tam, "The Venture Capital Tangle," *The Wall Street Journal*, May 8, 2007, p. C1.

4. Jim Hopkins, "Corporate Giants Bankroll Start-Ups," *USA Today*, March 29, 2001, p. 13A.

5. Edward Iwata, "Funds, Internet Projects Linked to Superstar Players" *USA Today*, February 25, 2000, p. 1B.

6. "Angel Investor Market Rebounds in 2010, UNH Center for Venture Research Funds," University of New Hampshire, April 12, 2011.

7. Laura Petrecca, "Creative Sources of Seed Money," *USA Today*, May 9, 2011, pp. 1B and 2B.

8. Communications from the National Business Incubation Association.

9. www.ceebic.org.

10. Eleena De Lisser and Rodney Ho, "Barter Exchanges Say Future Looks Promising," *The Wall Street Journal*, November 12, 1997, p. B2.

11. C.J. Prine, "A Fair Trade," *Entrepreneur*, October 2003, pp. 59–60.

12. Chris Penttila, "Bartering in Business", *Entrepreneur*, July 2005.

13. www.craftsreport.com.

14. SBA Office of Advocacy, *The Facts about Small Business*, 1997, at www.sba.gov/ADVO/stats/fact1.html. p. 4, accessed March 18, 1998.

15. Marshall Eckblad, "Debunking the Myths About SBA Loans," *The Wall Street Journal*, May 16, 2011, online wsj.com.

16. Except where otherwise noted, this discussion is based on the SBA publications *Lending the SBA Way* and *Your Business & the SBA*. Because Congress periodically passes new legislation that determines the kind of assistance the SBA provides, contact the nearest SBA district office to ascertain what types of assistance are currently available to you, or visit the SBA website at www.sba.gov.

17. J. Tol Broome, Jr., "Borrowed Time," *OfficeSystems97*, December 1997, p. 14.

18. Michael Selz, "Venture Capitalists Fear the U.S. May Renege on SBICs," *The Wall Street Journal*, February 3, 1995, p. B2.

Chapter 8

1. "Secrets from the Market Pros," *Small Business Reports*, January 1994, p. 27.

2. Phred Dvorak, "Seeing through Buyers' Eyes," *The Wall Street Journal*, January 29, 2007, p. B4.

3. Pam Lontos, "How to Get the Media to Notice Your Business," *Home Business Journal*, November/December 2003, p. 62.

4. Bob Levy, "The Prime Offender: Business Itself," *Washington Post*, May 12, 1988, p. D20.

5. George Anders, "I Think I Can, I Think I Can," *The Wall Street Journal*, March 12, 2007, p. R8.

6. Alex Miller, *Strategic Management*, 3rd ed. (New York: McGraw-Hill, 1998), pp. 14–21.

7. Jeffrey F. Rayport and Bernard J. Jaworski, *Introduction to E-Commerce*, 2nd ed. (New York: McGraw-Hill/Irwin, 2004), pp. 3–5.

8. "Edsel and Friends: Ten World-Class Flops," *BusinessWeek*, August 16, 1993, p. 80.

9. Magrid Abraham, "Getting the Most Out of Advertising and Promotion," *Harvard Business Review* 68 (May/June 1990), pp. 50–52.

10. Paul Lucas, "Card Sharps," *Fortune Small Business*, February 2004, p. 96. © 2004 Time Inc. All rights reserved.

11. Dhruv Grewel and Michael Levy, *Marketing*, 3rd ed. (New York: McGraw-Hill/Irwin, 2012), p. 273.

12. Joe Follanbee, "From Brochure to Pickaxe: How to Turn Your Web site into a Prospecting Tool," *Home Business Journal*, January/February 2004, pp. 10–12.

13. AP Bulletin, "Caller I.D. Aids Businesses," *Mobile (Alabama) Press Register*, January 30, 1995, p. 7B.

14. Lorrie Grant, "How Harried Shoppers Can Take Control at Supermarkets," *USA Today*, June 7, 2001, p. 1A.

15. Karen Dybis, "Teens' Shopping Styles Change," *USA Today*, February 4, 2004, p. 5B.

16. Theresa Howard, "Dylan Ad for Underwear Generates Lingering Buzz," *USA Today*, May 17, 2004, p. 8B.

17. Stephanie Clifford, "Cash and Controversy," *Inc. Magazine* (29:5), May 2007, p. 23.

18. U.S. Census Bureau, *Statistical Abstract of the United States: 2011*, 130th ed., Washington, DC, 2010, p. 54, table 59.

19. U.S. Census Bureau, *Statistical Abstract of the United States: 2011*, 130th ed., Washington, DC, 2010). p. 11, Table 7.

20. J. Allen Tarquinio, "King of Grits Alters Menu to Reflect Northern Tastes," *The Wall Street Journal*, September 22, 1997, p. B1.

21. Sakina Spruell, "Hot Stuff," *Fortune Small Business*, February 2004, p. 47.

22. Meera Somasundaram, "Red Symbols Tend to Lure Shoppers like Capes Being Flourished at Bulls," *The Wall Street Journal*, September 18, 1995, p. B10a.

23. Anne Lowery, personal interview, July 14, 2004.

24. Kitty Bean Yancey, "Grandkids Mean a Great Deal—as in Discounts," *USA Today*, September 19, 2003, p. 1D.

25. William Rabb, "He Scrubs Up Sites No One Else Wants to Touch," *Mobile (Alabama) Register*, April 19, 1998, pp. 1B, 5B.

26. Nichole L. Torres, "Game On," *Entrepreneur*, April 2004, p. 22.

27. Author's discussion and correspondence with Ms. Brown.

28. Reprinted from Norm Brodsky, "Street Smarts," *Inc.*, March 2004, pp. 59–60. Used by permission of the author.

Chapter 9

1. Theresa Howard, "Subway Sees Success with Low-Carb Campaign Sandwiches," *USA Today*, January 9, 2004.

2. Bruce Horovitz, "Subway Teams Up with Atkins," *USA Today*, December 26, 2003, p. 3B.

3. Jim Hopkins, "Pretzel Makers Shoot for Big Dough," *USA Today*, January 23, 2004, p. 4B.

4. Jefferson Graham, "Web Sites Test Local Search Marketing,," *USA Today*, February 5, 2004, p. 3B.

5. U.S. Census Bureau, *Statistical Abstract of the United States: 2007*, 126th ed., Washington, D.C., 2006, p. 656, Tables 1023 and 1024.

6. www.hoovers.com, accessed July 13, 2011.

7. "A Perfect Vacation," *The Wall Street Journal*, February 27, 2004, p. A3.

8. "Aflac gets a Minnesota accent," *USA Today*, April 27, 2011, p. 3B.

9. Thomas Petzinger, Jr., "Druggist's Simple Rx: Speak the Language of Your Customers," *The Wall Street Journal*, June 16, 1995, p. B1.

10. U.S. Census Bureau, *Statistical abstract of the United States: 2011*, 130th ed., Washington D.C., 2010, p. 14, Table 10.

11. William M. Bulkeley, "Rebates' Secret Appeal to Manufacturers: Few Consumers Actually Redeem Them," *The Wall Street Journal*, February 8, 1998, pp. B1, B2.

12. Christopher Hosford, "Avoiding Trade Show Faux Pas," *Inc. Magazine*, June 2007, pp. 33–34.

13. "William Wrigley and Family," *Forbes 400*, October 16, 1995, p. 136.

14. U.S. Census Bureau, *Statistical Abstract of the United States: 2007*, 126th ed., Washington, D.C., 2006, p. 48, Table 51.

15. www.longotoyota.com, accessed June 23, 2007.

16. Chris Woodward, "Multilingual Staff Can Drive Up Auto Sales," *USA Today*, February 1, 2005.

17. Kim T. Gordon, "In the Mix," *Entrepreneur*, April 2004, p. 86. Reprinted with permission of Entrepreneur Magazine. www.entrepreneur.com

18. Its hotline can be reached at 800-872-8723.

19. "PMO53." United Parcel Service of America, Inc., 2003.

20. Andrea C. Poe, "Shipping 101," Entrepreneur.com/ accessed May 6, 2010.

21. Letter from Virginia Scoggins to Suzanne Barnhill, May 1987.

22. Author's correspondence with Professor Russell Eustice, Husson College, Bangor, Maine.

23. "Telemarketing after 'Do Not Call'," *Inc.*, November 2003, p. 32.

24. Jerry Fisher, "Quick Study," *Entrepreneur*, April 2004, p. 88.

25. Walter Kiechell, "How to Manage Sales People," *Fortune*, March 14, 1998, pp. 179–80.

26. Published by Career Press.

27. Distributed by Nightingale-Conant Corporation.

28. Barry Farber, "Get Over It!" *Entrepreneur*, October 2003, pp. 88–89. Reprinted with permission of Entrepreneur Magazine. www.entrepreneur.com

Chapter 10

1. Thomas A. Stewart, "A New Way to Think about Employees," *Fortune*, April 13, 1998, pp. 169–70.

2. Jim Hopkins, "Fewer Small Businesses Plan to Hire," *USA Today*, March 8, 2004, p. 1B.

3. Jonathan Katz, "Labor Shortage Hits Global Markets," *Industry Week* 256:6, June 2007, p. 16.

4. Darryl Haralson and Keith Simmons, "Most Job Seekers Willing to Start Anew," *USA Today*, May 13, 2004, p. 1B.

5. U.S. Census Bureau, *Statistical Abstract of the United States: 2011*, 130th ed., Washington, D.C., 2010, p. 402, Table 622.

6. Emily Brandon, "Retirees Consider Returning to Work," USNews.com, August 6, 2009.

7. Kerry Hannon, "Inspiration for an Emerging New Post-midlife Generation," *USA Today*, April 25, 2011, p. 6B.

8. U.S. Census Bureau, *Statistical Abstract of the United States: 2011*, 130th ed., Washington, D.C. 2010, p. 391, Table 612.

9. Dory Devlin, "What to Consider When the Hire Is Temporary," *Mobile* (Alabama) *Register*, March 1, 2004, p. 6F.

10. Gary M. Stern, "New, Views, and Tools for Small Business," *MyBusiness*, March 2004, p. 11. Used by permission of the author.

11. "Internet Expedites Employee Recruiting," *The Rotarian*, April 1998, p. 8.

12. Henry Canaday, "A Better Test," *Selling Power*, March 2004, pp. 100–4.

13. Michele Leder, "Is That Your Final Answer?" *Working Women*, December/January 2001, p. 18.

14. Dave Anderson, "Ask Good Questions, Get Good Hires," as published in *Floral Management*, November 2003, p. 20. Used by permissions.

15. Jerry McLain, "Practice Makes Perfect," *OfficeSystems95*, April 1995, pp. 74, 75, 77.

16. G. David Doran, "Revving Up Students," *Entrepreneur*, September 1997, p. 189.

17. "Two-Day Suede and Leather Class Coming in March," *National Clothesline*, March 2004, p. 29.

18. Sandra Swanson and Diane Rezenders Khirallah, "Online Training Helps MetLife Develop, Keep Its Staff, *Information Week*, August 8, 2000, p. 119.

19. Jeffrey R. Young, "Maryland Colleges Train Professors to Teach Online," *Chronicle of Higher Education*, August 10, 2001, vol. 47: 48, p. A48.

20. "Enterprise Training and Skill Soft Partner for Online Training to SSA Workers," *Lifelong Learning Market Report*, 4: 24, p. 5.

21. Diane Rezenders Khirallah, "Veterans Agency Turns to Online Training," *Information Week*, March 27, 2000, p. 183.

22. Kym Gilhooly, "Making E-Learning Effective," *Computer World*, July 16, 2001, p. 52.

23. See, for example, Lynn Beresford, "McSchool Days," *Entrepreneur*, August 1995, pp. 200–202.

24. "New Managers Get Little Help Tackling Big, Complex Jobs," *The Wall Street Journal*, February 10, 1998, p. B1.

25. U.S. Census Bureau, *Statistical Abstract of the United States: 2011*, 130th ed., Washington, D.C., 2010, p. 362, Table 558.

26. Susan B. Garland, "Finally, a Corporate Tip Sheet on Sexual Harassment," *BusinessWeek*, July 13, 1998, p. 39.

27. Nadine Heintz, "There's No Perk Like Home," *Inc.*, December 2003, p. 42.

28. Jim Hopkins, "Rising Benefit Costs Hurt Small Businesses' Financial Health," *USA Today*, June 4, 2004, p. 1B.

29. Bryna Brennan, "Small Firms Dropping Pension Plans; Laws Too Complex," *Birmingham* (Alabama) *News*, December 17, 1989, p. 2D.

30. U.S. Census Bureau, *Statistical Abstract of the United States: 2007*, 126th ed., Washington, D.C., 2006, p. 421, Table 641.

31. U.S. Census Bureau, *Statistical Abstract of the United States: 2007*, 126th ed., Washington, D.C., 2006, p. 421, Table 641.

32. Katherine Sayre, "OSHA Cites Millard Refrigerated Services," *Press-Register*, March 2, 2011, p. 1C.

Chapter 11

1. Douglas McGregor, *The Human Side of Enterprise* (New York: McGraw-Hill, 1960).

2. For more information on this topic, See Rosemary Stewart, *Managers and Their Jobs* (New York: Macmillan, 1967); and Henry Mintzberg, *The Nature of Managerial Work* (New York: Harper & Row, 1973), p. 38.

3. Owen Thomas, "At Shell Everyone's the Answer Man," *Business 2.0,* January/February 2004, p. 55. © 2004 Time Inc. All rights reserved.

4. Mark Vickers, "Hire or Train: The Growing Conundrum," American Management Association, www.amanet.org, accessed July 15, 2007.

5. Paul Spiegalman," Deliver Value to Your Employees— Your Most Important Stakeholders," *INC.,* July 18, 2011.

6. Clarence Francis, "Management Methods," speech given in 1952; reprinted in *Management Methods Magazine*, 1952.

7. H.H. Meyer and W.B. Walker, "A Study of Factors Relating to the Effectiveness of a Performance Appraisal Program," *Personnel Psychology*, August 1961, pp. 291–98.

8. U.S. Census Bureau, *Statistical Abstract of the United States: 2011*, 130th ed., Washington, D.C., 2010, p. 429, Table 633.

9. Jamie Roberts, "Learning Curves," *MyBusiness*, December/January 2004, p. 48. Used by permission.

10. Thomas Petzinger, Jr., "A Couple Rescues Waremart from Throes of a Clash of Cultures," *The Wall Street Journal*, February 6, 1998, p. B1.

11. Dan Armstrong, "Six Degrees of Project Management," *Baseline*, February 2004, p. 85.

12. Chris Penttila, "Out with the 'In'," *Entrepreneur*, April 2004, pp. 73–74.

Chapter 12

1. Jan Norman, "How to Find the Perfect Location," *Business Start-Ups*, February 1998, pp. 54, 56.

2. Michelle Conlin, "Rolling Out the Instant Office," *BusinessWeek,* May 7, 2007, p. 71.

3. Joyce M. Rosenberg, "Independent Retailers Still Can Stay Viable," *Mobile* (Alabama) *Register*, July 8, 2001, p. 3F.

4. Danielle Reed, "A Tale of Two Leaves: Outlet Shopping," *The Wall Street Journal*, October 17, 1997, p. B12.

5. George Talbot, "Across the Water," *Mobile* (Alabama) *Register*, December 10, 2003, pp. 1A, 4A, 7A.

6. K.A. Turner, "Telecommuting Redefines the Work Day," *Press Register*, August 20, 2006, p. 1F.

7. Deroy Murdock, "For a Holiday That Honors Work, Labor Never Had It So Good," *Mobile* (Alabama) *Register*, September 2, 2001, p. 14A.

8. Linda Duval, "Decorating the Home Office," *Mobile* (Alabama) *Register*, March 2, 2001, p. 1D.

9. "Faculty Connections: Wired In," *USA Today*, June 28, 2001, p. 14A.

10. Aliza Sherman, "Power Tools for Women in Business." Used by permission of the author.

11. Consult any basic industrial engineering or production/operations management text for a more detailed discussion of this process. There will probably be some sample forms you can use.

12. Yuniko Ono, "Would You Like That Rare, Medium, or Vacuum-Packed?" *The Wall Street Journal*, January 6, 1997, pp. A1, A14.

Chapter 13

1. Donna Fenn, "Growing by Design," *Inc.*, August 1985, p. 86.

2. Robert Jacobs and Richard Chase, *Operations and Supply Management: The Core,* 2nd ed., New York: McGraw-Hill Higher Education, 2010.

3. Author's conversation with Alan Lowe, Department of Product Planning and Development, Sharp Corporation.

4. Erick Schonfeld, "The Big Cheese of Online Grocers," *Business 2.0*, January/February 2004, pp. 60–61.

5. Scott McCarthy, "A New Way to Prevent Lost Luggage," *The Wall Street Journal*, February 27, 2007, pp. D1 and D6.

6. Mary Roach, "43 Minutes and Holding," *Readers Digest*, July 2002, p. 31.

7. Author's correspondence with Craig Taylor, Director, Business Programs, Disney Institute.

8. Leslie Chang, "Eating Their Lunch: Coals to Newcastle, Ice to Eskimos; Now, Noodles to the Chinese," *The Wall Street Journal*, November 17, 1997, pp. A1, A10.

9. Jacob Hale Russell, "Unhappy Feet: Ballerinas' New Lament," *The Wall Street Journal*, December 23/24, 2006, pp. P1, P11.

Chapter 14

1. Paul DeCeglie, "Reality Check," *Business Start-Ups*, March 1998, p. 12.

2. Roger Ricklefs and Udayan Gupta, "Traumas of a New Entrepreneur," *The Wall Street Journal*, May 10, 1989, p. B1.

3. Paul DeCeglie, "Cut It Out," *Business Start-Ups*, February 1998, p. 14.

4. Philip Piña, "Organic Can Mean Profits for Farmers," *USA Today*, September 19, 1995, p. B1.

5. Dan Reed, "More Passengers Fly, but Revenue Lags," *USA Today*, March 12, 2004, p. 5B.

6. Dan Reed, "Jet Fuel Consumes Airlines' Projected Profit," *USA Today*, March 29, 2004, p. 5B.

7. Bruce Horowitz, "Fast-Food Restaurants Herd Angus Beef Burgers onto Menu," *USA Today*, March 24, 2004, p. 1B.

Chapter 15

1. George Talbot, "Money Changes Things," *Mobile* (Alabama) *Register*, December 8, 2003, pp. 1A, 4–5A.

2. George Talbot, "Farewell to Fairhope," *Mobile* (Alabama) *Register*, December 9, 2003, pp. 1A, 4A.

3. Henry Canaday, "The Sky's No Limit," *Selling Power*, March 2004, pp. 71–72.

4. Jacquelyn Lynn, "Damage Control," *Entrepreneur*, March 1998, p. 37.

5. Missy Mastel, "Ringing Up Profits," *Small Business Opportunities*, May 2004, p. 12.

6. Larry Luxner, "Trade Zones Mark Strategy Shift," *The Wall Street Journal*, October 9, 1997, p. B20.

7. *Starting a Business and Keeping Records.* Publication 583, www.irs.ustreas.gov.

8. Patrick McMahon, "Seattle Voters to Decide on 10-Cent Tax on Expresso Drink," *USA Today*, September 15, 2003, p. 4A.

9. Bernie Kohn, "Toe-to-Toe with the IRS," *Tampa Tribune*, March 29, 1998, pp. 1–2, www.rampatrib.com.

10. Karen J. Bannan, "Don't Take It Personally," *MyBusiness*, February/March 2004.

11. Miriam Jordan, "Even Workers in U.S. Illegally Pay Tax Man," *The Wall Street Journal*, April 4, 2007, pp. B11–12.

12. John R. Emshwiller, "Handing Down the Business," *The Wall Street Journal*, May 19, 1989, p. B1.

13. Information found at onlinebc.gov, accessed June 23, 2004.

14. Roger Yu and Charisse Jones, "Foreign currency conversion fees annoy many," *USA Today*, March 22, 2011 p.7B

15. Jilian Mincer, "Despite Risks, Debit Card Use Rises," *Dow Jones, San Jose Mercury News*, July 7, 2007.

16. Robin Sidel, "As Card Fees Climb, Merchants Push PINs," *The Wall Street Journal*, January 16, 2007, pp. A1, A18.

17. Federal Reserve Bank of Boston. "The 2009 Survey of Consumer Payment Choice." http://www.bos.frb.org/economic/ppdp/2011/ppdp1101.htm. Accessed August 1, 2011.

18. "Café Just Keeps on Rockin'," *USA Today*, June 12, 2001, p. 1D.

19. Richard Gibson, "Planet Hollywood Reels as 'Entertainment' Fades," *The Wall Street Journal*, January 23, 1998, pp. B1, B7.

Chapter 16

1. Adapted from an interview with Allen Kirksey, owner of the Rose Bud Flowers & Gifts.

2. Jim Hopkins, "Smaller Firms Spend Faster on Tech than Corporations," *USA Today*, October 29, 2003, p. 1B.

3. David H. Freedman, "Plenty of Challenges, No Rules," *Inc. Technology*, Summer 1995, p. 9.

4. Innovation Life Cycles, www.innovation-point.com.

5. Chilton Tippin, "Cell Phone Usage Statistics 2010, *Signal News*, September 23, 2010.

6. Jon Swartz, "Gadget Explosion Leads to Niche Business Where Tech-Savvy Make House Calls, *USA Today*, June 2, 2003, pp. 1E–2E.

7. Roger Yu, "More Hotels Use Tech To Track Linens," *USA Today*, July 28, 2011.

8. http://www.aimglobal.org/technologies/rfid/, http://electronics_howstuffworks.com/smart-label.htm, http://www.wired.com/wired/archive/14.05/rfid.html, http://www.rfidvirus.org/, http://www.themanufacturer.com.us/content/5547/A_guide_to_selecting_an_Active_RFID_tag, http://www.morerfid.com/details.php?subdetail=Post&action=details&post_id=25&step=show, http://www.fortherecordmag.com/archives/ftr_07102006p18.shtml, http://www.ezpass.com/.

9. Byron Acohido, "Hackers Target Small-Company Sites," *USA Today*, July 5, 2011.

10. Jim Kersetter, "What It Costs to Vanquish Viruses," *BusinessWeek*, April 5, 2004, p. 14.

11. Kevin Coughlin, "What's Bugging Computers," *Mobile* (Alabama) *Register*, June 20, 2004, p. 3F.

12. Jon Swartz, "Spam Can Hurt in More Ways Than One," *USA Today*, July 8, 2004, p. 1B.

13. Andrew Blackman, "Spam's 'Easy Target'," *The Wall Street Journal*, August 10, 2004, pp. 1B, 4B.

14. Darryl Haralson and Marcy E. Mullins, "Companies Hit by More Cybercrime," *USA Today*, July 8, 2004, p. 1B.

15. Stephanie Mehta, "Older Business Owners Ponder the New Technology," *The Wall Street Journal*, May 27, 1994, p. B2.

16. Ibid.

17. Evan Ramstad, Defying the Odds: Despite Giant Rivals, Many Tiny PC Makers Are Still Doing Well," *The Wall Street Journal*, January 8, 1997, p. A1.

18. Brittany Shammas, "Some Retailers Test E-Mailing Customers' Receipts," *USA Today*, July 7, 2011.

19. Kate Westbrook, "6 Secrets of eBay Sales Success," *MyBusiness*, December/January 2004, p. 46.

20. Melissa Campanelli, "Seller's Market," *Entrepreneur*, August 2004, p. 41.

21. Jane Imber and Betsy-Ann Toffler, *Dictionary of Marketing Terms*, 3rd ed. (city of pub, state: Hauppauge, N.Y. Barrons Business Dictionaries, 2000).

22. Rafi Mohammed et al., *Internet Marketing*, 2nd ed. (Burr Ridge, Il: McGraw-Hill/Irwin, 2004), pp. 3–4.

23. Jeffrey F. Rayport, *Introduction to e-Commerce*, 2nd ed. (Burr Ridge, IL: McGraw-Hill/Irwin, 2004), p. 151.

24. Isabella Trebond, "On Target," *Entrepreneur*, August 2004, pp. 88–94.

25. Darryl Haralson and Sam Ward, "Electronics Shoppers Prefer Bricks-and Mortar Stores," *USA Today*, February 2, 2004, p. 1B.

26. Chris Foresman, "Wireless survey: 99%of Americans use cell phones," *Ars Technica,* http://arstechnica.com/telecom/newa/2010/03/wireless-survey-91-of-americans-have-cell-phones.arr.

27. Delia Garvilescu, "Local Businesses Fight Groupon with Mobile Marketing," *Everything PR,* August 8, 2011, http://www.pamil-visions.net/local-businesses-groupon/229518/.

28. Laura Ruane, "QR codes are everywhere – even on grave markers," *USA Today*, July 19, 2011.

Chapter 17

1. U.S. Census Bureau, *Statistical Abstract of the United States: 1994*, 114th ed., Washington, D.C.: U.S. Government Printing Office, 1994, pp. 254, 415; and Margaret Isa, "Pet Practice's Coming IPO May Not Have Much Bite," *The Wall Street Journal*, July 31, 1995, p. C1.

2. "Citibank's Test of Paying to See Tellers Doesn't Pay," *The Wall Street Journal*, May 26, 1993, p. 6.

3. Adapted from Shelly Reese and Ellen Neuborne, "Malls Sell Shoppers on Security," *USA Today*, December 20, 1994, p. 2B.

4. Conversations and correspondence with Alfred C. Corina, CLU, ChFC.

5. "Get It Covered," *Entrepreneur*, August 2006, p. 93.

6. "Ask Inc., Inc. Magazine" *Inc. Magazine*, May 2007, p. 63.

7. James Hannah, "Rising Insurance Costs Take Toll on Small Business," *Mobile* (Alabama) *Register*, May 6, 2001, p. 4F.

8. Luladey B. Tadesse, "Many Farmers Can't Afford Health Insurance Coverage," *USA Today*, March 23, 2004, p. 6B.

9. Personal interview with Alfred Corina, CLU, ChFC, Financial Services Professional, October 25, 2011.

10. Jane Easter Bahls, "Inside Jobs," *Entrepreneur*, June 1995, pp. 72–75.

11. Sandra Block, "Want the best insurance rates you can get? Do these five things," *USA Today*, March 25, 2011.

12. Personal interview with Alfred Corina, CLU, ChFC, Financial Services Professional, October 25, 2011.

13. Steven C. Bahls and Jane Easter Bahls, "Safe Harbor," *Entrepreneur*, April 2000, pp. 98–100.

14. "Store Safety," *USA Today*, April 29, 1998, p. 1B.

15. Pat Carr, "How to Make Your Workplace Safe," *Mobile* (Alabama) *Register*, August 29, 1994, p. 1D.

16. Greg Farrell, "Employee Theft Grows for Retailers," *USA Today*, November 10, 2000, p. 2B.

17. *Justice Files*, program for May 26, 2001.

18. *Security Management* magazine, as reported in *The Wall Street Journal*, November 11, 1986, p. 39.

19. John Goff, "Labor Pains," *CFO: The Magazine for Senior Financial Executives*, January 1998, pp. 36–44.

20. Amanda Kooser, "Feeling Insecure," *Entrepreneur*, April 2004, pp. 54–55.

21. Allison Weiser, "Protecting Your Business Secrets," *The Rotarian*, August 1997, p. 14. See also Steve Casimiro, "The Spying Game Moves into the U.S. Workplace," *Fortune*, March 30, 1998, pp. 152, 154.

22. Greg Farrell, "Kraft Sues Schwan's, Putting Spotlight on Corporate Spying," *USA Today*, February 19, 2001, p. 13.

23. "Cracking Down on Corporate Crime," *Citizen Works*, www.citizenworks.org, accessed October 7, 2004.

24. Baseline Software Inc., www.baselinesoft.com, has a package for writing such policies. It is *Information Security Policies Made Easy Version 9*, priced at $795, and consists of a book and CD-ROM providing companies with written policies. Access October 7, 2004.

25. Stephanie Armour, "Retail Anti-Crime Steps Spur Debate," *USA Today*, May 6, 1998, p. 5B.

26. Ibid.

Photo Credits

Frontmatter

Photo courtesy of the University of Mobile.

Chapter 1

Page 3. Filters-Now Corporate offices. Photo courtesy of Cory Poff. *Page 4.* Veridiana Reyes. Photo courtesy of Cory Poff. *Page 8.* ©Corbis Stock Market/Jose L. Peleaz Inc. *Page 11.* Main Street America. Photo courtesy of MHHE Digital Image Library. *Page 26.* Tom Segwald. Photo courtesy of Jane Byrd. Page 29 Sheridan Livery Inn. Photo. Courtesy of Cori Byrd.

Chapter 2

Page 33. Ferris-Feuerborn Memorial Chapel. Photo courtesy of Joseph S. Blake, Jr. *Page 34.* Ruben and Dudley, Dudley and Rueben and Rueben and Payton. Photos courtesy of Leon Megginson.

Chapter 3

Page 55. Barkley Shreve. Photo courtesy of Cori Byrd. *Page 56.* Cheesewafers sign. Courtesy of Spring Hill Kitchens, LLC.

Chapter 4

Page 75. Gerald Byrd and Sarah Wicker. Photo courtesy of Cori Byrd.

Chapter 5

Page 97. Photo of Albretson. Courtesy of Brynn Albretsen. *Page 104.* Carpe Diem.

Chapter 6

Page 127. Courtesy of Teresa Davis.

Appendix B map

Page 166. Courtesy of Tom Keith, Keith Map Service.

Appendix C map

Page 167. Courtesy of Tom Keith, Keith Map Service.

Chapter 7

Page 179. Sarah and Cary Coxwell. Photo courtesy of Cori Byrd.

Chapter 8

Page 201. David and Karen Pilliod. Photo courtesy of Brynn Gilbreath. *Page 213.* ©Reg Charity/CORBIS.

Chapter 9

Page 233. Springdale Travel. Photo courtesy of Cori Byrd. *Page 235.* Todd DuBose. Photo courtesy of Cori Byrd.

Chapter 10

Page 263. Michael Levy and Mary H. Partridge. Photo courtesy of Michael Levy and Mary H. Partridge.

Chapter 11

Page 295. Cathy Anderson-Giles. Photo courtesy of Cathy Anderson-Giles.

Chapter 12

Page 323. Koi and Lilies. Photo courtesy of John Boydstun. *Page 324.* Inside Koi and Lilies. Photos courtesy of John Boydstun. *Page 329.* ©Robert Holmes/CORBIS. *Page 335.* ©L. Clarke/CORBIS.

Chapter 13

Page 345. Anders Book Store. Photo courtesy of Cori Byrd. *Page 346.* Anders Book Store owners, Bob and Kathy Summer. Photo courtesy of Jane Byrd. *Page 359.* Photo Barnatsky Betts. Photo courtesy of Cory Poff.

Chapter 14

Page 367. Carpe Diem owners. Photo courtesy of Cori Byrd. *Page 368.* Carpe Diem barrel. Photo courtesy of Cori Byrd.

Chapter 15

Page 387. Allen Smith. Photo courtesy of Jane Byrd.

Chapter 16

Page 417. Photo courtesy of Martin Smith, MBA.

Chapter 17

Page 443. Dr. Jeffrey F. Van Petten. Photo courtesy of Jeffrey Van Petten. *Page 449.* Daniel Feldkamp and Randy Sowash. AP photo by David Kohl. *Page 450.* Insurance logo. Photo courtesy of Cori Byrd. *Page 451.* Alfred Corina. Photo courtesy of Cori Byrd.